INSIDE EARLY MUSIC

INSIDE
EARLY MUSIC

Conversations with Performers

BERNARD D. SHERMAN

New York   Oxford
Oxford University Press
1997

Oxford University Press

Oxford   New York

Athens   Auckland   Bangkok   Bogotá   Bombay
Buenos Aires   Calcutta   Cape Town   Dar es Salaam
Delhi   Florence   Hong Kong   Istanbul   Karachi
Kuala Lumpur   Madras   Madrid   Melbourne
Mexico City   Nairobi   Paris   Singapore
Taipei   Tokyo   Toronto

and associated companies in
Berlin   Ibadan

Library of Congress Cataloging-in-Publication Data
Sherman, Bernard D.
Inside early music : conversations with performers /
Bernard D. Sherman.
p. cm.   Includes bibliographical references (p.) and index.
ISBN 0-19-509708-4
1. Performance practice (Music).   2. Style, Musical.
3. Musicians—Interviews.   I. Title.
ML457.S52   1997   781.4'3—DC20   96-6341

1 3 5 7 9 8 6 4 2

Printed in the United States of America
on acid-free paper

To my family

CONTENTS

PREFACE AND ACKNOWLEDGMENTS

Many readers will wonder why I chose these specific artists to interview—and, more to the point, why I didn't choose others. Some decisions were obvious: anyone would include pioneers like Anner Bylsma, William Christie, or Gustav Leonhardt. But where, you ask, are . . . ?

One serious constraint was space: to do justice to all the branches of the historical-performance scene would take a book at least twice this size. I would have been happy to write that book (my editor will attest to that), but you would have had to pay twice as much for it. Some interesting interviews were sacrificed to reduce the book's length. I was distressed that we couldn't include the fascinating interview that Monica Huggett granted me, because this outstanding artist has not received all the recognition she deserves. But her interview had too much overlap with Anner Bylsma's; since hers was published elsewhere,[1] his was kept. The gifted soprano Judith Nelson and the distinguished harpsichordist Christoph Rousset had to be left out, with just as much regret, for similar reasons.

Other factors entered into my choice as well. One—not the least of them—was sheer accident. Had I searched internationally for a Bach expert, I would probably not have chosen the as yet little-known scholar and keyboardist John Butt. But after spending three fascinating hours with him, I believed that a more insightful interviewee would have been impossible to find. The "sheer accident" in this case was geographic: Butt was a neighbor of mine. And geography partly explains why there are too few Continental musicians in the book.

The choices also reflect, inevitably, the accident of my tastes and interests, though I did try to go beyond that. And some interviews weren't possible. Mary Springfels was too busy; Jordi Savall was disinclined; Nikolaus Harnoncourt won't do telephone interviews, and I couldn't afford air fare to Austria. The exceedingly busy Christopher Hogwood had just invested a great deal of time in interviews that were never published, and I didn't yet have a publisher at the time I approached him. I would have liked to include more women. I could argue, accurately, that even in the 1990s, men dominate the early-music field; but several serious attempts I made to do more interviews with women (in ad-

1. Bernard D. Sherman, "Monica Huggett," *Strings* 10 (March/April 1996), pp. 54–61.

dition to the ones I've mentioned) fell through. I also wanted more Continental musicians, such as Reinhard Goebel and Eduardo López Banzo; that, too, just didn't turn out to be feasible.

For all these reasons, a number of artists I admire enormously were not even approached. And many important areas are omitted. There are no instrument makers, for example. Perhaps a future volume will fill some of the gaps, but for now I hope this one gives a reasonable sense of the current scene and its issues. (This book, by the way, does not attempt to give a history of the historical-performance movement; a good one is Harry Haskell's *The Early Music Revival* [London: Thames and Hudson, 1988].)

Instead of just giving my own opinions, my discographic notes often quote other critics. If I were reading this book, I would prefer to get an idea of the critical consensus, instead of just one listener's opinions (although some of those are present as well). Also, I rarely attempt to provide a full critique of an artist's recordings, but instead suggest what I think are high points and good places to begin investigating.

Performers are now playing Mahler with historical styles and instruments, so the term "early music" is no longer quite apt. For convenience, though, I will use it as well as "historical performance."

In preparing this book, I have been a great borrower; my voracious need for books and scores was fed by such uncomplaining borrowees as Belle Bulwinkle, Jonathan Harris, Julie Jeffrey, James Meredith, Zoë Vandermeer, and Rick Weller. On occasion, Joseph Spencer and Anna Shtutina lent me CDs. My thanks to all of them for their generous loans, which, I am relieved to say, have all been returned.

I can't see how the music library at the University of California could be surpassed. If something I needed was unavailable there, I could usually find it at the excellent public libraries in Berkeley and Oakland and the private one at Mills College (late in the book's preparation, the University of Iowa library was very helpful). Julie Jeffrey and Jim Bates provided expert last-minute reference aid. Many record companies helpfully sent me review copies of CDs.

Many experts were kind enough to answer my queries about specific issues. They included Wye Jamison Allanbrook, George Barth, Katherine Bergeron, Jane Boothroyd, Alfred Brendel, John Butt, Mary Cyr, Laurence Dreyfus, David Fallows, Donald Greig, Ralph Holloway, D. Kern Holoman, Chris Hunter, David Lasocki, Carol Lems-Dworkin, Hugh Macdonald, Daniel Melamed, William Meredith, Donald Mintz, Herbert Myers, Marc Perlman, Lawrence Rosenwald, the late Max Rudolf, Sally Sanford, Howard Schott, David Schulenberg, and Richard Taruskin.

Finally, let me thank all those who took time to comment on the book's contents. To the interviewees themselves, of course, my thanks for putting what was in some cases considerable time and energy into their interviews. Thanks also to their agents or concert contacts for helping me gain access. Reviewers at Oxford and one other press gave me valuable and much-appreciated feedback; I can thank Oxford's reviewers by name—Fallows, Taruskin, and Tess Knighton—as they all revealed their identities to me. I didn't have the chutzpah to ask anyone else to read the whole manuscript, but many people took valuable time (something they don't have a lot of) to look at and comment on chapters or subsections of them. I'm very grateful for their feedback. These readers included, among musicians and musicologists, Allanbrook, Barth, Butt, Bulwinkle, Michelle Dulak, Virginia Hancock, Tamara Loring, William S. Newman, Perlman, Vandermeer, and Robert Winter; among non-musicologists, Bryan Aubrey, Steven Bensinger, Gerald Geer, Beverly Hill, Leon Honoré, Christopher Minkowski, James Obertino, Amy Sherman, Brian Stains, and Elizabeth Van Schoick. Stains and Van Schoick also served as sounding boards whenever asked, and were so perceptive that I asked more than once. Several non-musicologists read the Postscript to the Christopher Page interview and gave valuable input: Silvine Marbury Farnell, William Jankowiak, James Karpen, Lee Kirkpatrick, Steven Pinker, Dane Waterman, and Robert Wright. Harmon R. Holcomb III wrote a detailed critique of an early version of that Postscript; I am indebted to him for that, and for having (in the process) suggested the angle taken in the final version. Jonathan Harris not only gave me helpful feedback but, along with Myrna Melgar, devoted an extraordinary amount of time to helping prepare and then translate questions to be sent to the elusive Jordi Savall (who, through no fault of theirs, never responded). Elliot Hurwitt and Jerome F. Weber generously gave discographic input. Joel Flegler kindly granted permission to use material in the Jeffrey Thomas interview that had previously appeared in *Fanfare*. I'm grateful to Oxford University Press for honoring my request that Eric Van Tassel be asked to copyedit the book, and even more grateful to him for agreeing to do so, and for doing so expert, thorough, and helpful a job of it. I'm also grateful to Kimberly Torre-Tasso of Oxford University Press for being so helpful throughout the production process. Finally, special thanks to my editor, Soo Mee Kwon, for her enthusiasm for this project and for her unfailing patience and skill.

Berkeley, California/Fairfield, Iowa
1995/1996

INSIDE EARLY MUSIC

INTRODUCTION:

AN ATMOSPHERE OF CONTROVERSY

Torniamo all'antico: sarà un progresso [Let us return to
old times: that will be progress]—Giuseppe Verdi

The "early-music revival" has been around for a whole century, but it was only in the 1980s that its recordings suddenly began to top the *Billboard* charts. A decade later those who called "historical performance" a fad have been proved just as wrong as those who called it a revolution. It shows no signs of disappearing. But even now, it can still make us wonder, "Why do they play like that?"

That question inspired this book. Musicologists have published whole libraries of historical evidence, but few performers have put their experiences into print. Yet they have special insights to share. Charles Rosen says that "musicology is for musicians, what ornithology is to the birds."[1] While some of my interviewees do say a good deal about musicology, the musicologists can't tell us how it feels to fly.

The relationship between musicologists and early-music performers might seem to be a simple matter: musicologists do research, performers put the research into practice. In fact the relationship is complex,[2] because the two disciplines make an uneasy match. Music history tries to restrict itself to what is supported by data, but performance suffocates under that restriction. Music historians try to find out what happened in the past, performers try to make something happen now. In some ways, the purposes conflict: as Rosen says, "Paradoxically, in so far as the purpose of a performance of a Mozart concerto is reconstruction of eighteenth-century practice rather than pleasure or dramatic effect, just so far does it differ from an actual performance by Mozart."[3]

1. Rosen, *The Frontiers of Meaning* (New York: Hill and Wang, 1995), p. 72.
2. Discussed by Joseph Kerman, *Contemplating Music* (Cambridge, Mass.: Harvard University Press, 1985), chap. 6; Laurence Dreyfus, "Early Music Defended Against Its Devotees," *The Musical Quarterly* 69 (1983), pp. 297–322; and Richard Taruskin, "On Letting the Music Speak for Itself," reprinted in his *Text and Act* (New York: Oxford University Press, 1995), first published in the *Journal of Musicology* 1/3 (1982), pp. 338–49.
3. Rosen, *The Classical Style* (New York: Norton, 1971), p. 107.

But a performance can, of course, try both to reconstruct early practice *and* to give pleasure or dramatic effect. The results can be surprisingly vital. Still, the tension between the goals may explain part of why the early-music movement has, as Joseph Kerman says, "always flourished in an atmosphere of multiple controversy."[4] This book presents insiders' views of many of the controversies—what they are about, and why they might matter. Without such views, we can't really understand why these artists play as they do.

Some of the controversies arise within the realm of musicology, but others reflect the tension between scholarship and art. The crux of this book can be expressed in a question: How can you use historical information to enliven modern performance? Answers to that question fall on a spectrum from ignoring the evidence to following it to the letter. Those two responses, and others less extreme, underlie the most obvious of the controversies—what Kerman called "disputes over turf."

"Manichean Struggles": The Turf Wars

The turf wars have usually pitted mainstream musicians against the history-minded upstarts who encroach on their territory, as in, "Now they're playing *Brahms?*" or, from the other side, "How can they still play Bach on the piano?" If the "war" image is extravagant, it does at least suggest how strong the emotions could become on both sides. When historical performers of the 1970s and '80s compared using old instruments to cleaning a dirt-encrusted Rembrandt, it was more than an analogy; it implied that the ignorant mainstreamers were trashing the classics.[5] The historicist pronouncements often involved not just art, but also morality. Bernard Holland recalls "fierce Manichean struggles of good versus evil."[6] I remember an early-music advocate describing her colleagues' work as "the responsible performance of Baroque music." Another, expressing the zeal many of his colleagues felt in the 1970s, argued that musi-

---

4. In "The Early Music Debate" (an edited transcript of a symposium featuring Kerman, Laurence Dreyfus, Joshua Kosman, John Rockwell, Ellen Rosand, Richard Taruskin, and Nicholas McGegan), *Journal of Musicology* 10 (Winter 1992), pp. 113–30.

5. It was, moreover, a problematic analogy. It assumes that underneath all the accumulated grime there is an authentic musical "original" waiting to be restored to pristine condition. This conceives of a piece of music as a timeless *thing*—a concept that raises enormous problems when applied to an active, temporal process like music, as several writers have discussed, such as Lydia Goehr in *The Imaginary Museum of Musical Works* (Oxford University Press, 1992). Another problem is that the analogy, in comparing tone color to the pigment in paintings, exaggerates the importance of tone color in pre-nineteenth-century music; this is discussed in the Gardiner interview, Chapter 19. However, the charge that historical performers put an anachronistic emphasis on tone color ignores the fact that many of them justify the use of period instruments not in terms of sound, but in terms of the clues that the instruments give performers about style and articulation. But the analogy itself misses this point.

6. Bernard Holland, "A Streak in the Heavens Has Become a Straggler," *The New York Times*, Sunday Arts and Leisure section, 31 October 1993, p. 31.

cians are [my italics] "under an *absolute* injunction to try to find out *all* that can be known about the performance traditions and the sound-world of *any* piece that is to be performed, and to try to duplicate these *as faithfully as possible*." So much for Horowitz, Gould, and Rachmaninoff, who violated that injunction without apology, and for other mainstream performers, who also violate it (if less audaciously). It's not surprising that mainstreamers often accused the historical performers of pedantry—of "restraining any and all of the interpreter's natural urges."[7]

As that shows, mainstreamer charges could be belligerent and moralistic in their own way. The historicists were accused of amateurism, and—to turn the tables—of trashing the classics. Although historical performers did sometimes take speed, lightness, or inflection to the point of mannerism, the critiques went beyond that. One critic wrote of the unfamiliar instruments, "it is impossible to listen without discomfort, nausea, without clenching one's teeth," and urged that performers "guilty of musical outrages" be given prison sentences.[8]

The turf wars sometimes seem a textbook case of "ingroup and outgroup" psychology.[9] Psychologists have found that people in an ingroup tend to see the outgroup in terms of simplistic stereotypes—and while historical performers are a varied group, you wouldn't know it from many of their critics. Similarly, the "mainstream" has eddies that historicists sometimes ignore.[10] Also, ingroups tend to see themselves as virtuous but beleaguered, and the outgroup as malevolent and powerful. Both camps have been known to describe each other in such terms: I recall a review of the Cecilia Bartoli/June Anderson recording of Pergolesi's Stabat Mater, which praised the two popular divas for bravely reclaiming the piece from the early-music mafia.

Of course, both sides also make substantial points. Regarding the mainstream complaints, even the most sympathetic observer must admit that historical performance did have its phases of both amateurism and pedantry. Both phases, however, were necessary. Regarding amateurism, it has often been hard to make a living at historical performance, so those who tried to master it had to earn their keep doing something else. Besides, even in supportive circumstances it takes a while to master an instrument. In 1963, Nikolaus Harnon-

---

7. Donald Vroon, *American Record Guide* 56 (March/April 1993), p. 220.

8. Gérard Zwang, *A contre-bruit* (Paris, 1977). The translation comes from Laurence Dreyfus's "Early Music Defended Against Its Devotees."

9. Marilynn B. Brewer and Roderick M. Kramer, "The Psychology of Intergroup Attitudes and Behavior," in *Annual Review of Psychology,* vol. 36, ed. Mark R. Rosenzweig and Lyman W. Porter (Palo Alto: Annual Reviews, 1985), pp. 219–43.

10. Hermann Danuser argues that there are actually three modes of performance in art music today: the "traditional" mode, which includes what I call "mainstream" musicians; the "actualizing" mode, which interprets old music in light of modern compositional styles, and includes such artists as Glenn Gould and Pierre Boulez; and the "historical-reconstructive," which includes the artists interviewed in this book. See Danuser's *Musikalische Interpretation* (Laaber: Laaber Verlag, 1992).

court's fledgling Concentus Musicus recorded the *Brandenburg Concerti* in ten-second takes, because the period winds could stay in tune only that long;[11] but in 1993, John Eliot Gardiner's Orchestre Révolutionnaire et Romantique recorded three Beethoven symphonies in live concerts, and the winds stayed in tune throughout. As for pedantry, it too was an inevitable phase. It takes time to unlearn old habits, and a longer time before new practices become ingrained. In the gap between the old habits and the new ones, musicians play pedantically. In addition, sometimes the pedantry was deliberate; a program note circa 1950 said that "Early music was a highly aristocratic art and restraint governed even the display of emotion."[12] In 1994, however, Clifford Bartlett writes of British Baroque playing that "what was at first a fairly stiff, somewhat puritanical approach has become much more free";[13] and that applies elsewhere (though not universally—medieval performers, who often have links with folk music, sounded anything but puritanical in the 1950s, and the old Harnoncourt Baroque recordings were not exactly stiff either). In any case, I don't find much evidence for pedantry in my interviewees' playing, or in their words. Several of them praise historically uninformed moderns from earlier in our century. Anner Bylsma admires Fritz Kreisler; William Christie loves Sir Thomas Beecham's recordings, and doesn't mind at all that Beecham detested musicology and insisted on using corrupt editions. These interviewees have no fetish about historicism, but they do object to an undiscriminating obsession with smooth, powerful surfaces, a fault many music critics observe in "competition-winner" mainstream playing today.

In general, the turf wars appear to be subsiding in favor of what Alfred Brendel calls "true cross-fertilization."[14] Period string sections, once famous for astringency, are now sometimes praised and even criticized for *sweetness* of tone[15] (which, according to Michelle Dulak, proves that the astringency was not determined by the instruments but instead reflected the performers' choices).[16] Wendy Carlos uses historical tunings in her electronically synthesized Bach, some mainstream conductors explore period styles,[17] and many

---

11. According to the producer, Wolf Erichson, in James Keller, "Wolf Erichson," *Historical Performance* 6 (Spring 1993), p. 32.

12. Erwin Bodky, program notes for the Cambridge Society for Early Music, quoted in Harry Haskell's *The Early Music Revival* (London: Thames and Hudson, 1988), p. 178.

13. Clifford Bartlett, "Pandolfi Mealli and Others," *Early Music* 22 (August 1994), p. 521.

14. Alfred Brendel, *Music Sounded Out* (London: Robson, 1990, and New York: Farrar, Straus and Giroux, 1991), p. 224. See also Michelle Dulak, "The Quiet Metamorphosis of 'Early Music,'" *Repercussions* 2 (Fall 1993), pp. 31–61.

15. Stanley Sadie praises Trevor Pinnock's strings for their sweetness in *Gramophone* 72 (January 1995), p. 50; Raymond Knapp, in an informative review of Norrington's Brahms First Symphony, praises the strings' sweet tone but faults their "reluctance to abandon" that tone in some passages (*American Brahms Society Newsletter* 11 [Spring 1992], pp. 4–7).

16. Dulak, "The Quiet Metamorphosis," p. 39.

17. For example, Yehudi Menuhin, David Zinman, and Michael Morgan; Sir Charles Mackerras and Sir Simon Rattle have even conducted period-instrument groups.

players in both camps cross over regularly. Gardiner conducts the Vienna Philharmonic, and Yo-Yo Ma, who has performed the Beethoven Triple Concerto with Itzhak Perlman, Daniel Barenboim, and the Berlin Philharmonic, has also played it with Ernst Kovacic, Robert Levin, and Roger Norrington on historic instruments (Ma using a gut-strung cello). Even eminent singers cross over: Bartoli has recorded Mozart with Christopher Hogwood (using period instruments), and Dame Joan Sutherland is featured in Hogwood's period recording of Handel's *Athalia*. When told that the recording would involve old instruments, she is said to have replied, "That's all right, I'm a bit of an old instrument myself."

Listening tastes, too, seem less segregated. Today, writes James Jolly, the editor of *Gramophone*, "a Mozart opera almost has to be performed on period instruments to make reasonable headway in [the CD] catalogue."[18] He notes that recent exceptions, by Harnoncourt and Sir Charles Mackerras, have explored period styles, if not period instruments. At the same time, a few performers of pre-mainstream repertoire—the monks of Silos, Anonymous 4, the Tallis Scholars, Jordi Savall, and some others—have reached audiences far larger than the usual medieval/Renaissance music subculture. These performers may even cross over to contemporary classical music (as in Paul Hillier's work with Arvo Pärt, or Fretwork's commissioning of new music by Gavin Bryars) or, to everyone's surprise, to popular musics (as in the Hilliard Ensemble's disc with the saxophonist Jan Garbarek).[19]

Nonetheless, it would be mistaken to declare either a victory for early music or a cease-fire in the turf wars. The later interviews in this book contain plenty of salvos against the mainstream. On the other side, some critics still speak of "the authenticity craze['s] . . . arid [music making,] the often out-of-tune instruments [sounding] ghastly."[20] As for performers, in a recent interview the violinist Pinchas Zukerman said that historical performance is "asinine STUFF . . . a complete and absolute farce * * * AWFUL," and adds, "Nobody wants to hear that stuff. I don't."[21]

The Authenticity Debates: What Is Possible, What Desirable?

As large audiences began to want to hear that stuff and historical performers began to make money, new controversies arose, often within the historical ranks. Beneath the disputed turf lay certain assumptions; as the historicists gained ground, they began to question those assumptions. For example, many

18. Editorial, *Gramophone* 71 (April 1994), p. 1.

19. *Officium* (ECM New Series 445 369).

20. Sedgwick Clark, in "North American Retrospect," *Gramophone* 70 (May 1993), North American edition, p. A3.

21. David K. Nelson, "An Interview with Pinchas Zukerman," *Fanfare* 13 (March/April 1990), p. 38.

flinched from their critics' mockery of the use of the term "authenticity" to mean historical accuracy, so that the term has become virtually taboo among historicists (unless it's enclosed in ironic quotation marks; though some artists who sneer at the term don't seem to be able to stop their record companies from using it). Other disagreements (often still internecine) continue, reflecting the tensions between art and scholarship—and, some would say, between artistic idealism and marketplace pragmatism. And these disagreements, like the historicists' disputes with the mainstream over turf, reflect a further tension: between the past, when the music was written, and the present, when we're playing and hearing it.

For example, many doubt that reviving old playing styles is entirely possible today. The goal of historical performers is something like playing Strauss waltzes with the special rhythmic lilt that makes the oom-pah-pah uniquely Viennese; but the equivalent of *echt* Viennese style may be forever lost to us in Dufay or Monteverdi. Admittedly, our growing knowledge of performance practice lets us "resolve certain problems about how various musical notations were meant to be rendered."[22] But evidence about early playing styles is almost never complete. We must fill in the gaps with our imaginations, and we have twentieth-century imaginations.

To honor St. Patrick's Day, a small Iowa town once hosted an Irish-accent contest. A visiting Dubliner—the only authentic Irishman in town—signed up and seemed certain to win. He lost, to an Iowan. To Iowan judges, the real thing didn't have enough of the ould sod to it. Perhaps when we fill in the gaps of authentic Bach or Beethoven style, our sense of what's authentic is just as biased.

What might also make historical re-creation impossible is that performing contexts influence music-making, and old music is almost never performed now in the contexts it was written for—chapel, feasting hall, music room, salon.[23] Even music written for the concert hall has to contend with radically different concert-hall sizes, acoustics, and audience behavior.[24] In a subtle example of a context shift, Robert Philip observes that a modern audience's main listening context is recordings, which are "perfect."[25] If a concert performer, in the heat of inspiration, flubs a few notes, many of his listeners, recalling their CDs, will say not "How inspired!" but "Why should I pay good money to hear someone who hasn't practiced?" Cowed by such responses, most modern performers

22. Neal Zaslaw, *Notes* 8 (March 1994), p. 948.

23. See Charles Rosen, "The Shock of the Old," *New York Review of Books,* 19 July 1990, pp. 46–52, and *The Romantic Generation* (Cambridge, Mass.: Harvard University Press, 1995), pp. 383–85.

24. Nicholas McGegan and Robert Levin discuss the changes in audience behavior in their interviews. Julianne Baird, in her interview, discusses how hall sizes have affected singing technique.

25. *Early Recordings and Musical Style* (Cambridge University Press, 1992), pp. 230–31.

spend hours practicing a concerto so that they get the notes exactly right, and make that a higher priority than the flight of inspiration, which the orchestra might not be able to follow neatly. This attitude is the opposite of those held by many performers in even the relatively recent past (as early recordings show); to the extent that recordings have changed our outlook, some critics say, we can never play as artists played in the past.

Some historical performers try to "recontextualize" old music—for instance, by embedding a Renaissance mass in re-enacted liturgy, or preceding a Mozart concert by giving the audience minuet lessons. Such approaches, however, may not quite bridge the chasm that divides us from the past. They do not solve a deeper problem that is often raised: that our musical aesthetics reflect our emotional, intellectual, and spiritual lives, which differ from those of past eras. Even if we embed a Dufay mass in its liturgy, we probably won't feel, as Dufay's listeners did, emotional associations between the chants and specific religious holidays (as Susan Hellauer explains in her interview). Even if we learn to dance a few Mozartian dances, they probably won't signify class distinctions for us as they did for Mozart and his listeners; unless we're told, we won't understand that the Count would dance a minuet but not a "relatively rowdy" contredanse.[26] And the problem might go deeper: If a passage in Mozart expresses yearning, says the fortepianist Steven Lubin, we should know that eighteenth-century yearning was different from twentieth-century yearning: it was "more innocent and trusting" than the sort habitual to us, who have fewer "hospitable realms" to yearn for.[27] If such "otherness" applies to Mozart, a contemporary of Thomas Jefferson, how much more to Hildegard, who predates Thomas Aquinas?

Lubin believes, however, that we *can* re-create eighteenth-century yearning, through historical immersion and through searching within ourselves. I myself wonder whether yearning in Mozart's day was all that "innocent and trusting." Mozart's father constantly warned him that "all men are villains," that "all friendships have their motives," and that he should "trust no one"; Mozart ended up "[s]keptical, wary of easy solutions, doubtful of men's motives, disdainful of panaceas."[28] Wye J. Allanbrook is right, I think, to say that we value the dark side of Mozart more than did he or his contemporaries, who didn't share our post-Romantic "ingrained assumption that profundity and melancholia go hand in hand":[29] we do seem more prone to melancholy than

26. See Wye J. Allanbrook, *Rhythmic Gesture in Mozart* (University of Chicago Press, 1983), chap. 2, and p. 81.

27. Lubin, "Authenticity Briefly Revisited," *Historical Performance* 4 (Spring 1991), p. 46.

28. See Maynard Solomon's *Mozart* (New York: Harper Collins, 1995), pp. 8 and 90 on Leopold Mozart and trust, and p. 355 on Mozart's skepticism.

29. Allanbrook, "Mozart's Tunes and the Comedy of Closure," in *On Mozart*, ed. James Morris (Cambridge University Press, 1994), pp. 169–86; quote, p. 176.

Mozart's contemporaries,[30] and our era is clearly less optimistic than theirs was, with its faith in the triumph of reason and the perfectibility of humanity. But a close look at the joys and sorrows of both eras suggests that underlying human emotional equipment has changed little since then.[31] So the claim that "otherness" makes historical re-creation impossible may be exaggerated (we'll return to this in Christopher Page's interview). Still, there's no denying that we differ in some ways from our predecessors, and that it affects how we hear or play their music.

For all these reasons, almost no one today makes bold claims about playing music exactly as it was played in the past. Attaining that goal seems too difficult.

Of course, a goal might still be worth seeking even if it's impossible to attain. If 100 percent historical accuracy were really ideal, 50 percent accuracy would be better than none at all; and while a minuet lesson might not give us eighteenth-century ears, it could still enrich our understanding. And the argument that our imaginations must fill in some factual gaps can apply to any historical enterprise (and doesn't invalidate it). But some critics argue that even if perfect historical reconstruction were possible, it would not be worth the effort. We can hear Elgar conducting his music on early recordings and could re-create his performances accurately. But why should we play Elgar as Elgar did, these critics ask, if we prefer it played differently? Why shouldn't we use Mozart to express twentieth-century yearning? That may be what we need Mozart for. And some listeners might prefer a Dufay mass with as little liturgy as possible.

The original early-music view was, of course, that music sounds best when played as the composer expected it would be played. In this spirit, the interviews in this book include many specific claims that historical practice improves performance. If, for example, the composer wrote down only a bare skeleton and expected the performer to flesh it out with ornamentation, then learning how to ornament in the composer's style will generally give better results than playing the bare bones. And (though this doesn't arise in the interviews) seventeenth-century keyboard music has proven to be vastly more interesting when played with historical instruments and tunings.[32] These and other arguments can be convincing; but in the end the principle is not as universal or as self-evident as it may seem.[33] No one, for example, has tried to revive the French

---

30. Or Ravel's: in recent decades, rates of serious depression appear to have doubled every ten years in many countries. See the Cross-National Collaborative Group, "The Changing Rate of Major Depression. Cross-National Comparisons," *Journal of the American Medical Association* 268 (1992), pp. 3098–105.

31. This is discussed in the Postscript to the Christopher Page interview.

32. John Butt pointed this out; personal communication, 1996.

33. Sometimes an informed critic even applauds the bare-bones avoidance of ornamenta-

Baroque practice of conducting by beating time on the podium with a large wooden staff. And when we imagine shivering Thomasschule students, at seven-thirty on a winter morning, performing a virtuoso chorus written three days earlier, we might ask whether we could tolerate *truly* historical Bach.

Whether or not the original way is best may also depend on who's listening. I once saw a Chicago production of *Under Milk Wood* with an English friend. She informed me afterwards that most of the actors had vaguely Gaelic accents, and that only Captain Cat's was truly Welsh. His was the only accent I'd found difficult to understand. Perhaps Chicagoans are better served by ersatz Welsh. Such thinking, some fear, might lead a musician to pander to an audience rather than challenge its preconceptions; but principle may have deeper musical applications. Joshua Rifkin is far from alone in noting that a typical performance in the eighteenth century or earlier was what we would call a barely rehearsed run-through. We could re-create that, he says, but maybe an eighteenth-century audience, hearing a piece for the first time, needed only a run-through, while we, who have heard Mozart and Bach so often, need an interpretation. And the fact that performance context has changed also raises questions about why we should want historical accuracy. Charles Rosen points out that much of Bach's keyboard music was written for private use; if we tried to play it in public in the same way that an eighteenth-century musician would have played for himself—that is, without trying to project the musical events to an audience—we would defeat the purpose of concert-giving.[34]

Such examples suggest that even if you believe that historical evidence matters, you still have to decide whether each *particular* historical practice does. Is it important to making the music work today, or is it a meaningless accident of history—irrelevant or even harmful from a musical standpoint? The "meaningless accident" is what Donald Tovey had in mind when he said that if we want to be truly authentic in performing Bach cantatas, we would have to "flog the ringleaders of the choir after an atrocious performance."[35]

The distinction is by no means lost on most historical performers. Of course, making the distinction is not an objective science; sometimes a conclusion (one way or the other) is all but inescapable, but more often it depends on the performer's assumptions and priorities—and those of the performer's era. Our era is more likely to consider historical practice important than the nineteenth century was. And as we'll see, historical performers themselves draw the line in a variety of places, from near-purism to near-rejection of the historical ideal.

The question of the accidental versus the relevant distills some of the "authenticity" issues into the kind of practical problems a musician faces every day.

---

tion; see Richard Taruskin's praise of Artur Schnabel's unhistorical Mozart in *Text and Act*, pp. 290–91.

34. Rosen, "The Shock of the Old," p. 50.

35. Tovey, *A Musician Talks* (Oxford University Press, 1941), p. 66.

It applies, for example, to the original calling-card of historical performance—period instruments. Harnoncourt now focuses on modern-instrument groups; an instrument, he says, is "a tool, not a religion." Nonetheless, when he conducts modern orchestras he often uses historical brass and percussion instruments, which he thinks have an inimitable effect. Anner Bylsma sometimes plays Bach with instruments other than those specified, or with a modern bow; but he considers using gut strings crucial to Boccherini's cello music.

As that suggests, how much of period practice is important might differ in different sorts of music. "[It] is more acceptable," wrote Howard Mayer Brown, "to play Bach's music on modern instruments than Rameau's,"[36] and Bach seems robust in many other ways. But French Baroque music often requires period instruments and a firm grounding in historical style even to be interesting, much less effective.

The issue of accidence versus importance relates also to a major trend among musicologists today, which seeks to understand music by reference to its larger contexts—social, political, economic, religious, and so on.[37] Such musicologists often seek to understand what music meant in its own time, which makes their project seem, at least at first glance, like a natural ally to historical performance. In fact, historical context comes up often in the interviews. I suggested earlier that changes in performance context may make it impossible (or undesirable) for us to play as people did in an earlier century; here we may ask which aspects of larger *historical* contexts must be considered when trying to make the music live in modern performance.

The discussions in this book often suggest an ecological web: change one part of the system, and you change what is incidental to the music and what is necessary to it. An authentic historical performance practice may no longer fit, because we or our contexts have changed. If you re-create the exact size and layout of the orchestra that premiered a Mozart symphony, but put it in Carnegie Hall, it will sound puny. The "necessary" element is an adequately powerful sound; the "historical accident" is the size of the premiere's orchestra, which made a big sound in the small, resonant halls of Mozart's day.[38] Some historical performers, perhaps, have focused on accidental features—such as the exact size of an ensemble—rather than the important ones. My interviewees are often more discriminating.

Should We Care about the Composer's Intentions?

Some doubt that even selective historical accuracy is a worthy goal. In particular, they question whether performers should be concerned with honoring

36. Brown, "Pedantry or Liberation?" in *Authenticity and Early Music,* ed. Nicholas Kenyon (Oxford University Press, 1988), p. 30.

37. Discussed briefly in the Postscript to the Page interview.

38. See Neal Zaslaw, "Mozart's Orchestra," *Early Music* 20 (May 1992), pp. 204–5.

composers' intentions on how to perform their own music. During the nineteenth century this ideal became widespread,[39] and today, says Robert Martin, "In general, the best performers have a strong sense of their roles as servants of the composer."[40] Admittedly, some critics believe performers' subservience to the composer is lip service—John Butt has called it little more than "crocodile humility"—but few would agree. In any case, many in the early-music movement (for example, Malcolm Bilson and Robert Levin) share Martin's "strong sense."

Others in the movement appear to serve a slightly different purpose: they try to play as the composer's contemporaries did. This may seem to make arguments about composer's intentions somewhat less relevant to the authenticity debates, but critiques of the composer's intentions raise arguments that, if accepted, could undermine this approach as well. For example, Richard Taruskin argues, to paraphrase him, that what really counts in the arts is the experience delivered to the audience; what doesn't count is *who* comes up with the means of delivery.[41] A distinguished critic has denounced conductors who, like Barenboim, at the chorus's first entry in Brahms's *German Requiem* ignore the *p* marking and instead have the chorus enter *pp*. Barenboim might respond by pointing out that in his later years Brahms told a choral conductor that the chorus should enter with "the softest *pp*."[42] But this argument against intentions is different: it would say that if the effect is beautiful, it doesn't matter who thought of it—Brahms, Barenboim, or Brahms's contemporaries. Another argument against privileging the composer's intentions distinguishes between a performance art and a textual one, and thus between the composer's intentions regarding performance and those regarding notes. As Peter Kivy says, it's easy to disprove the simplistic belief that the composer always knows best how to *play* his or her music;[43] and the composer's contemporaries could be equally fallible.

Of course, as Kivy notes, composer's views on how to perform their own works deserve special consideration—and sometimes composers *do* know best. In previous centuries, composers were often great performers, so their performance instructions reflect their expertise in that area as well as in composition; and their compositions may have been partly determined by performance con-

---

39. José A. Bowen, "Mendelssohn, Berlioz, and Wagner as Conductors: The Origins of the Ideal of 'Fidelity to the Composer,'" *Performance Practice Review* 6 (Spring 1993), pp. 77–88.

40. Martin, "The Quartets in Performance: A Player's Perspective," in *The Beethoven Quartet Companion*, ed. Robert Winter and Robert Martin (Berkeley: University of California Press, 1994), p. 140.

41. See Taruskin, "Tradition and Authority," reprinted in *Text and Act*, p. 190, originally published in *Early Music* 20 (May 1992), pp. 311–25.

42. The conductor was Siegfried Ochs; see Max Rudolf, "A Recently Discovered Composer-Annotated Score of the Brahms Requiem," *Quarterly Journal of the Riemenschneider Bach Institute* 7/4 (October 1976), p. 13.

43. Kivy, *Authenticities* (Ithaca, N.Y.: Cornell University Press, 1995), pp. 162–87.

siderations. One must then distinguish between a performance instruction that is part of the piece's identity (just like the notes themselves), and an instruction that is, to quote Virgil Thomson, "not part of [the composer's] original creation, but rather one musician's message to another about it, a hint" on how to put it over.[44] If you play the slow movement of the "Hammerklavier" Sonata at a *presto* tempo, you are not only contradicting Beethoven's performance instructions, you are, in a sense, creating a new piece. On the other hand, if your slow tempo is slower than Beethoven's metronome marking, you may be choosing what is (in your particular situation) a better tempo for the movement. You may be serving one of Beethoven's intentions—winning over the audience with a great performance of the movement[45]—by overriding another one[46] (playing at eighth note = 92).

Arguments about the composer's performance intentions can get more complex than this, and the above is far from a complete survey. In practice, the resolution may be the same as with historical practices: it may boil down to case-by-case decisions by the performer about whether each performance instruction is essential, beneficial, insignificant, or inferior to some other alternative. Which category each intention ends up in will, again, depend on the artist's (and the era's) priorities. Furtwängler was at least as devoted to serving Beethoven's intentions as Norrington is; but Norrington, unlike Furtwängler, defines such service so that it includes the metronome marks.

Why Did the Early-Music Movement Happen?

This brings us to the most celebrated of the authenticity debates, those involving motivation. These take my originating question—"Why do they play like that?"—to a deeper level. They ask not "On what grounds does Norrington justify following Beethoven's metronome markings?" but "Why does Norrington think it important to do so?" If the goal of historical performance might not be completely attainable or desirable, why do so many people seem to share it? The simplest explanation, as we've seen, is that they just think the music sounds better played historically. That may seem an adequate reason, and in some cases it's undeniably convincing. But, in general, one can't get away with so simple an explanation of motives. A critic could, for example, respond, "You can get used to many things once you decide that you

44. Thomson, *The Art of Judging Music* (New York: Knopf, 1948), p. 296. See also Kivy, *Authenticities*, pp. 28–32.

45. Beethoven could show more concern for such things than we might expect. In an 1819 letter to his piano student Ferdinand Ries, he said that if the "Hammerklavier" Sonata "should not be the right thing for London," Ries could leave out the slow movement or reorder the internal movements. In *Beethoven's Letters*, with notes by A. C. Kalischer, trans J. S. Shedlock, ed. A. Eaglefield-Hull (London: Dent, 1926), p. 268.

46. Kivy, *Authenticities*, pp. 24–44.

should—but if performers ever run into a case where it sounds *worse* to them played historically even after they get used to it, would they ignore the history, or would they play in a style they didn't like?" In short, for historical performers is history a means or an end?

Some say these performers (many of them, anyway) do make it an end in itself. The motivation, they say, is antiquarian, like Civil War battle re-enactments and other "living museums." But that kind of historical accuracy, some add, should be an end only for scholars, not artists (the "uneasy match" idea). Of course, when a musical culture is as fixated on the past as ours has become, it might seem inevitable that some musicians would want to re-create history for its own sake. But is it? After all, the emphasis on past masterpieces needn't be antiquarian, since those masterpieces are believed to speak to all times. In fact, many musicians understand the composer's intentions as involving timeless elements of the work, which transcend historical circumstance.

Robert Morgan finds another explanation for our concern for historical accuracy. Most musicians before our era, he says, believed themselves part of a *living* tradition with a direct connection to the musical past, so they usually saw nothing wrong with playing Bach or Handel in the performer's own modern style. That attitude still holds today among, say, rock musicians covering a Beatles tune: there's no expectation that they will simply reproduce the original, because the tradition is still alive. In "classical" music today, though, when modern musical styles seem unconnected with those of the past, the musical past has become a museum. Its artworks are "no longer ours to interpret as we wish"—that would seem like painting airplanes over a Constable landscape—but "ours only to reconstruct as faithfully as possible." Morgan contends that "concern for historical authenticity represents . . . a situation characterized by an extraordinary degree of insecurity, uncertainty, and self-doubt"—that is, a fragmented musical culture, which lacks a strong identity of its own.[47]

Some go further and speculate that the concern with historical accuracy "may be a symptom of a disintegrating civilization."[48] Perhaps; regardless of whether eighteenth-century yearning really was more naive and trusting than ours, many of us yearn for a more naive and trusting world. Some listeners and players *want* music to take them out of our world and into Bach's or Hildegard's, whether that is impossible or not. A sense that our culture has taken a wrong turn (or even that it is "disintegrating") is no longer the preserve of fundamentalists, fascists, and reactionaries; as a college professor

47. Robert Morgan, "Tradition, Anxiety, and the Current Musical Scene," in *Authenticity and Early Music,* ed. Kenyon, pp. 57–82.

48. Donald J. Grout, "On Historical Authenticity in the Performance of Old Music," in *Essays on Music in Honor of Archibald Thompson Davison* (Cambridge, Mass: Harvard University Press, 1957), pp. 341–47.

wrote in 1994, "Nearly everyone I know lives with the sense of serious decline if not impending fall."[49]

Since Berlioz,[50] various people have questioned the assumption that modern instruments are necessarily better than their predecessors; but, with a few exceptions, such questioning has become a force in the musical marketplace only since the 1960s. That this date seems a watershed may reflect nothing more than the growth of the recording industry; but as we've just seen, it is tempting to speculate about deeper social causes. Such speculations are, of course, slippery. On the one hand, one could note that this rise in the market popularity of historical performance coincides with when Robert Heilbroner sees society on a large scale losing faith in human progress and perfectibility—and in particular, in technological progress.[51] (Obviously, he is aware that such doubts had arisen in the nineteenth century and in the early twentieth, but says that these doubts were localized to intellectual circles, and not nearly so widespread as those of our era.) This fits in with the idea that yearning for an Arcadian past motivates some historical performers. On the other hand, John Butt speculates that the shift toward historical performance could equally well reflect the "bombshell in late nineteenth- and twentieth-century historiography and hermeneutics: that one's viewpoint is not neutral and absolute" but is instead contingent on one's place in history.[52] Such an attitude could have made musicians less likely to assume that their "natural" way of playing music was the best way.

Indeed, some other suspected motives are not especially oriented to the past. Some see the motivation behind the early-music movement as simple competitiveness: if Karajan and Co. have already perfected mainstream style, the only way to make your mark is to stake out radically new territory. Other observers see this in a less cynical light. They think that historical performers are trying to inject a dose of novelty into a flagging concert life, in which a limited repertory and an increasingly uniform style have led to shrinking audiences.[53]

49. Joseph Epstein, "Decline and Blumenthal," *The American Scholar,* Winter 1994 (Epstein is a neo-conservative, but many liberals feel the same way). There are many optimists too, of course—for example, those who believe that computer technology will create a new golden age. But even some techno-optimists exhibit nostalgia for a golden past.

50. Berlioz, "Instruments Added by Modern Composers to Scores of Old Masters," from his *À travers chant* (Paris, 1862). In *The Art of Music and Other Essays,* trans. and ed. Elizabeth Csicsery-Ronay (Bloomington: Indiana University Press, 1994), pp. 148–49.

51. Heilbroner, *Visions of the Future* (New York: Oxford University Press, 1995). He sees a somber, "apprehensive" view of the future becoming common only during the last thirty years; the *fin-de-sièclism* of the 1890s was, he argues, localized, and should not be given undue prominence. (Whether or not the world is in fact in a state of decline today is a separate question, as he notes, and for purposes of the present discussion is irrelevant.)

52. Butt, personal communication, 1996.

53. See Nicholas Temperley, "The Movement Puts a Stronger Premium on Novelty than on Accuracy . . . ," *Early Music* 12 (February 1984), pp. 16–20; Will Crutchfield, "Fashion, Con-

With few newly composed works reaching a significant public, performers sought a more appealing brand of novelty—and the past provided plenty of neglected works and new ways of playing familiar pieces. But if novelty is all that historical performance offers, what will happen when the novelty wears out?[54]

Richard Taruskin argues that this novelty-making reveals some life in our musical culture. Historical performance, he says, is *not* about putting musicology into action—it's about trying to make old music suit our modern (and, he argues, modernist) tastes. Regarding the acid-test question—"if the music sounded *worse* to them played historically, what would they do?"—Taruskin documents cases of supposed historical purists ignoring inconvenient historical evidence. These performers, he says, privilege the evidence they liked and ignored or devalued the evidence they didn't. He concludes that by using evidence selectively, even the most uncompromising historicist performers unconsciously try to create the sound not of "then," but of now.[55] They are doing, in other words, exactly what Morgan says musicians at most times have done—playing earlier music in the style of their own day. The only difference is that because of the museum-curator ethos that Morgan talks about, historicists have to *pretend* (even to themselves) that they're being historically accurate. This makes it irrelevant to argue about the "impossibility" of re-creating the past: the past is something we construct to suit *our* needs. In many of his writings, Taruskin tries not to deplore this or to dismiss it as the equivalent of the Iowan Irish accent; instead, he calls it far more reassuring (and, in the deepest sense, more

---

viction, and Performance Style in an Age of Revivals," in *Authenticity and Early Music*, ed. Kenyon, pp. 19–26; and Joshua Kosman's section of "The Early Music Debate," pp. 117–19.

54. Peter Phillips, "Beyond Authenticity," in *Companion to Medieval and Renaissance Music,* ed. Tess Knighton and David Fallows (London: Orion, and New York: Schirmer, 1992), pp. 44–47. Phillips believes that this has in fact happened, and that historical performers must now win attention on "the strength of their musical vision."

55. In many of the essays reprinted in Taruskin's *Text and Act.* His claim that early-music style belongs to modernism—by which he means a Satie/Stravinsky-like concern with lightness, formalism, and impersonality—applied most effectively to some of the dominant British artists of the 1980s; it was, perhaps, a specific example of his general point, an example Taruskin was able to document at length. But even at the time, Taruskin acknowledged that some of the Continental early-music leaders, like Harnoncourt and Leonhardt, were not Stravinskyan objective modernists.

This does not necessarily disprove Taruskin's basic idea that historicists are creating a modern, not a historical, sound. Jordi Savall's gamba-playing does not reflect Stravinskyan modernism, but it does use more legato than French Baroque playing probably did (see Taruskin's "Of Kings and Divas," *The New Republic,* 13 December 1993, pp. 31–44; on p. 43 he discusses Savall with enthusiasm). This too may reflect Savall's modern tastes rather than history. Romantic though it sounds, it may not entirely escape the label of "modernism." Rosen writes, in "The Shock of the Old," p. 46, that modernism "has its neo-Romantic side"; Taruskin, in the introduction to *Text and Act* (p. 10–11), describes modernism as a late manifestation of Romanticism, not its antithesis.

authentic) than true antiquarianism would be. "Being the true voice of one's time," he writes, "is . . . roughly forty thousand times as vital and important as being the assumed voice of history."[56]

Despite the compliment, this argument has not endeared Taruskin to the early-music world. And, of course, Taruskin's argument seems overstated if it's put simplistically. Early-music performers have been known to ask instrument makers to use wood only from the very region used by the seventeenth-century instrument maker they want copied. Marcel Pérès tells me that at home he never uses electric lights, but only candles, in order to better understand the mentality of the Middle Ages. Telling such performers that they aren't *really* trying to re-create historical practice does not win their gratitude, even if you then tell them that what they're actually doing is forty thousand times more important.

This is part of why Taruskin is generally seen as early music's most ferocious detractor. That perception needs more discussion, because the published record suggests something more complicated. Taruskin agrees, after all, that "the fruits of scholarship can mightily assist the performer's purposes"; pursuing historical practice, he thinks, can free one from deadening habits. He even says that "the best specialist performers get much closer to their chosen repertory than their mainstream counterparts manage to do."[57] And as a reviewer he has warmly praised, in detail, the musicianship of many early-music performers—I count twenty in the reviews I've surveyed—and has attacked, according to my survey, only seven. But the impression that remains from his work is of a scathing denunciation. The reason may lie partly in Taruskin's rhetorical emphases, partly in his internal contradictions (his critics have noted some),[58] partly in what got published where (the praise has been buried in smaller-circulation magazines), and partly in how entertaining the attacks can be. But another part of it may lie in the fact that his praise for the playing is often mixed with complaints about claims of historical fidelity. Consider Taruskin's response to one of many angry letters.[59] Here he takes an approach different from the one I summarized: he says he admires early-music performers' idealism and musicianship, but continues, "What I am waiting for is an end to the pretense that what Early Music performers are doing is being [merely] historically correct. They are not ransacking history in pursuit of truth. What they are seeking is permission. . . . Being human, when they find

---

56. "The Modern Sound of Early Music," originally published as "The Spin Doctors of Early Music" in *The New York Times*, 29 July 1990, Sunday Arts and Leisure section, p. 1. Reprinted in *Text and Act*; the quote is on p. 166.

57. *Text and Act*, p. 306.

58. John Butt, "Acting up a Text," *Early Music* 24 (May 1996), pp. 323–32.

59. The letter is from James Richman, and was printed in the *New York Times* Sunday Arts and Leisure section letter column on 26 August 1990; parts of it are reprinted in *Text and Act*, p. 171, along with the commentary from Taruskin that I quote.

permission, they are apt to believe that they have found the truth and be-come 'certain.'"[60]

Just how apt they are to believe this you can judge for yourself as you read. Whatever you decide, this idea of "seeking permission" brings us to another proposed motive in historical performance. Needing permission reflects, of course, submission to authority. Perhaps thinking of the moral tone of the turf wars, Nikolaus Harnoncourt calls the authenticity ideal "very close to the kind of political dogmatism and religious fundamentalism that are so much part of our times."[61] Taruskin and the gambist/musicologist Laurence Dreyfus,[62] among others, argue more generally that the need to get "permission" is all but universal in classical performance today. This authoritarian need, Taruskin says, reflects the exaltation of the composer and the musical work over the per-former and the performance. Permission usually comes from the composer's score, he and Dreyfus say, but among early-music purists permission must also be granted by another authority: scholars of performance practice. Not sur-prisingly, Taruskin considers this "tyrannically limiting."

All the same, another motivation for historical performers might be the opposite of adding more constraints of authority: it might be to sidestep the conflicting demands that musical authority makes of performers today. Over the past few centuries, our art-music culture has given performers less and less latitude in determining what notes to play or how. But since about 1800 our culture has also put far more emphasis on individual expression and cre-ativity than in pre-Romantic times. Performers are supposed to express the composer's emotions and intentions, not their own; but they are also sup-posed to be original, insightful, and creative.[63] Some believe they can't win: whatever they do, someone will attack them, either for serving the composer too slavishly or for expressing themselves too willfully.[64] This conflict is at the root of the critics' arguments about inspirational artists like Bernstein and Furtwängler. Perhaps historical performance offers a way out of this dilemma. Historical performance obliges you to serve the composer's intention by learn-ing all you can about his era's playing style, including idiomatic features (like the Viennese waltz rhythm) that were never explicitly notated. (Let's overlook

---

60. *Text and Act*, p. 171.

61. Stephen Johnson, "Making It New," *Gramophone* 69 (May 1992), p. 26.

62. Personal communication, 1995.

63. The ethnomusicologist Marc Perlman, who is doing a study of the early-music scene, points out that there are other music cultures which give their performers little latitude in de-termining the notes but do not lavish attention on the figure of the composer. What makes us distinctive is that we lionize the composer and limit the performer's creative freedom but also value originality highly. We thereby sever the functions of composer and performer, and place them in a relationship of mutual dependence in which a certain tension inheres. Personal com-munication, 31 December, 1994.

64. For an example of the latter, see Bernard Holland, "When the Musician Upstages the Music," *The New York Times*, 24 May 1995, p. B2.

the inconvenient fact that composers sometimes ignore their own idiom, as in Bernstein's recording of *West Side Story*.) To regain the style of a past era means that you have to improvise, ornament, add notes—skills that are hardly recognized in mainstream conservatory training—and phrase and articulate quite differently than you learn to do in such a conservatory. As a result, you can creatively rethink how to play. Even better, especially if you play music about which there's little or no evidence regarding performance style, you can construct your own style more or less from scratch. An advantage of such stylistic creativity is that it is less likely than mere originality to get you accused of willful self-expression—after all, you are just doing what was done by the composer's contemporaries, and musicology says so. Historical performance, then, may let some performers have it both ways, by combining creativity and fidelity.[65] Michelle Dulak argues that the true defining characteristic of the historical-performance movement today is that it offers "radical freedom from mainstream convention"; its players "are expected merely to sound different and are given such wide latitude that they can be different in nearly any way that pleases them."[66]

It could be, of course, that all of the motivations I've mentioned—and others too—act on different historical performers, or perhaps on the same performer in varying degrees. It's not difficult to find evidence both for *and* against every one of these motivations somewhere in this book. And they hardly exhaust the possible motivations. For example, John Butt, at the outset of his interview in Chapter 9, gives some reasons for his interest in historical performance that are quite different from those suggested above.

Why Does It Matter?

> Das Beste, was wir von der Geschichte haben, ist der Enthusiasmus, den sie erregt [The best that history has to give is the enthusiasm it arouses]. (Johann Wolfgang von Goethe)

The musicologist Leo Treitler recently began an article about a Marcel Pérès concert by remarking on the "decline of Early Music Talk," by which he meant the controversies discussed above. He then proceeded to give a fascinating example of Early Music Talk.[67] It seems to me that the Talk is, if anything, get-

---

65. An argument against the proposals I've made in the preceding two paragraphs is that they may overestimate the prestige of the composer relative to the performer. After all, some say, it is the performers who are idolized and enriched, not the critics or composers.

66. Michelle Dulak, "Early Music Circles Its Wagons Again," *The New York Times*, Sunday Arts and Leisure section, 11 June 1995, p. 40.

67. Leo Treitler, "Remembering 'Early Music,'" in *Thesis* 8 (Fall 1994), pp. 32–33. "The decline of Early Music Talk" is a phrase quoted from Bernard Holland's "A Streak in the Heavens."

ting more interesting these days, interesting for what it says about both the past and the present. And I consider the extent of controversy surrounding historical performance to be a sign of artistic vitality.

All the same, the controversies may not convey why the fuss is worth it. Analyzing premises and hidden motives can obscure creative achievements. Two of the most vocal critics of the premises of historical performance, Taruskin and Rosen, concur about these achievements. Rosen says that through taking "the indefensible ideal of authenticity" seriously, historical performers have increased "our knowledge . . . and our musical life [has been] enriched."[68] Taruskin calls historical performance "the least moribund aspect of our classical music life";[69] it allows a musician to "remake oneself," to challenge all of his or her "knee-jerk habits."[70] (Laurence Dreyfus argues that it can impose uniformity and knee-jerk habits of its own;[71] but I don't find these faults afflicting the artists in this book.) I will be less circumspect than Taruskin and Rosen. As someone who has reviewed and played mainly modern instruments, I've found that the best historical performers provide some of today's most insightful, original music-making. Historical reconstruction has its own fascinations, but its ultimate justification has been in the moving performances of many artists like those interviewed in this book. Moreover, no one can deny that only historical performers have made it possible for us to live with great music—from such giants as Hildegard, Dufay, or Josquin—that had been buried for centuries.

I've spoken of the incompatibilities of musicology and performance, but the two share a common interest: the same works of music. The interactions of musicology and performance can reveal important things about those works, things that would stay hidden without the joint effort. Thus my interview subjects offer us entryways into composers many of us had never heard of, like the sixteenth-century Spaniard Alonso Mudarra; they share insights into some whose music may be less familiar than we think, like Palestrina; and they make us reconsider some whose music we thought familiar, like Mozart. And my interviewees often give revealing answers to my original question, "Why do they play like that?" In doing so, they often challenge assumptions that many of us make about music.

68. "The Shock of the Old," p. 52.
69. "The Modern Sound of Early Music," p. 170.
70. "The New Antiquity," p. 231.
71. "The Early Music Debate," pp. 114–17.

❧ I ❧

MEDIEVAL MUSIC, PLAINCHANT,

AND "OTHERNESS"

We have so little evidence about how medieval music was played that any performance of it becomes, as Jonathan Harris puts it, "something of a personal vision quest."[1] We are often unsure about things as basic as a piece's rhythm, and will probably never have anything but educated guesses about less intrinsic matters such as bowing, tonguing, and voice-production techniques. As my interviewees show, however, the dearth of evidence brings forth some ingenious sleuthing.

Perhaps because the era is so distant, medievalists tend to raise the question of why we bother playing this music at all. Sometimes their answers involve what we might call nostalgia—a sense that medieval music conveys a vision of the divine, or a connectedness to the rhythms of life, that the modern world has lost. But in one way or another, not necessarily nostalgic, all the medieval performers I've interviewed express the view that encountering music from this remote time and culture can enrich *modern* life; the later interviews raise this topic less often.

That medieval music might bear on modern life is suggested by recent record sales. In 1994, a reissued CD of Gregorian chant by the monks of Santo Domingo de Silos reached number one on *Billboard's* classical charts (as of mid-1996 it had never fallen below the number three rank) and number three on the magazine's *overall* charts. At last count the CD had sold over six million copies worldwide.[2] Dozens of other plainchant-related CDs—particularly

1. Sarah Cahill, Jonathan Harris, and Bernard D. Sherman, "Berkeley Festival Stretches the Boundaries," *Historical Performance* 7 (Fall 1994), p. 131.
2. David Littlejohn, "Chant Meets Culture," *Early Music America* 2 (Fall 1996), pp. 24–32.

those of Anonymous 4—are selling briskly, at least by the modest standards of classical records. This wave clearly reflects our era more than it does medieval music. As we'll see, plainchant served its first audiences, who were also its singers, less as music than as prayer; for modern CD buyers, it usually provides ambience. Medieval monks did a lot of praying; we, it seems, need a lot of background music.

But are prayer and ambience as unrelated as they seem? James McKinnon informs us that early Christian chant was "a form of meditation," sung by fourth-century monks "for extended periods in an effort to maintain a meditative state."[3] Later on, monastic life became more communal and regulated, but, says Christopher Page, chanting was still meant to calm the mind, body, and senses in order to create a "meditative quiet" in which "a monk could hear the voice of his Creator."[4] Such total involvement is obviously very different from background music; but there may be a connection. When we use chant for ambience, the only "meaning" involved seems to be a vague feeling of time-less, otherworldly purity and calm—which we hope will give temporary relief from the pressures of time and the world. Although chant seems to have conveyed more specific feelings and meanings to its monastic singers, didn't they also use it—as we do—to screen out such pressures?

The four interviews that follow all include attempts to understand what chant meant to its originators (the recurring emphasis on chant is not by my design). We'll see that theorists of the later Middle Ages discussed conventional associations between the elements of plainchant and specific emotions (though we could question whether such theory governed practice), and that many chants were associated in people's minds with specific liturgical events—associations that we lack. Still, as I've suggested, it might be worth asking whether what chant and other music meant to medieval people has any continuities with what it means to us, and what such continuities might be based on. As we've seen, "otherness"—the idea that the experiences of people from remote times and places have little significant in common with our own—has been claimed for a composer as recent as Mozart; how much more might it apply to a medieval hermit or minstrel? On the other hand, nostalgia may tempt us to exoticize those who were not really so different from us. Just how "other" *were* our medieval forebears? And would serious musicians bother with their "vision quests" if they believed that continuities with medieval experience were impossible?

---

3. James McKinnon, "Desert Monasticism and the Later Fourth Century Psalmodic Movement," *Music and Letters* 75 (November 1994), p. 507.

4. Page, "Musicus and Cantor," in *Companion to Medieval and Renaissance Music*, ed. Tess Knighton and David Fallows (London: Orion, and New York: Schirmer, 1992), p. 76.

1

A Different Sense of Time

Marcel Pérès on Plainchant

Newspaper reports on the monks of Santo Domingo de Silos have called their best-selling CD "an album of 1,000-year-old Gregorian chant" or even "1,500-year-old chant." But both estimates make the same mistake: they assume that the chants on the CD are unaltered relics from the Middle Ages. If anything in music can be shown clearly, it's that the chanting of modern monks bears only a general resemblance to what was sung a thousand years ago. The very concept of an "original form" of the chants is problematic.

Not that people haven't tried to find original forms. It can be argued that today's historical-performance movement began (like written-down Western art music itself) with plainchant. Like the CD's target audience, the nineteenth-century religious "[sought refuge] from the unwonted strangeness of the present" in ancient church music.[1] Among them were a group of Benedictines at Solesmes near Le Mans, whose attempt to resurrect ancient plainchant proved momentous. Like today's early-music performers, they wanted to get back to the way it was—in this case to a body of chant that, according to tradition, had been whispered by the Holy Spirit, in the form of a dove, into the ear of Gregory I, the pope who reigned from 590 to 614. Today it appears that Gregory had "virtually nothing to do with either liturgy or chant."[2] The misattri-

1. Carl Dahlhaus, *Nineteenth-Century Music*, trans J. Bradford Robinson (Berkeley: University of California Press, 1989), p. 181.

2. See James McKinnon's "The Emergence of Gregorian Chant," in his *Antiquity and the Middle Ages* (London: Macmillan, 1990, and Englewood Cliffs, N. J.: Prentice-Hall, 1991). This quote comes from earlier in his book, p. 19; the following discussion of the misattribution simplifies his explanation, which is given on pp. 115–17.

bution had several causes; for one thing, Gregory's sainted name lent authority to the Carolingian emperors as they replaced their subjects' many chant traditions with their single official one. They did this not only from political motives, however, but also because they believed their "Gregorian" chant to be the *authentic* early Roman one. They too wanted to get back to the way it was.

The Solesmes research into the so-called Gregorian repertory began in mid-century, and the monks eventually collected an enormous amount of original material. In 1903, after decades of internecine struggle, Pope Pius X threw his authority behind their project. Since then, the chant repertoire and style of singing developed by Solesmes has been canonized and used in most Catholic chant, including that of the monks of Silos.

But despite their stated goal, what the monks of Solesmes actually produced was very different from medieval Gregorian chant. Regarding singing style, for which evidence is scant, it seems that what they created reflects, as Joseph Kerman said, "the ideals of the Cecilian or Pre-Raphaelite movements more closely than anything that can conceivably be imagined from the ninth century."[3] It seems a textbook example of Taruskin's idea, discussed in the introduction, that historical re-creations unconsciously reflect the re-creator's taste. In recent decades, many elements of the Solesmes method, having to do with details such as ornamentation but above all with rhythm (which Susan Hellauer will discuss), have been vigorously debated and revised. Some of the best work has come from within the walls of Solesmes itself. An obvious question is whether a century from now it will seem to reflect *our* era or an advance in historical accuracy (or, perhaps, both).

Nor were the actual chants canonized by Solesmes historically accurate. Solesmes, as we've said, made the crucial assumption that there had been a pristine repertory of chant centered in Rome at the time of Gregory I, and that the rest of Europe sang distorted variants of it. But David Hiley speaks for most scholars today when he comments, "It is not at all certain that an 'original' form of this type ever existed. . . . The manuscript tradition is too variable for a single 'authentic' reading to be deduced even from a small group of the earliest sources."[4]

Since the Second Vatican Council in 1963, Gregorian chant has become a rarity in Catholic churches. As Mary Berry points out, this has proved a blessing in disguise for modern performers interested in re-investigating chant.[5] It

---

3. Kerman, "A Few Canonic Variations," reprinted in his *Write All This Down* (Berkeley: University of California Press, 1994), p. 47.

4. David Hiley, *Western Plainchant: A Handbook* (Oxford University Press, 1993), p. 628. McKinnon seems to disagree; see his "The Emergence of Gregorian Chant," pp. 111–17, where he speculates about the possibility of a stable core repertory dating from the time of Gregory the *Second* (pope from 715 to 731).

5. Mary Berry, "The Restoration of the Chant and Seventy-five Years of Recording," *Early Music* 7 (1979), pp. 197–217.

has encouraged them to pursue other approaches to Gregorian chant performance, and to explore the chant repertoires that were suppressed centuries ago in favor of the Gregorian. In these explorations, no one has been more adventurous than Marcel Pérès. Pérès has devoted his career to exploring such chant traditions as the Old Roman (which was sung in Rome, except perhaps for the Vatican, until the thirteenth century), the Beneventan (sung in southern Italy until the eleventh century), and the Mozarabic (forbidden in Spain at the end of the eleventh century, but still sung in some places until the fifteenth). Pérès has also explored Ambrosian chant, which escaped suppression and was sung in Milan—though not necessarily in its original form—until our own time, and various Gregorian "dialects," such as the seventeenth- and eighteenth-century plainsong repertoires of Auxerre, Paris, and the Italian Franciscans.

In approaching lost repertoires, Pérès has collaborated with distinguished modern representatives of non-Western chant traditions, especially the Greek Byzantine and the Syriac (Syria was the first Christian center outside Palestine). He argues that these repertories have important links with Old Roman, Ambrosian, and Beneventan chant, and that his collaborations have solved otherwise impossible performance problems. This approach, not surprisingly, has been controversial and has often been criticized by scholars. But the musical results have been, it is generally agreed, mesmerizing.

Part of the mesmerism comes, I think, from Pérès's choirboy background. He never forgets that chant was not music in the modern sense, but (since about the fourth century) the prayers of monks whose lives revolved, all day, every day, around the church liturgy. In this sense, the monks of Santo Domingo de Silos are authentic in a way that few non-monastic chant performers can be; as the interview makes clear, Pérès takes this very seriously. He emphasized this music's unmechanized, unhurried sense of the unfolding of time, and the idea that the West's experience of time has changed over the millennium. Perhaps the older sense of time, he implies, is part of what appeals to us in this music. Just how different, we might ask, was that sense of time from ours?

Gregorian Chant

For modern listeners, plainchant is usually taken to mean what we now call Gregorian chant. You've been exploring other aspects that chant has taken.

In a general sense, Gregorian chant means the chant of the Church of Rome. But in different times, places, and ideological centers, the content of this repertoire changed. Today it means essentially the repertoire that was printed in 1908 in what we call the Vatican edition, the official publication of Gregorian chant by the monks of Solesmes. In this edition, they collated most of the surviving manuscript versions of a specific chant and, using statistical methods, abstracted something they called the "authentic" version of the Gregorian melody. But they were deriving a specific chant from chants composed in different parts of Europe and different eras, ranging from early Christianity through the nineteenth century.

So a specific chant in the Vatican edition might never have existed before Solesmes.

Right. If you want to reconstruct how it was in the Middle Ages, you have to consider many other sources of information. Above all, you have to go back to the manuscripts themselves, because even the same melodies often vary greatly from one place to another. Also, in the Middle Ages each place had its own repertoire of polyphonic settings and tropes (poetic and musical comments on the canonical texts); in the Gregorian revival of the nineteenth century, they didn't want to deal with these important aspects of medieval music. Only polyphony in the style of Palestrina was held to express the "Catholic spirit in music."

Solesmes also canonized a specific style of singing, which we still hear today from most groups of monks.

Yes. Regarding Solesmes, we have to be precise about which aspect of this community we are talking about: the scholarly one, the liturgical one, or the aesthetic one.

First is the scholarly work they've done on collating manuscripts, which is very important; they were the first to publish a collection of manuscripts in facsimiles. Second is the liturgical aspect of their work, which has been focused on the idea that the Catholic Church must live in unity, having throughout the world the same liturgical practices, the restored Roman rite being the norm. So they wanted to get rid of the local traditions that still existed in the nineteenth century.

And third is the aesthetic side, whereby they developed a style that was just the opposite of the singing style of traditional church singers of the nineteenth century. These singers used to have a very strong and deep bass voice, and their chant was highly ornamented, just the contrary of what we're used to now. To Solesmes, that was an eighteenth-century tradition, and they could not imagine that that way of singing might have any links with medieval singing. We must be precise in noting that they were not at all interested in re-creating the medieval aesthetic; they wanted only to reconstruct a tradition they believed to be of the time of St. Gregory in the sixth century. The way of singing that the monks of Solesmes developed chiefly in the beginning of this century, then, was with a very high voice with an almost uncolored timbre and no ornamentation.

Their publication was not meant as a critical edition; it was a useful, practical book. It was to be used by an amateur parish choir, so they had to imagine a very simple method that would not require that the singer be able to read complex music. Dealing with theoreticians of the Middle Ages would have been too complicated. So they developed a method that most people could sing.

The Solesmes method of singing has been called "This very beautiful, very Romantic, and somehow very French tradition of singing [that] has never ceased to dominate our notion of Gregorian chant."[6] Could you explain why it might be considered Romantic and French?

Romantic, because the aesthetic beginning of this restoration was linked with the Romantic idea of a mythic Middle Ages, the "age of faith" as they used to say. Musically speaking, most of the elements of nineteenth-century musical performance are found in the Solesmes performances: the legato phrasing, the lack of ornamentation.

As for it being French, that is simply because Solesmes is in France. But we must keep in mind that all regions and cathedrals in France used to have their own styles, which disappeared after the normalization that the Solesmes style created at the beginning of this century.

Indeed, I don't try to find *the* authentic way of performing Gregorian chant. I am much too aware of all the different styles that coexisted throughout the centuries. For each manuscript, period, or repertoire, I try to create a specific performance. But above all, I try to remain open-minded and to change my interpretation if a new aspect I was not aware of comes into consideration. Each of my records shows a different approach to chant.

Reconstructing Ancient Chant

There was a range of different chant repertories and styles in Europe before Gregorian chant. Traces of some of them survive; and you've been the most active of anyone in resurrecting them for performance. How do you go about that?

I think the revival of ancient music is a sort of equation. On one side are the documents. On the other side is the performer, with his personality, voice, education, and skill in doing music and living with it. And then you have the understanding of the source. By that I mean all that the performer, and the scholars he refers to, have understood—not only of the music and its function, but also of the nature of the tools they are using today to re-create the past. That last aspect is why you must always work on the original notation, with good musicians who come from different worlds, and why you must have relations with researchers not only in your field but also in other subjects connected with yours.

In Ensemble Organum, we use singers who come from all parts of the musical landscape: from folk music, liturgical music, early music, opera, and so

6. Katherine Bergeron, "Chant, or the Politics of Inscription," in *Companion to Medieval and Renaissance Music,* ed. Tess Knighton and David Fallows (London: Orion, and New York: Schirmer, 1992), pp. 101–3. Mary Berry, "The Restoration of the Chant," describes Solesmes chant's "smooth expressive legato with its undoubted 'spiritual' quality . . . lilted accents, and the softening of the melodic peaks which gives the style its extraordinary elasticity."

on. Others are instrumentalists who come to me to learn to sing. For me the important thing is to work with musicians who can add something to what I think I've figured out. I try to be aware of my limits.

How about musicology: how do you use that?

I work from time to time with musicologists on certain specific subjects, but also with historians, philologists, liturgists, and ethnomusicologists. Since 1984, I have managed a center for the research and interpretation of medieval music at the Fondation Royaumont, near Paris. We work on research programs that may last one year or many. The role of Ensemble Organum is to make known the musical result of this research. We publish books, organize symposiums, and make instruments. We also invite a group for residence at Royaumont each year; they may also be musicologists or historians or instrument builders. We offer them the opportunity and the tools to study a specific problem. In this way, we try to be in touch with most of today's leading personalities in the study of medieval civilization.

For instance, we are engaged now in a three-year study of how aesthetics changed in relation to changes in political power, in different cathedrals in Europe. We aim to figure out how an aesthetic gained coherence in coordination with all the aspects that made up the life of the cathedral—the economy, patronage, architecture, painting, sculpture, music—that is, all the fields that work towards the celebration of the liturgy.

In the project, we are studying four cathedrals. In three of them they had a complete change of repertory at specific dates, while in the fourth, Sens, they were still singing from thirteenth-century books as late as the eighteenth century. Throughout the centuries, they wanted to keep the Carolingian traditions, because the Archbishop of Sens received his title of "Primat de Gaule et de Germanie" from Charlemagne. This shows us one of the problems often met in the history of music: how to appreciate the continuity of a tradition in one place while other musical events, sometimes very different, occur elsewhere. We tend to think, for instance, that at the time when Machaut composed his Mass everybody knew the work, and that everybody was doing music that way. In history it's been realized for several decades that this is nonsense, but in musicology you still find this way of thinking. The popularizing history of music tends to be much too factual.[7] And we lose what is, to my mind, one of the most important things we must be aware of, which is the persistence in some places of some practices in music. When you realize that in Sens Baroque music

7. On this point, see Reinhard Strohm, "Centre and Periphery," in *Companion to Medieval and Renaissance Music*, pp. 55–59, or in his *The Rise of European Music* (Cambridge University Press, 1993), pp. 62–105. Machaut's *Messe de Nostre Dame*, from c. 1360, is the earliest surviving cyclic setting of the Ordinary of the Mass to show "conception as a unit." As Philip T. Jackson writes, "In one of the ironies of music history, there is no evidence that Machaut's unparalleled work had any direct influence on future developments" (*Companion*, 120).

was coexisting with some forms of medieval music, it changes your conception of periods in music history.

I have the same kind of question regarding the changing of notation in the thirteenth century from neumes to square notation.[8] When they made this change, did they also change, in every place, the way they sang? A lot of scholars think so, but I am not so sure.

Rome is another good example of an aesthetic shift, when the Old Roman chant was forsaken and supplanted by the Gregorian at the end of the thirteenth century. One thing I have been wondering about for years, but have not been able to come up with an answer to, is this: When Rome changed from the Old Roman to the Gregorian chant, was there a change in their voice production and in the style of the music itself? The liturgy changed, but I'm not able, even after ten years of singing Old Roman chant, to define the difference in aesthetic between Old Roman and Gregorian chant, because some Gregorian chants can be understood in a certain way, in which the notation refers to certain ornamentation formulas very similar to Old Roman chant.

David Hiley notes that "the main difference between the Gregorian and the Old Roman chant concerns surface detail: Old Roman is more ornate,"[9] much more ornamented. He adds, "In many places the two versions [of a chant] are almost identical [in Gregorian and Old Roman chant] and there is evidently a close relationship between them." Scholars have argued over what this might mean.[10] What is your opinion on how the two repertories may have interacted?

At first glance, the Old Roman chant seems to be more ornamented. But in

---

8. From the ninth century to the twelfth, the term "neume" referred not to a form of notation, but to "a sounding melody, or phrase, in particular one which has no words" (Hiley, *Western Plainchant*, p. 345). Nevertheless, today the term has gained currency as a label for the kind of notation used from the ninth century to the thirteenth. Neumes did not record either pitch or rhythm precisely; their function was to indicate a melody's direction and contour, as well as certain nuances of performance. This partly reflected the orality of the tradition—the notation aided people who had already learned the repertory—and also the concept of the music, where "melodic identity meant identity of contour, not a literal identity of notes" (D. Fenwick Wilson, *Music of the Middle Ages* [New York: Schirmer, 1990], p. 25). This is true of many modal traditions elsewhere in the world.

Square notation, developed in the second half of the thirteenth century, used a four-line staff indicating the height of each pitch with square note heads (originally developed by Guido of Arezzo in the eleventh century); the notation gave some rhythmic indications as well.

9. Hiley, *Western Plainchant*, p. 532.

10. Scholars have contended that this could mean that the Roman style, in the two centuries before it was finally written down, grew more elaborate compared to the forms in use when Pepin, the father of Charlemagne, had the pope send Romans to teach their form of chant to the Franks (thus creating Gregorian chant); or that the Franks didn't understand elaborate music, so they simplified what they learned from Rome. There is also evidence that the Gregorian chant had influenced the Old Roman by the time the latter was written down. See Hiley, pp. 561–62, for a summary of scholarly arguments. Pérès argues for another interpretation.

the Gregorian neumatic notations, a lot of the signs can be performed as ornaments or even formulas.

So the traditional Solesmes concept of Gregorian chant underestimated how ornamented its early form was?

Yes. The paradox is that it's easier to know how to perform the Old Roman than the Gregorian chant. I have the impression that in most of the pieces (some are very different), we have in the manuscript of Old Roman chant a sort of recording of what a skillful and creative singer could do when performing what we call Gregorian chant. That is to say that in the Old Roman chant the ornaments and cadential formulas had been written down, but we have very few examples of notated ornaments in Gregorian chant.

The only thing we are sure of is that every important place had its own tradition. An example can help us to understand this. At the beginning of the twelfth century, the first Cistercians from Burgundy were sent to learn the Roman tradition from the singers of Metz. In music, as in all aspects of monastic life, the Cistercians wanted to go back to the original traditions, and for music this meant Rome. But the two Cistercians sent to Metz were shocked by what they heard there. They could not believe that it was the true tradition—which shows that chant singing in Burgundy was very different.

Now, their mission to Metz had been instigated by their abbot, Étienne Harding. Harding knew the Roman tradition because he had made a pilgrimage to Rome in his youth. Even if on paper the Gregorian version from Metz looks different from the Old Roman chant, it is interesting to notice that they sounded much the same, at least in the mind of Harding. So he decided, against most of his monks, to follow the Metz model. It was only after his death that the Cistercians made their reform of chant. The story reminds us that notation, even when we believe it's precise, conveys only part of the musical event. It never tells you the sound of the voices. By this I refer not only to the voice production, but also to the value of the intervals, and especially to musical practices that include the way of doing ornaments. Two melodies with different notes can be perceived as the same if they are sung with the same vocal style, and two melodies written with exactly the same notes can, if they are sung in different styles, be perceived as different.

Old Italian Chant and Non-Western Traditions

I'd like to ask you about your work in reconstructing Old Italian chant.

I started to study the Old Roman chant in 1984. When reading this music, I realized I was missing something. I couldn't understand the aesthetic of this repertoire. You can't catch it with a standard modern Western approach; you need something else. Most of the scholars who described the Old Roman chant talked about tedious, boring, unimaginative music, chiefly because it contains a lot of apparently repetitive formulas. It uses a different logic from the Gregorian one, and some musicologists, who didn't understand the way it works, concluded it was a decadent system.

I noticed that this repertoire preserved until the thirteenth century some pieces in Greek. To try to understand what was going on in this music, I thought it would be interesting to work with a Greek singer and a Greek musicologist. So I contacted Lycourgos Angelopoulos; it was really intuition, because I had heard him in concert in Barcelona a few years before, and I had a sense that he was living a lot of the things I was trying to understand—it was everyday to him. I asked him if he could be interested in working with me on the Old Roman repertoire. He told me, "I know nothing about Gregorian chant; I cannot be useful to you." I said, "That's exactly why I wanted to get in touch with you, because you don't have preconceptions. You'll come to Old Roman chant like a virgin but with all your own background."

And it was a revelation, maybe the biggest of my life. After three or four difficult days, he was able to get into the music; he brought a different mentality to dealing with the modes, the rhythms, the intervals, and so on.

You argue for a strong Byzantine influence in Old Italian chant. But David Hiley, after reviewing the evidence, argues that the "overwhelming impression is that Roman chant developed largely independently from Greek models," and that "Byzantine musical influence can be seen to reduce itself largely to a number of individual instances." (He saw more examples of Byzantine borrowings in Milanese and Beneventan chant.)[11] How would you respond?

First of all, we must consider the words we are using to talk of the past. In your question you use the words "Byzantium," "influence," and "Italian." From the beginning you assume that Byzantium and Italy had two distinct cultures and that the first influenced the second. But let us consider the facts from the beginning. From the second century B.C., the Roman and Greek cultures not only had relations, but very quickly the Greek model and its opening on Eastern cultures became the reference for Rome. And when we go to the first centuries of the Christian era, it's impossible to locate the boundary between the Roman and Greek liturgical cultures. The Roman liturgy was exclusively in the Greek language until the fourth century, and it retained a lot of Greek until the ninth century. Even in a twelfth-century manuscript of Old Roman chant you find seven Alleluias with Greek verses.[12]

11. Hiley, *Western Plainchant*, p. 527. Leo Treitler rejects the connection of Old Roman and Byzantine chant too, in that the oldest records of Byzantine chant were written down in the twelfth century and bear no resemblance to Old Roman chant. As for *modern* Byzantine chant, he says it originated in 1300, when the Old Roman chant repertory was no longer sung, and he adds that it has since been influenced by centuries of Turkish occupation. See "Remembering 'Early Music,'" in *Thesis* 8 (Fall 1994), pp. 32–33.

12. See Hiley, p. 538.

In the mind of Boethius, the sixth-century Roman philosopher and theoretician of music, there is no distinction between Roman and Greek music. For him, it's very clear that the theory of music is Greek. This conception will stay the norm among most of the medieval theorists; even if some authors are very far from the Greek original, they will go on using Greek terms in order to look educated. This community of culture is obvious not only in music but in many other fields.

After the Gothic domination, Byzantium reconquered Italy in 533, and its domination, although merely symbolic from the eighth century on, lasted until Charlemagne's coronation as Western Emperor. During the seventh and eighth centuries, fourteen popes were Greek, most of them from Sicily, where there was a very strong Greek community from antiquity until the thirteenth century. Also, the iconoclastic persecution in Byzantium in 726 sent many of the Greek religious to Italy. Let us keep in mind also that the Emperor of Byzantium had the title of Roman Emperor.

Once this has been settled, it's possible to observe how with time the Italian and Greek churches and chants evolved in different ways. Western, Eastern, and Greek aesthetics must not be considered homogenous blocks. The different styles found between and within the three Italian repertoires show us that important diversities existed.

To come back to our subject, which is musical performance, we are in the same situation as a linguist who tries to find the sound of medieval Latin by studying today's Romance languages. Of course, for centuries there have been differences between all these languages and the original Latin. But some words have not changed, such as *sol* for "sun" in Spanish, *stella* for "star" in Italian. We could find thousand of examples like them. In music it's the same process. You find in the Italian repertoires—the Roman, the Milanese, and the Beneventan—some formulas or ornaments that are still living in Byzantine, Syriac, or Coptic pieces. The process in experimentation is not to imitate the models slavishly but to use their information to figure out the dynamism of these dead musics. The common roots of Eastern and Western chant should be studied, but not in order to prove anything.

One repertoire you've recorded did survive in a living form until our time: the Milanese "Ambrosian" chant. But in your CD notes you point out that it was much influenced over the centuries by Gregorian chant, and that originally it had been sung, according to Ambrose, "in the manner of the East." You worked on that, too, with Eastern collaborators.

Yes, there we went further in our experiments. The Milanese liturgy had roots in the Antiochan [Syrian Christian] liturgy, and at different times in its early history Milan had been in relation with Syria and even had Syriac bishops. We tried, as a working hypothesis, to distinguish traces of Syriac chant in the Milanese repertoire. I worked not only with the same Greek singer, but also with experts in Syriac chant, with the Lebanese singer/musicologist, Sister Marie Keyrouz, and with the Lebanese musicologist Elie Kesruani. They opened another field that I had not imagined at all, because Marie Keyrouz had another approach to music, to modality, and to the value of intervals. From the beginning, she told me something very important: "This music [Milanese chant] is a music of intervals." That means you really have to be aware of the value of each interval, because it's what creates the mode; the ornamentation is there to throw the intervals into relief. This was something quite new to me. Western musicians, when singing monody, are too little aware of the quality of intervals—but that is what produces the real character or mood of the mode.

Could you give an example?

In the offertory of the Milanese Christmas mass, *Ecce apertum est,* there's a mode that alternates B♭, low B♮, and high B♮. When this formula reaches its highest point on a low B♮, the A is sharpened. When the formula reaches its top on the C, the B♮ is high. So you can imagine the complexity of the music. In each formula, you must always discern which note exercises a power of attraction that redefines the value of the intervals of the scale.

And regarding the role of ornamentation she mentioned?

Marie Keyrouz is very sophisticated in the art of ornamentation. This is something we have lost in the West. Even in Baroque music, most singers don't have enough imagination to go very far in ornamentation. Some jazz players do it, and some Baroque players, like Jordi Savall, have a freedom in ornamentation and a quality of nuance that you don't find in many singers. Singers like Marie Keyrouz have this knowledge. I think what will be really important in early music in the next few years will be the progress of singers in the art of ornamentation. In old traditions that's what made the quality of a musician: someone was a distinguished musician because he had his own way of ornamenting.

Ornamentation has been one of the hallmarks of your work, but in some repertory it has been controversial; for example, some argued that there was no evidence for what you did in your reconstruction of the Gradual of Eleanor of Brittany. How would you respond to such critics?

That they should improve their knowledge of the thirteenth century. In fact, it's from that century that we have the first precise description of ornamentation, with the treatise of Jerome of Moravia, a Dominican friar. I have managed to do two books on him.[13] As I said, ornamentation is the big lacuna in

---

13. *Jérôme de Moravie, un théoriticien de la musique dans la milieu intellectuel parisien du XIIe siècle* (Paris: Créaphis, 1992); and *Jérôme de Moravie, Traité sur la musique,* ed. Christian Meyer, trans. Esther Lachapelle, Guy Lobrichon and Marcel Pérès (Paris: Créaphis, 1996).

the early-music revival. Now it's accepted for seventeenth- and eighteenth-century music, but not yet for Renaissance and medieval music. I feel like saying to those who believe people started to add ornaments on New Year's Eve of 1600: Wake up!

One other interesting area you've explored is the use of microtones—tones that fall between the usual twelve pitches used in the modern Western scale. You say microtones were used in early chant traditions?

There are two approaches to this problem: the manuscripts, and the oral traditions that still exist. From the written documents, we know that microtones were known, because a lot of theoreticians talked about them, and we have at least three manuscripts that refer more or less explicitly to some microtone practices. To my knowledge, the first mention of microtones in Western writings, after Boethius, are in Remigius of Auxerre (d. *c.* 900), a Frankish theorist. In one of his texts he uses a Greek musical vocabulary, meaning that at this time the Greek vocabulary was in use among educated musicians. He uses this vocabulary to talk about quarter tones and thirds of tones: so such intervals were known, though we don't know how they occurred in the music. After that, the next book to give us this information more precisely is the Montpellier Treatise [copied *c.* 1100]. In this manuscript you have a dual notation: one form uses neumes, and one uses letters of the alphabet from A to P to cover a two-octave range. In this notation you have two ways of signifying the quarter tone. The two other manuscripts I referred to—a twelfth-century antiphonary from Utrecht and another one from Cluny—have the same kind of chromaticism, often at the same places. But as they are just neumatic manuscripts, they use different neumes' shapes to express these variations.

Now, all this is useful information, but the problem is how to deal with it. For some examples we were able to find some correspondence with Byzantine or Arabic theory, but for some examples we were not. The latter cases may have involved things that had disappeared in Byzantine tradition, or that occurred in Latin music only.

Another practice you've taken from Greek tradition in singing Old Roman chant is the use of ison *singing—the use of a vocal drone pedal point—which is first documented in Byzantine chant in the fifteenth century, but of course may be older. Many critics find it hypnotic, but nonetheless it is controversial; how would you respond to critics?*

There is some evidence that this practice might come not from the Greek but from the Latin. As you said, the use of the *ison* seems to be known in the Byzantine tradition around the fifteenth century, but not in other Eastern churches. The first clear description I know of this technique, though, comes from a Western source, the *Micrologus* by Guido d'Arezzo in the eleventh century. For him it was a sort of organum.[14] He teaches us that this practice was common in Rome. We know from the *Ordines Romani* that by the seventh and eighth centuries there were traditions of organum singing in the pontifical chapel.[15] Later the anonymous author of the *Summa Musice*,[16] a treatise written around 1200, describes the sort of organum that consists of a drone. He calls this manner *diaphona basilica*: that's very interesting, because the term *basilica* in liturgical matters often refers to the Roman tradition. So in the thirteenth century there was still in the vocabulary of singers a word that seems to referred to the Roman Basilican tradition and that means a vocal drone. It is very possible that the Greeks borrowed this practice from the Italian singers. We find in some fifteenth- and sixteenth-century Greek sources, written in Byzantine notations, some instances of polyphony in this style with parallel fifths and contrary motion. In one manuscript a rubric says, "This is done in the Italian way." We know that from the thirteenth century the Italians, chiefly the Venetians, had a very strong influence in some regions like Crete and in Byzantium itself, where there existed a strong Latin government for almost seventy years. So there is a strong basis for this scenario.[17]

But, you know, above all it is important when you make a theory to experiment and see how it works. In this matter, the big question is, Why do we have so few recorded instances of drone singing? Was it so common that it was not necessary to talk about it? Or maybe some people did not consider it a form of polyphony at all, as is the case today in Greece, so that maybe it was assimilated into monody. Or maybe it existed in only a few places. But musically speaking it works, and that helps us to better hear the modal structure of a piece.

14. "Organum" meant several things, but in this context it meant, in general, singing two or more related lines, as opposed to just the single line of plainchant. See Sarah Fuller, "Early Polyphony," in *New Oxford History of Music,* II, rev. ed., ed. R. Crocker and D. Hiley (Oxford University Press, 1990), pp. 484 et passim.

Guido describes several organum practices, and he notes that practices varied from one locale to another. His text has been published in English translation in Warren Babb's *Hucbald, Guido, and John on Music* (New Haven: Yale University Press, 1978). The section suggesting what we call *ison* singing is on p. 80 (section 211).

15. The *Ordines Romani* were "Frankish reports of Roman practice." See Richard Crocker, "Liturgical Materials of Roman Chant," in *New Oxford History of Music,* II, rev. ed., p. 139.

16. *Summa Musice,* ed. and trans. Christopher Page (Cambridge University Press, 1991). The description of *diaphona basilica* is on p. 124.

17. Pérès recommends Michael Adamis, "Some Instances in the Byzantine Manuscripts Indicating a Relation to the Music of the West," in *Polyphonies de tradition orale: Histoire et traditions vivantes,* ed. Michel Huglo and Marcel Pérès (Paris: Créaphis, 1993). On the other hand, Dimitri Conomos's "Experimental Polyphony in Late Byzantine Psalmody," in *Early Music History* 2 (Cambridge University Press, 1982), pp. 1–16, suggests that *ison* was introduced into Greek singing several decades after any Italian influence—which was in any case quite "isolated"—had run its course.

Time and the Nature of Plainchant

Katherine Bergeron writes: "It may be well to ask from the start whether chant can properly be considered 'music' at all. . . . [It had] an eminently practical purpose: to make ritual words audible, memorable, and powerful . . . in this sense a particular chant is hardly different from a spell or incantation, a set of specially pronounced words designed to bring about a certain magical result."[18] Could you comment on this, and on how that affected both the way chant was composed and sung in earlier centuries and the way you perform it?

The answer is very simple. To really restore these musics, and clarify their vocal aesthetics, it's better to reconstruct the liturgies they belonged to and to believe in what you are doing.

This is what I found, for example, when I started working with Lycourgos Angelopoulos. He has another way of approaching time. This is because he is a real church singer. He is used, for instance, to singing for liturgies that go all through the night. So he really has experience of the pace of the liturgy, and that's very important. The biggest criticism I would make of many reconstructions of medieval music is that, listening to them, I don't feel the atmosphere of the ancient liturgies. I think you must be able to visualize all the stages and the movements of the liturgy whose music you are singing. To know the Eastern liturgies can help us, since today the Catholic traditions are almost dead. I had a traditional Catholic education; and fortunately I work with Syriac and Byzantine church musicians.

For your concerts, you dress liturgically.

Only for our liturgical dramas. It is really necessary to play dramas because it's the best way to get into the spatial and temporal dimensions of these musics, as it's very rare to have the opportunity to perform them in true liturgies. It is also fundamental to get used to working with candlelight. That was a constituent part of the liturgy. With candles, you have lights around you, but large parts of the room are darkened. Today, due to electric light, people have lost the habit of living with the night. When people have lost the habit of living with the night, the night doesn't exist. To live surrounded by the night gives you another way of understanding the mentalities of the past. The candle is a living light as fragile and powerful as human life. It always reminds you that light is not to be taken for granted; you have to be conscious of it.

Contemporary Catholic clergy have lost the sense of light and sound. Even in Europe, where we have old churches planned according to the position of the sun, they use electric lights during the day. For today's Christians that's a secondary, even nonexistent matter, but in the tradition of the Church of all centuries it was a crucial point. It's a disaster that the Roman Church aban-

---

18. "Chant, or the Politics of Inscription," in Knighton and Fallows, *Companion*, p. 101.

doned the liturgy in Latin, because all the people who were able to transmit the tradition are now very old, so we'll have a break in the transmission. But I think Latin could come back to the liturgy because young people have an attraction to plainchant . . .

As the monks of Silos found out . . .

Yes, and it's significant that the age range of the customers in Europe was 18–25, because these people did not grow up with the Latin liturgy and plainchant. That suggests that the Church made a mistake.

The earliest notation of plainchant had to do with the melodic gestures' motion, rather than with the exact pitches or rhythms:[19] the time wasn't notated exactly. That was because of the oral nature of the tradition; but does it fit in with your view of liturgical time?

Yes, and that's why we're a little bit lost with these notations. Now we are used to a mathematical division of time, but we must remember that this has been true only since the end of the thirteenth century. Before that, people had no way to write these things down.

Is this why you've been opposed to singing Notre-Dame organum with strict proportional rhythm?[20]

Yes! In the polyphony of the twelfth century, we know from the notation that this note is longer and that shorter, but not exactly *how much* longer one note is than another. We can get a sense of what this might mean from music we still have that reflects a mentality that treats time differently than we do in the West today. For example, in Corsican polyphonic singing they don't have a tempo with a beat, they just have the time of the chords, and when the energy of the chord starts to diffuse it changes. Time becomes a succession of focuses of energy each with a period in itself, and almost every chord has its own period. When you feel the end of the period of this chord you move; it's not something you can divide arithmetically, saying this chord is two times longer or three times longer than the last one.

So it seems that there are two ways of perceiving time—qualitative and

19. See above, note 8.

20. Organum at Notre Dame in the thirteenth century seems to have been sung using what are called "rhythmic modes," codified around 1240, whereby notes had specific durations relative to each other. There were six rhythmic modes, all in triple meter; they were developed for singing polyphony, but their interpretation is not entirely clear. (Their application to monophony is much more troublesome still.) Hendrik van der Werf writes that a belief in the omnipresence of modal rhythm in Notre Dame polyphony "is now waning." He specifically notes that in polyphonic passages in "sustained pitch" style—as opposed to "pitch against pitch" style—the note lengths were probably not modal; his interpretation is congruent with Pérès's (van der Werf, "Early Western Polyphony," in *Companion to Medieval and Renaissance Music*, p. 112).

quantitative. The quantitative manner began to be created during the end of the thirteenth century and developed in the later centuries. But the older way of thinking about music co-existed as well. It's funny, because the trend in all the spheres of social life and science of this time is to rationalize things. For example, the first mechanical clock was invented at the end of the thirteenth century.[21]

We did a symposium on this four years ago,[22] in which we tried to figure out how in a place like Paris many thinkers in different fields intended to give a description of time and to find a tool to describe it. In that century many different authors proposed a system, but the systems don't all fit together. The most exciting of the treatises was that of Jerome of Moravia, who wanted to put in a book all the musical knowledge of his time. Writing of polyphony, he says, "Many different authors have their own way of describing the rhythm, and I think the best thing to do is to present all these treatises and let the reader make up his own mind." At this time, around 1265, they knew they were on the verge of reaching something, but it was only in the fourteenth century that a notational system would be standardized.[23]

Even when this notational system was standardized after the fourteenth or fifteenth century, the old mentality continued to exist. Although the mechanical clock was invented at the end of the thirteenth century, it doesn't mean that a few years later there was a clock in every home. In the country today, farmers still have to live with the seasons; for them, in the winter and summer 8 o'-clock doesn't mean the same thing.[24]

Music is a tool that can help us to better understand history, how human beings used to be, used to live. It also can help us to increase our sensibility, our aesthetic sense. When we learn the ancient arts, we start to develop our sensibilities to be able to perceive more things in the reality of our human relationships and ways of living. Quality of life is one of the most important things we can learn from people of the past, because one thing we have to learn from the past until the nineteenth century is that people had a different qual-

21. See David Landes, *Revolution in Time* (Cambridge, Mass.: Belknap, 1983), p. 53, though he considers references to clocks from before the fourteenth century a little uncertain.
22. Proceedings published in *La rationalisation du temps au XIIe siècle* (Paris: Créaphis, 1995).
23. Christopher Page's essay "Ars Nova and Algorism" in his *Discarding Images* (Oxford University Press, 1993), pp. 112–39, relates the rise of measured music to scientific trends of the era, especially the wider adoption of Arabic numerals—but not to the clock. Page also discusses the issue of time and notation in his interview, and arrives at conclusions opposite to those of Pérès regarding medieval polyphony.
24. I am not convinced that clocks had much impact on the development of quantitative rhythm; see the Postscript to the Christopher Page interview, where I mention my reasons briefly. This is not to say that I think Pérès is necessarily wrong about rhythm in Pérotin or in Corsican chant; but that the explanation for the change to more quantitative rhythms in music might lie elsewhere.

ity of life—one that, at most social strata, had certain cultural advantages that we have lost, in spite of all the technical progress . . .

   . . . sometimes because of it . . .
   . . . yes, but we make poorer the quality of everyday life. For instance, in churches, even in Europe, they use microphones for the liturgy. That means we have lost a quality of hearing and of voice production. The same thing for lighting; I talked before about candles. If you light the church with candles, the mood you create—the quality of the space and time—is really something different and is worth the experiment. There is no reason to lose these things.

SELECTED DISCOGRAPHY

Marcel Pérès has made a number of recordings for Harmonia Mundi, and even readers with little interest in plainchant might find them fascinating. The best starting points may be the discs that include non-Western singing, especially the one featuring Beneventan chant (HMC 901476) and the second of those featuring Old Roman chant (HMC 901382). Both feature Lycourgos Angelopoulos, with his extraordinary microtonal ornamentation and un-Western voice production; the results in both cases are hypnotic—a word many enthusiastic critics have applied to it. The same adjective is often applied to his recordings of other repertory discussed above—e.g., the Milanese chant CD (HMC 901295), which includes Marie Keyrouz.

   It would be misleading to imply that the reviews have been unanimous in praising Pérès's chant CDs. One persistent critic has been Jerome F. Weber, who thinks that many of the performance practices used have no scholarly basis; he often objects, for example, to the use of drones and of "Eastern" ornamentation. Reviewing a recent Pérès CD of Mozarabic chant, Weber says that it sounds "less like any other recording of Mozarabic chant (few as they may be) and more like [Pérès's] own recordings of Gregorian, Cistercian, Old Roman, Ambrosian, and Beneventan, and Neo-Gallican chants." (He says this same criticism applies to another wide-ranging director of plainchant, László Dobszay.)[25] Weber is, however, enthusiastic about Pérès's recording of the Mass of Tournai (HMC 901 353), which he thinks is clearly the best realization of that manuscript.[26]

   From the chant recordings, one might turn to Pérès's recordings of later repertoire. These bring up a theme that recurs often in the other medieval and Renaissance interviews in this book, and even in some of the Baroque ones— English versus Continental singing styles. Fabrice Fitch describes the difference well in his review of Pérès's Ockeghem Requiem (HMC 901441): "The tenors'

25. Weber, *Fanfare* 19 (November/December 1995), p. 453.
26. Personal communication, 1996.

emphasis on chest-tone clearly differentiates them from their English counterparts. It is as though English ensembles match their lower voices to the high partials of the choirboy and the countertenor, whereas ensembles like Organum start from the basses' rich, deep low Cs and build upwards."[27] Despite reservations regarding a few pitch standards and tempos, Fitch is enthusiastic about this recording. Pérès interpolates plainchant, treating the Requiem as the Mass for the dead it was meant to be, and while Fitch usually experiences such interpolations "as so many distractions from the polyphony," here he finds them "literally awe-inspiring." He also calls Pérès's recording of Josquin's *Missa Pange Lingua* (HMC 910239) "superb."

FOR FURTHER READING

Plainchant has inspired an extremely active and wide-ranging body of research over the last generation. To do justice to it all in one book would clearly be impossible; David Hiley has done the impossible in his *Western Plainchant: A Handbook* (Oxford University Press, 1993). This *magnum opus* is indispensable for anyone interested in chant.

I don't know of a better introduction to chant than James McKinnon's chapter, "The Emergence of Gregorian Chant in the Carolingian Era," and Hiley's "Plainchant Transfigured," both in McKinnon's *Antiquity and the Middle Ages* (London: Macmillan, and Englewood Cliffs, N.J.: Prentice-Hall, 1991), the single best introduction to medieval music. For those wanting more musical detail than McKinnon aims to provide, David Fenwick Wilson's *Music of the Middle Ages* (New York: Schirmer, 1990) is excellent. All these books also discuss non-Gregorian chant; those seeking a more advanced discussion might try the *New Oxford History of Music*, II, rev. ed., ed. Richard Crocker and David Hiley (Oxford University Press, 1990), Part II.

Katherine Bergeron's essay on the nature of plainchant in *Companion to Medieval and Renaissance Music*, ed. Tess Knighton and David Fallows (London, Orion, and New York, Schirmer, 1992), quoted above, is a high point in a very stimulating book. Her essay on Pérès and the Silos monks, "The Virtual Sacred" (*The New Republic*, 27 February 1995, pp. 29–34), has been controversial partly, I think, because it has been misread: her real subject is not early music, but what the chant phenomenon says about spiritual life in the 1990s.

David Landes's *Revolution in Time* (Cambridge, Mass.: Belknap, 1983) is a first-rate history of the clock and its impact on Western civilization. Paul Fraisse's "Rhythm and Tempo" in Diana Deutsch's *The Psychology of Music* (New York: Academic Press, 1982) summarizes a wealth of research on time perception in music.

---

27. *Early Music* 22 (February 1994), p. 155.

2

You Can't Sing a Footnote

Susan Hellauer on Performing
Medieval Music

Medieval composers rarely expected their sacred music to be listened to for its own sake. They designed it to accompany church services—events of solemn meaning for medieval worshippers, but not for modern concert audiences. On top of that, they set texts with little appeal or resonance for most modern listeners. For these reasons, their music translates to the modern concert hall with difficulty. Anonymous 4 have been unusually successful in this act of translation; my discussion with Susan Hellauer focused on how the group approaches it.

We also discussed their extraordinary popularity, their appeal to a "crossover" audience whose usual interests do not include medieval motets and sequences. Popularity, the group told me, was something they had neither sought nor expected. At the time of the interview, February 1994, their first two CDs were bestsellers, and they had appeared on Garrison Keillor's radio show and in an interview in *USA Today*, a publication not known for the height of its brow. But it wasn't until a few months later that the four singers, all veteran performers of medieval music, felt secure enough to at last become full-time musicians. Their musicianship deserves no less; but what exactly was its large-scale appeal? Their pure, celestial sound might be at least a factor. I discussed that sound, too, with Hellauer.

Historians writing about American beliefs at the end of the second millennium may note that in 1994 at least a score of angel books were published, that two of them made the *New York Times* bestseller list, and that angelic images adorned T-shirts and college dorm rooms, side by side with posters of death-rockers.[1] All of this, too, may be relevant to understanding the wave that Anonymous 4 has caught; as a German critic wrote of them, "They sing like angels."

Offstage, these singers are wonderfully down-to-earth—and humorous, as suggested by their group name (though the name is, as our interview shows, a meaningful one, it is actually a play on the designation given by modern scholars to a medieval theorist whose name is not recorded). I met with Susan Hellauer on the morning before an Anonymous 4 concert, and began by asking her about their new-found (and still baffling) celebrity.

An English Ladymass reached number three and On Yoolis Night reached number one in the Billboard charts. [So did, since then, their third release, Love's Illusion; it was Billboard's "Classical Disc of the Year" for 1994, as Ladymass had been for 1993.] You've said that this took you by surprise; why do you think it's happening?

We may not be the right people to ask! Perhaps the answers lie in the hearts of our listeners, and in the minds of the record company executives, who keep their fingers on the popular pulse far more than we do. An audience member at a recent concert suggested that our performances create a space for contemplation, an opportunity often lacking with the frantic nature of most daily routines. Much of our repertoire is contemplative in nature. Perhaps there's something in that explanation . . . In any case, we are mystified and delighted at the response to our recordings and performances.

Many people think that the repertoire you sing, and also the music of Arvo Pärt and John Tavener, taps into New Age spirituality—just like angel books, for example. Have you or Harmonia Mundi USA done anything to reinforce a connection to these things?

We have never tried to tailor either the repertoire we sing or the way we sing it to any particular audience. As an ensemble, we have not attempted to connect ourselves to New Age spirituality. Whatever our listeners' religious or spiritual leanings may be, there would probably be a common belief among us that creating and appreciating beauty are food for the spirit. As for Harmonia Mundi, they give us free rein in terms of choice of repertoire and its performance, and they fully support our musical decisions. We leave the marketing to them.

Much of your music was written for a liturgical context, but now it's listened to in a concert or on a recording. Those are very different listening contexts—we go to concerts not to worship in a service that's supported by music,

1. "Angels Everywhere," *The New York Times,* editorial, 4 September 1994.

but primarily to listen to the music. How do you translate music written for one context to others that are very different?

It's a very complex issue, one that has been on our minds from the very start in 1986. There are several possible solutions. To illustrate one extreme, some ensembles present medieval music in the tradition of the nineteenth-century song recital. They wear formal dress. They begin their concerts by bowing to the applause of their audiences. They sing a number of pieces, receiving applause after each work or "set." Their concerts include an intermission, and may be followed by one or more encores. Some groups use this format very convincingly. The other extreme is the complete reconstruction of, say, a liturgical service with everything but the priest—as, for instance, Ensemble Organum does so superbly. (Of course, the liturgical drama is a different category: the music, its order, and the dramatic continuity at least are provided within the structure of the work.)

One of our first ideas about how we were going to structure our programs came from an uneasy feeling we had all occasionally had when hearing or performing in concerts of this music presented recital-style. These might be programs of wonderful music, well performed, but they consist of a succession of beautiful miniatures, often with little connection beyond their all being from more or less one time or possibly from one place. After about the tenth or fifteenth similar piece, it can be almost impossible to absorb any more. And when the pieces share little similarity, it can be hard to concentrate, or to come away with a feeling of completeness. From the very start, our most important objective has been to make stylistically cohesive programs, each built around a thematic concept, but including enough internal contrast to show off each work to its best advantage. This might occur naturally in a liturgical service, but we didn't feel that the answer for us was in going all the way to complete reconstruction.

The development of each of our new programs is a major effort—much more work, we believe, than making a recital program. Each one needs quite a long gestation. We begin with the concept: a particular manuscript (the music for *Love's Illusion* comes from the thirteenth-century French Montpellier Codex); a historical liturgical practice *(An English Ladymass* is an evocation of the thirteenth- or fourteenth-century votive mass to Mary as it might have been sung at the Cathedral of Salisbury); or a portrait of a historical or legendary figure *(The Lily and the Lamb* is a depiction of the intensely personal suffering of Mary at the foot of the cross). Once we have decided on the theme for a particular program, we have to find and select the music. We look for both continuity and variety in the music, and for musical texts which help to illuminate the theme in question.

Some of those texts involve concepts modern people can relate to—devotion, romance, suffering—but others are more difficult. An extreme case is when a medieval text is objectionable to us in some way. I'm thinking of the anti-Semitic passages in medieval and Renaissance sacred music and in chant; and secular songs that treat wife-beating or rape as a huge joke. How do you deal with such texts?[2]

Depending on the situation, we've dealt with it in several ways. For example, texts about rape (or attempted rape) do occur in the motets from the Montpellier Codex, the source for our program *Love's Illusion*. Luckily, we had so many other pieces illustrating aspects of courtly love that we could simply ignore the most repulsive ones. However, the four of us didn't always respond identically to what I would call "borderline" texts, which denigrate women in various ways but don't go all the way to force or violence. It was a matter of negotiation, based on the shape and requirements of the program, and on our own feelings. I don't think any of us would sing a song trivializing rape or wife-beating.

We've also come up against anti-Semitic texts. If a work is strophic and the anti-Semitic text is in isolated verses, as in Pérotin's monophonic conductus *Beata viscera*, we omit the offending verses in performance (although we haven't yet found a solution for recording such a work). Where the anti-Semitic text consists of only a few words, we actually change the Latin and explain in our program notes what we have done.

The way we choose to handle these problems is very personal; we wouldn't presume to mandate it for anyone else. Of course, we recognize that these pieces, with texts that are in some way objectionable to us today, are important historical documents, reflections of their times. But we don't want to contribute in any way to a pervasive sense that women are things or that hate is an acceptable way of life.

Getting back to the program-development process: once you've decided on the theme and chosen the music, what next?

We use either our own transcriptions or good modern editions, and prepare the music to our satisfaction. The order of the pieces and their key relationships are crucial, as are variations in texture and voicing. We complete the design with poetic or prose readings, which add a sense of the unfolding of a narrative, bringing the program to about 75 minutes in length. Our programs have no intermission, and we request that our audiences not applaud between pieces. The result feels to us more like a story than a concert. This story-like function, with continuous communication and dramatic flow, is really at the center of everything we do.

2. This topic was discussed by Lawrence Rosenwald, "On Prejudice and Early Music," *Historical Performance* 5 (Fall 1992), pp. 69–71, and by a number of respondents to his essay, including Barbara Thornton and Richard Taruskin, in the pages that followed and in the following issue of *Historical Performance* (Spring 1993). Taruskin has since written about it elsewhere, notably in "The Trouble with Classics: They're Only Human," *New York Times*, Sunday Arts and Leisure section, 14 August 1994, pp. 25 and 31, reprinted as the title essay in his *Text and Act* (New York: Oxford University Press, 1995), pp. 353–58.

Of course, your earlier observation is correct about liturgical polyphony not being meant for concert performance as we know it. There are some similarities, in that in the medieval church service there was an audience listening (attentively, one presumes), undistracted by food, conversation, or other pursuits. But there are three principal differences between medieval sacred music and music intended for concert performance: context, anonymity, and textural rhythm.

First of all, the medieval audience for liturgical polyphony was listening in a very different context than most modern audiences. As you said, these listeners were there primarily to worship and only secondarily to hear music (although there undoubtedly were exceptions!), and the meaning of the particular feast being celebrated created a context and emotional framework for the music. In the U.S., at any rate, only one Christian feast still has this kind of power, and that is Christmas. If you grew up in—or in close contact with—Christianity, you know what strong emotions a hymn like *Adeste fideles* can create on Christmas Eve. But hearing that hymn on a hot summer day is like finding shoes in your refrigerator—completely out of place. In the Middle Ages there were many feasts besides Christmas: each one had its identifying music that was heard only once a year and that had tremendous emotional power. We feel that it is our job, through the selection and arrangement of musical texts and poetry or narrative, to create something approaching that emotionally powerful context for the music we sing.

The second point of difference is the lack of acknowledgment for the medieval composers/performers themselves: what we would call anonymity. Medieval church musicians composed and sang as do their modern counterparts; but it was *soli deo gloria* [to God alone the glory]. This is why so few of their names have come down to us. And the singers were not supposed to be the center of attention in a liturgical service (although there were certainly instances of church singers in the Middle Ages receiving reprimands for their tendency to show off).[3]

We try to evoke this sense of anonymity by structuring our programs in a continuous flow, and by avoiding extensive solo singing, suppressing applause between pieces, and refraining from encores, all elements which tend to draw the audience toward the performers and away from the narrative. The only star in each of our programs is the program itself.

The third element of difference is the naturally occurring textural contrast or rhythm in a festive medieval liturgy. We frequently use liturgy—both Mass and Office—as a structural framework; we find that it helps to provide us with the right balance of continuity and contrast. Along with varied textures and types of polyphony during the celebration of the feast, there was also plenty of

---

3. References to vocal "excess" by clerical singers in the thirteenth century can be found in chap. 6 of Christopher Page's *The Owl and the Nightingale* (Berkeley: University of California Press, 1989) and in his interview, below, p. 74.

chant—in fact, the service was mostly chant—and it varied greatly, from the simplest psalm tones, prayers and readings to long, elaborate, and virtuosic graduals and responsories. And so from the beginning we were determined not to neglect chant, either in the amount we include in our programs or in the attention we give to its performance.

Even an all-chant program needs textural contrast. While developing our program of music of Hildegard von Bingen, we found that alternating her strongly expressive, pungent works with plainer chant in something like their original liturgical order greatly heightens their effect and, we think, comes closer to reproducing the startling first impression they must have made. We think of Hildegard's virtuosic chant, or virtuoso polyphony, as exquisite gourmet dishes. As wonderful as they are, we wouldn't think of serving them alone; we prefer to serve them with good plain rice to clear the palate and act as a foil to their complexity.

I wanted to ask you about your performance of chant. For one thing, if one doesn't know anything about chant, one assumes that it's easy to sing, whereas, oh, Wagner and Berg are hard to sing. But people who sing chant assure me that it's difficult both to understand and to sing.

The assertion that singing chant is easy is based on the assumption that increasing vertical and harmonic complexity in music represent definite progress along a continuum from primitive to civilized, from immature to mature. The truth is that the medieval chant from western Europe that has survived, and that we can decipher, is the flowering of a long and marvelous development, and its masterworks are as subtle and artfully crafted as any polyphonic work could be. The means of communication are different, but the performance of these works deserves and requires no less skill and devotion. On average, it takes us longer to prepare a substantial work of chant than it does a polyphonic work. We must first pay close attention to nuance of verbal accentuation, musical line, and phrase relationships; only then can we begin to make music—but it is music of the highest level, very exposed, very intimate, very rewarding. There is a kind of ego submersion that is necessary as well—to create something that becomes greater than the four of us, yet remains part of each of us. It's a mystical thing in its own right, bringing together four very different voices and four very different personalities, so that in any particular chant, the listener hears a sound that is all of us and none of us. Singing chant is great training for the kind of ensemble consciousness that we strive for when we prepare and perform all of our repertoire, both monophonic and polyphonic.

That could be part of the popularity of chant—maybe it appeals to those who want to experience something communal, as opposed to isolated individualism. Anyway, there's another issue: expressiveness or not in singing chant?

Aha! There's a word—"expressiveness." We throw it around easily, like the word "progress," but what does it really mean? Singing expressively can mean different things in different vocal repertoires. The uninflected delivery of a traditional Scottish ballad singer telling of blood-curdling deeds is just as riveting as the vocal intensity of Tosca pouring out her anguish.

There are some who believe that it is inappropriate to respond to word stress, accentuation, and meaning when singing chant. However, we feel that our individual emotional responses to the music and texts of chant contribute to the ensemble's artistic interpretations. For us, the key to expressiveness lies in definite nuances in rhythm and dynamics in response to the text and its meaning, and to word stress and musical line. In a leaderless group like ours, it's the response that's tricky, because no two people (let alone four) respond to a musical line or a text in the same way. Working out the nuances that reflect our emotional and artistic responses to a work is just as important as working on pitch and rhythm. We hope that comes across.[4]

Some people have remarked to us that our singing seems much more flexible and emotionally involved than do recordings of chant performances by monks or nuns, and they ask what theory of chant performance we follow. We don't subscribe to any particular modern theory, but we are probably closest in spirit to one of the earliest leaders of the Solesmes chant revival, Dom Joseph Pothier (1835–1923), who favored a free, oratorical rhythm, based on speech. It was the later Solesmes-movement leaders who devised the basically equalist, "ictus"-ized rhythmic guidelines, in an effort to create uniformity of performance.[5] In fact, the earliest Solesmes editions from the 1880s don't contain the ictus and other phrase marks so characteristic of the mod-

4. For a somewhat different view of expressiveness in chant, see Christopher Page's interview, pp. 79-81.

5. Solesmes was discussed in detail in the Marcel Pérès chapter. One enormous challenge Solesmes faced was reconstructing the rhythm of early Gregorian chant. The Solesmes edition of 1905, which set the monastic chant-singing style for much of this century (as heard in the recordings of monks and nuns that Hellauer mentions), included a number of rhythmic indications; these included accents to mark the "ictus"—that is, in this usage, the first pulse in what Solesmes understood as groups of two of three pulses. As Hellauer notes, these indications are now considered misleading and without historical justification. In the last forty years, new scholarship—particularly that of a Solesmes monk, Dom Eugène Cardine—has led to some advances. (See David Hiley's *Western Plainchant: A Handbook* [Oxford University Press, 1993], pp. 373–85, for a detailed discussion of rhythmic notation of chant.) Among the schools that have been somewhat discredited are the mensuralists, who argue that "the notes of chant have various fixed time-values, or that some system of strictly proportional measurement is to be applied to the performance of chant," and (as Hellauer notes) the equalists, "who hold that all notes of Gregorian chants are more or less of equal duration so that there is a single basic time-value" (the definitions quoted are by Mary Berry, in her "The Restoration of the Chant and Seventy-five Years of Recording," *Early Music* 7 [1979], p. 217). Cardine's views are similar but not identical to those of the equalists: "a theory of syllabic equivalence, relating the length of notes to the normal delivery of a syllable with a single note" (Hiley, p. 382).

ern Solesmes books—with a few exceptions, these markings are not at all medieval.

This brings up a broader authenticity issue. Scholars need to doubt their convictions or at least test them against the evidence; but performers, to really perform well, need complete conviction, beyond all doubt. To reach such conviction, they have to go beyond the evidence. How do you deal with these issues as artists performing music of the past, music that today is so involved with scholarship?

Since it's impossible to know what medieval music originally sounded like, no one can ever claim that they know exactly how to perform it. Scholars can argue and argue; they may even throw knives at each other—early in this century, one French musicologist challenged another to a duel over whether or not troubadour music should be transcribed in rhythmic modes.[6] But since our job is to present this music in performance, we are forced to make *musically* viable choices. As I often say, You can't sing a footnote.

That's a great motto—but could you say a bit more about it?

Well, I don't mean to imply that the performers can do without the scholars; they need to work together in order to make informed decisions about performance. We've had important help from several outstanding scholars, and they've been as generous and understanding as they have been meticulous in their work.

The facts that scholars have uncovered are the firm foundation on which our imaginations can build. But sometimes the facts are insufficient to complete the picture, or scholars disagree about what they mean. Then we have to make choices that convince us, and that will convince our audiences. Our working goal is very simple: to gather the sources and the available interpretations of the facts and, with those in mind, to come to an agreement about how to present each piece. Then each of us can express whatever it is she wants to express within the boundaries we've set. Each piece is very carefully worked out, but it has to sound effortless in performance. That's where the hours and hours of rehearsal come in.

It shows. For one thing, your intonation is amazing.

We'll never stop working on it. We don't follow a particular theory of tuning, but we do have to take care in tuning certain intervals.

___

6. Actually, the two musicologists, Jean Beck and Pierre Aubry, both agreed that the troubadours had used the modes (six specific rhythmic patterns used, at least sometimes, in thirteenth-century Parisian polyphony); the argument was over which of the two had thought of it first. Ironically, it is now felt that the troubadours did *not* use the rhythmic modes. The duel never came to pass: while practicing his fencing, Aubry was fatally wounded. It should be noted that in France in 1910 literal dueling was still possible; today's musicologists stick to verbal swordplay.

In the full triads found in later music, there is a wider acceptable range for the placement of the harmonic third. But for medieval repertoires, we need to adjust the size of our thirds according to the melodic mode. And in twelfth-through fourteenth-century polyphony, in which many of the nodal points (such as cadences) consist of an open fifth (with no third), the intonation bull's-eye is very small.

Accuracy of tuning is especially crucial in pieces that are very dissonant, such as thirteenth-century French motets. We sometimes sing ten beats in a row with seconds or sevenths occurring vertically, and if we're not perfectly in tune they all sound like mistakes; but when they're right, they sound really spicy. It's similar to some twentieth-century music, where the intonation has to be very crisp and clean so that sense can be made out of dissonance.

Singing in tune is both an individual and an ensemble skill. In order to bring our tuning to its finest point, we have to examine the way in which our individual voices work together. For example, we often have to modify one person's pronunciation or shaping of a vowel sound so that even our overtones will match.[7] That's where more hours of rehearsal come in!

Could you discuss one issue that musicologists disagree about: the role of women in the music of this era? Scholars have argued, for example, over whether or not women sang fourteenth-century English sacred polyphony.[8]

Women in convents probably sang chant just as much as men in monasteries did. Hildegard of Bingen and her community certainly provide evidence of that. We don't know whether or not women sang sacred polyphony; but since much of this music is for equal voices (and since *we* can sing it), we think it's possible, and even probable, that they did. Of course, women were not welcome to sing in cathedrals (unless they disguised themselves as men, as they did for other reasons). With regard to secular music, there are many paintings and illuminations, as well as literary references (Boccaccio's *Decameron*, for one), that depict women participating both as singers and as instrumentalists in the high Middle Ages.

7. Christopher Page writes about a related issue: "In every language there are dark vowels and bright vowels, and the dark ones must often be sung slightly sharp in order to avoid giving an impression of being more than slightly flat. (The radical vowel in British English 'father' is an example of a dark vowel; it accounts for the flatness which is often heard when performers of plainchant sing the final note of a melisma on the word 'Alleluya')": in *Performance Practice: Music Before 1600*, ed. H. M. Brown and S. Sadie (London: Macmillan, 1989, and New York: Norton, 1990), p. 84.

8. For example, Frank Ll. Harrison argued that a certain fourteenth-century English motet was sung by nuns, but Roger Bowers has strongly disputed this point. See Bowers's "English Church Polyphony, c. 1320–c. 1390," in *Studies in the Performance of Late Medieval Music*, ed. S. Boorman (Cambridge University Press, 1983), p. 188. In any case, the narrow pitch-range of medieval music, discussed in Christopher Page's interview, allows a quartet of women to sing it without revision.

Apart from historical issues, do you think there are any purely musical advantages to having polyphony sung by women's voices rather than by men's?

One of our reasons for starting Anonymous 4 was to experiment with the sound of this music as sung by higher voices. And some of our listeners have commented that the individual lines of polyphony sound more clearly etched in our voices than in lower voices. We've been told that this might be explained by the fact that low voices singing polyphonically produce more acoustical combination tones in the audible range than do our higher voices. But, of course, the study of acoustics is not our area of expertise!

Clearly the women's voices appeal to audiences. So many of your reviewers say that you sound like angels. Care to comment on that?

The acoustical phenomenon may help to explain it. Also, since its revival in this century (until quite recently), it's been outside the norm for women to sing medieval music. Of course, in real life we're not exactly angels.

SELECTED DISCOGRAPHY

Since their first release, Anonymous 4 has been recording new CDs for Harmonia Mundi at least annually. The releases so far have been consistently fine. Of their first, *An English Ladymass* (HMU 90 7080), David Fallows writes, "There may be some question of whether it is historically appropriate to sing the English polyphony of the years around 1300 with women's voices only; but that is not the point. What is clear is that some of it sounds magical that way on their record. . . . This is because the higher voices help to clarify the texture in a way that pays enormous dividends for complicated music."[9] As an example he mentions the four-voice motet *Salve mater redemptoris,* "where the details and textures are far more transparent than in any all-male performance and the music comes across with an irresistible swing." Most critics have greeted the group's other CDs with similarly warm praise.

The only criticism of the group I've encountered, in fact, is Tess Knighton's concern that in *The Lily and the Lamb* (HMU 90 7125) "the harsh and dramatic nature of the texts is here too often belied by the beguiling performances."[10] She says the group provides "the ethereal qualities of The Tallis Scholars . . . further disembodied." Knighton singles out *Jesu Christes milde moder* as the only piece that conveys "the emotional and physical asperity of the Crucifixion." Nicky Loseff says of the same performance that it "evokes the pain of the crucifixion . . . intensely." But she considers this typical rather than exceptional, saying that in general "it is this direct connection between poetic meaning and musical interpretation in polyphonic items which most sep-

9. Fallows, "Quarterly Retrospect," *Gramophone* 71 (December 1993), p. 33.
10. Knighton, *Gramophone* 73 (September 1995), p. 98.

arates Anonymous 4's approach from that of other high quality ensembles."[11] The two critics' disagreement may reflect nothing more than differences in subjective response; but it may also reflect different ideas about the nature of expressiveness in medieval singing. Hellauer discusses this in her interview, and the issue returns in the Christopher Page interview.

One item in the group's discography is an example of the crossover, mentioned in the introduction, between medieval/Renaissance performers and contemporary composers. Richard Einhorn's oratorio *Voices of Light* (Sony SK 62006) uses Anonymous 4 to collectively represent the voice of Joan of Arc. The piece refers to early music in terms both of idioms (e.g., parallel organum and plainchant) and of instruments (viola da gamba).

FOR FURTHER READING

A good introduction to the English medieval repertory—which Anonymous 4 has recorded on three of its discs—is found in the relevant sections of David Fenwick Wilson's *Music of the Middle Ages* (New York: Schirmer, 1990). More detail can be found in chaps. 9 and 14 of *The New Oxford History of Music*, II, rev. ed., ed. Richard Crocker and David Hiley (Oxford University Press, 1990). More detail still can be found in John Caldwell's *The Oxford History of English Music*, I (Oxford University Press, 1992).

---

11. Losseff, "Anonymous 4, an Ensemble Apart," *Early Music 24* (February 1996), p. 176.

3

Vox Feminae

Barbara Thornton on Hildegard
of Bingen

Hildegard (1098–1179), the founder and abbess of a Benedictine nunnery in Bingen, Germany, first came to the attention of modern America in a book about headaches. Oliver Sacks's 1970 book *Migraines* included an essay[1] arguing that Hildegard's mystical visions were "indisputably migrainous," although with characteristic open-mindedness he has also written that this "does not detract in the least from their psychological or spiritual significance."[2] What is significant for my discussion, though, is that in describing Hildegard's "exceptional intellectual and literary powers"—shown in her work as, among other things, a mystic, poet, naturalist, and playwright—Sacks made no mention of her music. This oversight was by no means unusual; even many music historians in 1970 knew little about Hildegard.

Today Hildegard is known chiefly for her music. What brought about the change was a pair of 1982 CDs, Gothic Voices' *A Feather on the Breath of God*, and Sequentia's *Ordo Virtutum*. Both still stand among the best-selling recordings yet made of early music. Several factors have been suggested for the discs' popularity, among them Hildegard's appeal to the rising interest in women's spirituality, the feminist search for great women composers, and—a factor we have already encountered—the quest for transcendence, by the same audience that has since made best-sellers of the monks of Silos and Anony-

1. The essay, "The Visions of Hildegard," is reprinted in Sacks, *The Man Who Mistook His Wife for a Hat* (New York: Summit Books, 1986), pp. 166–70.

2. *Ibid.*, p. 130; the comment comes from Sacks's introduction to the section of the book that contains the Hildegard essay, and applies not only to Hildegard but to others discussed in the section.

mous 4. All these factors intertwine, no doubt, with an essential one: Hildegard's musical and poetic genius. No one can reasonably claim that her works need any special pleading based on her gender.

Hildegard's "everflowing, rapturous outpouring of melody"[3] seems unusual even to those who know little of her contemporaries' music; according to Barbara Thornton, who knows a great deal of such music, Hildegard's musical language surpasses that of her contemporaries in "intensity and breadth."[4] Thornton's own contributions to the Hildegard revival include scholarly articles and the reconstruction of the *Ordo Virtutum* (The Play of the Virtues), an allegorical music-drama, which she has not only recorded but has also published, staged, and had filmed; above all, they include her performances, which convey Hildegard's vision with special fervor. Thornton is now recording Hildegard's complete works, a process to be completed in time for Hildegard's 900th birthday in 1998.

Thornton, an American-born soprano, began working on medieval music with her partner, Benjamin Bagby, in 1974, when the two were graduate students at the Schola Cantorum Basiliensis in Switzerland. In 1977 the pair founded Sequentia, which performs a wide range of medieval music, from Occitan troubadour songs to Old English sagas to early polyphonic motets. The group is based in Cologne, about 75 miles (as it happens) from Bingen. Our discussion of Hildegard reveals Sequentia's general approach to preparation: an uncompromising immersion in the music, language, texts, milieu, and cultural as well as musical sources. It includes using only the original medieval notation, and memorizing everything performed, for reasons that become clear when Thornton speaks about orality in medieval culture.

I interviewed Thornton when she was touring with Sequentia's ensemble of five women, Vox Feminae, in a program of music by Hildegard. Their concert the next day was in San Francisco's Grace Cathedral, a Gothic structure with a reverberation time of about six seconds. The architecture was appropriate— the Gothic style emerged during Hildegard's lifetime—and with its stained-glass light reflected Christendom's turn toward subjective, personal religious feeling, which finds such strong expression in Hildegard's music. The acoustics proved appropriate, too: while a twelve-part Renaissance Mass would have been lost in the echo, Hildegard's "ecstatic devotions" (as the program notes called them) seemed all the more celestial.

Hildegard's era, the twelfth century, was innovative and transitional—the era when Europe began to rediscover Aristotle, when modern scientific thought began to emerge, when Christian piety became more personal and emotional

3. Mary Berry, *Gramophone* (May 1995), p. 94

4. Thornton, "*Vox Feminae*: The Ecstatic Devotions of Hildegard von Bingen," (program notes, 1993), p. 3.

as opposed to sacramental, when the Virgin Mother really took a central place as a figure of devotion, when the idea of "courtly love" emerged, the seeds of humanism were sown, and so on.[5]

In many areas of thought, certainly in those of literature and music, the eleventh and twelfth centuries demonstrated an enormous burst of energy which modern writers have often called a renaissance of sorts.[6] However, I think it is now accepted that "renaissances" are actually very carefully prepared in previous times: for example, the great surge of so-called Marian worship, which came to pervade every aspect of twelfth-century art, had been gaining momentum since the ninth century.

Musically, the twelfth century seems to me in a way the apogee of the archaic mind. In it the mind has not yet become technological in our modern sense, but has reached an enormous imaginative flowering according to pre-existing rules. In this sense, twelfth-century music fits a certain modern approach to the idea of what an avant-garde is: in its search for innovation and new expression, it takes even the most archaic forms and uses them to make new music. Our era has become interested in so-called primitive ways of life and of thinking—African art, modal music of all varieties, shamanistic traditions, etc.—as it has, in a sense, exhausted the rationalistic way of doing things; our era has also discovered that there is an attractive radicalism in so-called archaic world views.

The musical/poetic spirit of the twelfth century entails both tradition and innovation. It is very forward-looking and avant-garde, because creators considered their own creations as utterly new; but the older rules of operation were never abandoned. There's an insistence in certain musical and poetic repertories on the idea: "This is *nova cantica*," "this is new song." Of course *nova cantica* is a term that comes from the Bible, in several different contexts, but it also reflects the sense in which we today say "this is new music"—this is the latest, this is the hottest, this is the newest, this is refreshing, this is going to wake up parts of your spirit that have been asleep. And yet there is no sense at all of "to do this we have to cut off from what came before." It's rather very

5. For more thorough discussion, see the relevant chapters in Norman Cantor's introductory history, *The Civilization of the Middle Ages* (New York: Harper Collins, 1993), notably pp. 306–56. To quote another writer, A. C. Crombie, it was in the twelfth century that "men of philosophic temperament began to turn away from the vision, given them by St. Augustine, of the natural world as a symbol of another, spiritual world, and to see it as a world of natural causes open to investigation by observation and hypothesis." In Crombie, *Science, Optics, and Music in Medieval and Early Modern Thought* (London: Hambledon Press, 1990), quoted in Christopher Page's *Discarding Images* (Oxford University Press, 1993), p. 11.

6. See Christopher Brooke's *The Twelfth-Century Renaissance* (New York: Harcourt, Brace and World, 1970); *Renaissance and Renewal in the Twelfth Century*, ed. R. L. Benson and G. Constable (Oxford University Press, 1982); and Dom Jean LeClerq's *The Love of Learning and the Desire for God*, 3rd ed., trans. C. Misrahi (New York: Fordham University Press, 1982) on monastic life in the period. Finally, the "dark underside" of the twelfth-century renaissance, the increased persecution of groups such as the Jews, is discussed in R. I. Moore's *The Formation of a Persecuting Society* (Oxford University Press, 1987).

much in the spirit of this era to imagine a tree of Jesse, coming from deep roots and spreading infinitely from its fertile origins.

How did Hildegard, with her huge range of accomplishments, fit into this era?

There were not many people like Hildegard in her era. There were some other "universal geniuses," however. One, for example, was the theologian and poet-composer Peter Abelard, who added a great deal of original work to the tradition and was an accepted though controversial master. Another was the poet-theologian Alan of Lille. Hildegard can easily take her place among those two. She's also been compared to the Arab philosopher-encyclopedist-healer Avicenna [980–1037].[7] She was well known in her period, though not as well known as Abelard or as widely read as Alan of Lille. But unlike Abelard, she took the necessary steps to ensure that she not fall into disfavor with the higher political powers of her day and that her position stay secure within the Church. Over time she also gained official recognition of her gifts as a prophetess and visionary. Without that official recognition, she probably would have had more clashes with authority than she did have. In fact, toward the end of her life the prelates of Mainz decreed a temporary ban on music in her cloister, in response to a perceived disobedience on her part.[8] But in general, she knew which important steps to take to ensure her creative freedom. If she had come under the shadow of serious suspicion, the authorities would presumably have cut her off very quickly.

In Hildegard we also see someone who, within that secure position, saw to it that her works were documented. She seems to have had scribes of the highest caliber, copyists with great expertise in music notation, even very gifted illustrators; she was obviously in a position to call on the best people. In this she resembles composers of later centuries such as Guillaume de Machaut and Oswald von Wolkenstein, poet-musicians who also supervised the creation of manuscripts of their works.

Could you say something about her background?

At the age of eight, she entered a Benedictine double cloister—a monastic community consisting of men and women, where all labor and forms of wor-

---

7. By Peter Dronke, *Women Writers of the Middle Ages* (Cambridge University Press, 1984), p. 144. He also compares her to Goethe.

8. "Many wealthy people" buried family members at her convent. One such burial, in 1178, was of a nobleman who had been excommunicated, though in the end he was reconciled with the Church. The prelates of Mainz alleged, however, that he had died excommunicate, and they ordered Hildegard to remove his remains or be excommunicated herself. She refused, and also defied (and challenged in writing) their ban on music in her convent. Her nuns chose to remain with her and thus be excommunicated as well. During this episode, the Archbishop of Mainz was in Italy mediating between the Pope and the Emperor Frederick Barbarossa; in 1179 the Archbishop made it possible for the ban and excommunication to be lifted. See Dronke, pp. 196–99.

ship were carried out equally but separately—called Disibodenberg, near to her birthplace. This cloister must have been very aristocratic, and intellectually of very high standards. For most of her early life, Hildegard was cloistered alone with an older woman, Jutta of Spondheim, who taught her in isolation for many years. Her education must have included a formidable body of religious knowledge. Apparently, this woman was also her teacher in areas such as healing—what we would call medicine—and in what we would call natural sciences. A recent article by the medieval scholar Peter Dronke[9] identifies some of the more obscure writings that Hildegard must have known when she was putting her own writings together. He concludes that she had one of the better educations available at the time, if we can speak in such terms. Perhaps the terms "privately tutored" and "self-educated" might be appropriate for describing how she came to command such a breadth of knowledge and originality of thought.

Dronke in this article refers to some very esoteric works known to Hildegard. She seems to have had access to some quite progressive and up-to-date material whose Latin was rich and full of images, as was fashionable then. More general influences came from her lifelong familiarity with the Bible and its commentaries, and the writings of the Church fathers. In addition, twelfth-century thinkers were drawing on much Platonic literature, and on many sources of music and drama from Antiquity. Perhaps the most pervasive influence of all came from religious rites at the convent, and all the types of contemporary music and poetry that would have been heard in a well-to-do, mainstream monastic institution of the time.

So this cloister presumably had a large library, and a source of new books?

Yes; but it seems, according to newer assessments of medieval intellectual life, such as those of Mary Carruthers and her school,[10] that in this era books were crucial to the tradition but were not used in a manner we are accustomed to. A book, as a repository of thought and wisdom, was almost a symbol of the intellect's ability to store words in memory so that they could be used at will for reasoning, speaking, and composing. It has been crucial for us, dealing with all periods of the Middle Ages no matter how advanced, to be sure that we understand that basic premise. It was common that in one's education the available works of Plato and other philosophers, the Bible, commentaries, and other favored works, were interiorized through active memorization more than just being read off the page. An intellectual would have memorized—using certain systems for facilitating the process—vast amounts of knowledge in his lifetime. Therefore learning, certainly of music and literature, took place mostly on an oral basis.

9. Dronke, "Platonic-Christian Allegories in the Homilies of Hildegard von Bingen," in *From Athens to Chartres: Neo-Platonism and Medieval Thought, Studies in Honor of Edouard Jeaneau,* ed. J. H. Westra (Leiden: E. J. Brill, 1992).

10. Carruthers, *The Book of Memory* (Cambridge University Press, 1991).

How does this orality apply to Hildegard?

Hildegard wrote some very intriguing things about her own processes of musical creation. As you know, she claims to have heard her songs directly from the Spirit with her "inner ears," although (she explains) she did not "know neumes"—meaning she did not know how to notate music. Some modern writers have taken this statement to be an expression of false modesty on her part, or a way of strengthening her claims to having "mystic" or direct connection to divine inspiration, which would seem to use her ignorance as a medium for reaching her senses. I have no way of knowing in exactly what spirit she makes the claim of "seeing" and "hearing" Divine Light. I do not think it beyond imagining that she would assume a humble personality as a literary device, or attempt to create a mythology out of her gifts and works in order to give them authenticity. She may, indeed, have created an acceptable persona for her peers, in order to remain in a position to continue her various enterprises. In any case, what is significant from the practicing musician's point of view is that her claim is, in fact, a plausible statement from any accomplished musician of the period. The realms of theorizing about or notating music were separate from that of actually producing sounding music. In both cases we're dealing with skills of a highly specialized nature reserved for very few people. In general, the class of the musically active was not musically literate (this situation changed over the next few centuries).

Once you take that premise of orality seriously, it changes very fundamentally all your opinions and feelings about the evidence that comes from the period. In particular, people had interiorized their knowledge to such an extent that adding a commentary or contribution of one's own to the body of knowledge was already an enormous step. For us today it's easy to say that an intellectual contribution should be above all "original," but for twelfth-century thinkers originality would be expressed differently. Probably the majority of one's intellectual life consisted of exchanging and transmitting knowledge with other individuals who had the same sort of deeply stored textual information; exchanging ideas on this material was already one vital level of intellectual creativity in the period. To take the next step, then, and document in written form one's original opinion or commentary upon the basic body of knowledge would imply that a very creative contribution was being made. While to us it may seem that commentators of this type were adding minimal amounts of information and new thought, it is actually because we approach "knowledge" with a fundamentally different philosophy from intellectuals of that period. We tend to "project" knowledge into books; they stored it, had it readily available, *used* it to build their souls. When we see representations of monks laboriously copying books and adding their commentaries, we are actually in the presence of those people who were recognized as masters in their tradition.

In musical situations as well, the risk, the audacious step, of adding melodies to the existing canon was one taken only by a master.

Regarding Hildegard, what was the body of existing music that she was working from?

Her compositions are strictly religious, and seem to be very much based on the ideas and traditions of Gregorian chant; they take the elemental ideas, such as modes, formulas, and subject matter, and widen the scale of the whole experience both technically and emotionally.

So Gregorian chant is the tree of Jesse you spoke about at the outset?

That would be a way of putting it, yes. To people who are involved in the notation and realization of Gregorian chant, tenth- through twelfth-century new music must seem very simple, actually. The complexities in notation and in theology and literary exegesis are heavily concentrated in Gregorian chant; twelfth-century pieces add a certain transparency, certain "performance qualities" if you will. Such pieces are usually intended to embroider central events in religious services, be it a Mass or an Office. This embroidery creates new forms and attitudes, and gives an outlet for contemporary feeling and thinking. On the level of real composition and experience, our pieces are elementary compared to Gregorian chant—they were intended to be that way. Anyone who's interested in the molten core of this whole process needs to look at Gregorian chant, its notation, its history, its performance, its repertoire. Then the newness of our music becomes apparent.

From modern writers we might get the impression that there is something simple and cute about medieval melody; this is a fundamental misunderstanding. There is enormous power implied in these kinds of modal melodies, but only with a great deal of study can a modern person add the imagination necessary to understand what is implied and to realize the intended effects. Although we do have direct evidence about instrumental music—we know there was an art and tradition of arranging notes without texts—the heart of medieval tradition is liturgical, which is preserved as an untouchable and unalterable repertory of chant. As a composer, you didn't try to *change* that repertory; you spent your life trying to realize it. Then, if you wanted to entertain yourself and your friends and have literary/musical experiences of a new sort, you might, based on this intense relationship to certain themes, add individual arrangements and pitches and so on, but drawing from an enormous reservoir of communally interiorized associations. Modal music lives from these kinds of associations, just as language does.

So you're talking about associations with specific Gregorian formulas and melodies from a standard repertoire?

Yes. All modal musics seem to enjoy this fluidity, this protean quality which allows a gesture to take on one meaning within one context and a different one in the next context. People are writing very interesting things in ethnomusicological circles[11] about how modal or proto-modal music systems work which shed light on these processes. In our experiences in Sequentia, we have found that a modal gesture does not unfold uniquely on the "horizontal" level as a melody might. A modal system is much more a matter of defining some very simple constructive principles, attaching meaning to those simple elements, and then learning to combine them significantly.[12]

Now, the modal system is always significant, but it's relatively undogmatic despite its elemental laws. It is also open to exceptions (here too it is a lot like language and grammar). But one must build up associations to the elements and combinations in order to understand the next level of significance.

Now, I don't suppose there is an essential difference in this respect between modal and tonal music. I suppose they could be considered ancient and modern versions of the same language, the only difference being that the average listener has built up these associations only for tonalities and not for modalities. As a result of our lack of associations, though, when we hear a modal figuration we make an inner judgment as if it were a melody. Because we're so busy with the melody on the horizontal level, we can't appreciate the very specific messages of modes. Each gesture shows a new understanding of how to combine elements and colors. If we don't relate to the fundamental colors, we won't hear the individual shadings.

What do you mean by color? You don't mean timbre, obviously.

I don't, you're right. The "color" is the emotional effect of the relative placement of pitches in a modal gesture. It means, for example, that *intervals*, especially imperfect ones,[13] are never "absolute" but always derive their significance from their modal context. On the other hand, the actual *pitches* of the *gamut* (the known spectrum of pitches) do have some "absolute" associa-

---

11. Leo Treitler cites the ethnomusicologist Robert Ridgely Labaree's studies of troubadour songs, which suggest applying to plainchant ideas developed in the study of Irish music. See section VII of Treitler's "Sinners and Singers: A Morality Tale," *Journal of the American Musicological Society* 47 (Fall 1994), pp. 137–71.

12. See Leo Treitler's work, for example "Centonate Chant," *Journal of the American Musicological Society* 28 (1975), pp. 1–23. Treitler differs with some predecessors who argue that chant composers put together pre-existing formulas into an artistic whole; he says instead that as all these chants were memorized, it was natural that certain "well-defined moments in the progress of chants (openings, cadences, continuations after cadences, settings of words with particular syntactical functions such as conjunctions)" would tend to become standardized within a genre of chant, and that what was in between would be less fixed (I quote from "Sinners and Singers," p. 149).

Regarding oral cultures, see Walter Ong, *Orality and Literacy* (London and New York: Methuen, 1982), chaps. 2 and 3.

13. The "perfect" intervals are the octave, the fourth, and the fifth; all the rest are "imperfect."

tions. The composer plays with both levels when he sets up an arrangement of modal gestures.

Not surprisingly, I think one's real associations to modes develop through practice, not through descriptions such as I've tried to give. Medieval modal music, like other modal musical cultures, is a very practice-oriented tradition. You can't learn to associate from music theory books, or from schemes that show modes in a scale, because a mode doesn't exist in a scale. Presenting a mode in a scale is the worst thing you can do to it. It would be like writing a treatise on painting by saying, Here is the row of pigments—red, orange, yellow, green, blue—now you understand how to combine them. It doesn't tell you anything about, for example, how modal colors relate to emotions.

This is part of why text is so important to our music, for the emotional world of the text constitutes the fundamental color of a musical composition. We have also found some old treatises, such as ninth- through eleventh-century handbooks for cantors, to be helpful in revealing contemporary ways of looking at "Gregorian" modes.[14] The authors of such books developed a tradition of terms and affects associated with the several modes.[15] For example, what we call Dorian mode—the D-oriented or "protus" mode—for them had the quality of *gravitas* (it was grave in the sense of solemn) and also had the association of *nobilitas*, nobility. It was called *fons et origo*, the source and origin of all other modes. If you superimpose these ideas upon a string of pitches in this mode, you also get a concrete result. Superimposing upon the music the emotional idea of a text then represents another level which must be interiorized in a given piece.

You mentioned text as a color. It's sometimes asserted that in medieval music the text was primary, and the music decorated it; and sometimes the opposite is claimed.[16] How do you apply this question to Hildegard?

I think that in making music of any sort, but especially in singing religious music, the process which results when text and music combine cannot be analyzed in this way at all. I can't see that one element in this process could possibly dominate the other. Leo Treitler, whose writings have influenced our work, uses the term "text carrier" or "text vehicle" for medieval music. That usage has been interpreted as relegating music to a subservient role; but I think that perhaps demonstrates a certain lack of understanding of how medieval people thought of "word." Word *(logos)* is practically the Tao of Western civilization.

That fits in with what you've been saying about its being an oral tradition: Walter Ong writes that oral cultures commonly, and probably universally, con-

14. See Harold Powers, "Mode," III, 1, in the *New Grove Dictionary of Music,* vol. 12 (London: Macmillan, 1980), pp. 397–401.

15. See Christopher Page's interview, p. 80–81, for a more detailed discussion of this.

16. See Page's interview for his views—very different from Thornton's—on text expression in medieval music.

sider words to have enormous power,[17] *though that implies the primacy of the word—as in* "in principio erat verbum," *in the beginning was the Word.*

But ascribing great power to words doesn't necessarily grant them primacy. It is hard to convince modern people of one basic truth: that the medieval poems *are* music in and of themselves. This idea is fundamental to the classic definition of poetry—"words set to music" (with or without pitches). It depends on how intensely you relate to the poetry to know just how the music of a text operates. So to say, as some people do, that the word comes first and the music comes second is an absurdity, because to the medieval person the concept of music is an all-encompassing idea; it's the most divine thing a human being has at his or her disposal. It's even more divine than Word, because it reaches above human words to superhuman WORD, and it's thoroughly inexplicable in its origins and effects (although it obeys certain laws). In the mind of a medieval person, it comes as close as anything can to giving an image of what cosmos and soul are like. Augustine's treatise *De Musica* deals with music, as such, in terms of texts because, he says, one experiences the proportions of all types of harmony more clearly through texts. This was the accepted way of looking at music in the Middle Ages. So to combine the music of word and the sounding music of pitch represents an extreme potency in and of itself; we ought not try to pull it apart and say which should come first, word or music, because it puts us in the wrong frame of mind.

Moreover, a medieval cleric heard and sang vast amounts of music in the Latin language in his lifetime. Clerical musicians experienced music and text in the highly integrated form of Gregorian chant, and it formed the psychic background of their own music-making. So the question of which comes first would be meaningless to them. They'd have lived with the power of chant all their lives.

Regarding Hildegard's own use of the word, Peter Dronke writes, in the liner notes to your Symphoniae *CD, that her* "poetic effects are often strange and violent," *not smooth like those of most of her contemporaries, and that her anaphoras, superlatives, exclamations,* "daring mixed metaphors," *and intricate grammatical constructions make her Latin stand out in her era.*[18]

All I could add from the performer's point of view is just how effective these metaphors and images (and even the strange things she attempts) really are. In his article about her influences, Dronke traces the origins of some of these obscure images. He quotes a passage where Aristotle says that the merit of a poet lies in his metaphors. A more pragmatic statement might be that the merit of a poet is tested by how much life is in the images he or she creates. One cri-

17. Ong, *Orality and Literacy*, p. 32. On p. 93 he discusses this with reference to societies where writing is restricted to certain sectors, as in Hildegard's time.

18. *Symphoniae*, Deutsche Harmonia Mundi (DHM) 77020–2–RG; booklet, p. 9.

terion of poetic merit from the memorization treatises of Antiquity and the Middle Ages is the vividness of a given allegory or image, making it suitable for memory. Their theory of memorization had to do with making one's soul receptive to the energy of imaginative material. A creative person was an image maker, and the effectiveness of a creation could be judged by the relative ease or difficulty with which one could interiorize the images. If they were easily interiorized and seemed to live within one, both immediately and over the long term, then perhaps one could say that the poet was very good. Without question, Hildegard is such a poet-creator-musician. You never tire of her images. They're very specific, very intricate, very alive!

Could you give an example?

One might be her imagery for Wisdom from her antiphon *O virtus sapentiae:* "You power of Wisdom/ that circled circling/ and embracing all/ in a course that is filled with life—/ You have three wings:/ one soars into the heights,/ another has moisture from the earth,/ the third flies all around."[19]

As that example may show, the ways her images are chained together always has an extremely organic logic that the body and the mind are more than willing to follow, and there's something so musical and pleasing about the process of interiorizing these images. Of course, the music facilitates that. It bring these image-experiences into the self in a very specific—modally specific—way. Everything is crafted to the utmost, so that one is very quickly in a position to live what's being composed. I think that's a good criterion for judging a poet-composer.

You said that in music she derives her procedure from the tradition of Gregorian chant, but expanded it. Could you give an example?

Remember, Hildegard was by no means unique in having based her flights of imagination upon the stable repertoires of her experience. It is the power and scope and degree of surety in her flights that contributed to her individual, recognizable musical style, and this is extremely rare in the Middle Ages. As an example, one might look at the (presumably) tenth-century antiphon *Alma Redemptoris Mater* and a composition of Hildegard's called *Ave Maria, O auctrix vite.* Her piece could be called a composed improvisation upon all the elements found in the older liturgical piece—its mode, its message, its individual gestures, its overall curve and construction. One can truly appreciate the inexhaustible source of invention which was Hildegard's when one sees how skillfully she has embroidered upon the original material.[20]

19. The piece is recorded on Sequentia's *Symphoniae* CD.
20. These two pieces are presented in succession on Sequentia's CD *Canticles of Ecstasy,* DHM 05472–77320–2.

Regarding the element of musical craft, in describing how you developed the Ordo Virtutum, *one thing you mentioned was that to Hildegard different instruments represented different things—the strings earthly striving, the harp heavenly blessedness, the flutes the presence of God. You used this information in scoring the piece.*

That was based on her other theological works, which were very helpful to our preparation because she expresses herself so vividly—and repetitively, so that certain ideas gain stable associations in the mind. And her feeling for music is prevalent no matter what she's writing about.

We still take the poetic license offered to us by her poetic vision of seeing everything, including instruments, in terms of the divine scheme. She gives very specific information about how she thought various aspects of music affect the soul. This is completely in keeping with other things you can read from the period, that all disciplines—rhetoric and grammar, arithmetic and so on—are intended for the enrichment of the soul. Therefore, instruments, by their very natures, communicate diverse modes, emotions, and symbolic associations, in addition to being embodiments of *musica instrumentalis.*

We don't use instruments nearly as much now as we did when we recorded the *Ordo,* which was over ten years ago. Instruments were very helpful for singers not initiated into modal thinking, and we're a little more secure in our feeling for modes. Instruments—or should I say instrumentalists—realize these things so quickly and clearly. Instruments stimulate imagination: they are very potent, and they should be used as judiciously as possible, so that the word and the modal gesture, whether realized by voice or instrument, remain the main sources and means of impregnating the imagination.

That brings to mind Hildegard's mysticism; does it influence your approach to her music?

One must probably take seriously her accounts of how she had visions and heard music; she says that her compositions are not, strictly speaking, her works, but that she functioned as a medium for them. I do take that seriously, even if I don't always understand what it might actually imply. Today the creative personality is made the object of a cult and is exalted as such; in her era that concept of the solitary creative genius hadn't developed to such an extent. Her claims of being a medium are not really that different from what many people today are saying about the creative process generally, but hers are ultimately bigger claims.

Sometimes one is tempted to feel she is justified in claiming "mystic" inspiration—her music is so perfect in certain ways. She's a first-rate composer by any criterion of composing. This is not an instance of having to bend around the issues because she's a woman or because we are dealing with music from the remote twelfth century—hers is first-rate music by any definition or method. Many things in her upbringing explain the coherence of her concepts, but if mystical inspiration is how she explains or defines her personal genius, then by taking it seriously we are also taking the religious content of her poetry seriously when it isn't second nature for us to do that at all. I don't know anyone today whose own history prepares them for the kind of detail and intensity of her religious experience. In that respect, her claim has helped us put ourselves in a position to receive this music as we might not have done otherwise—as we do have a rather secular way of looking at creation and inspiration nowadays. She made sure with her explanations of her creative process that we not secularize her works.

Dronke writes in those notes about her world view, which was definitely not secularized.

In all eras, there are probably prevalent, archetypal views of the world that people generally share with varying degrees of consciousness, and then there are learned world views which might be built up on a system of central and secondary texts or belief systems. The learned world view in the Middle Ages might take various forms but seems to have had as its basis a synthesis of sacred disciplines and systematically rational ones (which they called "scientia"). One author who influenced this synthesis greatly was Plato—and he came into the medieval spheres of knowledge through various channels. For example, a Platonic-Boethian theory of music is based on a vision of the cosmos in which three "musics" are recognized: a music of the spheres, or harmony in the heavens (*musica mundana*); an unexpressed harmony above that, the harmony of God; and below it the harmony of the soul (*musica humana*). Sounding music (which medievals called *musica instrumentalis*) brings these together in a manifestation, so that the soul which "hears" it becomes "symphonic," expressing itself in the inner accord of the soul and the body; thus music-making is both earthly and heavenly.

In our day, this cosmic scheme seems like an archaic myth. Some call it the myth of Timaeus, from Plato's dialogue of that title.[21] But that's where the term "myth" falls short. In the twelfth century, people didn't think of this scheme of things as myth; they thought of it as reality, just as we consider it reality that we turn a light switch and have the lights go on, or that the earth goes around the sun. For them, the harmony of the celestial spheres and its mirror on earth in the soul was just as real as what we call scientific fact.

Some people say that medieval people had a degree of faith in their religious beliefs that went beyond most modern believers' experiences.

21. According to David Hiley, medievals knew the *Timaeus* in a reworking by the fourth-century writer Calcidius; see Hiley's *Western Plainchant*, pp. 443–44. The formulation of the three types of music came into medieval thought from Boethius, the Roman statesman and philosopher (c. 475–524), in his book *De institutione musica*.

Well, textbooks call the Middle Ages the Age of Faith, but even that term doesn't explain the phenomenon well. Even the word "faith" has something Protestant about it. We are all post-Reformation people, and also post-Inquisition people. The Church as an organization discredited itself over the centuries. It hadn't yet reached that turning point in the twelfth century, so there was little necessity to isolate "faith" from any other phenomena in the intact world view of that period.

We live in an era where things have become much more relative. We embrace thousands of different realities in a given day. Consider all the styles, periods, and types of music we listen to in a given day, all the different traditions, epochs, and experiences we confront through TV or film or books. In a sense, there are elements to living within an intact world view that we will never understand.

How does her world view influence your work on Hildegard?

For me, she was a very important gateway to all medieval thought. Her intensity and immediacy, and that quality to her work that one could identify as feminine, made it a lot easier for me to come into a profound medieval experience. Working on Hildegard's music is demanding, and that is part of the intensity of the experience, part of the reason one says, in retrospect, "I think I really lived through something doing this." Yet we don't necessarily have time to think about these things when we're performing it. It is extremely hard work to sing her music: not in the sense that it is drudgery, but because we must know where to put our concentration at all times. Her music provides a strong incentive to learn the craft of medieval song. And that's also a reason why she was a pivotal experience for me, because she helped me identify my craft and make such a full identification with it that a lot of other issues fell away afterwards.

You spoke about the feminine elements of Hildegard; her spending her life in an abbey was presumably a basic part of this? I think of texts where she exalts virgins, an important theme in her work.

You know, I spent a lot of my early life among women, in school and at home, and I think I do have an inkling now of how female religious communities might function. I've been doing professional work with women for quite a while, and I really enjoy it. I can easily identify with what Hildegard is aiming for in writing music to be sung by women. There is something normal and everyday about valuing women—if you spend your time with women, you come to understand their special natures. I suppose it's the same for any man who spends his life married to a woman; at a certain point womanly things become treasured and yet "everyday." Hildegard von Bingen has been able to express certain of these treasured feminine things through the themes she chooses: Mary, praise of the virgins, stories and meditations based on the Saint Ursula legend, Wisdom literature, and so forth. From Hildegard, I've learned a lot about women's musicality, women's relationship to their own spirituality. It sounds trite, but it is worthwhile to seek out "feminine Divinity" in addition to the all-pervasive Father principle; feminine spirituality is something very natural, uncomplicated, and yet intense, in my experience.

Is it just her themes, such as the ones you mentioned, or is it something beyond that?

Certain poetic "paintings" of the idea of womankind, even in the way she composes around it, are very lovely and revealing of her profound feelings about womanhood. Look at pieces like *Quia ergo femina* or *O tu suavissima virga.* She uses standard medieval images like comparing women to flowers, but the distinction of her style is in the exalted way she does it. She makes it easy to feel high and sensuous things, and, based on these good feelings, she will try to insert grander ideas about archetypal womanhood as well (drawing on established Judeo-Christian tradition), so that suddenly imagining something like a beautiful Mother principle governing the world becomes conceivable to the singer, where it was not conceivable before. Such ideas had previously been presented in contexts I absolutely could not accept.

This is often spoken of as an era when, as in most of history, women were subjugated; and people like Norman Cantor have applied that idea to Hildegard.[22] But some argue that this was also the era in which the seeds of the eventual recognition and emancipation of women first emerge—the adventure-romances like the Arthurian cycles that were written in that century put women and feminine qualities in a more positive light than before.[23]

I would certainly want to distance myself from Cantor's statement about Hildegard's creative motivations being frustrated and rebellious. There's something glorious about the twelfth century that you can feel in many male writers as well as female writers (of which there are surprisingly many):[24] an admiration for women's spontaneous musicality and spirituality. Many spiritual men were able to recognize, pay homage to, and aspire to that quality without feeling any conflict. Their homage is couched in specific terms. For example, in our program tomorrow, one section is formulated with the feeling and vocabulary of the biblical Song of Songs, which has been a pivotal text for musical composition in all eras (after all it's the song of *songs*). The work can be seen as a dramatization of what is *yin* and *yang* in the universe, of how beautifully

---

22. Cantor, *The Civilization of the Middle Ages,* p. 356. He argues that Hildegard's creations were "a form of women's revolt against the male-dominated society. Confined and frustrated . . . she single-handedly created an alternative culture in her imagination . . . [in which] religious women have a special claim to articulate God's word in the world."

23. Cantor, pp. 354–56.

24. See Dronke, *Women Writers of the Middle Ages.*

they move together in nature and in reality, and how desperately it hurts the soul when they're forced apart. These were conscious issues in the twelfth century, and the fact that this text served as such an important basis for theological discourse as well as for lyric art says a lot about the imaginal quality of the period.

SELECTED DISCOGRAPHY

Andrew Porter, in a review of a Sequentia concert, asserted that "singing more beautiful than theirs is not to be heard today" and followed this with a catalogue of virtues that is worth quoting at length: "pure, steady tone from open throats; supple movement through the phrases; pure intonation, with precise intervals; verbal force and clarity, with vowels distinctly colored; rhythmic liveliness serving at once the sense of the word and the musical structures." He concluded, "[T]his was a demonstration that bel canto—beautiful, eloquent singing that by its sound can move listeners to rapture—is an art not lost."[25] One might compare Porter's list with one that Christopher Page gives, near the end of the next chapter, of his own desiderata for medieval singing; both the overlaps and the differences are instructive. Sequentia attempts to express the text more in its singing style; that, plus the fact that it uses instruments more (although, as Thornton says, they use them less now than they once did), has sometimes caused controversy in the British musical press.[26]

Of the group's many recordings for Deutsche Harmonia Mundi, the most relevant to this chapter are, of course, those of Hildegard. Their 1994 *Canticles of Ecstasy* (DHM 77320) gives a good idea of what I heard at Grace Cathedral. It is described as the first in the projected complete Hildegard series, which suggests, Jerome F. Weber writes, that "the ensemble recognizes how far it has come since their" early 1980s Hildegard recordings—though some regarded their *Symphoniae* (DHM 77020-2–RG, rec. 1982–83) as having surpassed other available Hildegard recordings at the time of its release. Weber praises the "ecstatic interpretations" in *Canticles* and in the second CD of the series, *Voice of the Blood* (DHM 77346-2).[27] In her *Gramophone* review of *Canticles* (May 1995, p. 94), Mary Berry praises the singers' ability to "give a real shape and meaning" to Hildegard's soaring phrases, and adds, "Their vocal quality is very much what I would like to think Hildegard herself would have expected from her own company of nuns—firm, unwavering, exultant."

Sequentia's many other CDs display their wide range of sympathies. A sense of this range can be gained from *Vox Iberica*, their three-CD set (DHM 77333)

---

25. Porter, "Reanimations," *The New Yorker*, 22 October 1990, p. 100.

26. See, e.g., David Hiley's review in *Early Music* 13 (November 1985), p. 597, and Benjamin Bagby's essay, written in response, "Musicology and Make-Believe?" *Early Music* 14 (November 1986), p. 557.

27. Weber, *Fanfare* 19 (May/June 1996), pp. 167–68.

of Hispanic repertoire, since it covers many medieval styles: polyphony, improvised polyphony, monophony, popular music, troubadour songs, and so forth. The discs are available singly as *Sons of Thunder* (DHM 77199) for men's ensemble, *Codex Las Huelgas* (77238) for women's ensemble, and *El Sabio* (77173) for mixed ensembles. *El Sabio* is probably the disc to start with if you buy them separately; Ivan Moody especially praises the "marvellous 'Bulgarian' folk sound (and, indeed, harmony) of the women's choir in the incantatory *Sobelos fondos do mar.*"[28]

FOR FURTHER READING

A good biography of Hildegard is Sabina Flanagan's *Hildegard of Bingen: A Visionary Life* (London: Routledge, 1989). Hildegard's own words are available in Barbara Newman's *Symphoniae* (Ithaca, N.Y.: Cornell University Press, 1988) and Joseph Baird and Radd K. Ehrman's translations of *The Letters of Hildegard of Bingen* (New York: Oxford University Press, 1994). Newman's *Sisters of Wisdom: Hildegard's Theology of the Feminine* (Berkeley: University of California Press, 1987) provides a different approach. Norman Cantor's *Medieval Lives* (New York: Harper, 1994) contains an enjoyable short story featuring Hildegard, though many people, including Thornton, might take issue with it.

Peter Dronke's work on medieval poetry includes some important discussions of Hildegard. See especially chap. 6 of his *Women Writers of the Middle Ages* (Cambridge University Press, 1984), and also his *Poetic Individuality in the Middle Ages* (Oxford University Press, 1970).

Regarding the effects of oral tradition on plainchant—its structure, creation, and transmission—the pioneering work in English is that of Leo Treitler. As I write, this has not yet appeared in book form but is spread over many journal articles; the best summary is "'Unwritten' and 'Written' Transmission of Medieval Chant and the Start-up of Musical Notation," the *Journal of Musicology* 10 (1992), pp. 131–91. Peter Jeffery's *Re-Envisioning Past Musical Cultures: Ethnomusicology in the Study of Gregorian Chant* (University of Chicago Press, 1993) is an important book, especially for its voluminous bibliography. Two critical reviews of the book have been Treitler's "Sinners and Singers: A Morality Tale," *Journal of the American Musicological Society* 47 (Fall 1994), pp. 137–71, in essence a defense of his work against Jeffery's, and Edward Nowacki's review in *Notes* 8 (March 1994), pp. 913–17.

28. Moody, *Early Music* 21 (August 1993), p. 491.

4

The Colonizing Ear

Christopher Page on
Medieval Music

Christopher Page first ruffled the early-music world in the late 1970s, when he
(and, independently, the American scholar Craig Wright) put forward a radical
hypothesis. It held that the instruments popularized by Noah Greenberg,
Thomas Binkley, and David Munrow—their shawms, rebecs, nakers, and the
rest—were modern impositions; that medieval polyphony was usually performed with voices taking every line and with little or, more often, no instrumental accompaniment; and that even monophonic music may often have been
sung unaccompanied.[1] Audiences and performers had come to love those
shawms and rebecs, and scholars had supported their use, so it's not surprising that the idea was hardly welcomed—except, significantly, in Britain, with
its wealth of cathedral-trained singers.

1. Page's "Going Beyond the Limits: Experiments with Vocalization in the French Chanson, 1340–1440," *Early Music* 20 (August 1992), pp. 447–59, begins with a review of the evidence for this hypothesis. See also David Fallows's crucial paper "Specific Information on the
Ensembles for Composed Polyphony, 1400–1474," in *Studies in the Performance of Late Me-
diaeval Music,* ed. S. Boorman (Cambridge University Press, 1983), pp. 109–59; Page's "The
Performance of Songs in Late Medieval France," *Early Music* 10 (October 1982), pp. 441–50;
and Craig Wright's "Voices and Instruments in the Art Music of Northern France during the
15th Century," in *Report of the Twelfth Congress [of the International Musicological Society]*
(Berkeley, 1977), ed. D. Heartz and B. Wade (Kassel: Bärenreiter, 1981), pp. 643–49. Especially useful are Fallows's "Secular Polyphony in the Fifteenth Century," in *Performance Practice: Music Before 1600,* ed. H. M. Brown and S. Sadie (London: Macmillan, 1989, and New
York: Norton, 1990), esp. pp. 203–12, and in the same volume, Page's "Polyphony before
1400," esp. pp. 92–99. See also Reinhard Strohm, *The Rise of European Music* (Cambridge
University Press, 1993), pp. 357–58.

The musicologist Howard Mayer Brown, reviewing Page's early recordings, dubbed the new hypothesis "the English *a cappella* heresy." In the last fifteen years it has overcome its heretical status and become the majority position among scholars. Not that all performers have given in: they tend to fall, roughly speaking, into two camps, instrument-abstainers (mainly British) and instrument-users (often American or Continental, e.g., the Newberry Consort and the Ensemble PAN). The latter camp seems, if anything, to be gaining strength—although it also seems to be using instruments more selectively than before the *a cappella* ideal was mooted.

Page is far less absolute about that ideal than are some of his followers; he told me that he is sure that all options were used in the Middle Ages, but that *a cappella* performance was a common and sometimes standard one. And he doesn't consider instruments a sort of enemy—he is also a lutenist and an important scholar of medieval instruments. Still, it was Page who published the *a cappella* hypothesis first, and Page who has been the most influential in establishing it. This was in part because he is also a distinguished performer. As the leader of Gothic Voices, he has recorded a great deal of medieval repertoire in the *a cappella* style, and those recordings, more than any documentation, have proven how well the approach can work.

Page is one of the most influential of musical scholars, but he is not a musicologist. He is a philologist who teaches Anglo-Saxon, Middle English, Old French, and Latin in the English department at Cambridge. The combination of philological expertise with a direct, deep involvement in music has been central to his work. It has allowed him to look at musicological issues in a fresh manner. It has focused him on literary evidence that had been ignored, and has allowed him to read that evidence skillfully. It has prompted him to look at the field of musicology itself from an outsider's perspective.

It has also prodded him to consider, perhaps more than full-time performers would, how the agendas of scholarship conflict with (or support) those of performance. His published thoughts about the relations between performance and scholarship—particularly his views on the English choral tradition and its relevance to early vocal music—have evoked new controversy, making some performers hopping mad, as we discuss late in the interview. Another of his suggestions has galled some scholarly critics: that performing medieval music today can tell us something about musical experience in the Middle Ages. This idea was almost certain to be controversial, as Page explains, given the academic trends of our day. The fact that my other interviewees said almost nothing about these trends is symptomatic of how far the concerns of academics and non-academics have diverged. But in this case the academic concerns brought out some core issues of historical performance.

In your writings I find clues to what the medieval experience of music might have involved. Could you discuss this?

It's a treacherous issue, but I'll try. For one thing, the music of Latin Christendom probably gave its listeners a clear awareness that a piece, whether monophonic or polyphonic, was not occupying the full range of frequencies that it could occupy. The compass of most medieval pieces lies within two octaves. Listeners probably sensed that a piece they heard had the hue of a certain area in the larger spectrum of usable pitches. In other words, when they heard a piece they were aware that it could be sung significantly lower or higher, because the compass of human voices from the lowest men to the highest women or boys is much greater than two octaves. By the later fifteenth century the range employed had expanded significantly; when we listen to Josquin we begin to feel that the composition has colonized much more of the available space. With Tallis, and other members of the English School, we marvel at the sheer expanse of the musical territory.

Of course, when Josquin and his generation were colonizing the whole musical range their patrons were colonizing the world,[2] but before that "Latin Christendom" colonized a lot of territory in Europe. Why did the medieval musicians stay within a narrow spectrum?

Because the medieval music which survives to us suggests a dependence upon the human voice as the means of colonizing territory for the ear to rule. Theorists of the Middle Ages state that the absolute limit of one human voice is two octaves or less. Medieval singers were clearly not required to exercise in anything like the gymnasium of the modern singing lesson. The theorists frequently say that musical instruments can ascend considerably further upwards (I cannot think of one who says they may descend considerably further *downwards*), but this clearly did not affect their conception of the voice as the central resource of artistic music.

Which has of course been reflected in your work on secular song performance. To consider another element of this, though, what do we know about the specifics of how they listened to music?

The evidence is even sparser than the evidence about performing practice, but it would be worth putting together. I think we need not only a discipline of performing practice, but also a discipline of listening practice. It would be good to know more, for example, about the patterns of attention that a performer could expect. Did people gather together specially to hear music, or was

---

2. Edward Lowinsky, over fifty years ago, found connections between the Renaissance expansion of musical space and the expansions of the Renaissance concept of physical space produced by Copernicus and Columbus; see his "The Concept of Physical and Musical Space in the Renaissance," reprinted in his *Music in the Culture of the Renaissance* (University of Chicago Press, 1986), pp. 6–18. In one of a number of parallels, Lowinsky points out, for example, that the medieval scheme of the solar system not only was geocentric, but also placed the planets much closer to the earth than in the Copernican scheme, because empty space was considered useless, and nature did not include anything useless.

music essentially inserted into what was another kind of occasion? And how consistently did people pay attention? There is more evidence about that than one would expect. As early as the thirteenth century there is a reference, from troubadour sources, to listeners who have started to chatter by the time a singer reaches the third word of his song.

What would be the listening practice for those complex three-texted motets?

The one person who says anything about that is Johannes de Grocheio, and he is quite remarkable for *c.* 1300 in that he specifies something of the audience for each kind of practice. For the motet, which in his day is on the way to transmuting itself to a precious *ars nova* creation, his comment is that it should be performed before the *literati*, which I think means the clergy, or a little more than that—the more conscientious clergy, those who take seriously their duty to know Latin and to study books of theological and pastoral importance. That suggests that the listening practice for something like a motet of *c.* 1300 could well be the following: the bishop in his palace—every bishop has one, although the word "palace" may be rather grand for what it actually is—has dinners to which he invites clergy from his diocese, possibly another bishop, and quite possibly some leading guildsmen or the mayor. One can imagine that an occasion like that might have a motet. The context for so much music-making in the Middle Ages is festive in the strict sense of the word: a feast, actual dining. Meal times are probably the only times when people in a medieval household converged, and therefore there was a tendency for music to gravitate towards them.

As for the listening practice of sacred music, you once described chant as being not so much a performance as an incantation or prayer among monks.[3] At what point do sacred musicians become performers, as of course they were by the time of, say, Monteverdi?

By the fourteenth century, there are clear references, most of them disparaging, to singers in England who sing elaborate polyphony so that they will be congratulated afterwards by laypersons. One thing involved here is the natural vanity of people who have good voices, which I imagine is simply irrepressible and always has been. But there is another factor. We see it in the twelfth century, with the Parisian organum of Léonin and Pérotin. One of the striking things to emerge from Craig Wright's *Music and Ceremony at Notre Dame*[4] is that much of the organum of Notre Dame is processional: it was performed with the full theatricality of a procession. Now, if lay men or women were impressed, the more wealthy amongst them would endow masses or give

---

3. In "Musicus and Cantor," in *Companion to Medieval and Renaissance Music*, ed. Tess Knighton and David Fallows (London: Orion, and New York: Schirmer, 1992), pp. 74–78.
4. Cambridge University Press, 1989.

money to raise the rank of the liturgical feast so the organum could be sung. Most of the polyphonic singing was done by deputies, some of whom were free-lance performers, the so-called "masters of organum."[5] One could say to them: "I am the bishop of Amiens, and we do not have anything like this at the moment. So I will buy your services; I will give you a benefice of so many florins per year if you will come and sing it in my church." This was a living for some young singers—even if probably not a very good living, and one they rejected once they found some better job in the Church. So here there is a link between organum and money. Sometimes when organum is performed very vigorously, as it was by David Munrow, it seems to me that I can almost hear turned into sound one of the great themes of twelfth- and thirteenth-century history: *ambition.*

This suggests an approach to understanding their experience: how music related to other social developments. We discussed the colonizing spirit, but you've also written about connections between music and mathematics and science—for example, how the introduction of Arabic numerals led to notational advances that made ars nova possible.[6]

It's clear that the idea of measurement does intrigue medieval musicians, and of course there are two things you can measure—how far apart notes stand (their intervals) and how long they last. The idea that the materials of music might be objectively and scrupulously calibrated, with regard to both the height and the duration of the notes, bit deeply into Western musical consciousness in the thirteenth century, and retained its intensity for a very long time indeed.

One obstacle to our understanding their experience, though—and this applies, I suppose, to any period—is that you have to compare what contemporaries *say* about their own art with what they appear to *do* within their art. The example I use in *Discarding Images* is that if we were to form our assessment of Geoffrey Chaucer's poetry on the basis of what fifteenth-century readers praise in it, we would end up with a very different Chaucer from the one we have now—and probably a poet that Chaucer himself would find surprising. Fifteenth-century readers praise him for all the virtues that they have terms for—his "high sentence" and "moral learning" and so on. They don't praise him for the things we praise—for irony, for humor, for realism, and (to come more up to date) for a sympathetic and complex attitude to women. But when fifteenth-century poets try to imitate Chaucer, often to complete the incomplete *Canterbury Tales*, they show by their pastiches that they understand things which they did not have terms to explain. To attach great importance today to what medieval theorists say about measurement is to lean heavily upon what

5. Page, *The Owl and the Nightingale* (London: Dent, 1989, and Berkeley: University of California Press, 1990), chap. 6.

6. See Page's *Discarding Images* (Oxford University Press, 1993), chap. 4.

medieval people were able to say about what they found in music. I suspect that what they actually found was broader than what they could name. It is surely the same with us.

Your mention of ambition and of marketing oneself at Notre Dame brings Hollywood deal-making to mind, and you say now that appreciation of Chaucer by the generation that followed him was much more like ours than their critical writing suggests. This brings up a key issue in this whole exercise I've tried to involve you in: how much can we understand and relate to them— are we just too different, as some today believe?

If there were no such thing as "transhistorical humanness," then trying to write a history of fifteenth-century music by composers like Obrecht would be like trying to write a history of the parrot community in Australia on the basis of interviews with living parrots. We can't understand what the parrots are saying, and we don't know how they structure their experience or what memory they have of the past. Obrecht does not sound to me like a parrot.

Regarding the question of transhistorical humanness and performance, *a particularly hot debate has arisen over your suggestion that "sustained expo- sure to the sound of medieval music [today] contributes to a vital sense of pro- portion (in the colloquial sense of those words), not only in the analysis of spe- cific musical details but also in conceiving what the music may have meant"* (Discarding Images, *p. xxiv). That is, you seem to say that our playing the music now can give us insight into what it meant to them then. What would you say to critics of this view?*

Anybody who denies that listening to the music of the past is a vital part of studying the music of the past will never write a book or article that I want to read. Why, though, has this issue become so controversial? It may be partly because we live in an academic milieu where anyone who follows a critical practice of any kind is required to clarify the "theory" of what they do—which usually entails the presentation of an argument that can be recognized as methodologically sophisticated and self-aware by those who, wittingly or un- wittingly, espouse some form of post-structuralism, deconstruction, discourse theory or whatever it may be. Many influential literary critics argue that in speaking of texts—or, some would say, of anything—it is not legitimate to take a particular standpoint and try to discredit other standpoints. It is not legiti- mate to insist upon a particular value judgment; when we admire texts we are really only reacting to the fact that they seem flattering to us, that they tell us what we already know. If you are to substitute "listener" or "performer" for "reader" or "critic" in statements of that kind, you will end up with something like the position which some modern scholars have taken on the question of historical performance.

It would be one thing to state that certain performances now are actually recovering something that was done then; I've never published such a view. But it's another thing to say that some performances are more historical than others. If they're all equal in their historicity, then the historicism disappears. It's only when you can have some kind of a scale of judgment that you can invoke a notion of historical performance at all.

That "scale of judgment" is exactly what critical theories would try to dismiss.

My conception of what we do in Gothic Voices implicitly rejects some major developments in critical theory during the last thirty years. Up to a point, perhaps, this is true of any committed early-music ensemble, and is not just a matter of the inevitable slippage between theory and practice. From the vantage point of the later 1990s, it is obvious that thinking of the kind found in various kinds of post-structuralism was bound to corrode the notion of "authenticity," so often invoked in the 1970s as the pursuit of "what the composer intended." During the last three decades, various forms of deconstruction have attacked the belief that a coherent, individual subject—an author—endows an artistic creation with meaning. Further, many critical theorists have tended to silence discussion of ethical issues. One may now read sophisticated presentations of the view that the study of ethical issues is the study of what an individual society finds acceptable or expedient, or that it is the study of a certain way in which language operates. A short step takes us from here to the assertion that there is no such thing as "human nature," and that we have no firm ground upon which to stand in judging the promptings of conscience. To bring the matter down to the level of historical performance, it means that, as you said, there would be no way of talking about continuities of musical taste or understanding from the Middle Ages to the present.

I am far from clear where I stand on some of these issues at this point. But I do wish to state boldly here that I believe the modern performance of medieval music to be an ethical concern, and that any "historical performance theory" which tends to silence ethical issues can have no interest for me. By invoking "an ethical concern" in this context, I mean that my answer to the question of why we should perform medieval music is a part of my answer to the question of how we should live.

This may seem too portentous an edifice to build on waste ground that is strewn with old reviews, performer profiles in newspapers, CD booklets, record company publicity, and all the other ephemera which sometimes cause professional scholars such alarm. I hope it is not. An alert and compassionate approach to the arts of other civilizations, including the arts of one's own civilization in the past, is a great human good. The aim of people in many areas of cultural life, as we approach the year 2000, is to inspire what might be called "compunction" in this regard: a sudden turning of the mind's attention to the existence of something that has beauty where one might not have expected to

find it, or that offers a challenge where one might not have expected the resources for mounting a challenge to be present. I hope that recordings and concerts by medieval ensembles, Gothic Voices included, may do something to promote such awareness. That is an enterprise which is independent of scholarly
progress or controversy, because it does not depend upon a belief that one's
own artistic solutions have scholarly support.

*True, but when you talk about a compassionate approach to the arts of
other civilizations and the value of encountering them, it returns us to the issue
of what these performances can tell us about the experience of people in these
civilizations—presumably, that's part of their value to us. Can our performances tell us about such things, specifically about our own past eras?*

Yes, why not? Music is part of our evidence about the past. It is certainly
possible for performers to influence in subtle and powerful ways what the
public (and that includes scholars) hear in the music, and to define what
scholars think could have happened in the past. If modern performers are unable to produce a certain kind of result, it will often produce a consensus
among scholars that the result could *not* have been achieved in the past. A
specific instance of this is the performance of French secular music with voices
only. One of the reasons why the idea was rejected in the late 70s, when it
was first proposed, was that at the time no performer had done it successfully. When performers learned how to do it, the idea became acceptable. So
in that sense, if there is a change in performing style, it can affect the way
we hear the music.

However, that's not necessarily the same as saying that one is discovering
something about the music. One may be discovering something for oneself, a
possibility one didn't think was there, but the question is whether performance
can imply something about the musical past. I would agree that it can't verify
anything. I would still suggest, however, that some performances are more historical than others, and that those that are more historical should be able to
imply something that the less historical performances don't.

*That seems reasonable, but I suppose a crucial question then is how we de-
cide which performances are the more historical ones—who decides, and on
what basis?*

Let me give an example to illustrate how one might approach it. Accuracy
of tuning is something that performers of the 1940s, as one can tell from their
recordings, simply couldn't accomplish in their performance of medieval music.
It's just a plain fact; they couldn't do it, partly because they were using various vocal techniques that prevent the listener's ear from seizing and savoring
true, clear pitch. Nor could they sing some of these very syncopated rhythms
of Machaut, for example, in correct time. Now it seems to me that everything
one can deduce about medieval performance style from what theorists say and

from what composers write suggests that performers who can do those things are being more historical in their approach than performers who can't.

I suppose the safest position to take is that performance can be educative. I think we're all agreed on that. Like most performers, I have certain intuitions that some things are correct and others are not. Now, that's a very shaky basis on which to go into print, and it may be that as a scholar one should keep out all such intuitions and deal only with what can be deduced from the evidence in a positivistic way, but I still do believe that progress has been made in the performance of medieval music in the last thirty years.

One thing that dramatizes the uncertainties, and that is more likely to arise in medieval than in, say, nineteenth-century repertoire, is when two performers come to opposite conclusions. An example has to do with meaning in medieval music: whether texts should be sung expressively. Here your views as you've written about them seem to conflict with those of some others, including some interviewed in this book.[7] Could you address this?

To take an extreme view for the moment, one could say that medieval musicians set a text as neutral syllabic material, while Renaissance musicians, imitating what they imagined to be classical example, discovered the power of music to express the meaning of text, not only by adopting more "rational" methods of word-setting but also by attending to particular moments of verbal meaning. Medieval writers on chant—with whom any consideration of this matter begins—sometimes say that composers of new chants should ensure "that the music seems to express what the words say."[8] Notice that this is a reference to how a composer should compose, not to how a performer should perform; expressiveness in that regard is something which medieval theorists of music do not so readily discuss. As I read the several hundred words which our twelfth-century author has devoted to the composition of new chants, I cannot find anything that is easily recognizable as a summons to what a modern singer may intuitively regard as "expressive" means. Indeed, this author thinks that the best way to make music project the sense of the words is to lead every mu-

7. Page, *Discarding Images*, pp. 85–86. See the interviews with Barbara Thornton and Susan Hellauer.

8. Page informs me that he was referring to the treatise of Johannes (*c.* 1100); see J. Smits van Waesberghe, ed., *Johannis Affligemensis De Musica cum Tonario,* Corpus Scriptorum de Musica 1 (Rome: American Institute of Musicology, 1950), p. 117. As early as the ninth century, in the liturgical-music treatise *Musica Enchiriadis,* we read, "In peaceful subjects let the notes be peaceful, happy in joyous matters, grieving in sad ones; let cruel words or deeds be expressed with harsh sounds—sudden, loud, and swift—shaped according to the nature of events and the emotions." In line with Page's view that this has to do with composition only, this passage has been called "rather irrelevant to actual singing technique" (David Hiley, in *Performance Practice: Music before 1600,* p. 44) and "an elegant formulation of the medieval aesthetic of the affections" (J. Dyer, "Singing with Proper Refinement," *Early Music* 6 [April 1978], p. 211).

sical phrase towards the final of the mode at a point where the text completes
a sentence or other major unit of sense. This is an analytical—even a grammatical—approach to the idea of projecting meaning, not a synthetic or dramatic one. It is also striking, I think, that one of the most influential of all
plainsong theorists, Guido of Arezzo [whose treatise *Micrologus* was finished
c. 1030], describes a way of composing new chants in which the composer is
to write the five vowels of the Latin alphabet in one, two, or three sequences
beneath the gamut, and to produce a new composition by matching the vowels of the syllables to their corresponding notes. This is a system which suggests a remarkably undramatic conception of how words and music might be
married.

The plainsong modes bring us a little closer to the kind of expressiveness
that a modern singer is perhaps most likely to wish to discuss. Although there
can have been no standardized pitch in the Middle Ages, the system of eight
plainsong modes was not regarded as a way of defining eight different sequences of tone and semitone steps within the same notational octave but was
conceived as a movement in which those sequences were assigned to various
areas in the voice from the lowest usable region to the highest. To say, for example, that a chant is "Authentic Phrygian" (and the plainsong theorists are
overwhelmingly concerned with such classifications) is to say roughly where it
should lie in the voice. One sang the Plagal Dorian (mode 1) lowest of all, for
example, and the Authentic Mixolydian (mode 2) the highest of all. Let me repeat, this has nothing to do with actual sounding pitch: men and women could
establish this system of differentiation within their voices at quite different
pitches. The eight modes were therefore associated with a move upwards from
a thicker, darker region of the voice to a thinner, brighter tone, and this is the
language which medieval writers repeatedly use to describe the sonorities of the
human voice as pitch rises. This movement from darkness to brightness was
naturally associated with the most fundamental association that the human
mind makes between emotion and musical sound, namely that a high, bright
sonority befits a mood of exaltation. (The words "gravity" and "exaltation"
both have etymological roots which display the potency of the simple concepts
I am describing.) Medieval writers on plainsong say exactly this; and while it
is clear that there are lamenting texts set to higher modes and joyous texts set
to lower ones, the association between vocal pitch and meaning that I have just
described exists in their minds and is described in several treatises. Once again,
however, this is an expressiveness which is created in a general fashion by a
major resource of the entire piece—its place in the voice—and not by a response to certain individual moments in the text.

The association of modes with certain states of feeling—an association that
a number of plainsong theorists make with exuberant metaphor—is more than
a matter of vocal color, however. The modes were not just scalar patterns of
an octave associated with certain regions of the voice; a mode was a complete

stylistic grammar for all the melodies cast in it, involving certain characteristic melodic movements, especially at the beginnings and ends of phrases. These aspects of mode also seem to have been associated, at least in the minds of theorists, with certain emotional states.[9] I have tried to illustrate in my edition of the thirteenth-century *Summa Musice* how references to "the haughty prancing of the third mode" and so on do make sense in terms of brief, recurrent melodic configurations characteristic of the modes concerned.[10] I emphasize once again, however, that this is a system of expressiveness which relies upon the singer's (and the listener's) internalization of the whole modal system of plainsong; it is not something that can be approximated by the modern singer who reads the text of a piece, forms an idea of its "meaning," and then proceeds to project it rhetorically moment by moment. There is certainly evidence in medieval monophonic settings that composers might respond to verbal moments in a text, but the crucial difference between their practice in this regard and what a modern listener might intuitively expect is that the medieval composer does not actually "mime" the affective meaning of the word with some musical figure which he considers a correlate for it; when he draws attention to a word or words, it is by exploiting something—a melodic formula, a particular intervallic step—that is part of the general resources of the piece.

How does this relate to expressiveness in later medieval repertoire, especially polyphony?

The question of whether such "expressive" resources were ever transferred to measured polyphony, whose melodic modal character (when it had any) was clearly of a very different sort, is easy to ask but probably impossible to answer. My own suspicion is that when the interests of composer and theorists shifted to mensural music and to the endlessly intriguing (and exasperating) problems of its notation, the older language for talking about expressiveness in general terms of the plainsong modes was simply dropped from the agenda of trained musicians, together with the issues broached in that language. One achievement of the fifteenth century will be to reinvigorate that language and to apply it to polyphony. (In this regard, as in some others, the Renaissance in music is not so much a rediscovery of Antiquity as a rediscovery of twelfth-century teaching about plainsong, now applied to polyphony.[11]) I have never read a medieval treatise that cites a set of polyphonic pieces for their contrasting "affects" in the way plainchant theorists cite items of plainsong from at least *c.* 1100 on.

9. Harold Powers, "Mode," III, 1, in *The New Grove Dictionary of Music,* vol. 12 (London: Macmillan, 1980), pp. 397–401.

10. *The* Summa Musice: *A Thirteenth-Century Manual for Singers* (Cambridge University Press, 1991). The passage Page refers to here is from chap. 22, on p. 118; his discussion and illustrations are on pp. 18ff.

11. Powers, "Mode," III, 1, b.

Of course, you've already discussed the discrepancy between what theorists talked about in Chaucer and their pastiches of Chaucer.

Absolutely, and there's another factor to consider as well. All of what I've said about chant and polyphony is true, I hope, but it is also a delaying tactic; for I am at last compelled to admit that I often find performances of medieval monophony or polyphony unsatisfactory if singers are zealous "to make something of the words." I cannot endure performances of any medieval music in which singers act, and singers who do perform in that way are, in my view, making a grievous mistake. "Expressiveness," as most modern singers are inclined to interpret it, often includes a pervasive and subtle (or not so subtle) rubato which is in my view fundamentally opposed to the ethos of *musica mensurabilis*, an art which thrived upon the scrupulous calibration of durations and intervallic steps, and which is constantly praised by its devotees for its innate resistance to waywardness and caprice.

This brings up another area of divergent opinion: accuracy of duration. Marcel Pérès has a different attitude: his view is that because they weren't used to the clock in the twelfth century, they may have notated duration precisely but still didn't think of time arithmetically—instead, they thought of it qualitatively.

It's definitely a different attitude. Certainly the rise of measured notation in the late twelfth century and its increasing elaboration in the thirteenth and fourteenth centuries has been linked to the rise of mechanical clocks, and indeed to the establishment of civic, mercantile time as opposed to contemplative monastic time.[12] But I don't think that this has anything to do with issues of performance or notation at any time. I can quite well believe, however, that performances of some kinds of polyphonic conducti in the twelfth century had a wondrous flexibility, and that by the fourteenth this had all changed. When one is investigating the music of, say, Machaut, one surely discovers that the sonorous events are calibrated against a pulse with great scrupulosity, and that the placement in time of each note, not before and not after, so that the dissonance is precisely disciplined, is an essential part of the medium.

Here I must declare my affiliation. My genealogy as an interpreter of medieval music goes back through singers such as Margaret Philpot to Michael Morrow and John Beckett of Musica Reservata, the ensemble whose recordings I first heard as a schoolboy. How does this affect me? For one example among many, I take it to be absolutely fundamental that unless a crescendo is planned, a note should begin with as much commitment and tone as it is ever going to possess; but that's something that Michael Morrow taught John Beckett who taught it to Margaret Philpot who taught it to me. So perhaps it be-

---

12. Jacques Le Goff, *Time, Work, and Culture in the Middle Ages* (University of Chicago Press, 1980).

hooves me to stand back a moment before I reach for medieval theorists whom I might cite to support my views in this regard—theorists who insist that tenor parts, for example, be sung "in a firm and rigorous fashion." Influences reaching back long before I had heard of the medieval theorists must have influenced the uses I find for their statements.

After twelve years, the ensemble Gothic Voices has evolved a style. Our stylistic ideal—one which it is quite beyond us to achieve with any consistency—is this:

> All the polyphonic music of the Middle Ages must be sung with scrupulously accurate tuning (would that it were always possible!). Standards of ensemble must be of the highest order. In most cases polyphony should be sung one voice to a part, by singers with a natural ability to phrase and an ability to move very cleanly from one note to the next. Blend is vital. Close attention to tactical tuning—the widening and narrowing of intervals for artistic effect—is of great importance, and for most French, Italian, and Franco-Flemish music before the mid fifteenth century tuning should normally follow Pythagorean principles. Next, the music must be sung with a meticulous sense of pulse, with a light, transparent tone, and (for the most part) with bright, clean vowel sounds produced quite far forward in the mouth.

Here are some of the difficulties I believe I encounter in performing medieval music. Some of what I said to describe the Gothic Voices' stylistic ideal can be classified at once as personal artistic preference (the bright vowels, the clean movement from note to note), vital to any sense of style in the performance of music but not demonstrable by reference to the surviving evidence. However, it is only by the most laborious self-scrutiny that I can begin to glimpse how many of the remaining matters are what I *know* and how many are what I *believe*. Up to a point, questions of scoring (one voice to a part) rest upon literary and documentary evidence, although the testimony is far from unanimous. The claim about scrupulosity of tuning can also be urged, if not actually proved, on the basis of the obsessive interest which the musical theorists of the Middle Ages show in the calibration of musical intervals, not to mention the strictures of someone like Jacques of Liège (c. 1325), who cannot abide singers who, when they are required to sing an octave, "ascend more, or ascend less, than the full five tones with two minor semitones." As for blend, we have Jacques again, who says that in polyphony the various parts should resolve as if into one voice (this was an ideal carried over from plainchant). But I can't claim that any of this is conclusive.

Your distinction between house style, knowledge, and belief indicates caution about claims that your approach is more historical than others', even if you posit that such a thing is possible in principle. However, you've been criticized for (your critics say) suggesting not only that English musicians are distinctive in some respects, but that their priorities are like those of medieval and Renaissance singers, which, you said, might "complicate (but not confute)" the argument that some ideals of historical performance are "a projection of certain 20th-century musical ideas and tastes."[13] Some non-British musicians take this to imply a Kiplingesque assertion of British privilege and, also, of historical accuracy in this domain of music. How would you answer such charges?

When the article to which you refer was still in typescript, it was read by more than a dozen English musicians, scholars, and critics. As I remember, none of them quite foresaw the reaction of the "non-British musicians" whom you mention. Indeed, the general view of the English readers whom I consulted was that the article offered a timely deconstruction of the English *a cappella* scene and one liable to offend many working within it, not a complacent or somehow political vindication of what is being done there. Perhaps the non-British readers whom you mention do not realize what is implied by saying (as I do in the article) that the English *a cappella* scene might be described as "the musical equivalent of the Whitehall civil service." That is *not* a compliment.

I think I now see it this way. The medieval writers who discuss measured music sometimes say that expertise in plainsong is the basis of an expertise in polyphony. At least two things are involved here. A training in chant was usually the way in which a singer learned to read from staff notation and came to recognize note shapes. On the other hand, however, those writers also mean that no singer can be a skilled performer of measured music until he has acquired long experience of the choral discipline of performing chant. We possess many attempts by medieval writers to codify good practice in the performance of plainsong. They emphasize that each singer should listen carefully; they require that all pauses should be executed in a neat and unanimous way; some

---

13. Page's "The English *a cappella* Renaissance," *Early Music* 21(August 1993), pp. 453–71 (quoting p. 470). This article should not be missed by anyone interested in this issue. It argues that the English preference for *a cappella* singing of medieval and Renaissance music—and the proliferation of groups such as his, the Tallis Scholars, the Hilliard Ensemble, and many more—reflect partly a scholarship that has mostly originated in England and, more than that, reflect an English tradition of *a cappella* choral singing cultivated in a tight network with hubs at Oxford and Cambridge. He summarizes his theory, early on: "It begins from the premiss that English singers performing *a cappella* are currently able to give exceptional performances of medieval and Renaissance polyphony from England and the Franco-Flemish area because the ability of the best English singers to achieve a purity and precision instilled by the discipline of repeated *a cappella* singing in the choral institutions is singularly appropriate to the transparency and intricate counterpoint of the music. From that premiss we proceed to the theory that, in certain respects, and especially in matters relating to accuracy of tuning and ensemble, these performances represent a particularly convincing postulate about the performing priorities of the original singers" (p. 454). It was the last proposition especially that touched off controversy; for one argument, see Donald Greig's "Sight-Readings: Notes on *a cappella* Performance Practice," *Early Music* 23 (February 1995), pp. 125–48.

authors, such as Jerome of Moravia, insist upon a blended sound, and sets of regulations for the conduct of religious life sometimes emphasize the essentially self-effacing nature of the ideal chant performance: "Let one voice be scarcely distinguishable from another." All of these stipulations must be read with care, needless to say, for their ultimate goals are spiritual and not aesthetic; moreover, many of them are specifically concerned with psalmody. None the less, their regulations sound like a call for something which can be described, I believe without grievous anachronism, as "good consort singing." By this I mean an essentially non-soloistic manner of singing that values blend and good ensemble, honed during the daily discipline of preparing music for the day's services. England is a country where singers are still trained in a discipline of this kind—so is America, if you relax the point about "preparation for the day's services" and then count some of the vocal ensembles in the soul and close-harmony traditions. The performers of Take Six are by far the best consort singers I have ever heard, and it was Rogers Covey-Crump, a doyen among English early-music singers, who first introduced me to them.

As I've said, for me, working with an *a cappella* group in England, there is already a danger that hidden preferences are making themselves felt even as I speak about the meaning of medieval evidence. For various reasons, the tradition of consort singing in England has produced (by general agreement) standards of excellence in intonation, blend, and ensemble, and this provides a very suggestive—perhaps a very seductive—context for understanding what Jacques, Jerome, and others are referring to. I attempted to scrutinize that context in the article you mentioned, even going so far as to say that, because most of the English ensembles have a very strong (indeed overwhelming) Oxbridge contingent, their singing "turns the memories and dreams of a social class into sound."[14]

And here is the heart of the problem. All serious musicians, I take it, have something we may call their artistic integrity; it is a specialized working of conscience that they bring to what they do. When musicians are involved in historical performance, however, they must scrutinize the relationship between their artistic integrity and their intellectual integrity—the relationship between what they *believe* about the music, and can satisfactorily express in no other way than by performance, and what they *know* about the music. The problem for many performers is that it may be difficult for them to distinguish what they believe about the music from what they know about it. I do not believe that the modern performer has privileged access to any special way of knowing; but, as I said, I believe that our understanding of the technical resources required to make early music musical can improve with time, and has done so in medieval music. As a scholar, my greatest difficulty has been to find a rhetoric with which to express that idea while acknowledging the need to scru-

14. "The English *a cappella* Renaissance," p. 458.

tinize the means that have enabled me to conceive it, namely the English choral tradition. As a performer, my greatest difficulty has been, in a Yeatsian phrase, to acknowledge that I "lack all conviction," for most of what I do to make the music musical rests upon nothing that can be called evidence, and yet I am "full of passionate intensity" about what we do.

You mentioned Kipling. Well, the *a cappella* renaissance in England will not last forever. During the next twenty years the universities of Oxford and Cambridge, with their choral foundations and chapels, are set to change a great deal. Nobody knows what effect that will have on the choral scene. Come back in 2015, and you might well find me quoting Kipling to myself:

> "Over then, come over, for the bee has quit the clover,
> And your English summer's done."

SELECTED DISCOGRAPHY

Page and Gothic Voices have made over a dozen recordings for Hyperion. In a review that includes an index of almost all of them through 1993, the musicologist Lawrence Earp says that "no recordings are more eagerly awaited by enthusiasts of medieval music."[15] Page feels that the group hit full stride in 1991 with their ninth CD, *The Medieval Romantics* (CDA66463); it was the first in which, according to Page, the group had solved the problems of how to vocalize non-texted parts and had found two bass-baritone singers appropriate to the music. One of its songs, Solage's *Joiex de cuer,* inspired Pierre Boulez to approach Page after a concert and say, "This Solage—it is extraordinary!" The disc and the two that followed, *Lancaster and Valois* (66588) and *The Study of Love* (66619), explored the French repertoire of the fourteenth and early fifteenth centuries; any one of them would be a good place to start exploring Page's work. Even better might be his most recent (as I write) series, *The Spirits of England and France,* since its Volume One (66739) is an anthology that surveys several areas of repertory. Volume Two (66773) is one of the finest extant recordings of trouvère songs; Volume Three (66783) is an acclaimed sampling of the fifteenth-century composer Binchois and his contemporaries.

Howard Mayer Brown criticizes the performances of chansons on the CD *Castle of Fair Welcome* (66194) as "a bit too perfect, slightly without individual personality or nuance. One cannot tell, for example, just from listening whether the performers are singing a happy or a sad song." Brown notes, however, that this is "clearly intentional."[16] Page's view is that the music itself would tell one nothing about whether a song is happy or sad (only the lyrics would) and that the performance needn't either; what the original performances

---

15. Earp, *Early Music* 21 (May 1993), pp. 289–95; quote, p. 289.
16. Brown, *Early Music* 15 (May 1987), p. 277–79; quote, p. 277.

expressed was the "social register" of a piece—whether it is in high style or a lower one. Richard Taruskin, heartily praising the same CD, paraphrases Page's views on expressiveness in late-medieval songs, saying that "what is 'expressed' in these chansons, in short, is the quality of *hauteur*, that is 'elevation' . . . in tone, in diction, in delivery, all reflecting the elevated social setting in which the performance took place." He says that Gothic Voices' application of this approach, in one piece, gave him "goose bumps," adding that such "historical gooseflesh is 'authenticity' at its best and [in existential terms] its most authentic."[17] That two prominent musicologists could differ on this issue suggests how challenging the historical evidence can be.

I am especially fond of *The Voice in the Garden* (66653), which takes a very different approach to the Spanish *cancioneros* repertoire from the more popular one of Jordi Savall. Savall's colorfully orchestrated versions are infectious, but I was surprised to find that the same is true of Page's mostly vocal approach. Page's approach appears to be more musicologically sound.[18]

FOR FURTHER READING

Page's own writing not only is among the most important in this field but is some of the most readable. His own favorite among his books is *The Owl and the Nightingale* (London: Dent, 1989, and Berkeley: University of California Press, 1990). The book's importance goes beyond details of music: it is really a social history that considers such issues as the role of music in the life of a society, and how that role changed during a time and place crucial in Western history. Page also discusses the period in an excellent brief essay, "Court and City in France, 1100–1300," in *Antiquity and the Middle Ages,* ed. James McKinnon (London: Macmillan, 1990, and Englewood Cliffs, N.J.: Prentice Hall, 1991), pp. 197–217.

Page's *Voices and Instruments of the Middle Ages* (Berkeley: University of California Press, 1987) includes a fascinating discussion of the troubadour repertoire and its use of instruments. Some of his other writings on the use of instruments and voices are listed in note 1, above.

Page's most controversial book, *Discarding Images* (Oxford University Press, 1993), is about musicology's construing of the Middle Ages. One important record of the controversies it evoked is an exchange between Page and two musicologists, Margaret Bent and Reinhard Strohm, which appeared in *Early Music* 21 (November 1993), pp. 625–33 (Bent); 22 (February 1994), pp.

17. Taruskin, "High, Sweet, and Loud," originally published in *Opus* (June 1987), pp. 36–39, reprinted in *Text and Act* (New York: Oxford University Press, 1995), pp. 347–52; quotes, pp. 350 and 352.

18. See Tess Knighton, "The *a cappella* Heresy in Spain: An Inquisition into the Performance of the *Cancionero* Repertory," *Early Music* 20 (November 1992), pp. 562–81, and Kenneth Kreitner's "Minstrels in Spanish Churches, 1400–1600," in the same issue, pp. 533–44.

127–32 (Page's reply); 22 (November 1994), pp. 715–19 (Strohm's comments). Incidentally, Strohm's *The Rise of European Music: 1380–1500* (Cambridge University Press, 1993) may be challenging (Alejandro Enrique Planchart's review began with the memorable line, "This book is not for wimps"), but it is fascinating. Far more accessible is Strohm's article "The Close of the Middle Ages" in *Antiquity and the Middle Ages,* ed. McKinnon, pp. 269–312; Page discusses earlier eras in light of (and in contrast to) Strohm's book in his article "Towards: Music in the Rise of Europe," in *Musical Times* 136 (March 1995), pp. 127–34.

Page's essays in other books give accessible entries into his thought: see for example "Instruments and Instrumental Music before 1300," chap. 10 in *New Oxford History of Music,* II, rev. ed., ed. Richard Crocker and David Hiley (Oxford University Press, 1990); and "Polyphony before 1400," in *Performance Practice: Music before 1600,* ed. Howard Mayer Brown and Stanley Sadie (New York: Norton, 1989), pp. 79–104.

Postscript: Medieval Music, Plainchant, and "Otherness"

In the preceding chapters, we've heard Marcel Pérès speak of an era before clocks and electric lights, Susan Hellauer discuss medieval associations between plainchants and holy days, and Barbara Thornton emphasize the oral nature of Hildegard's tradition.[19] Page, too, argues that the era's idea of musical expressiveness differed from ours.

Yet he also disputes those who proclaim the "otherness" of medieval people. Unabashed humanist that he is, Page asserts that beneath the obvious differences lies a "transhistorical humanness," which he has described elsewhere as "an appreciable continuity of human thought and feeling from age to age."[20]

This assertion has caused a flap. In a critical essay, the musicologist Rob Wegman dismisses Page's "transhistorical humanness" as an expression of the "Enlightenment ideal of universalism." Like (among others) many postmodernists, Wegman has no sympathy for that ideal. He mentions its "deeply problematic legacy"[21] and calls it "a typical product of a society that appropriates the thoughts and artifacts of other societies while it tries to understand them. Not surprisingly, it was closely allied to imperialism and nationalism in the 19th century."[22]

19. A longer version of this essay will appear in *Early Music* in February 1998.
20. Page, *Discarding Images,* p. 190.
21. Rob C. Wegman, "Reviewing Images," *Music and Letters* 76 (1995), pp. 265–73; quote, p. 270.
22. Rob C. Wegman, "Sense and Sensibility in Late-Medieval Music," *Early Music* 23 (1995), p. 312.

We could question the tone of moral condemnation; almost any idea, including the ideologies Wegman seems to prefer, can be used for harmful purposes. We could also question whether ideas of transhistorical humanness could express only "Enlightenment" concepts. But I will ignore all that, and note just that if we were to grant Wegman the point about hidden agendas it would settle nothing. It would tell us about the biases that predispose people to see the world a certain way, but it would not address the real question here: whether Page's way of seeing things is, in the instance of transhistorical humanness, more plausible than its rivals.

To help determine that, we must consider the relevant empirical evidence. Theory-laden though it may be, it can at least disprove faulty ideas. Wegman, too, is interested in empirical evidence. He says it "persistently denies" the idea that medieval people "heard and felt just like us." The phrase "just like us" makes this hard to challenge; it may also be unfair to Page, who speaks only of "appreciable continuities." "Continuities" demand not exactness (hearing *just* like us) but similarity. Does the empirical evidence really show that we have *no* appreciable continuities of thought and feeling with people from other times and places?

Wegman does not say which empirical evidence he means, but his references suggest he's thinking of anthropology.[23] In mid-century, almost any generalization about humanity could be countered by a report of a people so different from us as to seem almost another species. There were Polynesians with no sexual attachment or frustration, Chinese without romantic passion, Chambris with reversed sex-temperaments, "gentle" Arapeshes without aggression, Hopis with no sense of past, future, or temporal flow (they sounded a bit like Alzheimer's patients), tribes with few color terms and, it was assumed, just as few colors experienced, and so on. A common explanation was that human beings were, in Margaret Mead's words, almost unbelievably malleable, with the molding process done entirely by culture and language.

But in recent decades every one of the above reports, and some of anthropology's other exotica as well, have turned out to be myths.[24] A few anthropologists have begun to complain about their field's tendency to overly exoticize

23. For example, in discussing transhistorical humanness in the *Music and Letters* review, p. 270, Wegman quotes the anthropologist Clifford Geertz.

24. Donald Brown, *Human Universals* (New York: McGraw-Hill, 1991) chaps. 1 and 3; Helen Harris, "Rethinking Heterosexual Love in Polynesia: A Case Study of Mangaia, Cook Island," in *Romantic Passion: A Universal Experience?*, ed. William Jankowiak (New York: Columbia University Press, 1995), pp. 95–127; Jankowiak, "Romantic Passion in the People's Republic of China," in *ibid.*; Derek Freeman, *Margaret Mead and Samoa: The Making and Unmaking of an Anthropological Myth* (Cambridge, Mass.: Harvard University Press, 1983); Ekkehart Malotki, *Hopi Time: A Linguistic Analysis of the Temporal Concepts in the Hopi Language* (Berlin: Mouton, 1983); Brent Berlin and Paul Kay, *Basic Color Terms: Their Universality and Evolution* (Berkeley: University of California Press, 1969). The "Alzheimer's" comparison is from Jankowiak (personal communication, 1996).

"others" and to overstate cultural determinism;[25] and over a hundred behavioral or psychological traits many once thought to result from "Western acculturation," have been shown to be universal.[26] For example, human beings in all cultures have words for logical relations, including "not" and "same," and "equivalent" and "opposite"; and all cultures make binary distinctions, including "male and female," "black and white," "nature and culture," "self and others," and "good and bad."[27] None of these cultures, obviously, subscribe to deconstructionism, which teaches that "oppositional thinking" is a Western hang-up.

It's unlikely that any of these human universals have changed since the Middle Ages. That alone gives us reason to take the idea of transhistorical humanness seriously.

Wegman's complaint may reflect an influential mode of thought, which holds that there is "not such a thing as human nature" and that "socialization, and thus historical circumstance, goes all the way down—that there is nothing 'beneath' socialization or prior to history" in any of us.[28] We are entirely "socially constructed." Some even imply that we are born blank slates. In view of these ideas, transhistorical continuity has to seem an outmoded concept.

This viewpoint has little place for universals; and it is true that a given cross-cultural universal doesn't necessarily imply an inborn detail of human nature; but consider the other evidence this mode of thought must answer to in the mid-1990s. Some examples are:

- Universals discovered by psychology. An extensive research program has shown that certain basic emotions (happiness, sadness, anger, fear, disgust, contempt, and surprise) are expressed by the same facial expressions in cultures as disparate as Japan, the United States, Europe, South America, and preliterate New Guinea.[29] This basic repertoire of expressions is widely agreed to be an inborn universal. Our culture may affect our sense of when it's *appropriate* to smile, but it does not create our association of smiling with happiness. This is evidence of our coming into the world with at least some unlearned content and detail built into our psychologies. A more complex example of universals in psychology involves certain patterns of mate preference found in every culture so far.[30]

25. Brown, *Human Universals*, p. 155, and chap. 1. See also Freeman, *Margaret Mead and the Samoans*, and Maurice Bloch, "The Past and the Present in the Present," *Man* 12 (1977), esp. pp. 283–85.

26. Brown, *Human Universals*, chap. 6.

27. Brown, *ibid.*, p. 134 and elsewhere.

28. Richard Rorty, *Contingency, Irony, and Solidarity* (Cambridge University Press, 1989), p. xiii.

29. E.g., *Emotions in the Human Face*, ed. Paul Ekman (Cambridge University Press, 1982).

30. David M. Buss, "Sex Differences in Human Mate Preferences: Evolutionary Hypotheses Tested in 37 Cultures," *Behavioral and Brain Sciences* 12 (1989), pp. 1–14; reprinted in *Human Nature: A Critical Reader*, ed. Laura Betzig (New York: Oxford University Press, 1997), pp. 175–90.

• Some patterns of behavior are found not only in all humans but in many other species—which raises the possibility that they are not entirely the result of human acculturation.[31] An example involves social status: both the body language used to signal status and the biochemistry that accompanies changes in status are found not only among humans but also among other primates.[32]

• Some preferences may be present from birth, before one can be socialized[33]—including, possibly, a preference for consonant over dissonant intervals.[34]

• Instances exist of "prepared learning," where animals (including us) are innately "primed" to learn certain things and not other things. An example is certain phobias: it has been shown that monkeys are pre-wired to develop fear of snakes;[35] and human phobia patterns suggest that we, too, are primed to fear, among other things, snakes, heights, and spiders—but not more significant modern hazards like, say, electrical outlets.[36] These instances may provide evidence for innate mental "modules" designed to process specific kinds of information in specific kinds of ways.

• There is evidence of genetic bases for highly specific cognitive or mental problems, e.g., impairments in language and in visual-spatial cognition.[37] Again, these may suggest inborn mental "modules."

• Evidence of brain-cell specialization. Although the development of the brain

31. Some examples are research on incest-avoidance mechanisms in humans and other sexually reproducing species, discussed in chap. 5 of Brown's *Human Universals*; on family dynamics in vertebrate species, in Stephen Emlen, "An Evolutionary Theory of the Family," *Proceedings of the National Academy of Science*, USA, 92 (August 1995), pp. 8092–99; on sex differences in violence, e.g., intra-sex homicide rates, discussed in Martin Daly and Margo Wilson, *Homicide* (New York: Aldine de Gruyter, 1988), chaps. 6, 7, and 8; and on sexual strategies, reviewed in Robert Wright's *The Moral Animal* (New York: Pantheon, 1994), chap. 2.

32. This evidence is reviewed in Wright, *The Moral Animal*, pp. 236–62.

33. E.g., Judith H. Langlois, Lori A. Roggman, Rita J. Casey, Jean M. Ritter, Loretta Rieser-Danner, and Vivian Jenkins, "Infant Preferences for Attractive Faces: Rudiments of a Stereotype?" *Developmental Psychology* 23 (1987), pp. 363–69; Curtis A. Samuels, George Butterworth, Tony Roberts, Lida Graupner, and Graham Hole, "Facial Aesthetics: Babies Prefer Attractiveness to Symmetry," *Perception* 23 (1994), pp. 823–31.

34. Marcel Zentner and Jerome Kagan, "Perceptions of Music by Infants," *Nature* 383 (5 September 1996), p. 29.

35. Susan Mineka, "A Primate Model of Phobic Fears," in *Theoretical Foundations of Behavior Therapy*, ed. Hans J. Eysenck and Irene Martin (New York: Plenum, 1987), pp. 81–111.

36. Martin E. P. Seligman, "Phobias and Preparedness," *Behavior Therapy* 1 (1971), pp. 307–20; D. R. Kirkpatrick, "Age, Gender and Patterns of Common Intense Fears among Adults," *Behaviour Research & Therapy* 22 (1984), pp. 141–50.

37. Studies indicate genetic linkages for Specific Language Impairment; see, for example, Dorothy Bishop, et al., "Genetic Basis of Specific Language Impairment: Evidence from a Twin Study," *Developmental Medicine and Child Neurology* 37 (1995), pp. 41–55. Genetic linkages have been found for developmental dyslexia, and for visuospatial skill impairments in Williams Syndrome. Regarding the latter, see "Gene Connected to Human Cognitive Trait," *Science News* (20 July 1996), p. 39.

allows for a great deal of plasticity, damaging a specific section of a mature brain often results in the loss of a very specific function. This might be said to provide evidence that the mind includes not just general mechanisms, but also specialized ones. That some of these brain-cell localizations (as well as some elements of neurochemistry) are found across species suggests that these may be built-in, not the products of learning.

This is far from a complete list. But it's hard to see how the belief that "there is nothing beneath socialization" could possibly account even for this subset of the evidence. Rather, the full range of the evidence seems better explained by the viewpoint that we are born with at least some shared content built into all of our brains. How *much* content is built in, what its exact nature is, how it operates, and how it got there in the first place are matters of debate and of active research programs.[38] And whatever the answers are, they clearly will not equate to "genetic determinism"[39]—when genes influence behavior it's usually through complex interactions with culture and environment. We *are* astonishingly malleable, and culture has an enormous influence on how we think and act. But enough evidence exists to cast grave doubt on the idea that we have no inborn natures at all. Even the more moderate idea that we have only a minimal human nature, consisting of a few general mechanisms and basic drives—a view common among social scientists—would find it hard to account for all of the above evidence (it's not obvious that it could). At the very least, then, "transhistorical humanness" has earned something more than a curt dismissal.

(By the way, the political and ethical implications of the findings I've listed are by no means clear. Robert Wright says that to the degree that the emerging picture of innate human nature has "reasonably distinct political implications—and as a general rule it just doesn't—they are about as often to the left as to the right. In some ways they are radically to the left."[40] None of what I've covered implies Social Darwinism. Also feminists have tended to object to arguments for innateness, but today many leading researchers in this field are avowed feminists. And many thinkers in this field dismiss racial differences as insignificant. I think we should try, therefore, to base our verdict not on politics but on the weight of the evidence.)

It's harder to say how all this applies to music. The musical universals we know about (involving such things as phrase grouping) are so basic and gen-

---

38. See *Human Nature: A Critical Reader,* ed. Laura Betzig; also, Harmon R. Holcomb III, *Sociobiology, Sex, and Science* (Albany: State University of New York Press, 1993). See also *The Adapted Mind: Evolutionary Psychology and the Generation of Culture,* ed. Jerome Barkow, Leda Cosmides, and John Tooby (New York: Oxford University Press, 1992).

39. For a sophisticated discussion see Holcomb, *Sociobiology, Sex, and Science,* pp. 132–48.

40. Wright, *The Moral Animal,* p. 13.

eral that they don't usually bear on issues in early music. An example: it seems likely that the "natural intervals"—such as the octave, fourth, and fifth—have affected the development of scales in many cultures;[41] and it has been suggested that we tend to prefer these intervals because they play a role in how the brain analyzes sound in natural environments.[42] But I can't think of any early-music performance issues that this could illuminate—especially since research suggests that tuning and intonation, as opposed to scale structure, are determined by culture, and that even scales can deviate from the natural intervals.[43] On the other hand, it's possible that evidence for inborn elements of rhythm disproves Pérès's idea that strictly measured quantitative rhythm developed as a result of our ancestors becoming used to the clock. Instead, such rhythm seems to reflect innate timing and motor mechanisms.[44] (This also may account for why quantitative rhythms can be found in some cultures that have no clocks.) But such reasoning doesn't take us very far.

The evidence I reviewed for a trans-cultural, transhistorical human nature may have another kind of relevance to the quest to understand early music. In recent years many scholars have emphasized how social elements bear on and shape musical meaning.[45] Some of their work has been unconvincing, and some can even seem laughable; but some has demonstrated that at times we misunderstand early music because we fail to recognize how differently people saw things in previous eras. This book includes many examples of how culture has influenced the meaning of music—say, the meaning of different dances in Beethoven's day (in addition to whatever meaning those dances may convey intrinsically). But we should take care not to exaggerate the "otherness" of those who did the dancing. Several myths of medieval "otherness" have been debunked in recent years: it is no longer reasonable to say that medieval people

41. Edward M. Burns and W. Ward Dixon, "Intervals, Scales, and Tuning," in *The Psychology of Music*, ed. Diana Deutsch (New York: Academic Press, 1982), pp. 241–69.

42. Do the component frequencies that strike our ears at a given moment come from separate sources in our environment, or are they parts of a single sound from one source? To figure this out, one of the tricks the brain uses is to analyze whether any of the frequencies belong in the same harmonic series. If some do, the brain guesses that these ones are parts of a single tone—and in the natural world, this is usually accurate. Steven Pinker relates this to our response to musical intervals, in a brief section of his forthcoming *How the Mind Works* (New York: Norton, 1997; page numbers unavailable as I go to press).

43. Burns and Dixon, "Intervals, Scales, and Tuning," pp. 258–59.

44. See Paul Fraisse, "Rhythm and Tempo," especially pp. 151–55, in *The Psychology of Music*, ed. Deutsch.

45. Richard Leppert writes, "[Meaning] develops not only, and maybe not even principally, from what's 'in' the music . . . but more from the purposes or functions to which music is put (inevitably different for different people at any given moment, *and* inevitably changing in historical time)." "The Postmodern Condition and Musicology's Place in Humanistic Studies," *Journal of Musicological Research* 12 (1995), pp. 235–50.

A caveat regarding these attempts is Charles Rosen's "Music à la Mode," *New York Review of Books*, 23 June 1994, pp. 55–62.

had no idea of childhood as a separate stage[46] or, as I'll discuss below, no experience of romantic love before the twelfth century. (And in music it is no longer reasonable to say, as once was said, that medieval people had only a weak sense of harmony.[47]) If music's human context influences its meaning, then we had better understand humans as accurately as we can. We need to recognize not only the historical differences, but also the transhistorical continuities.

To illustrate why this might be worthwhile, consider one of the most central aspects of musical meaning: emotion. Wegman may be right that we do not "hear just like" medieval people; and there's no denying that our world views, lifestyles, technologies, economies, political structures, class structures, and—to return to music—listening contexts differ markedly from theirs. So do our aesthetics and our pool of artistic experiences. Some of these things affect musical experience. But given the research I've summarized, it is no longer naive to suspect *pace* Wegman, that we *feel* more or less as medieval people did. Many psychologists now accept that emotions often have functional origins in our species' evolution, and are not purely a matter of acculturation.[48] Some of our emotional "calls" (such as crying and laughing) are like the facial expressions I discussed: they convey the same emotions in all cultures. Romantic love was once written off as an invention of the West in the twelfth century,[49] and anthropologists portrayed certain cultures as being free of it;[50] but it is now regarded as a human universal.[51] Of course, different cultures place different valuations on romantic love. In our culture, it's considered one of life's highest achievements, but some cultures regard it as something to avoid or at least hide. But even in those cultures romantic love erupts regularly, with all the intensity (and all the components) that it has for us.[52]

Thus, the longing of a medieval song may not be so "other" from modern

46. See, for example, pp. 462–63 of Michel Rouche, "The Early Middle Ages in the West," in *A History of Private Life, I: From Pagan Rome to Byzantium,* ed. Paul Veyne, trans. Arthur Goldhammer (Cambridge, Mass.: Harvard University Press, 1987).

47. As was shown by R. Crocker, "Discant, Counterpoint, and Harmony," *Journal of the American Musicological Society* 15 (1962), pp. 1-21.

48. *The Nature of Emotion: Fundamental Questions,* ed. Paul Ekman and Richard Davidson (New York: Oxford University Press, 1994), pp. 15–25, 146–77; and Richard Lazarus, *Emotion and Adaptation* (New York: Oxford University Press, 1991).

49. Denis de Rougemont, *Love in the Western World,* trans. Montgomery Belgion, rev. ed. (New York: Pantheon, 1974).

50. Re the Chinese, *ibid.,* p. i; re Polynesians, Margaret Mead, *Coming of Age in Samoa* (New York: Morrow, 1961 [1928]); Donald Marshall, "Sexual Behavior in Mangaia," in *Human Sexual Behavior,* ed. Marshall and R. Suggs (New York: Basic Books, 1971), pp. 103–62.

51. *Romantic Passion: A Universal Experience?,* ed. Jankowiak; Jankowiak and Ted Fisher, "A Cross-Cultural Perspective on Romantic Love," *Ethnology* 31 (1992), pp. 149–55.

52. Helen A. Regis, "The Madness of Excess: Love among the Fulbe of North Cameroun," in *Romantic Passion,* ed. Jankowiak, pp. 141–49.

longing. Of course, that and other basic emotions may be embedded in belief systems we find foreign and in musical idioms we don't speak fluently. Still, it seems reasonable to suppose that transhistorical emotional resonances have something to do with why old music means more to us than wild parrot squawks. They may also give the historical performer a bit of hope that what he or she is expressing can be, if not identical, at least closely related to what the music was expressing in its own day. At the very least, they provide one more reason for giving the idea of transhistorical humanness a careful hearing.

∞ II ∞

THE RENAISSANCE, OXBRIDGE,

AND ITALY

In 1994 a lecturer in the music department at Cambridge University asserted, in a memo to his students, that "Recent recordings [of Renaissance music by British artists] are in many cases unspeakably dull and performed with a desperate absence of historical awareness." He went on to damn most of the prominent English ensembles. The leader of an ensemble that was treated fairly leniently—Christopher Page, who teaches in another Cambridge department—relayed the document "in amazement" to the readers of *Gramophone*.[1]

A couple of months later, the author of the document, the music historian Roger Bowers, responded with a letter backing up his complaints.[2] He compared using women's instead of boys' voices to using "members of the violin family for music conceived for viols." He called upward transposition by a tone or a third "a pretty miserable experience" (such transposition is now discredited, largely by Bowers's own work, but is still employed by some British performers). Beyond that, he argued that "the performances are far removed from the spiritual and aesthetic sensibilities of the period. . . . Rather, they tend to respond to the wholly alien concepts of the modern Anglican tradition. . . ."[3]

1. Christopher Page, "The Listening List," *Gramophone* 72 (December 1994), p. 8.
2. Roger Bowers, "The Listening List," *Gramophone* 72 (February 1995), p. 6.
3. American readers may wonder what Bowers means here. Chris Hunter (personal communication, 1995) answered my query by saying that it probably refers to a performing style in which the chorus dramatizes the text—e.g., slowing down for the Crucifixus or speeding up for the Et resurrexit. This approach grew out of the Victorian revival of the Anglican chorus, and appears not to have been part of church music performance in the Renaissance. The issue is discussed briefly in the Peter Phillips interview.

The large and resonant tone production of the singers and its expansive projection conflicts with the conditions under which the music was originally conceived and performed—namely, the sense of intimacy and introspection generated within a late medieval chancel or chapel by singers performing for themselves and for their deity alone, there being no congregation in attendance to edify or entertain."

All of which may be valid—though the success of the Tallis Scholars suggests that many people find a little upward transposition far from "miserable," and reminds us that when Bowers sets out aesthetic judgments he can no longer claim to be speaking objectively. But what strikes me most is that Bowers objects mainly to practices that present the music in modern conditions. If you use boy choristers, forget about grueling international tours. And if you are performing for an audience, you may well find it impossible to sing like people who didn't have one. If you do manage not to project to your audience, you may not have one for long. If it comes down to it, which would you sacrifice: the history or the audience?

This is an issue that recurs throughout early music: how far should (and can) we go toward the past, as opposed to trying to bring it toward us? Peter Phillips argues cogently for the latter orientation; Bowers and others, also with good reasons, argue for the former. And Paul Hillier argues that the issue itself may be anachronistic.

If we do want to go toward the past, one obstacle we face is that much of what musicians did in the past they did not write down. Some of the notes they performed were improvised; others were written down without all the information we'd need about inflection and even pitch. Modern classical training enjoins us to honor the written notes, so (as Andrew Lawrence-King observes) learning to go beyond the notes is in some ways subversive, or at least *terra incognita*. Paul Hillier mentions another problem: even when we feel that all the notes we need *were* written down, modern forms of notation differ from older forms so profoundly that it can change how we sing the music.

Finally, "Renaissance" is a more likable term than "Middle Ages": most medievalists object to their period being labeled as a "middle" ground lying between other, implicitly more interesting times; but who could dislike a rebirth? And unlike "medieval," "Renaissance" does seem to apply to a real historical development. But for musicians, the latter term is problematic. For one thing, compared to art or literature, it's harder to say just what is so "Renaissance" about the era's most prominent music, the polyphonic vocal works. Christopher Page speculates about this in his interview, and Peter Phillips adds further observations on the issue. In Andrew Lawrence-King's chapter, definition again proves troublesome, in that we find the dividing line between "Renaissance" and "Baroque" to be a little arbitrary. Not long ago, Monteverdi was usually described as the father of the Baroque, but an influential recent book called him "the foremost Italian composer at the end of the Renaissance."[4] I include his chapter here, rather than in the section on Baroque singing, because it relates to the issue of "Oxbridge" style, discussed by Hillier and Phillips, and to the views of Italophiles who would prefer that Britons find other work for their vocal cords.

4. Gary Tomlinson, *Monteverdi and the End of the Renaissance* (Berkeley: University of California Press, 1987), p. ix.

5

There Is No Such Thing as a Norm

Paul Hillier on Renaissance
Sacred Music

The mainstream repertory is so heavily Germanic that a novice of an earlier generation might easily have imagined that classical music had always been Teutonic territory. But in the art music of the Renaissance, the crucial region was what is now Belgium and northern France. Franco-Flemings like Dufay and Ockeghem dominated the fifteenth century, and their follower Josquin Desprez established the polyphonic style that dominated the sixteenth century. It's true that the English were an early stimulus to these Franco-Flemish masters—the sweet, thirds-dominated "English countenance" of Dunstaple was a crucial influence on Dufay and Binchois—but England usually remained somewhat separate from developments on the Continent. As far as the sixteenth-century Franco-Flemings and Italians were concerned, England was a musical backwater.

Thus there is a certain irony in today's early-music revival: the great Franco-Flemish polyphonists have been popularized mainly by English groups, such as Pro Cantione Antiqua, the Clerkes of Oxenford, the Sixteen, the Taverner Choir, the Oxford Camerata, and various cathedral and university choirs. An irony; but not an accident. The choral tradition in England's colleges and churches, has, as Christopher Page points out, produced an astonishingly large pool of skilled choral singers, who can read difficult music at sight, stay perfectly in tune even when singing challenging harmonies, and blend skillfully with each other. No other country has such a resource concentrated in so small a geographic area. Moreover, much of the classical recording industry is in London, around which this brigade of singers stands on call, and recordings have long been the main means of propagating early-music performance. Thus, most listeners have heard their Dufay, Ockeghem, and Josquin with a new English countenance, called by many the "Oxbridge style" in honor of its main propagators' alma maters.

As Page noted in his chapter, on the Continent this style has won approval but far from universal acclaim. Even within Oxbridge it has detractors, as the Roger Bowers controversy shows. All the dissent, though, is at least in part a reaction against enormous success. David Fallows writes that, although the situation is changing, since the early 1970s "it has looked very much as though British musicians were the almost unchallenged leaders in the performance of music before 1550."[1]

Our next chapters feature two leading representatives of the Oxbridge style who have taken opposite paths. Peter Phillips, an Oxford graduate, founded the Tallis Scholars in 1978 (though the group had been singing without the name before then); Patrick Russill writes that the group has always seemed to him "not so much a product of the 'early music and authenticity' movement, but rather a perfectly logical development of the English choir-stall tradition."[2] In 1974, the baritone Paul Hillier, a graduate of the Guildhall School of Music, co-founded something rather different to perform much the same repertory: a quartet with three other singers, two of them Oxonians. (The group was named after the sixteenth-century miniaturist painter Nicholas Hilliard—not, as many assume, after Hillier.)

Phillips shows no inclination to do anything but continue exploring the Renaissance repertory with the Tallis Scholars, using London as his home base. Hillier, though, left the Hilliards in 1990 and moved across the Atlantic. He first joined the music faculty of the University of California at Davis, where he formed a new ensemble, the Theatre of Voices. Then, in 1996, he took the directorship of the Early Music Institute at the University of Indiana (a post previously held by the late Thomas Binkley, a pioneer of the early-music movement). Hillier has also worked closely with the Estonian composer of mystical minimalism, Arvo Pärt—an interest that Phillips, as we'll see, doesn't share.

Phillips and Hillier have differed on many musical issues: choral size (the Tallis Scholars use ten or so singers; the Hilliards sing one-per-part, as the Theatre of Voices occasionally does); pitch (the Tallis Scholars transpose upward); pronunciation (Phillips has little interest in regional differences in Latin pronunciation, Hillier finds them crucial); use of *musica ficta* (Hillier applies these unnotated sharps and flats more freely); the use of a conductor (the Hilliards don't have one, the Tallis Scholars—and, usually, the Theatre of Voices—do;

---

1. "Quarterly Retrospect," *Gramophone* 71 (December 1993), pp. 33–34. The article is a stimulating survey of the rise of non-British groups who are performing this music.

2. *Gramophone* 73 (June 1995), p. 104.

Renaissance choirs generally had no conductor, relying on rehearsal, stylistic empathy, and, probably, eye contact to stay together). Above all, the two men differ more than one might expect in their basic aesthetic orientation—compare Hillier's doubts about "seraphic refinement" to Phillips's admiration for the Berlin Philharmonic, or the two men's views on "Continental" versus "Oxbridge" sound.

As these differences demonstrate, "English" ideas of style and taste can vary considerably—though that's influenced by (among other things) the inconclusiveness of much of the evidence, and by questions about how carefully we should attend even to evidence that is firm. These were the first issues I raised when I interviewed Hillier in his office in the music building at Davis.

When singing a Renaissance piece, we usually have less certain information about performance practice than when we perform a Classical or Romantic piece.

Yes, but I think the music in itself contains virtually all the information you need to unlock its beauty; and while the particular way in which this beauty manifests itself is obviously not unimportant, it is liable to adaptation according to the means used to perform it.

Definitive realization—the idea that there's one right way to orchestrate and perform a piece—is a much later concept.

I think the most important thing to remember regarding this music is that there is no such thing as a norm to which we must try to adhere, which means that the question is very open. It is important to avoid assuming that this music should sound the way it has always sounded to us—in other words just adopting a standard choral format and singing style, and assuming that the sound and balance they're producing is the right one for the music.

I'd like to deal with various areas of uncertainty one by one. One of them is the size of the ensemble. There's evidence of group sizes ranging from a total of four through fifty or more.

It's pretty obvious, as you say, that choral sizes varied tremendously, and not only to fit the size of the given building they were singing in, but also to reflect different tastes about what the music should sound like. The same piece would surely have been performed differently in different places.

My approach to this may be excessively pragmatic, but I believe that the music is there for us to use and to suit to the forces we have, rather than always requiring that we play around with the forces to try to suit the music. We may feel there is an ideal grouping for a given piece or genre, but that doesn't mean to say one should never perform it with groups of different sizes—large choirs, small choirs, one to a part. Of course, it also depends on the piece you're talking about. But I think that one can be very open-minded about it, allowing for the fact that the more you do a certain repertoire the more you're likely to develop a relatively fixed sense of your ideal.

Is there music you prefer with small or, for that matter, large ensembles?

Well, for example, when I work on Dufay and his period, I've been interested in the research of scholars who are trying to work out the size and balance of his ensembles. The evidence seems to point towards a larger number of singers—falsetto male sopranos—on the top lines, and fewer on the lower lines.[3] That music tends to have a strongly melodic upper line that clearly can take a certain amount of emphasis. This seems to tell us what to do; but then we also have to remember that our chorus members surely sing in a different way than people did four hundred years ago. Today, the singing voice is "placed" in a way that differs radically from the placement we use when we speak, but I (and others) suspect that back then it wasn't[4]—as it still isn't, for example, in folk singing. Today's singing technique creates a legato stream of sound and breath support that tends to increase the size of the voice. So maybe our falsettists, for example, produce an individually stronger sound than their fifteenth-century counterparts did; if so, maybe the need for greater numbers is obviated. Even if we can establish exactly how many singers there were then, we still don't know if we're reproducing the sound of the original, because our ways of singing have changed.

So you're left, really, relying on your own musical intuition as to what the ideal balance is, how the music works best. You can't really get away from that.

To give another example, I'm very interested at the moment in the music of Byrd, and there have been a lot of very fine choral recordings of his music. But I'm convinced that the *Gradualia*, which is a very significant part of his output, was performed by solo voices, one per part. The music was probably performed at secret Catholic services,[5] and though they could perhaps have had more than one singer per part, it's unlikely. And if you look at the music, the nature of the individual part-writing is often much more florid, sometimes only in one part at any given time, and I find it sounds much more effective with one singer to a part than with a whole choir. Again, I want to avoid a blanket assertion that I don't think it should be sung by a choir; but I just think it's

3. See especially David Fallows's essay, "Specific Information on the Ensembles for Composed Polyphony, 1400–1474," in *Studies in the Performance of Late Medieval Music,* ed. S. Boorman (Cambridge University Press, 1983), esp. pp. 120–33.

4. See John Potter, "Reconstructing Lost Voices," in *Companion to Medieval and Renaissance Music,* ed. T. Knighton and D. Fallows (London: Orion, and New York: Schirmer, 1992), pp. 311–16.

5. See Joseph Kerman's essay (aptly described on its book jacket as "moving") entitled "William Byrd and Elizabethan Catholicism," in his *Write All These Down* (Berkeley: University of California Press, 1994), pp. 77–89.

time we had a look from the other end of the telescope. There, you see, you have a special case, Byrd and the position of the Catholic Church in England at that time. It's not a rule you can apply indiscriminately.

How about Byrd's Anglican works, such as the Great Service?

That's different again. We know the standard Anglican choir of today is quite appropriate for that—at least in terms of overall size.[6] It's a different kind of music, too; it doesn't have those little virtuosic moments in quite the same way that you find in the *Gradualia*.

Another area of uncertainty is instrumental accompaniment. For example, written-out organ parts exist for Victoria, among others.

Again, the probable answer is that there were varying practices. There is strong evidence for instrumental participation in Isaac, for example, in the court of Maximilian, where he worked, and in Lassus too. It seems somewhat more common later in the Renaissance than earlier. But I happen to be biased towards the sound of *a cappella* singing: it's as simple as that. So even where there's strong evidence for using instruments, both for practical reasons and for reasons of personal taste I usually opt for *a cappella*. I suppose it's a case of liking what I know. But there is some music—for example the Lassus *Penitential Psalms*—which I've recorded using voices and instruments. And I can still imagine doing that music in both ways and getting a great deal of pleasure out of it. They're different, but both options seem to me equally viable, and in either case the character of the music is altered—though not fundamentally.

You mentioned voice production in Dufay's time; what do we know about Renaissance voice production? I'd imagine this would be especially hard to reconstruct. And do you have any comments about using vibrato in this music?

What we "know" is actually very little. What we can imaginatively reconstruct depends on cross-referencing all sorts of information (from linguistics, the nature of instruments, the history of liturgy, etc.)—none of which is remotely conclusive from the singer's point of view. The reason I would give for not using excessive vibrato is that it obscures the counterpoint and muddies the tuning, making the music of the era quite simply less effective—disastrously so in some cases.

Another area where information is incomplete is the use of unwritten accidentals—the convention of musica ficta, *as it was called. It suggests that some*

---

6. Eric Van Tassel, however, observes that many Anglican choirs today have a higher proportion of trebles than in the sixteenth and seventeenth centuries. See, e.g., his "Purcell's Sacred Music on Record," Part 2, *Early Music* 24 (February 1996), p. 92 n. 11.

of the accidentals that the composer assumed would be sung in a piece weren't written down, but were understood by convention.

I'm going to have to generalize, but providing you're using a good edition (and there are a lot of them nowadays) that issue will have been taken care of. The best advice, then, is to follow the editorial suggestions (usually written above the notes) unless you really know what you're doing. It's a very involved issue, since the more you deal with that kind of music, the more you will want to introduce changes, and the more you'll be in a position to do so. But it's important to know clearly what is original and what the editor has added. Different editors will solve the same *ficta* issues in slightly different ways.

There's been a tendency in the past years towards adding more *ficta* so that, particularly in the middle Renaissance period, the music is not so "modal."[7] Also, the guiding principle gives weight more to the logic of the individual line as against the resulting harmony. We have to remember that in earlier centuries each singer had only his own part in front of him—they didn't sing from a score. So their initial response would have been based very much on their own part first, and then the other parts and the total harmonic picture afterwards.

That brings up something else that maybe you're going to ask me about—the appearance of that part, as opposed to the way it appears in a modern score. Modern notation puts a bias on the information you're receiving that is very different from what the original notation tells us. It's not only that early notation usually presents a single part by itself rather than a score. It's also, first of all, that you do not have barlines, which divide the music up far too frequently: you get a long line of sound, which in a modern edition is broken up into little segments of $\frac{4}{4}$ or $\frac{3}{4}$ or something. The barline not only divides it up, it also suggests a regular emphasis or a beat which is inappropriate to the music most of the time. Visually, the flow of the line and phrase is impeded by these barlines. And the second thing that's different is the nature of the note values that we use, as opposed to the originals—all this does affect the way we sing the music. As just one example we might consider a well-known motet by Byrd, such as *Ave verum corpus*. Looking at the familiar editions used by most choirs, we can see straight away that the editor has responded as well as he can to the music's demand for a flexible sense of meter, changing frequently throughout the piece between duple and triple time signatures. The problem is that there are still many, many passages where the voices either are in a mix-

---

7. One group that has tended to add *ficta* very sparingly in earlier repertoire is the Tallis Scholars (I failed to ask Peter Phillips about this). While their practice may represent an anachronistic preoccupation with the written text and may not re-create period practice, it may not be entirely unrelated to Renaissance musical philosophy. Charles Rosen says that the very term *musica ficta* ("fictive music") suggests that a version that was never actually sounded—the purely modal one on the page—was considered "real" (Rosen, *The Romantic Generation* [Cambridge, Mass.: Harvard University Press, 1995], pp. 28–29). That "real version" is what the Tallis Scholars are sounding in some of their recordings.

ture of duple and triple rhythms, or else simply have their "downbeats" at different times. No system of barring can do justice to this, and the result is a mixture of seemingly displaced accents and superfluous syncopations. Even taking a line at a time, the use of barlines, however flexible, imposes a set response in place of the wonderfully supple and expressive ambiguity of the original. Skeptics will argue that the sounding result is pretty much the same in either case, but I beg to differ. We hear the same sequence of abstract notes, certainly, and the difference may be rather subtle at any given moment, but the net result is like viewing the music through tinted glasses. Ultimately, we lose a sense of rhythmic freedom and "natural" phrasing, replaced by a kind of foursquare security borrowed from the conventions of a different age.

It would be wonderful if people wanting to perform early music could use either a facsimile of the original or a transcription (known as "diplomatic") using a more readable adaptation of the original style of notation. It might be impractical to do that all the time; but it would be a very informative experience if singers would once or twice work their way through a piece in the original notation, and just learn the kinds of information that are conveyed by that notation. Sometimes the differences are very subtle; one wouldn't want to insist upon them too heavily. But then it would, I think, be possible to go back to using modern editions armed with this information and not simply having been told by someone like me that the trouble with these editions is that there are too many barlines. It's one thing to say that, and another to have the experience of singing that music without the barlines.

When do you feel that the barline becomes a musically significant element, as opposed to a modern intrusion?

I suppose, loosely speaking, the middle to late sixteenth century. It seems to develop first in lute songs; soon after, in polyphony and larger court music, the barline is more clearly related to an audible metrical emphasis. There is a fairly clear division in the polyphonic field, at least in my mind, and I suppose it falls right around the end of the sixteenth century, where suddenly the use of the barline makes sense and doesn't get in the way.[8] But with Palestrina and all those people it doesn't really help. It helps *us* because we're used to it, but it doesn't help the music.

Returning to the theme of incomplete information, I wanted to ask also about transposition—the possibility that a piece was meant to be heard at a higher or lower pitch than the notation appears (to us) to imply.

I think the important thing is to be clear that there was no such thing as a fixed pitch standard, that it varied from place to place—maybe not wildly,

---

8. For an explanation of why the barline became musically important after this point, see the interview with John Butt, Chapter 9, in the section on "grammar."

though maybe more than we might expect. And because they didn't use extreme key signatures—in the Renaissance, usually at the most two flats or sharps—the concept of color that later centuries attach to keys just did not exist. So it's perfectly appropriate to perform a piece at more or less any pitch. In practice, one's talking about transposing a half-step or so, depending upon what your choir needs. Again, I would say, let practical considerations rule: make sure it's pretty much in the range of your choir or your singers, and then you can't go far wrong. Obviously, there are pieces where low registers are being exploited, so you wouldn't want to transpose them from low to high—though you could argue that as long as it sounds low on the spectrum of whatever voices you have, then the relative sense of depth has been retained.

There is a separate issue with regard to certain combinations of clefs. It seems that in sixteenth-century polyphony, some pieces were actually sung a third or a fourth lower, and certain clefs were used to avoid the necessity of unusual key signatures. You may have a collection of motets in which suddenly there's this motet where every voice is at the top of its range, and it all seems very impractical; you look at the clefs, and sure enough, the bass part is in the baritone clef, and so on. If you transpose it down, it's in line with the range of the other motets. In modern editions, usually the original clef is printed before the new one, so that even if everything is transposed into "normal" clefs you can see at the beginning what the original was.

Then there's another side issue, the question of English polyphony of the early sixteenth century, which certain scholars[9] are sure sounded a minor or even major third higher. I'm not totally convinced by this, just because I feel that the result is wonderful for five minutes but then is quite tiring. I'm not saying it shouldn't be done, but I don't think we need all follow in that direction. Instead—and this would again be a pragmatic approach—we might keep in mind the possibility that generally the music needs to be shifted up, say, a half-step or so.

Another topic of uncertainty: intonation systems. Modern equal temperament, of course, hadn't developed yet, so one reads about just and mean-tone and Pythagorean tunings.

Well, again, unfortunately, it's a very large topic, and the application of it changes as you move through history. Ultimately I would argue that it's im-

9. Notably David Wulstan: see his "The Problem of Pitch in Sixteenth-Century English Vocal Music," *Proceedings of the Royal Musical Association* 93 (1966–67), pp. 97–112. Wulstan's view has been countered by Roger Bowers, who demonstrates that (as Hillier says) there were no established pitch standards at this time; see his "The Performing Pitch of English 15th-century Church Polyphony," *Early Music* 8 (January 1980), pp. 21–28; "Further Thoughts on Early Tudor Pitch," *Early Music* 8 (August 1980), pp. 368–75; and "The Vocal Scoring, Choral Balance, and Performing Pitch of Latin Church Polyphony in England, *c.* 1500–58," *Journal of the Royal Musical Association* 112 (1987), pp. 38–76.

portant not to rehearse with a piano. The choir will probably settle on their own naturally into a good tuning system, all other things being equal—if they aren't tired, if the music isn't too high for them, if they're reasonably good singers, and so on.

Talking about unaccompanied polyphony, one thing I've found very helpful when there's an intonation problem is to transpose the music up or down a half-step (so we return to the topic of transposition). In other words, you're moving the music from the white keys of the piano to the black keys. And for some reason—and I have no idea what it is—that very often solves all the intonation problems. Now this shouldn't be the case, unless we have the piano's tempered tuning so ingrained that we can't get away from it. For example, F major is a very problematic key when it comes to tuning, so I move F major a half-step up and usually it falls into place. That's totally unscientific, but it just seems to be something that works.

I think that, beyond that, the most important thing in the question of intonation, rather than worrying about given systems, is to give very close aural attention to the principal intervals, the octave, the fifth, and the fourth; also, the note just above the tonic is worth watching. If those are in tune, everything else will probably follow. Just to get a choir to practice tuning a perfect fifth is actually quite an interesting exercise. There are lots of other little practical tips that one can follow up with. For example, basses generally need to think a little bit higher, particularly in a descending phrase. So if the basses think more like high baritones, even when they're singing at the bottom of their range, and the higher voices are a little bit more deeply rooted, then they can begin to come together. This is verging more on choral music generally—these are important considerations for any period of music, not just the Renaissance—but given the relative lack of chromaticism in Renaissance music, those principal intervals become that much more crucial.

Another area of uncertainty is the question of improvisation. It's been suggested that there were two kinds of music in the High Renaissance: what the composer had put on paper, and then what was performed, which was heavily ornamented.[10]

The fact that polyphony was probably ornamented some of the time does not make *me* want to ornament it, unless I am performing one to a part—and even then, quite frankly, not very much. I also think that if anyone is going to concern themselves with ornamentation they need to spend a considerable amount of time not only practicing it but exploring the treatises themselves and thoroughly absorbing the kinds of configurations that were used.[11] I have to be

10. John Butt, personal communication, 27 April 1993. See Howard Mayer Brown's *Embellishing Sixteenth-century Music* (Oxford University Press, 1976).

11. In his interview, Robert Levin makes a similar point with respect to Mozart.

honest: it's something that holds very little interest for me. With a lot of people—especially singers who come to Renaissance music from Baroque music—almost the first thing they want to know is how to ornament, but I would say it's the last thing they should worry about. Yes, it undoubtedly played a role in performance, but there's so much else to learn that it seems to me it's putting the cart before the horse, or whatever the appropriate saying is. Especially in polyphony, apart from an occasional cadential thing, I have to be honest: it just doesn't interest me. It's a purely personal reaction. When you go into the Baroque, that's different, of course. But I've often heard it done so badly.

Bovicelli, Rogniono, and others wrote down examples of how singers ornamented Palestrina motets, but there were complaints from contemporaries about this practice. More recently, Alfred Einstein said the Bovicelli versions were "monstrosities," and Howard Brown said they show that "bad taste is not the exclusive property of the present century."[12] This relates to the debates about authenticity: one ideal of authenticity is to play the music the way it was played in the composer's era, but could this be a case in which the modern style of playing it, unornamented, would—at least to our ears—serve the music better than the historical practice?

Maybe. Music that wasn't virtually contemporary in those days didn't get performed, or, if it did, we can be sure that it was reworked according to the tastes of the day; so this whole notion of authenticity is thrown out the window by the very people we're trying to emulate. They lived and breathed one style of music essentially, which was the style of their contemporaries. This is something we have no idea about; I think we have no conception of what that could feel like. If we grew up hearing one kind of music then we might be in a position to start embellishing it authoritatively. But I still say, though I've heard some very good performances of sixteenth- and seventeenth-century music that used embellishment, many have been awful. Another important thing to remember is that embellishment exists for only one performance. It shouldn't be reproduced exactly from performance to performance, otherwise it's going to become rigid. So, again, if it's done very well, I'm interested, certainly. In fact, in the Theatre of Voices we've had Drew Minter singing, and he's someone who embellishes as naturally as he breathes; you don't hear the extra notes as "ornaments," but as part of a natural response to the music. Done like this, it works—but now we're talking about one-to-a-part singing.

All the same, are there any places where you find ornamentation or embellishment necessary?

Before about 1600, I wouldn't say so. Again, I would take any given version on its own merits. There's a school of thought that says the use of fer-

12. Brown, *Embellishing Sixteenth-century Music*, discusses this on p. 73.

matas in some passages in Dufay indicates a place where someone could embellish the notes. Fine: let's hear someone do it. But it takes a lot of know-how and just sheer application over a period of time to get inside the music and the history of it—and not just the history, but also the kinds of things that might have been done to make the embellishment work.

The theme we've been returning to here, with embellishment being one example [and *ficta* another], is that the music on the page is not necessarily quite representative of what was actually heard.[13] I totally agree with that; but I would also say that it allows one to take other kinds of liberties as well, and not just the addition of extra notes. And these concern articulation, expression, tempo, all the things that we don't really hear about in Renaissance music.

Let me ask you about them, then. Can any general principles be stated about articulation in Renaissance music?

No, I don't think so. I don't think that one can lay down any specific guidelines as to how to perform a piece of Renaissance polyphony in quite the way you can for some later music. And even for later music there are lots of ifs and buts. There are a number of things that can be said on this subject, and the more you perform this music the more possibilities you see in it. The only general statement I can make is that, again, you shouldn't assume that what you've been hearing is the way it should be. I don't think one should automatically turn on the all-purpose church legato when there are so many other possibilities.

Again, it has to be ultimately a matter of taste, as to how you treat the fast figuration versus the slow notes, whether it's clearly articulated, whether you should ever use what we would call a staccato, and so on. Unfortunately, without specific examples it's very hard to talk about this issue, which I think is one of the most important.

Can you give an example?

In the music of one of my favorite composers, Ockeghem, there are often many different things happening at once. And I don't think there should ever be any dead ground. So even the slower-moving phrases should be phrased in an expressive way, whatever that may mean. I'm thinking also of the music of Dufay, where the slow-moving parts should be sung with just as much care for their shaping as the more obviously expressive fast-moving parts. This

---

13. James Haar suggests another angle to this: that notated music, e.g. some florid lines in Josquin Masses, attempted to capture something of how skillful singers might have improvised. This, he argues, suggests a different approach to performing such pieces than that which is common today—a more improvisatory, less solemn manner. See Haar, "Monophony and the Unwritten Tradition," in *Performance Practice: Music before 1600,* ed. H. M. Brown and S. Sadie (London: Macmillan, 1989; New York: Norton, 1990), pp. 240–66; reference, p. 260.

brings the music into sharper relief, and makes it more interesting and more expressive. I have no idea whether it was performed that way, but that's the way it interests me.

How about specific issues of articulation per se, *though?*

Your first clue, I think, has to come from the text. The nature of the language, in so far as you can understand how it was pronounced and used, has to have a strong influence on the way in which you sing and enunciate the text through the music.[14] If you go back to styles of polyphony where one syllable stretches over a long period of time, you lose that particular crutch, obviously. But in less florid music, clearly it's important to understand how the language that you're singing was pronounced. This refers not only to the vernacular languages—French, English, Italian, and so on—but also to Latin, which we know varied quite considerably from country to country. It still doesn't give us nice easy solutions, hard and fast rules, but it certainly is a way of opening up our ears and minds to what kinds of possibilities are available. It is generally accepted that Latin pronunciation in sixteenth-century England lacked the smooth Italianate quality that we give Latin today. Its pronunciation and vocal placement were probably much closer to that of the spoken English of the time. As a result, the Latin pronunciation would have had a "lived-in" quality—and of course for some people Latin was still potentially a second language of communication.

Can you give an example of how it differed from modern Latin pronunciation?

Certain consonants and vowels were different. The diphthongs, for example, were emphasized differently. We tend in Italianate Latin to iron them out, making the vowels as "pure" as possible; singers are trained to extend the first half of the diphthong and then slip in the second half as briefly as possible. By contrast, my philology teachers tell me that the first element of a

14. Hillier discusses this issue in more detail in his essay "Framing the Life of the Words," in *Companion to Medieval and Renaissance Music,* ed. Knighton and Fallows, pp. 307–10. He says that modern voice production "is significantly different for singing than for speech"— modern vocal technique being designed to sustain sounds for "quite long periods" at "considerable volume." As a result, when we sing "the physical properties of the language do not seem to be felt . . . as they are when the language is spoken. Instead there is a barrier of produced sound, a continual deposit of 'expressive' sonority, between the singer and the words." Most early-music singing technique is modern, but "the singer is told not to use vibrato, not to do this or that with regard to dynamics, tempos, tone-colour, contrast, and other expressive devices. Thus, the natural connection between emotion and voice, thought and its expression, words and music is inhibited and enveloped in a set of cautionary restrictions." He argues that period pronunciation can provide a positive framework for enlivening early-music singing.

Regarding the "authenticity" of period pronunciation, Hillier notes that Josquin's music was sung in many different parts of Europe, where Latin pronunciation was far from uniform.

diphthong would have been sounded quite briefly, giving longer emphasis to the second element. In thickly texted polyphony this is going to make a big difference.

Can you give an example of a work where this makes a difference?

Well, we've already mentioned Byrd. So you could experiment, in his Latin works, by pronouncing the Latin with a heavy regional English accent (as opposed to the standard BBC accent that's preferred today). First just notice the difference that produces, and then try to sing it in the same way. This is not producing a "correct" result, but it's producing a different result (similar in kind to the one I'm talking about) and, hopefully, opening one's ears to the idea that there are more than one or two ways of doing it.[15]

It's a difficult issue, because merely the fact of making something strange—in this case the pronunciation—might cause you to overreact and say, "Oh yes, the music has to be very different here like this." And we haven't proven anything. All we've done is to create a different set of possibilities. That's all, but I think that's important.

Also, you have to accept that the result won't seem so comfortable. The kind of thing that's regarded as proper blend, the smooth homogeneity we are so used to, will disappear out the window. In its place will be something uncompromisingly active and grainy, a sense of real people singing about something that is real to them. How does this square with the beatific view we all have of Renaissance church music? Not very easily, at first anyway. And you can be sure that the critics, even those who are supposedly "informed," will be alarmed at the sound of something actually new.

After articulation, you mentioned tempo as another thing that's not notated but that is important.

Obviously, the key—perhaps the most important key—to a piece of music is finding the right tempo. It applies to all music, actually, and it applies no less to the fifteenth or sixteenth century. My feeling—it's a very general observation—is that there's a tendency to adopt tempos that are too fast in this music. I used to take Renaissance sacred music rather slowly, partly because of the singers I was working with. Now I'm enjoying a somewhat different approach. But I never like doing a piece exactly the same way twice—sometimes I'll adopt a different approach just to avoid solidifying my approach and to see if something fresh and interesting will emerge. As a general observation, I would say that when choirs take this music "too fast," even just a little too fast, they tend to skate across the surface of it, rather than go right through the middle. Par-

15. An example of how Byrd's Latin may have been pronounced is given on pp. 60–61 of *Singing Early Music,* ed. Timothy J. McGee (Indiana University Press, 1996). The text given is also recited on the book's accompanying CD; it does indeed sound like Latin with a heavy regional English accent.

ticularly in America, I've noticed a tendency towards that in college choirs, making the music sound a little bit flippant. It's very beautiful in an airy-fairy way, but it doesn't seem to have any guts. That's what I miss too often. Of course, the other extreme is to become too self-indulgent, and the music dies a different kind of death. But I think that in Renaissance music one can experiment by taking it too slowly to start with, so that you're really brought face to face with what's going on inside the music. And then you can somehow retain that intensity but take it at a more flowing tempo.

Your mention of American choirs and guts, and before that of "blend"—an Anglican choral virtue—versus graininess, brings up another often-discussed issue, that of the Oxbridge/Anglican dominance of Renaissance and medieval performance in recent decades, and how that has affected our perception of this music.[16]

It certainly has had a clear impact on the accepted sound of this music today, because these are the people who have mostly been recording it. And from a purely musical point of view it is perhaps a shame that there is so much duplication of personnel from one well-recorded group to another. But it's inevitable. You have a resource of very skilled singers who can virtually perform this music at sight. There is a danger there, of course, that the results will be a little superficial unless they do actually spend time on a given piece; but the disadvantages are outweighed by the advantages in purely practical terms. It's true, there are groups in France and Belgium that are also performing this music, like the Ensemble Clément Janequin, the Huelgas Ensemble, and the choirs conducted by Philippe Herreweghe, and although they use a few English singers one can clearly hear a different kind of timbre, one that's more grainy or personalized than the more ethereal Oxbridge sound. I'm very interested in that: in fact, I prefer it! Perhaps it's just that I'm so used to Oxbridge that it's nice to go and hear something different, something fresh. I'm interested in hearing the music sung by different kinds of choirs. It's the same with plainchant: you hear different countries bring a totally different sound to music which is on paper exactly the same. It's like hearing the music of Victoria sung by a Spanish choir; although there the point is a little bit disproved, because Westminster Cathedral has recorded some Victoria very beautifully, very powerfully, and doesn't sound at all like Oxbridge.

They have a more Continental sound . . .

Well, what we English call a Continental sound, though it's hard to find it on the Continent. It's something different again. But, yes, relative to the English tradition, it *is* more Continental.

16. See Christopher Page's interview, above, and Howard Mayer Brown's "Pedantry or Liberation?" in *Authenticity and Early Music,* ed. N. Kenyon (Oxford University Press, 1988), p. 47.

Your Theatre of Voices is American.

Mostly American, though even there I have a couple of English people! But the overall sound is definitely different; and anyway, the sunny California climate gives one a different feel for things than all those gray English skies!

SELECTED DISCOGRAPHY

Paul Hillier's talents are represented on disc in music from the eleventh century through our own day (the latter notably in the music of Arvo Pärt, on a number of ECM releases). The earliest repertoire is featured in two of Hillier's best recordings—and in one of his most controversial ones. The two acclaimed ones preserve gripping performances of eleventh- to thirteenth-century troubadour songs (Hyperion CDA66094, and *Proensa*, ECM 21368—on the latter disc he deploys a less smooth singing style, perhaps in line with the ideas he discusses toward the end of his interview; of the two discs, I prefer it). But when he and the Hilliard Ensemble recorded music of the twelfth-century Parisian master Pérotin (ECM 21385), Mark Everist found it "a misguided attempt to perform this music as if it has no surface interest," due to Hillier's "attempts to interpret Pérotin's music in terms of a post-60s minimalist aesthetic."[17] That he and Hillier have such different views on the music may—as we've seen in earlier chapters—be symptomatic of (or is at least allowed by) the incompleteness of the evidence.

One's response to the Hilliard Ensemble depends in part on one's response to its individual voices; but describing the group collectively, Richard Taruskin says its strengths in Renaissance music include "a wonderful sense of line," a "phenomenal" level of intonation, and a knowledge of "what relative harmonic tension is, and what it can contribute to keeping music of slow tempo afloat."[18] The ensemble made numerous recordings during Hillier's tenure with them. Naturally, not all the recordings are successful, but many are first-rate, including CDs of Dufay (to Gareth Curtis, "by far the most satisfactory recording of any of Dufay's Masses at present available"[19]—EMI 47628); Josquin's *Missa Hercules Dux Ferrarie* (according to Todd McComb, it is "uncommonly rich in sonority and color" for the Hilliard, and "may be their best recording, among many excellent ones"; EMI 49960);[20] music from the Old Hall Manuscript (to Mary Berry, the CD is "a major service to early music"[21]—EMI 54111); and what David Fallows calls the "blandly titled but stunningly performed"[22] *Sacred and Secular Music from Six Centuries* (Hyperion 66370).

17. Everist, *Early Music* 18 (August 1990), p. 486.
18. Taruskin, *Opus* (October 1985), p. 42.
19. Curtis, *Early Music* 16 (February 1988), p. 127.
20. From his online database, whose URL is http://www.medieval.org.
21. Berry, *Gramophone* 69 (January 1992), p. 90.
22. Fallows, *Gramophone* 69 (January 1992), p. 39.

Hillier has made two recordings of Byrd's great Mass for Four Voices. The earlier one, with the Hilliard Ensemble (EMI 63441), has detractors (Eric Van Tassel calls it "low-temperature to a fault, with excessively slow tempos and lacklustre phrasing," though he liked the Mass for Five Voices, on the same CD),[23] but it also has strong advocates (Jerome Weber not only likes the tempos but thinks the performance has a subtlety and depth that no other recording has matched).[24] Hillier's later recording of the Mass for Four Voices (ECM 21512) was among his first with the Theatre of Voices—which, in this recording, consists of a solo quartet. Tess Knighton writes that its American soprano and countertenor have noticeable vibratos that obscure the counterpoint, and voices that don't blend with those of the Englishmen who sing the lower lines.[25]

By contrast, the Theatre of Voices' more recent larger-ensemble recordings, on Harmonia Mundi, have garnered quite a bit of praise. Regarding their Josquin *Missa de Beata Virgine* (interspersed with beautiful Marian motets by Jean Mouton; HMU 907136), Fallows calls the singers "effortlessly clear, wonderfully in tune, beautifully balanced," and comments on their control of "a range of vocal timbre, from the sweetest to something really quite direct." Beyond that, he adds, "there is an energy in the performances that keeps everything marvellously alive."[26] (By the way, I bring up the idea of interspersing Renaissance masses with motets in the next chapter to Peter Phillips, who prefers a different approach.) Patrick Russill praised the Theatre's Tallis collection (HMU 907154) for the singers' "dark-browed *gravitas* and warmth of feeling" and their realization of "the sombre harmonic undertow so characteristic of Tallis."[27]

Clearly, Hillier's move toward new sounds proceeded step by step. His (I believe) first American recording, from 1991, was of the Cornago *Missa de la mapa mundi* (HMU 907083) with an *ad hoc* group of American singers—who, according to Fallows, sound like Englishmen. And not just any Englishmen: "Anyone on a blind tasting," he says, "is likely to conclude that this is indeed The Hilliard."[28]

FOR FURTHER READING

Howard Mayer Brown's *Music in the Renaissance* (Englewood Cliffs, N. J.: Prentice Hall, 1976) is an excellent introductory text on Renaissance music. For a discussion of what is known about Renaissance performance practice, the indispensable starting point as I write this is *Performance Practice: Music before*

23. Van Tassel, *Early Music* 13 (August 1985), p. 463.
24. Weber, personal communication, 1996.
25. Knighton, *Gramophone* 72 (September 1994), pp. 86–87.
26. Fallows, *Gramophone* 73 (November 1995), p. 137.
27. Russill, *Gramophone* 73 (July 1996), p. 91.
28. Fallows, "Quarterly Retrospect," *Gramophone* 71 (December 1993), p. 34.

1600, ed. H. M. Brown and S. Sadie (London: Macmillan, 1989 and New York: Norton, 1990); the chapter on sacred polyphony by Christopher Reynolds is especially relevant to this interview. Alexander Blachly and Alejandro Planchart provide more practically oriented guides for Renaissance vocal ensembles in chaps. 2 and 3 of *A Performer's Guide to Renaissance Music,* ed. Jeffrey Kite-Powell (New York: Schirmer, 1994); they, too, are first rate.

Regarding historical pronunciation, the essays by Hillier and by Alison Wray in *Companion to Medieval and Renaissance Music,* ed. T. Knighton and D. Fallows (London: Orion, and New York: Schirmer, 1992), are stimulating introductions. The best complete book on the subject is *Singing Early Music,* ed. Timothy J. McGee (Bloomington: Indiana University Press, 1996), which also includes a helpful CD with texts recited using historical pronunciations.

For a discussion of William Byrd's sacred music, the most important book is undoubtedly Joseph Kerman's *The Masses and Motets of William Byrd* (Berkeley: University of California, 1981); and there are four fascinating essays on Byrd and Tallis in Kerman's *Write All These Down* (Berkeley: University of California, 1994). An excellent book about another composer Hillier discusses is David Fallows's *Dufay* (London: Dent, 1982).

6

Other Kinds of Beauty

Peter Phillips on the Tallis Scholars
and Palestrina

One could locate an endless number of beginning points for the early-music revival, from late-eighteenth-century Handel-reverence[1] to early-twentieth-century clavichord making. Wherever the revival first sprouted, though, one could argue that it was foreshadowed by the sixteenth-century composer Giovanni Pierluigi da Palestrina. Palestrina was the first composer to remain influential not just for a few decades after his death, but for at least 300 years.

His influence lay not in his works, though they went on being performed sometimes, nor even in his style, which was drawn upon mainly in some religious music or in the odd work of, say, late Bach or Beethoven.[2] Instead, what kept Palestrina influential was something that theorists *derived* (more or less) from his music—a set of rules of counterpoint. These became central to musical education and remain so today. In our interview, however, Peter Phillips observes that these rules of counterpoint have distorted our concept of Palestrina: they represent only one aspect of his style.

Palestrina foreshadowed today's early-music revival in another way: in the nineteenth century, both Catholic and Protestant musicians restored his music to more frequent performance. That they sang it at what we would now regard as half speed was due partly to their misreading of his notation and partly to

---

1. Ellen T. Harris, "Handel's Ghost: The Composer's Posthumous Reputation in the Eighteenth Century," in *Companion to Contemporary Musical Thought,* vol. I, ed. J. Paynter et al. (London: Routledge, 1993), pp. 208–25.

2. See Christoph Wolff's "Bach and the Tradition of the Palestrina Style," in his *Bach: Essays on His Life and Work* (Cambridge, Mass.: Harvard University Press, 1991), pp. 84–104.

their longing for the seraphic purity of the lost age of "true church music."[3] We sing the music closer to an appropriate tempo now; but Peter Phillips believes that we may be even further from its aesthetic. Perhaps this legendary composer needs a re-evaluation.

Phillips thinks so and has done his part to contribute to one—above all through his group, the Tallis Scholars, who, he says, perform Palestrina more than any other composer in their vast repertory. Moreover, he says that the Tallis Scholars' style "is, to a considerable extent, formed on Palestrina."[4] If you wonder how a group of twentieth-century British men and women can claim to sound like a group of sixteenth-century Italian males, read on. As you'll see, Phillips has never aimed to re-create original performing styles, and was among the first in the early-music world to publicly question the goal of doing so.

Phillips also spoke about the Tallis Scholars' popularity. Musicians often consider such questions crass, but few issues could be more urgent today. One possible factor in their success is something they share with Anonymous 4, another group with rare market appeal: a celestial sound. We discussed the Tallis Scholars' sound as well.

I interviewed Phillips a few hours before he led a sold-out Palestrina concert. The program was similar to one the Tallis Scholars had given a few weeks earlier in Rome, in the church where Palestrina was trained. It's interesting that when the Accademia Nazionale di Santa Cecilia scheduled this commemoration of the 400th anniversary of the composer's death, they invited an English group to sing. Even Italians, it seems, loved the Oxbridge achievement in this music and were, like Phillips, not convinced that natives had come up to snuff in it yet. We'll see something quite different in the next chapter, on Monteverdi.

On Performing Renaissance Music

You once wrote that the issue of authenticity didn't really apply to the choral music of the Renaissance, partly because there's no way of ever knowing what it sounded like in the first place.[5]

Well, I haven't changed my view. I'm uncomfortable, though, with the implication that because we can't know exactly how they sounded we are therefore absolved of all responsibility to try to find out.

3. Carl Dahlhaus, *Nineteenth-Century Music,* trans. J. B. Robinson (Berkeley: University of California Press, 1989), pp. 181–82.

4. Hilary Finch, "The Road to Rome from Oxford," *Gramophone* 72 (September 1994), p. 17.

5. Peter Phillips, "Performance Practice in 16th-century English Choral Music," *Early Music* 6 (April 1978), p. 195.

But you also made the point that you think the evidence suggests that we may sing it better *than they did—their archives show some very old singers, who probably would have become woolly in voice production.*[6]

That does follow—we may be doing it better in our own terms. Again, I don't think that's necessarily a reason for not trying to find out as much as we can about how they would have sounded. But it stands to reason that a choir some of whose members are quite old and have been in it almost the whole of their lives probably didn't sound fresh, agile, and youthful, as we like the music to sound now. Moreover, the older singers probably were not careful about their tuning and in control of their voices, as we think essential.

Of course, there's always the converse question of what Palestrina would think if he heard us. But what I'm really saying is that we have to carry on in making the sound good in our own terms. I don't think there's much future in making it disagreeable to our ears to satisfy some theory, even on the rare occasion when we can substantiate the theory, because then modern audiences won't go for it and we as performers will cut the ground from underneath our feet. I do think that occasionally groups make an error of judgment, in a way that I would hope to avoid, of not trying to appeal to modern people. I won't go into huge detail about this, because it sounds as though I'm swiping at my colleagues; but just to give one example, I am struck by a recent recording of the Allegri *Miserere* that in all five verses leaves out the top C that everyone wants to hear. Predictably, it wasn't very successful in commercial terms. I say this only to illustrate that we try hard to interest people in what interests us. I hope we communicate with people; and I think that the numbers of records sold and of people who come to our concerts all over the world mean that we're getting this intellectually difficult, taxing music across to many who would never have believed that they would like it.

It's not only difficult; it's also written for liturgical purposes quite different from the concert experience.

At least half the time we're performing in churches; but even then it's not a service, it's a concert. We're singing to people who've come and paid to hear it. To bridge the gap between our performing contexts and the original ones, I think we—deliberately—and the audience—also deliberately—turn this music into something they're more familiar with. So a Mass setting, which lasts half an hour and has five movements, begins to turn into something like a symphony. I'm normally quite careful to program one big work, which will prob-

6. This problem clearly existed and caused consternation in the papal choir in Palestrina's time; see Richard Sherr's "Competence and Incompetence in the Papal Choir in the Age of Palestrina," *Early Music* 22 (November 1994), pp. 607–29. Sherr concludes, "we may not really want to hear the music the Sistine choir sang in the Age of Palestrina in the way that they sang it. (So much for 'authenticity.')"

ably take up the first part of the concert, so that people can come away with the feeling that they've had to grapple with something substantial. A Requiem Mass is ideal—even longer than a Mass, even more of a grapple in many cases, and potentially highly emotive. I don't like to program too many short items. The same principle applies to records. So new guidelines come into play in modern circumstances.

An issue that has been raised in this respect is, to quote Richard Taruskin, "A Palestrina mass done as a five-movement choral symphony defeats the composer's purpose, which is to unify the service of an hour's duration or more by periodic inspiring returns to familiar and symbolic sounds." The sections were made to sound similar, with a single cantus firmus or head motif, so people would recognize each return as part of a unity. "In hearing them in the artificial context of a recording, it's like hearing a gigantic rondo with the episodes removed. Why not record cyclic masses with motets interspersed?"[7] How would you answer that?

I would answer by saying that I think we've changed the terms of reference under which these pieces are being sung. We're singing either in concert or on disc, but not in a service. Now, Richard Taruskin suggests a sort of halfway house there, which would be very interesting.

His concern is partly musical—he thinks it's too repetitive to hear the same ideas again and again for five movements in a row, when they're meant to be interrupted with other ideas.

Well, I think he has a point. But I *like* listening to the Masses straight through. There's a musical argument in so many of them that doesn't necessarily benefit from having long interruptions between movements for liturgy. It would perhaps be even worse, in a sense, to interrupt it with other pieces of music that distract you from the musical argument that is unfolding from movement to movement. You can argue this either way; I think he has a point, but it doesn't worry me, nor does it seem to worry the people who buy our discs. I invite him to look at the sales figures.

Regarding that last point, I'm sorry to argue from the point of view of "it's a great success and that's all there is to it." It may cease to be a great success in ten years' time, in which case the argument will be turned around on me. In any case, even if it ceased to be a great success I would not change the way I do it, because I actually believe it presents the music to best advantage.

One question regarding performance of masses has been that of dramatizing certain sections by such things as tempo variations, slowing down for the

---

7. Richard Taruskin, "A Glimpse of the New British Choral Sound at Its Best," Opus (October 1986), pp. 21–25—an interesting (and generally very enthusiastic) discussion of the Tallis Scholars' early recordings.

Passus et sepultus est and speeding up for the Et resurrexit. This is something that people often disapprove of. What are your views on that?

My views on that have in fact changed—among the few that have. (I don't mean to say that my views on this music haven't matured, but we have been quite consistent in what we've done as far as sound goes, as you can hear from the old recordings.) This business about changing speeds is difficult, because we're so used to pulling out the phrases for the Miserere and speeding up for the Quoniam; we do it because the words suggest to a modern mind that something should be slower or faster. But I'm no longer prepared to do such things, and I think the change came with more understanding of what polyphony is really about. If the polyphonic lines are going without a break through one of what we used to call "slow" sections into one of the "fast" sections, I'm not prepared now to speed up in the middle of a phrase. That's what used to happen, but I now think it spoils, and must spoil, the nature of the counterpoint.

After a double bar, when it is possible to start again, I may take on a new tempo, provided that at the end of the new passage the tempo fits satisfactorily with what follows afterwards. But this question is wrapped up in a very complicated issue about whether you maintain strict tempo relationships between all the time signatures from the start to the finish of a whole Mass, not just from the start to the finish of a movement.

So you wouldn't go to a strict proportional tempo ideal, with all the tempos based on an unchanging tactus?[8]

I *am* prepared to do that within a movement. By and large, we try to keep to the proportions implied within a movement, so that the triple times relate to the duple times and the duple times relate to each other. What I'm *not* prepared to do is then start the next movement at exactly the same speed, especially not in the Credo and Sanctus.

You could argue that this has come about through concert performance. If you're doing five movements on the trot without any interruption, you're more inclined to vary the speeds, to give variety to the audience, than you would be if the movements were broken up. In fact, under the "gigantic rondo" liturgical situation that you spoke about, it would actually help the audience to understand what's going on in the music if you maintained the same speeds, because then they would hear all the connections undisturbed. Whereas in a concert performance, running things against each other, you can get new perspectives on the head motif and so on by taking them at slightly different speeds.

We try to throw off what might be called a nineteenth-century view of in-

---

8. For a discussion of this, see Alejandro Enrique Planchart's "Tempo and Proportions," in *Performance Practice: Music before 1600*, ed. H. M. Brown and S. Sadie (London: Macmillan, 1989, and New York: Norton, 1990), esp. p. 134, where he writes, "It appears that the *tactus* was meant to stay constant throughout a composition, though there is a small amount of evidence that it could vary slightly."

terpreting certain passages when it clashes with what I think the polyphony requires. And it's *very difficult* to do so, however hard you try, especially in pieces that you're used to doing in the old way and, indeed, using editions that insist that you do it in the old way. In Palestrina's *Missa Papae Marcelli* I've discovered that there should be no double bar before the Et incarnatus est—you should go straight on without any break at all. I can't do it; I've done it for so many years from bowdlerized old editions that have always had double bars there. And even if I were able to make myself do it, the singers would have to as well; I would just be asking for instant trouble. You ask yourself what's gained.

If we had come to it fresh, we would have gone straight on, but I also bet that however much we tried to keep the speed up for the Et incarnatus est, we would actually have gently slowed down even if we'd never sung that piece before, since this is what people expect at those words. This is the astonishingly difficult process of undoing received opinion in all our training. It's difficult to do this and make the music live.

That of course is exactly what historical performers of Beethoven or Bach must do every time they play; as you say, in some repertoire, Renaissance performers can run into it too. But to return to the tempo issue: how do you choose your speeds? Has this anything to do at all with such elements as dissonance, and suspensions⁹ being prepared and resolved?

We adopt speeds that are convenient to ourselves in the singing, so that we can make the phrases breathe, make them expressive to people, and let people hear how the music is constructed.

Speed is largely in the hands of the singers. You have to find a compromise—you can't go so slow that the singers can't breathe the phrases so that they fall naturally, but you can't go so fast that the suspensions sound rushed and lack their full weight. If you want to take a passage fast, the singers have to know the music well, so that they stand a chance of being able to feel it, phrase it, and make it sound convincing. Otherwise you need to slow it down, and then they'll be in trouble because they can't breathe. And then you have to take into consideration the building that you're singing in. If it's very dry you don't want to take things too slowly because then the voices get dried out and they can't sing the phrases. Performance is a living art, and you have to take all these little factors into consideration.

There has been a lot of discussion lately of the Oxbridge sound, which has dominated modern performance of Renaissance music, versus the so-called

9. A suspension is a note that begins as a consonance but is held over (suspended) when the other voices change, creating a new harmony in which the suspended note is dissonant. At this point the suspension must be resolved onto a consonant note, which it almost always does by moving up or down a step. The suspension is a basic source of expressiveness in Renaissance polyphony, and indeed in most later music as well.

"Continental" sound.[10] *You've described the "traditional" English sound: "variously described as hooting or floating, depending on the commentator's point of view, with indistinct words and good, if rather hazy blend and balance."*[11] *And you've noted that this is different from what you do—using women instead of boys, for example. Richard Dyer called your sound "Phillips's great imaginative creation. It is a sound that requires [acoustic] coddling because it is so bright and piercing in Tudor tessitura."*[12]

That's amusing, because the criticism that's made of the Tallis Scholars in England is that we're narcissistic in the sound we make: that we're just wallowing in beautiful noises. And I think that ties up with what you just quoted about the English choral tradition. The King's sound in its heyday was a very beautiful basic sound. It was much helped by the acoustics of King's Chapel, but in addition, certain things were done to cut off the sharp edges of the sound and round it off into a mellifluous ensemble. The Continental sound is much edgier, less purely beautiful, more dramatic and arresting.

I think it's true that we try to make beautiful sounds. Having said that, I can't see the problem with it. What is the matter with making a beautiful sound? It's extremely difficult to do. It's like complaining that the Berlin Philharmonic sounds too beautiful.

Which people do.

Yes, well, they're nuts. It's significant probably that I have a vast collection of Berlin Philharmonic recordings, because I think that they are the best orchestra. They have exactly the same aim that we do, a blended overall sound, in which every different timbre has its place, but not so that it dominates or distorts. In purely musical terms, you can get wonderful effects with this. The crescendo, for example, is a remarkable thing, a thrilling opening-out of the sound in completely seamless stages—that's something, for a start.

I think this blended sound suits the nature of the polyphonic writing, which is always my concern. The lines in polyphony need to be equal, but distinguishable from each other. You could make a nasty noise on each line and they would then be equal, but I think to be able to distinguish them all in a seven- or eight-part texture there has to be a background out of which the lines emerge, rather than a nasty up-front jangle, which I think is perhaps the danger with Continental-sounding choirs. The lines are highly distinguished in timbre from one another, but the ear can't always get to them because of

10. A thorough discussion of this can be found in Christopher Page's essay, "The English *a cappella* Renaissance," *Early Music* 21 (August 1993), pp. 453–71, and, of course, it is discussed in his chapter above.

11. Peter Phillips, "The Golden Age Regained," Part II, *Early Music* 8 (April 1980), pp. 180–98; quote, p. 180.

12. Dyer, "The Boston Early Music Festival and Exhibition," *Historical Performance* 4 (Fall 1991), p. 126.

what's up front. And the tuning may be bad, which is always a disaster for picking out individual lines in the polyphony.

The beautiful sound is also consistent with your concern for reaching large audiences.

Yes, many people have told us that what recommended polyphony to them has been the basic sound: before they've actually listened to any piece of music very carefully, they've been seduced by the sound. I don't object if anybody comes to polyphony that way, but I would go on to say that there's more to it than that. If they want to make an effort, if they can be bothered to buy a second or third record, they won't get bored by it, as they may get bored by modern religious minimalism. In twenty or thirty years we'll see where we stand vis-à-vis Górecki, Tavener, and Pärt. I suspect that Palestrina et al. will be listened to just as much, if not more, while the minimalists will lose appeal.

In her review of your Isaac record, Tess Knighton said that your sound had "developed over the years into something much more direct and full-blooded."[13] Have you noticed such a change?

Yes, certainly since the amateur days. Nowadays we use fewer singers who make more noise. Because they have trained voices, our ten singers today sing more powerfully, more excitingly, and with more varied dynamic control than the twenty amateur singers we used to have. I've always encouraged people to *sing*; however it blends and tunes, new singers must sing out, and then I can tell them what to do. There's no good holding back or singing half-voice. In a concert, if you stand next to these singers it's deafeningly loud. It's just that it's a certain sort of voice, one that is not operatic.

On another issue, using women instead of boys, you said, "one of the most blatant contraventions of the ground rules of historical accuracy is perpetrated by chamber choirs who claim, while using female sopranos and altos, to come nearer to what the composer had in mind than our cathedral choirs that consist entirely of male singers."[14]

Exactly, this is one of the hypocrisies of the whole thing. Boys in the sixteenth century sang differently from the way women sing now—I'm sure of that. But they also may well have sung differently from boys now; boys' voices crack much sooner today, so the old treble sound may be biologically unavailable to us. It would have been very interesting to hear the treble voices of the sixteenth century, but we've got to get on with it now. And using female singers is much better than using boys in terms of, among other things, concert touring.

I feel that our job in the Tallis Scholars—what it comes down to—is to introduce the public to as much of this unknown repertoire as we can perform

13. Knighton, *Gramophone* 69 (October 1991), p. 165.
14. Phillips, "The Golden Age Regained," Part II, p. 180.

well. That is a pioneering stage, and I'm aware of it. The next stages should be more varied. For example, if enough people get interested in Renaissance polyphony, then the market will support many more groups doing what we're doing. When that happens, those groups will be able to specialize even more than we can. We have a wonderful role at the moment, which is to roam around doing whatever attracts our attention. But the next stage is obviously going to be more specialized than that.

I think many other things should be tried out that never are. We can't do them because we can't do everything; we already have a lot to do. One example, briefly, is that I wish a professional Italian choir would sing Palestrina according to reasonable rules of Renaissance performance practice. That would be fascinating, to hear the Italian spirit behind fully committed performances of Palestrina. Maybe one day this will happen, but it certainly hasn't yet.[15]

On Palestrina

Please comment on Palestrina, since we're observing the 400th anniversary of his death.

Palestrina is unlike every other Renaissance composer: it's not that he was unfairly neglected but that he was unfairly pushed forward. Being pushed forward, in his case, meant that certain aspects of his style were studied very carefully and others were ignored. What was studied especially was his writing in the quasi-Franco-Flemish style, because that was a style that could be imitated. There's a mathematical basis to good counterpoint that students can study and regurgitate: examiners would presuppose a missing line, or give students one line and leave them to compose two or three more, largely according to mathematical principles. It would have been very much more difficult to teach a student to write a pastiche of homophonic music.

But this obscured the fact that Palestrina changed his style at least once and possibly, I think you could argue, twice, in the direction of homophony. He did vary, like Tallis. Basically, both were fine craftsmen who did what they were told. And what they had been told, whichever side of the argument you were on, was that music had been too elaborate, and that it should come down to earth, with the words to the fore. Palestrina managed to do that: famously, that's the *Missa Papae Marcelli* story.[16] But what is ignored is the music that came out of it.

The *Missa Papae Marcelli* is a sort of halfway point. Some of the move-

15. Since this interview took place, some Italian recordings of Palestrina, on the Bongiovanni label, have received enthusiastic praise (see Jerome F. Weber, *Fanfare* 20 [September/October 1996], p. 283). But the ensemble, led by Sergio Vartolo, doesn't actually address Phillips's "wish": it sings one-voice-per-part with discreet organ accompaniment (which may well, however, be historically correct).

16. An account of the Counter-Reformation legend that with this Mass Palestrina "saved polyphonic music" for the Church—alas, not true—can be found in the Norton Critical Score of the *Missa Papae Marcelli,* ed. Lewis Lockwood (New York: Norton, 1975).

ments are in the old Franco-Flemish style, but some are looking towards the
Baroque and are much more homophonic. After that come all the double-choir
motets and other Mass movements which are so chordal, so homophonic, that
it's clear he's thinking entirely from a harmonic starting point—which shows
that he's looking forward to the next musical period, the Baroque.

Now, that's almost never said about Palestrina. People go on about how
progressive Gesualdo was, but Gesualdo was a freak. No one else was like
Gesualdo: of course he looked forward. And some of Lassus's music looks forward. But Palestrina was not so conservative as is made out. That's one thing
that I think needs serious correction.

From this perspective, you can make up interesting programs with early,
mid-period, and late Palestrina. The *Missa Papae Marcelli* is the quintessential
mid-period work, because you can see the way the style is changing. You've got
the two beautifully elaborate Kyries, and especially the second Agnus, which is
canonic—an old-fashioned technique. It's not a difficult canon by some standards, but it's very effectively worked out, and it's a substantial movement. And
then you've got some other sections where he's obviously come right down on
the style and cleaned it out. Then you can go on from there to the late-period
works, especially the double-choir motets. A particular instance is the double-
choir Magnificat *primi toni*. There's not a note of counterpoint in it—well,
that's an exaggeration, but basically it's so. And it's such a clever piece. I have
looked at it on the page and thought, We can't do this, this is boring compared
with all those wonderfully elaborate florid lines that overlap each other so
beautifully in his earlier works. And yet when you come to sing it you realize
that every element of the composition is under perfect control. The progression
of the chords is so finely calculated that it thrills audiences; I'm so impressed
because you really can't *see* why. It's almost inexplicable when you just look at
it on the page.[17]

The other thing I'd like to say about Palestrina, which is more offbeat, I suppose, is that the word "Renaissance" is a problematic one to describe music.
After all, there was no rebirth of interest in Greek and Roman music to inform
anything that happened in Renaissance polyphony. It's a convenient term to join
music with the other arts. All I can say about this is that if ever there was a tie
to be made between Renaissance choral music and classical thought, Palestrina
would exemplify it, because he always does remind me of magnificent classical
edifices. It's with architecture that the comparisons can be made. Palestrina has
Roman grandeur in his style. I don't think this is just fanciful. His music is beautifully sonorous, like a large classical arch, if you like, or a large classical struc-

17. In writing to a ducal patron who had asked the composer to critique some of his own
compositions, Palestrina emphasized, in James Haar's words, "that the sound of the music is
much more important than scholastic rigidity of technique." From "Value Judgments in Music
of the Renaissance," in *Companion to Medieval and Renaissance Music*, ed. Tess Knighton
and David Fallows (London: Orion, and New York: Schirmer, 1992), p. 20.

ture. It's cool, as these facades were, really big and massive, and that's caused by his clever use of sonorities perfectly contrived to give a solid basic sound. My experience of Palestrina is that if you take him too fast it seems as though you're making the edifice squat; it's reduced, spoiled, in a way that other composers of this period are not necessarily spoiled. This has a lot to do with the sonority, the grandeur in this music. If you take it too fast you spoil it—it's as if a Roman architect had got the proportions wrong in a building.

To continue with this comparison, people speak of Palestrina using words like "serenity," "moderation," and "balance." Musically, that means, for one thing, dissonances and suspensions being carefully prepared.

He's more careful than most. The telling comparisons here are not really with madmen like Gesualdo, but with the style that Palestrina grew up with, the Franco-Flemish style. I wouldn't say his suspensions are more bizarre than Josquin's; he is a true successor to Josquin in some important respects. And you can compare him with the Franco-Flemish composers who lived at the same time as he—the really great men, Clemens and Gombert. The Palestrina/ Gombert comparison is a beautiful one to make, though it would be more illuminating if more people knew any of Gombert's music. But there's no doubt now that Gombert was one of the great polyphonic thinkers of those decades, for all that his lines work completely differently from Palestrina's. He prepares his suspensions, but he's much more cavalier with the way they resolve; yet it's a cavalier attitude that's completely the opposite of Gesualdo's. The music seems to grow organically out of itself. There's something in Gombert's style which marks him out as an original thinker, and not just a quirky one. He was a very great composer, consistently so over his entire output, which can't be said of some of the more way-out names. I think Lassus[18] was as good as Palestrina when he was writing sonorous music; but he was prepared to experiment (which one admires him for), and some of the experiments didn't work. Palestrina seems not to have done that; there's a much higher average in Palestrina, a craftsman-like technique that maintained a minimum level. Like Bach, he had an absolutely rock-solid technique that rarely let him down.

To return to the descriptions of serenity and balance, they may be rooted partly in melodic aspects of the "Palestrina style"—avoiding leaps beyond a fifth except in rare instances, and preferring stepwise motion, and immediately reversing the direction of the line after intervals of more than a third[19]—almost plainchant-like.

18. Phillips discusses Lassus in detail in the essay "Great Men Think Alike," *Musical Times* 135 (June 1994), pp. 357–63; the article includes comparisons with Palestrina.

19. These characteristics, as discerned by Knud Jeppesen, are discussed clearly by Howard Mayer Brown in *Music in the Renaissance* (Englewood Cliffs, N. J.: Prentice-Hall, 1976), p. 286.

This is partly because he's a very vocal composer. Palestrina is grateful to sing; he's an ideally vocal writer. Lassus is not. Lassus thought of things from an instrumentalist's standpoint very often, which is why some of his effects don't work—or at least why you have to impose yourself on the singers to make them work, which in the long term, at the hundredth performance, is not ideal. We give up Lassus pieces sooner than we give up Palestrina or Tallis, both of whom were singers and thought like vocalists, so that their lines are convenient lengths and tend not to do anything bizarre or pose technical problems that have no expressive meaning. So to return to your question, yes, it doesn't help to have to sing a major sixth or major seventh in a melody line. It's difficult to do; you can practice until you get it right, but in the end—as I say at the hundredth time—you'd rather have a composer who was sympathetic to the basic needs of the performers, which Palestrina certainly was.

Another comparison might be with Victoria, and this might connect to the question of Palestrina's relationship to words. Howard Mayer Brown remarks that Palestrina would seldom go to great lengths to imitate or paint the meaning of an individual word; he didn't want to disturb the continuous stream of music in a dramatic way by abrupt changes of pace or texture, for example, in order to insist on the priority of text over music. Victoria, on the other hand, "was willing to disturb the even flow of counterpoint; to emphasize a word or a phrase he would tolerate an 'ungraceful' leap of a major sixth, for example, which Palestrina would have avoided, or he would allow a strong melodic line to proceed without immediately reversing its direction."[20]

Victoria wasn't a contrapuntist like Palestrina, so what you say about his interrupting the counterpoint doesn't necessarily apply. Maybe; but you always feel with Victoria that he didn't have the same ability to hold in his head six lines in genuinely independent counterpoint. His effects are consistently more Baroque than Palestrina's. He groups voices against each other, and his phrases are generally shorter, more harmonically conceived. Wonderful music; I actually think Victoria produced the greatest single work of the whole period, his six-voice Requiem. And his Responsories for Tenebrae—I'd take that set over the Gesualdo any day. I think Victoria was a very great musical thinker, who also is appreciated only in part.

And yet Palestrina doesn't bang on in a six-part texture page after page after page—Clemens does, as a real Franco-Flemish composer would have done, where they get going and stay going, point after point unworking itself, never stopping, never cadencing fully. Palestrina is almost never like that. He cadences fairly frequently; he's prepared to group. In his motet *Tu es Petrus*, he's constantly grouping and regrouping, not using imitation as the only means of starting a phrase. There is a seamlessness to Palestrina's writing which distinguishes

20. *Ibid.*, p. 315.

him from many late Renaissance composers, but he's like a halfway house between the Franco-Flemish and the late Renaissance/Baroque composers, amongst whom I would put Victoria, Andrea and Giovanni Gabrieli—especially Andrea—and the early Monteverdi of the *In illo tempore* Mass. Palestrina was a crucial halfway house, a man of utmost importance even in his own lifetime. Victoria was completely in awe of him.

What did Palestrina transmit to the later generation?
I think a lot of scholars would say he was overtaken by events; this is the argument that Palestrina was essentially a conservative composer. I would say, instead, that he was required by his employers and by the Council of Trent to update or change his style, and this encouraged him into a harmonic way of thinking.[21] This harmonic approach is so gently done, so unobtrusively done, that most people now don't notice it, and I wonder whether it was noticed then. But there are books' worth of great works by Palestrina which are essentially homophonic pieces; and I really think it must have made a difference to people at the time. It showed them how to organize their thought.

A difference between him and early Baroque composers seems to be this issue of imitating and painting the text.
The words do come out more in later Palestrina than in early Palestrina. He was always reluctant to be obvious about word painting, though there is word painting in early works as well. But I don't think his musical thought depended on the words, not in the way that certain composers throughout history needed words to get their musical thought processes going—one thinks of Gluck, Wagner, and Verdi, for example. There's another type, a pure contrapuntist like Josquin, Bach, or Gibbons, who could turn anything into a beautiful succession of interrelated melodies, which is what polyphony is. Palestrina was one of those.

A further difference between Palestrina and Victoria is that Victoria seems to have taken a much more impassioned view of the text; Palestrina was a cooler composer, a more understated composer, as understated as Clemens and Gombert in the Franco-Flemish tradition. It makes one wonder if Palestrina was fully Italian in the way we now view the Italians.[22] He maintained a certain distance; I think his intention was to give a sort of overall picture of the

---

21. See Phillips's article "Reconsidering Palestrina," *Early Music* 22 (November 1994), pp. 574–86, for another discussion of this point.

22. On this point, Phillips has written: "Yet although Palestrina's Italianness is now less familiar to us than the other, more vaunted kind, what he represented is just as typical, and, of course, can be found throughout the mainstream of Italian intellectual life. Perhaps the best visual proofs of it are contained in the paintings of Botticelli: a directness of expression, artlessness, even naivety of effect, a certain ineffable sweetness." Phillips, "Fürst der Musik aller Zeiten," *Musical Times* 135 (February 1994), pp. 74–79.

words, a dignified one. And if that puts modern people off, then I'm sorry, there's nothing to be done about it. I think his is a position which is full of interest; it's just rather untrendy. I was told by a BBC interviewer that Palestrina was "cold and sexless," and that she preferred Victoria because it made her sob. Now, I'm sure there's a lot of truth in what she says. But why is it that music must be sexy, tear-inspiring, and warm (a particularly nasty concept) in order for us to be moved by it? I don't say that *all* music should be cold, remote, and understated—rather elitist, one might almost say aristocratic. But some elements of that are in Palestrina and I think have their expressive force.[23]

If you want to be an instant success in the modern world, it's best if you're experimental, obviously human, and obviously suffering, which Lassus was. The very fact that Lassus produced some bad pieces, as I think he did, only adds to his image now. The idea of the perfect Palestrina is not attractive to people; that's a modern problem. Yet I'm sure Palestrina is great enough that in another fifty years he'll be a trend again. In this we are saying that we hope his moment will come; but his moment, compared to any other composer of his period and later, has come and come and come. It's never stopped coming.

When people say they can't love Palestrina's music, I say, "Just listen to it without any preconceptions about whether it's warm and sexy; imagine other kinds of beauty and other forms of enjoyment." Then he comes into his own. On this tour we are doing a whole program of Palestrina, and people are coming up to me and saying, "This is it; this is the greatest music of the period that I can imagine." So it is for me.

SELECTED DISCOGRAPHY

In the Palestrina issue of *Early Music* (November 1994), Graham Dixon concludes that one-per-part may have been the most common configuration used in contemporary performance of Palestrina; ornamentation of his lines may have been common; and the organ and other instruments may have played more of a role than we usually recognize (though not within the *a cappella* Sistine choir). Yet in the same issue Richard Sherr, who has done much of the research on these issues, notes that the original performances may not have sounded very good even to contemporaries' ears. It's hard to imagine Palestrina not enjoying what the Tallis Scholars do with his music, even if (as Philip might acknowledge readily) it sounds like nothing he ever heard in his own day.

23. About which Phillips writes: "[Palestrina's] contribution to the palette of expression through music was to broaden it in ways which most composers have found unsympathetic. Few writers have gone unreservedly for happiness, since it is much easier to make an effect through its opposite. . . . movement after movement of irrepressibly positive, hopeful music is an experience to be valued, all the more for being rare" (*ibid.*, pp. 78–79). Phillips also writes about the power of understatement in Palestrina's setting of penitential or despairing words.

Indeed, for investigating Palestrina, there may be no better starting point than the recording that was made of the 400th anniversary concert mentioned in this chapter's introduction (Philips 454 994; the concert is also available in video and laser disc). In it the Tallis Scholars sing the *Missa Papae Marcelli* and other works; it is essentially the same program that Phillips discusses in our interview. The Tallis Scholars have recorded six other Palestrina Masses, which, says Michael Oliver, are "most beautifully, but not too beautifully, sung."[24] Tess Knighton praises their "flexible, expressive, and at times overwhelmingly beautiful" performances of the Masses *Sicut lilium* and *Assumpta es Maria* (Philips 454 920).[25] Noel O'Regan, however, complains about the same expressive qualities, calling these performances "somewhat overshaped," with more a "concert" than a liturgical feeling—though that is, as we've seen, Phillips's intention. O'Regan also says that the singers' perfect blend "entails a loss of contrasts between registers," and says that their underuse of *musica ficta* in *Sicut lilium* gives it an "unjustified antiquated feel."[26] But he finds that their attention to detail "gives the listener a constant insight into Palestrina's compositional process."

In apparent contrast to O'Regan, Patrick Russill finds the Tallis Scholars "on occasion . . . blandly under-inflected,"[27] and Fabrice Fitch speaks of their "cool and rather detached interpretive stance."[28] As this shows, for all their success, the Tallis Scholars evoke varying responses from early-music aficionados, ranging from devotion to dismissal. But critical consensus seems to be that the Tallis Scholars' recordings are of reliably high quality and are sometimes inspired (Russill's and Fitch's remarks come from their enthusiastic reviews of the Tallis Scholar's CD of White, 454 930). Three outstanding ones are their beautiful CDs of Isaac (454 923)—which, by the way, includes chant interpolations—of Cardoso (454 921), and of Shepherd (454 916). Their CD of Josquin's Masses *Pange lingua* and *La sol fa re mi* (454 909) was the *Gramophone* "Record of the Year" in 1987—the first time in the history of the awards, we are told, that all the critics "who voted in a category placed the same record first"—and their Rore CD (454 929) won the *Gramophone* 1994 Early Music Award (according to Iain Fenlon, it is "moving and beautiful . . . the best record [Phillips has] ever made").[29] On the other hand, in the Victoria Requiem (454 912), Jerome Roche says that the Tallis Scholars, though beautiful and not cold, are "less overtly expressive" than the Westminster Cathedral Choir (Hyperion 66250), which is "well imbued" with the "plangent, intense" spirit of Victoria[30]—more likely to make one weep, perhaps.

24. Oliver, *Gramophone* 71 (January 1994), p. 86.
25. Knighton, *Gramophone* 69 (December 1991), p. 49.
26. O'Regan, *Early Music* 19 (February 1991), pp. 136–38.
27. Russill, *Gramophone* (June 1995), p. 104.
28. Fitch, *Musical Times* 136 (September 1995), p. 495.
29. Fenlon, *Gramophone* 72 (November 1994), p. 40.
30. Roche, *Early Music* 16 (February 1988), p. 137.

FOR FURTHER READING

The November 1994 issue of *Early Music* is a very good introduction to current issues in Palestrina performance. Another good starting point is Phillips's own articles on Palestrina—in the same issue of *Early Music* and in the *Musical Times* for February and June 1994. Howard Mayer Brown's *Music in the Renaissance* (Englewood Cliffs, N. J.: Prentice-Hall, 1976) contains a very useful chapter on Palestrina. The idea of three creative periods in Palestrina's output was, as far as I know, first broached in a 1971 monograph by Jerome Roche (Oxford University Press), *Palestrina*, which is an excellent introduction to the composer.

7

Singing Like a Native

Alan Curtis, Rinaldo Alessandrini, and Anthony Rooley on Monteverdi

I read once about a blues musician who claimed he could immediately tell a recorded blues singer's race. On a blind listening test he scored perfectly, until he mistook the white Englishman Eric Burdon for a black American.

I wish I had thought of a similar test for Alan Curtis and Rinaldo Alessandrini. I wouldn't have bet on the outcome. Both are gifted keyboardists who have founded vocal groups to explore the madrigals of Monteverdi and other Italian composers. The gist of their efforts is to have the music sung not by the early-music specialists, often British, who have dominated the field, but by native Italian speakers. No one else, the two believe, can equal Italian singers in this music.

That may suggest nationalism, and in the 1990s many of us find ourselves recoiling from nationalism, or to be more precise, from the ideal of ethnic purity. Yet most of us do like local color. When I challenge the ideal of keeping a national culture "pure," I like to mention that Italy got pasta from the Chinese, tomatoes from the New World, and pizza from Sephardic refugees. But if I ever get to Italy I will be distressed if I have to eat at a McDonald's or, more to the point, a Pizza Hut. I fantasize about "pure" *cuccina Italiana*, not the American mass-market culture that so much of the world is adopting.

Which, then, of the two faces of nationalism show in the Monteverdi debates: the bad essentialism, or the good—what shall I call it—cultural integrity? (I mean something like a culture that assimilates valuable input from other cultures, but without losing its own best features.) Certainly, getting the local color right pays dividends in some music. Chopin played his mazurkas in Polish

133

dance rhythms that were so different from the notated 𝅘𝅥 that sometimes they could be counted in 𝅘𝅥.[1] Played as written, many mazurkas lose something.

But just being Polish wouldn't equip you to re-create Chopin's rhythms; some Polish pianists (clearly not dancers) have played the mazurkas without ever straying from 𝅘𝅥. The music of Monteverdi, however, involves a cultural legacy more basic than dance steps. Monteverdi wrote some of the most text-centered music in Western history. In sections of a few madrigals, he notated no rhythms at all: clearly, the rhythms are to come from the words. If this demands native fluency, as some argue, that would rule out a lot of us. Gaining native fluency in a language usually requires mastering it before puberty,[2] which usually means being a native. Perhaps that's why connoisseurs of art song, which is also text-centered, have argued that such songs respond best to native speakers.[3] And even in the eighteenth century it was sometimes said that only Italians could give Italian vocal music its "true accents and expressions." Thus I can't dismiss Curtis's and Alessandrini's preferences for Italian singers in this music.

And yet Ivan Moody writes that his earlier conviction that "it was almost impossible for the secular song repertory of Europe to be sung by ensembles from countries other than those in which they were created" was shaken by "highly idiomatic performances of Italian madrigals" by some non-Italians.[4] To my ears British Monteverdi of the 1990s can be far from the musical equivalent of Pizza Hut, and needn't sound "Anglican," "restrained," or—well, any of the things that Alessandrini accuses it of. It is fair, in an ironic way, that I give the last word to a British Monteverdi pioneer, Anthony Rooley. Just as the main audience for the blues in the late 1970s was college-age white kids, the main impulse for today's Monteverdi revival originated not in the Italian sunshine but in the English fog.

"Every Detail of This Music Has Something to Do with Language"

Alan Curtis

After graduate study at the University of Illinois in the late 1950s, the harpsichordist/conductor Alan Curtis went to Amsterdam to work with Gustav Leonhardt, whom he has called his "chief mentor." In 1960 he joined the faculty of the University of California at Berkeley. There, in 1966, he conducted his first

1. Jean-Jacques Eigeldinger, *Chopin: Pianist and Teacher as Seen by His Pupils,* trans. Naomi Shohet with Krysia Osostowicz and Roy Howat (Cambridge University Press, 1986), pp. 110–12.
2. Steven Pinker, *The Language Instinct* (New York: William Morrow, 1994), pp. 290–91.
3. Alan Blyth, *Gramophone* 68 (February 1991), p. 1546.
4. Ivan Moody, *Early Music* 20 (November 1992), p. 685.

opera (and Monteverdi's last), *L'incoronazione di Poppea*. Since then he has been in some ways the work's most important advocate. He has published the pre-eminent modern edition of it, recorded it twice, and, in an influential study, shown that some of its music, including the celebrated final duet, was not written by Monteverdi.[5]

Over the years, Curtis's work has centered more and more in Italy; he now lives in Venice, and conducts opera regularly in Italy and elsewhere in Europe. He has conducted at, among other places, Spoleto, La Scala, the Rome Opera, San Carlo, Bologna, the Netherlands Opera, the Lisbon Opera, and the Innsbruck Festival.

Curtis has pioneered several elements of Baroque performance practice. He was (as far as he can tell) the first person since the seventeenth century to have a chitarrone built, for use in a 1962 Monteverdi recording. He was the first since the eighteenth century to use lutes in the continuo[6] group in Handel operas, a practice that is now common. He was also the first to revive Rameau operas and ballets with period instruments and choreography. More relevant to this chapter, he has been the leading advocate of what was at first a radical approach to performing Monteverdi's late operas: without any added orchestration, but with just the documented band of a few instruments[7] playing mainly just the notes indicated. This challenged what had long been the dominant view, espoused by (among many others) Nikolaus Harnoncourt, who wrote,

> In contrast to the all-too-liberal arrangers, there are those representing the opposite extreme: super purists who only want to realize the handed-down, skeletal score and reject any additions. This sort of loyalty to the work does not serve the intention of the composer, since it negates the presuppositions on which he has based his work. It is just as incorrect to reveal only the "skeleton" which was written down by Monteverdi as to cover it with inappropriate "flesh" of a much later age—as frequently happens.[8]

5. The edition was published by Novello, 1989. The recordings were made in 1962 (Vox) and 1980 (Nuova Era). The article is *"La Poppea impasticciata,* or Who Wrote the Music to *L'incoronazione?" Journal of the American Musicological Society* 42 (1989), pp. 23–54.

6. In the "continuo"—essential to the Baroque style from mature Monteverdi through Bach and Handel—a keyboard or plucked instrument both played the bass line and filled out the harmonies above it throughout. Often a melody instrument (gamba, cello, bassoon, etc., depending on the era and location) doubled the bass line.

7. In his preface to his edition of *Poppea,* p. xii, Curtis explains that the typical seventeenth-century Venetian opera orchestra consisted of three to five string parts, often with one on a part and usually with a violone or other 16-foot instrument doubling the bass. Occasionally trumpets, cornetts, or recorders were added. The continuo used, Curtis says "two harpsichords and one or two instruments of the lute family, such as an archlute and theorbo (or chitarrone)." *Poppea* and *Ulisse* were scored for such small groups; *Poppea,* Curtis says, should not have trumpets added, though he seems to approve of a recorder or two.

8. Nikolaus Harnoncourt, article on Monteverdi's *Ulisse* in *The Musical Dialogue,* trans. Mary O'Neill (Portland, Oregon: Amadeus, 1988).

How do you respond to Harnoncourt's critique of "super purists" in Monteverdi?

The notion that early opera must be orchestrated comes from the period when it was rediscovered. When Vincent D'Indy conducted the Monteverdi operas early in our century, he found it necessary to orchestrate them, because no one then could conceive of opera without a modern orchestra. When I came along, around 1960, there were people who believed that in Venice they didn't use an orchestra but who would invent some excuse or historical fantasy to the effect that "Of course, they must have improvised, and probably improvised accompaniments to the singing." I took the stance that we don't have to do anything beyond simply reconstructing some missing parts in the ritornellos [repeated instrumental sections that come between the sung sections].

Why do you think it's wrong to do more?

I stick to what I believe was Monteverdi's notion, which we see lasting on into Alessandro Scarlatti in the early eighteenth century. When Scarlatti writes an aria that is delicate, he might specify one violin to a part and then write those parts only when the voice is resting. He's writing an accompanied aria, which Monteverdi almost never did—Monteverdi alternates the ritornellos with the voice—but even though Scarlatti could have written obbligato counterpoint to the voice, he doesn't, because he doesn't want to cover the voice. He still wants the voice to be able to have its subtle expression.

Subtleties, as a form of expression, are later replaced by virtuoso display, which is much less related to the text. With that, of course you can have instruments. We hear of [the eighteenth-century castrato] Farinelli having a contest with a trumpet to see who could do the most coloratura. But that's not Monteverdi. It's just as wrong musically to put that kind of eighteenth-century concept back a hundred years as it is to put a Respighi concept back three hundred years. That's what I would like to convince Harnoncourt of. Not only is it hard to imagine what would have been improvised, but I'm simply not convinced that it would have been tolerated for a moment for a trumpet to be improvising while the singers were trying to sing expressively about fortune or fate or the gods. Harnoncourt has this idea that whenever the gods speak or whenever there's something godlike in the text, it's Baroque to have a trumpet in the background. So when Jove makes a pronouncement, in the background you hear military trumpet arpeggios. To me, that's distracting. What I object to in the versions by René Jacobs, Harnoncourt, Leppard, and others is that their composed additions (let us all confess that we are not really talking about true improvisations!) do not—indeed, cannot—follow the voice but rather tend to cover it, distract from it, impede its rhythmic freedom—in short, lessen the potential dramatic impact of Monteverdi's musical line.

What I think we really have to do is not orchestrate, but find out why this music was so interesting without an orchestra. What would make it interesting to a modern audience with only a continuo accompanying it? That is still what we are struggling to find out. We must continue to seek expression that is so complex and gripping, immediately gripping, that it will fascinate a wide audience—not just scholars who get all the complexity on the first hearing (if there are any such people), but also people who've never been to an early opera or heard any early music.

The solution to this, in my view, is that if we're going to revive early Baroque Italian music we have to revive the notion that language is the most important element. The libretto comes first, and the libretto is then set to music. This is opposed to the notion we've inherited from the nineteenth century, when people came to believe that the libretto wasn't very important, and that music was all that really counted.

Now, if you don't have singers capable of bringing off a Monteverdi opera with the subtle response to the words that it needs, then you're probably better off orchestrating it or doing something like what Harnoncourt does: using instruments that don't cover the voices completely, or that give color to voices that don't have color, or that interest the audience in singers who wouldn't be interesting otherwise. What I prefer, though, is to find singers and teach them to be expressive in terms of the vocal writing itself—that is, not as they would be in Wagner or Puccini, but as they are relearning to be specifically for Monteverdi—so expressive that they knock people off their feet.

What's your view of how one learns to sing specifically for Monteverdi?

I try not to be dogmatic, which doesn't mean that there aren't some things I like and some I don't like. Among the things I don't like are the extremes. One extreme, of course, is obvious: I wouldn't want to use Birgit Nilsson or Montserrat Caballé. In my opinion, as in that of the majority of early-music people, the standard opera singer of today—with the Wagnerian unending line and lack of articulation, plus the volume (at times bordering on shouting) and the vibrato that seem to be felt necessary for large halls—is not suitable for music that requires such subtle inflections. But where I differ from the vast majority of early-music buffs is that I also think the light-voiced, pure, "non-vibrato" (often English) "early-music voice" is not on the whole appropriate for the *dramatic* music of the Baroque, although it may be ideal for other Baroque music. For opera, we should try to explore more things in between.

What I try to do is to get potential future Fischer-Dieskaus before they've become too expensive and, more important, too inflexible to be persuaded to do something other than the modern style. If you find young people who have enormous talent, and I'm finding quite a few of them coming up now in Italy, you can get them to do practically anything. I like to work with young opera singers: the result can be voices that are good enough, and dramatic enough, to be on the stage, but that also have control of vibrato and intonation, and of the stylistic patterns and the flexibility needed for the style.

You mentioned that the late-Romantic "unending line" and so on would be out of place in Monteverdi. Can you give an example of why?

Again I turn to what we all say, the text. Let's take Monteverdi's setting of the words "Lasciatemi morire" ("Let me die"), which opens the Lament of Arianna. If you say the words simply and nobly, it can be very touching, but it may not really grab you. On the other hand, if you say more vehemently, as I think you should, [emphasizing the consonants] "La-SHA-te-mi mo-RIR-e," with enormous intensity, it can be overwhelming. But suppose you say it with intensity and great beauty of sound, but with an absolutely smooth legato, huge volume, and wide vibrato—"LAASHAAAATEMI-I-I MORI-I-I-I-RE-E"—with that much unvarying volume, legato, and vibrato, it can't have the same kind of effect. It may overwhelm you with Caballé's vocal strengths, but not with the meaning of the words, so the power and expression have to come from somewhere else.

This relates to another issue—and here too I differ from many of my early-music colleagues: I strongly favor the idea that the singer's native language is very important.

What advantage would Italians have in singing Monteverdi—couldn't pronunciation, for example, be developed by a good Italian coach?

Pronunciation, as you say, is not so crucial, and perhaps its importance is more for Italian audiences. But what comes across to everybody is the particular relationship between the text and the music, and the emotions that arise from that relationship. This includes such things as extremes of diction and coloring and accent, and freedom of rhythm, and knowing where the rhythm should be free and where it can be more metrical. Also, knowing which words need to be strongly accented and which are ambiguously accented (not that there are many in Italian, but there are some); the color of the vowels; where you would make a crescendo and decrescendo—every detail of this music has something to do with language.

Now, all of that can be taught to a foreigner, but it just doesn't come together in the same way. Listen to certain foreign-born singers in your own native language; you hear a very clever mimicry, but not the substance. You can't even say specifically what they're doing wrong. But there's something essential that's not there.

How about when the singer is fluent, flawlessly fluent, in the foreign language? Can't they get the same result as a native?

No, although they can get very close. Now, anything that I say could be contradicted demonstrably, because you can find Italians brutalizing their own language. In fact, many Italians don't care about or even know the texts they're singing. And they don't necessarily declaim the words instinctively; but even when they do, it would be better if they would pay more attention to these things. That's what I focus on, as a conductor working with singers.

Of course, your own example could be said to prove that a foreigner can *master the subtleties of Italian.*

It would seem that way; but a famous Italian critic once noted that I demand from my singers much better diction than I could produce myself.

What is also important for the conductor is to hear subtle relationships (that are present or are added appropriately) even in the accompaniment, because everything should revolve around the text. By "text" I mean not just the words, but also the meanings and above all the emotions that go with those words. And there, too, I think Italians have an advantage. What does "ahi, lasso" mean? Well, you can explain to a non-Italian that it not only means languishing and exhaustion but also can have certain sexual connotations. But unless that understanding has been there from the beginning, it won't be there in the same way. There are many such instances where nuances persist in the language, unstated but implicit. It's not just a matter of reproducing the sound, the pronunciation and phrasing of a sentence; it's knowing the subtle connotations of those words.

I've read that what has become modern Italian was, in Monteverdi's day, just one of many regional dialects, some of them mutually unintelligible (some of these persist today). Elsewhere in Italy this dialect, Florentine Tuscan, had great prestige as a literary and courtly language, but "only the highly educated could master [it], and they used it almost exclusively in writing or on very formal, solemn occasions."[9] Do historical and regional dialects—such as those no doubt spoken by Monteverdi's singers, for whom Italian was probably not the first language[10]—have any bearing on your argument that native Italians speakers have an advantage in Monteverdi?

No. For one thing, Monteverdi's singers would have understood "Florentine Tuscan" perfectly—as any educated audience would have—even if educated ears might have been able to detect a slight accent (and remember that regional accents are much less noticeable in singing than in speaking). And I've said that pronunciation is not the main advantage of using native speakers. Still, sometimes pronunciation does matter: when "historical" pronunciation is significant to Monteverdi's music, as occurs sometimes, then I retain it. But one can often modernize the pronunciation without doing any harm to the music or the verse, and in those cases, I prefer to modernize for the sake of native listeners.

9. Gianfrenzo P. Clivio, "Italian," in *Singing Early Music,* ed. Timothy McGee (Bloomington: Indiana University Press, 1996), pp. 187–88; he also points out that because modern Italian was primarily a written language until the nineteenth century, it has changed very little since the fourteenth century, unlike English or French.

10. Tuscan "would not have held any real sway amongst the singers in Mantua and Venice." Alison Wray, "Restored Pronunciation for the Performance of Vocal Music," in *Companion to Medieval and Renaissance Music,* ed. Tess Knighton and David Fallows (London: Orion and New York: Schirmer, 1992), p. 296.

Your arguments about the text-centered nature of Monteverdi may be qual-
ified by something you said about the rise of virtuosity, when you mentioned
Farinelli and the trumpet. People argue that even in late Monteverdi there's
some move away from the primacy of the text; and when you get to Han-
del you get coloratura that's not text-based. Wouldn't that reduce the ad-
vantage of native speakers?

I don't see that happening significantly in Monteverdi, although Monteverdi
does something different, even more dramatic: he becomes less word-oriented
and more emotionally oriented. Here I disagree with Gary Tomlinson.[11] I
would go along with Gary and others in saying that the text-centered style
starts to die out with later Monteverdi and with Cavalli; but it's only the very
slightest beginning of its demise.[12]

Now, text-centeredness dies very gradually, and it gets revived regularly—
such a revival in Hugo Wolf is one reason he was a great song writer. Still,
you can't deny that the overall trend is away from text-centeredness. To me,
the real change comes after Mozart, in the 1790s.[13] Cimarosa starts doing
things that actually cover up the voice, like having an offstage band, or choruses that try to outshout the lead singer. All these things become part and
parcel of nineteenth-century opera, carrying on from Gluck. For me, the big
change is then, just as there's a big change in history with the French (and
other) revolutions followed by the industrial revolution.

In terms of patronage, what happens with both revolutions is that the aris-
tocracy is no longer reliably the main employer and supporter of musicians,
and the audience is more and more middle class. But the beginnings of that
change are at least slightly hinted at in the Venetian opera of the 1630s.

Oh, yes, everything is gradual; you can trace everything backward and for-

11. Gary Tomlinson, *Monteverdi and the End of the Renaissance* (Berkeley: University of
California Press, 1987) argues that Monteverdi's early works reflect Renaissance humanism as
it flowered in a moment of Italian prosperity and liberalism *c.* 1600, but that his later works
reflect an economic collapse, a more repressive Church, and a withering of culture toward a
preoccupation more with surface and less with ideas. Thus, *Orfeo's* recitatives "aspire . . . [to]
something like the sustained persuasive force of Ciceronian oratory" (p. 237), whereas many
of Monteverdi's later madrigals exhibit "a loosening of the tightly woven fabric of musical
and poetic rhetoric he had spun in earlier works" (p. 172). Tim Carter reviews Tomlinson's
book scathingly in *Early Music History 8* (Cambridge University Press, 1988), pp. 245–60,
but in general it has been applauded.

12. Several authors, including Tim Carter and Gary Tomlinson, have discerned in Monteverdi last years a "Third Practice," in which musical concerns dominate textual ones to a
greater degree. In "From Madrigal to Cantata," in *Music in Late Renaissance and Early
Baroque Italy* (London: Batsford, and Portland, Oregon: Amadeus, 1992), p. 253, Carter
writes, "The new role given to the aria prompts the notion of a 'terza prattica'"; Julianne
Baird sees this as a broader Italian trend (in the second part of her interview, below).

13. For an interesting discussion of (among other things) the changing relationship between
words and music in the eighteenth and nineteenth centuries, see Charles Rosen's *The Romantic
Generation* (Cambridge, Mass.: Harvard University Press, 1995), pp. 58–78, esp. p. 66.

ward. But any historian would have a hard time denying that a lot changes in the 1790s.

Some people say that the opening of the opera to paying customers in Venice was part of the reason Monteverdi changed his style[14] (as opposed to what he wrote for a noble audience in Mantua). Do you think there's any fruit to be plucked off that tree?

Not a lot. I think it's been overplucked. It's an idea that we like because we like any chance to exalt democracy and put down the "decadent aristocracy"—which has become almost one hyphenated word. More recently, it's become fashionable to paint a rosy picture of the aristocracy, which of course is equally false. They *were* scoundrels. But you can't say they were uncultured scoundrels.

I think a historian has to realize that many of the horrors of the modern operatic environment—the things that singers do to composers and their music—were there almost from the beginning. Nevertheless, there are big changes from the early Baroque to the nineteenth and, especially, the twentieth century.

"People Say, 'It's Incredible to Hear Monteverdi Sung by Italians'"
Rinaldo Alessandrini

I first heard Rinaldo Alessandrini's group, Concerto Italiano, after their CD of Monteverdi's Fourth Book of Madrigals won the 1994 *Gramophone* Award for best Baroque vocal recording. In a brief review accompanying the announcement, the Monteverdi scholar Iain Fenlon said, "These are performances infused with such a strong sense of the drama of the text that it is almost overwhelming," and concluded that "this is the finest recording of Monteverdi madrigals ever made." That last sentence is what made me take notice; experienced reviewers like Fenlon rarely allow themselves absolute superlatives.

I arranged an all-too-brief interview, which took place by transatlantic telephone and required that I rouse Alessandrini at daybreak in his hotel room in Nice. I didn't have time to ask about his background, but according to Fenlon, it involved some study with Ton Koopman, and beyond that a great deal of self-education.[15] He has directed Concerto Italiano, whose changing personnel is always all-Italian, since the late 1980s.

14. However, Iain Fenlon argues that the Venetian audience was, to judge from the high price of tickets, probably also aristocratic; what made Venice different from Mantua, where *Orfeo* was written, were other factors, such as Venice's long-standing interest in spectacle. Fenlon, "Monteverdi, Opera and History," in *The Operas of Monteverdi*, ed. N. John (London: Calder, and New York: Riverrun, 1992), p. 11.

15. Iain Fenlon, "Their Way," *Gramophone* 72 (October 1994), p. 27.

People often argue about Monteverdi singing style. The latest example I've seen is Jeffrey Kurtzman's in the second Monteverdi issue of Early Music *(February 1994). He says that in Paul McCreesh's award-winning recording of Venetian sacred music, the singers "substitute loveliness and elegance for affect. I find the expressive devices in this performance too limited—the vocal sonority is the typically English 'white' sound, and tempo and dynamics are the principal sources of 'affect.' I would like to hear the singers utilize consonants more as vehicles for vocal expression . . . [the performers are] too concerned with re-finement and too little with the manifold means of emotional expression available to them." What would you say about that?*

I think it's typical of the culture of English musicians that, having been trained in choirs from childhood, they have a very collective approach to singing. Often, they sing the solo repertoire in the same style that they'd use in choral music. For me this is not good, of course: the voice is not flexible or elastic enough for expressing the mood of the madrigal. In the madrigal we have a lot of musical changes as the text calls for different emotions. I have the feeling that the color and dynamics of many English singers is too often un-varied.

I also have the impression that English performances tend to be anti-Ro-mantic—that they are performing in the opposite style from that used in Brahms or Verdi. If vibrato is right for Verdi, than it must not be for early music. To me, this shows a lack of historical awareness about early Baroque singing. We have a lot of documents about singing in the seventeenth and eigh-teenth centuries from which we can realize that the style of singing was very rich; and I feel that the English tone of voice is not a rich style. We have no interdiction against vibrato, or against using all the possibilities of the human voice in order to express all the different things we find in the text.

One fine English singer, Richard Wistreich, has examined a Monteverdi let-ter and some other documents and finds that singers were praised for their abil-ity to articulate in the throat, to support gorgie *(rapid virtuoso passages) from the chest, to do a trill, to sing loud enough to fill a church, to declaim clearly. And they were praised for subtle shadings and for their ability to make audi-ences weep.*[16] *What would you say about the Monteverdi singing style?*

It seems that the most important ability was to express the mood of the text, in the largest way possible. About the technique, the *gorgie* in fast pas-sages [where the voice can't be as loud], we have to consider that the theatres were not as big as those of today. We have to use a very elastic voice; it does-n't need a powerful voice so much. Perhaps it's better if a voice is not so pow-erful, because it lets one pass from a declamatory style, in which the voice is

---

16. Richard Wistreich, "'La voce è grata assai, ma . . .': Monteverdi on Singing," *Early Music* 22 (February 1994), p. 7–19.

used at the maximum of its power, to a style in which we need a more elastic voice—with very little breath, because in the *gorgie* the breath is beating against the glottis.[17] We have to consider a lot of possibilities for the voice, not just power—though all of it is supported by the breath from the diaphragm. Of course we don't need the same volume as for Verdi; that's historical, absolutely. But it's without sacrificing from the voice any possibilities, such as vibrato and portamenti, because they are so characteristic of the voice. We cannot find any vibrato indications in the music, but that doesn't mean we can't use vibrato. We do find a lot of portamento indications in the music. When we find slurs in the music, they indicate that we have to sing *portato*. But do you hear English singers sing *portato*? Never.

[See Anthony Rooley's interview, below, for an opposite view.] Nowadays opera singers have a wide vibrato; is it certain that the seventeenth century favored a narrower, faster vibrato?

I think that vibrato is different in each voice; every voice has its own characteristic vibrato. Of course the vibrato that's good for Wagner is not for Monteverdi. So we have to find a vibrato agreeable for the music—not so large. And it's also true that vibrato was a sort of ornamentation.

In reviewing your recording of the Fourth Book of madrigals, Iain Fenlon found that your being native Italian speakers was a crucial advantage in terms of your "strong projection of text geared to a determination to allow each detail of the words to speak with due force."[18]

We've had the same reaction from many listeners; they say, "It is incredible to hear Monteverdi sung by Italians."

For us, it was a sort of rediscovery of the possibilities of the Italian language. We take a lot of care in that, especially in the pronunciation and the artistic declamation of the text. Of course, being Italian, we don't need a language coach! Also, we know that before rehearsing the music we have to do enormous work just to conceive a sort of theatricalization of the text. Normally, we consider each madrigal as a sort of opera scene. Before we rehearse the music, we try to identify a certain theatrical rhythm in the text with pronunciation, declamation and so on. After that we add the music.

So the text solves musical problems. Does the music ever solve textual problems?

One of the most important sources regarding declamation in music is the

17. See Julianne Baird's chapter for a further discussion of early Italian singing style. In Iain Fenlon's "Their Way," Alessandrini is quoted as seeing aspects of the (modern) Italian vocal sound and technique as "distinguishing features of a tradition which has not changed since the sixteenth century"; Baird discusses this issue in more detail.

18. Fenlon, *Gramophone* 71 (December 1993), p. 106.

score of *Orfeo*. I think it was a personal study by Monteverdi of the possibilities of declamation in music. Monteverdi is very precise in notating the different rhythmic values in the score. So it is possible from the score of *Orfeo* to create some rules for realizing declamation. For example, some words are always very important. If you find in a phrase certain words, especially adjectives, that are very powerful in expression, they must be pronounced slowly. So for me that was the first source about old declamation. It is so clear, especially in the solo music. Normally I try to respect the relationship between the different values of the notes. Even if the general rhythm is a little bit more elastic, and even though the bar must be really elastic, still if we read a half note and an eighth note and a sixteenth note, that relationship must be more or less conserved. This is very good for getting an idea of the declamation.

When we understand the structure and power of the text, we find regularly that the music is clear. But if we start from the music, the music alone is not always clear. When we consider the music without the text, we can come up with multiple solutions; if we start with the text, we have only one solution.

The new seconda prattica, *Monteverdi said, made music the servant of the words, whereas the older practice had it the other way around. Yet in Denis Arnold's view, many of Monteverdi's finest works were backward-looking ones.*[19]

This is true. Especially in the sacred music, you find a lot of pieces in the new *concertato* style and a lot in the older contrapuntal *prima prattica* style, and it's true that much of the latter is very special. Still, I think in either style Monteverdi realized the enormous power of the word. We have to consider that before the music; and we have to realize that the music must be servant to the words. This is the story of history. There's no sense in defying it in any way.

In fact, Tim Carter points out that the emphasis on text that defined the seconda prattica *was not necessarily something that emerged around 1600; it had been part of Renaissance humanist thought for a while, and the dividing line may not be so clear.*[20]

The relationship with the Renaissance is very difficult to define. We cannot

19. Arnold, *Monteverdi Madrigals* (London: BBC, 1967), p. 44.

20. In "Renaissance, Mannerism, Baroque?" in his *Music in Late Renaissance and Early Baroque Italy,* Tim Carter suggests that "many of the aesthetic ideals of the *seconda prattica*—for example, its emphasis on the close relationship between music and word—had their roots in the Humanist movement so characteristic of the Renaissance. Similarly, the rise of opera in Florence was claimed to be a product of that typical Renaissance activity, looking back to the Greeks and Romans. Even the supposed shifts in compositional style and performing practice at the end of the sixteenth century may be more apparent than real, being rooted in improvisatory procedures that had developed over the preceding century. It would be ironic if those new musical styles were in fact 'Renaissance' styles in their most representative form" (p. 20). When I read this to Andrew Lawrence-King, he strongly endorsed it, but he noted that what was new about the *seconda prattica* may have been, first, that it allowed written music to take liberties that unwritten music had been taking for years and, second, that composers like the later Monteverdi and D'India deliberately set texts that involved more extremes of emotion.

say where exactly is the dividing line between Renaissance and *seconda prattica*. But at the beginning of the seventeenth century, especially with the first operas, by Caccini and Peri, we do have a sort of reaction against the *prima prattica*. I think it was a real shock when the *seconda prattica* came along, to get people to sing in this elastic way, and especially to move between singing style and reciting style in a single passage. We have to wait for a musician like Monteverdi to create really artistic results from this revolution; I think the first opera we can listen to is *Orfeo*. Personally, I find the music of Caccini or Peri a little bit boring; at the time it was quite important, but at the beginning of the seventeenth century polyphonic madrigals are more interesting than solo music.

Why do people regard Monteverdi as greater than, say, Grandi?

For me, he's not greater; for me, he's one of many great Italian musicians. I love Marenzio, and Marenzio was composing in exactly the same style as Monteverdi. We know that he created *seconda prattica* music before Monteverdi. I recorded Marenzio some months ago, and it was a surprise to see that there are elements in the style of Marenzio that are sometimes more amazing than in Monteverdi.

Generally speaking, the standards of Italian musicians were very high. So perhaps the problem is that we know only Monteverdi and know so little by Grandi, Marenzio, and others. For me, the seventeenth century had so well-formed and complete a musical language that in a certain way it was very easy for composers to speak in that language. Monteverdi's role was very important, but every time we do music by other composers we are astonished by its quality. Monteverdi is very well known—okay, I'll grant that he is the greatest Italian composer of the time—but as we have the possibility of discovering other music, perhaps we will be obliged to place Monteverdi in a larger cultural context.

Kurtzman [in the review I quoted earlier] says that in these other composers' sacred works "there is invention of melody and musical figures fully comparable to those of Monteverdi. What is lacking, however, is Monteverdi's masterly structural sensibility; his melodic shapes, as they unfold through a motet, have a more pronounced sense of direction and purpose, and the succession of figures and styles in his large-scale psalms have a similar sense of solidity and direction, even with his sometimes violent juxtapositions. . . . Monteverdi generates a greater perception of inevitability than any of the others." Do you agree with regard to the secular music?

Not totally. I repeat that Marenzio is for me one of the greatest composers of madrigals. I cannot imagine how we can listen to the early madrigals of Monteverdi and not see that Marenzio is at exactly the same level. Especially in the early madrigals of Marenzio, there are very individual, very fine ideas about structure, and about the relationship between words and music. It's like Monteverdi, and sometimes more complex than Monteverdi.

"It's Like the Difference Between Oils and Acrylics"
Anthony Rooley

I interviewed Anthony Rooley when he and the Consort of Musicke were on a 1995 tour of the United States, giving Purcell anniversary concerts. I had hoped the justly renowned soprano Emma Kirkby, a member of the Consort, would join us, but she declined to engage in what we discussed as "the debate" over English versus Italian Monteverdi singing (besides, she had errands to run on the only free day of the tour). Rooley, indeed, had agreed only reluctantly to address the topic. In a letter to me (20 December 1994) he said that he respected Alessandrini's work and wanted to avoid polemic. Besides, Alessandrini's "stated aims (fidelity to the text, return to source materials, freedom from tactus, etc.) are all entirely in accord with my aims and intentions and are not new at all."

In the end, fortunately from my standpoint, Rooley gave in. His views do have quite a few points of overlap with those of Curtis and Alessandrini: Rooley has, for example, worked for years on the music of Marenzio, Arcadelt, Rore, Wert, and other composers who help us see Monteverdi in context; and he strongly emphasizes the primacy of the text. But in other respects, his perspective differs—he mentions, for example, his long-standing interest in the esoteric neo-Platonic philosophy of the Italian Renaissance.

Rooley, a lutenist, founded the Consort of Musicke in 1969 to explore the secular repertoire of the late Renaissance and early Baroque. The group was originally oriented toward instrumental music, but began to focus on madrigals in 1978, when a British Arts Council bursary and a British Decca recording contract made possible several months of rehearsal. Since then the group has brought a wide range of long-hidden vocal repertory to the record-buying public. As Rooley points out, the group's large (and often pioneering) discography can obscure how it has evolved over the years.

Some critics and artists are claiming that Monteverdi is best served by Italian singers. How would you respond?

If Monteverdi is as great as we all say he is, there is room for at least a dozen ways of approaching him. I don't want to add one word to a debate based on vehement polemic; I don't believe that that's what music is about. Music is fundamentally about harmony and bringing health and well-being to the soul. That's how it started out, and that's why the Gonzagas were paying Monteverdi for it in Mantua. It was entertainment, but underneath it's about well-being and harmony. So I would like any contribution I make to carry something of that feeling. I'd like to embrace any "competitors" who appear to be there and congratulate them for what they're doing and encourage them.

With that as a primer, then it's possible to say some things that I believe, because I don't mean to say that I'm losing my critical faculties.

Let's talk about it historically for a moment. It is great for Italians now to be desiring to explore Italian repertoire. To this end I and my colleagues in the Consort of Musicke have been encouraging Italian singers, including many of Alessandrini's singers, for about fifteen years, by teaching courses, coaching, and so on. They needed encouragement. There was sense of failure on their part, partly because of the strength of the living tradition of Verdi and Rossini—they felt unconfident about anything before then—and this also affected economic resources. When you have so much of a nation's money poured into the culture of the nineteenth century, "real" singing becomes Verdi singing, not Monteverdi singing. From officialdom downwards, pre-Rossini culture was not really praised. You had to be somewhat unusual, even eccentric, to take an interest in that repertoire.

We were welcomed in Italy with open arms, because we gave a fresh account of this repertoire and, to some extent, brought back with it a sense of Italian self-respect and self-esteem. They liked us for it, and they thanked us for it and for the care we had taken with the Italian pronunciation. For the first time the Italians were able to hear the words to these things, because we put the language first—always did and continually have done.

Now, another historical perspective. The musical lingua franca throughout Europe around 1600, outside of liturgical music, was Italian repertoire. The whole of Europe, if it was sophisticated at all, had an awareness of what was happening in Italian courts. Anyone who claims that this is a repertoire for the Italians alone is clearly drawing a false conclusion from the myriad of evidence that shows the spread of Italian culture across Europe.

The argument that's given, though, is not historical but linguistic. People say that Monteverdi is so incredibly word-oriented, so responsive to every syllable, that you can't do him justice if you're not an Italian native. Otherwise, they say, you won't know that this word has hidden connotations, that that syllable needs a special weighting, and so on.

It *is* incredibly word-oriented, but of course people all over Europe were struggling with the very same problem then. But they were determined to work with it. In most places they had a few Italians on hand. And the English, in a way almost more than the Italians themselves, nursed an interest in some of the most esoteric things that were happening. A lot of the Italian repertoire would not have been transmitted to us were it not for these English students, as it were, of Italian music. The English had a sense of the special quality of the Italian repertory being created at that time, and they took care of it, nurtured it, studied and learned from it. Now that, I would suggest, is a relationship that I have attempted to continue. We have nurtured an awareness of Italian culture, albeit transmitted through the eyes, ears, hearts, and minds of English people, but with real love and care. We have never for one moment pretended that we are Italian or could do what an Italian group could do. We've listened to what Italians have to say and learned from it, I hope. Yes, there will always be passages for which we can learn about the Italian language, and how it should be accented and nursed. But I would suggest that some of what's being done now by Italians has learned a great deal from what we've done in the past.[21]

Regarding which, another historical perspective to recall in this "debate" is that our performing is a continuing journey. Because we have recordings going back almost two decades, I can now put on my CD player something we recorded in 1980 and compare it to what we're doing presently. The changes are absolutely phenomenal. Our first recording project was, believe it or not, Gesualdo's Fifth Book of Madrigals. What a place to step in! When I listen to that now, I hear that it's a study project. It's full of effort. The fact that it sits in the bins and looks as current as the thing we did last year is just in the nature of the CD industry.

What makes a very interesting little experiment is to compare our 1984 recording of Monteverdi's Fourth Book, Concerto Italiano's [1993] recording of the Fourth Book, and our 1992 version of some of the madrigals from the television film we did in the Gonzagas' Palazzo Te in Mantua. That is a fair comparison, and brings this dialogue rather more up to date. Anybody who listens to those recordings will hear them as if there were three different ensembles approaching this repertoire, not just two.

Because we've recorded so frequently, others can listen to what we've done and react to it and in dialogue with it go a step further. You can hear Alessandrini reacting to something we've recorded before, and because we did it *this* way, he's going to do it *that* way—which is perfectly natural. You can also take a step back from where we are now. Indeed, we've gone so far since then that there are others now who are saying "Oh, the Consort have gone too far, they're too theatrical, they're *too* dramatic." You can't get it right, of course. People either like where you're coming from or they don't, and can find all kinds of reasons to criticize it.

In the beginning, too, you were exploring new ground for the early-music movement. You were, for example, the first group to record integral books of madrigals.

The reason I was doing that was that if a composer had felt there was a certain integrity to bringing together a collection of separate works and pre-

21. In Fenlon's "Their Way," Alessandrini is quoted as saying that twenty years ago, "all Italian singers of early repertoires wanted to sound like Emma Kirkby; their efforts were doomed to failure from the start, he believed, since they inevitably involved the destruction of cultural backgrounds and traditions." On the other hand, in some Monteverdi recordings by Italians (not Alessandrini's, obviously, or those of some others) the singing has been too Romantic in style. These instances support the view that non-Italians like Curtis and Rooley have played a role in fostering the current *risorgimento* of Italian early-music singing.

senting it as a monument to his patron, or whatever other impulse it was, that was an integrity worth honoring.

We were also pacemaking in our choice of singers. They were all singers capable of singing with great clarity, with a voice that's centered and relatively vibrato-free, so we could start from that and then use colors as they came from the various consonant and vowel sounds of the language and from the mood and sense of the poetry. You could build out, in almost a sculptured way, a performance that was molded and bent in terms of vocal color and vibrato. If you start with a voice that has a directness and simplicity about it, it allows expressive additions to have meaning, rather than starting with a voice that is so fruity in itself that what you'd have to do is bring it down rather than allow it to expand.

Some specific charges that Alessandrini made about English singing were, indeed, that "they don't use vibrato" and that they don't use portamento. Yet I heard both yesterday in your concert and on, for instance, your Musica Oscura CD of Monteverdi.

In good measure, and used with some considerable skill, so it's clearly not something that we've just taken on recently.

Another complaint is that "the English" don't make enough of the vowels and, especially, the consonants of Italian.

It has nothing to do with being English or Italian, I believe. We've got some pretty exciting consonants in English too, and when you get to a writer like Dowland or Purcell, they're using the English consonants as well as the English vowels. How you use consonants depends upon your awareness as a performer of the space you're in, and of the mood and mode that you're presenting in that space. Then it devolves on the director, if there is one, as to how far he or she wants to take explosive consonants and their use. I like them, and I use them quite a lot, and we are pretty theatrical in our approach. You won't hear that in our 1984 recording of Monteverdi's Fourth Book, but you will get it if you look at our film from 1992. If you listen to our performances in concert today, you will find that the consonants are as alive as those coming from anybody else. We've stepped out; we've learned how to handle it. And we're learning all the time.

Another thing people criticize "the English" for in this music is suppressing solo expression in favor of ensemble.

Well, we don't search for "blend." I hear that word used a lot with regard to English vocal ensembles in general. The King's Singers, for example, is an ensemble famous for blending. We couldn't be further apart on the spectrum, because what we want is to have four, five, or six voices as individuals, more like flutes, violins, oboes, and violas interweaving together. Certainly it has to be an ensemble. My model was to bring my group's work to the level of consistency you expect of, once again, a string quartet, but using the voices and their special qualities individually. Emma Kirkby's soprano voice against Evelyn Tubb's—there's a wonderful difference, and I've wanted to exploit it.

Now, to compare this approach not to the King's Singers but in the other direction, I'd suggest listening to *Rimanti in pace,* from Book Three—one of Monteverdi's best compositions, hardly known, but a masterpiece, absolutely sublime. Listen to our recording, and then to what the young Italian groups have been turning out recently; it clarifies the contrast. I find that hearing the Italian recordings is like enjoying the powerful effect when you first see acrylic colors. You think Wow! I've never seen colors like that! They're so bright, they're so vibrant, they're so alert, they're so up-front! But contrast that to painting in oils. The oils take you deeper and have a sense of chiaroscuro, subtleties of shading. Now I would say our *Rimanti in pace* is Titian using oils, and some of the Italian recordings have a more slightly edgy quality, belonging more to acrylics.

The reason is partly to do with recording technology. Almost all my recordings since 1982 have been done in Forde Abbey in the West Country in England. It's a medieval space, with a stone flag floor well-worn by centuries of feet going across it, so that it's an undulating surface. There are no flat surfaces in the room, really, except for some glass. It gives a most magical experience of sound. It's vibrant, it's alive, it's warm, it's sweet, and the sound seems to present itself in the middle of the room for you to view and enjoy, and then gently evaporate to make room for the next sound. When we record, I try to use the natural dynamics and ambience of the room and capture as much of that as possible on the final tape. These things form part of the alchemical mix that performance is. If you cut out an awareness of the acoustics of the room, you've cut out an essential ingredient.

But you believe "the Italians" don't record that way.

What we're hearing nowadays increasingly goes right into the midst of the voices. Because the recording engineers are having a bigger and bigger say in how the end sound comes around, we're getting a closeness of recording where you hear the warts and all of each individual voice. At first this is incredibly exciting to the ear. It can be mind-blowing, because the ears have never heard it like this before. But it's the aural equivalent of using a microscope, or a television lens that can go so close to the mouth you can see almost the larynx of the singer. Nobody in Monteverdi's time would have heard it sung this way, because if you're in an ensemble you've got your own space in which you're singing, and you're hearing your colleagues in their space—but that is not like an independent microphone sitting in the middle.

It may have not been a historical experience, but what about its musical costs or benefits?

I feel it produces anti-polyphony. Polyphony is about the melding together (and, again, I'm not talking about "blend") of the various elements to make a dialogue of equals. What we get with close microphone technique is anything but a dialogue of equals. It causes the breakdown of polyphony, because it puts the emphasis on magnified detail rather than on the whole. Once you've got accustomed to the brilliance and sharpness of sound and the bright colors assaulting your ears, you begin to hear the strengths and weaknesses of each individual voice as it comes and goes into the line. This is highly distorting to your ability to keep an overall picture of where the composition is going. And there are very few singers, I would suggest, whose technique is sufficiently, consistently under control to be able to give us a line that can stand that degree of close inspection all the way through. It's certainly not true of some of these rather inexperienced young singers who are being used to present these over-vivid realizations. You hear the flaws, they're disturbing, and it's not fair to the singers. It is vivid, but it's a very modern experience. It's almost a surreal experience.

Now, it's a style of its own. And it may be that some of us want to go in that direction in the future. But it's important to state that this is not how anybody could have heard it previously. The squeaky-clean CD technology has now taken us so far that we can in fact begin to distort our perspective of how music should sound, because the technology begins to interfere. We've stepped into a new technology and a new use of polyphony (which, again, I happen to think is anti-polyphony). Then when you step back from it again you're in great danger, because you lose the brightness and clarity which was so exciting to the ear at first. It's like being used to music being turned up several degrees too loud: when you turn it back down, it sounds tame.

As you say, though, some might prefer it even if they acknowledge that it is unhistorical.

Of course. And even stating the contrast as I have is making too big a case, because when you come to compare the recordings they're often not that far apart. Very often the difference is, "What's the big difference?" So let us get all these elements out of the way; then we can begin to have a proper dialogue about niceties of emphasis here or there, taking more the overall architecture of a work and seeing how the parts of it can be expanded and compressed. A shift of perspective would take the debate further in.

One thing that CDs don't convey is something we see in your concerts, and also in the film you made in the Gonzagas' pleasure dome: acting and choreography to accompany the madrigals. Could you talk about this?

Contemporary sources tell us that madrigals were performed with suitable facial and hand gestures and so on. They became theatrical. The works themselves have theatrical implications and possibilities. So the film I made was a serious attempt to marry all of those things together, with the rider that in the end there's a degree of compromise because it is for television—just as you have to decide what kind of sound you want for polyphony when you're making a record. This is not for the Gonzagas' ears.

Still, in making the film, and when recording a CD, I have in mind the response of a group of the kind of people the Gonzagas, or any other patron, would have gathered together. People who were cognoscenti; people who knew not only about the music and the poetry, but also about the philosophies of performance lying behind them. People who knew why the arts were there: to raise one's mind upwards. It wasn't simply for entertainment; it wasn't just dainty music to adorn. It was music which was there to some extent to improve and educate and lift up. It was a music which was addressing not only the mind, not only the literate intellect, but the soul as well. It was a music which was created—as was all music, in Renaissance thought—in order to create a sense of harmony and well-being, and also to carry, to some extent, a divine *furore*, such as Orpheus's divine frenzy represented. All music-making had that behind it. It would be so taken for granted that it would not always necessarily be forward consciously in the mind, but it would be there in the background of thought: that it's impossible to divorce musical performance from the quality of Orphic frenzy that we find expressed by Ficino[22] and his like. So it was just there, a given, which it isn't for us. We have to work hard to remind ourselves of it, and that sophistication of awareness is something we find very hard to reproduce today.

How do you relate that, then, to modern audiences, who don't have the background you describe, and usually will not catch all the classical references that might have been meaningful to contemporary Academy members?

I think that an attuned performer is going to adapt his or her performance differently to each audience and space. When you gather people in a space for a performance, the moment of creativity is very exciting. It's like watching an artist about to put the first brush stroke onto a plain bare canvas. The audience witnesses that taking place; it's a special moment.

Now, a seasoned, subtle performer will adapt to that, and in that is the translation for modern audiences of the Renaissance ideal I described. For that's really where art becomes life. It's not a seeming of life, it's not a play, it's the being of life. I think therein is the great shift. How far is this art? How far is it just a play, and how far is it truthful? How far is it a reflection of the human condition in one aspect or another, be it meditative or theatrical or whatever else? And I feel that this is why the seemingly over-esoteric debates of the academies of Monteverdi's time are very important for us to tune in to. Because life is too short just to play. Life is too short to say, "My approach to Monteverdi is better than yours." In approaching the music, you raise curiosity and you

---

22. Marsilio Ficino, a Florentine Platonist (1433–99) whose translations and commentaries were extremely influential. He is discussed in depth in Gary Tomlinson's *Music in Renaissance Magic* (University of Chicago Press, 1993), esp. chap. 4, and from a performer's standpoint in Rooley's *Performance* (Longmead, Dorset: Element Books, 1990).

entertain, but it's saying much, much more than that. If it doesn't have that dimension, then I think I've been in the wrong business!

SELECTED DISCOGRAPHY

Alan Curtis—whom Andrew Porter calls "an interpreter with a rare instinct for living rhythms, pulses, and inflections"[23]—has been ill served by the record companies, and many of the recordings he has made are out of print. His finest opera recording is probably Handel's *Floridante* (CBC SMCD5110); but the disc preserves only excerpts. Still, many listeners will not really mind that in *opera seria*; and Stanley Sadie, a leading critic of Handel opera performance, says that the recording "sets new standards in the presentation of Handel as a dramatic composer." Sadie praises Curtis's "full-blooded . . . alert, knowledgeable direction," and "a cast who show a real grasp of how to convey powerful emotion through this idiom." He also mentions "a good deal of music of supremely high quality."[24]

As for Monteverdi opera, Curtis's *Il ritorno d'Ulisse in patria* (Nuova Era 7103, 3 CDs) gives a sense of the kind of singing he discusses in his interview. It is, moreover, a powerful performance. It is indeed a performance; it was recorded live in (I am told) essentially one night at the Siena Opera. As one would expect of live opera, it has moments of out-of-tune singing and must not come as close to Curtis's ideal as a studio recording might. For listeners who share my disdain for the modern preoccupation with polish, though, it is strongly recommended. I have not been able to procure Curtis's 1980 *Poppea* (Fonit Cetra LMA 3008/A-D); Thomas Walker admires it but complains about its recorded sound and its cuts, while Ellen Rosand praises its conviction and Curtis's deep understanding of the work.[25] Among recent releases are an interesting exploration of Neapolitan chromatic seventeenth-century harpsichord music (Nuova Era 7177), and his first recording with his new group, I Febi Armonici (Symphonia SY 93S25), featuring pieces by d'India, Marenzio, and Monteverdi. Margaret Mabbett finds the Monteverdi the "least secure performance," but says that "this fine group . . . otherwise gives Concerto Italiano some real competition."[26]

Having expressed reservations about the priorities of the recording studio, I should note that in a review of Monteverdi madrigal recordings Eric Van Tassel argues that recordings may allow us *closer* access to madrigals than modern concerts do: madrigals, he declares, depend on intimate subtleties that are lost in today's concert halls.[27] Van Tassel's review is the most balanced comparison I've read of the two "rival" groups whose leaders I interviewed. An-

23. In *Music of Three Seasons* (New York: Farrar Strauss Giroux 1978), p. 373.
24. Sadie, *Gramophone* 70 (January 1993), pp. 58, 60.
25. Both quotes are from reviews in *Historical Performance* 4 (Spring 1991), p. 53 (Walker), p. 73 (Rosand).
26. Mabbett, "Monteverdi and Other Italians," *Early Music* 24 (May 1996), p. 359.
27. *The New York Times,* Sunday Arts and Leisure section, 9 April 1995, pp. 31–32.

thony Rooley's Consort of Musicke, Van Tassel says, sings with the "bold elasticity of dynamics and phrasing" that the historical evidence calls for, and its "singers spur one another on to interpretive flights of fancy more daring than any of them might have ventured on their own." Rinaldo Alessandrini's Concerto Italiano "[declaim] and [act] out the words without inhibition, with swooping glissandos on words like 'alas' and unabashed accelerandos as climaxes . . . approach; some pauses between phrases are so generous that we lose track of the meter altogether." In the Second Book (Opus 111 30–111) and Fourth Book (Opus 111 30–81) of Madrigals, "there are abrupt staccatos where Monteverdi writes whole-notes; spectacular changes of tempo; an almost lubricious rallentando on 'squeeze me till I faint.'" He believes that Concerto Italiano is "imperfectly housebroken in matters of 'authenticity,'" but holds that "even the most extravagantly overdone moments spring from an authentically madrigalian concern for the words." Their great strength, in fact, is their fluency in the Italian language; they can sing "just the way they speak across a dinner table." But the group's youthful voices "do not yet interweave as gracefully as the Consort's"; the "interplay among the voices still needs work." Van Tassel concludes by dismissing the rivalry: "these groups are complementary, not competitive."

Concerto Italiano has also recorded some Monteverdi sacred music (Opus 111 30–150)—an interesting case, since the music is in Latin, not Italian, so their linguistic advantage is irrelevant. Iain Fenlon, who has called their Fourth Book "miraculous," and generally much prefers the group to English rivals, finds the sacred music disc brimming with "revelations and surprises—no serious Monteverdian can afford to be without it."[28] The group's many other recordings have generally been quite warmly received. This is also true of Alessandrini's solo keyboard recordings; a good sampler of his work in this field is his "150 Years of Italian Music" (Opus 111 30–118). His harpsichord recordings of Böhm (Astrée E 8526) and Buxtehude (Astrée E 8534) show how superbly an Italian can play German music, should anyone doubt that.

When we talked, Rooley gave frank assessments of his own earlier recordings of Italian music (those of English composers have been almost universally praised). The earliest he considered "study projects." He liked the group's Virgin recordings of Monteverdi—particularly, the first three books of madrigals (Book One, Virgin 45143; Book Two, 59282; Book Three, 59238)—but he was less pleased with the *Balli* of Book Eight, in which the microphones caught the Consort on an off day. He has recently reissued some recordings (many made in the 1980s by West German Radio) on his own label, Musica Oscura. Among those relevant to this chapter are the CDs of Marenzio (many consider this one of the group's best recordings; Musica Oscura 070992), Monteverdi (Jonathan Freeman-Attwood notes that it is "more overtly impassioned"[29] than their mid-

28. Fenlon, *Gramophone* 74 (July 1996), p. 90.
29. Freeman-Attwood, *Gramophone* 71 (March 1994), p. 94.

1980s recording; 070995), and Notari (Fenlon describes some of the performances on this disc as "quite breathtaking both literally and metaphorically";[30] 070983). On the other hand, Mabbett says that their CD of Pallavicino (07096) shows the group "tiring of late 16th-century repertoire" and reluctant to "attack the harsher sounds of the text." She complains that the radio recording constricts their true dynamic range, and in general prefers the group's "exciting live performances."[31] Yet this same CD stirred Anthony Pryer to praise the Consort for providing an object lesson in how to avoid "the dangers of habit in a life of music-making, in how to expand the personality of a group to fit the music."[32]

FOR FURTHER READING

Excellent discussions of Monteverdi's operas and of their performance can be found in *The Operas of Monteverdi*, English National Opera Guide no. 45, ed. Nicholas John (London: Calder, and New York: Riverrun, 1992). A good general introduction to Monteverdi can be found in *The New Monteverdi Companion*, ed. Denis Arnold and Nigel Fortune (London: Faber and Faber, 1985). A good introduction to the madrigals is the BBC Music Guide by Denis Arnold (London, 1967).

The foremost discussion of early Italian opera today is Ellen Rosand's *Venetian Opera in the Seventeenth Century* (Berkeley: University of California Press, 1991). Some provocative recent work on Monteverdi includes Gary Tomlinson's *Monteverdi and the End of the Renaissance* (Berkeley: University of California Press, 1987), although I recommend reading the critical review by Tim Carter in *Early Music History 8* as well. Carter's own book of essays, *Music in Late Renaissance and Early Baroque Italy* (London: Batsford, 1992; Portland, Oregon: Amadeus, 1992) contains fascinating material as well.

A scholarly discussion of Renaissance Neo-Platonism and music is Gary Tomlinson's *Music in Renaissance Magic* (University of Chicago Press, 1993). His discussions, in chaps. 3–5, of Ficino et al. are fascinating, whatever one makes of the Foucaultian philosophizing that occupies the outer chapters. Tomlinson has disavowed any interest in performance; Rooley, of course, is preoccupied with it and even called *his* book on Renaissance musical mysticism *Performance* (Longmead, Dorset: Element Books, 1990). The book relates Neo-Platonic Renaissance ideas to the modern performer's problems; its New Age slant puts off some readers, but others find it engagingly personal. Rooley has also published a fascinating article on passion in Monteverdi singing, called "L'humore universale," in *Musical Times* 134 (September 1993): 490–95.

30. Fenlon, *Gramophone* 73 (August 1995), p. 117.
31. Mabbett, "Monteverdi and Other Italians," p. 357.
32. Pryer, "Assuming Personalities," *Musical Times* (September 1995), p. 493.

Postscript: Nationalism and Early Music

The debate over who can best sing Monteverdi gives an example of the influence of nationalism in the early-music revival. If Bach scholarship has flourished, it was at least originally through the work of German scholars; if Handel scholarship lagged behind for decades, it was, as Winton Dean noted,
because no one country claimed Handel—a Saxon who immigrated to London—as a national asset.[33] As for performers, England would probably not have
emerged as such an important center for early music if its own music hadn't
reached an apex before 1700, and if modern Britons had been less fascinated by
their own earlier history. Conversely, as Rooley points out, Italy might have
emerged sooner if it hadn't been intoxicated with Verdi and Puccini.

But if nationalism has been beneficial for early music, national borrowings
and interactions have been even more salutary.[34] Think of Bach, whose mature
style depended crucially on Italian and French influences. Such interaction has
raised the current level of Monteverdi madrigal performance in both England
and Italy to a new high. The Italian/English controversy, however absurd it may
seem, will probably continue to bear artistic fruit in both countries.

33. Dean, "Scholarship and the Handel Revival," in *Handel Tercentenary Collection*, ed.
S. Sadie and A. Hicks (Ann Arbor: UMI Press, 1987), p. 3.
34. A classic discussion of this with respect to folk music is Béla Bartók's "Race Purity in
Music" (1942; reprinted in *Music in the Western World*, ed. Piero Weiss and Richard Taruskin
[New York: Schirmer, 1984]). Bartók shows that borrowings back and forth between Slavic
and Hungarian folk music repertoires have almost always improved upon the "pure" originals.

8

Emotional Logic

Andrew Lawrence-King on
Renaissance Instrumental Music
and Improvisation

Conventional wisdom holds that during the Renaissance, instrumental music was a sideshow. Vocal music, such as that discussed by Peter Phillips and Paul Hillier, had such prestige that only after 1600 did instrumental repertory come into its own. But according to the harpist-keyboardist Andrew Lawrence-King, conventional wisdom is wrong.

It became the conventional view anyway, he argues, partly because of the modern preoccupation with written scores. In Renaissance instrumental music, much of what was important was not written down but was improvised. This raises, he points out, a paradox at the heart of the early-music movement: to be faithful to the spirit of the past often means being unfaithful to the written notes that survive from the past.

It also points to another issue. Structure has been a critical element of Western art music; composers like Bach, Haydn, and (most influentially) Beethoven used large-scale structure as a powerful expressive device. Music theorists in the past century or two have focused much of their attention on understanding large-scale integration in music. But it has been argued that this focus has led us to undervalue local, non-structural musical elements—most ornamentation, for example—and to overestimate the emotional significance of structure. Meaning and emotional power, some argue, reside on the music's surface at least as much as in its undergirding. The way a jazz singer bends a note may have as much expressive significance as the way a composer provides catharsis by bringing back an unresolved musical progression and at last resolving it. Lawrence-King's discussion of how he improvises gives a sense of why we shouldn't ignore local elements: compared to written music, he says, improvisation is structurally much looser, yet in concert it compels an audience just as much as pre-composed music does.

Preoccupation with perfect musical integration may be a later development, but composers from Vitry[1] to Mozart gave structures—often remarkably tight ones—to their music. The tendency to seek order in experience is one of the deepest of the human mind. But Lawrence-King reminds us that in music, order can take different forms, some of them quite fluid.

Lawrence-King acquired his first harp, a medieval Irish model, during a party at a harpmaker's house. Because no one knew how to play the instrument well enough to teach it, he taught himself. He then mastered the Italian Renaissance double harp and other historic harps as well. He has been in demand ever since as an accompanist or continuo player for many leading artists, including several in this book, such as Christopher Page, Paul Hillier and Gustav Leonhardt; and as a soloist, he has won high praise from the critics. His solo playing shows us why the harp was in the Middle Ages no variety-show act, but the most prestigious and admired of instruments, and was in the Renaissance an instrument for master virtuosi only.

Perfect Instruments

It's widely held that the prestige of vocal music militated against the development of purely instrumental music in the sixteenth century, except for dances, and that it was in the seventeenth century that true instrumental genres developed. What do you think?

I'd like to answer that by sidestepping the question. The important question to ask is subtly different: not Where is Renaissance instrumental music? but, rather, What did Renaissance instrumentalists play? The answer has to be in the first place that they mostly played vocal music. That doesn't downgrade what they did; it's simply that they took vocal music as their repertoire, which is very similar to what happens today in popular music. If you go into a restaurant, you'll hear a lot of instrumentals being piped in, which are really vocal pieces in instrumental arrangements. Of course, the ideal that instrumentalists strove for was to have the same flexibility and expressivity

---

1. The fourteenth-century French composer Philippe de Vitry, who coined the term *Ars Nova* for his era's new style, devised one of its main forms, the isorhythmic motet. About this Reinhard Strohm says, "In order to absorb the world into its own structure, music had first to acquire such a structure, at least in principle. This happened—only on the level of written art music, to be sure—in the theory and practice of the French Ars Nova"—specifically, Strohm then explains, in the isorhythmic motet. Strohm, "The Close of the Middle Ages," in *Antiquity and the Middle Ages*, ed. James McKinnon (London: Macmillan, 1990, and Englewood Cliffs, N. J.: Prentice Hall, 1991), p. 270.

in an instrumental version of a piece that one could hope for in a vocal version. That was, in fact, one of the roles of ornamentation in some of the instrumental repertoire.[2]

But did this general picture change in the seventeenth century?

It is the conventional view that the early seventeenth century brought a change: instrumental pieces are independently published with titles, the two significant ones being *canzona* and especially *sonata*—which means "what is played" as opposed to *cantata*, "what is sung." In fact, though, these early sonatas are more parallel to vocal music than might be assumed. I don't think there's a great splitting away of explicitly instrumental music from vocal music; I think, rather, that the early sonata repertoire is a way of translating the new gestures of vocal music into instrumental terms. So all the new development that was taking place in vocal music around 1600—monody, the new reciting style, and the episodic style of writing vocal pieces according to the text, which meant that from phrase to phrase the music changes radically from recitative style to arioso style, or changes speed or mood—all of this episodic style was taken over by the sonata.

There's a second reason why I don't think 1600 is such a sharp dividing point. True instrumental styles actually developed earlier, in a different genre—namely, the various styles of writing for what they called the "perfect instruments," that is, instruments that could play polyphony as well as a single melodic line.

Such as the lute, harp, and keyboard instruments?

Also the viola da gamba, which I think had a special place because its early history was so associated with a lute-like Spanish instrument, the vihuela. The vihuela could be played either with the hand, like the lute, or with the bow; and the later viola da gamba was a descendant of the bowed vihuela. From that point of view it had an especial association with polyphonic playing and with the style of the perfect instruments.

So the perfect instruments are really where the interest begins with instrumental music.

Yes, because they're instruments that have a lot of functions. They can of course play single lines, and we know that ensembles existed where these instruments would play single lines (or, at most, thickened-up versions of single lines). But because they could play polyphony, perfect instruments could accompany a solo voice or instrument by taking the remaining voices of a composition and combining them into one accompanying part. Many solo-voice-

2. See Lawrence-King's essay "Perfect Instruments," in *Companion to Medieval and Renaissance Music*, ed. T. Knighton and D. Fallows (London: Orion, and New York: Schirmer, 1992), esp. pp. 356–58.

with-accompaniment publications were in fact arrangements of four-part vocal pieces, based on exactly that approach.

And this pre-dates the seventeenth century?

The first printed works of this kind are right at the beginning of the sixteenth century, in Petrucci's publications.

Of course, the other function of the "perfect" instruments, besides accompanying, is that once you can play polyphonic lines you can play an *entire* polyphonic solo on one instrument: you can play vocal works as solo instrumental pieces.

So I'm making a different distinction here than vocal/instrumental. As I suggested at the outset, one can't simply make a distinction between vocal and instrumental music, because vocal music was routinely played by instruments as part of their normal repertoire. And, equally, instrumental music could be sung.[3] But as we begin to get published sources of instrumental music in the sixteenth century, we find polyphonic pieces that are certainly related to the normal styles of vocal polyphony, but that have a number of distinctive features that are not only non-vocal but are also non-consort. These features come about because the music is to be played on one instrument. The usual practice may be for vocal consort music to be played by an instrumental consort; but there's something else involved when one person, on a perfect instrument, can play music that normally involves several people. It's that special capacity which led to the development of particular instrumental styles for these instruments.

What are some of the distinctive features of these instrumental styles, and what capacities of perfect instruments led to their emergence?

Some key features are liberties that a soloist can take with the polyphony that a consort can't take. An important such liberty is playing around with the number of voices in a free way, so that on a particular chord, or for a few notes, you add extra voices simply for more resonance or sonority. You haven't created that voice strictly polyphonically, nor do you lose it polyphonically: it just appears as needed. You do occasionally see this in vocal writing, especially in English sources where the top part splits into what is called a "gimell," but you see it very often in the perfect-instrument pieces, in ways that would not be practicable even if you had a couple of singers on one of the parts who could separate to sing chords.

A second uniquely instrumental feature is a way of creating polyphony that sounds stricter than it really is, where the number of parts stays constant but

---

3. Stewart McCoy, "Edward Paston and the Textless Lute Song," *Early Music* 15 (May 1987), pp. 221–28, describes an English practice whereby a piece that appears to be for lute and solo instrument could also be performed by lute and solo singer, with the singer either vocalizing or using solmization syllables.

a part may exit as a bass part and reappear as a high soprano part. That's very convenient on one of these perfect instruments; you're only holding down three or four notes at a time, so your three- or four-part polyphony can stay strict. You see that a lot in early organ music, for instance that of Tallis. But if you attempted to realize this in ensemble music you'd be faced with a bass singer having to make a high soprano entrance; even in an instrumental consorts, the bass instrument would have to make an entry that is impossibly high in its range.

I think even more significant is something you see in the first published source of vihuela music, a book of 1536 called *El Maestro* by the Valencian composer Luis Milan, in the many pieces that he calls either *fantasia* or *tiento*. This is the style that Milan calls *consonancias y redobles,* consonances and re-doubled lines. The *redobles* are fast passages and scales, which run up and down the whole compass of the instrument. This is virtually impossible to do by combining several instruments or several singers, each of which works in a limited range; but it's simply an idiomatic style for a single instrument with an extended range.

The *consonancias y redobles* style leads to another point that I think de-serves emphasis. Because the cutting edge in instrumental composition was with these perfect instruments, and because these kinds of instruments did a lot of accompanying, I see numerous links between accompanying techniques and solo instrumental techniques. To connect this to the specific example of *conso-nancias y redobles,* the correspondence is with the styles for the so-called *ro-mances,* where the instrument plays simple chords while the singer is singing. Every time the singer pauses at the end of a phrase, the instrument takes over, and instead of playing back something similar it plays something of great con-trast—you have simple chords accompanying the singer, and then you have fast scale passages in between the phrases. The fast scale passages employ the whole compass of the instrument, often including chords in unusually high positions, so it's something that displays the abilities of these perfect instruments, in par-ticular their ability to cover the whole compass. The style of these *romances,* with their alternations between the vocal passages accompanied by simple chords and the instrumental passages of fast scales, seems to be what is mim-icked in the *consonancias y redobles* style of fantasia.

Another thing you see in the fantasia are tantalizing hints of the improvis-ing style, a style sometimes consciously imitated in these works. The most fa-mous example of this is by the Spanish composer Alonso Mudarra: a piece for vihuela, dated 1546, written in imitation of the improvising style of the Span-ish harp player Luduvico. It has features which are clearly imitations of the sound of the harp, features which seem to be those of the improvising style, and features that break the normal rules of polyphony by the inclusion of strange notes. It also exhibits a much freer way of writing, neither strictly poly-phonic nor strictly melodic, but a combination of melodic fragments and chords. These features are very characteristic for any one of these perfect instruments, but very uncharacteristic of polyphonic music whether vocal or instrumental, where you're writing for a certain number of singers or players with limited ranges.

Finally, what we also see in the Spanish sources, right from the beginning with Mudarra, is an interest in *falsas*, which usually means illegal harmonies that disobey the normal rules of polyphony. These give you particularly interesting chords and sounds. We then see *falsas*—called *stravaganzas* in Italy—in the Giovanni Trabaci and Giovanni de Macque generation of keyboard and harp compositions in Naples around 1600, and we see similar dissonances later on in Spain in sources for the guitar. That is quite extraordinary, because the guitar—with, at that time, five courses and a rather narrow compass—is in some ways quite a limited instrument. It is particularly important in this examination of instrumental music, because it uses styles which are purely instrumental and solo, with no vocal imitation. Originally, the guitar didn't play in the polyphonic style, it only played chords which could be made rhythmic by strumming. As the guitar repertoire developed, this interest in strange harmonies was always well to the fore.

The guitar was at the time a purely harmonic, non-polyphonic instrument, and it was not the only one—another one to emphasize was the lyra. Such instruments indicate an awareness of harmony in the mid-sixteenth century which we tend to overlook. The conventional wisdom used to be that music was conceived entirely polyphonically until the invention of the continuo, at which point composers and players for the first time begin to think harmonically, whereas before the harmonies were something that resulted from the accumulation of polyphonic lines. I think the use of instruments like the guitar and lyra show that this wasn't always true. The players of those instruments were entirely harmonically aware, and both of those instruments abandoned polyphony in the sense that they abandoned the regular movement of the bass line. It's normal on the guitar—since it doesn't have a very large bass compass—to play chords as they arrive, without requiring that the bass note be the lowest sounding note of the chord. A G chord with D as its lowest note didn't bother the guitarists at all and was not perceived as inverting the chord position.

It's interesting that among the early sources that talk about continuo playing is one that describes the sound of an entire piece being re-created from the realization of the continuo line. That suggests to me that even in the "Renaissance," and right at the beginning of the Baroque, musicians were able to recognize a piece by harmonic content as much as by the polyphonic lines that supposedly made it up.

Did these elements from the styles of perfect instruments influence other genres of music writing? An essay of yours refers to Haar and Pirrotta specu-

lating that the sound of the Italian fourteenth-century madrigal derived from improvisatory organ playing, and you suggested that the Burgundian chanson might have been influenced by the kind of accompanying you spoke about.[4]

With the idea that the three-part chanson was influenced by instrumental style, I'm referring particularly to the level of quick activity that you often find in the tenor and, especially, the contratenor parts of these chansons, where fairly static harmonies are kept on the move by the voices repeating or exchanging the notes: the harmony doesn't change, but the two voices keep active. That seems very reminiscent of the way a plucked-string player keeps the harmony sounding, just by repeating notes, exchanging parts if necessary, and using rhythmic repetition to keep harmonies in the air. That has the effect of giving music rhythmic impulse and rhythmic life, which is why it would have been interesting to take it into vocal music.

You're talking about fifteenth-century chansons—Dufay, Binchois et al.?

Yes, the standard Burgundian chanson, which typically has a vocal style in a texted upper part, and two lower parts which appear to be less what one might call vocal in style. Of course, the trend nowadays is to perform these works entirely vocally, with those lower parts either texted or sung to solmization syllables. Yet we know that those parts were also played instrumentally, in such a combination as lute and harp accompanying a singer, or with the two lower parts combined for one lute or one harp.

Perfect instruments also influenced vocal styles in the sixteenth century. The four-part *frottola* style of the early Petrucci prints was derived from lute improvisation in essentially two-voice polyphony.[5] These frottolas were then rearranged as lute songs, bringing the vocal style back to the perfect instruments.

How about influences on music for purely melodic, non-perfect instruments?

Although at the outset I asserted that early instrumental sonatas are less a novelty than an instrumental equivalent of what was happening vocally, it's true that they begin to explore elements that are non-vocal. These include the extended use of the kind of instrumental figures that suit a particular instrument—particular combinations of notes, ornamentation, and tricks and turns of phrase. That's one aspect, the use of special effects for instruments. But, yes, the other aspect is the copying by melodic instruments of the kinds of non-consort effects that were being used a long time before by the perfect instruments. An example is the use of strange tunings for the melodic instruments, tunings that give you more harmonic and solo possibilities, such as Biber's for the violin. Violins experimented more and more with double stops, allowing the re-

4. Lawrence-King, "Perfect Instruments," p. 355.

5. W. F. Prizer, "The Frottola and the Unwritten Tradition," *Studi Musicali* 15, ed. Leo S. Olschki (Rome: Accademia Nazionale di Santa Cecilia, 1986), pp. 8–12.

alization of polyphony in forms specially adapted to the violin. That I think is a very clear example of something that was happening with many of the melodic instruments. Seeing the freedom and the possibilities open to the perfect instruments, they explored the possibilities of working in that direction.

One thing that I think is very important in this regard is the so-called *style brisé* which evolved from the lute, where you play a piece which is progressing in a completely normal polyphonic way with a melody and a bass, and polyphonic parts sitting in the middle, but instead of playing the chords vertically and simultaneously, you play the notes one after another, sometimes in a very subtly varied order. You don't just play the arpeggio up from bass to treble or down from treble to bass, but you pick the notes out one by one in a subtle and subtly changing way. It produces a very rich texture and all kinds of subtle and jazzy syncopated rhythmic effects, although the underlying music is quite simple. It's obviously a very idiomatic technique for any instrument that arpeggiates, like the lute or the harp. But it was taken over by the harpsichord and even by the organ in, for example, some Buxtehude and Bach organ pieces. Moreover, this technique of playing a polyphonic texture by playing the notes one after another allowed instruments that weren't polyphonic at all to create the illusion of polyphony. Thus we even have quasi-polyphonic works by Telemann and Bach for unaccompanied flute—the instrument is purely melodic, but you can make a solo suite for a flute by imitating the solo perfect instrument's *style brisé*.

Another issue: later instrumental music is usually for specific instruments— sonatas for piano, or for flute, harp, and violin. When did this specificity come in?

There's a growing body of evidence to indicate that instrumental music went on being unspecific much later than we used to assume. The harp, for example, had a small repertoire of music specifically *"per l'arpa,"* and an enormous repertoire of pieces shared with singers and other instruments. We certainly know for the Baroque period that the repertoire of harp players was identical to that of keyboard players. There recently was discovered a mid-nineteenth-century library belonging to a harpist in Wales, which contains mostly vocal and keyboard music. And that points out a consistent factor from at least the Renaissance through the Baroque, which is that instrumentalists of all kinds mostly played vocal music, and otherwise shared a common repertoire of keyboard music. This instrumental repertoire, especially in the earlier eras, was playable either by consort or by any of the perfect instruments. Specificity was the exception rather than the rule.

The lists of instruments we see on title pages of printed works in the seventeenth century are determined more by market forces than by anything else. They are an indication of performances by the—mostly—amateur players or the lower-ranking professionals who would be the target of that kind of marketing, rather than very precise information about performances by the top ranks of performing virtuosos. Record companies searching for repertoire for specific instruments lead to an inauthentic concentration on music performed by "original" forces as described on title pages. Literary descriptions of performances suggest that instrumentalists spent more time playing "cover versions" than "original hits."

To digress: you've mentioned Spain several times—a country widely ignored in popular histories of music. You've written elsewhere that there was a well-trodden path from Spain to Naples to Rome to Paris, taken by many of these aspects of instrumental composition, and taken by the harp.[6]

And by the guitar. Those clearly are the routes taken by the improvisatory styles of composition—fantasia, toccata, prelude—and by the large double harp and guitar. It may be no more than coincidence, but I find it a strong one, especially given the link between the harp and improvisatory music, and given that the harp and the guitar as perfect instruments make very particular instrumental colors rather than only trying to imitate the voice. This route is also that taken by the chaconne and the passacaglia. Their descending four-note bass theme is definitely Spanish—it's what the whole of flamenco is based upon! It takes the same route through Naples up through Rome, and there is Roman repertoire entirely based upon it, in Luigi Rossi for instance. And then the chaconnes and passacailles become associated with the high Baroque French keyboard composers, moving from there even to Bach.

On Improvisation: "Emotional Logic"

I want to ask you about improvisation, because it has to do with the nature of music as we think of it. It's not done in the mainstream classical world.

The theme in our time has been a separation between improvisation and the performance of great masterworks of the past. It's a separation particularly painful for early musicians who are trying to deal with a paradox in being faithful to the great masterworks of the past, because half of their fidelity must include what was called *sprezzatura*, the willingness to disdain, not to take too seriously the object that you're dealing with.[7] In other words, to be faithful to the spirit of the music one must be prepared to alter the written notes. In a way, it's a paradox that impinges on all period performances, since they require ornaments, but it's particularly important when thinking about instrumental music and the perfect instruments, because these, being able to play completely solo, are the instruments that are most convenient to improvise on. Obviously, it's easier for one player to improvise as a soloist than it is for pairs or larger

6. In the notes to the CD *The Harp of Luduvico* (Hyperion 66518).

7. The idea was expounded in Castiglione's 1528 *Il libro del cortegiano* (*The Courtier*) and applied to music by, among others, Caccini in *Le nuove musiche* (1602).

groups to agree on ground rules for improvising together, although they did that too.

We know that Renaissance performers added improvisation to their complete performances. For example, if a performer played a suite, he'd probably improvise a prelude to begin that suite. In fact, "suite" means "that which follows on." It's the continuation, and the thing it continues is the prelude. Of course, there are written preludes, but the best performers would usually improvise their own, which could be as long as the whole rest of the suite. (That gives you a nice balance between this first piece, which is in the improvised and solo instrumental style, and what followed—a group of dance pieces which tend to symmetry and fixed forms, and perhaps more strict polyphony.)

Today we tend to venerate the great written masterpieces and see music made up by performers as irreverent, but in the past that certainly was not the case. Improvisation had a parallel status to written music, even in the fairly recent past: some of the great nineteenth-century pianists were admired as much for their improvisations as for their composed works. Many of the great master composers were actually the main performers of their music, sometimes being the only ones who could play it at the time: the separation between composer and performer was a lot less strong. And this was much more so in the Baroque era. We know of J. S. Bach improvising at considerable length and in fact taking part in a competition to improvise; and that skill was valued for its own sake. We know also of the French art of preluding, from surviving written preludes that attempt to give a sense of the freedom, and the different way of structuring, found in improvised preludes. As I mentioned, regarding those preludes and the toccatas/fantasias and so on, I think improvisation had a very important effect on written music.

I think that in general music history tends to place too much emphasis on the first notated evidence of each new departure in music, simply because it's more easily traceable and so more convenient to write about. But many of the important developments were already happening way before the notation was established. Consider, for example, the notation of basso continuo as a way of accompanying music: I think the sound of basso continuo was happening long before the notation was developed. And I think that's especially true for the question of instrumental performance and the kinds of freedom that were notated just by chance in the Mudarra piece imitating the improvising style of Luduvico. This was clearly a recognizable improvising style, because that was the point of the piece: people could say "Aha! Yes, that's how Luduvico used to sound." In the written repertoire, apart from this one piece, we don't see these harmonic and structural freedoms for decades afterward; but they clearly were there among improvising instrumentalists.

I think that's a particularly important point: the structural freedom. If you're improvising, it's very hard to keep hold of a formal design, where you remember a phrase well enough to repeat it, for instance, or where you work out a long, elaborate formal pattern. The planning of the piece tends to be inspirational: what you play at this moment gives you an idea of what to play in the next moment. This "organic" development is very satisfying for an audience; they'll follow the piece along with you. It's very different from the kinds of formal organization we see in written pieces. We see this kind of inspirational planning in some of the fantasias, in particular the Mudarra piece. We don't see it again in written music until we get to the very late ornamented versions of madrigals, where the ornaments themselves develop in this inspirational rather than formal way. These pieces have the formal underpinning of the original piece on which the ornaments are being written, but the ornaments themselves develop in this more organic, less formal way. Otherwise we see it best in monody, where the structure of the piece follows the poetry and its emotional development, rather than formal elements. And of course the monodists tended to choose particularly emotional and dramatic texts, which justify an emotional logic for a piece rather than a formal logic. When they were setting arioso or dance movements, they'd choose texts with a more coherent structural form. As I said, this is imitated in the solo sonatas at the beginning of the seventeenth century.

That point is made concrete by Frescobaldi, who says his toccatas should be played like the modern madrigal, by which he means that you should vary the *Affekt* [predominant emotion], vary the speed, and feel free to omit certain passages if you want to—again, a lot of freedom for the performer. The point he's making there is that the formal organization of the piece is not based on strictly instrumental forms but, rather, is copied from the vocal recitatives, which themselves take their organization from the emotion of the text. So you have this emotional logic behind the piece rather than a formal logic. You're able to hold it together by performance rather than by composition. If you have a piece which is unified by emotional development, rather than by fixed formal elements, then, assuming the performer can supply this emotional content, it isn't damaging to the piece to leave out one of the sections as long as the emotional development is still coherent. Whereas in a piece designed in a fixed form such as a dance—let's say a galliard, with three strains, each of which is repeated—it would be quite strange to leave out one of the strains. It would have an odd feeling, because it's upsetting a fixed formal progression.

You improvise yourself in concert and even on your CDs.

Yes, I think that this is very important. In the same way, over the last twenty years we've come to realize that adding ornamentation to Baroque music isn't being sacrilegious to the great masterworks, but is rather what was intended and must be done. Many performers now have learned the delight of making that added ornamentation spontaneous.

I see the revival of the Renaissance art of fantasia not as a radical new departure but simply as the next stage on—from improvising ornaments for the dances, to improvising the prelude which would normally begin a suite of dances. Of course, it's quite a challenge to be free enough to improvise but remain within the style boundaries, especially when one knows that improvisation is where the style boundaries were stretched the most anyway.

You mentioned that they also improvised in groups.

I think that one of the important things to consider in the earlier period is that opinion is beginning to shift now with regard to large-scale works, to see (for example) the Monteverdi Vespers not as a choral and orchestral piece, but rather as concerted music sung by a team of soloists. And seeing these large works in this way means that the possibilities for spontaneous ornamentation and other kinds of improvisation are greater than they appeared to us before.

To give another example of how supposedly large-scale pieces could still incorporate improvisation, there seems to have been a practice in Rome, which is preserved in a few pieces now in the Uppsala library, involving the continuo players who accompanied a four-, five-, or six-voice canzona—which likely was played by a violin band—with a continuo of perhaps a couple of harpsichords, a few harps, and a couple of lutes. There are certain sources which between the sections of the canzona give passages that have simply a very slow-moving bass line as a basis for improvisation for each of the accompanying instruments. In fact, in some of the sources, even the violins get a passage like this to improvise over. And it seems probable that the few sources that notate this practice are the tip of a performance-practice iceberg, in that this would normally happen even when it wasn't notated. So in the middle of, say, a Frescobaldi canzona, the violin band or the wind band would stop and take a breather while their continuo improvised for a few bars.

Have you experimented with group improvisation?

Actually, with my new group, the Harp Consort, the idea is to take varied ensembles of perfect instruments—harp, keyboards, viola da gamba, lutes, and guitar—and explore the links between improvised and written music. We are all continuo players, and obviously continuo is one such case, where the player has a written bass line but the realization is improvised. We're attempting to take the continuo player's mind set—where one is trying to produce a realization that is free and spontaneous, but also very historically informed and appropriate to the period, and apply it to other areas of performance besides continuo—if you like, taking continuo thinking as an inspiration for carefully stylized improvisations. There are enough indications in period sources that show that they too saw this link existing between continuo improvisation and solo improvisation.

It's fun. It's quite a challenge, because of this paradox of trying to be as free as possible, as spontaneous as possible, while also trying to remain carefully within the style boundaries. It's not enough to play anything and say, "Well, that was free." But the advantage that continuo players have, aside from the fact that they're playing the very instruments that used to improvise, is that they're used to dealing with this paradox in the job of continuo playing. From there it's a relatively short step to doing it in the context of solo playing or group improvisation away from accompanying, as well as improvising in ricercars and canzonas.

To what degree does improvising well depend on education in composition and theory?

I think this again brings us to the paradox we spoke about earlier, that to improvise you need as much technical information as possible about the compositional style of the period, the rules of composing. But you also need to combine that with the freedom to just play. I do quite a lot of teaching of improvisation, and I usually start with the second of those, the freeing up, as the first phase. Then, as a second phase, I go almost in contradiction and try to refine it somewhat. Usually I've got ten people who are terrified of improvising; but once they have the feeling for it, I change tack and, for example, teach about how to cadence within a particular style, since once you get going on an improvisation one of the most important things is to know how to stop! It really does need an awareness of styles, whether that comes from training in composition or training in analysis, or simply from playing a lot. I certainly wouldn't want to underemphasize that side of it, the awareness of style that one couldn't describe formally but nevertheless is very strong. That's how all jazz players improvise. They know what sounds right and what sounds wrong, based on a very subtle and complicated set of style rules that few of them would want to articulate but that they're all extremely aware of. The challenge is trying to get that same sort of deep-down awareness of a Renaissance or Baroque style, so that you can bend the rules but not break them.

SELECTED DISCOGRAPHY

Lawrence-King and his Harp Consort have both signed long-term recording contracts, so it is likely that many more CDs, both solo and group, will be available by the time you read this. As I write, Lawrence-King's solo discography consists of two CDs on Hyperion. The second of them, *The Harp of Ludovico* (Hyperion 66518), has better sound and freer performances; it includes the Mudarra fantasy spoken of above. It's an extraordinary CD that I recommend strongly (though the earlier CD is certainly recommendable too).

Lawrence-King has appeared on over eighty recordings by various ensembles. He plays on several of Christopher Page's CDs, which include some of his harp solos, and on some of Jordi Savall's. In addition there are his Teldec recordings with the group Tragicomedia, which he formed with two other continuo players, Stephen Stubbs and Erin Headley. The high point of their discography may be a selection from the Notebook of Anna Magdalena Bach (Teldec 91183). Elliot Hurwitt, reviewing the disc in the November 1994 *Fanfare*, called it his "CD of the year . . . and I imagine of the decade as well." Hurwitt called one of the disc's numbers, an arrangement of Couperin's *Les bergeries*, "quite simply the most delicious single performance of a piece of music that I can remember ever hearing."

Lawrence-King's new group, the Harp Consort, has released two CDs as I write: *Musick's Hand-maid* (Astrée Auvidis E 8564), a "colourful and inventive"[8] Purcell program; and *Spanish Dances*—"a joyous experience, not to be missed"[9]—which offers selections from Ruiz de Ribayaz's 1677 collection *Luz y norte musical* (Deutsche Harmonia Mundi 77340).

FOR FURTHER READING

Companion to Medieval and Renaissance Music, ed. Tess Knighton and David Fallows (London: Orion, and New York: Schirmer, 1992), has several short essays on Renaissance instrumental music (chaps. 22–26, 32, and—most stimulating, to my mind—Lawrence-King's own chapter, "Perfect Instruments," chap. 49). *Performance Practice: Music before 1600,* ed. Howard Mayer Brown and Stanley Sadie (London: Macmillan, 1989 and New York: Norton, 1990), contains Brown's rigorous surveys of what is known and not known about instrumental performance in the Middle Ages and Renaissance. Brown also wrote a very good introduction to the subject of *Embellishing Sixteenth-Century Music* (Oxford University Press, 1972). Finally, *A Performer's Guide to Renaissance Music,* ed. Jeffrey Kite-Powell (New York: Schirmer, 1994), contains valuable background and advice on a number of instrumental genres, including the plucked strings. Herbert Myers's chapter on harps (pp. 154–60) is concise and useful, as is Paul O'Dette and Jack Ashworth's section (pp. 201–14) on "proto-continuo."

---

8. Jonathan Freeman-Attwood, *Gramophone* 73 (January 1996), p. 76.
9. John Duarte, *Gramophone* 73 (January 1996), p. 76.

∞ III ∞

THE BAROQUE

Robert Benchley once remarked that there are two kinds of people: those who divide the world into two kinds of people, and those who don't. In recent decades, two national schools have dominated Baroque performance: the Dutch, whose style has been described as more inflected (or, if you don't like it, mannered), and, again, the English, whose style has been called more direct and energetic (or, if you don't like it, boring and modernist). Yet talking with musicians suggest that this oversimplifies. The Londoner Monica Huggett, for example, developed her unique, imaginative style in the Netherlands, and the Dutchman Anner Bylsma considers swelling on most long notes (which some consider a "Dutch" trademark) tasteless.

A second oversimplification is that this ignores other nations. Austria played an influential role in fostering early-music Baroque style, thanks to Nikolaus Harnoncourt (Julianne Baird is one of many artists who studied with him). In more recent years, some critics believe, Cologne has displaced Amsterdam and London as the international capital of early music.[1] Yet I represent Cologne only by the American expatriate Barbara Thornton, and—regretfully—I neglect its father figure, Reinhard Goebel. Also regretfully, I haven't covered the exciting scene that is emerging in Spain, though the one in Italy has already been represented by Rinaldo Alessandrini, who of course argues that Italians sing Monteverdi best. By contrast, the French scene is represented by a non-native,

1. James Oestreich, "The New Sound of Early Music," *The New York Times,* Sunday Arts and Leisure section, 21 July 1996, pp. 1 and 32.

William Christie—the American who, more than anyone, catalyzed its current excitement. Home-based Americans are represented as well, but as to whether there's an "American" Baroque style, as the record producer Wolf Erichson argues,[2] I would suggest that if maestros Gardiner and Norrington were Americans, people would describe their styles as "very American."

Along with the by-now-familiar issue of nationality, Baroque playing brings up some new issues. Renaissance players don't need to defend the use of historic instruments, for example, but in repertoire that people had been playing for decades or generations on modern instruments—Bach, Vivaldi, and Handel—the issue does arise. (The first three interviews delve into various aspects of using early instruments.) For similar reasons, vibrato (or its absence) becomes more controversial. Improvisation and ornamentation, which have been broached in some of our discussions of Renaissance and medieval music, become central concerns; a number of references are made to jazz. And a new analogy surfaces repeatedly in this section (and later, too, in discussions of the Classical era). Musicians in the seventeenth and eighteenth centuries often compared music-making to speech. Joshua Rifkin, however, sounds a cautionary note later in the book: was the Baroque concern with rhetoric just a way of describing what good musicians of any era have always done?

2. In an interview by James Keller in *Historical Performance* 6 (Spring 1993), p. 34. After saying that many of the best players are American, he adds, "I don't want to sound critical, but it is a typically American characteristic to be rather extroverted. A bit of what you might call a 'Juilliard Style.'" Queried on that—since Juilliard pretty much neglects early music—Erichson answered, "But the musicians are coming from there, or at some point they're trained by people who did. . . . It's a different aesthetic."

9

Consistent Inconsistencies

John Butt on Bach

In 1827, Goethe wrote that the *Well-Tempered Clavier* sounded "as if the eternal harmony were communing with itself, as might have happened in God's bosom shortly before the creation of the world." In 1950, Pablo Casals spoke of Bach's ability to "strip human nature until its divine attributes are made clear, to inform ordinary activities with spiritual fervor, to give wings of eternity to that which is most ephemeral." It was such expressions, perhaps, that led the composer Lou Harrison ("a Handel man myself") to grumble, "Why don't they simply canonize him and be done?"[1]

To which many would respond, Good idea. To his devotees, Bach's mystique originates in his music: one feels that there's much more to it than meets the ear, and that the extra something is profound. His mystique may be heightened, though, by our tantalizingly limited knowledge of his life and his performance style. These limitations have given rise to a field of research distinguished by cunning detective work and ongoing ferment. As one leading Bach scholar, Christoph Wolff, said, "There hardly exists a more fascinating and rewarding subject in the history of art than the music of Bach."[2]

For an example of the challenges of Bach scholarship, consider Bach's ar-

---

1. Lou Harrison, "Cloverleaf," in *Companion to Contemporary Musical Thought*, vol. 1, ed. John Paynter et al. (London: Routledge, 1993), p. 254. The Goethe quote is from the postscript of a letter to Karl Friedrich Zelter, 17 July 1827; the translation is from Robert Marshall, *The Music of Johann Sebastian Bach* (New York: Schirmer, 1989), p. 71. The Casals quote is from an essay written for the 1950 Prades Festival.

2. In his *Bach: Essays on His Life and Work* (Cambridge, Mass: Harvard University Press, 1991), p. ix.

ticulation marks. These slurs and dots may have aided Bach's contemporaries, but they flummoxed modern scholars for decades. The confusion lay in what Erwin Bodky called the markings' "incredible discrepancies";[3] for example, three simultaneous parts playing the same notes may have three different slurrings. Attempts to find a consistent interpretation of the markings kept failing, a fact that Bodky found "bitterly disappointing."

A 1987 Cambridge University doctoral dissertation yielded more palatable results. Through an exhaustive survey of Bach sources and Baroque performance treatises, the author, John Butt, discerned some of the motivation behind Bach's markings. He showed, moreover, that the markings give special insight into how Bach understood his music. A book based on the dissertation won the William Scheide Award of the American Bach Society in 1992.[4] Those findings formed the center of our conversation. Eventually the discussion moved on to Bach's metaphysics—which, Butt showed, connects meaningfully with Bach's perfect technique.

The conversation took place in Berkeley, where Butt was serving the University of California as associate professor and University Organist. (He has since then accepted a position at his alma mater, Cambridge.) We spoke in Butt's basement, which he had converted into an office with the usual equipment—computer system, fax machine, etc.—as well as the specific tools of his trades of scholarship and performance: at the periphery, taking up every square foot of wall space, shelves crammed with books and scores; near the center of the room, a harpsichord and a piano.

On Using Original Instruments

You've written that even when Bach's music is played on synthesizers, "if the notes are correct and played in the right place, Bach's genius is still somehow there."[5]

I was partly paraphrasing Bach's own words.[6] One conception of Bach, which I think is valid, is that his music is there whatever you do to it interpretively. It's very hard to play Bach well, but if you get the notes right it's very hard to ruin. With Handel, on the other hand, you can get the notes right and nothing else and it will sound absolutely terrible—there's nothing there at all. But with Bach, such is the tautness and tightness of the writing that if you are

---

3. Erwin Bodky, *The Interpretation of Bach's Keyboard Works* (Cambridge, Mass.: Harvard University Press, 1960), p. 214.

4. John Butt, *Bach Interpretation: Articulation Marks in Primary Sources of J. S. Bach* (Cambridge University Press, 1990).

5. John Butt, recording review, *Early Music* 17 (February 1989), p. 116.

6. Bach, when complimented on his organ playing, is reported to have said, "There is nothing remarkable about it. All one has to do is hit the right notes at the right time, and the instrument plays itself." From *The Bach Reader*, ed. Hans David and Arthur Mendel (New York: Norton, 1966), p. 291.

inclined to appreciate it, you'll get something out of it. More than with virtually any composer up to our time, you can appreciate it however bad the performance is. From that point of view it doesn't matter in the slightest how it's
played, or on what instrument.

So why bother with historical information?

What interests me in terms of historical performance, if we're talking about
Bach, is that the performer can perhaps gain some insight into the way this
music was created in the first place—the tradition of improvisation, the tradition of performance, the traditions relating performer and composer in terms
of their professions and practice, and so on. As a historian and a performer, I
like to put my two disciplines together and try to recover and experience something of the creative process behind the music.

You see, one error I think there is in historical performance is the emphasis on what the first performers did, when they encountered this music. I think
historical performance has been rather superficially concerned with what's the
right way to play and the wrong way to play, with what should be "done to"
the work, which itself is taken as a given. As far as I'm concerned, I never know
what's right or what's wrong, but I'm always keen to look for new ways of discovering the music. I'd rather go beneath the surface and ask, "How did this
music come to be written like that in the first place?" What are the origins of
this particular kind of form, this particular kind of figure, this ornamentation,
this note, and so on? I think questions of historical performance should be
placed in the realm of the original creation of the music, rather than merely the
original reception of the music.

Where, then, might you start?

Well, for one thing, it's nice in some ways to be able to see Bach's music almost from the perspective of the seventeenth century. As a performer, I like to
see this music emerging out of the raw material of seventeenth-century musical
practice—the musical figures, performance conventions, and so on. Almost all
of the ingredients are there—not quite the formal structures, such as the concerto ritornello, but most of it. By limiting yourself like that historically, and
putting yourself notionally in the positions of the creator of that music and the
creator of the original performances—the two roles I think were very close,
closer than we often imagine for Bach, anyway—you can get a particular insight, as a performer, into music that has a lot of colors, levels, and implications in it. Now what I do as a performer might not come across to any listener (indeed, it doesn't to some!); and even if it does, I can't prescribe how
one listens to Bach. But this is how I like to approach it.

*So to understand Bach you immerse yourself in the music of Buxtehude,
Reinken, and other seventeenth-century composers he would have known?*

Definitely, and in the general things that Bach would have been thinking about. Above all, the function—what is this music for? What is he trying to do in this music? How is he trying to use conventions in new ways? That is central to a lot of Bach's compositional thought. It's inventing nothing new, virtually, but constantly using conventional musical ideas, conventional forms, mixing them up, and combining them in new ways.

Robert Marshall[7] gave the example of Cantata 78's first movement—which unites different, apparently incompatible Baroque conventions, the chaconne en rondeau, the Lutheran chorale, and the cantus firmus. Which means you need to know all those conventions, and all the other ones too.

Yes, and what was on his mind—was he concerned with me, the performer, when he wrote this? Sometimes he might not have been.

As in some late contrapuntal works.

Right. In other words, what were the issues involved in creating a piece of music? What was it meant to be doing, what was it doing, and how does it relate to other pieces of music?

The playing techniques have a place, but I think that if there's any mileage in historical performance, it's in other issues, such as the issue of what counts as a "piece of music." Is it the notation as we see it today? Is it the original manuscript? Or is it something more subtle than that?

Such as?

A combination of influences: the historical prejudices on the part of a particular composer, and the resources available to him, the limitations of any particular performance medium. I think historical performance can help us understand the intricacies of what actually counts as being a musical work.

Which is more than the notes, or than the notes played well.

Yes. To put it differently, where does the work stop? That's like asking where the human being stops: is it a single person, or is it a whole range of cultural and genetic influences?

The Goldberg Variations might be a good example. We can look at them as a self-sufficient structure, or we can look at them as a range of culturally derived genres—sarabande and Scotch snap, fughetta, French overture, quodlibet, and, of course, canon.

Yes, the later works of Bach are often trying to encompass everything. You might look at the *Goldbergs* as a compendium of all the different styles of the age, or you might look at it as a compendium of all the harmonic implications

---

7. Marshall, *The Music of Johann Sebastian Bach*, pp. 76-79.

of one particular bass line—you can appreciate it very deeply on one of these counts while ignoring the others, and still get an incredible amount out of it. And there's also some sense of thoroughness, particularly in the way the canons work, of going full circle, of almost creating a curved universe.

So historical instruments (getting back to that issue) would relate to one of those ways of looking at Bach—the cultural and creative origins—but not to others.

Well, historical instruments might correspond to the conditions under which he wrote the music. So in some ways historical instruments can help show you how he came to conceive of writing music in one particular way rather than another completely different way. It gives you something of the context, just as in order to understand a human being you might look at their parents and their family.

On the other hand, you can appreciate human beings apart from their parents; whether they have problems or not, you can appreciate them on their own merits in relation to where they happen to be now. And the same might be true of the music. Where does the music happen to be now? How does it relate to other music that we're using today? How does it fit into that equation? From that point of view, original instruments, logically speaking, are irrelevant.

As far as I'm concerned there are strong intellectual problems with a strict insistence on using original instruments. I have a subjective affinity to using historical instruments, because I find that their limitations are analogous to the limitations the composer knew in his own age, which may have influenced him to write in a certain way, to create works in one way rather than some other way. So again it's bringing us back to the creative process.

On Bach's "Inconsistent" Articulation Marks

One avenue we might use to enter Bach's creative process is explored in your book on Bach's articulation marks. In the past, they hadn't seemed to admit of any consistent interpretation. You found that they do, if one understands the historical context.

There are consistencies within the inconsistencies, in various ways. For example, inconsistent articulation marks within the same piece sometimes reflect differences in the instruments used. That's the case in the gamba sonatas, where a harpsichord using a specific slurring would produce a result different from a gamba slurring the same way. In those circumstances, what might superficially seem a different slurring could produce the same musical result.

On the other hand, sometimes I feel that Bach just wanted a basic slurred idea and didn't really care how it was realized. So that's another issue, that quite often he's not consistent because he doesn't consider it essential—or even, perhaps, thought it counterproductive. An example are those movements where the basic ⁷⁄₈ meter is broken into triplets. In the last movement of the A Minor Violin Concerto, for example, it's not clear whether these are to be slurred 2+1 or 3. Quite often the player's technique or choice will determine it. Of course, some may argue that the markings are ambiguous only to us, and that the original players would have known from local convention what Bach desired. But if they knew what he wanted all along, why did he bother to mark virtually every slurring in the autograph solo violin part? Just one or two slurs at the outset would have sufficed. In other words, it was crucial to him that a slurred style be adopted—three slurs per bar—but the details were not to be notationally carved in stone.

So the exact details of the slurring weren't critical to him there? You've given the last chorus of the St. Matthew Passion *as a related example—as in, say, the last bar, where the voices have no slurs, the first violin a four-note slur, and the second violins two-note slurs.*

Yes, that's an example of where he wants a general slurred effect to make the strings more of a background to the voices. So it's just a device to make the strings quieter or less forward at that point, and he's not concerned about how you do it (there are similar examples in the B Minor Mass, among other works).

So part of my view on the inconsistencies is that you have to be very careful about whether the slurring is actually important at a particular point. Sometimes there's every evidence that to Bach it didn't matter. Of course, it's hard to convince people today that different players in an ensemble should play something differently or completely randomly!

We're more concerned than most past ages were with ensemble unanimity. But how do you tell whether the exact slurring does matter in Bach?

It might depend on the music. For one thing, if it's an inner part or an accompanying part, I would say he was not concerned as much with motivic cohesion as with foregrounding certain elements in the texture and not others. In that context, slurring acts as a way of shading out certain areas of the texture. So one has to decide, within the overall texture, how important the music is that's being slurred.

Well, one of the trends of twentieth-century performance has been to remove the differentiation between foreground and background material. Yet it appears to be an important element of Bach interpretation.

Oh, certainly, yes, very important. I think in Bach's music, and that of many other composers of the time, you need to see the music as a simple structure which has been ornamented at several overlapping levels, each of which might bring out other relationships within the music. You shouldn't see the music as cast iron, note after note after note, as you would in Brahms, where every note is of the same importance—to a certain extent—within the larger lines.

In other words, within the music you need to see hierarchies of pulse, dissonance, and so on, all the way through to the overlaying of different types of figures and ornamentation. Now, this is a theory I've drawn from a variety of historical data, and there's no book I can point you to from, say, 1715 that puts it exactly as I do.

It seems that performance-practice studies of a generation ago were often algorithmic—when you see X, do Y—about such things as ornamentation and rhythmic alteration. You're saying that you can't read Bach's articulation marks simply, as if they were algorithms.
Right: you first must understand something of the music, its structure and its various historical implications.

Can we discuss that, beginning with the nature of its structure?
The simplest hierarchical level, you could say, is perhaps the grammar, and then there are other aspects of syntax, rhetoric, emotion, and decoration which go above that.

Like verbal language? Let's begin with grammar.
The "grammar," the first of several parameters that might define articulation—the first level in the hierarchy—is the way the music is put together in terms of meter, accent, and bar. These provide the *metrical* hierarchy of the music. From that point of view you come up with a fundamental style of articulation in which what Baroque theorists called "good notes"—notes on strong beats, like the first beat in a bar—are stronger than what they called "bad notes." And that concept always seems to be in the background of Bach's music.

Why was the downbeat stronger in this era?
You only have to know the rules of harmony as they were codified from the early seventeenth century, up until Mozart and beyond, to understand that the downbeat is assumed to have a function that the upbeat doesn't have. This is in the very structure of music, in the way dissonance is used. You prepare a structurally significant dissonance, like a suspension, on the weak beat, sound it on the strong beat, and resolve it on the weak beat. That's there all the way through, and if the suspension is done in the wrong place, unless it's skillfully handled, it's a compositional anomaly.

So the strong beat gets the dissonance.
Right. But if you're learning to write a *passing* dissonance, one that carries less structural weight, the first dissonance you learn is the unaccented passing tone, which comes between two harmony notes and *mustn't* be on the strong part of the beat.
In some sense, then, melody and harmony have rhythmic dimensions. You cannot understand meter unless you understand dissonance, and vice versa. And dissonance is perhaps the very substance of tonal harmony. Particularly in

late Baroque harmony, the control of dissonance is really what gives the music its power. Directly connected to that, of course, is where you hear the dissonances and where you learn to put the dissonances; and that brings us right back to the hierarchy of beats.

I'd like to return to the dissonance issue later, but first get back to the articulation marks. One thing you spoke about in your book is how Bach's marks relate to metrical stresses.

Or bring out contrasts in metrical stresses, or deviations from metrical stress, as in the slurs in the Kyrie theme of the B Minor Mass.[8] The articulation of that piece is tied in with the appoggiatura[9] on the offbeat. It rubs against the meter—it's a metrical and melodic dissonance although not strictly a harmonic dissonance.

Your book mentions some other slurs and dots that indicate deviations from the basic grammar of "good" and "bad" beats.[10]

It also suggests that when the articulation marks themselves are inconsistent, that may be when the hierarchy of good/bad beats is in routine operation.

Not all Bach performances, especially mainstream ones, observe that hierarchy of beats—a lot still play Bach as Proust's "divine sewing machine," with all the beats more or less equal in importance. Sometimes even early-music groups do that. Other early-music groups have gone to the opposite extreme, and have been attacked for bashing the downbeats.

The divine sewing machine was characteristic of the 1950s; it was a Stravinsky- and Hindemith-influenced approach. As for downbeat-bashing, you find it for example in some of the Teldec [Harnoncourt/Leonhardt] cantatas, in the chorales, in the manner of attacking the words. So even within the early-music movement, you can get the whole range, from the totally undifferentiated ticker-tape approach to the downbeat for children's dance class.

The big problem of downbeat-bashing is the view that the barline is sacrosanct, when quite often it's just a notational aid, and in fact the grouping might

---

8. Bach, Mass in B Minor, BWV 232: subject of Kyrie I.

9. An appoggiatura is an ornamental note that leads melodically into the main note that follows, usually from a half-step or whole step away. In this example, the first note under each two-note slur is an appoggiatura.

10. E.g., *Bach Interpretation*, pp. 179 and 176; the latter concludes: "players—unless otherwise informed—geared their articulation to the natural hierarchy of pulse, and to their knowledge of harmony and figuration."

well go beyond that bar. In this regard, dance patterns can be of crucial importance, even in pieces which are not specifically labeled as dances.[11] The other point regarding the grammar, this metrical hierarchy, is that it's much more important that you have the *idea* of it than that you play it out rigorously. By analogy, we manipulate grammar rhetorically when we're speaking. Sometimes we use standard grammar more or less unconsciously, but sometimes we follow the strictest grammatical rules conspicuously for a specific effect, and at other times—for example, when we're being poetic—we might flout the rules.

You mentioned Bach's syntax as the next level in the hierarchy; could you define it?

You might think of the way a musical phrase is structured as being the syntax of the music. "Syntax" is a question of how Bach ties all the various devices—the figures and so on—together. It's concerned with what's appropriate at any particular point of the musical sentence, as it were. By contrast, "grammar" helps us to know how various musical "words" fit into a background metrical scheme—whether you stress this note or that note.

While syntax deals with putting those words together into sentences.

Right. And with syntax you can blend together several issues at once: the question of metrical and harmonic underpinnings (the grammar), the question of phrasing, the "rhyming" of various motivic figures with one another, and so on. So it's a complicated issue, but it's crucial to how the music works.

It relates to the inconsistencies of articulation marks as well. For example, Bach's syntax often involves the interaction of several lines; their slurs might well agree on the strong part of the beat and differ on the weak parts.[12] The articulation marks of the different lines in these cases may just be meant to create resonance and underline metrical accents—to remind the players that there should be three accents per bar, let's say—rather than to enforce a particular articulation. (If these lines are involved in a subtle interplay of contrasting figuration, though, the slurs might be meant more exactly. And we could also discuss the "melodies" that emerge from the interaction of multiple lines.)

Also, the role of a motivic figure is often ambiguous—does it relate to what preceded it or to what follows, or both? That influences the player's articulation. Now, these ambiguous notes often come at the weak part of the bar. In other words, you could look at any weak note in Bach, whether on a weak beat or a weak subdivision of a beat, and ask yourself whether it prepares the

11. Butt discusses this in chap. 6 of his Cambridge Handbook *Bach: Mass in B Minor* (Cambridge University Press, 1991). Some examples are the Gloria in excelsis deo and the Osanna, which use a two-bar rhythmic grouping derived from a pair of similar dance types, the Gigue and Passepied. For more extensive discussion see Meredith Little and Natalie Jenne, *Dance and the Music of J. S. Bach* (Bloomington: Indiana University Press, 1991).

12. *Bach Interpretation*, p. 132.

way for the next strong beat or is the dying breath of the strong beat before it. Or you might play it both ways. In the Second Organ Sonata, the figure (a) could relate to the previous downbeat, or to the following one:[13]

And, as I said, I like to have it both ways, if possible. To be able to point to that ambiguity in the way the music emerges within notation and bring it out in performance is a very great challenge. Here I'm talking as a performer rather than as a listener. I try to preserve the ambiguity when I play such figures.

The next levels you mentioned are those of rhetoric and emotion. You've been talking about music by analogy with language in terms of grammar and syntax, but Baroque theorists often talked about music-as-language in terms of Latin rhetoric and oration. How does that relate to understanding Bach's creative process and his articulation marks?

First, I should say that I think the connection between rhetoric and music is often overstated. Some modern writers believe that a study of rhetoric enables them to discern specific meaning in the music—holding, for example, that the various musical figures each had a specific meaning[14]—but rhetoric is a very different field from semantics. It deals with the power of persuasion, and the nuances of figurative speech. Most people, including Bach, had been taught rhetoric at school[15] (though not necessarily to a very sophisticated level), so the idea of how to construct a persuasive speech would have been clearly in their consciousness—the basic building-blocks of a speech, the order of the arguments, and their elaboration. Moreover, they clearly would have understood the different levels of rhetorical delivery: *inventio*, the invention of the basic idea; *dispositio*, laying out the idea; *elaboratio*, filling in or "elaborating" the laid-out idea; *pronuntiatio* and *enunciatio*, the actual performing of that idea.[16]

Its "pronunciation" and "enunciation"? Where do the articulation marks fit into this sequence of stages in making a persuasive speech?

13. Bach, Trio Sonata No. 2 in C Minor, BWV 526: opening.

14. Butt writes, in *Bach: Mass in B Minor*, "Most figures, like words, create different *affekts* in different contexts, so it is certainly a mistake to interpret them as fixed tokens of meaning"(p. 85). This flexibility, he notes, accounts for the ease with which Bach could reuse his own music with different texts.

15. One of Butt's books studies musical education in German Baroque schools: *Musical Education and the Art of Performance in the German Baroque* (Cambridge University Press, 1994).

16. See *Bach Interpretation*, pp. 15–19, for detailed source references on how these terms, derived from Cicero, were used in the German Baroque. On the other hand, as Butt points out, this can be overstated: see Peter Williams, *The Organ Music of J. S. Bach*, vol. III (Cambridge University Press, 1984), pp. 69–72, and Joshua Rifkin's interview later in this book.

Articulation marks deal primarily with the levels having to do with performance, how you "enunciate" and "pronounce." But they also relate to the previous level, called *decoratio*, decoration. Decoration is part of the way you "elaborate" the basic "inventions," which in music are more like musical themes or ideas for the potential development of the entire piece. Decoration is taking that elaborated form of the invention and, in music, adding little motivic figures to it, the little ornamental figures that help convey the work's specific mood or character. These decorations were, by the way, one of the things that distinguished Baroque music from Renaissance music, which at least on paper allowed only a few "primary" figures—"exceptions" that eventually, in the Baroque era, became a new "rule."

So the decoration *is the* detailing *of the elaborated idea, and it's with this level that the articulation marks in Bach primarily deal.*

Right. Now, in music decoration is the level (in terms of ornaments and diminution) which is often added by the composer but can also be added by the performer. And that's why it interests me—you can think of decoration as being the hinge between what's notated and what's performed.

You note in your book that Bach's articulation markings are concerned with bringing out the roles of the decorations, the motivic figures, in the musical argument, and that this differs from later eras' markings, which have to do more with indicating longer phrases. You also said that if one articulates the decorations in the detailed way Bach's markings suggest, it clarifies his contrapuntal textures.

That's right. I would emphasize that while articulation marks belong to the same mode of thought as the decorative level of the music, they don't always simply deliver these motivic figures—indeed they might sometimes contradict a simple motivic analysis.

In fact, the role of figures in the musical argument is *changeable*, and this bears on the question of inconsistencies in articulation marks. For example, sometimes changes in slur markings are meant to highlight a moment when a figure begins to play a different role in the musical design. At one point in the first movement of the A Minor Violin Concerto,[17] a three-note figure (a) is slurred four times, but not the fifth time (a¹): The dropping of the slur at this fifth occurrence disguises the way that the three-note figure is suddenly incorporated into a long sequence.[18] In that sequence the three-note slur then be-

17. Bach, Violin Concerto in A Minor, BWV 1041: first movement, bars 24–30.
18. Butt, *Bach Interpretation*, p. 197–99.

comes a musical element in its own right—it is transferred to the first beat of the bar over a different figure (b).

This reminds me of a review you wrote, where you contrasted Leonhardt's Bach playing—in which a given motif may be played slightly differently in different contexts—with that of a harpsichordist for whom each note in a Bach theme or motif "is definitively legato, staccato or midway."[19] *So it seems that with Bach the decoration interacts dynamically with the structure.*

To understand this, I would suggest that in Bach—to an extent that's unusual for his era—the basic idea or *inventio* of any particular piece is played out in all the levels right up to the figures, the decorations. For example, quite often the little figure might be the *subject* of the piece of music, as in the Two-Part Inventions. In No. 1, for instance, it becomes a subject that is discussed and developed in the course of twenty-two measures.[20] In fact, Robert Marshall finds that Bach usually began a piece by composing the essential figures in the primary melodic voices.

So one has to think on several levels—not just in a sequential line from invention to performance, but backwards and forwards and sideways. The smallest element of decoration might in fact be the seed to the invention, and so on.

This connecting of the different levels in Bach—where the seed idea is also the surface ornament—does this account for your statement that although it's very hard to play Bach well, something of Bach always comes through if the notes are all there?

Yes. In some ways I like to think of Bach's music as being a notated form of performance—that he's actually recording in notation almost what he did as a performer. And, yes, that's why even if you play the notes of Bach's music without any interpretative intent at all, you're bringing out a performance of the music, because the performance is already there in the notation itself. It's already ornamenting itself; there's already an aspect of what the performer might have done.

Indeed, it's always assumed nowadays that in the Baroque era the performer played the ornaments, and the composer wrote the "real" music. But with Bach, and with many Baroque composers for that matter, the boundary between notated ornamentation and improvised ornamentation is hard to define.

From that point of view, the articulation markings extend the idea that the performance is in the notation. The articulation markings bring out more and

19. Butt, *Early Music* 17 (February 1989), p. 117. In this review of Davitt Moroney's *Musical Offering* recording, Butt does note that the approach taken by Moroney may be appropriate for Bach's late works, which were written when the general style of keyboard articulation was moving in this direction. This relates to Butt's comment that in Leonhardt's Bach playing the hierarchy (discussed in this chapter) is always clear.

20. "[Baroque] music [was] understood as a complex discussion of motives and figures very much like classical rhetoric." Butt, *Bach: Mass in B Minor*, p. 84.

more of the implications of figures and ornamental patterns of the music. The articulation is actually a part of the interpretation, which is why I called my book on articulation marks *Bach Interpretation*.

Earlier you related dissonance to grammar—*which notes one stresses in a bar. But now that you're discussing the rhetorical element, where does dissonance fit in?*

Many dissonances are just part of the substance of the music—what motivates it—and you don't notice them particularly. But others give you a specific emotional effect. I think the Kyrie I theme in the B Minor Mass is a good example—its character comes partly from its dotted rhythm, but more importantly from the melodic dissonance. It's the progression of various kinds of dissonance and the implication of dissonances that give it its character, its emotion. If you stripped it of that and made it a continual line, it wouldn't have any character at all. In general, you might think of particular notes that stick out—stand out as dissonances or for other reasons—as being rhetorical.

They're "decoration" as well as "invention"? The Kyrie theme relates to a point in your book, where you say that some articulation marks have to do with bringing out the emotion, the affect.

In these marks, a particular slurring may be associated with a particular affective figure and therefore brings it out (as in the Kyrie theme), or there is the idea of a slurred affect, where everything is somewhat slurred to give a particular mood (as in the *St. Matthew* example).

That reminds me of your statement that the dissonances are what give this music its power.

Yes. To bring in metaphysical issues, which are common in the writings of the time, there was the idea of introducing dissonance as a way of appreciating consonance. You must have the opposites, you must have the yin to appreciate the yang, you can't have one without the other. If it's just a continuous consonance, you don't know how "good" consonance is.

You can relate this to religion. You have to appreciate evil in order to understand good. I don't think the Baroque use of the terms "good" notes and "bad" notes is casual thinking: there's an analogy here that they were conscious of at the time. Bach's cousin J. G. Walther, who was a theorist, said, "You must think of dissonance as night and of consonance as day." And so on: the interplay of the two concepts.

On How Bach's Metaphysics Influenced His Music

The understanding of Bach's religiousness has gone through a big shift since 1950, from the idea of a "devout Lutheran, his art and life wholly directed to-

wards the improvement of church music," to a more confusing picture.[21] *Still, his religious faith would seem to be an entryway into his creative process. What would you make of the connection between the two?*

The traditional way of looking at this, particularly by those who have a religious ax to grind, is to find religious symbolism and all sorts of levels of piety in what Bach does. Some of these findings seem too convincing to be fortuitous—the emphasis on "threeness" in *Clavierübung* III, for instance, or the ten entries for the Ten-Commandments fugue[22]—but of course it's in the nature of Baroque music to paint or gloss on a text, so from that point of view there's not a tremendous difference between Bach and many of his contemporaries (and not just those in the sacred field). I think it's more or less a dead end to try to make Bach's music a medium for hidden esoteric messages, merely on account of his superlative quality as a composer and his evident piety.

In your book on the B Minor Mass you dismiss attempts to apply numerology, Old Testament prophecies, and the like to the composition of the Mass; you say that "there is at once no supporting evidence for verification [of this approach] and, on the other hand, no possibility of refutation." But is there a fruitful way to use Bach's religion to understand his creative process?

One approach towards answering this question is to get to the main religious dispute of his age, which was between the Pietists and the Orthodox Lutherans. It has become quite clear, perhaps only in the last ten years or so, that Bach was very definitely an Orthodox Lutheran, not a Pietistic one. That doesn't mean that he lacked piety, but he wasn't part of the movement of Pietism with a capital "P," which looked towards a very direct relationship with God, one which didn't require the Church—congregations, buildings, altars, and such things—as intermediary. They wanted a personal relationship that could be expressed in the language and discourse of the early Christians. In many ways, it's like a modern, homespun Evangelical movement, where the great emphasis is on worship at home, with the singing of sacred songs. From that point of view, the Pietists shunned the whole apparatus of the church year and church music.

It's quite clear that throughout Bach's career he was escaping the Pietists. His second post, at Mühlhausen, fell through in a couple of years because of what was very clearly the Pietistic attitude of certain authorities, which didn't allow complex church music. Now, you can articulate this issue from two angles. First of all, you could say, "Bach liked to write great music, and therefore

21. Malcolm Boyd, *Bach*, The Master Musicians (London: Dent, 1983, and New York: Viking, 1987), p. xiii, in explaining the ongoing Bach revolution.

22. Fughetta on "Diess sind die heil'gen zehn Gebot'" ("These Are the Holy Ten Commandments"), BWV 679. The "threeness" of *Clavierübung* III (BWV 552, 669–89, and 802–5), which represents the Holy Trinity, is evident in (among other things) the collection's having three settings each of the Kyrie, Gloria, catechism, and sacrament movements.

sided with the Orthodox"—that Bach was really only interested in music, and therefore chose the wing of Lutheranism that favored music. But I suspect it was the other way around: that Bach was an Orthodox Lutheran and therefore believed in the order of the church year and the order of the church ceremony, the history of the church ceremony and liturgy, and the indisputable history and place of music within that liturgy as part of the mechanics of religious faith.

This brings us beyond his theology to his metaphysics. Bach sees music as being part of a mechanical process by which humankind comes to terms with the divine. And that mechanical process involves aspects of liturgy, going through all four Gospels day after day, week after week in a specific order, covering the Bible and the Psalms in an ordered way throughout the course of the liturgical year. It's organization, what you might think of as cultured religion, as opposed to personal and immediate religion, religion that's based on one's immediate reactions, feelings, and notions of faith. So from this point of view there's an aspect of his music that falls into a larger picture of what a religion is concerned with.

So Bach's beliefs might have influenced the way he approached the task of composition in a more abstract sense than that of theology. What he might communicate more in his music is his sense of order, which is in fact more a metaphysical concept than a religious one. His type of faith is one that looks for Godly order on earth. It's not a million miles from Pantheism in some ways, but it would never have been articulated thus in his time.

Could you say more about this metaphysics?

Well, one thing that interests me is the natural philosophy of the time. Whether or not Bach was familiar with the work of, say, Leibniz, I think there's a strong connection between that naturalistic philosophy of Bach's age and the way Bach's music works. Leibniz sees the smallest substance in the universe as being a microcosm of the greatest—the concept of the windowless monad. You could infer the whole of creation from a single monad and vice versa—he infers monads from looking at the whole of creation as he knows it.[23] I myself am particularly fond of linking Bach with the thought of Spinoza—not that this is plausible historically. But Spinoza seems to come closest in describing the "one substance" of Bach's music, and the "immanentist sacrality" of music—

23. Bach's analogies with Leibniz were discussed in a 1963 paper by Edward Lowinsky, "Music and the History of Ideas" (reprinted in his *Music in the Culture of the Renaissance* [University of Chicago Press, 1989], pp. 67–86). Lowinsky footnotes earlier discussions of the relationship, and points out that Bach's student and advocate Lorenz Mizler studied with Christian Wolf, a translator of and authority on Leibniz. Regarding Butt's idea that there are even deeper analogies between Bach's metaphysics and Spinoza, see his "'A Mind Unconscious that It Is Calculating'? Bach and the Rationalist Philosophy of Wolff, Leibniz and Spinoza," in *The Cambridge Companion to Bach*, ed. Butt (Cambridge University Press, 1997), pp. 60–71.

the idea that Bach expressed in his jotting in the margin of his Bible, "Where there is devotional music, God is always present with His grace." Spinoza's term "the intellectual love of God" seems remarkably appropriate for Bach.

There are other historical streams feeding into Bach's metaphysics; you might even think of the Lutheran sense of the mystic function of music as being a late manifestation of medieval thought. The conception of music as mirroring God's universe, and having mathematical proportions and mysterious aspects that mirror the human soul, is in some ways a medieval conception all along.[24] On the other hand, humanism brings in classical texts in which the power of art is more human-based than God-based. So in some ways the phenomenon in Bach and the late Baroque is a sort of combination of these two. The God-based medieval conception and the more human-based Renaissance conception melded together in what we think of as Orthodox Lutheranism. Pietism is a more progressive movement; it's actually pointing more towards Enlightenment types of thought, where the individual is responsible for his own salvation, his own faith. It's more immediately put down to the personal, the individual.

Regarding the Pietist movement, wasn't Bach criticized in his own lifetime for the over-complexity of his writing?

Oh, yes, by Scheibe in 1737. Scheibe is in some ways speaking for a later age, the early Enlightenment age, in which simplicity, of melody and of affect, is thought to be more natural than complexity in music. And, as you said, here is another relation to the Pietistic movement. Scheibe was not a Pietist as such, but the artistic side of the Pietistic movement (if you can think of it as having an artistic side) was very much that of mid-eighteenth-century mainstream music, which favored lightness, simplicity, and directness.

Like American classical radio today. Or Rousseau, a little later . . .

. . . the same sort of thought. Anything that apparently confuses and makes complex was thought of as being bombastic. Indeed, one of the things which Scheibe criticizes is the way Bach notates every little ornament. He puts down every little figure that the singer would normally sing completely naturally himself, and much more gracefully than this ghastly fixed notation of Bach allows.

That points to my view that Bach wanted a lot of control over the performance, and that part of that control was gained by writing down ornamentation. In his mind, this made the music that much more complex and cohesive, because it always relates to other aspects of the structure which an improvising performer would surely miss. It's a particular conception, not unlike that of

24. Lowinsky points out that Bach's student J. P. Kirnberger was still writing about the medieval classification of *musica mundana, humana,* and *instrumentalis* (see Barbara Thornton's interview for a discussion of these ideas in Hildegard of Bingen). Lowinsky also mentions Mizler's advocacy of Pythagorean principles.

twentieth-century modernists such as Stravinsky or Schoenberg. Both of those composers have a very similar view of control over the performer, and control of the insignificant; the insignificant is to be as significant as the significant.

That seems to indicate a limit to improvisation, namely that you can't get perfect integration of the parts and the whole (though, of course, not all music aims for that).

That's right: there's going to be a sense of chance, or a sense of diffusion. Bach in some ways has a more nineteenth-century aesthetic, that the music must form its own coherent whole. That means, on the other hand, that as a performer you must play the piece as if for the first time, as if you were just discovering it. It doesn't mean you take away the spontaneity. You can keep the spontaneity and have the sense of the coherent whole, which is the best of both worlds.

And Bach's concern for coherent wholeness derived from the metaphysics you described.

Very certainly, yes. He had an attitude that everything human, natural, and musical existed in a neatly ordered hierarchy. This included even his patrons and the aristocracy—he felt that the domination of the upper classes was strictly analogous to the domination of God. It's hard, particularly for religious people, to accept today that Bach must have believed in the divine right of the aristocracy as much as he believed in the greater divine right of God. But the two do belong together.

That concern for coherent wholeness also may account for why Bach has been so fully accepted into the canonical mainstream of music. He had no intention of being up there with Beethoven, Mozart, and Co.; he couldn't conceive of that sort of thing in his day. But it's no surprise that he's the one composer from that era who's been taken into common practice.[25]

Because his contemporaries' music is less coherent, and coherence is what we value now.

In other words, in Bach's time it was not so important to write music that was really tightly organized.

So his pre-Enlightenment metaphysics helped bring him into the post-En-

---

25. This is a nice twist on Lydia Goehr's argument that Bach did not conceive of his pieces as "works of music," which she considers a nineteenth-century concept (though she does not deny that his pieces can legitimately be considered "works"). See her essay "Being True to the Work," *Journal of Aesthetics and Art Criticism* 47:1 (Winter 1989), esp. pp. 56, 57, and 61. Butt's next remark does seem to concur with her belief that in Bach's *era*, musical practice "was not regulated by the idea of the work." Recall also Butt's thoughts on what constitutes a "piece of music," in the early pages of this interview.

lightenment canon. Richard Taruskin[26] points out the irony that twentieth-century composers like Stravinsky have taken Bach as the standard for treating music as a purely formal arrangement of sound, of pure form, abstracted away from the rest of life—his music is so perfectly wrought that he can be taken as "the formalist supreme"—when to Bach music was not that at all.

In some sense, Bach was something even more extreme than a formalist; Bach more or less saw music as reflecting the whole substance of everything around him: substance and form, actually. And he very much believed that music has value in its own way. His underlinings in his copy of the Bible are all under texts that mention music as being crucial to God's creation, to showing God's work.

In your notes to your CD of the Trio Sonatas, you say that Bach's "religious faith probably led him to believe that the musical language of his time was divinely developed and fixed; all he needed to do was to understand its deepest implications to discover the unity behind the diversity, but also to create something fresh and unique each time he composed." So that mixing of Baroque genres we talked about—the way he melds so many different conventional genres into unified forms, as in Cantata 78—was motivated by his religion.

I suspect it was the religion, not the metaphysics, that he thought about, because that's what you were supposed to think about; the metaphysics was a given. In a thoroughbass method he wrote down for his students in 1738, Bach said, "The end or final cause of all music, and also of thoroughbass, is the glory of God and the permissible enjoyment of the spirit. Wherever this is disregarded, there is no longer actual music but a devilish bawling and singsong." In other words, following the rules of music as he knew it was almost like following an ethical rule, a cosmological rule.

I would repeat, though, that it's a mistake to reduce the music's quality and effect to the religious values he held, as some people have tried to do. After all, there are religious composers who don't have that kind of effect, and some non-religious composers, like Debussy, whose music is highly ordered. I think a lot of writings on Bach miss the fact that his religious faith rests upon certain metaphysical premises, of order, of connection, of thoroughness—that his faith rests upon those premises, rather than supporting them.

SELECTED DISCOGRAPHY

John Butt's research into articulation tells throughout his recording of the Bach Trio Sonatas for organ (Harmonia Mundi HMU 907055), whose articulation

---

26. Taruskin, "Facing Up, Finally, to Bach's Dark Vision," in *The New York Times*, Sunday Arts and Leisure section, 27 January 1991, pp. 25, 28, reprinted in his *Text and Act* (New York: Oxford University Press, 1995), pp. 307–15.

marks are especially detailed. Reviewing the CD, David Mulbury praises Butt's "splendid instinct" for the "most problematic of instruments," the organ, and says that "a strong musical personality permeates his music making."[27] Mulbury thinks his articulation works well in the "buoyant" fast movements, but is disturbed by the "rhythmic Quixotism" in some slow movements; this refers to Butt's use of rubato, which I think is eloquent.

Butt has also recorded music that may have influenced the young Bach. This includes Pachelbel's *Hexachordum Apollinis* (on organ; Harmonia Mundi HMU 907029), and two recordings of music by Kuhnau, Bach's predecessor at the Thomaskirche: the *Frische Clavier Früchte* (on harpsichord; HMU 907097) and the *Biblical Sonatas* (on harpsichord, organ, and clavichord; HMU 907133). Nicholas Anderson says, "Butt's Kuhnau playing is fluent, rhetorical and virtuosic and he makes more sense of these extraordinary, often theatrical pieces [the *Biblical Sonatas*] than I have previously experienced."[28] Butt's recording of the organ composer Cabanilles (HMU 907047) appears regularly on lists of the best CDs of Spanish Baroque music. As for his recording of the complete organ music of Purcell and Blow (HMU 907103), Marc Rochester likes it but finds it "somewhat remote";[29] by contrast, the organist Haig Mardirosian praises Butt's ornamentation, rhythm, and "verve and grace" in these works. He concludes, "Butt plays Bach and earlier organ music with unchallenged expertise."[30]

With the violinist Elizabeth Blumenstock, Butt has also recorded Bach's complete violin and harpsichord sonatas (HMU 907084). Reviewing the set, Anderson calls Butt's playing "impressive" and praises Blumenstock's "invigorating, perceptive, and often very sensitive" playing, which "reaches the heart of the music."[31]

FOR FURTHER READING

Butt's *Bach: Mass in B Minor,* a Cambridge Handbook (Cambridge University Press, 1991) is an excellent general introduction to Bach's formal techniques and procedures, especially in the vocal works. Donald Francis Tovey's 1937 essay on the Mass in B Minor is also a superb introduction to the ritornello in Bach; it is reprinted in his *Concertos and Choral Works* (Oxford University Press, 1989). Butt's *Bach Interpretation* (Cambridge University Press, 1990) is important, even essential, for performers and scholars. His *Musical Education and the Art of Performance in the German Baroque* (Cambridge University Press, 1994), an important work for specialists, sheds light on the one-per-part

27. Mulbury, *American Record Guide* 55 (May/June 1992), p. 22–23.
28. Anderson, *Gramophone* 73 (March 1996), p. 71.
29. Rochester, *Gramophone* 72 (June 1994), p. 87.
30. Mardirosian, *Fanfare* 17 (March/April 1994), p. 282–83.
31. Anderson, *Gramophone* 71 (October 1993), p. 60.

debate (see Chapter 15 below) among other performance-practice issues. Malcolm Boyd's *Bach* in the Master Musicians series (London: Dent, 1983, and New York: Viking, 1987) is the best introductory biography at present. Robert Marshall's *The Music of Johann Sebastian Bach* (New York: Schirmer, 1989) is illuminating. Best of all, perhaps, is Christoph Wolff's *Bach: Essays on His Life and Music* (Cambridge, Mass.: Harvard University Press, 1991). Regarding Bach's metaphysics, see Robert Marshall's essay "On Bach's Universality" in his book, and Butt's two essays—chaps. 4 and 5—in a book he edited, *The Cambridge Companion to Bach* (Cambridge University Press, 1997).

10

"One Should Not Make a Rule"

Gustav Leonhardt on Baroque
Keyboard Playing

In the 1950s and 1960s, a group of Dutch musicians created one of the world centers of what we now call the early-music movement. Through the work of—among many—the Kuijken brothers, the recorder virtuoso Frans Brueggen, and my interview subjects Gustav Leonhardt and Anner Bylsma, the Netherlands became to Baroque performance what Switzerland is to chocolate, watches, and banks. Just as young musicians had long flocked to the Schola Cantorum in Basel for instruction, they now came from all over the world to Amsterdam.

Leonhardt and his associates raised their instrumental technique to new heights. More significantly, they developed a new approach to playing Baroque music. In contrast to the motor-like "sewing machine" style prevalent in preceding decades, these players emphasized the metrical hierarchy that John Butt explains in the last chapter; and their playing, says Laurence Dreyfus, sounded "strikingly speech-like by mimicking ever-shifting patterns of thought."[1] Their approach has had enormous influence, either by being adopted elsewhere or by being reacted against.

In the next two chapters, Leonhardt and Bylsma speak about their approach to performance and to the exploration of early instruments.

"The harpsichord is perfect as to its compass and is brilliant in itself," wrote the great French composer François Couperin in 1713, "but as it is impossible to swell or diminish its tones, I shall always be thankful to those who, by means

---

1. Dreyfus, in "The Early Music Debate," *Journal of Musicology* 10 (Winter 1992), p. 115.

of infinite artistry borne up by good taste, shall succeed in making the instrument capable of expression."[2] He might have been especially grateful to Gustav Leonhardt.

Harpsichord playing in the middle of our century (in reaction against the pioneering romantic, Wanda Landowska) was often rigid and prickly. My pianist friends still occasionally say things like, "But the harpsichord can only play staccato, right?" More than anyone else, Leonhardt has developed a battery of techniques that allow the harpsichord to speak and sing, to create an illusion of rich variety in both sound and touch. How he did this was one of the topics we discussed when I telephoned him at his seventeenth-century Amsterdam house—"a dwelling," says Howard Schott, "filled with beautiful old furnishings and fine instruments."[3]

Leonhardt, born in Amsterdam in 1928, grew up playing piano and cello, and after the war he studied harpsichord and organ at the Schola Cantorum in Basel. He returned to his native city in 1954 to take up a professorship at the Conservatory. Since then he has played a key part in the extraordinary development of Dutch Baroque performance. He has been, beyond question, the most influential harpsichordist of our time. Name a leading harpsichordist, and the chances are good that they studied with Leonhardt. Among his pupils are Bob van Asperen, Lisa Goode Crawford, Alan Curtis, John Gibbons, Pierre Hantaï, Ketil Haugsand, Christopher Hogwood, Ton Koopman, Edward Parmentier, Skip Sempé, Colin Tilney, Anneke Uittenbosch, Glen Wilson, and many others. The French harpsichordist Christophe Rousset says that it was a master class with Leonhardt that liberated him at the keyboard:

> I learned all I know about harpsichord technique in Holland. They know everything about the harpsichord there. It's amazing how Gustav Leonhardt has thought about everything, every little reaction of the instrument, the action of the keyboard and the plectrum and the string. . . . after I took a master class with Leonhardt, I finally understood . . . what is possible on a harpsichord and how to make it sound.[4]

Some harpsichordists become a bit lost in the "infinite artistry"—the subtle techniques that Leonhardt pioneered. Alfred Brendel writes that "nowadays we hear Couperin on the harpsichord played in a way that amazingly resembles the 'romanticism' of Paderewski's records: no chord without an arpeggio and

---

2. "Le Clavecin est parfait quant à son etendüe, et brilliant par luy même; mais, comme on ne peut enfler ny diminuer ses sons, je sçauray toûjours gré à ceux qui, par un art infini soutenu par le goût, pourront ariver à rendre cet instrument susceptible d'expression." Couperin, Preface to the Premier Livre of the *Pièces de clavecin*.

3. In an interesting tribute to Leonhardt, "Ein vollkommener Musik-meister," *Musical Times* 133 (October 1992), pp. 514–16.

4. Bernard D. Sherman, "Finding One's Own Recipes: Christophe Rousset Ponders the Ingredients," *Piano and Keyboard*, May/June 1994, p. 29.

the left hand constantly anticipating the right."[5] In fact, a "straighter" school of period-instruments Baroque playing, which emerged in London in the 1970s, developed in conscious reaction against what its players considered the "highly mannered style" of Dutch (and Austrian) Baroque playing. In our interview, Leonhardt discusses how he integrates his subtleties into a natural whole.

Leonhardt clearly feels uncomfortable with the roles of *éminence grise*, doyen, or guru; "I don't regard myself as a pioneer," he once told a German interviewer.[6] It is equally characteristic, and a tribute to his teaching, that many of his students have distinctive styles of their own. Rousset, for example, doesn't play in what he would call a "Dutch" interpretative style, as described above by Dreyfus; as he told me, "If Leonhardt does something, it's not a recipe. It's good for him; it's convincing, but as a system of interpretation which works every time, I don't believe in it." Neither, as you will read, does Leonhardt.

In the Baroque, three keyboard instruments—the harpsichord, the clavichord, and the portative organ—were in common domestic use. To what degree were they interchangeable, or to what degree specific in a composer's mind?

In general, it's difficult to say; but I think they were largely overlapping, and the composers couldn't care less. Someone at home would use indifferently whatever was practical (of course, the large organ is a different matter). It's rare to find specifications that make it dead certain that the composer wanted a piece played on this or that instrument. Sometimes we think that we know that *this* must be an organ piece, and *that* a harpsichord piece, and it cannot be anything else; but usually we cannot prove it. And I think it's rather good that we cannot prove it, because it should remain rather flexible.

Regarding this interchangeability, Charles Rosen argues that few of Bach's fugues "exploit the resources of any particular instrument"—harpsichord, clavichord, organ, or piano; most were meant to be playable on whatever instrument one had at home.[7] If, as he says, "the type of sonority . . . is rarely a matter of interest," why not use the piano?

I don't agree at all with the conclusion. I think the historical facts surrounding the composer are much more important than that argument suggests. It's a unity; you can't break it up, although there's a lot of liberty within it.

Of course, one should not say the harpsichord is always the thing to use, because so often it might be a small organ or a clavichord. But they, unlike the piano, all belong to a certain way of thinking.

5. Alfred Brendel, *Music Sounded Out* (London: Robson, 1990, and New York: Farrar, Straus and Giroux, 1991), p. 221.
    6. Arnd Richter, "Ich fordere nichts vom Publikum," *Neue Zeitschrift für Musik* 147/9 (1986), pp. 34–38; quote, p. 34.
    7. *Bach: The Fugue,* ed. Rosen (Oxford University Press, 1975), Introduction, p. 3.

What defines that way of thinking?

Well, it also depends on the particular pieces, but most pieces of the seventeenth and eighteenth centuries seem to want to speak instead of sing—though this is too simplistic a statement—whereas in the nineteenth century one thinks primarily about singing in long, sustained phrases.

I think the nineteenth century, to put it roughly, is for sustained sounds, which are always under tension and always nourished; but I think before that it was exactly the contrary, it was more like speaking, which means wave-like, constantly rising then loosening up even within a single sentence. In this music, you push it from a "good" beat,[8] and then the following group of notes goes by itself. Unlike later music, you don't have to push a phrase all the time; it often rolls by itself.

Put differently, there is more attention to the details of the phrase, as opposed to projecting a long, sustained line, which is what the modern piano is designed for.

Pianists will always play Bach; so what would you say to a pianist regarding what, if anything, they can learn from harpsichordists? Some pianists have tried to use harpsichordistic techniques.

I think such imitations are useless, because the piano only sounds worse if you try to imitate the harpsichord. The piano has its own ideals and capacities; you can't mix the two instruments. I don't want to be a policeman, but I think that's not the right approach.

Harpsichord technique has changed dramatically since World War II, and you've been very much involved in that. What are some of the ways developed since then through which one creates a sense of speaking and dynamics on the harpsichord?

I cannot say that it's a secret, but it's almost impossible to describe with words; it's even difficult to show at the keyboard. Essentially, it must be based on a dynamic *wish*. The imagination of the player, fed by analysis and by study of the whole period in which the music was written, must have become very dynamic. Again, I cannot describe how one puts that on the keyboard, but it must be based on the musical imagination.

8. A "good beat" was defined in John Butt's discussion of Bach in Chapter 9. What Leonhardt is discussing here exemplifies Butt's point that the music of Bach and his contemporaries has a hierarchy of different levels, so that all notes are not equally important. Here Leonhardt discusses what Butt calls the "grammar," the hierarchy of strong and weak beats. Regarding the idea that the music "rolls by itself," Butt again offers some support: in reviewing Leonhardt's second recording of the Bach Partitas (reissued on Virgin VER5 61292), Butt mentions Leonhardt's attention to the "grammar," coupled with his insight into longer-term matters— motivic development, voice-leading, and harmonic tension—and says that together these lead to "a performance where the music provides its own momentum" (*Early Music* 17 [February 1989], p. 117).

Indeed, I think that the changes made in the last fifty years are based on the fact that the imagination has changed. Ignoring for a moment the kinds of instruments the earlier harpsichordists were playing, which were not historical at all, the crucial element behind the wish of some players not to play Bach on the piano was that they wanted to get rid of that dripping Romanticism they did not like (for good reasons, we now think). But they then threw out the baby with the bath water; their approach was only negative, with no expression, no dynamic levels. They had the idea that the music should "speak for itself." So the Helmut Walcha school, the *neue Sachlichkeit*,[9] put everything at zero.

In the last fifty years, we have gradually begun to see that Baroque music is, if anything, *more* expressive than Romantic music, but in detail rather than in large lines. With that, a technique developed, but not by itself; it's only that the wish has changed, that our imagination of the music has changed completely.

That's fascinating. Nonetheless I would like to ask a little about the ways technique has developed: for example, subtleties in how the plectrum strokes the string.

Yes, through the harpsichord's key we can feel the plectrum touching the string, so we can rest the plectrum on the string before we pluck, and then pluck quickly, slowly, overlapping with other notes, or with a range of other subtleties. The pianist never has this really close contact with the string, because with the piano it's all indirect. He can of course compensate with dynamics and little rhythmic subtleties, but he can never caress the string.

Let me take that technique as an example: how did you learn to do it?

I can't remember that I learned it. Once again, by studying so many fields of this period, not just music but all of the arts, you see that the Baroque is the most expressive period we have had in the whole history of Western civilization.[10] So I thought the music cannot be dull like a block of concrete, without any life in it, without any undulations. And then, one reads in historical sources about such techniques as overlegato—in which you release a note later than it is marked—and other techniques, all used in order to achieve dynamic subtleties. But again, it's based on the wish. I have never worked on technique as such. It came by expanding one's understanding of the music

9. The "new objectivity" or "new actuality"—a post-World War I aesthetic movement that radically rejected nineteenth-century Romanticism.

10. Compare, e.g., Joseph Kerman on the Baroque's "exhaustiveness of emotional effect": "[high Baroque] music hammers away at a single feeling, intensifying it and magnifying it to a remarkable extent. . . . The Baroque theater concentrated on grandiose gesture and high passion. . . . Theatricality is the key to the emotional world of Baroque art, whether in music, the visual arts, or poetry" (*Listen* [New York: Worth, 1980], p. 197).

I was going to ask about overlegato: holding some notes longer than written. To anyone familiar with older harpsichord playing, the effect was of an almost Impressionist wash of sound. It's another tool for making the harpsichord expressive.

If not overdone.

What determines whether it's overdone—is it a matter of harmonic tension, or what?

It's very hard to say, and one should not make a rule. It is one of the means. But again, you use that means in order to achieve a dynamic effect. Now, on one instrument in one hall you do it a little, and in another you do it a lot, in order to achieve the same effect. So the circumstances play an enormous role. Pianists usually find that with the sustaining pedal they can make the surroundings more or less the same; we cannot, so we depend much more on the hall's having good acoustics, and we must adapt our way of playing very much to the circumstances of the acoustics. So that changes the technique. You use different tricks hoping to achieve the same results.

Another crucial element of your style has been the use of timing—delaying an important note a little, or holding it a little longer than written—to clarify which beats are strong beats and which are weak. Can you discuss that?

Well, it's not that I don't want to speak, but it's too subtle to explain. Again, one doesn't make up one's mind, for example, to delay a certain note. Rather, the wish is to stress that note, and delaying it is one of the means which sometimes one hopes will work. And you can delay to make a note weaker, or to make it stronger, anything you like; but it's not with the thought of delaying.

When one is a student one does things consciously, but when one is more experienced one does not play intellectually any more. One doesn't *think*; one *has thought*. You must have done so before, but when you perform it is too late to think; you are only making music, without any thought of "now delay here" and "now articulate there." The only thing is music. It is like when we speak; we don't think, "Now this 'S' must be strong," or "Here let's pause." Those things are done automatically, depending on what you intend to say.

How does one learn to integrate these things? And can the ability to integrate the parts into a whole be taught?[11]

No; I think it comes from two things. The first is a gift. You are born with it, and then you must develop it; but either you can develop it or you can't. The second is probably experience or age, if you like. It takes time, I think. A young person usually has not that feeling for integration. You see that in all

---

11. On this topic, I recall something Leonhardt said at a lecture in Berkeley about Frescobaldi; he cautioned against over-emphasizing repeated motifs, quoting Oscar Wilde's last words (delivered in a characteristic Parisian hotel room): "The wallpaper is killing me."

the creative arts, especially the visual arts. I don't know of any great artist who in his youth was sloppier than in his old age—sloppy not in the negative sense, but in being more concerned with the whole than the details. Think of Titian or Rembrandt; they were meticulous when they were young, but rough—concerned only with the major things and forgetting about small details—when they were old. So I think it's a general tendency in a human being: when you get older, the whole becomes more important than the details.

I'd like to ask you about some specific performance issues. One is so-called early fingerings.

The question is, what do we know of good fingerings of important pieces by important players or composers? Hardly anything remains except by François Couperin. The other fingerings are not necessarily written by the composer, but either by a slow pupil or by a good teacher for a silly little student learning the piece and doing the thing wrong. So they wrote out, "Here use the second finger." Now we write a whole book on the second finger being on that note. So it's dangerous; one must consider it, but it doesn't explain things.

In fact, we see the whole thing in an inverted way. They used a certain fingering in order to achieve a certain effect in the easiest way. Now we go backwards; we see a fingering and try to see what effect they meant by it. That is why it can be dangerous—worth doing, but not to be followed absolutely.

Of course, I've studied early fingerings as much as I could, but the inconsistency of early written fingerings is incredible. Even in one piece, with all the fingerings written by one person, the same motif recurring gets totally different fingerings, suggesting totally different articulations. It's a very common thing. Sometimes, a certain articulation is determined if you use a certain fingering, and it seems to make sense. However, other early fingerings, which a modern pianist would never use, *can* indicate articulation, but not necessarily so. These things are easily exaggerated; one can get pedantic.

Generally, then, I think the early fingering is hardly ever known. Even in Couperin, I'm not sure in my heart that he himself used his own fingerings all the time. Of course, his fingerings are cleverly thought out and are marvelous to know; and I probably use them most of the time, because they make sense, and fall easily for that clear, gentle, clean speaking style of his.

Temperament is another issue. Howard Schott writes that you tune the harpsichord "as the tonalities and enharmonic notes in [your] programme require, seeking to preserve as many pure, or at least less than very wide, thirds as possible."[12] I take it that you don't feel the need to adhere rigidly to a specific historical tuning system?

12. Schott, "Ein vollkommener Musik-meister," p. 516. Schott tells me that Leonhardt pioneered the use of historical tunings, and was recording with them in the early 1960s (personal communication, 1996).

Yes, on the harpsichord I adapt my tuning, depending on the program. The temperament is unequal, but how unequal and where it is unequal I cannot standardize. Indeed, as Howard Schott said, the main issue is the major third—the purer it is, the better it is for that music—but inevitably there are conflicts and practical drawbacks. All the various systems were just attempts to answer the question, "How do I get around the conflicts? How much can I suffer on one side in order to enjoy the other side the more?" Anyway, as soon as the audience comes in, the room heats up and the tuning is already gone a little, at least the very fine things.

Another issue is registration. A person who hadn't heard an organist play Bach since 1950 would notice that some of the current players change registration much less.

I think the very active registration shifts came into being in the late nineteenth century because the organs were so awful, so totally unhistoric, that it was unbearable to hear most sounds for any length of time. So in a way, it was a musical thing. But since one has discovered better organs, and I think also looked at the music very precisely, one sees that many of the registration changes suggested by Widor or Dupré or whomever are not clean; they break up one voice in order to make another voice's entry clear, so they butcher the piece. I think the most important thing is that if you make a manual change it must be clear in all parts. And then, yes, of course, why not? They had four-manual organs in the Baroque era.

Can you give an example of where and where not to change manuals?

Well, it depends on the piece. In the big B Minor Prelude of Bach [BWV 544] you cannot change manuals properly; more specifically, while you can get out of the opening registration properly when the opening ritornello ends and the first episode begins, you never can come back properly from the episode to the returning ritornello. You have to break a thematic element in the middle. On the other hand, today one often hears the Passacaglia in C Minor [BWV 582] played in a roaring *fortissimo* from beginning to end; I think that, first of all, it is unbearable that way and, second, it is contrary to the character of several of the variations. So one can make a very clean change of manuals between variations in that piece, which is typical for variations anyway.[13]

Harpsichord registration raises similar issues. For example, what do you think about varying registration in repeats?

13. See Christoph Wolff's "The Architecture of the Passacaglia," in his *Bach: Essays on His Life and Music* (Cambridge, Mass.: Harvard University Press, 1991), pp. 306–16. A detailed discussion of manual changes is in Peter Williams, *The Organ Music of J. S. Bach,* vol. 3 (Cambridge University Press, 1984), pp. 171–82.

Well, I may *think* something about it, but I don't *know* anything about it. To my knowledge, it is never written about in early sources. I think it is not so important.

You are much more sparing than many harpsichordists in taking repeats—in many recordings people take them all, while you often take few or sometimes none.

Again, I think there are no rules. One does what is required, and a repeat that may make the piece too long in one setting is just right in another. One doesn't know the historical practice, really, but I think it has always been like that. There was no "You must," ever. I think it's a bit modern and pedantic when people think that way. And recording is a rather unhuman thing. I find that repeats can be pedantic on a recording.

This brings up the issue of recordings. They have been central to the early-music movement, but of course nothing could be less historical. And yet they do allow the harpsichord more intimacy than a large hall does. In your experience of recording, how does it influence the music-making?

Music-making? That I don't want to say. It has influenced enormously the spread of what I consider good taste in music. This is apart from the fact that it can offer some bliss to people in the middle of the Sahara who want to hear some music; for people in the middle of a big town it's not so necessary. But the influence of recording has been enormous, and I think beneficial on the whole. Though that's not what you wanted to know.

I suppose the question is, in making a recording is there a conflict between inspiration and technical perfection? Would you let a take go out with wrong notes because it was inspired or had the right feeling?

For me, a recording is quite a different thing from playing a concert. That's the reason why I refuse to combine them. Often people, either the radio or someone else, want to record a concert: I always refuse, because my playing is totally different from concert to concert. In a concert I adapt my wavelengths to how large the hall is, how far away the audience is, the relationship with that audience at that moment, and, of course, what the acoustics are. And also it's only for once, so I take risks. Whereas on record, a risk is a silly thing. You have to do it over if it doesn't go. So I play neatly, and as well as I can on the record, and in the concert I try to play beautifully.

Is something lost from the music in playing neatly?

If you do outrageous things which may perhaps be fine in a concert, they are ridiculous if you hear them several times in a recording. So I think it should be a sort of quasi-ivory-tower perfection on record—not too much, not too little; exemplary in your own mind. It's a document, really.

Regarding the concert experience: Charles Rosen differentiates between playing an organ fugue written for public performance—in which "the entrances of the theme . . . are easily heard and appear with dramatic effect"— and "private" keyboard fugues written to be played mainly just for oneself. In these, the entrance of the theme is often hidden, "its opening note tied to the last note of the previous phrase." Because it was being played in private, however, these entries of the theme "needed no illustration or emphasis from the performer," who could "hear [the theme] himself as he knew where it was, and, even more, he could feel its presence in his fingers." But now, when one plays in a concert hall, it becomes "imperative to allow the listeners to perceive what [goes] on in the fugue, to give them an idea how the individual voices move." At its worst, this leads to the pianist who will always bring out the subject to the detriment of everything else; but for any performer, Rosen says, it creates a unavoidable tension between modern concert life and "what the composer wanted or what he expected to get."[14]

Well, I think it's a nice idea. It may be a bit of a modern idea to make a distinction between private and public works; I'm not aware that Bach or anybody else thought in these terms, though I must say I cannot deny it either. But I suspect it's a new thought, which may be a bit overdone. I quite agree that there are some hidden entrances, but I don't know if the reason is that it was only for oneself; the thought is nice, but I would not like to say that that's the reason. That's definitely one of the pleasures of polyphony, that there are some surprises, subtleties, that make you think "Ah!" because they are hidden at first. You may say these are literary private jokes, for the connoisseur, but such people may also sit in a large hall. And I think the general music lover, who is not really listening closely to what happens, may enjoy a piece that is full of hidden entries without ever noticing them. It may be a bit academic to make the distinction, but the fact happens that there are clear-cut and hidden pieces.

In discussing the change in harpsichord playing, we set aside the unhistorical instruments of fifty years ago, but one of the developments of the last thirty years has been the historical re-creation of specifically Baroque harpsichords, and of national styles of harpsichord—the French, Italian, and German instruments for example. You've been very much involved with the revival of these. How much does it matter to have say, a French harpsichord for French music? What's your experience?

I think the whole development, which I consider a sound one, leads to more refinement. One discovers little things that are more important than we thought, so they don't remain little things—well, in the whole view perhaps they are still little things, but the refinement means that more and more one hears and experiences how certain instrument types may have inspired com-

14. Rosen, "The Shock of the Old," *New York Review of Books,* 19 July 1990, p. 50.

posers of that period. Things that did not sound well, or even that were dull on one instrument, would, with the proper instrument, all of a sudden start to live. So that, indeed, an instrument of the composer's period and country is certainly the best. There's no doubt about that; it's been proved for people with a refined ear. On the other hand, with modern concert life, which is different from anything before the 1800s, we should not be too stubborn, so I personally think that although it is perhaps not perfect to play Bach on a French eighteenth-century harpsichord, it *doesn't matter* so much. On the other hand, to play Frescobaldi [an early-seventeenth-century Italian] on a Kirckmann [a late-eighteenth-century English builder] is so unsuccessful that I don't do it. But, then, I'm not angry if somebody else does.

Organs also varied greatly from place to place. You've recorded on quite a variety of organs; has that had similar benefits?

Organs are of such individuality that I find it impossible sometimes, technically, to play certain music on certain organs. For example, French music is thought out for French instruments with certain standard registrations; you hardly ever play any of them on organs of another country. And even Italian organs are, again, so specific and standardized in layout that most of the pieces only come off on that kind of organ. So there we are much more restricted. I think the idea of taking one specific type of instrument is the only good solution to arriving at a better understanding of the music.

Finally, I want to ask about national styles in the current music scene. The Netherlands has produced an unusually large number of prominent early-music players, like Italy producing opera singers; do you have any theories to explain why that might be the case?

No, just chance. Although a thing that happened by chance may perhaps spread because there's an example.

I think of the main examples as coming from yourself, and Brueggen, Bylsma, and the Kuijkens. Are the kinds of performance practices one associates with the Netherlands—the metrical hierarchy, rhetoric, and so on—the sorts of things you were thinking about?

Oh, we never thought about them. We never thought about developing anything much. We never talked about any issues. We didn't make a point of anything, ever. We played, and each one studied the pieces. We played—we had no theories. Perhaps in secret; but no, I never had theories. I was investigating all the time, but from a tradition to a wealth of general concepts. And maybe it [our style] is all wrong; I don't know, it could be.

Is there anything else you would like to add to what we've discussed?

No, I have nothing to say, I am only a player.

As opposed to?

To a real musician, which is a composer.

SELECTED DISCOGRAPHY

What Leonhardt says about playing in an exemplary way on recordings may sound off-putting, and some of his discs do seem to lack the spark of live performances; critics have been known to comment on this (e.g., Teri Noel Towe considers his B Minor Mass "almost completely devoid of excitement"[15]—though some critics appear to have found more of it; Deutsche Harmonia Mundi 77040–2–RG, 2 CDs). But listeners with a taste for Leonhardt's intensive approach may find many of his 200-plus recordings gripping, and sometimes overwhelming. For example, Nicholas Anderson writes that the Dies irae of the Biber Requiem à 15 (DHM 77344) "inspires Leonhardt and his musicians to deliver it with fearful fervour," and says that Leonhardt "makes a good deal more of the drama" of the work as a whole than Ton Koopman does in his recording.[16] Below are listed a few of Leonhardt's best recordings, with no further attempt to give a balance of pro and con.

For a sample of Leonhardt's keyboard work, you might start with his second recording of the Prelude, Fugue, and Allegro in E♭ (BWV 998) on an excellent 1986 Philips Bach recital (416 141). This is one of my favorite Bach performances—Leonhardt has a unique feeling for this work's mysteries. It's interesting to compare it with his 1965 recording of the same work (DHM 77013–2–RG, 2 CDs) to see how his conception of the Prelude changed over two decades. Bach lovers should definitely hear the other works on the earlier CD, especially the *Art of Fugue* (his second recording of it, from 1969). Leonhardt has since the 1950s argued that this work was intended for the keyboard—an argument that today is widely accepted—and his performance here (as well as his booklet essay) makes a strong case for that position.

Leonhardt has recorded almost all of Bach's keyboard works and most of the concertos and chamber works, plus many of the choral pieces (discussed in the discography of Chapter 15) and organ works. A good example of his Bach keyboard recordings is the late-1970s French Suites (RCA Seon GD 71963, 2 CDs): the Allemande of the Fourth Suite, for example, has a mystical *gravitas*, Scott Cantrell describes the Gigue of the Fifth as "limpid," and about the Courante of the Second he says he has never "so viscerally *felt* the momentum."[17] Leonhardt has recorded the English Suites and Partitas twice. Howard Schott prefers the earlier version of the English Suites (no longer

15. Towe, "J. S. Bach: Mass in B Minor," in *Choral Music on Record,* ed. Alan Blyth (Cambridge University Press, 1991), p. 58.

16. Anderson, *Gramophone* 73 (August 1996), p. 81.

17. Cantrell, "The Multifaceted Mr. Leonhardt," *High Fidelity,* March 1979, p. 85.

available, on Philips-Seon);[18] I have heard only the second version (Virgin 61157, 2 CDs), recorded in 1984, and I find it excellent. The Prelude of the Fourth Suite, for example, is an exhilarating rebuttal to critics who think Leonhardt is at home only in sober, grave music; so, for that matter, is his lyrical Allemande and his smiling Menuet I. The First and Third Suites also stand out particularly. Leonhardt doesn't take many repeats (the earlier recording takes many more, I am told), but those he observes show his skill at ornamentation.

Alan Curtis calls Leonhardt "certainly the greatest living improviser in Baroque styles of accompaniment as well as in solo organ and harpsichord playing, [who] far surpasses in both authenticity and imagination anything I can remember having heard before."[19] We in the public are unlikely ever to hear Leonhardt's solo improvisations, but we can at least hear his outstanding work as an accompanist, sometimes improvising from a bass, on a number of recordings. Listen especially to his recordings of Bach chamber works with the Kuijken brothers, on Deutsche Harmonia Mundi. Of the Flute Sonatas with Barthold Kuijken (DHM 77026-2-RC, 2 CDs), Richard Taruskin writes, "Those attuned to subtlety will find more of it in these poised, deeply considered renditions than in the work of any other flutist," and praises the "warmth and scope" of Leonhardt's playing.[20]

Leonhardt was a pioneer in recording the music of keyboard composers before Bach. One of his best is of Georg Böhm, Bach's friend and possibly his teacher (Sony SK 53114); Kevin Bazzana writes, "Order and improvisation are expertly balanced here: Leonhardt preserves distinctive rhythmic profiles in the dance movements while injecting a considerable amount of perfectly judged *rubato*."[21] Another highlight is a profound 1989 recording of the seventeenth-century giant Johann Jacob Froberger (DHM 7923-2-RC). A recital of French Baroque music (DHM 77924-2-RC) conveys, according to Julie Ann Sadie, a range of emotions and displays a "superb sense of timing [that is] unrivalled today."[22] Another notable harpsichord CD is a 1988 recital featuring various composers (Philips 426 352), which gives an idea of Leonhardt's range, both stylistically and expressively.

"Leonhardt's recordings as an organist," writes Patrick Russill, "are all too rare. No other player can draw such poetic intensity . . . from just a single stop."[23] Only one Bach organ CD is readily available (DHM 7868-2-RC), but it includes some of the most masterful organ playing in my collection.

18. Schott, "Ein vollkommener Musik-meister," p. 516.
19. In Curtis's edition of Monteverdi's *L'incoronazione di Poppea* (London: Novello, 1989), p. xv.
20. Taruskin, *Musical America*, May 1990, pp. 69–70.
21. Bazzana, *Fanfare* 17 (November/December 1993), p. 193.
22. Sadie, *Gramophone* 69 (May 1992), p. 79.
23. Russill, *Gramophone* 72 (October 1994), p. 164.

Another fine recital (Sony SK 66262) is titled *North German Organ Masters*; Haig Mardirosian praises its "remarkable freshness and admirable insights."[24] Leonhardt has also recorded an entire CD on the clavichord. The 1988 recital on Philips (422 349) is a classic, with inspired performances of C. P. E. and W. F. Bach—whose polonaises, in Leonhardt's hands, are heartbreaking—and of their father's Second French Suite, played with a piquant touch and eloquent rubato.

FOR FURTHER READING

Richard Troeger's *Technique and Interpretation on the Harpsichord and Clavichord* (Bloomington: Indiana University Press, 1987) is excellent, as is Peter Williams's article "Keyboards," the first entry in *Performance Practice: Music after 1600,* ed. Howard Mayer Brown and Stanley Sadie (London: Macmillan, 1989, and New York: Norton, 1990). An approachable discussion of performance-practice issues, including many of those Leonhardt speaks about, is Peter le Huray's *Authenticity in Performance: Eighteenth-Century Case Studies* (Cambridge University Press, 1990).

In recent years, several guides to Bach's keyboard works have appeared. David Schulenberg's superb *The Keyboard Music of J. S. Bach* (New York: Schirmer, 1992) is at the moment the indispensable handbook for anyone seriously interested in the repertoire. Peter Williams's three-volume *The Organ Music of J. S. Bach* (Cambridge University Press, 1980–84) is masterful and, once again, indispensable; the first two volumes analyze the works one by one, and the third is a brilliant discussion of performance-practice issues. Paul Badura-Skoda's *Interpreting Bach at the Keyboard* (Oxford University Press, 1994) contains stimulating ideas about interpretation from a leading performer, but must be used with caution: it does not clearly distinguish between current scholarly findings and the author's personal solutions, and its scholarship is not always reliable.

---

24. Mardirosian, *Fanfare* 19 (July/August 1996), pp. 376–77.

11

Aladdin's Lamp

Anner Bylsma on the Cello
(and Vivaldi, and Brahms)

William H. Youngren, who writes frequently about Wagner recordings, complains that most modern string performances "have a certain oppressive mo-
notony. . . . Almost every phrase, regardless of content or context, is delivered
in the same big, luscious, vibrato-ridden tone. . . . a thick wall of throbbing
sound come[s] between us and the music."[1] A different complaint was lodged
by no less mainstream a musician than George Szell: "Any subtle function of
the wrist and fingers of the [bowing] hand is practically unknown to [most
modern violinists]. . . . They have never been told that the bow has to articulate the music."[2] For these and other reasons, Hans Keller, the music analyst,
string-quartet coach, and devotee of Furtwängler and Casals, concludes that
"contrary to official, professional views, modern [string] technique has actually
narrowed down our expressive range."[3]

Obviously, these critics (who are not in the early-music camp) don't mean
to damn *all* mainstream players. Only extremists would dismiss such talents
as—to mention only cellists—Jacqueline Du Pre or Yo-Yo Ma. And I've read
about the violinist Anne-Sophie Mutter making extensive use of non-vibrato in
the Sibelius Concerto. Still, the group to whom the complaints about vibrato
and bowing most clearly don't apply are the outsiders—the period-instrument
players, about whom mainstreamers are quick to lodge their own complaints.

---

1. Youngren, "Vocal Violin," *The Atlantic*, November 1992, pp. 144–48. The article is an
appreciation of Josef Szigeti.
2. Ibid, p. 148.
3. Keller, "Whose Authenticity?" *Early Music* 12 (November 1984), p. 517.

Whichever side you take, when you discuss the Baroque cello you have to put Anner Bylsma on the shortest of lists. Bylsma took up the Baroque cello in the 1960s, by which time he already had a distinguished career as a modern cellist (which we discuss below). In the ferment of the early-music scene of Amsterdam, he says, it was inevitable that he would be drawn to the early cello. That he still plays both instruments makes him a sharp observer of their differing challenges, and of current issues in their use.

He also spoke about a favorite composer of his, Vivaldi. Vivaldi was the most influential Italian composer of his day, and the only one of his time and place to become truly popular in ours. But serious musical thinkers often dismiss him. The modern Italian composer Luigi Dallapicola uttered the most famous put-down: "Vivaldi wrote a great concerto, 500 times." Charles Rosen thinks it wasn't even a great concerto. Bylsma, however, thinks that musicians play and hear Vivaldi wrong; he believes that the key to Vivaldi is his interest in depicting character.

This point may reflect changes in musical aesthetics.[4] The nineteenth century, as John Butt said in Chapter 9, placed new emphasis on the tight integration of musical works; and in our century some have regarded music as a set of formal structures and nothing else. People may not have really believed that even in the high modernist era, but it may lie behind some of the Vivaldi-bashing. Looking at Vivaldi in purely formal terms may impoverish him, which it does not do to Bach, who, Butt said, wrote music that was unusually integrated for its time—and who, ironically, discovered how to handle large-scale form by studying Vivaldi.

Another obstacle for Vivaldi is that later in the eighteenth century thinkers began to emphasize musical genius and innovation, while in Vivaldi's time a musician was, above all, a craftsman[5] (he prided himself on being able to turn out a concerto in minutes). Borrowing from one's own work was normal. Admittedly, Vivaldi reused the same patterns to a degree unusual even for his own day. But he was often brilliantly inventive within his form's parameters—parameters that to a significant extent he created himself.

Bylsma and I met briefly in an airport coffee shop while he was waiting for a flight; we spoke again later by telephone. Both conversations exhibited

4. See Carl Dahlhaus, "The Metaphysics of Instrumental Music," in his *Nineteenth-Century Music*, trans. J. Bradford Robinson (Berkeley: University of California Press, 1989), pp. 88–96; and "Theme and Character," chap. 6 of his *Ludwig van Beethoven*, trans. Mary Whittall (Oxford University Press, 1991).

5. Edward Lowinsky says that Rousseau was the first to write about the concept of genius in music, as opposed to the older ideal of craftsmanship; Lowinsky, "Musical Genius: The Evolution and Origins of a Concept," in his *Music in the Culture of the Renaissance* (University of Chicago Press, 1986), originally published in *Musical Quarterly* 50 (1964), pp. 321–40, 476–95. Charles Rosen observes, though, that "the late eighteenth century does not mark the first appearance of the concept of the temperamental genius in music"; he points to a fifteenth-century Netherlandish composer like Josquin, and says that in the arts in general Michelangelo provided the "basic model of the temperamental genius." In "Did Beethoven Have All the Luck?" *New York Review of Books*, 14 November 1996, pp. 57–63, quote p. 58.

Bylsma's gifts for figurative language and for aphorism, and his originality of thought on many aspects of music—among them the issues raised by Keller, Youngren, and Szell.

Performance Practice

You started out on the modern cello, winning the Casals Competition in 1959 and playing first cello in the Concertgebouw Orchestra.

I still do play the modern cello. And of course, everybody played the modern cello at that time. I played in the Concertgebouw in the 1960s, and left about twenty-five years ago. I never regretted leaving, although I like the orchestra very much.

I began working on the Baroque cello during my days at the Concertgebouw, because playing early music with musicians who were playing Baroque instruments made it a natural thing to do. Playing with instruments like the harpsichord and recorder, which were so clear and at the same time so fast and soft, made it hard to deliver on the modern cello. I was always having to play between *pianissimo* and *pianississimo*. It sounded so horribly unnatural that experimenting with Baroque cellos came easily.

You, more than anyone, developed the prevailing style of Baroque cello playing. How did you go about doing this—using Baroque treatises, or what?

Well, I think the mastering of an instrument never goes through reading first, and then playing. It goes through playing first, and then reading—and having good colleagues, especially people who play other instruments.

One aspect of the style heard in your playing and that of your colleagues, such as Leonhardt and Brueggen, is an eloquent use of rubato. Could you speak about that?

The word "rubato" means "robbed"—you rob from the bar. Rubato is possible only if there is a very keen sense of the pace of the music. If you see a film, and somebody is in a cell, and he grabs the bars and wants to get out because the government wants to shoot him, the whole audience wipes its brow in sympathetic anguish. Now, if this fellow were standing in an open meadow there would be nothing to grab—there'd be no rubato. There's no feeling of having to get out of anything.

It's the tension of freedom versus order.

It is the individual against law. One person's rebellion against restrictions.

There seem to be different approaches to rubato in different eras. Is there such a thing as a Baroque approach to rubato, as opposed to a Romantic rubato?

No, the thing is that there's no "Baroque" in the first place. There are so many variations. What is a twentieth-century man? Just look around and you see so many types; some would fit very well in the eighteenth or nineteenth century. Or the thirty-first, but we don't know that.

The Gramophone *reviewer of your Sony recording of the Bach Cello Suites was enthusiastic, but also remarked that "if Pierre Fournier had allowed himself the expressive licence demonstrated by Bylsma he would most probably have been roundly condemned for excessive romanticism."*[6]

All these things go in waves. First, people do too much rubato, and then somebody comes up with the new idea—don't do any at all. And it's the same with vibrato and portamento,[7] and all these things. It's like fashion—if everyone is wearing long skirts, you can be sure that the next thing will be short skirts. And to be honest, after so many long skirts you'd like to see some leg.

How about vibrato and portamento? Those are two other aspects of string playing that have gone in and out of fashion. There's confusion over how much they used vibrato in the past.

I have at home a method by Kummer, a cellist, written about 1840, saying, "Formerly, people vibrated much too much; the modern style of playing demands that we also be able to draw with clear lines." And you can find this kind of thing time and again; we think that something is quite new at a certain point, when generations before people were saying it was old-fashioned. Praetorius in 1619 said the instruments of the violin family sound best with iron strings. Gambists vibrated on the frets, flutists in eighteenth-century France used a vibrato that sometimes covered almost a whole tone. And you can tell that some string players vibrated a lot and some not at all. Geminiani in his violin school of 1751 said you should vibrate as often as possible.[8]

Though since he didn't hold his violin under the chin, he couldn't have meant a constant vibrato, like that of Fritz Kreisler—it would have been too difficult.

True; but violinists were very good at using their chins when needed, and of course it depends on how long your neck is. And Kreisler was not such a vibrator; it's more the American and Russian violinists of today. Have you heard Kreisler's recordings? What a beautiful player, and his vibrato is not so like an electric bell, the way many people sound now. And great rhythm! [Sings the opening of the finale of the Brahms Violin Concerto as Kreisler played it.] Kreisler and his contemporaries grew up playing gut strings, and on gut strings vibrato works quite differently. One does not have to hide the ugliness of steel strings.[9]

So it's difficult to give a straightforward answer, like "they vibrated not at all in the seventeenth century, a little in the eighteenth, and more in the nine-

6. Nicholas Anderson, *Gramophone* 70 (January 1993), p. 49

7. "Portamento" is the audible sliding from one note to another.

8. Francesco Geminiani, *The Art of Playing on the Violin* (London, 1751), p. 8.

9. The top (E) string on the violin remained pure gut until about 1920, when steel strings generally took over—though gut E strings did not entirely disappear from mainstream play-

teenth, and most today." That would not be true at all. Joseph Joachim [1831–1907] still vibrated very little, while the cellist David Popper [1843–1913] vibrated much more than his contemporaries. The cellists around Brahms, Robert Hausmann and Alfredo Piatti [1822–1901], vibrated very little. It would be a pleasure if people were to start using less vibrato in Brahms, because you get so tired—you hear string players in Brahms and in five minutes you are already at the end of what you can digest.

How about in orchestral playing?
Well, my 91-year-old father-in-law, who is a very fine violinist, had his first orchestral job in 1916, in the second violin section. He was a poor boy and was so happy to have a job that he tried to play as well as he could. They had just started playing when the conductor stopped and said, "Hey, young fellow, no solo tone here." Because he was vibrating. So all the comments by people in the early-music world about how the mainstream players are applying nineteenth-century style to old music are ill-informed—they use a twentieth-century style, one that developed between the world wars.

The older recordings prove it.[10] *On them, even the soloists use vibrato only on expressive notes, not in passages or background material.*
That we now vibrate all the time is a pity. It feels as if people are afraid that their neighbor in the orchestra will say behind their backs, "He cannot vibrate correctly." It seems as if people don't use their judgment and don't listen to whether a particular passage or note is dissonant or consonant, but just keep vibrating.

To be specific, would you stop vibrating on dissonant notes, to increase the discomfort? Or do I have it backwards?
I think one should not vibrate on the *consonances*. A consonance is uninteresting . . . you never read in the paper about father putting on his slippers and lighting a cigar, except when the house, being full of petrol fumes, blows up. A good time for vibrato.[11]

---

ing until later. The two middle strings remained (for the most part) pure gut until about 1950. Sir Adrian Boult, who was conducting during the transition, lamented that the adoption of steel E-strings had ruined orchestral string tone.

The lowest string on the violin has been "overspun" since the eighteenth century, though authorities differ on when this started being done with *metal* winding; Robin Stowell says metal winding was "increasingly common" in the late eighteenth century ("Strings," in *Performance Practice: Music after 1600*, ed. Howard Mayer Brown and Stanley Sadie [London: Macmillan, 1989, and New York: Norton, 1990], p. 239).

10. See Robert Philip's *Early Recordings and Musical Style* (Cambridge University Press, 1992). These matters are discussed in the Postscript to the Norrington interview.

11. In Chapter 12, below, Julianne Baird suggests the opposite; this probably reflects the differences between the way most Baroque singers use vibrato (as a continuous style of tone production, which can be varied) and the way most Baroque instrumentalists use it (as an occasional ornament).

How about vibrato in Bach's or Beethoven's time?

Again, it is difficult to make generalizations. For instance, in Berlin in Beethoven's time there were three cellists with quite different styles of playing— Jean-Louis and Jean-Pierre Duport on the one side, and Bernhard Romberg on the other. Romberg, who was a friend of Beethoven (and you may take it that his playing was an example for most of what Beethoven wrote for the cello—so we'd better mind that), hardly vibrated, and you can see that from the way he held his fingers at a slant, like a violinist.[12] Jean-Louis Duport, who wrote a very important essay that has since been the basic text for all cellists on fingering, held his hand in a more perpendicular way, where one could vibrate easily. I'm sure there must have been quite a difference in the way these two people played.

So when you play Beethoven, you follow the non-vibrato approach of Romberg?

I try, because I like it very much. If you don't vibrate, you're much more alert about your bowing;[13] also, instead of vibrating you can use portamento— slides—as another way of enlivening a note. And it leaves you with vibrato as a trick up your sleeve, so that if you really feel you have to do something, you can vibrate all of a sudden. That is often in the places where a modern cellist would *stop* vibrating all of a sudden. In the first movement of the Second Sonata of Beethoven, in the coda, there's a place where people tend to stop vibrating, eight long notes at the end; I like to suddenly use vibrato there, and it's just as special.

And how about portamento?

That was always there, of course. In the naughty or sad times of one's life, one's shifts [of a finger from one note to another] tend to become a little more pronounced. I personally like fingerings which use the same finger more times in a row, which naturally brings forth more portamento. You often find these fingerings in nineteenth-century texts.

But the comparison of Romberg and Duport shows that, in general, because string instruments have so many more possibilities than a recorder or a harpsichord, the styles of playing must have been vastly different not only over the years, but also within the same era. We know that Corelli, in Naples, told Han-

---

12. David Watkin details Romberg's "preference for expression through the varied use of the bow rather than vibrato." Romberg appears to have used vibrato only as an ornament, and then only in the first one-third of a note. Watkin, "Beethoven and the Cello," *Performing Beethoven*, ed. Robin Stowell (Cambridge University Press, 1994), pp. 110–11.

13. See previous footnote. Hans Keller observes that in coaching young string quartets his instructions to play passages non-vibrato often produced regrettable results: "Owing to the narrowing down of our expressive range, the player's right arm is, in most cases, no longer capable of producing the tone modulation required for his vibrato-less execution . . . his right arm has grown up behind the screen of a vibrato" ("Whose Authenticity?" p. 518). Bylsma's remarks suggest that the converse also applies: playing without vibrato forces one to bow more subtly.

del he couldn't play French music. Now, that is only the difference between two major styles, the French and Italian; but the artists within each style must also have been very individual.

One Italian played very differently from another Italian.
Oh, I am sure of that. And how can we tell? Well, we have a sentence here or there saying how this or that one played, but also we have their compositions and the way they use slurs in notation. And sometimes they wrote books—like Geminiani or Leopold Mozart. The most outspoken were the French composers, who were more schoolmasters than the Italians. The Italians would generally rather *not* write a treatise, for fear someone else would steal their secrets, but the French were obsessed with what they called "good taste," to the point that you think good taste is another word for "jealousy," because somebody else has more invention than you have—the Italians certainly had more imagination than the French. Even the native French suites are often less interesting than French suites written by Italians, let alone those written by the Germans, who mixed the two styles together and made out of them the incredible thing we find in Bach.

The French and Italian styles were dominant at the time of Bach. Can you discuss how the French and Italian string-playing styles differed?
One example is the downbow rule, an especially French rule. If you look at Muffat's introduction to his *Florilegium Secundum,* you'll see how he says that the French do a downbow on the first beat of every bar, and that the Italians go back and forth. It's a very interesting statement. You should keep in mind that in France, the famous orchestra of the twenty-four violins of the king played a great deal of ballet music, for which it's wonderful if you have a strong accent on the first beat. The French possibly also had shorter bows.

I think the famous story of Lully dying of gangrene after hitting his foot with his big staff, with which he beat time loudly, shows that it must have been hard for all these guys to have their bow on the right spot, barline after barline. It must have had to do with this French technique where you have to go back to the frog of the bow on every downbeat.

In the notation of rhythm, the eighteenth century saw imprecise conventions, like the French notes inégales—where the first note in each pair is held longer and the second note shortened—and also overdotting.
No, I think the French were very precise about where their *inégalité* was applied, and they gave you all the exceptions to it also. *Inégalité* is always pairs of notes slurred together, in runs like scales; there are many, many exceptions.[14]

14. See Stephen Hefling's *Rhythmic Alteration in Seventeenth- and Eighteenth-Century Music* (New York: Schirmer, 1993). Chaps. 1 and 2 discuss French practice; later chapters discuss controversies concerning the application of this practice outside of France, and also the issue of overdotting. See also note 13 in the William Christie interview, below.

On the other hand, the Italian style of "Lombardic" notation,[15] which is the opposite of *notes inégales,* is mostly not very precise as to where it should be applied—and I'm sure Italians like Geminiani did everything they liked in the French style as well. *Inégalité* is like shaking someone's hand with a very soft handshake, while the Italian Lombardic style—where the first note is short and the second is long—is vigorous and proud.

What about the issue of assimilating dotted notes to triplets?

One must decide case by case, but mostly, to make these things equal seems dull. The clashing of triplets and duplets can also be found in later music; for example, in Beethoven's "Moonlight" Sonata, where the right hand is playing triplets and the left hand is playing dotted rhythms, you wouldn't reconcile them.

The French and the Italians ornamented differently?

The French would have notated all the ornaments, while the Italians would mainly have just ad-libbed it; that's the general modern opinion.

Is that why Quantz said that the Italian style required good knowledge of harmony to extemporize ornaments, while the French didn't?

All good players must understand harmony in adding ornaments, because an ornament must express an excess of emotion. Too often now people add ornaments like babbling at the mouth; they add runs and chords that don't mean much, and take away from the real character of the piece. Indeed, one very nice way of ornamenting is to leave out notes. Often a single note, a dissonance resolved late, is a much better ornament than a whole exercise of scales. Ornaments must come from the heart, not from the fingers.

To get back to Quantz's point, the reason the French notated the ornaments and the *inégalité* so precisely, I think, is that the French were so concerned with *comme il faut*; Marin Marais played all of his pieces through every two weeks, and I think it was just to make each one a little more meticulous and precise, not different. Give me Vivaldi any time, his incredible amount of fantasy, imagination, and daring. And give me Vivaldi a thousand times over Corelli, who I think tried to make music palatable for the upper classes, the bored rich, of his day. I think Vivaldi must have hated him; the violin sonatas, Op. 2, of Vivaldi are like Corelli, but there's a little kick in the pants here or there—not that it's wrong, actually, but it's like a finger in the eye. It's very interesting—Corelli seen in the light of Vivaldi.

15. The "Lombardic" rhythm is described by Johann Joachim Quantz, Frederick the Great's flutist, in his treatise on flute playing, *Versuch einer Anweisung die Flöte traversière zu spielen* (Berlin, 1752): *On Playing the Flute,* trans. Edward R. Reilly, 2nd ed. (New York: Schirmer, 1966), p. 323. Quantz and other Berliners thought that the rhythm derived from Corelli, Torelli, and Vivaldi.

Vivaldi

Vivaldi is the most often dismissed among the major composers. Stravinsky, for example, called him "greatly overrated—a dull fellow who could compose the same form over and so many times over."[16]

Stravinsky's remark—or is it Craft's?—is very superficial, and a pity for somebody buried in Venice. I feel shy about daring to criticize a genius like Stravinsky; but could it be that (if it was not unfamiliarity on his part) he felt irritation in meeting a spirit in many ways like himself: wit, irony, a certain "coldness" or, at least, professed coldness?

Of course, in Stravinsky's time Vivaldi was played like a tenth-rate Brahms,[17] without any idea of how to characterize all the *commedia dell'arte* figures, plus those one could encounter on the streets of Venice. This is the most surprising thing about him—the endless variety of characters depicted and caricatured. All of his music is always depicting a character.

Can you give an example?
The first movement of the G Major Cello Concerto seems like a fat fellow walking down the street, enjoying himself immensely:[18]

16. Igor Stravinsky and Robert Craft, *Conversations with Igor Stravinsky* (Garden City, N.Y.: Doubleday, 1959), p. 76.

17. Stravinsky did complain about "sewing-machine performances of Vivaldi." Robert Craft, *Stravinsky: Chronicle of a Friendship, 1948–1971* (New York: Knopf, 1972), p. 178.

18. Vivaldi, G Major Concerto, RV 413 (recorded by Bylsma on Sony SK 48044), opening.

The famous E Minor Cello Sonata is somebody wallowing in an opera on stage.[19] But Vivaldi is always theatre; it's always characterizing, as you would do in a play. Also, his love of color and sonorities reflects the splendor of Italy.

Nowadays, he is not just misinterpreted; too often he is uninterpreted. Many modern soloists when playing Vivaldi do not seem to have ever looked at any caricatures by, say, Ghezzi, Tiepolo, or Guardi. People often just play scales and chords, with no feeling for that period or nationality. There is so much more there than you think. I once got a compliment after I played a concert of Vivaldi, Frescobaldi, Gabrielli, and Boccherini: an Italian colleague said, "I loved your Boccherini, because it was exactly the dialect of Lucca." This didn't make me feel so safe—I thought, "What about the dialect of Venice, the dialect of Rome, the dialect of Bologna?"

For all the bad-mouthing he gets, Vivaldi was the most influential composer of the first half of the eighteenth century. Even older composers like Albinoni modified their styles in mid-career to be more like his. Vivaldi had a decisive influence on Bach, who adopted the ritornello principle from him. Bach told his sons, apparently, that studying Vivaldi "taught him how to think musically."[20] *Could you comment?*

He was an incredible form-maker: witness what Bach said about him. And Vivaldi, apart from being a great contrapuntist, and apart from the many ways of bowing and left-hand virtuosity, is an unfailing stage-setter. And what invention!

Eleanor Selfridge-Field writes that "Vivaldi's talent for extracting a succession of motivic variations, or the process of Fortspinnung, *from sedate opening phrases distinguishes him and enables soloists to enter with an air of drama rather than of mere duty." Any comments?*

One main kind of *Fortspinnung*—literally, "spinning out"—is of course the

19. RV 40; recorded by Bylsma on Deutsche Harmonia Mundi 7909.

20. Bach was introduced to Vivaldi's music when he was serving the young music-loving Duke Johann Ernst at Weimar in 1713. The ritornello principle derived from Vivaldi's concertos became the basis for the large-scale organization of most of Bach's music thereafter. In this design, an opening section for the whole orchestra (tutti) returns in full at the end of the movement, and in part, in different keys, at intervals in between. These ritornellos ("little returns") tie together the "episodes," which are played by solo instruments and often involve changes of key. A clear discussion of the Vivaldi ritornello, by Walter Kolneder, appears in *The New Oxford History of Music*, vol. VI, pp. 302–39. For discussions of the influence of the ritornello on Bach's concertos, see Malcolm Boyd's *Bach: The Brandenburg Concertos* (Cambridge University Press, 1993), chap. 5; on Bach's choral works, see John Butt's *Bach: Mass in B Minor* (Cambridge University Press, 1991), chap. 5. For a discussion of the more subtle influences that Vivaldi had on Bach's style, see Christoph Wolff's "Vivaldi's Compositional Art, Bach, and the Process of 'Musical Thinking,'" in his *Bach: Essays on His Life and Work* (Cambridge, Mass.: Harvard University Press, 1991), pp. 72–83.

sequence.[21] In itself it's a boring device used to modulate, but in Vivaldi's hands it is full of wit. For instance, sometimes he'll put in one sequence too many, as a caricature.

Michael Talbot wrote that Vivaldi can be seen as a "harbinger of musical Romanticism" partly because of "the higher value he placed on expression than on perfection of detail."[22] Could you comment?

I think Vivaldi certainly had a better sense of what the important and unimportant notes were in a bar, and definitely played the important notes in the melody more in tune than any of us do now. To hell with the perfection of the highway tarmac!

It's the same issue in playing any of the great composers. Imagine what goes through your body when you have composed a piece like the *St. Matthew Passion*, and you lead it. Or imagine that you're Maurice Ravel, and you're sitting in the hall and hearing *Daphnis et Chloé*. It must be so much made out of your own soul that it must be hard to take. All these great people, our demi-gods, are so much greater than we realize. I've worked on the Bach cello suites for over forty years and keep coming back to them, and still they don't get boring—still there is more depth.

The Baroque Cello

The obvious differences between the modern and the Baroque cello are the gut strings, the bow, and the endpin. I'd like to ask about each of them in turn.

Technical changes are never only technical. They always are more than just that and give new possibilities where other ones mostly are not perceived to disappear. The steel string of course is not just technical. The heyday of the steel string is the time of the big swing orchestras, especially the Glenn Miller band—everything smooth and round.

People argued that steel strings were more powerful and more reliable.

The arguments for steel are mostly cheap—cheapness, for instance, ease of use, loudness, and, worst of all, equality across all the strings.

---

21. A sequence, in Baroque and later music, means the repeating of a musical phrase at a different pitch; it was the primary means that high Baroque composers used to keep their music moving forward harmonically. The term *Fortspinnung* is a modern one, first coined to describe the second (of three) sections of a typical ritornello tutti. The ritornello's introductory section, usually a few bars long, establishes the home key but cadences on the dominant; the *Fortspinnung* section then modulates through various keys (usually through sequences); and the third, final, section is an "epilogue" in the tonic.

22. Talbot, "Vivaldi", §7, in *The New Grove Dictionary of Music and Musicians* (London: Macmillan, 1980), vol. 20, p. 38.

Can you give an example of why equality of strings is so bad?

One example is that they make it very hard to play Boccherini on modern instruments. I hardly can do it. And it's so easy on an old instrument. The main reason is that Boccherini makes use of the different unequal sounds from string to string. When you play high notes on low strings with gut, the sound is a bit muffled—and Boccherini uses this effect like a stopped horn. Boccherini is a sound-oriented composer anyway. Almost all of the main notes in his melodies are bolstered in sound by the harmonics of the other open strings. It's all made on sound.

How about the endpin, which Baroque cellists today often don't use and mainstream cellists do use—although nineteenth-century cellists generally did not use it?[23]

I don't know why up to our century most cellists played without endpins. Imagine—great nineteenth-century cellists like Popper, Hausmann, and Piatti playing Brahms without an endpin, when an endpin definitely makes the instrument louder and also easier and more stable.

What do you do about endpins?

I have two cellos, one with, one without.

It's not like gut strings, which really do make a difference?

It may perhaps make a difference, but I have never been able to form an opinion about it.

How about bowing? It's been said that in the Baroque "the bow, to a much greater extent than in modern playing, became the primary source of expressive inflection."[24] What would you say about that?

All good artists with any kind of bow at any time have their primary source of expressive inflection in the bow. I did say, though, that when you vibrate less you have to be more alert about bowing, and also that you don't feel the need to vibrate as much on gut strings. So perhaps those are factors.

How about the different bows themselves—the modern "Tourte"-style bows versus the earlier pre-Tourte bows?[25]

Of course there were many different bows—the great violin makers also

23. Tilden A. Russell, "New Light on the Historical Manner of Holding the Cello," *Historical Performance* 6 (Fall 1993), pp. 73–78. This also bears on the question of vibrato, by the way: "Without the security of an end-pin, cellists had to rely on the contact of the left hand with the neck and strings for certainty of intonation, and a continuous, fierce vibrato was less practicable." Watkin, "Beethoven and the Cello," pp. 92–93.

24. Peter Walls, "Strings," in *Performance Practice: Music after 1600*, ed. Brown and Sadie, p. 52.

25. Named after the French bow maker François Tourte (1747–1835). According to David

made their own bows. But I think one should not play with too many different bows. Your bow is your magic wand, and you need to know it well. So if
you have a good old bow and a modern Tourte-type bow, that's enough. For
that reason, I don't know whether you should also have a so-called transition
bow, a Classical bow. It's interesting to note that Duport in his *Essay* wrote,
"The best bows made now are those by Tourte. That's not a compliment, it's
true." It's the last line in his book. One of the Duports was the man who played
the Op. 5 Beethoven sonatas for the first time; that was in 1795, so from that
date onward there's no doubt that you can play Tourte bows, modern bows,
but possibly in the old-fashioned way.[26] For some time, the cellists in France
went on holding the modern bow in the old-fashioned way, as you often see in
caricatures of French cellists.

*The earlier bows had a much thinner band of hair, had no ferrule to keep
the band of hair flat, and lacked an even balance. How do such things affect
one's approach? Do they relate to the style of articulation?*

Yes, the old bows are made much more for speaking, the modern bow much
more for singing. But when you use the modern bow in the old-fashioned way,
the difference is not so great as when you hold it the modern way, at the frog.
And, of course, you should not think too much of instruments, because for a
good player, what his inner ear hears his hands can do. So if you know what
you want, then you can usually do it quite nicely with a modern bow and instrument. But first you have to know what you want. And therefore I would
say, take an old instrument and keep using it—but this is just part of one quest;
in fact, an independent thinker is always developing his ideas.

*This question of speaking versus singing, of a rhetorical understanding of
music, seems crucial to Baroque and Classical approaches to music.*

Yes; and the dynamics when you speak are much more detailed than when
you sing. When you say four words you have four *mezzoforte*s, one or two
*forte*s, and several *piano*s, and then it diminuendos into nothing. So if you tried
to notate your own speech, you'd need all the dynamic signs in a matter of two
bars. That's also the pleasure of it. Sometimes somebody has engaged the
wrong singer for a Baroque piece—if you're used to a more speaking style, it's
horrible when somebody just bellows. With these opera bellowers, you cannot
hear the words anymore.

Boyden, "the type of bow he established about 1785 has continued (a few details apart) to be
the standard 'modern' type." It was not a radical innovation; rather, Tourte's design "succeeded
in . . . combining the best features of his predecessors in so satisfactory a manner that it set a
standard for bowmaking." Boyden, "Tourte," *The New Grove Dictionary*, vol. 19, p. 100.

26. This includes, among other things, not holding the bow at the end (the "frog"), as
modern string players do, but a little way up from it. The universal supremacy of the Tourte
bow, by the way, was attained not overnight but over the course of the nineteenth century.

One reflection of that more inflected, speaking style is the ornament called messa di voce—*the gradual crescendo and decrescendo on a single long note. Some say that was overdone in some of our era's earlier experiments in Baroque string playing.*

Yes, that was notorious. To be sure, there's also the *mezza* di voce, where each note starts very soft; most modern string players use that too *little*. Both groups are too extreme: those early-instrument players who swell every note in the middle, and those modern players whose notes have no real beginning. To start a note is a thing that woodwinds always practice and strings never practice. And they should. If you listen to an orchestra warming up, and stand over near the horns, you'll hear them do all these things—a note without a beginning, a note with a small beginning, a note that is a hundred percent from beginning to end, a note with diminuendo, a note with a swell in the middle. If you go to the oboe section, you'll hear the same things. But when you stand near the violin section, you'll hear all the violin concertos at the same time, but you won't hear anybody try to start a note well. I am always surprised when I hear famous cellists and violinists who, it seems, do not know how to start a note—they seem to speak a language without consonants.

So starting the note well relates to the aesthetic of speech—like enunciating a consonant.

I think this idea of speech is so fruitful that you can apply it to almost all music. The better the music, the more it speaks.

Historically, there was a change from thinking of music in terms of speech to thinking of a long, unbroken singing line. How did that change in aesthetic come about?

A lot of later music does need more speaking and less singing, such as Brahms. The influence of Wagner is rather strong. The interesting thing is that, historically, players have almost always slurred a chromatic figure. Think of the famous *Musical Offering* theme of Bach—actually Frederick the Great. It starts with "words" and "syllables," but when it descends chromatically, you would not think of syllables: you slur it together. And because Wagner is so chromatic, that might have contributed to the triumph of the long line.

Another influence is the modern conductor, with this totally inadequate musical instrument, the baton, which cannot show motifs in any detail—maybe once every ten seconds at most. Just try to show with a stick all the inflections you can make with your bow or your voice or your flute. The provenance of the long line in music is the conductor's, because it's easier to conduct that way. Conductors always want to beat slow pieces in four that are written in two, and fast pieces written in four in two; it damages music very much, but then they can conduct it. The answer, of course, is to never look at these guys.[27]

How would you relate this to early-music conducting?

I sometimes doubt whether there should be a conductor. Of course, what you can't show with the baton you have to talk about in rehearsal, so in that case it's not the baton that speaks but the voice.

Could you comment more about the state of modern string playing, particularly soloists?

When I heard a modern violinist in Khatchaturian the other day, I thought the playing was fantastic. But often you hear Brahms played too hot, too slurred together, too egocentric. When you hear Beethoven, it's worse, because it's all in the same vein; and when you hear Mozart and Bach, it gets worse and worse. And when you hear a famous violinist play Debussy, it's mostly horrible too.

The thing is that so many of the famous players of today are too dependent on their teacher; they are not their own man. They are great pupils, fantastic pupils, without a voice of their own. Give me an amateur anytime—a good amateur, hearing what he thinks he does with tears in his eyes—super!—rather than a famous pupil. All these pupils' fingerings come from their teachers— Galamian, or somebody in France or in Russia. And of course you'll never find any of the teacher's fingerings in the playing of Kreisler, or Josef Szigeti, or Bronislaw Huberman, or Adolf Busch. It's personal playing. Those were masters.

Some people might be surprised to hear you praise early-twentieth-century violinists like Kreisler, because they would expect you to be terribly concerned about "historical authenticity."

I'd like to say something about being authentic. "Authentic" means "just as alive as it ever was." Being authentic is, most of all, Aladdin rubbing his lamp: we rehearse some music, and all of a sudden we have the feeling, "Hey! *This is right.* This is the way it must go." And I guarantee you that in a year's time, when we hear the tape of that, we will agree that it's not at all how it should go. But it's a very wonderful feeling—"*This* is how it should go!"—and *that's* authenticity. And I think it's worthwhile. But it has nothing to do with being historically correct. Maybe the motive behind what we do today *has* something

27. It may be worth noting, in light of Bylsma's remarks, that two of the conductors most often lionized in our century had an *unclear* beat, namely Toscanini (according to an admiring Sir Adrian Boult) and, especially, Furtwängler.

In their interviews below, Julianne Baird, William Christie, and Philippe Herreweghe all comment on the conducting of Baroque music, and Robert Levin talks about playing Mozart concertos without a conductor. A fairly consistent picture emerges.

to do with history—"This is how it must have been." But one's view of history changes with the times. When you see some buildings from the 1880s, such as our Central Station in Amsterdam, where the architect fully believed that he had conceived a medieval castle, what *we* see is definitely 1880; it would not fool anyone now.

SELECTED DISCOGRAPHY

Anner Bylsma's feeling for the Italian Baroque has been captured deliciously on record. You might begin with his Deutsche Harmonia Mundi selection of rarely played seventeenth-century Italian cello music, which in his hands is captivating (DHM 7978). His Vivaldi concertos on Sony with the excellent Canadian group Tafelmusik (SK 48044) are an antidote to the kind of Vivaldi playing he complains about, and his recording of the composer's cello sonatas (DHM 7909) gives, among other things, a vivid demonstration of the element of "caricature" he speaks of.

Reviewing Bylsma's recording of Boccherini Sonatas (Sony SK 53362), Stanley Sadie praises his "high spirits and nervous energy," "quite extraordinary rhythmic vitality," "sharp and precise" articulation, and "close to reckless abandon." In the slow movements, he says, Bylsma plays with much intensity, eloquence and a "natural feeling for . . . expressive tension"; but these movements, he adds, could occasionally benefit from "a little more relaxation (not his strong point), warmth, and grace."[28] Bylsma's recordings of Boccherini concertos with Tafelmusik (on DHM 7867 and Sony SK 53121) have met with enthusiasm; several critics speculate that Boccherini himself might have sounded like Bylsma.[29]

Bylsma has recorded a great deal of chamber music, much of it with L'Archibudelli, a group he formed with his violinist wife Vera Beths (admired for her work in contemporary as well as early music), Lucy Van Dael (the most unjustly neglected of today's Baroque violinists), and the unsurpassed violist Jürgen Kussmaul. Among many fine recordings, some highlights are three sublime quintets—the Schubert (Sony SK 46669), the Bruckner (SK 66251), and the Mozart Clarinet Quintet (and Trio, with Charles Neidlich and Robert Levin, SK 53366)—and Mozart's great Divertimento K. 563 (SK 46497).

Bylsma's comments about how Bach's solo cello suites keep changing for him are verified by his two recordings of them, made only a decade apart yet differing significantly. Each set has its supporters, and I suggest that you compare for yourself (unfortunately, as I write the earlier set [RCA RD 70950] is not distributed in North America). Some critics describe the later set (Sony S2K 48047) as mannered, but others find it especially imaginative and individual. I

28. Sadie, *Gramophone* 71 (March 1994), p. 69.
29. E.g., Alan George, "Classical and Romantic Chamber Music for Strings," *Early Music* 23 (November 1995), p. 342.

side with the latter group. Bylsma, by the way, uses a modern bow in Sony's first five suites: no listener, no matter how expert, could have guessed that it's not a Baroque bow, which suggests that the instrument matters less here than the player.

His Beethoven Cello Sonatas with Malcolm Bilson (Elektra-Nonesuch 79152 and 79236) have been said to "stand beside the finest on modern instruments."[30] In Brahms's Second Cello Sonata Op. 99 (Sony SK 68249), Bylsma's tempos are the fastest I've heard. In the first movement this is bracing, but Joan Chissell finds him "marginally too fast for [the slow movement's] *affetuoso* to speak as it can."[31] Chissell praises the disc's Schumann performances for allowing "fantasy its full, free rein" and the Brahms First Cello Sonata for "its unflaggingly strong and purposeful sense of direction"; still, she suspects that "there has never been a real love-affair between Bylsma and Brahms."

She might reconsider—or suspect that one has been kindled—after hearing L'Archibudelli's Brahms string sextets (Sony SK 68252). The first movements of both sextets have prominent solos for the first cello, and Bylsma plays them with passion. An example is the second subject in Op. 18's first movement, marked *espressivo* and *animato*; Bylsma picks up the tempo a little, with a sense of surging emotion (tr. 1, 2:11–2:21). In an enthusiastic review of the disc, James Oestreich says, "L'Archibudelli responds brightly and with seeming spontaneity to each peculiar turn in the scherzos but gives full scope to more meditative or passionate moments."[32] In these CDs Bylsma doesn't really sound like the string players Brahms knew, some of whose recordings survive[33] (he uses less portamento, for one thing); but sounding like them is not what he seems to be after. Instead, this performance gives an idea of what he means by "rubbing Aladdin's lamp."

FOR FURTHER READING

Michael Talbot's *Vivaldi* in the Master Musicians series is a first-rate biography (London: Dent, 1992, and New York: Schirmer, 1993). Vivaldi's critics deserve a hearing as well; a representative might be Robert Craft, in his review "Women Musicians of Venice and the Red Priest," *New York Review of Books* 27 (2 November 1995), pp. 58–59. Regarding Brahms, see the reading list after the interview with John Eliot Gardiner. As for historical cello practice, Klaus Marx's article "Violoncello" in the *New Grove Dictionary* (vol. 19) is very

30. David J. Fanning, *Gramophone* 69 (April 1992), p. 93.

31. Chissell, *Gramophone* 73 (January 1996), p. 69. "Affetuoso" means "affectionate" or "tender."

32. James R. Oestreich, "Critic's Choice Classical CDs: Brahms' New Day in the Sun," *New York Times*, 8 August 1996, p. C2.

33. See Will Crutchfield, "Brahms by Those Who Knew Him," *Opus*, August 1986, pp. 13–21, 60, esp. pp. 15–16.

good, as are the discussions in the essays on "Strings" by Peter Walls and Robin Stowell in *Performance Practice: Music after 1600,* ed. H. M. Brown and S. Sadie (London: Macmillan, 1989, and New York: Norton, 1990). David Watkin's "Beethoven and the Cello," in *Performing Beethoven,* ed. Robin Stowell (Cambridge University Press, 1994), is thorough and informative.

Finally, David Blum's *Casals and the Art of Interpretation* (Berkeley: University of California Press, 1977) is one of the great books on musical performance. Its significance extends well beyond string playing—though Casals's views on that relate in certain ways to those expressed by Bylsma. See, for example, the discussion of vibrato (pp. 133–37), which includes a detailed analysis of how Casals would vary his. Says Casals, "When you hear all the time a beautiful vibrato—well, you've had enough!"

12

Beyond the Beautiful Pearl

Julianne Baird on
Baroque Singing

More than anything else in music, the art of singing can turn reasonable people into red-faced absolutists. That by itself guarantees that the most controversial area of Baroque performance today is singing. It probably explains why outsiders often have problems with early-music singing: after years of bathing in rich, warm voices like that of Jessye Norman, critics often can't adjust to the small, light, clear voices of many early-music specialists. And after the opulent beauty of the singing of Renata Tebaldi, they often object to such elements as limited vibrato—though it's a mistake to assume that Baroque singers never use any vibrato. Such objections sometimes remind me of Paul Hindemith's remark, "I don't know how, with no vibrato, Bach could have had so many sons."

But as the next half-dozen interviews (and, for that matter, those of Alan Curtis, Rinaldo Alessandrini, and Anthony Rooley) all demonstrate, the early-music community itself argues over Baroque singing. Reconstructing historical singing styles has proved more challenging than reconstructing instrumental styles. We have more or less the same kinds of vocal cords and larynxes that Baroque singers had, but our singers don't necessarily use them in the same ways; and our vocal priorities can be quite different from those of past eras. Unfortunately, it didn't occur to singers or critics in earlier centuries to make their priorities clear to us. And in the field of singing, far more than in the world of the harpsichord or the gamba, modern mainstream style weighs heavily upon us. It's not necessarily easy for a cellist to adjust to limiting their vibrato, but for a singer the effort can be far more difficult. Will Crutchfield writes, "Most pedagogues agree that a fully developed singer cannot continuously suppress his customary vibrato without some kind of unhealthy tension of the vocal mechanism."[1]

The debates about Baroque singing also reflect an aspect of the Baroque itself: there was more than one style of singing. In the following four chapters, we look at the various schools from different angles. William Christie explains the French style; John Butt, Philippe Herreweghe and Jeffrey Thomas look at the German, as represented in Bach. But all agree that the style that dominated the era was the Italian. In the next chapter, Julianne Baird proves a knowledgeable guide to Italian style and to its impact outside Italy. In the chapter following hers, Nicholas McGegan discusses Handel, a Saxon who spent his mature years in London, but whose vocal writing was essentially Italian.

It might surprise some to learn that Julianne Baird, the American Baroque specialist, was attracted to singing because she loved Maria Callas and Mirella Freni in *verismo* opera. It might not surprise Baird's admirers. Tom Moore, for example, praises her in the same terms used for Callas: he writes of Baird's "uncanny ability to connect with the emotional core of the music she sings, so that every thought or mood of the poetry finds a compelling musical response, the phrase hastening or alighting on a word made special, the voice sighing, dying . . ."[2]

Baird's soprano voice is far from the *verismo* type, and its vernal beauty blends perfectly with early instruments. As with Callas, though, it's what she does with the voice that makes her work matter. In Will Crutchfield's judgment, "hers is the most perfect integration of style and sense, of period practices and dramatic persuasion, that I have yet encountered in Baroque opera." Crutchfield, an authority on vocal ornamentation, praises her as one of the few singers to have mastered the art of decorating extempore, again emphasizing the emotional basis of Baird's art: "It is not just that the ornaments are wonderfully apt, stylish and fluent, but that they are dramatic. Not, as one sees all too often, that they have been tagged to some obvious dramatic concept . . . but rather that Baird herself is charged with an emotional certainty that floods through the theatre, and the ornamentation flows out as an unselfconscious means of expressing the feeling."[3]

Baird herself has said that she prefers "a more personal, more dramatic approach" that "tries to express [the character she is portraying] in the music."[4] Not that she neglects scholarship. Baird has a doctorate in music history from Stanford and holds a tenured faculty position at Rutgers. When we spoke on

---

1. Crutchfield, "Voices," in *Performance Practice: Music after 1600,* ed. H. M. Brown and S. Sadie (London: Macmillan, 1989, and New York: Norton, 1990), p. 295.

2. Moore, *Fanfare* 16 (November/December 1992), p. 410.

3. "Handel Opera: A Tercentenary Report from New York," *Early Music* 14 (February 1986), p. 149.

4. In Octavio Roca, "A New Authenticity," *Gramophone* 68 (January 1991), p. 1351.

a sunny July day in a church in California's Marin County—she was singing Bach that night—she was engaged in preparing her doctoral thesis for book publication.[5] It deals with two major eighteenth-century singing masters, the Italian Tosi and his German translator and commentator, Agricola, the latter of whom she made available in English for the first time. Tosi, in an attitude typical of his era, defended the singer's right and even obligation to embellish—that is, to create part of the music. Agricola, however, takes an attitude that, as we've seen, has become the modern orthodoxy: he insists on the primacy of the composer and the score. (As this shows, the "composer's intention" was by no means a brand-new idea in the nineteenth century.) Though Baird has obviously learned a great deal from Agricola, it is to Tosi's philosophy that she subscribes. In doing so, she challenges the essence of today's text-based performance theory, and I took up that point early in our conversation.

You've told me that Callas and Freni inspired you to become a singer. What attracted you to them?

I admired the assurance of Freni's *impeccable* technique and the sheer beauty of her voice. Of course, Callas's voice and technique could hardly have been more different. To me, what was especially impressive in Callas was an absolute fearlessness that let her overcome vocal faults by her sheer drama and passion.

But wouldn't the modern approach to their repertoire—the idea that we sing just what the composer wrote—conflict with some of what you now do: specifically, improvising ornaments?

But that is exactly what singers were still doing in the early Romantic era—especially among the Italians, where singer-dominated traditions held on from the high Baroque. In Verdi's day, as in earlier times, performances were often a rather "seat of the pants" affair, with the music geared to whoever was available to sing. When Verdi, for example, was involved in a production he, like his predecessors, made alterations to accommodate the voices available. From Handel to Verdi, composers didn't dare fashion arias without intimate knowledge of the abilities, both technical *and* dramatic, of the singers waiting to be fitted. Almost like tailors—to whom they sometimes compared themselves—composers made alterations to reveal the strengths and hide the faults of the singer the aria was being written for. At least in the early part of Verdi's career, the primacy of the singer was still respected.

5. *Introduction to the Art of Singing, by Johann Friedrich Agricola,* trans. and ed. Julianne C. Baird (Cambridge University Press, 1995). Agricola's *Anleitung zur Singekunst* (1757) is a translation of and commentary on Pier-Francesco Tosi's *Opinioni de' cantori antichi e moderni* (1723), the most influential treatise on singing in the first half of the eighteenth century. Baird's version is cited in the following notes as "Agricola/Baird."

When did this start to change?

During the middle of Verdi's career—the middle of the nineteenth century. The usual contractual arrangement with the opera house at the beginning of Verdi's career required the composer, like his predecessors in the Baroque era, to be available for the first few performances. He was to be in the pit, to be available at the keyboard, to help direct, and to give various kinds of assistance, such as page turning. Only after the first few performances did he get paid for his work. Following the publication of his text, which occurred usually around the time of the first performance, Verdi frequently lost control over what the singers did with his music. Without his presence in the pit and his availability to tailor the arias to individual requirements, singers refashioned them to their own needs and whims, sometimes (to Verdi's dismay) even inserting passages with no basis whatsoever in the published texts—such as arias created by other composers!

To see the situation from the singers' point of view, they were merely exercising their prerogative, their right, their obligation to embellish so as to emphasize their own virtuosity—to produce the most stunning performance possible and to ensure the success of the opera.

The modern idea of the sanctity of the composer's score simply didn't exist in the Baroque tradition, especially among the Italians. Music was a living art, created anew by the singer in each performance. It was not a dead artifact. When the composer in the Italian tradition set down his directions on paper, he was not killing possibilities: he was creating possibilities. He was providing a sort of blueprint for an artist who would then realize the music in his or her own creative way.

That is what the Baroque era was all about: uplifting not just the creativity of the composer but also the creativity of the singer, honoring what an individual might bring to something that was already partly fashioned. If one thinks of written-down music as a blueprint, the singer or instrumentalist was a co-designer; this is a very sensible and human approach. These days, the conductor is entrusted with the "re-creation" of the music, and the singer is relegated to one category or, in the widely used German term, one *Fach*. Even though forensic medicine and criminology recognize the individuality of voices in voice prints, the prevailing attitude in opera is that the singer must fit into a *Fach*. If the coloratura *Fach* includes the roles of Zerbinetta, Constanze, the Queen of the Night, and several others, God forbid that the singer be anything other than just the perfect tomato for each of those boxes.

One result today is that many opera singers feel compelled to take on "big" roles that do not suit their voices, and this contributes to the voice's early demise.

Exactly. This development, of making the score primary and suiting the singer to it, is rather recent. For example, in remounting an opera in Paris,

Verdi had to adapt the tenor role for the star tenor of the Paris Opera, who had damaged his voice by trying to sing full-voice high Cs. Because the tenor had lost all of his range above the staff, Verdi transposed or rewrote the part to eliminate every note above the staff.

How would you explain the rising power of the composer and reverence for the score?

It comes largely from the German philosophy of singing that had its roots among such personages as Frederick the Great, who forbade added ornamentation among his singers. Gluck and other musicians and theorists of this persuasion (Agricola, for example) were offended by the extravagances of the all-powerful virtuoso singers, and sought to rein them in and effectually deprive them of their creative spontaneity. The insistence on the *Urtext* [the score as the composer wrote it, free of any editor's additions] reminds me of what we learn from nineteenth-century German philology, where the term was coined. Scholars were concerned with establishing valid original texts for the written-down epics, sagas, and chansons that are believed to have originated in the oral tradition. Once committed to paper and then rigidified as "the text," an oral tradition is dead in its tracks. It has become a *written* tradition. A vital, creative singing tradition is somewhat similar to the oral tradition of literature in that each performance is something of an original creation.

In the course of his career, Verdi became more and more powerful, more able to control what singers did with the score.[6] By the end of the Romantic period, the balance of power had shifted almost entirely to the composer's corner, but this arrangement still worked so long as the composer fitted his music to the individual singer. In the twentieth century—with its atonal compositions, which discourage both singers and audiences—has arisen a predilection for the performance of music of earlier eras and the unhappy situation in which a singer is forced to fit his or her body into the body (the larynx) of another person in a role that was tailored specifically for that other person. The singer can be judged harshly for not being another person. That is the problem.

This textual rigidity diminishes music as a living art; it denies singers the full power of their creative potential; it pigeonholes them; it creates vocal athletes; and sometimes it even ruins singers' voices. I am a staunch advocate of singers' rights and of a more sensitive and, I think, effective relationship between composer and performer.

This is why I subscribe to the Italian philosophy. This is why I chose the Baroque era.

6. As Will Crutchfield has shown, though, until the end of his life Verdi expected the singers to add ornamentation of a characteristic sort. For details, see "Vocal Ornamentation in Verdi: the Phonographic Evidence," in *19th Century Music* 7 (1983–4), pp. 3–54.

Let me ask you for some details about Italian Baroque singing. Is it true that Italian vocal writing changed from the early Baroque—the Monteverdi period—with its ideal of the music following the words very closely, to the middle Baroque, which put more emphasis on melody, and to the late Baroque, when ornamental display becomes most important?

I once had the opportunity to look at five Italian Baroque recitatives setting the same text. The later the setting, the more formulaic it was, and the less interesting harmonically and melodically. The text of the recitative was very powerful: "Oh Heaven! In one instant, I have lost my country, my family, and my father." In the earliest setting, pre-1700, the anguish of the text is represented both in the harmony and in the leaps over dissonant intervals and appoggiaturas in the melody. The later settings have much less poignancy. There are fewer large melodic leaps, fewer dissonant intervals: it is a flatter, more formulaic workaday style. The vocal part contains mostly consonant leaps, and the harmony is nondescript; it almost sounds as if the text could be, "Oh Heavens, I've lost my hairbrush."

In later opera composition (about 1720 to 1750) there were many conventions—opera-goers presented with the first line of text would recognize the chief sentiment or affect of the aria. Examples might be the *aria di bravura* and the *aria di pathetica*. Some arias were structured around specific metaphors, such as nightingale arias or shipwreck arias—"Poor me, I'm like a little vessel that gets tossed from one wave to another; I'm in love with two people, and I can't decide between this port and that port." The audience really wouldn't pay attention to the text any more; they were satisfied with knowing the general affect.

Did this loss of interest in the words reflect in part an increasing priority placed on showing off the singers' virtuosity?

Yes. In fact, as singers gained in prominence, librettists began to be severely limited as to the words they could use. By the late eighteenth century the prominent librettist Pietro Metastasio complained[7] that in his time, the librettist had become limited to two vowels, *a* ["ah"] and *o* ["oh"], for the final vowels of lines set to coloratura passages—and that, eventually, even the latter vowel had been eliminated. Thus, all the final syllables had to be *a*, which limited the rhyme and thus the choice of words.

Early Baroque Italian singing was genuinely text-centered, but it also involved very florid embellishment. Robert Greenlee wrote that "when performed with the vocal techniques commonly taught today, these embellishments are unwieldy, often resulting in phlegmatic tempos and awkward phrasing."[8] Could

---

7. Charles Burney, *Memoirs of the Life and Writings of Abate Metastasio,* 3 vols. (London, 1796; reprint, New York: Da Capo, 1971), vol. 2, pp. 135–36.

8. Greenlee, *"Dispositione di voce:* Passage to Florid Singing," *Early Music* 15 (February 1987), p. 47.

*you talk about the technique that allowed Italian singers of the early Baroque
to sing these tricky passages?*

In the period from 1580 to 1640 or so, dominated by such composers as
Monteverdi and Caccini, Italian singers negotiated the fast passages with a
lightning-quick kind of glottal articulation, which was performed on the soft
palate. The air percussed against the soft palate the way it does in a giggle. Several treatise writers called this technique the *dispositione di voce* or "disposi-
tion of the voice," and said it gave the voice the ability to move quickly or with
agility.[9]

In vocal writing, these fast notes were alternated with long-held notes. Flexibility in the alternation of the fast notes with the sustained notes, in passages,[10]
was considered the essence of good singing throughout the seventeenth and
eighteenth centuries. A singer was considered accomplished if he could exhibit
both types on every note in his range: that is, to sustain a note while making
a *messa di voce* (crescendo-decrescendo on a long-held note) and to trill (to effect a rapid alternation between two notes that are one full tone apart).[11] When
Roger North, a contemporary of Pepys, suggests that one begin instruction on
the viol by playing long-held notes with a *messa di voce,* I believe he was imitating singing instruction. This way the voice is kept in balance, and maintained in health.

*In contrast to that glottal articulation, singers nowadays are often taught to
treat the throat as if it were a hollow tube through which air passes. When did
the change in attitude occur?*

The old style of glottal articulation became unpopular when, in the late seventeenth century and the eighteenth century, performance moved out of
princely chambers and private rooms and into larger spaces such as the opera
houses and concert halls. Glottal articulation became unpopular because it is
difficult to hear at the back of a larger space, even one that holds just 500 people. During the high Baroque (1700–1750), in every nation, singers had largely
discarded this technique. By 1723, it was derisively called the *sgagateata* (cack-
ling like a chicken). Agricola, a student of Bach's on whom I did my doctoral
thesis, explains the acoustical factor behind the demise of glottal articulation.
Agricola recommended instead a detached articulation of passages, or *battuta,*
as Tosi names it. (The term is not commonly used by modern musicians.) According to the 1757 translation of Tosi by Agricola (who rendered this term

9. *Ibid,* pp. 47–55.

10. "Passages" here refers to "fast-moving, stereotyped melodic formulas" substituted for
longer notes or groups of notes (as opposed to "specific ornaments applied to single notes"):
also called *diminutions.* The definitions come from Howard Mayer Brown's *Embellishing
16th-Century Music* (Oxford University Press, 1976), p. 1.

11. The trill is a difficult ornament to master; it was highly prized in the Italian Baroque
but is rarely emphasized in modern voice instruction. See Julianne Baird, "An 18th-century
Controversy about the Trill: Mancini v. Manfredini," *Early Music* 15 (February 1987), pp.
36–45.

gestossen), it involves re-articulating the vowel on each note. To avoid the effect of giggling, detached articulation required a diaphragmatic impetus for each note, together with a light throat articulation for the sake of clarity. This style of articulation, Tosi's *battuta*, was used for most passages of the Italian and German high Baroque.

What about what we think of as Italian style now, which joins the notes in a legato?

The smoother articulation of the legato, which was discussed by both Tosi and Agricola, not to mention other Baroque writers, was far less common in the seventeenth and eighteenth centuries than it is now. In this type of articulation (according to Agricola), the singer articulated the vowel only once, at the very beginning of the passage or division.[12] The legato was typically employed in pieces in the "pathetic" style, pieces with an affect that was sad, tender, expressive or nobly serious.[13]

So was articulation more marked in Baroque singing, generally, than today?

While that is true, it should also be noted that Tosi enthusiastically praises slurred articulation or the "drag," for which he uses the term *strascino* (the Germans called it *Das Ziehen*). The technique is like a glissando.[14] It did not appear suddenly in the high Baroque. It was already being employed in the works of Monteverdi and D'India, particularly upon affective words like *piango*, "I cry," or *lagrime*, "tears." It is often notated on a rising note—for example, on a B♭ going to a B with a slur mark connecting the pitches. In the drag, the singer was expected to slide by almost imperceptible increments from one note to the next, touching all the pitches in between.

How does this relate to what we call portamento? Wasn't portamento a part of the Italian cantabile *style of singing in Mozart's era, too? Didn't Corri discuss it as well?*

Portamento is a more difficult concept to explain. Tosi's phrase "portamento di voce" literally means "carriage of the voice," and Hiller uses the term to mean "good use of the voice." Corri, a student of Porpora, for example, calls it "perfection of vocal music" and "the refinement in elegant pronunciation in speaking." In general usage, portamento refers simply to the process of "singing well."[15]

But wasn't portamento more specific than that?

12. "Divisions" decorate a melody by replacing each long note with livelier melodic movement in shorter note values.
13. See Agricola/Baird, p. 196.
14. *Ibid*, p. 279. Baird says that there is no good English equivalent of *strascino*, and that she adopted "the drag" from John Galliard's 1742 English translation of Tosi, *Observations on the Florid Song*.
15. Agricola/Baird, p. 271.

Yes, in fact it was. Corri is getting to the essence of the concept when he says that the "good use of the voice" involves the "sliding and blending [of] one note into another with delicacy and expression." To improve portamento, Mancini provides exercises designed to "connect the voice from one note to the next with perfect proportion and union in ascending and descending motion alike." He warns that no "unpleasant slide or dragging through smaller intervals" must be heard, so that the singer brays or howls. Mancini says that when the singer attacks the tones too strongly and pushes them forward, because his chest is too weak to sustain the tones evenly, he brays; when he produces an intermediate note that does not have a harmonic relationship to the notes on either side of it, he howls.

Students were encouraged to work on the portamento only after they had mastered music reading and eliminated the defect of "singing through the nose."

I've heard it said that there was a continuity of the Italian singing tradition from Caccini to Rossini.[16] *Do you think there was a continuity of the* bel canto *style over the centuries?*

A few years ago I saw a televised La Scala production of *La Cenerentola* with Frederica von Stade.[17] In that production, two native Italian male opera singers used glottal articulation when performing the fast passages—the *battuta* of Tosi or *gestossen* of Agricola. I remember wondering at the time about an unbroken tradition of *bel canto* teaching in Italy, particularly because glottal singing is usually discouraged today in the USA. The music of Bellini, Donizetti, and early Verdi certainly required agility and a good trill (as did eighteenth-century music—which might indicate continuity of technique). In Italian Baroque singing, the trill was stressed as not only as the *hallmark* of agility, but also as the *source* of the agility—one practices the fast notes in order to get the trill to happen more evenly, and vice versa.[18] And usually a light voice production was also a component.

16. The issue of continuity from Caccini to Rossini is discussed in an evenhanded way in John Rosselli's *Singers of Italian Opera* (Cambridge University Press, 1984) pp. 103–4. He cites a 1968 doctoral dissertation by E. V. Foreman at the University of Illinois, "A Comparison of Selected Italian Vocal Tutors of the Period from 1550 to 1800," as arguing for such a continuity, but he neither endorses or dismisses Foreman's conclusion.

According to Owen Jander, the term *bel canto* was not used until the mid-nineteenth century, and referred not only to a beautiful voice but to "effortless delivery of highly florid music," as opposed to the more stentorian *verismo* style that followed. (See his article "Bel Canto," in *The New Grove Dictionary of Opera*, vol. 1, ed. Stanley Sadie [London: Macmillan, 1992].) It is anachronistic, Jander says, to apply the term to mid-seventeenth-century lyrical singing (in, say, Carissimi) that reacted against the "representative" style of, say, Monteverdi; I do so with that disclaimer. Also, the early-nineteenth-century Italian style was distinct from earlier singing in at least some known respects. For instance, Manuel García II observed in 1840 that a lowered larynx position was a new development in his generation; it has since become standard operatic technique.

17. The laser disc is available on Deutsche Grammophon 072502.

18. Agricola/Baird, chap. 3.

*Unlike today, where we value warm, rich timbre and sheer size of voice
more than anything else.*

Listening to the recordings of Galli-Curci, Jenny Lind (a Manuel García student), and other famous singers from the early twentieth century, one is struck
by their light production, much like that of today's early-music singers.

Was it the Wagnerian influence that changed things?

Perhaps, but I think it was more the size and acoustics of larger performance
areas such as today's opera houses, and the decibel levels of today's orchestras.
It's much like the conditions that caused the changes in use of glottal articulation in the Baroque. The old Met was a horseshoe-shaped theater with excellent acoustics; it was like an Italian opera house, easy to sing in and project in,
much better than huge rectangular halls. Now we have halls like the 3,300-seat
San Francisco Opera [built in 1934] and the 3,800-seat Met [built in 1966].
And we have louder orchestras, with instruments (like steel-string violins and
larger-bore brass) that can produce greater volumes. Many voices break down
early because of the stress caused by singing at the volume necessary to be
heard in such conditions.[19]

Today, in some operatic circles, few words are so damning as "small voice";
but the "large voice" has not always been needed or even relevant, and attempts
to develop or keep on using a large voice can sometimes ruin it. One might compare the voice to an earthquake-proof building, with a lot of architectural give
and take so that it adjusts to seismic shocks. The vibrato enables the voice to
sustain a volume that's audible in a huge hall over a loud orchestra. In these circumstances, singers need to rely on a wide vibrato to avoid hurting the voice.

*This brings up a much-debated question: how much was vibrato used in
Baroque singing?*

Vibrato was and is used as part of the singer's sound vocabulary. It is difficult for a singer to execute a *messa di voce* or crescendo without some vibrato at the top. One indication that vibrato was used are the many organ stops
called the *vox humana,* which always had vibrato (the earliest are in fifteenth-
century Spain).[20]

Whether or not vibrato was employed constantly by seventeenth- and eigh-

19. Another factor demanding more vocal volume is that conductors have moved up in
the operatic pecking order, and often want more of the limelight in performance. Many have
their orchestras play much louder than previous generations of conductors did, making it even
harder for singers to be heard.

20. The leading study of Baroque vibrato is Greta Moens-Haenen's *Das Vibrato in der
Musik des Barocks: Ein Handbuch zur Aufführungspraxis für Vokalisten und Instrumentalis-
ten* (Graz: Akademische Druck- u. Verlagsanstalt, 1988). It is not available in English translation; but Moens-Haenen's entry on "Vibrato" in the *New Grove Dictionary of Opera,* vol.
4, pp. 982–84, makes points similar to Baird's. Eighteenth-century opera singers seem to have
had a basic vibrato, but it appears to have been small and almost inaudible, allowing for the

teenth-century singers is a different question. The writings of the eighteenth century indicate an aesthetic in which a singer was most prized for the ability to change his or her sound to express the words. By contrast, many teachers today promote an even vibrato with an equal width and speed on each note, to create a series of "beautiful pearls." You make your beautiful pearl, and it doesn't matter what the words are.

Many opera singers today don't do much with varying their sound and color to suit the words—though Callas did, of course, as well as Fischer-Dieskau and Schwarzkopf. You've praised Fischer-Dieskau and Victoria de los Angeles for their use of non-vibrato.[21]

Yes. One of the things that made Callas's singing so exciting was that she wasn't afraid to make an ugly sound. While that may sound like a back-handed compliment, I applaud her willingness to go to great lengths to portray her characters dramatically and to move the audience. For her, it was most important to play the part, rather than to produce a "pearl." Vocal beauty as such should not always be prized; the "pearl" is not always appropriate.

How does this "beautiful pearl" issue apply to the use of vibrato?

There are places—on a dissonant note, a leading tone, a chromatic tone, or a *tonus diabolus* (an augmented fourth)—which are better sung without vibrato, because the vibrato softens the effect, makes it a beautiful pearl, as if

---

application of more vibrato (though still narrow) as an ornament, and the suppression of vibrato as an effect.

Interestingly, Moens-Haenen concludes that "vibrato was used less often in early Romantic opera than in the opera of the late 18th century"; singers still used it as an ornament. The increased size of orchestras and opera houses and the development of the *verismo* and Wagnerian styles of singing led to increased use of vibrato over the century. Continuous vibrato, however, is "a 20th-century phenomenon," she says; the same can be said of the wide, slow continuous vibrato that has come to signify "operatic singing" for many listeners.

Robert Philip points to one bit of evidence for this last assertion—early recordings, in which "distinguished singers" use a vibrato that is usually "too fast and too shallow to be perceived as a fluctuation in pitch. What is clear from recordings is that many singers of the early years of the century used a shallower vibrato than singers later in the century" (Philip, "1900–1940," in *Performance Practice: Music after 1600*, ed. Brown and Sadie, p. 477). In the same book, p. 453, Will Crutchfield has a good deal to say about these recordings; he mentions Adelina Patti, an adherent of the older *bel canto* style, who was praised in 1886 for "her judicious 'refusal to sing tremolos' in spite of the growing [*verismo*] vogue for them." Recordings show that her vibrato was indeed minimal.

In the opposite historical direction and in a different country, John Butt finds that the surviving German Baroque documents suggest that vibrato was used as an ornament rather than something continuous: see his *Music Education and the Art of Performance in the German Baroque* (Cambridge University Press, 1994), pp. 70, 138, and 144.

21. "Fischer-Dieskau commonly uses non-vibrato, and we just think of him as an extremely expressive singer without examining why he does it. And Victoria de los Angeles is the same." Baird, quoted in Roca, "A New Authenticity."

the singer is oblivious to the affect of the words. The modern aesthetic is very
different from that of the Baroque. Another example is the appoggiatura. Three
rules apply to the appoggiatura: it is longer than the main note, louder than
the main note, and performed with less vibrato.[22]

*Does the appoggiatura get less vibrato because it's dissonant? Wasn't a mo-
mentary increase of vibrato itself used as an ornament? If so, how and where?*
Some good examples in the music of Bach are the soprano aria "Zerfliesse,
mein Herze" in the *St. John Passion*—which involves a *Bebung* (vibrato), indicated with a long chevron sign on the word "Tod"—and a similar passage on
"timentibus ejus" from the alto–tenor duet "Esurientes" in the Magnificat.

Also, many Italian composers from around 1580 to 1630 employed an ornament called the *trillo*, a type of intensity vibrato.[23] It was performed both
quickly in glottal fashion and slowly *von der Brust* (in the chest), or from the
diaphragm.

How about the width and speed of the vibrato?
Early-twentieth-century studies showed that the average speed of vibrato in
modern singers is around six or seven cycles per second.[24] Vibrato speeds were
probably not *very* different in the seventeenth and eighteenth centuries—although I do think there is a correlation between speed in singing divisions in
rapid passages and speed of vibrato, and rapid passagework was far more important in Baroque music than in Wagner or Puccini. But as I suggested, the
width of today's vibrato, sometimes approaching a minor third, is quite another
matter. It is a product of volume and stress or pressure on the voice.

*Another technical question is how much singers blended the head and chest
registers in the Italian Baroque style. Is it true that they* distinguished *the*

22. Agricola/Baird, pp. 92–93.
23. "The trillo is a tone repetition which can be the distinct (almost staccato) articulation
of one note or can be a more legato pulsing on the same note" (Agricola/Baird, p. 246). There
is some controversy about this: see David Fuller, "The Performer as Composer," in *Performance Practice: Music after 1600,* ed. Brown and Sadie, p. 124, and Brown, *Embellishing
16th-Century Music,* p. 10.
24. A number of these studies are collected in Carl Seashore's *The Vibrato* (Iowa City: University of Iowa Press, 1932). Studies of famous singers of the first part of the twentieth century found that the average speed of vibrato was about 6.5 cycles per second. The speed could
vary, however, both for an individual singer and between singers. The most extreme case was
that of Giovanni Martinelli, whose vibrato ranged from 5.5 to 12.5 cycles per second; but he
too averaged around 7 cps. Vibrato width averaged about a half-step, though it could vary
from a quarter-step to (rarely) more than a whole step. The minor third that Baird mentions
was very rarely approached by the earlier generation. Among these singers, 95 percent of their
tones had some vibrato; these studies found that among untrained adults only about 20 percent had a vibrato. This last finding shows that vibrato is not as "natural" as some claim.
(The further assertion that it is impossible to sing without vibrato is misleading: it is based
on a redefinition of "vibrato" to refer to the vibrating of the vocal cords, but in common
usage "vibrato" refers to the sound as heard, not to its source.)

sounds of the different registers, instead of trying to minimize the differences as modern singers do?

The Italians recognized two registers, the head and chest, with the falsetto evidently included in the head voice. The Germans, such as Agricola, distinguished the falsetto from the head and chest voices. *Blending* the registers around the break between them is mentioned in singing treatises of every era. The singer is encouraged to practice certain notes around the break both in chest voice and in head voice, in order to make the transition between them gracefully. When the chest voice is extended into the domain of the head voice a sound occurs that is the same as belting in Broadway singing. Eighteenth-century writers discouraged the singer from extending the chest voice too high because of possible damage to the voice.

It's said that eighteenth-century singers were encouraged to not *belt out the high notes, but to hit them lightly, which is the opposite of what we admire now.*

That's absolutely true. Tosi said, "Let the singing master be careful not to let the student who's seeking to attain the high notes shout them or scream them." He adds, " . . . lest he not only lose his soprano voice . . . "

. . . as happened to Verdi's tenor . . .

Right, " . . . but also lose his health."[25] One may ask, what does singing loud high notes have to do with general health? There is, however, an account of a castrato singer who died of a hemorrhage from singing too loud in the high register.[26]

Which, however, indicates that it was done.

It was done. Not every singer is aware of his or her limits. There are other examples. The treatises admonished singers not to memorize cadenzas—they were supposed to listen to those of the best singers, study composition, and improvise in the style of the aria. But some of the most famous male and female singers of the day had collections of cadenzas, and probably drew from them, mixing and matching, so to speak. Perhaps they operated somewhat like a good jazz musician, who can begin with various standard riffs.

Similarly, the books warned against memorizing and simply reusing the same ornaments in a *da capo*.[27] But in the memoirs of Madame Mara, Elizabeth-Gertrud Schmelling, we learn that she prepared by writing many different

25. Tosi, *Opinioni de' cantori antichi e moderni*, chap. 1, section 9. The translation is an informal one by Baird.

26. Agricola/Baird, p. 263, n. 37, tells of the strange end of Luca Fabbris in 1765.

27. The *da capo* form, a common high Baroque form (it is used often in Handel and Bach arias), has an elaborate first ("*A*") section, followed by a contrasting second ("*B*") section in a related key, and then repeats the *A* section. The second appearance of the *A* section is called the *da capo* (lit., "from the beginning"); it was used to demonstrate a singer's skill at ornamentation.

ornamentations, from which she would pick and choose. This gave the impression of improvisation even if the audience heard repeat performances. Mara attributes her triumph over her rival, Brigida Banti, to this trick.[28]

Your mention of the sopranos brings up another topic I wanted to mention. Wasn't it in the Italian Baroque that women singers first emerged as star soloists?

Yes. Not that their paths were always lined with roses. Many married their impresarios—managers—in order to avoid gossip about their personal lives, or traveled with their mothers. And a great number died in poverty.[29]

To return to singing style—and interpretative freedom—how was rubato used in Italian Baroque singing?

One of the first mentions of the rubato is in Tosi's treatise. He specifies two kinds of rubato, one in which time is lost in order to be gained, and the other in which it is gained in order to be lost. Our first response is to wonder what he could mean by that; I think it means one type was rushed and then dragged, the other dragged and then rushed. The point is that the rubato is not a slowing down of a whole section, only to have the tempo resume later; the bass stays pretty much in the original tempo, and the bass and melody come together eventually on a downbeat.

It sounds like what is said of the piano playing of Mozart and Chopin—both of whose approaches to melody were clearly derived from Italian operatic singing.

Yes, the rubato clearly did find its way into keyboard playing. For an earlier example, Carl Philipp Emanuel Bach in his *Sechs Sonaten mit veränderten Reprisen* (Six Sonatas with Varied Repeats) writes out this kind of rubato, giving sometimes seventeen in the right hand against four in the left, or twenty-three against six. Similarly, Mozart writes it out in the Rondo in A Minor, K. 511. In both cases, it's clear that the right hand plays more freely while the left is more steady.

This is one of the reasons why a singer was taught to accompany himself:[30] so that the right hand can be free while the left hand stays steady. Rubato was one of the things a singer was expected to learn. Skill in using rubato was another little tick on the chart as to whether the singer was triumphing that night or failing.

I'd like to ask you about Italian influences in England and Germany. You've written that English composers kept to a simpler, less florid style,

28. Agricola/Baird, p. 28.
29. See Rosselli, *Singers of Italian Opera,* chap. 3.
30. Agricola/Baird, p. 252.

where the words were paramount, until the Italian style took over in the sev-enteenth century.[31]

Yes. For example, in many pieces by Campion or Dowland, the word set-tings, involving one syllable per note, makes the music subservient to the text and makes it much more difficult to sing. Campion was of course a poet, and he wrote even his second and later stanzas so that they would fit the music. But once the English fell under the Italian influence, especially with Nicholas Lanier [1588–1666] and Robert Johnson [1583–1633], we start to see a slow-ing down of the harmonic movement. Instead of a chord every beat in a $\frac{4}{4}$ piece, they use a chord every bar, or every two bars. So the harmonic movement gets much slower, and this means that the singers get much more active with a great deal of florid expression of the text—sometimes, curiously, on those words where you would least expect it.

Suppose, for example, you have the phrase "loss of breath." You might think that the way to make a joke on it would be a florid run on the word "loss," so that the singer almost runs out of breath on it. But, in fact, what we typically find in English music of this period is that the coloratura passage is on the word "breath."

Because a florid run on an insignificant word turns out to help make the text more understandable, it helps listeners get a *double entendre*. It's a little hat-tipping to the ideal of understanding the words. It doesn't fulfill that ideal completely, but it does help. You'll find it also in Johnson's *Care-charming Sleep*, where long elaborate ornaments occur on very insignificant words, like "in," "of," and "to."

By contrast, among Italian composers the ornamentation is on poignant words. But the result is that the minute the singer starts the wild ornamenta-tion, it becomes hard to hear the text. Although in theory the ornamentation is meant to develop the meaning of the word it occurs on, in practice the lis-tener misses both that word and the point of the ornamentation. You hear the notes but you don't understand their function. So the English didn't simply ape the Italian manner.

You mentioned that as the line got more florid, the harmonic rhythm slowed down. Could you say more about the connection between harmonic rhythm and floridity?

Regarding that, I think of the most influential composer in England, the Ital-ianized German Handel, and of the Italian singers who came to London to sing his music. Some of them were annoyed because his instrumental parts had too much busy-ness, whereas in Italy it was often the singers who provided all the melodic interest, perhaps with instrumental doubling. Handel's writing for the accompanying instruments was far more complex than what Italian singers would have received from Galuppi or Torelli. And the more complex and

31. Booklet note, Dorian CD 90109, *The English Lute Song*.

rapidly changing harmony makes it harder for the singer to ornament—you have to really know what the bass is doing. You can't assume anything.

When Handel wrote a strictly continuo aria, that was one of his highest compliments to a singer, because then the singer was completely on her own. By the way, I'm always a little piqued when I get a Handel aria that has the violins in unison with me. My first thought is, "The soprano must not have been very good." But in fact, it wasn't necessarily a slur on the singer. Quite often the Italian opera orchestras were brilliant in their ability to do *chiaroscuro*[32]—a hundred violins may have been accompanying a singer, but when the singer started soloing the violinists knew how to cut back so far as to be almost an ambience around the singer, to support without competing. But that's a concept that most modern orchestras don't have, and they often have to be told over and over again to cut back.

In eighteenth-century Germany and England, Italian singers were hot commodities.

This is still true. Agricola writes that there were probably ten or fifteen good German singers who left Germany to make their careers in other countries, sometimes even changing their names—so great was the prejudice against them in their own country and the preference for Italians. The Irish singer Michael Kelly—Mozart's first Don Basilio—changed his name to Michele Ochelli!

It's like our own country now!

That's very true!

When Frederick the Great founded the Berlin Opera, he insisted on having only Italian singers—which resulted in angry editorials complaining that Graun[33] had been sent by Frederick to Italy to once again audition Italian singers for the Berlin opera, and "because of such circumstances, our best performers leave the country in shocking numbers, while wretched Italians are accorded great honor."[34] And the castrati made so much more money than the average singer that it's like comparing Pavarotti to a church singer. The English, Spanish, and German courts employed so many castrati and other Italian singers that when Frederick was getting his opera going in the middle of the eighteenth century Italy was practically depleted of her best singers. And although Graun returned with second-rate talent, they nonetheless earned far more than the native German singers.

Dresden had its stable of Italian singers, including the famous Faustina Bordoni, Johann Adolph Hasse's wife.

32. Varying the loudness. Agricola/Baird, p. 279, n. 4.

33. Karl Heinrich Graun (1703–1759), Royal Kapellmeister to Frederick the Great, as well as chief composer to the Berlin Opera.

34. Quoted in Agricola/Baird, p. 254, n. 3.

Yes. By the way, Agricola and Quantz both have a lot to say about Faustina's technique, particularly her ability to sing divisions loudly but with glottal articulation. Agricola notes this as an exception to his ban on glottal articulation.

Your main interest regarding singers seems to be to promote the exception—the not fitting into boxes.

My general thought is that modern music teachers, and I am one, should respect the particular strengths and weaknesses of the singer standing before us to be taught. We must resist the pressure to fit the singer into some procrustean bed inimical to his talents. We must teach him the first principle: Know thyself. We must realize that there are important values—wit, ingenuity, feeling, for example—to strive for, other than the large voice and the plastic sameness in quality of sound for every note—other than the "beautiful pearl."

SELECTED DISCOGRAPHY

Julianne Baird's relative absence from British Baroque recordings can be puzzling. One explanation might be that Newcastle already has so much coal; but Baird suggests, in an *Opera News* article by David Patrick Stearns, that another reason is "the individualistic approach that I take—that rubs them [conductors, if I read correctly] the wrong way. It's hard to be a singer when you're supposed to stumble from one Svengali figure to another, being molded in their own image."[35] Nicholas McGegan, in the next interview, seems to oppose the "Svengali" approach.

Baird's way with much of the repertory she discusses is preserved on CD thanks mainly to American independent labels. Dorian, an audiophile company, has released a number of her CDs. Among the best are two of early Italian Baroque music: *Musica Dolce* (Dorian 90123)—the one praised by Tom Moore in the introduction to this chapter—and *Songs of Love and War* (Dorian 90104), in which, says Stearns, her handling of the ornamentation "gives a repeating sequence of notes an element of surprise . . . that drives home the architectural variety and unity." Regarding her *The English Lute Song* (Dorian 90109), David Fallows remarks that Baird's "dramatic sense pays rich dividends."[36] Nicholas Anderson find her "particularly beguiling" in Handel solo cantatas (Dorian 90147).[37]

She has also recorded for Newport. Her *Bach Arias with Flute* (Newport NDP 85530) has, according to Stearns, "great rhetorical variety, color and immediacy." Her *Handel Arias* (Newport 85530) demonstrates her mastery of the art of ornamentation; says Stearns, "one doesn't realize how effortful much

35. Stearns, "Baroque Rebel," *Opera News* (October, 1995), p. 33.
36. Fallows, *Gramophone* 67 (April 1990), p. 1858.
37. Anderson, *Gramophone* 69 (April 1992), p. 126.

modern Handel singing is until one hears an almost complete absence of this quality" in her singing on this CD.

Baird's recorded Handel opera and oratorio roles are mostly on the Newport and Vox labels. Stanley Sadie objects to the conductor's cuts in *Imeneo* (Vox 115451), but praises the "really lovely singing of Julianne Baird, an exceptionally tasteful artist and in excellent voice."[38] In *Muzio Scevola* (Act 3; Newport 85540) Nicholas Anderson dislikes Baird's vibrato, but calls her characterization "imaginative" and says that she "brings a coquettish sparkle" to her role.[39]

In Alessandro Scarlatti's oratorio *Ishmael* (Newport 85558/2), her singing of the final scene, says Stearns, is "one of the most convincing portrayals of physical exhaustion since Maria Callas's recording of Mimi's farewell in *La Bohème*." Her "most fully realized opera portrayal," says Stearns, is on Omega OCD 1016: Pergolesi's *La serva padrona,* in its century the most celebrated and influential of opera buffas. Finally, her *Lullabies and Dances,* with Bill Crofut's ensemble of folk instruments (Albany 048) is an ideal starter album for young children, though I'm hardly the only grownup to enjoy it.

FOR FURTHER READING

As far as I know, no good one-volume introduction to Baroque singing is yet available. I look forward to Sally Sanford's and Baird's chapters in Schirmer's forthcoming *Performer's Guide to Seventeenth-Century Music,* edited by Stewart Carter. Sanford's article, "A Comparison of French and Italian Singing in the Seventeenth Century," in the on-line *Journal of Seventeenth-Century Music* 1 (1995)—its URL is www.sscm.harvard.edu/jscm/v1/no1/sanford.html—conveys a great deal of information in an accessible style. Baird's edition of *Introduction to the Art of Singing by Johann Friedrich Agricola* (Cambridge University Press, 1995), especially her commentary (in footnotes), is a good entryway into the primary sources. Will Crutchfield's two essays on "Voices" and David Fuller's essay "The Performer as Composer," in *Performance Practice: Music after 1600,* ed. H. M. Brown and S. Sadie (London, Macmillan, 1989, and New York: Norton, 1990) are indispensable. John Rosselli's *Singers of Italian Opera* (Cambridge University Press, 1984) is an excellent historical study of that nation's singing traditions, and John Steane's *The Grand Tradition,* 2nd ed. (Portland, Oregon: Amadeus, 1994) is an excellent study of singers on record, including early recordings.

38. Sadie, *Gramophone* 71 (August 1993), p. 79.
39. Anderson, *Gramophone* 70 (March 1993), p. 96.

13

You Can Never Be Right for All Time

Nicholas McGegan on Handel

Christoph Willibald Gluck, the reformist opera composer, kept a full-length portrait of Handel by his bed so that it would be the first thing he saw when he woke up. Mozart, three decades after Handel's death, said that "Handel knows better than any of us what will make an effect." Beethoven called Handel "the greatest composer that ever lived," and added, "to him I bow the knee."[1]

Handel was the first composer in history whose works never fell out of the concert repertory. A few of his works, at any rate: in spite of the reverence for him, only a little of his music was actually performed in the nineteenth century. *Messiah* was one of them, of course, sung with increasingly gargantuan choruses and orchestras, and so were *Samson, Israel in Egypt,* and *Judas Maccabeus.* But such masterpieces as *Theodora, Giulio Cesare, Jephtha, Orlando,* and *L'Allegro, il Penseroso, ed il Moderato* occupied few beyond the occasional scholar.

It was in our century of revivals that these works returned to the stage and concert hall. The Göttingen Festival in Germany began staging Handel opera in 1920, and over time these pieces (and the less well-known oratorios) have received more frequent performances. Since the Second World War, the growth of the Handel discography has been vastly accelerated by the early-music revival.

---

1. For a discussion of Handel's posthumous influence, see Ellen T. Harris, "Handel's Ghost: The Composer's Posthumous Reputation in the Eighteenth Century," in *Companion to Contemporary Musical Thought,* vol. 1, ed. John Paynter et al. (London: Routledge, 1993), pp. 208–25.

The British conductor Nicholas McGegan has recorded more of Handel's operas than anyone else, as far as I know—as I write, at least nine of them, out of a total of thirty-nine. As artistic director of the Göttingen Festival, he has helped bring that Handelian mecca into line with current ideas about Handel playing. As Music Director of the Philharmonia Baroque Orchestra, he has fostered its emergence as one of North America's few world-class period-instrument orchestras, and the majority of his recordings with them are of Handel. He has also recorded Handel with a Hungarian group, the Capella Savaria. In addition, he leads Sweden's Drottningholm Festival and is principal guest conductor of the Scottish Opera.

The coincidence of the Handel revival with the historical-performance movement has raised a number of issues. Consider, for example, the Baroque convention of the *da capo* aria, in which a long first ("*A*") section is sung again after the shorter second section—the repeat lets the singers show off their ability to ornament. Handel singing in recent decades has (in the words of Winton Dean) "moved from a period when all da capos were literal repeats . . . to a fashion where decoration is allowed to sprout anywhere, even in *A* sections, and da capos release salvos of rockets in the style of Rossini or Bellini."[2] Doubts also arise about the Anglican purity of much early-music singing: does it really fit the music that Handel wrote for Italian opera singers? Then there are the roles Handel wrote for castrati, a voice type whose cultivation was illegal in Italy even in its heyday. The castrato voice is, we can rest assured, a historical instrument that won't be revived; but who, then, should sing the parts written for it?

A more basic issue is the works themselves. When certain works by a widely revered composer are almost never played, one might be forgiven for suspecting that these works are of lesser quality. Such suspicions have faded in recent decades, but doubts about the stageworthiness of the operas persist.

I discussed these and other issues with McGegan in his home office, which overlooks a scenic canyon from atop the Berkeley hills. McGegan's gift for wit and vivid language and his congenial manner all somehow fit the subject matter, for Handel's personality inspired an exceptionally large fund of anecdotes—some of which came up in our conversation.

People sometimes complain that using countertenors for the operatic roles Handel wrote for castrati is a sort of spurious authenticity. Handel, they say, always used a woman for such roles when a castrato wasn't available, because the voices were more similar: like a castrato, a woman uses both chest and head registers, whereas a countertenor typically uses only head voice.

2. Dean, "Scholarship and the Handel Revival, 1935–85," in *Handel: Tercentenary Collection,* ed. Stanley Sadie and Anthony Hicks (London: Macmillan, and Ann Arbor, Michigan: UMI Press, 1987), pp. 1–18; quote p. 17.

I accompanied the countertenor Paul Esswood in a recording of Schumann's *Dichterliebe*, which no one would have thought of singing in countertenor voice in Schumann's day. What mattered, I think, was that Esswood sings it very well. In Handel opera, I'm so grateful to find singers (like Drew Minter) who can hold the stage as well as sing the notes that I don't hesitate to use them if they're countertenors. To me it doesn't really matter. There are plenty of people who can sing but can't act, and plenty who can act but can't sing, so if you find any who can do both you use them. It's a question of giving a really good and exciting performance. Sarah Bernhardt could play Hamlet.

Someone called her Hamlet the "Princess of Denmark"—that suggests a theatrical advantage of using countertenors, men playing male roles.

On the other hand, it's a little odd to hear Alexander the Great sing in the range of Dame Janet Baker. And women can be great in trouser roles.

People have raised objections to "early-music singing" in Handel. Do you have any comments on that?

I don't think that you should make singers too uniform. They certainly weren't in the eighteenth century. Ultimately, a really successful singer, apart from having good technique and so on, is a total package. The personality, the technique, the diction, the way they sing, the way they put it across—it's all part of *them*. I don't think you should say that Madame Cuzzoni[3] was necessarily the most perfect singer in the whole universe, but I think all of Handel's singers were great personalities and sounded like themselves. There were criticisms of them—one had too much vibrato, another didn't have a very good trill—but it seems that they had a lot of color in their voices, and sang to the maximum range available, and weren't too Anglican.

You can don a cloak of authenticity in some spurious way, but if that cloak doesn't fit, it's a disaster. Still, there *are* quite clearly certain things that you can learn from early singing treatises, which singers have to pay attention to. A singing teacher of the late eighteenth century named Domenico Corri,[4] for example, provides breath marks, which are a lot more expressive than most singers' breathing now. Modern singers like to sing very long phrases, but a lot of Corri's breath marks are for much shorter phrases—it's breathing for expression. On the other hand, his written-out ornamentation gives you an idea

3. Francesca Cuzzoni (*c.* 1698–1770), a leading Italian soprano of Handel's day, "an eccentric and temperamental artist, neither beautiful nor a great actress. Her voice was her gift . . . [her] intonation, ornamentation and breath control were extraordinary; the sheer expressive power of her voice was praised by Tosi [et al.]" (Julie Ann Sadie, *Companion to Baroque Music* [London: Dent, 1990, and New York: Schirmer, 1991], p. 83).

4. Domenico Corri (1746–1825), whom Will Crutchfield calls "the most valuable single theorist" of his era for modern scholars to study. From Crutchfield's essay "Voices" in *Performance Practice: Music after 1600,* ed. H. M. Brown and S. Sadie (London: Macmillan, 1989, and New York: Norton, 1990), p. 293 et passim.

of how ornamentation was done fifty years after Handel, so while some of it is great, most of it is not particularly useful.

One thing that *is* useful is what Corri said were the three things a singer needed: the *messa di voce* (the swelling and diminishing on a note), the trill, and a thorough understanding of harmony and counterpoint so as to be able to improvise cadenzas and ornaments. And you can tell that people like Lorraine Hunt can improvise ornaments, or can make them sound that way even when they're not improvised.

How?

Ornaments that are written out often sound as if they're part of the text, instead of something added spontaneously; for instance, they may be too rhythmically correct, without enough rubato. Of course, somebody who's a very good performer can make you think they're improvising even when they're not, just as a really good actor can make you think he's scratching his ear because it itches, even though the scratch was rehearsed to the last detail.

I've always thought that every conservatory should have a compulsory jazz course for all keyboard players so they can learn to play continuo, and for all singers so they can free up their singing. What you learn at most conservatories is how to play music that's put in front of you—preferably sight-reading it, but not necessarily listening to it. If you turn to an orchestral player and say, "Now, why don't you play Mozart's Flute Concerto in G, and can you just improvise the cadenza?" they've had no training in that, which is absolutely one of the most important things in all music up until Verdi. This seems to me a whole dimension of music teaching which is a desperate failure.[5] It's a great shame that it's a failure in the States, because this is, after all, the land of jazz. Whether you like jazz or not, it still has that free spirit that was expected of musicians in the eighteenth century, the ability to improvise.

This reminds me that you once said a Baroque orchestra is in some ways jazz-like.

It's very much continuo- and bass-section-led, in the same way that the rhythm section and bass form the foundation of a jazz group. In both, the treble parts are the free parts which sit on top of that. A Baroque piece is very much like a classical building, where you have structure, which the bass gives you, and ornament, which is provided by the melodic instruments on top. And if the structure is strong, then the ornaments can float freely. It's the same in a good jazz piece; it's *not* the same in a Tchaikovsky symphony, which is very often driven by the tune. Even the cellos are often playing the tune. It's just the double basses that are providing the harmony, limping along underneath.

When I conduct Baroque music with modern orchestras, one thing I do is to ask the cellos and basses to drive it a bit more, and I ask the violins simply

5. See the interview with Robert Levin for a discussion of this.

to relax. You can often get very good results that way. It's the opposite of what they're used to. The cellos and basses love it.

How do you get such orchestras used to the element of improvisation?

I was doing Handel's *Ariodante* at the English National Opera, and asked the oboe player and the bassoonist to make up some twiddles if they felt like it. At the first couple of performances nothing happened, but by the end it was encrusted, and I actually had to ask them to put less in. In the other Handel operas they'd done, the conductor or editor wrote everything out that he wanted added, which I think is not the spirit of the thing. Somehow it betrays a great lack of trust in the performers.

Is your trust ever ill-placed—do you ever find that singers or players improvise ornaments badly, and if so what do you do? Or do they overdo it, as Winton Dean complains happens nowadays?

Well, occasionally you get that. Sometimes people put more than enough ornamentation in and expect you to edit it out. And there's also the question of whether what works in the theatre, where it's tied to something physical, will work in a recording. And those of my singers who improvise, like Drew or Lorraine, will sometimes just try things out and say, "Well, that one didn't work"—though as far as I'm concerned, the attempt is itself laudable. Also, I think in general you'd use more ornamentation in opera than in oratorio. This was partly because of the needs of the operatic singers: opera was more about brilliant effects by prima donnas, oratorio more about making sense of the dramatic situation.

Do you ever use the ornamentation that Handel wrote out for his singers?[6]

I always ask my singers first. In one case the singer simply didn't want to do them. This was in a Handel opera, *Ottone*, where he once had to use a mezzo for a soprano part, and this mezzo obviously was hopeless so Handel had had to write out the ornaments for her. But her arias were transposed down a fourth or a fifth, and when you put it back up to the soprano range, the ornaments sound like the Chipmunks. It was simply too high. So we did a couple of them, but basically not.

In general, such ornaments were tailor-made for a particular singer. So I tend to show those ornaments to a singer, and then say, Go and do thou likewise, but not necessarily copy. Also, I think some of those ornaments are too much.

It's said that rising to high notes in ornaments and improvisations is a modern idea, that eighteenth-century singers weren't so enamored of heights.

6. See Winton Dean, *G. F. Handel: Three Ornamented Arias* (Oxford University Press, 1976), and "Vocal Embellishment in a Handel Aria," a 1970 essay reprinted in his *Essays on Opera* (Oxford University Press, 1990), pp. 22–29.

It's very hard to say, because I'm not sure that we have enough evidence to know what every eighteenth-century singer did. We often read that a singer had a particular range, but when you actually see the music written for them it doesn't go nearly that high; so if they had a range that went up to there, when did they use it?—perhaps in the cadenzas. You can generally assume that if a singer had a good top C, Handel would use it. Maybe a lesser composer wouldn't. But, yes, Handelian tenor parts don't have as many high notes as a lot of modern performers would like, so they do tend to throw in extra high notes. There's some evidence that sopranos used rather more head voice at the top of their range, and tenors too, rather than belting things out at full voice as nowadays they're trained to do. Sometimes the tendency to do that always, and end everything like the Toreador Song, is a little unsubtle. But I don't think we can ever say that nobody ever did a particular thing, because we just don't know.

You quoted Corri as saying that knowing harmony was crucial to ornamenting well.

Well, this business of knowing harmony is extremely important. When I was teaching at the Royal College of Music, I was amazed that the singers were often excused from harmony classes on the grounds that they didn't need it, when in my view they're precisely the people who do need it. Most string instruments can provide harmony of their own, and wind instruments can at least get a sense of what harmony is about, but singers generally sing only one line, and if you're a tenor or soprano singing the top line you don't really get any idea of structure and harmony. But you really need that fundamental knowledge.

The other thing you need, which is also very poorly taught to singers, is rhythm. I find when I'm working with singers who were or still are good instrumentalists—Lorraine Hunt, for example, used to play the viola professionally—that their sense of rhythm is so much stronger, which means that when they want to depart from the beat they know what they're doing. Some singers merely sing out of time because they've never been disciplined to sing in time. Somehow the normal rules don't apply to voices. But the great thing about the eighteenth century is that they did.

Cuzzoni was known for her wonderful rubato.

The biggest problem with all those things is not in performing them but in putting them on record, because they're very fragile things. If you start to put too much on record, what tends to happen is that it starts to sound fixed and structured, especially when you've listened to it three or four times. What you really need is some wonderful machine that you attach to your CD player that can change all these things; you would record a basic performance and a bunch of ornaments and program them randomly.

With LPs, by the time you listened to them three or four times they were so scratched that you'd never listen anyway. I wish that CDs would self-destruct in the same way after five years, so you'd have to make them all over again. I was horrified that a record I'd made in 1974 was reissued on CD recently. I think of those pieces totally differently now than I did then. All I could say was, Thank God there wasn't a photograph inside, because I feel about those CDs the way I feel about photographs of myself from fifteen years ago: "Was there really so much hair? God, those sideburns are awful." Maybe some of it is okay, but a lot of it isn't and you'd like to redo it.

The recording issue is also related to responding to the audience. If an audience is dreary and sleepy, you have to pull all the stops out not to be dreary and sleepy yourself, but if there's a lot of energy coming from the audience it can inspire you to great things. And everything we hear about eighteenth-century audiences says that they were very participatory. If they didn't like something, they threw things. If they did like something, they followed you all over town, giving you diamonds. It was much more Italian in that sense than, say, going to an opera in Washington, D.C., where they tend to just applaud politely. (In Italy, the difference between a crowd at a football game and at the opera is that the football game crowd is maybe a little louder.) The audience can certainly inspire you to do your best. So if you extend that principle into the recording studio where there's no audience, you're having to produce the music in a way that it was never intended to be produced. You have to fake it. It's a very different art, especially if you have to do the same thing five times so they can edit it.

Your recordings often have a sense of live-ness.

Well, recording in the United States is much more expensive than in a lot of places in Europe, so we make our American recordings in one-third to half the time of many recordings in Europe. One European recording of a Handel oratorio took eighteen sessions; we did the same oratorio in six and a half. Therefore what you're getting very often *is* one take. Often I'm happy to let the odd mistake stay in, because it seems to me more important that the spirit is there, even if there might be one little plonk from the oboe; otherwise, everything might be perfectly manicured but perfectly dead.

In a metaphor I've used before, there's a great deal of difference between a butterfly flying about and a butterfly in a collection, which is beautifully colored but has this bloody great pin through it. It's as dead as it could possibly be. What you're trying to do at the recording is to fake the live butterfly, not the dead one. And you maybe can't see the details of the live butterfly so colorfully as you can the one in the collection; on the other hand, it has all the beauty of the live creature. We have a rule that we only record pieces we've performed. In the Handel operas, we've performed them on stage three or four times before we even take them to the studio, and the singers usually sing from memory. We recorded Handel's *Susanna* live, and *Messiah* in whole acts, where we started with the beginning of the act and went to the end of it as one enormous take, and then went back and patched that. The base take is actually sort of a performance without the audience, so you get some of that tension and drama, and some of the feeling of taking the energy from the previous piece—the sort of bleed-through from one movement to the next that inevitably happens in a concert.

So you've tried to turn the limitation of studio time in America into a virtue.
Yes. Correct the odd mistake here or there, but generally get that sense of making people tap their feet, at least in a happy piece.

It relates to that spirit you've talked about: technical perfection is a twentieth-century concern.
We assume that they were just as persnickety about ensemble as if the CD microphones were on in their day; yet there's strong evidence that not every string player even bowed in the same way. I think you can say that on certain matters in certain acoustics in certain times and places they were being maybe a little more careful, but in general I think we can be a little holier-than-thou about it.

One rehearsal was the norm for a new instrumental piece. Early recordings support your point; even well-rehearsed chamber groups play in what we would consider a sloppy way.[7]
You can hear it all the time on those recordings. If you want perfection, buy a synthesizer. Get the human element out of it altogether. And there are some people who think that's exactly what they should do. That's absolutely fine; but it's completely counter to the eighteenth century. The fun thing about doing so much eighteenth-century music is that it has this free spirit about it.

This also relates, perhaps, to the controversies about Handel's rhythmic notation—whether dotted rhythms and so on should be read literally?
Yes, one has to be very careful of the assumption that we read notes in the same way they did in the eighteenth century. I think that the danger of asking, "Do you dot this precisely, and do you make this a sixteenth as opposed to an eighth?"[8] is that it implies that they tried to be as mathematically precise as we try to be playing Boulez. Perhaps it was more like taking a Charleston, which

7. Robert Philip, *Early Recordings and Musical Style* (Cambridge University Press, 1992), chap. 9 et passim. For example, even the four players in a quartet didn't all apply portamento in the same places and didn't bow or use vibrato uniformly. The rhythms, in particular, are much less literal than modern performers would allow. All of this occurred in orchestral recordings as well.

8. McGegan is referring to a controversy (driven in recent decades by the musicologist Frederick Neumann) about "overdotting"—playing certain notes longer or shorter than the notation indicates. Neumann tended to favor playing the notes as written, a view that put him at odds with most musicologists. I discuss this at length in note 13 of the William Christie interview.

looks dead written down, but is lively and fluid when played in the authentic Charlestonized idiom. (I think a close study of Baroque dance would teach us a lot more about how to do a lot of these little rhythmic things.) In general, it's dangerous to assume that everybody had that very mathematical approach to writing down music; some people obviously did, and many people obviously didn't. Indeed, if you can assume that people knew how to ornament, you can assume that they weren't tied to the notes or the rhythms as they were written. We talked about Cuzzoni doing rubato; she obviously could sing in time but sometimes chose not to.

How do you handle overdotting?

What we do is based on the fact that if you do a crescendo, the dotting naturally gets a little sharper.[9] I'd almost rather that the notes were written out equally and you just played them a lot: I think if you played Lully overtures all your life, you'd find a way of playing them. It's fine to read a treatise saying the second note should be a sixteenth note, but ultimately, you just have to play a lot.

I have a computer next door, which lets me play into it and notates exactly what I play. I think I'm being incredibly accurate, but very often I'm a sixteenth note early or a thirty-second note late—and I'm just trying to play *Frère Jacques* or something. Because we don't actually play in time.[10] I think to reduce it to this sort of organ-loft mentality is ultimately pedantry. A Hungarian musicologist, László Somfai, did some work on Bartók's recordings of his own piano works, works for which he notated every timing, every pedal mark, every slowing, and every metronome mark. He found that not a single performance by Bartók conforms to what he wrote.[11] If the composer doesn't do it, why should we?

To return to opera performance, you once said that you could conduct Verdi's comic opera Falstaff *but not his* Otello;[12] *but one of the big areas of*

9. It's relevant to McGegan's point that performers in the first third of our century overdotted routinely in most music—not just Baroque music, and not in obedience to theoretical exhortations—and that the overdotting was more pronounced in loud than in quiet passages (see Philip, *Early Recordings,* chap. 3, esp. p. 84, last paragraph, and p. 90, second paragraph).

10. The Swedish psychologists Ingmar Bengstsson and Alf Gabrielsson have done extensive studies that found that when classical musicians play rhythms in a 2:1 ratio (say, a quarter note and an eighth note), even though it *sounds* like two to one, it is never mathematically precise (it's usually less than 2:1). Their work is published in *Studies of Musical Performance,* ed. Johan Sundberg (Stockholm: Royal Swedish Academy, 1983), p. 58.

11. Though it's not the study McGegan refers to, Somfai's *Béla Bartók: Composition, Concepts, and Autograph Sources* (Berkeley, University of California Press, 1996), pp. 279–95, discusses Bartók's recordings and what they tell us about his performance style—and, for that matter, about the inadequacy of musical notation systems. Bartók's playing goes well beyond what he notated, and that includes the rhythms and even sometimes the notes; one could not determine from the notation what Bartók actually plays.

12. Eric Van Tassel, "An Interview with Nicholas McGegan," *Fanfare* 13 (January/February 1990), pp. 76–84; quote p. 83.

your Handelian repertoire has been his operas, which are in the vein of opera
seria—*does that contradict your first statement?*

Not really. I find Handel's operatic characters—not as titled figures, the king
of this and that, but as actual people—a lot more interesting than those in the
really bourgeois operas of the nineteenth century. Wagner is very bourgeois in
terms of his plots and characters. In *Tannhäuser* and *Dutchman* the women are
really suburban, these dreadful singing Hausfraus. They always have to have
the *House and Garden* virtues: they all cook and spin (and sing top C). And
the men, it seems to me, are perfectly fine to begin with, but they all have to
be redeemed in some ghastly way. It's a problem in Wagner that I don't find
interesting. There was a wonderful cartoon in the *New Yorker*, showing the
end of one of these Verdi or Wagner operas, with everyone lying dead on the
stage; two blasé people are sitting in a box, and one of them says to the other,
"You know, with a little early counseling, all of this could have been avoided."
You don't get that so much in earlier opera.

*A question often raised about these operas (though, admittedly, it has sub-
sided) was whether they held the stage. You've conducted them in the opera
house; what do you think?*

I would say that you can say the same about Bellini, or about any Rossini
opera seria. The problem is not whether it's Baroque music as opposed to *bel
canto*. I think there are a number of ways through which you can make them
work on the stage.[13]

First, as far as cuts in the text go, sometimes you can trim a little bit, but
where it becomes a mistake—which has often been made—is when you simply
trim the arias of the lesser characters. Usually, these characters are the ones
who make the plot flow. Handel's own cuts, too, can riddle the plot with *non
sequiturs*, but they were often made in desperation, sometimes because he did-
n't have a good singer for a role.

One thing I think is extremely important in these operas is to cast grandly
enough. When Handel did an opera he was casting for the best, the most famous—almost as you would cast a Broadway musical now. These people were
known offstage as well as on, so when that particular famous person walked
onstage all the audience would go "Oooh!" just as you would if Barbra
Streisand walked onstage.

Another thing is that the stagings were often spectacular. A lot of opera
houses now decide that if they do a Handel opera it's going to be their cheap
show of the season. It's only got a cast of five, no chorus, so let's just save all
around, shall we? But actually, those shows should be gaudy and expensive and
glorious.

Another thing that I think is the death of Handelian opera is the orchestra

---

13. McGegan goes into this topic in more detail in his article "Movements by Candlelight," *Musical Times* 135 (April 1994), pp. 210–15.

pit, which is a nineteenth-century invention. In the eighteenth century the orchestra was at the same level as the stalls,[14] or maybe a foot lower, and the most important players faced the stage, so that they could accompany the singers directly just as they would in a concert. That's why you have these fantastic oboe and violin obbligatos: they are actually making music with the singers, without the silly medium of the conductor doing semaphore to relay between two people who can't hear or see each other.

Another thing is that you have to be very careful about doing these operas in large opera houses—theatres where you can't see the whites of the singer's eyes. Handel's opera house held about 1200 people, and we're very short of such houses. To get a feeling of intimacy, a sense of being very close to the scene, is very important for most of these operas. Of course, doing these operas in a small house isn't a terribly good idea financially, because the tickets have to cost too much—though in Europe there's generally government subsidy.

Another issue regarding Baroque opera performance: Paul Griffiths recently commented[15] *that Baroque staging and gestures seem stilted to modern audiences, even though Baroque performance practice in music has proven quite appealing.*

I don't know that any of us have seen Baroque gestures really done. We've seen some attempts, but if you don't do them under candlelight there's no point in doing them. Once you start raising all the light, the gestures remind you of that Monty Python skit of doing *Wuthering Heights* by semaphore. The only reason Baroque actors used those gestures was so they could get across what they wanted to get across in the dark. A gesture is of a certain size in order to be seen, and if you can see everything so clearly that all you need to do is raise your finger a little, then everything else is overacting. I think the only way in which Baroque gesture works is if it's part of a total package. The proportions of the stage, the sets, the costumes *and* the lighting all have to be right.

Another issue: Handel would revise a part, you've observed, to suit whatever particular singer he had on hand. Would you?

No. But you can put a part up or down with ornamentation—you can fudge it a little in that way. I think it's better to try and find somebody whom the part does fit, since so often the roles are dramatically somewhat generic.[16] Funnily enough, the heroes in these operas are usually the most boring people; it's

14. The American term is "orchestra seats."

15. *New Yorker,* 5 July 1993, p. 98.

16. Charles Rosen, in *The Romantic Generation* (Cambridge, Mass.: Harvard University Press), p. 605, writes that in eighteenth-century *opera seria* "the psychology, if that is the word for it, is . . . simplistic, even primitive: there were rarely any characters at all in *opera seria,* only a succession of dramatic situations which allowed the singers to express a series of emotional states."

the villains who have all the fun, and they're usually basses or baritones. The heroes are often not heroic. The lead castrato role, let's say, is a Roman emperor; but he doesn't do anything except moon about the stage in love. It's the women and, as we've said, the lesser characters who do everything in the drama.

Regarding another genre you've worked in, the English-language oratorios, one issue might be period pronunciation. Was Handel writing for a specific English pronunciation we no longer have?

He was: there are certain words that have changed. If I were to speak eighteenth-century English I could say that I am part of the audience at a dray-ma, and listen to air-ias (instead of arias) and sit in the bal-CO-ney. One of the American critics made a big stink because when Philharmonia Baroque did *Judas Maccabeus* one of the singers didn't make "hands" and "commands" a full rhyme, but in eighteenth-century England they weren't.

On the other hand, there hasn't been a standard English pronunciation until this century. If you had a regional accent you kept it. And beyond that, from what one can tell half of the oratorios, although they're written in English, were not sung entirely in it. At least six arias in *L'Allegro* were sung in Italian, because the singers were Italian. And even when the Italians sang in English, one critic said, "I thought they were singing in Hebrew." The famous story is about the revival of *Esther*, where an Italian singer made "I come, my queen, to chaste delights" sound like "I comb my queen to chase the lice." And there were Italian singers in almost all the oratorios right up to Handel's death.

It's a nice argument against the idea of authenticity being "re-creating just what they did at a performance in the composer's time."

Yes. When we did *Judas Maccabeus* we got roundly criticized because Guy de Mey's very good English was not absolutely perfect. I wrote to the critic and pointed out that most of Handel's singers were foreigners.

This question of authentic re-creation becomes, in the end, meaningless. In *Ariodante*, which I've just edited, there's an aria for the bass where Handel removed quite a lot of the coloratura for the first performance, and it's in this simplified version that the piece is now printed. If you do the simple version you're doing what Handel did in his lifetime, so it has a certain cachet of authenticity. But the only reason it exists is because that particular bass couldn't sing the more difficult original version. At Göttingen we have a singer who can sing the more difficult version, and we prefer that version, so it's what we're going to use. The great thing about performance is that you can never be right for all time, the way a scientist can be right about the earth going around the sun. These things are much more fluid. In the arts, one thing you can never be is absolutely right.

SELECTED DISCOGRAPHY

Nicholas McGegan's catalogue of Handel operas on Harmonia Mundi has grown at the rate of one per year. As I write, the best of the 3-CD sets are the most recent: the *Gramophone* Award-winning *Ariodante* (HMU 907146.48), which "may be the crown jewel of the series" according to David Johnson, who praises the "generosity, verve, and elegance" of McGegan's conducting;[17] *Giustino* (HMU 907130.2), in which, Johnson wrote earlier, "McGegan surpasses himself";[18] and the previous entry, *Radamisto*, which Stanley Sadie called "[McGegan's] best by far. . . . as compelling as any Handel opera performance I have heard"[19] (HMU 907111.3). Sadie, an expert on Handel opera performance, has not always admired McGegan's work in this repertory: writing of the 1990 *Floridante* (Hungaraton HCD 31304.6) Sadie calls it lively but emotionally detached and musically mannered, with "persistent and ultimately irritating little swells and squeezes and . . . coldly abrupt phrase endings."[20] But Sadie has recently called McGegan's *ariodante* "the best Handel opera recording we have yet had."[21]

Like the middle-class London audiences of the 1740s, I prefer the oratorios to even the best of the operas. Thus my favorite McGegan Handel recording is of the late masterpiece *Theodora* (HM 970060.62, 3 CDs); Colin Tilney calls the disc "impossible to recommend too highly."[22] McGegan's performance of the early cantata *Clori, Tirsi e Fileno* (HM 907045) is, in Tilney's words, a "lesson in style and joie de vivre." As for *Messiah* (HMU 40 7050.52, 3 CDs) McGegan's recording has the distinction of including almost all the variants from Handel's many versions, so that you can program any (or your own) version. The performance itself has proved controversial: *Classic CD* named it the best *Messiah* on CD, but Nicholas Anderson (among others) is disappointed by its "undercharacterization of Handel's music"; he misses "Handelian grandeur and nobility."[23]

McGegan has recorded a good deal of other Baroque music, including Corelli and Vivaldi. Among the best-received have been his CDs with a chamber ensemble, the Arcadian Academy, consisting of McGegan and three members of Philharmonia Baroque—Elizabeth Blumenstock, David Tayler, and Lisa Weiss. Their recordings of Matteis and especially of Uccellini (*La Bergamasca*, HM 907094) are exquisite examples of Italian Baroque chamber music. Of Philharmonia Baroque's recording of instrumental suites from Rameau's *Naïs* and *Le temple de la gloire* (HM 901418), Jan Smaczny writes that "The first

17. Johnson, *Fanfare* 19 (May/June 1996), pp. 163–64.
18. Johnson, *Fanfare* 19 (January/February 1996), p. 217.
19. Sadie, *Gramophone* 72 (June 1994), p. 109.
20. Sadie, *Gramophone* 70 (January 1993), p. 61.
21. Sadie, *Gramophone* 74 (November 1996), p. 54
22. Tilney, "Theodora: Two Views," *Historical Performance* 5 (Fall 1992), p. 91.
23. Anderson, *Gramophone* 69 (October 1991), p. 162.

forty seconds of the overture to *Naïs* should be enough to persuade anyone that they are listening to perhaps the most thrilling sounds of the late Baroque."[24]

FOR FURTHER READING

Handel had a strong personality but, as Donald Burrows points out, we have "surprisingly little firm evidence about his private life and many aspects of his personality."[25] Nonetheless, many fine biographies exist; the best so far is Burrows's *Handel* (London: Macmillan, and New York: Schirmer, 1994). Christopher Hogwood's *Handel* (London: Thames and Hudson, 1984) is also good, and Otto Erich Deutsch's *Handel: A Documentary Biography* (London: A. and C. Black, 1955) is a still a valuable resource (as Burrows notes, we do have detailed records of Handel's public and professional life). For a shorter biography, the *New Grove Handel* by Winton Dean (New York: Norton, 1983) is one of the most appealing in that series.

As for discussions of the music, Winton Dean's *Handel's Dramatic Oratorios and Masques* (Oxford University Press, 1959) and, with John Merrill Knapp, *Handel's Operas, 1704–1726* (Oxford University Press, 1987) are classics of scholarship and style. Those who want to read more about Handel's own surviving ornamentation might consult Dean's edition, *G. F. Handel: Three Ornamented Arias* (Oxford University Press, 1976), and his 1970 essay "Vocal Embellishment in a Handel Aria," reprinted in his *Essays on Opera* (Oxford University Press, 1990).

---

24. Smaczny, *BBC Music Magazine* (December 1995), p. 69.
25. Burrows, *Handel* (London: Macmillan, and New York: Schirmer, 1994), p. ix.

14

At Home with the Idiom

William Christie on the
French Baroque

A *Gramophone* critic, praising a French Baroque opera recording, noted that it was "a distinct improvement on what has been [the French conductor's] rather dodgy past." But how much of the improvement, he asked, was due to the "standards of technical and dramatic excellence which William Christie has helped to establish?" He pointed out that the singers, and for that matter those in the other French Baroque recordings under review, had all been trained by Christie, an American harpsichordist/conductor. "Do we have then," he asked, "a French school of performance or a Christie one?"[1]

The answer could be, both. *The New York Times* says that Christie is "chiefly responsible for reviving interest in French Baroque music,"[2] and few would disagree. After studying the harpsichord with Ralph Kirkpatrick at Yale, Christie moved to Paris in 1971; there he immersed himself in the available documentation on French Baroque music, culture, and performance practices. From this he extracted not only a wealth of details but also the essence of a living style. He has managed to share that style with a pool of young musicians, many of them his students at the Paris Conservatoire, where he was the first American ever to be given a professorship. His group, Les Arts Florissants (named after a Charpentier opera), and his protégés, such as Christophe Rousset, have been at the core of the recent explosion of activity in the French early-

1. Lindsay Kemp, "Quarterly Retrospect," *Gramophone* 71 (September 1993), p. 33.
2. Alan Riding, "Where Is the Glory That Was France?" *The New York Times*, Sunday Arts and Leisure section, 14 January 1996, p. 1.

music world—an explosion that led one critic to call Paris the current "hotbed" of early music.[3]

It may seem puzzling that France, the country that gave us the word "chauvinism," would adopt an American to teach it how to sing in the true French Baroque style. It's not as uncharacteristic as it seems, though. The French arts scene, even at its most *florissant*, has usually welcomed foreign talent (think of Chopin or Picasso). It may be especially welcoming in its less-than-flourishing present state: many people believe that what's exciting in the arts in France right now is, for the most part, the work of immigrants like Christie.[4] Whether that's true or not, France's reception of Christie is poetically just: Jean-Baptiste Lully, the father of the French Baroque style—a style that self-consciously distanced itself from the Italian style—was himself Italian.

Christie has become welcome enough to have been awarded, in 1993, the rosette of a Chevalier de la Légion d'Honneur (the award led the immigration office to at last grant him a permanent visa). The award honored his resurrection of French Baroque opera, an achievement that Richard Taruskin calls "perhaps the finest" of the early-music movement, the only one to which even Taruskin "would willingly grant the freedom of the term" restoration.[5] To accomplish that restoration, Christie's musical and theatrical gifts, though exceptional, weren't enough; they had to be allied to his unwavering quest for an ensemble that all but breathes in a unified, idiomatic style—precisely what had been hardest for performers to attain in French Baroque music.

Some musicians, such as the pianist András Schiff, complain about "so-called stars of early music . . . [who go] through the literature of music at the speed of a Concorde, maybe performing it once: this week it's Mozart, next week, Bach, then it's all of Monteverdi. In a couple of years they cover the field from William Byrd to Stockhausen. Nobody can digest that much music."[6] The critique may be valid in certain cases—you can judge that for yourself—but the majority of the artists interviewed in this book are specialists. Christie, for one, rarely ventures beyond the seventeenth and eighteenth centuries, and his focus has most often been French. In his interview (conducted by trans-Atlantic telephone) he argues that specialization is a path to musical freedom.

Many people, including yourself, have said that the French Baroque is the most difficult style for modern performers to master. Can you discuss why?

I think it's partly because you must have a linguistic approach to French Baroque music. The basis of all French musical art is declamation; you have to

---

3. Tim Pfaff, "Les Talens Lyriques: The Next Generation," *Strings* 9 (March/April 1995), p. 74.

4. Riding, "Where Is the Glory?"

5. Richard Taruskin, "Of Kings and Divas," *The New Republic,* 13 December 1993, p. 40.

6. Quoted by Harriet Smith, "Far from the Madding Crowd," *Gramophone* 72 (October 1994), pp. 22–23.

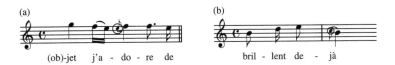

EXAMPLE 1   (a) A *port de voix* is a short added note that *ascends* to the main note; it usually repeats the preceding note. This *port de voix* (circled) moves from unstressed to stressed syllable. (b) A *coulé* is a short added note that *descends* to the main note, here seen moving from unstressed to stressed syllable, with *coulé* to the latter. From Rameau's *L'impatience*, realized by Mary Cyr, "Performing Rameau's Cantatas," *Early Music* 11 (October 1983), p. 485.

understand French declamation and declamatory patterns to understand, for example, all the baggage of French Baroque ornamentation, which is grammatical to a large degree.

This has to do with what the French call syllabic quantity, which essentially is a way of giving stress to certain syllables and not to others. Now, linguistic patterns that stress specific syllables can conflict with musical patterns that stress specific notes. You can have a conflict sometimes between the text and a musical line, where the musical value of the note is not the real value of the syllable upon which it's placed, especially in strophic music. The trill, *port de voix*, *coulé*, and other ornaments, which one finds in all Baroque music, in France become essentially ways of lengthening syllables to resolve such conflicts. Used this way, the ornaments and so on give the listener a better comprehension of the text. One might sum up their use in the following recipes. When leaving an unstressed syllable to go to a stressed syllable in a rising melodic line, one uses the *port de voix* in one of its various manifestations (Ex. 1 [a]). When leaving an unstressed syllable to go to a stressed syllable in a descending melodic line, the musician can use the *coulé* (Ex. 1 [b]) or the *port de voix* on the stressed syllable.

Why would stressing certain syllables lead to better comprehension of the text? I had understood that in French, stress and vowel length are not usually fixed factors in a word, and don't help one pick out the word in a sentence.

That's true in modern French, but in seventeenth- or eighteenth-century French, stress was an extraordinarily important factor. (These patterns generally changed about the end of the nineteenth century.) You can't have syllable emphasis without syllable quantity; and for that, vowel length is critical.

Syllabic quantity is important not only in the matter of ornamentation. Phrasing, too, becomes a question of long or short syllables, and non-legato treatment of music also arises out of this. These are difficult questions for people to solve, because essentially what you're doing is putting something into the music that isn't in the score. There's a lot you must put into French music, which is not the case in Bach or some other composers, where the music seems to be more indestructible—which of course is why their music is played more.

You've praised Beecham's Messiah, *Horowitz's Scarlatti, and Casals's and Landowska's Bach, saying that while they weren't historically informed, they had a grandeur and eloquence missing from much modern historical performance.*[7]

Yes. Incidentally, Beecham's 1938 recording of *Die Zauberflöte* is one of the best things in the world.

But what you were saying earlier brings up a question: is historical information more important for French music than for Bach and Scarlatti? Would Beecham have a harder time in Rameau?

One doesn't know, of course. But as for the first question, yes, I'd have to agree. French music dies when one doesn't have the tools to bring it back to life. As I said, to bring it back to life is largely a literary consideration, in many ways, having to do with declamatory and linguistic questions.

That raises another question: how do these linguistic concerns apply to French instrumental music?

To such an extent that A. Phérotée de la Croix said that all dances have texts—imaginary texts in some cases. Any allemande, any courante, any dance form (with a very few exceptions) is essentially a dance with specific numbers of syllables per line; one could say that instrumental dances are always accompanied by imaginary texts.[8] Indeed, all good instrumental styles have the voice as their model.

Almost everything has a verbal basis. We also have a kind of paradox, though, which singers don't like to hear: while instruments are supposed to imitate voices, we've got to recognize the fact that in France, Italy, and Germany and elsewhere, voices were sometimes asked to behave like instruments. A Mondonville psalm for harpsichord obbligato, *ad libitum* violin, and voice requires the voice to behave in a completely instrumental fashion. This is true of some Rameau and Handel arias as well, and Bach cantatas, of course. That's just something that one has to do in Baroque vocal music. There is a kind of extraordinary mimicry between voices and instruments. Voices have to identify themselves with the instrumental context to make coherent music.

Why do I like certain voices? Because they essentially know how to sing

---

7. Jean-François Labie, *William Christie: Sonate-Baroque* (Aix-en-Provence: Alinéa, 1989), pp. 86, 91. This work features extensive interviews.

8. A valuable discussion of this point can be found in Patricia Ranum's "Audible Rhetoric and Mute Rhetoric: The 17th-century French Sarabande," *Early Music* 14 (February 1986), pp. 22–39.

with a harpsichord or how to sing with a Baroque oboe or violin. It's a question of technique, it's a question of writing, and it's a question of *sound*—of mimicry. That's very important. It's true, also, that instrumental schools were bound and beholden to obey the same principles that singers were. An interesting thing is that the prototypes of instrumental ornamentation, as codified by people like d'Anglebert in the 1680s and 1690s, are vocal prototypes. We're aware that singers were already using these. There's an extraordinary sharing of ornamentation, vocal and instrumental.

The declamation, and emphasis on words, I understand reflected the prestige of French theater—Italy had nothing to compare with it; and to the seventeenth-century French, the Italian opera seemed weak from a dramatic standpoint. Is that correct?

There are all kinds of styles. You're talking about the *tragédie lyrique*, of course, and there that's true. But not everything in France comes out of Corneille and Racine. The big stuff does, of course, the big vocal forms and, by a kind of inevitable extension, the recitative—which was already being declaimed in the theatre in a very sung style. Lully essentially developed something that was already happening amongst the actors, the desire to burst forth into song.

He is said to have sat with the great actress Champmeslé and studied her declamation of Racine; Racine apparently wrote down pitches for her to use in declaiming.[9]

That was a constant of French declamation up until the end of the nineteenth century—there was something very sing-song in the way they declaimed. One hears it in the Sarah Bernhardt wax cylinders from the beginning of our century. The declamation patterns would be immensely complicated to graph, because they're so sing-song. And the French have had a kind of love-hate relationship with this. It was already criticized and defended back in the eighteenth century. This kind of grandiloquent way of declaiming is something I can sometimes hear nowadays in a bastardized form; one can still hear some echoes of it in modern-day public speaking. It's dying out now, but the older clergymen that I knew twenty-five years ago still had it.

An obvious corollary: the style of theatrical delivery was not naturalistic.

Well, it imitates nature: "nature" at the end of the seventeenth and early eighteenth century was very different from that word today. It meant, essentially, truth in terms of emotions and feeling. It's a way of heightening the pleasure by exaggerating speech and gesture.

---

9. See Lois Rosow, "French Baroque Recitative as an Expression of Tragic Declamation," *Early Music* 11 (October 1983), pp. 468–79.

When you prepared Médée, *you began rehearsals by having the singers first recite the text according to the rules of seventeenth-century French tragedy.*

Yes, though I can't claim that we're doing exactly what was done then. There are immense holes in what I do. I'm not seeking authenticity *per se.* For example, I don't really insist on historical pronunciation, though I recognize that eventually I have to get around to doing so. There are several reasons I don't insist, but one is that I've burned my fingers with it with French audiences many times; they simply balk at it.

It's like doing Shakespeare with Elizabethan pronunciation for English audiences.

Exactly, and people have tried that, you know.

With unfortunate results.

It goes back to what began all this: declamation and comprehensibility. I want to go further in terms of pronunciation, and I will. It is only a question of time.

You have used historical pronunciation, though, with Latin works by Charpentier and other French composers, using the seventeenth-century French style of Latin rather than the Italian style prevalent today. Can you say anything about how that benefits these works?

Pronouncing Latin texts as a Frenchman would have causes the singers to place their voices differently. This means you have a large number of half-closed vowels, which of course is not the case in Italian Latin, and they give a very particular kind of color to the piece, which you can use.

Let me ask you about the controversy over one very characteristic aspect of French Baroque music, notes inégales; *do you have a general statement about them in French music?*[10]

I'd say that if you don't subscribe to *notes inégales* you might as well stay away from French music. Anybody who has any notion of spoken French, even uncultivated twentieth-century spoken French, understands that one never pronounces a chain of monosyllables with equal insistence. Just listening in a student cafeteria, you understand very clearly why *inégales* exist. It's an extension of speech.

David Fuller questions the idea that notes inégales *are based on French*

---

10. As was observed in the Anner Bylsma chapter, in the French convention of *notes inégales* certain pairs of notes that were written at equal lengths were played unequally—more often long-short, long-short, but sometimes short-long, short-long.

declamation; he argues that they were mainly sung to diminutions on long syl-lables.[11]

I'd say that I hear inequality all around me, in modern-day French speech. I have a feeling it did come out of French declamation patterns, very much so.

Christophe Rousset says that applying notes inégales *to a sung text in French can have the same effect that you described with ornaments, that of making the text easy for listeners to comprehend.*[12] *And so it would be in-evitable in instrumental music with imagined text. What are your views on the awareness of* notes inégales *in Germany and England?*[13]

I can't imagine someone like Henry Purcell shying away from the practice. I mean, he's the most consummate Frenchman I know—the parallels, the bor-rowings, it's amazing. And all you have to do is listen to some of the eigh-

11. Fuller, "The Performer as Composer," in *Performance Practice: Music after 1600,* ed. H. M. Brown and S. Sadie (London: Macmillan, 1989, and New York: Norton, 1990), pp. 145–46.

12. In Bernard D. Sherman, "Finding One's Own Recipes," *Piano and Keyboard,* May/June 1994, p. 26.

13. The idea that Baroque musicians outside France generally did not know about such French rhythmic alterations as *notes inégales* and overdotting (sharpening dotted rhythms) was argued by the musicologist Frederick Neumann (see his *Essays on Performance Practice* (Ann Arbor, Mich.: UMI Press, 1982). Neumann's view that the notes should be played as written put him at odds with most early-music performers and scholars. A book by his student Stephen Hefling, *Rhythmic Alteration in Seventeenth- and Eighteenth-Century Music: Notes Inégales and Overdotting* (New York: Schirmer, 1993), demonstrates beyond a reasonable doubt that Neumann was largely mistaken about this issue. (See also the review of Hefling's book in the Fall 1994 issue of *Performance Practice Review* 7, pp. 120–32, by Neumann's principal critic, David Fuller.) Hefling summarizes his findings on *notes inégales* thus: "The available evidence suggests that French *inégalité* was certainly known to musicians in several areas of Germany as well as in the Netherlands and England, and also in Modena. . . . The custom was transmitted by Frenchmen who went abroad, as well as by visitors to Paris who subsequently imitated French style, and also by French musical writings. . . . Very likely in-equality was applied to music of French origin and to works that obviously emulated French style; to what degree [it was] extended to pieces less closely related to French models remains uncertain. . . . [However,] there seems to be no evidence that anyone outside France assumed inequality as a matter of course, with the exception of Quantz and possibly some of his col-leagues in Dresden and Berlin" (pp. 60–61).

In music by Bach in the French style, Hefling shows, overdotting and *notes inégales* were probably applied (see pp. 41–50, and chaps. 5 and 6, esp. pp. 98–100). In Purcell (in whose music Christie has been criticized for using *inégalité*), Hefling seems to find the evidence less clear; he argues that Purcell was probably familiar with inequality in French music, but that when Purcell wanted it used he may have indicated it with dotting (pp. 51–55).

While Neumann's positions on these issues have not held up under careful scrutiny, they did a service by forcing scholars to undertake that scrutiny. Moreover, his thorough critiques elsewhere have led to the relaxing of some early-music orthodoxies about ornamentation, such as beginning every ornament on the beat—as he showed, original practice was not so rigid. I would also mention that Neumann was not desk-bound; he was a fine violinist, and was mo-tivated by practical experience of playing early music, as well as by his distaste for much of the "early-music" style.

teenth-century English barrel organs that are still around to understand that the quirky rhythms—*inégales*, jerky lombards, scotch snaps—were very much present there.

As for Germany, again you have a predominant aesthetic. Good taste, *la mode*, was of course a kind of European disease in the eighteenth century, and the most important capital of *la mode* was France. If in fact this taste traveled, because French people did travel and were asked to travel to show people how to do these things, then everywhere—in St. Petersburg, in remote parts of Germany, in Edinburgh—you're going to find people doing things that were done in France in 1710 or 1730. It seems to me blatant: we have French musicians in Germany; we have German musicians who have spent time in France.[14] We have immense amounts of music being sent from France to Germany or being copied in Germany—Bach copying de Grigny, for example, or Couperin. It seems to me that it would be very difficult to avoid the essential features of French style. Ornaments we know they did—no one quibbles about that. The French ornament tables we know were in Germany from very early on. If that's the case, it seems to me that one would also have performance-practice ingredients like *notes inégales*, especially coming into forms that were essentially French to begin with. It's perverse to buy a bit of a product and not the whole product. But of course this is grist for the musicologists, some of whom have no more important things to talk about, and some of whom have no practical musical ideas.

I also want to bring up the distinction between the dominant style of Baroque singing, which was the Italian, and the French style. Although the Italians at the time of early Monteverdi spoke a lot about text, by the 1670s, when French opera gets going, the Italians are no longer paying that much attention to it.

Well, that happens to French opera in the 1750 and 60s: you lose text to melody and technique. I like the French Baroque immensely in the earlier periods, the 1670s and 80s, because there is that kind of equilibrium between text and music, and the fluidity that you find amongst the Italians fifty years before.

14. According to his obituary, the young Bach's excursion to Hamburg gave him the opportunity to "acquire a thorough grounding in the French taste," by allowing "frequent hearings of a then famous band maintained by the Duke of Celle, consisting mainly of Frenchmen" (*The Bach Reader*, ed. Hans T. David and Arthur Mendel [New York: Norton, 1966], p. 217). Peter Williams points out the significance of this by contrasting it to Bach's experience of Italian music. Exposure to Vivaldi scores influenced Bach's compositional style profoundly, but his music in this style often cannot be played at the rapid speeds for which Italian virtuosi were known, presumably because Bach didn't know about those speeds. See Williams's *The Organ Music of J. S. Bach*, vol. 3 (Cambridge University Press, 1984), pp. 91–102, for a subtle discussion of what Bach learned from France and Italy.

But would differences between the styles of singing, though—such as the use of legato in Italy but not in France—create a problem for modern singers, since most Baroque singers today are essentially singing in an Italianate style?

No, I think the basis for any kind of singing really is Italian. That was recognized even by the French. Rameau said if you want to have a good vocal education, go off to Italy. He was very much in favor of that. And you find the French nodding their heads towards the Italians, in terms of technique at any rate, from the beginning. It's funny that the French, whose singing style essentially goes counter to all that the bel canto aesthetic wants—legato, long-line singing—insist that you have to learn Italian style before you learn their style. To make coherent sense of the French music, of course, you have to do something different from the Italian; but just as you have to learn how to walk before you can run, you have to learn essentially how to sing legato before you can sing non-legato phrases.

The great error is that you get enthusiastic people who want to sing in the French style and have no vocal technique whatsoever, and that's been a problem in the States and in other places as well. I've had far more success with people in French music when they have a first-rate base in classical Italianate techniques—the support, the complete muscular freedom, everything that *bel canto* wants, essentially.

In the Labie book you expressed the thought that singing and dance were two areas of early-music style that had trailed behind.[15]

I think there's been improvement since then. Ten years ago, when that book was written, it was painfully obvious that the Baroque violin school, or flute playing or harpsichord playing or theorbo playing, had come a longer way than singing or dance. Now I have thirty young student singers working with me all over Europe, and they do things instinctively that professionals ten years ago wouldn't do. For example, in ornamentation they know exactly what I'm talking about and how to do it, in a way that already suggests a specialty approach. So that's enjoyable.

You mentioned back then that you felt the English singing style was vigorous and accurate but sometimes lacked the necessary passion for Baroque music.

I'm not wildly fond of a lot that I think is going on in England. I remember talking to one of the foremost early-music leaders from London, and we talked about apathy and routine, and these seem to be a kind of disease that's happening right now in London. Along with it comes a kind of lackluster way of dealing with style.

15. Labie, *William Christie*, p. 72.

Is it the training or the plethora of recording gigs? Is it because the same people play all the recording sessions?

Perhaps. Many no longer think about what they're doing, essentially. If it's in tune and it's together, that essentially satisfies what they're after. They don't take risks.

As for the training, though, I think the vocal education in England is fabulous, which is why oftentimes I'd rather use English singers—especially those coming out of the non-specialty schools, that is, coming from the mainstream repertories at, say, Guildhall or Northern College, where voices are given a good technique. There are some very fine countertenor voices from England; someone like Michael Chance is exquisite.

What I was harping on in the Labie book was this specialty "early-music" voice, which still sometimes gets my dander up. As it did back in the States too—people who somehow insist on squeaky, small, non-vibrato voices as the key to correct early-music style.

What is your view on vibrato in eighteenth-century singing?

My view is simply physiological. If you want to have a voice and a decent technique, and you want to keep your voice, you have to recognize that vibrato is an essential part of vocal production. You can't subscribe to good *bel canto* technique, you can't be a *bel canto* singer without vibrato. With a column of air with good breath support and no muscular tension—if it's free and easy—you are going to vibrate the two vocal cords. Aside from stentorian high-decibel *verismo* stuff, which is part of the twentieth century—the overblown American-monster style of singing where you blow your guts out—with the exception of that, sensitive singers of any kind of music have to know how to use the vibrato. Vibrato is more important in singing a Handel portamento aria, or Mozart, than perhaps in French music. But to say that one doesn't vibrate in French music is perfect nonsense.

One hardly talked about vibrato in the eighteenth century. You get occasional references: Rousseau[16] says that voices without *oscillations* can be just as pretty as ones that had them, which means of course that people were using vibrato. But it's very simple to fulfill all the requirements—conjunct-note singing, close-interval singing, obeying certain instrumental principles of vibrato and non-vibrato—if you are indeed a singer with vibrato. You just have to know when to turn it off or when to use less of it. If one is beginning a trill, since the trill itself is the beating of two notes, you want to make sure that the voice, if it is using vibrato, is using less of it. The key concepts are dissonance and good tuning, which are crucial parts of seventeenth- and eighteenth-century singing; these are things that require attention to vibrato. But to say that vibrato can't be used at all is nonsense.

---

16. Jean-Jacques Rousseau, *Dictionnaire de musique* (Paris, 1768), "Voix," pp. 541–42.

Was it used as something ornamental, to heighten or lessen, or as something constant?

Vibrato can be used as something constant, with non-vibrato being used as an ornamental feature. Or we can say—as instrumental schools did—that vibrato itself is an ornament, to be used, more of it or less of it, as an ornament.

Your work with Les Arts Florissants brings up the issue of specialization. David Fuller writes: "One does occasionally hear today what seem to informed ears to be fine, stylish idiomatic performances of this music, and the secret seems to be specialization . . . by steeping oneself in one repertory and all that surrounds it—cultural background, organology, the dance, matters of diction, prosody and gesture, physical surroundings, and above all large amounts of music in a narrow range of styles— . . . one discovers that features which could not be reconstructed on the basis of any documents are somehow shaped by the pressure of everything else that is right about the performance."[17] Do you have any view on this?

Yes, I talk about specialization a great deal. I use the word "specialization" far more than the word "authenticity," which I hate. I'm very specialized in my own way. I may conduct a *Missa Solemnis* or a *Zauberflöte*, but even then I feel very secure about all the components. I feel most at ease when I'm in a context, and that context has to do with specialization. For people at the end of the twentieth century who are dealing with music that's three centuries old, total immersion is very important. I've been with French style for a long time, and most of the pupils I work with are in this field because they love French music. They're not doing it because it's fashionable now, or because it's a good idea to do it; it's something they actively do themselves, and this you have to do. They probably can talk a great deal about what was going on elsewhere in the culture of France: they have notions of painting, sculpture, literature, history—all of these things are very important.

A case in point: I heard a production not too long ago of seventeenth-century French music. The cast was a motley crew that didn't have much style, but the biggest problem was a German orchestra that essentially had no notion whatsoever of playing in the French style. In many places, because the orchestra seemingly had no regard for the fact that they were playing texted music, it became unbearable to listen to.

Another thing you've done is emphasize ensemble, not famous divas or divos; you've had great interest in stylistic homogeneity.

Well, the greatest sin we're experiencing now, in a lot of new groups, is that they seem to think that with a big orchestra and fancy soloists you can

---

17. David Fuller, "Ornamentation," in *Companion to Baroque Music*, ed. Julie Ann Sadie (London: Dent, 1990, and New York, Schirmer: 1991), p. 433.

whip into shape Rameau's *Hippolyte et Aricie,* or give a convincing performance of a Charpentier/Molière, or do a marvelous Monteverdi *Poppea.* What's sadly lacking is the idea that you need homogeneity of style. It's so obvious when you hear any kind of group where people were doing just that. Just take a look at jazz of the 1930s or 40s or 50s: that's a real specialist medium. The people who created it knew only how to do that one style, but they did it instinctively, reflexively, with an extraordinary sense of ensemble. That always amazes me when I listen to old jazz recordings or to old tango people in Buenos Aires—this fabulous, extraordinary sense of fitting with each other, making a style which is so coherent, so easy, so effortless. The difference is enormous between that and what I heard a couple of months ago in a performance of *Hippolyte et Aricie* presented by a young colleague of mine, where there was no attempt to coordinate the main soloists in any stylistic sense, and there were wild differences of vocal style and technique. It doesn't work, because essentially it's as if the opera had become polyglot, as if people were singing in different languages. It's that blatant. And I said years and years ago that probably the most wonderful element of French art is its extraordinary unifying rhetoric and style. Given wildly differing interpretations, people were unified and linked by so many common things—rhetorical things, essentially. That's something I try to give off to the ensemble. And of course it's easier to do with younger people than it is with older people. If you have people who have wonderfully individual personalities, but who are united by a common aesthetic, it's far more interesting than the contrary.

I suppose one of the results of specialization may be the element of the improvisatory, which mastery would allow.

Of course, things become spontaneous and reflexive—two very important words, I think. And this imparts a sort of easy sense that one has with the score, especially scores that are incomplete—with these it becomes very apparent. Being at home with the idiom allows you to be fluid with it.

That's really the answer to the complaint that they couldn't have overdotted and stayed together.

Musicology of that type is living in the office, in the sense of looking at the score and not living with the reality of the score played. And one can open one's eyes so easily just by listening to ensembles that have been playing together for a long time. I can ask a choir with fifteen sopranos to sing very complex ornaments and they do it perfectly well. To get an entire orchestra playing *notes inégales* in a Rameau dance is not difficult.

The degree of documentation for French Baroque music is much greater than for Bach or Monteverdi. Could you summarize some of the areas in which this applies?

That would take hours to describe. But it's true that we have immense quantities of treatises from the 1680s through the entire eighteenth century about how to play and sing, and how not to play and sing. Some of these are quarrels, silly texts in which someone takes somebody else to task. Some are dreadfully simple, because they're written for provincial amateurs, who want to know how to do it as they do it in Paris; you get these sort of plain lessons. But some are much better. I have certain bibles I rely on constantly, such as the *Remarques curieuses sur l'art de bien chanter* by Bacilly (in 1681): a kind of primer for voices, and I use other texts to round it out. The resources are more complete, for example, than in Italy—absolutely. There are German treatises on the Italian style in the mid-seventeenth century, which are good but much less complete, of course, than one finds among the French.

There are German treatises about French style, too, of course, such as Muffat's. I want to ask you about the correspondence between Graun and Telemann (a lifelong student of French music) about French style.

It's a good text, because it's one of the rare documents where you really get a few glimpses of what staging was probably all about. Also there's the business about the quarter-tone and the portamento slides.

I was interested in its bit about how the frequent changes of time signature in the recitatives were necessary for putting the stresses on the strong syllables.[18] The issue I want to raise has to do with how much additional tempo flexibility is called for in recitatives, over and above notated signature changes; at least one musicologist has called for limiting that flexibility.

You can't sing recitative without an extraordinarily free sense of tempo. There is no fixed movement. The first thing I tell singers is that they've got to read what's on the page without confusing rhythmic precision as written by the composer with rhythmic freedom in terms of the overall line. You can't sing drama if everything is being beaten in a metronomic way. And that's a problem with a number of conductors today who—after we've spent years trying to get away from the conductor's tyranny—are being tyrannical with the Baroque groups. People are conducting three hours of recitative. Yet there are no indications whatsoever that the *batteur de mesure* beat time in the recitative; he was there to maintain order in the ballet and the large choruses. Remember also the division they had, the breakdown of the orchestra into a small improvising orchestra, the *petit choeur,* within the very large one, the *grand choeur.* That's essentially to allow the *petit choeur* to be supple and to hug on to the continuo during the recitative—without the intervention of a third party. Of course there would be immense tempo fluctuation.

Goldoni, on his first visit to the Académie Royale de Musique in Paris, was

18. Lois Rosow, "French Baroque Recitative," p. 468.

unable to tell when the arias were, and thought it was all recitatives—I'm won-
dering about tempo flexibility in arias.[19]

I think that because in the arias, the bass lines are far more organized, and
there is some element of melodic and rhythmic regularity, you are probably
going to have more regular rhythm. Goldoni had a problem because it is very
different from Italian music. Though arias could be long, an aria could often
be just five or six measures of more organized music and text—refrain texts or
moralizing texts—and might be over before Goldoni could notice it.

Along with material about orchestra size, bowing, tempo, and layout, don't
the treatises also discuss choreography, hand gestures, and so on?

I don't think we know much about hand gestures in France in 1670; we
know a lot more about hand gestures in Germany in 1780. That's a field that
is painful for me right now, I must say, the whole idea of gestural art, especially when it comes to the late-seventeenth-century style. We have a few good
iconographical references, and certainly the old adage about a good statue or
painting can be taken to heart. But as for how people *used* hands and bodies,
how they moved onstage, and the bigger issues of what do you do in terms of
staging—that's a terrible gray area. There are a very few things—a few French
burlesques, a few stage directions—and these essentially just tell you who came
in from the left and who came in from the right, and how long they stood onstage. Most of the information we deal with in terms of gesture and steps is
not French and is of a later epoch.

Do you think that much of what is done in the name of Baroque gesture is
conjectural?

I think that it has to do with conjecture, and I think that sometimes it applies, as I said, to a later date or to some other place. I think it's very necessary, but I also think that you simply can't come in a month before a performance and expect someone to learn the essentials of rhetorical gesture and then
make it convincing for the audience. In a lot of these productions I've seen people look like berserk windmills.

I think there's another side of the coin, too; there's a great need for many
of the stage directors to do some homework, to find out what remains of contemporary information about Baroque theatrical comportment, rather than
doing wildly excessive and exaggerated staging because that's what the twentieth century requires of stage directors. When the stage director becomes more
important than the music and more important than the composer, I have to
balk a great deal.

19. Carlo Goldoni (1706–85), playwright, librettist (to Galuppi, Salieri, and many others),
and "father of modern Italian comedy." He moved to Paris in 1762, and he recounted this
tale in his 1787 memoirs.

Could you discuss French Baroque opera's socio-political origins—the patronage of the aristocracy in the seventeenth century versus the growing influence of bourgeois audiences in the eighteenth?

I don't really want to comment on that—it's a very difficult issue to talk about, especially on the telephone—but I don't really believe simply that the *tragédie lyrique* and *tragédie* were exclusively aristocratic forms. The court commissioned the big Lully works—that's a historical fact—and Lully was the superintendent to the king, and he wrote a *tragédie lyrique* a year for the court. But the fact is that while you can call this music aristocratic, you can also call it in some ways popular. And certainly he wasn't aiming only at a very narrow part of society, the French court. The fact is that the music in its own time had this extraordinary popular allure. People said that every bootblack and chimney sweep was whistling a Lully tune on the Pont-Neuf a few days after the opera premiered. Don't forget, these things were also performed for a bourgeois audience in Paris—almost simultaneously in many cases. The parodies, the pastiches, all this gives you the idea that there's more to it than just aristocratic entertainment. Lully, after all, becomes a national figure very early; even forty or fifty years after his death he continued to be canonized, not only by the aristocracy, the literati, and the musically educated, but by everybody in France.

How about the idea that the opera was a way of propagandizing for the ancien régime?

Well, I think it obviously had that value. I think every society has a cultural appendage that helps it out and is its own mirror. But to think that Lully became famous and stayed famous for the better part of the eighteenth century just because he mirrored the aristocratic, Versailles court ideal is stupid. This music does have a very strong popular history as well: Lully as the man on the street. His was the song that everyone was humming. That's something one tends to forget.

As revered as Lully was in his day, today people often express a preference for Charpentier, and in the process patronize Lully. Are we missing something in Lully or was he overrated in his time? Is it our distaste for his personality, his political machinations, or for his music?

I haven't figured that one out yet, quite frankly. I find that there are times when Lully simply knocks me over, by his extraordinary sense of equilibrium between simplicity and doing essentially what the form wants him to do, in the *tragédies lyriques*, to give a wonderful meeting of words and music. There are other times when Lully bores me. There are times when I think, yes, Quinault has wonderfully well-wrought libretti in the *tragédies lyriques*, but there are others with very weak endings. I wouldn't want to do a *Phaéton* or *Bellérophon*, as I find that in a curious way they just collapse at the end. So there's very good and very bad. Sometimes the four-squareness of the music gets me down; I don't like it. But *Atys* and *Armide* I think are two of the finest examples of musical theatre in the world.

If I had to take ten scores of Charpentier or Lully to a desert island, I would probably take Charpentier. I think it's musically richer, more satisfying, and more individual. There's a musical personality that's more complex, more a musician. But then we're looking at these things very differently than they were looked at then. And Lully's extraordinary simplicity is something that the French revered. "Simplicity" is not a word that we like today.

This brings up the question of relating French opera to modern audiences. One issue is French audiences, who understand the words, versus other audiences; didn't you use supertitles in Médée *in New York?*

Yes, but I don't believe we used supertitles in *Atys* in the beginning. My impression was that *Atys* had an extraordinary success; you had people in England and France saying it was a milestone, a watershed—there's pre-*Atys* and there's post-*Atys*. And it was an enormous success not only in France but abroad, including the States. I think that essentially it has to do with its being a good show, well wrought, with fine singers and fine costumes and very good staging, and, again, this broad aesthetic coherence, a very tight structure, and a total bonding of the balance of dance and theater and music. People had given some thought to what they were doing and what their partners were doing. And that was with very good raw material. *Atys* and *Médée* are fabulous theatre pieces. They're very convincing. They deal with issues that are as relevant at the end of the twentieth century as they were at the end of the seventeenth. We adapted them, obviously; I don't claim for a minute that we were interested in doing a historical re-creation—by no means. But I think the essential is that there's a strong text to be communicated which includes very strong emotions which one tries to play upon and provoke among the audience.

SELECTED DISCOGRAPHY

The recent French Baroque revival rescued Charpentier from the library shelves; to many modern ears he seems its greatest discovery. To sample both him and Lully, ambitious listeners might invest in the 3-CD recordings of the *tragédies-lyriques* discussed above—Lully's *Atys* (Harmonia Mundi 901257–59; a single disc of excerpts, HM 901249, lets one hear the great "Sleep" scene) or Charpentier's *Médée*. In the Erato CD booklet for *Médée* Christie calls it the "most important of all [Charpentier's] works," while H. Wiley Hitchcock says it is generally agreed to be his "consummate masterpiece." Christie's 1984 Harmonia Mundi *Médée* (Harmonia Mundi 901139, 3 CDs) won a *Gramophone* Award; but he re-recorded the work ten years later in a performance that is widely preferred (Erato 96558, 3 CDs; excerpts, Erato 99486). The composer

Eric Salzman writes of Christie's second *Médée*, "You will rarely hear a dramatic work treated with as much depth and passion as this."[20]

Those wanting a gentler (or less expensive) introduction to Charpentier might sample some of his sacred works, such as the hauntingly beautiful Christmas *Pastorale* (HM 901082) or some lighter Charpentier, such as one of his Molière collaborations, the intermezzos to *Le malade imaginaire*. This recording (HM 901336) lets us hear Christie's own well-timed comic acting; he plays a part in Molière's still-funny satire of a medical-degree examination. The scene contains the famous exchange about why opium puts people to sleep: the "Bachelerius" impresses his examiners by answering that it's because "it has sleep-inducing powers."

Another beneficiary of Christie's work has been the greatest French opera composer of the eighteenth century, Rameau. You might begin with *Castor et Pollux* (HM 901435–37, 3 CDs; excerpts, HM 901501)—according to Barrymore Laurence Scherer, "a gem of its kind . . . melodically ingratiating, rhythmically vivacious"[21]—or with the *Gramophone* Award-winning *Grands Motets* (Erato 96967). The 3-disc *Les Indes galantes* (HM 901367) received an interestingly mixed review from Graham Sadler, who is enthralled by the work (it "raised the traditionally lightweight genre of *opéra-ballet* to a new level") and pleased with the performance—but with reservations. Sometimes, he says, the "polished and stylish" orchestral players "do not characterize the music as vividly as they might"; and he says that as with all modern Rameau performances, in this one "we have still to hear anything resembling a 'period voice' or the full range of vocal ornamentation."[22]

Christie has also recorded, on Harmonia Mundi, some neglected lesser masterpieces of the French Baroque, notably Campra's *Idoménée* (HM 901396–98, 3 CDs; excerpts, 901506), Montéclair's *Jepthé* (HM 901424–25, 2 CDs), Bouzignac's strange, fierce motets (HM 901471), and much else.

Also significant are Christie's forays into non-French repertoire, such as his Handel *Messiah* (HM 901498–99), with its unforced alertness to the implications of the words. Christie's Mozart is unlike that of anyone else either in the mainstream or the early-music movement. Stanley Sadie praises his Requiem (Erato 106972) for being "ready to make the most of changes in orchestral colour or choral texture, to mould the dynamics more than the (very sparse) original indications, and indeed to dramatize the music to the utmost," and for treating the music as "operatic, almost romantic."[23] Other critics have complained about this; Elliot Hurwitt found the performance "puzzling," with some "incredibly slow tempos."[24] Regarding Christie's well-cast *Magic Flute*

20. Salzman, "A Medea for Our Time," *Stereo Review* 60 (September 1995), p. 90.
21. Scherer, *Gramophone* 71 (North American edition), September 1993, p. A2.
22. Sadler, *Early Music* 20 (May 1992), pp. 353–54.
23. Sadie, *Gramophone* 73 (November 1995), p. 142.
24. Hurwitt, *Fanfare* 19 (January/February 1996), p. 265.

(Erato 12705, 2 CDs), Sadie writes of "light and soft textures and graceful phrasings," and says, "Some may find Christie less readily responsive [than some other conductors] to the music's quicksilver changes in mood, but this is part of his broad and essentially gentle view of *Die Zauberflöte*," which falls "more sweetly and lovingly on the ear than any I can recall."[25]

Christie's Purcell *Fairy Queen* (HM 901308–09, 2 CDs) was decried for its liberal use of French rhythmic conventions and both praised and blamed for its unabashed theatricality. Some Purcell lovers regard *King Arthur* as a greater work than *The Fairy Queen,* and Jonathan Freeman-Attwood regards Christie's *Gramophone* Award-winning recording (Erato 98535, 2 CDs) as making "the strongest case for this music to date."[26] Eric Van Tassel prefers Gardiner and especially Trevor Pinnock in this work, but praises Christie as offering "what I missed in [his] 1980s readings of *Dido and Aeneas* and *The Fairy Queen*: a true marriage of French and English seventeenth-century idioms, evidence that this group's long and passionate engagement with the music of Lully and Charpentier can throw new light on their greatest English contemporary."[27] This light is also present in Christie's vivid 1994 recording of *Dido and Aeneas* (Erato 98477).

FOR FURTHER READING

The basic English text on French Baroque music remains James Anthony's pioneering *French Baroque Music* (revised edition, New York: Norton, 1975); it may be time again for the author to update or expand it. French Baroque singing has not yet received a clear modern exposition in English, although rumor has it that Thomas Grubb includes a section on it in the as-yet unpublished third edition of his well-known textbook *Singing in French*. Albert Cohen's bibliography of recent writing in English (and other languages) about French Baroque music appeared in *Performance Practice Review* 1 (Spring/Fall 1988), pp. 10–24. This includes, among many other sources, some ambitious French-language books on French Baroque performance. The foremost study of French rhythmic conventions is Stephen Hefling's *Rhythmic Alteration in Seventeenth- and Eighteenth-Century Music: Notes Inégales and Overdotting* (New York: Schirmer, 1993).

25. Sadie, *Gramophone* 73 (May 1996), p. 119.
26. Freeman-Attwood,*Gramophone* 72 (May 1995), p. 110.
27. Van Tassel, *Fanfare* 19 (September/October 1995), pp. 282–84.

15

Triple Counterpoint

Jeffrey Thomas, Philippe Herreweghe, and John Butt on Singing Bach

"It is right, however tedious," writes Joseph Kerman, "that discussion of historical performance should always keep circling back to Bach. Musicians in general care as deeply about Bach's music as any other; they know they are attuned to its 'spirit' and consequently have strong feelings about its interpretation."[1]

Consider Bach's choral works. It's easy to forget the strong feelings aroused by Nikolaus Harnoncourt's pioneering mid-1960s recordings, using small choruses and period instruments;[2] among those who reviled them, quite a few were missing the grandeur and massiveness of large choruses, and the slow tempi they required. Today, though, it is large choruses that are often dismissed, with such terms as "elephantine," "gargantuan," and "bloated." Perhaps we might also call them "brontosauran," since their Bach performances have all but disappeared from the recording studios. New recordings of the B Minor Mass usually have choruses of about twenty-five, which a majority of historical performers have regarded as close to what Bach wanted. Many listeners (to judge from what the record companies think will sell) seem now to prefer the transparency and litheness of small groups, which serve Bach's polyphony and dance-based rhythms well—although early-music devotees sometimes forget that the older approach did yield some great performances.

---

1. *Contemplating Music* (Cambridge: Harvard University Press, 1985), p. 203.
2. For example, the musicologist Paul Henry Lang (*High Fidelity,* July 1969, p. 77) called one such recording "pitiful."

Small choruses may command the scene today, but Bach's choral works are still in some respects embattled terrain: the arguments keep circling back to Bach. For some listeners, historically informed performances "are so supple and elegant, so refined and light, [that] they miss the gravity" implicit in some of Bach's scores.[3] Among the historicists themselves, the performance-practice issues are by no means resolved. Chief among the problem areas (and I am ignoring minor ones, like those involving Bach's continuo group) are the very concepts of "singing" and, even more, of a "chorus." This chapter examines this pair of issues, and others, including the question of historical authenticity itself. The discussions bear out Kerman once again: the feelings stirred up can be, as you will read, quite strong.

"A Little More Direct"

Jeffrey Thomas and the American Bach Soloists

The tenor Jeffrey Thomas, a Juilliard graduate, did not begin his career in early music. He spent three years in the early 1980s with the San Francisco Opera, where he won a prestigious Adler Fellowship. Since then, he has performed with most of the major US orchestras, under such conductors as Zinman, Ozawa, Blomstedt, and Shaw; he has also been the dedicatee of new vocal works by such composers as Ned Rorem. But Thomas is now best known for his early-music work with Hogwood, Koopman, Leonhardt, McGegan, Norrington, Parrott, and many others. His central focus is clearly the American Bach Soloists (ABS), which he founded in 1988 with the organist Jonathan Dimmock, to give American early-music performers a domestic arena for exploring Bach cantatas. As a Bach conductor (and singer, for that matter), Thomas has demonstrated a special concern with conveying character.

In our interview, he discussed not only his approach to Bach performance, but the larger issue of authenticity. Many in the early-music community will bristle at his rejection of the ideal of historical re-creation—his attitude can lead, many would argue, to complacency—while others in the community will applaud it as a sign of the movement's maturity.

I began the interview by asking about Bach's Cantata No. 198, the *Trauer Ode*, the high point of an ABS cantata disc I had just received.

In your recording of Cantata 198, in the opening chorus, your singers sound as if they're really in grief—which is not the case with two other recordings I compared it to.

---

3. Edward Rothstein, "CDs in the Spirit of the Easter and Passover Season," *The New York Times*, 7 April 1995, p. B16.

I hope this is one of the things that come across about any of our performances. If critics want to blame us for something, let it be that we try to be much more emotionally direct, as in the first chorus of Cantata 198 when they scream [sings] "Lass, Fürstin" with all they've got. The same goal applies to the instrumentalists. We get them to really make some sound. It just kills me to hear what often happens with these beautiful old instruments—if people don't play all the way to the bottom of the sound the instrument can make, it seems like a waste.

In that same cantata, there's a recitative, "Der Glocken bebendes Getön," about death-knells and the terror of the soul. Unlike the other recordings I've heard, the feeling of terror comes through in your instrumental accompaniment.

I tend to ask them to play a lot more soloistically. It's a smaller group, but I don't necessarily think it should sound small. So I ask them to play a lot more deeply than they might in a different setting with a different conductor. Also, it's hard for the players sometimes, right off the bat, to play a phrase as long as I'd like. The opening of the Agnus Dei in the Mass in B Minor nowadays is usually played in half-bar phrases [sings, separating the aria's motivic fragments in an extreme way]—but in our recording, we're back to the four-bar phrases people used to play. We're not trying to romanticize it, but I don't think there's anything wrong with a phrase being a few bars long.[4]

I think that what an audience wants from a concert or a recording is to get something larger than life, something more than going to work at nine and coming home at five. I think that's the function of art in our society.[5] It's relief from the gray and the noise and the din. Now, there had been—necessarily so—a lot of careful and cautious playing in the early-music movement. They were trying to do something historically correct, and one doesn't want to be wrong in something like history. But one result is that in the singing world right now, and I think justifiably, there's more and more criticism of Baroque music

4. John Butt, in his Cambridge Music Handbook *Bach: Mass in B Minor* (Cambridge University Press, 1991), p. 61, points out that the aria's opening (ritornello) is binary—with "antecedent" and "consequent" halves—and that those halves are each four bars long.

5. According to Lydia Goehr, this demand has been widely made of Western art for only about two hundred years. She calls it the "separability principle"—art as "separated completely from the world of the ordinary, mundane, and everyday"—and discusses its emergence in her *The Imaginary Museum of Musical Works* (Oxford University Press, 1992), pp. 120–75. In a sense, the "separability principle" seems always to have applied in the church setting, as I suggested in discussing the meditative function of Gregorian chant, in the introduction to Part One of this book. What Goehr describes is the emergence of the principle into the secular sphere with the nineteenth century's "sacralization" of art—to be discussed in the Norrington interview. In this sense, there may be some continuity between what Thomas is trying to do in concerts and what Bach did in church. As Thomas pointed out to me, there are obvious and crucial discontinuities too: Bach's purposes involved encouraging the listener to be a better Christian.

singers. I think in Europe they've made some advances that we haven't yet here, in that singers there are singing with more voice now. We still have a lot of singers in the USA who sing stylistically very differently when they approach music from before 1760. I was certainly guilty of that for many years. A decade or so ago, when I started, I thought what conductors wanted was [he caricatures a very light-voiced tenor]. And I think they did want that. Now it doesn't sit as well. But we're evolving, and getting to be more direct about it.

Of course, the biases are hard to get over. A couple of people criticized our B Minor Mass for being very "romantic." The greatest compliment I got was from one local musician, who left at intermission because he hated the tempo of the opening Kyrie—it was too slow. And I said, "Just because they did it that way for the last eighty years doesn't mean it's bad." I personally don't want that piece to be over too soon.

The way you articulated the fugue subject was full of the emotion of pleading for mercy, and when you articulate that much, I suppose you need to give it time.

It has those ascending pairs of notes. I wanted there to be a sort of effort to get up to the top. We sort of elongated each note, "E-*le*-i-son."

How do you approach issues of phrasing and articulation—aside from the slurs Bach wrote?

There are two things that strike me about Bach's writing, whether in an aria or a recitative. One is the rhetorical element, which I think our approach to the Kyrie theme illustrates—though that's sometimes overdone nowadays. The other is the harmonic element. From the first time I opened up a Bach score, the vocal lines looked principally like arpeggiated harmonies, certainly in the recitatives but also in the arias. This was always a clue to me about how to sing Bach.

Imagine you're in a decent acoustic. And if you have B minor for two beats and then finally you get an A♯ or a E♯ or some other dissonance, that's the first interesting bit after two beats. So what I ask people to do is to sing harmonically. For example [singing both]:[6]

The first C♯ is just a passing dissonance, and the B and D that follow are still in the same B minor chord, so these three notes shouldn't be accented; it's the

6. Bach, Benedictus, from the Mass in B Minor: (a) as Jeffrey Thomas recommends singing it, (b) as it is sometimes sung.

C♯ in the second bar that's the harmonic event. That's made clear in the first way of singing it (a)—that C♯ should get the first accent since the initial D. This is obscured in the second way (b).[7]

On the other hand, I don't want to start reading into Bach all kinds of things that aren't there. I don't know how often Bach counted the number of notes or measures, and when he did, how much of that was in fun or seriously intended. In some cases I'm sure it was deliberate; in others . . . I mean, come on, he was very clever. I don't want to read too much into music that's not on the most immediate level, the level of the function it's trying to fulfill.

Regarding that function, there is of course an important distinction between Bach's church and our concerts. In Bach's church, people were meant to participate by taking the message to heart, not just by enjoying the music. His purpose in setting the words to music was to frighten or inspire the congregation, or whatever the text was supposed to do. He was being judged on how well he conveyed the Lutheran message. That was his job. We don't ask the audience to subscribe to the words; the modern Bach audience is usually interested in the aesthetic/artistic element. So what we're trying to do at ABS is take the immediate content of the music and make it come alive for our audiences.

But do you use musicological evidence in preparing performances?

Yes, but I've always felt that musicology and performance make strange bedfellows. Of course, their relationship in recent years has been very productive. But there is a point at which each must take its own path. To make a performance be about a work's stylistic aspects is to trivialize it.

Besides, musicology is one of those disciplines that can prove anything. You can take opposite sides of an issue and find treatises that support both. I don't want to get into the whole business of what's right and what's wrong— we're just trying to give really good performances. I'm not suggesting that other groups aren't doing that either, or are trying to prove points, but we're definitely not trying to.

Of course, there are certainly issues about which I've gone back and researched things—but again, the results are rarely conclusive. Consider the famous memorandum that Bach sent to the Leipzig Town Council in 1730[8] where he said that "it would be better if there were four subjects for each voice." Joshua Rifkin argues that he wanted those singers so he'd have enough to do motets when people got sick, and that he meant for his choruses to be sung one to a part. We've done it both ways, one to a part and with a cho-

---

7. The C♯ Thomas accents is on the first beat of the bar. This exemplifies the Baroque doctrine of "good" beats and "bad" beats—the first beat is the best of the "good" beats. It also concurs with the view that the doctrine reflects harmonic practice, so that significant dissonances fall on strong beats. John Butt discusses this in Chapter 9.

8. See John Butt's section of this chapter, below, for a thorough discussion of this and of Rifkin's hypothesis.

rus. Ultimately, I'm not concerned about what Bach did, but about the artistic results *now*.

How does your attitude apply to your continuo groups?[9]

Well, there's more and more evidence of rather large bottom-octave configurations in that period in other parts of the world, and plenty of evidence for it in Bach also, as Laurence Dreyfus has argued—not that, again, I try to follow him exactly.[10] I think nowadays people tend to under-balance the bass line very often. For a recitative, we almost always try to have a cello and sixteen-foot violone, *and* bassoon, *and* harpsichord, *and* organ; and yes, we even have lutes playing.

Have the lutes caused people to walk out?

I gave Roger Norrington a copy of our first record (we were doing Berlioz's *Roméo et Juliette* in Minneapolis). Sure enough, he played it that night in his hotel room, because the next morning at rehearsal he said he enjoyed it very much. Then he said, "Now tell me about this lute business. Are there historical reasons for that, or do you just like the way it sounds?" I said, "We-e-e-ll, you know, the famous lutenist Weiss visited Bach's sons for several months, and there were certainly instruments around, and Kuhnau, Bach's predecessor in Leipzig, is known to have used lutes in the continuo, and although there's nothing definite to say that it was a regularly played continuo instrument, um . . . yeah, I just like the way it sounds." Again, there are reasons to justify it, but they aren't the ultimate criteria.

Searching for the Balance
Philippe Herreweghe

Edward Rothstein says that one of Philippe Herreweghe's Bach CDs "manages to encompass the weightiness of the old [mainstream performances] and the highly refined language of the new [historical ones.]"[11] Reviewing another of the Flemish conductor's Bach recordings, Gerald Hansen puts it differently: he finds the delivery "romantic but ingratiating." He warns, however, "Purists, beware."[12]

In fact, some period-instrument experts cannot stand Herreweghe's work. His mainstream appeal does not result, however, from any ignorance on his

9. See note six in the Alan Curtis interview for a definition of "continuo."

10. Dreyfus, *Bach's Continuo Group* (Cambridge, Mass.: Harvard University Press, 1987), argues, among other things, that Bach sometimes used both harpsichord and organ in the continuo of his Leipzig cantatas. Dreyfus's conclusions are somewhat controversial, however.

11. Rothstein, "CDs in the Spirit."

12. Hansen, *American Record Guide*, March/April 1992, p. 20.

part about Baroque performance practice. Herreweghe, a former conservatory student in piano (he also has a degree in psychiatry), formed his chorus, the Collegium Vocale of Ghent, in 1975; it attracted the attention of Gustav Leonhardt, who used it in recording a number of Bach cantatas. In the process, Herreweghe served a kind of apprenticeship with Leonhardt, whom he admires enormously. Herreweghe is deeply concerned with the idea of rhetoric as the key to Bach, but he uses it in a very different way from Leonhardt and Harnoncourt. His style could hardly differ more from theirs, as our discussion shows.

You once wrote that "for many years the definition of Baroque style was shaped by harpsichordists and violinists who incited singers to imitate their manner of playing": a useful service, you thought, but causing "a certain loss of melodic line."[13]

I would only add that when people read eighteenth-century treatises about the interpretation of music, they can read into them what they wish. When an explanation about music is only in words, very often one can exaggerate, as people in the eighteenth century did about, for example, articulation. And if you're a harpsichordist, you might read it in a certain specific way that is different from how a singer might read it. I think this was the origin of a modern style of Bach performance. This style was necessary for getting us out of the previous styles—first the very romantic one, and then later the very motoric one. In this new style, though, many conductors were harpsichordists; and while they brought very important things into the playing of this music, from the beginning there was something in my opinion too edgy, too angular.

Of course, the approach has something useful in it, where you consider an architecture based on the addition of small elements—that is something that is special to Baroque music. My point is to find a balance between organizational cells that are too small and the overly long line. I think I'm still searching for that balance.

Also, I think that some instruments like voices, flutes, oboes, and even strings tend not to sound as they should when played with this overly static rhythmic approach. So you need a line, because I think that a line is a very important part of the architecture of the music, and also because without that line voices do not sound as they should.

I think Bach tried to write something that was a musical enlargement of how you speak the text. The verbal phrases tell you how you should phrase musically. Of course there are also small rhythmic impulses that come from the music. At the same time that it's a purely musical kind of architecture, though, the text gives exactly the right approach. I think you can make Baroque music with Baroque aesthetics and still pay attention to vowels and phrases. Now,

13. Booklet note to his recording of the *St. John Passion*, Harmonia Mundi 901264–65.

that's a matter of debate. Some people say that my approach is too romantic. But I'm convinced of it.

You've written that rhetoric is the only valid key to understanding the Baroque aesthetic.[14]

I always felt this by intuition when I worked on early music with other people, but gradually I came to feel it was really central, and then I read as much as I could about it. It's very obvious that rhetoric was central to Bach's manner of composition and also interpretation. The system of rhetoric took different forms over the ages and even over just two centuries of Western music; you can find these forms in theoretical books from the period. But I don't think it's just a theory: it's a musical reality. From the middle of the sixteenth century until Bach, it gives the key to what should be done in the music, especially music with a text.

For example, it can be useful in, for example, the first Kyrie from the B Minor Mass to know that Bach himself wrote the first chorus exactly like a classical speech. It helps your interpretation if you know that a certain section is the *confutatio*, which is a modulation—in a speech, the *confutatio* is done with more tension than when one is first exposing one's theme.[15]

Could you talk about the issue of boys' versus women's voices in Bach?

Yes, at the moment I'm convinced that we should use authentic instruments, because I find they are more appropriate to defining the sound and thus the message of the music. For the voices, I'm convinced in theory that boys' voices are the most appropriate for both soprano and alto arias in Bach. I could hear that twenty years ago, when there were very good boys' choirs singing Bach. Today, English boys' choirs are very good, but they cannot sing Bach well because the pronunciation of the German is so important. But in Germany, and in Belgium (where the language is Flemish, which is pretty close to German), the boys' choirs are simply disappearing, because the organization of society is very different now than it was twenty years ago. I think nowadays there are no boys who have the musical training that boys had in the time of Bach. The boy singers before may have been very narrow, because they didn't do sports

14. Booklet note to his recording of the *St. Matthew Passion,* Harmonia Mundi 901155–57.

15. I wasn't able to confirm this with Herreweghe (he did not comment on this footnote when he looked over this chapter), but he might analyze the Kyrie movement as follows: *introductio,* bars 1–4; *expositio,* bars 5–47 (the orchestral ritornello and vocal exposition, all in B minor); *confutatio,* bars 48–72 (the section where the voices continue while underneath them the orchestra repeats the opening ritornello—but in F♯ minor, the "dominant" key); *confirmatio,* bars 81–101 (vocal exposition repeated in B minor); *conclusio,* bars 102–26 (opening ritornello in the orchestra again, with voices continuing overhead—but this time in B minor.) See also Joshua Rifkin's discussion of rhetoric in his interview, and John Butt's in Chapter 9.

and so on, but they did the music very well. And now we don't have boys from the age of six or seven studying singing technique every day seriously, and singing every day three hours in church, and also studying harmony and counterpoint as some did in Bach's time.[16] A decade ago we could do it—with Leonhardt and Harnoncourt, the last of the tradition was there—but it's more and more difficult now. Of course, you still have boys with beautiful voices, but they're not really trained. And there are other factors: in the time of Bach, boys could sometimes sing soprano until age 16 or 17. Now, because of various changes including diet, the body develops much earlier, so the voice breaks before they are as mature as in Bach's time.

So I prefer to do Bach with girls who have special training. The women singing in Collegium Vocale do not have the normal vocal training for singing Brahms and Strauss, and while that may be a pity for them, it's good for Bach—they've developed their voices in the context of polyphony. When you only sing polyphony up to Bach, and you don't sing Mozart and certainly not Brahms or Puccini, then your voice develops in a certain direction. That is what has happened with the girls I work with. Of course, it's different from what Bach heard; but it's the best we can do, I think.

Joshua Rifkin argues that Bach didn't use a choir as we think of it, but had a solo quartet sing the choruses. What is your view?

I'm not a musicologist, and he probably can make better arguments, though I haven't studied them. From the subjective point of view, I think that using more than four sopranos detracts, because very often there's a dialogue between, say, the sopranos and the flute, and if there are too many sopranos it can no longer be a dialogue and the flute disappears. But when you have three people singing instead of one, the individual disappears and becomes something other than the individual. This for me is essential and is part of the emotion. Going between the individual singer singing the arias and three sopranos singing the choruses gives a very important emotional contrast.

You've advocated conducting later music as a way of improving one's conducting of early music.

If you're not able to conduct at all, like many specialists who never conduct except in early music, you can still do a good, interesting B Minor Mass, because in a way it's very simple from the conducting point of view. But I think that at a certain point being able to conduct well is an advantage. The rehearsal

16. The leading book on this subject is John Butt, *Musical Education and the Art of Performance in the German Baroque* (Cambridge University Press, 1994). It suggests that only the finest boy singers in Bach's time studied harmony and counterpoint. (By the way, it can't be assumed that Bach always used boys for alto lines; Bach's pool of alto singers in Leipzig included not only boys but also several males in their early twenties. See p. 6 of Joshua Rifkin's booklet note to his recording of Cantatas 80 and 147, L'Oiseau-Lyre 417 250.)

can go quicker, so you can give more time to essential points rather than spending a lot of time trying to get everyone together. Another advantage is that even for early music, when you have more than twenty musicians the beauty of the sound can be determined by the gestures of the conductor.

On the other hand, I think a lot of conductors of Romantic music face a danger in Bach and other Baroque music, because it's essential that this music come from the musicians themselves. It's essential in the architecture of the music that each musician has to be creative and make music himself. If you conduct "too well" in a certain way, you kill that. So it's a paradox: for conducting Bach, the ideal is to have a lot of technique and then to forget it and certainly not to use it; otherwise you kill what is essential in the music. In Bach, if something is not possible without a conductor, it's a sign that it's not a good interpretation.

On Singing Bach Too Well
John Butt

Bach's pupil J. P. Kirnberger, a theorist and composer, suggested in 1771 that students use the Italianate composer J. G. Graun as a model for writing melodies. They should not use Bach, Kirnberger said, because his works are so adventurous melodically and "require a very special execution that is exactly suited to his style; for, otherwise, many of his works sound hardly bearable."[17] What is this special execution? Julianne Baird and William Christie have shown us that the Italian style of singing was the mainstream of the Baroque; if Bach's style was "very special," how did it differ from (or relate to) this mainstream? And how might it have differed from (or related to) today's styles of Bach singing? These questions came up in the course of my Chapter 9 interview with John Butt (who is an experienced choral conductor). I asked about the same Herreweghe quote that I read to Herreweghe.

Philippe Herreweghe writes that "for many years the definition of Baroque style was shaped by harpsichordists and violinists who incited singers to imitate their manner of playing": he thinks this a useful service, but believes it caused "a certain loss of melodic line." What do you think about this?

To answer that, note first that there's not a great deal about the theory and physics of the voice in sixteenth- and seventeenth-century vocal treatises; but there is an incredible amount about ornamentation and articulation. In virtually all the singing technique books from 1560 to well beyond the time of Mozart, the emphasis over and over again is on ornamentation: how to sing a trill, how to sing a *messa di voce*, how to sing runs that are really articulated.

17. John Butt, *Bach Interpretation* (Cambridge University Press, 1990), p. 24.

And a very important point is that they were articulated in the throat—the epiglottis and glottis acted like a percussive device letting the air through. This is anathema to modern singing, so from that point of view, indeed, singers might learn a lot today from harpsichordists.

Now, you said in your book Bach Interpretation[18] *that in the Baroque singing was the basis for instrumental articulation, not the other way around, which seems to support Herreweghe's point. But you also said that singing in Baroque Germany was different from singing now. What do we know about Baroque singing?*

That's a huge question. I've tried to answer it to some extent in one of my books,[19] at least in the context of German church music and the very limited environment of choir schools; but I've also studied the more professional, Italianate styles of singing. From the late sixteenth century onwards, there was a very professional environment for Italian singers, with academies that taught them counterpoint all morning and vocal exercises all afternoon. From that point of view, I think Herreweghe is right to suggest that there was a quality to singing that's missing from a lot of early-music performance. Of course we're not talking about the whole of Baroque music here—just about the Italian mainstream of singing, which was a lot more professional than the amateur efforts you often hear in early music.

How about the German style, though?

Today, Italian opera singing and Wagnerian German singing are somewhat blended; it can be rather hard to tell the difference. But it's quite clear that well into the nineteenth century there was a difference between German singing and Italian singing. The Germans were always criticized throughout music history as being incredibly "vulgar" singers, not being able to tie their words together, declaiming, spitting and hissing and gutturalling, rather than actually singing.

How does that apply to Bach? Would he have preferred Italian singers like those in Dresden?

He was always very complimentary about the Dresden singers; I think he loved their capability because they could get around the notes so well. But whether he would have liked their style of declamation is a different matter. The music they would be singing, such as that by Johann Adolf Hasse, apparently a great friend of Bach's, would have been a different style from his.

Does this relate to one of the points from your book Bach Interpretation— *that when the little motivic figures are articulated, the polyphony is made more clear?*

18. Ibid., pp. 9–34.
19. Butt, *Musical Education and the Art of Performance in the German Baroque*.

Well, to me it doesn't makes sense to sing Bach either in the modern German declamatory way, in full voice, or in the traditional "early-music" sound of very light vocalization, often with hardly any sound at all and no edge to it; while perhaps the best Italian way of Bach's time would not be suitable for counterpoint. So in some ways, Leonhardt, and indeed Harnoncourt too, while they might be miles away from what was done in Bach's performances, might on the other hand come quite close to it: a mixture of rhetorical singing and enunciation with Italian flexibility.

Your point about "vulgar" Germans "not being able to tie their words together" and "declaiming" reminds me that when Leonhardt conducted your chorus in Bach's Magnificat he was criticized for having them break the words up so much.

Exactly. From that point of view, you might think of what Leonhardt does when he conducts a choir as being rather like bad Italian singing. In other words, it has many of the principles of Italian singing but all cut up into bits, into articulative fragments. In terms of what Herreweghe might do it *would* seem almost vulgar. The Italians, by all accounts, were more slick. They still had the same articulative power, particularly in runs, but there was always a great emphasis on *messa di voce,* on being able to sustain notes and not chopping things up. Even Schütz said, regarding some of his vocal "sacred concerti," that the players must listen to Italian playing because Germans cut the music up too much. There he was talking about violins rather than singing, but the same was true of singers.

The Germans were continually trying to emulate Italian singing. One of the first places this appears is in Praetorius, in the *Syntagma Musicum* of 1619: he says, "I'm going to give you a little guide to the new Italian fashion of singing." And you find Germans talking about the new Italian fashion of singing right into the mid-eighteenth century. Perhaps there were several "new" Italian styles of singing; or perhaps it always seemed new.

But in spite of that, the German style remained different in that they detached the figures and words more?

Yes, they certainly catalogued the components of Italianate ornamental figuration more carefully, suggesting (though never very clearly) that each requires a different method of articulation. Moreover, they were very concerned with enunciation and the textual aspects.

What factors gave rise to the differentiation between German and Italian singing styles?

Well, it has something to do with the central role of German music in Lutheran worship. There was more music in the Roman Catholic church, but it didn't play the same rhetorical role that it did in the Lutheran church. In the

Lutheran church you might think of music as being almost of the same status as preaching,[20] whereas in the Italian church the music is generally of the same status as the architecture; it's part of the building. If you're talking about opera, on the other hand, there are a few more things to think about, particularly the forms used in opera, and the cultivation of a presentation geared towards drama.

Does the difference in singing styles also reflect the difference between the languages—the melodious, vowel-rich Italian and the more guttural, conso-nant-rich German?

Yes, and by extension, those particular languages quite often reflect the culture, the way of thinking, as well. It's not a question just of the language, but also of the temperament that creates the linguistic community that will use language of a particular kind, both in terms of its grammar and of its sound.

There are many different cultural issues intertwined, but certainly if you just take the raw sounds of Italian and German they produce very different effects in singing.

How would you relate this distinction to modern Bach singing other than Leonhardt/Harnoncourt—the American Bach Soloists (ABS), for example?

I would say the ABS make a good attempt at showing how trained singers can bring out certain things in Bach's music. But on the other hand, like virtually any group using professionally trained singers, in some sense they're slightly *too* good.

What does "too good" mean?

Well, nothing can be too good from some points of view. The way the ABS, indeed all professionals, perform would probably have surprised Bach, in that everything is given its just deserts, everything is sung well; but I think there is a calculation in Bach's writing that some things aren't going to be performed as well as others. In fact, a point my colleague Richard Taruskin made,[21] which I think is a very strong one, is that Bach was quite aware that a lot of his church music was hard to sing and play. *I* would say that that brings out a lot of the light and shade of the music very well; Taruskin says that it brings out a particular spiritual point, that humankind is flawed. Either way, I think it's quite a good argument.

---

20. Unlike other Protestant reformers, Luther saw music not as undermining Scripture but as "a bearer of the Word of God"—thus the rhetorical role Butt speaks about. See the entry "Martin Luther," by Robin Leaver and Ann Bond, in *The New Grove Dictionary of Music*, vol. 11, pp. 365–71.

21. Taruskin, "Facing Up, Finally, to Bach's Dark Vision," in *The New York Times*, 27 January 1991, Sunday Arts and Leisure section, p. 1, reprinted in his *Text and Act* (New York: Oxford University Press, 1995), pp. 307–15.

But singing it that way presupposes that the music is going to be used in the same liturgical way that Bach used it, which is not the case. The audiences going to the ABS are expecting professional-standard music, and it's hard to explain to an audience that you're going to sing in a way that's slightly under par in order to make it good! On the other hand, if you get together a group of boys or university students who are not expected to sing well, and get them to sing well or at least convincingly, that's one way of approaching this particular issue.

Does that connect to your idea that Harnoncourt and Leonhardt, who used boys' choirs, may came close to the original style?

Well, they certainly bring something out that no one else does. Often it's intensely ugly and you feel like kicking in the loudspeaker when you hear it—particularly Harnoncourt; not so much Leonhardt. But you gain something in that terrible frustration. I can't stand some of the things I hear, but they're still very relevant.

We're in an age where we expect things to be finished and cellophane-packed. Some of the English performers, like John Eliot Gardiner, I think, are examples of this in Bach: extremely refined performances, which are always very lively but relatively safe. Jeffrey Thomas and the ABS go well beyond that in putting the guts back into the music. It's a very dynamic group, and there is a sense of unexpectedness about some of it. I've played on many of the records and am always struck by the grittiness of it.

What's your view on Joshua Rifkin's hypothesis that Bach meant for his choral works to be sung with one singer per part?[22]

I haven't looked at as many of the original parts as Rifkin has, but I have looked at more than most people have, and I find that virtually everything Rifkin says is very convincing. There is only one part for each choral line in most Bach choral works; applying Occam's Razor, you have to invent more hypotheses to support the idea of multiple users of parts than if you assume one voice per part.[23]

Of course, other people argue that there's a lot of outside contextual evi-

---

22. See Rifkin's "Bach's Chorus: A Preliminary Report," *The Musical Times* 123 (1982), pp. 747–51, and his shorter version, "Bach's 'Choruses'—Less Than They Seem?" *High Fidelity*, September 1982, pp. 42–44.

23. Rifkin's logic can be expressed in the following syllogism. The major premise is that in all but nine of Bach's surviving choral works only one part was written out for each of the choral lines; this premise is not seriously disputed among Bach scholars. Rifkin's minor premise, though, is controversial: that the parts are copied in such a way that each one must have been meant for one singer alone to use. If this premise is accepted, the conclusion is obvious: Bach used a solo quartet to sing those great cantata choruses.

As Butt points out, nobody has entirely refuted the assertion that these parts were copied so as to have been, in many works, difficult to share. Robert Marshall observes that Bach's parts are larger than most modern parts—which are routinely shared—and that his actual no-

dence of multiple choral voices.[24] I've done a lot of work in that area, probably as much as Rifkin, and my inquiries suggest that there was a great deal of variety in Bach's era.[25] Some people wanted multiple singers, some didn't. In most cases each singer did indeed get his own part to sing from.[26] What is certain is that there was a division between the *concertists*, the solo singers who were the number one in each of their parts [and sang throughout the piece], and the *ripienists*, the people that we would call the "chorus." That is crucial evidence about the way choruses are put together. But it allows the argument to go either way; it doesn't determine whether Bach had one per part or more. The wider context would allow you to do either, but his original parts, with a few exceptions, almost certainly suggest he used single voices.

Many people point to the 1730 memorandum to the Leipzig Town Council where Bach insisted that each chorus needed at least three singers on each part, and preferably four.

---

tation is "around twice as large" (Marshall, "Bach's Chorus: A Reply to Rifkin," *The Musical Times* 124 [January 1983], pp. 19–22; quote, p. 22). But Rifkin answers that it's not the size of the parts that leads him to conclude that they would be difficult for soloists and chorus members to share, but the shortage of cues about when the chorus should enter and exit. He argues that such cues might have been almost essential in some works, considering that surviving Bach works that use extra voices ("ripienists") tend to use them not to double throughout a movement but to join in or drop out at specific places; he adds that rehearsal time was limited. Marshall argues that these "ripieno" entries could have been cued by Bach from the keyboard; and others have argued that the boys may have memorized the parts rather than sight-read them, which might obviate the problem. Still, Rifkin would respond that Bach did have time to add articulation and dynamic marks to many cantata scores, and that he surely would have found choral cues valuable in at least some works; so his not writing them suggests that they were not needed. See Marshall, "Bach's Chorus: A Reply to Rifkin"; Rifkin's "Bach's Chorus: A Response to Marshall," *The Musical Times* 124 (March 1983), pp. 161–62; Marshall's "Bach's Choruses Reconstituted," *High Fidelity*, October 1982, pp. 64–66, and Rifkin, "Bach's 'Choruses': The Record Cleared," *High Fidelity*, December 1982, pp. 58–59. See also George Stauffer's review of Butt's *Bach: Mass in B Minor*, *Journal of Musicological Research* 13 (1993), pp. 257–72, and Rifkin's reply in the same journal, 14 (1995), pp. 223–34.

24. E.g., the distinguished scholar Hans-Joachim Schulze noted that musical forces at the Dresden court, with which Bach was directly familiar, were larger than those in Leipzig (see Schulze, "Johann Sebastian Bach's Orchestra: Some Unanswered Questions," *Early Music* 17 [February 1989], pp. 3–15). Rifkin replies, however, that we can't assume that what was done in Dresden was what Bach wanted in Leipzig; he adds that the Dresdeners still used one written part per singer and player, which supports his crucial minor premise (see Rifkin's "More (and Less) on Bach's Orchestra," *Performance Practice Review* 4 [Spring 1991], pp. 5–13). Schulze also quotes Mattheson's and Scheibe's denunciations of one-per-part singing; as Butt points out, however, the fact that both Mattheson and Scheibe felt compelled to denounce the one-per-part chorus so strongly indicates that "it was indeed still an option at that time" (Butt, *Musical Education*, p. 208, n. 55), as other evidence also indicates—see Andrew Parrott, "Bach's Chorus: A 'Brief yet Highly Necessary' Reappraisal," *Early Music* 24 (November 1996), p. 557.

25. This research is summarized on pp. 106–13 of Butt's *Musical Education*.

26. See *ibid.*, p. 111, for an exception.

Well, Bach didn't say that was the number of people needed to sing in his cantata choruses (the translation in *The Bach Reader* is misleading there).[27] For one thing, much of the memorandum is about double-chorus motets, usually not by Bach, which they sang every Sunday. More important, the topic of the memorandum is how many performers he'd need to operate a liturgical music establishment over an entire year. The memorandum gives the number of people who should be part of the *Kantorei* for each church.

And, says Rifkin, Bach, being a practical musician, would ask for some reserves in case someone had the flu when they had to sing a motet—he mentions frequent illness in that passage, and also observes that singers are sometimes needed to play instruments.

Right. If you were to ask Herreweghe or Leonhardt how many people were going to be playing in their groups this year, the numbers they'd give wouldn't all be playing in every concert. Now, if Bach had written, "For the chorus parts in my cantatas I need twelve singers," then the memorandum would be strong evidence.

I must say, though, that however convincing Rifkin's case may be, most of my favorite Bach performances use choirs; perhaps that relates to your comment [in Chapter 9] that Bach depends less than most composers on the specifics of realization.

Exactly. Groups such as the ABS succeed through their imaginative use of historical perspectives, not through a slavish devotion to greater or lesser "facts." That way, they can be creative within the framework of historical instruments and techniques of performance. Indeed, "fact" is almost a dirty word in contemporary intellectual thought. Historical performance, like "history" itself, should be always new.

---

27. In *The Bach Reader,* ed. Hans T. David and Arthur Mendel (New York: Norton, 1966), pp. 120–24, the crucial passage at issue is rendered thus: "it would be still better if . . . one could have 4 singers on each part and thus could perform every chorus with 16 persons"; Rifkin renders this " . . . one could have 4 subjects for each voice and thus 16 persons in each choir." (The original German reads: "Wiewohln es noch beßer, wenn der *Coetus* [student body] so beschaffen wäre, daß mann zu ieder Stimme 4 *subjecta* nehmen, und also ieden *Chor* mit 16. Persohnen bestellen könte."

One argument is that while the parts may suggest that Bach had only one singer per part, the memorandum shows that he *wanted* four per part; as Butt points out, however, the document does not unambiguously show that. We can never know for certain what Bach would have considered ideal, but we have no evidence that clearly demonstrates that he wanted "four singers on a part," or even, in most cases, that he wanted more than one per part.

Andrew Parrott raises an additional reason for doubting that the number refers to the performance size of each vocal group: of the musicians in each "choir," Bach normally had to assign at least three and sometimes several more to play instruments: Parrott, "Bach's Chorus: A 'Brief yet Highly Necessary' Reappraisal," p. 570.

SELECTED DISCOGRAPHY

Jeffrey Thomas's most widely acclaimed ABS recording is undoubtedly his B Minor Mass (Koch 7194, 2 CDs). Lindsay Kemp praises it for its "fresh ideas": "the opening bars lovingly sung instead of solemnly belted out; stabbed-out string dissonances driving home the nails of the Crucifixus; smoothly tender choral singing emphasizing the link between the more classically contrapuntal choruses and old-style polyphony. . . . some superbly musical instrumental playing—listen to the flute and muted strings of the 'Domine Deus.'"[28]

Two ABS recordings of early Bach cantatas have used the one-per-part approach. The first of them (Koch 7164) received poor reviews because its countertenor soloist was on bad form; but the second of them (Koch 7235; Cantatas Nos. 4, 131, and 182) was "warmly recommended" by Nicholas Anderson for the "expressive warmth" of its singing and for being "stylistically apposite and emotionally satisfying."[29] Thomas's recording of Cantata No. 198, which uses a chorus, is the one I praised in my first question to him (Koch 7163; the CD also contains Cantatas 8 and 156). Another starting point for sampling the ABS might be its first release (Koch 7138), with solo Bach cantatas sung by four American singers, among them Julianne Baird and Thomas himself.

Thomas's singing can also be heard as the Evangelist in Kenneth Slowik's recording of the St. John Passion (Smithsonian ND 0381, 2 CDs). Teri Noel Towe calls this "unequivocally . . . the best of period instrument [St. John Passions] overall."[30] Thomas Luekens says that Thomas, "entrusted with considerable freedom in forwarding the dramatic line, [gauges] the tempo fluctuations deftly while, over a crisp, clearly felt pulse, he captures the particular feeling of individual dramatic moments"; for example, in No. 12 his is "recitative singing at its finest, a verbally incisive, tellingly shaped line that tapers affectingly."[31]

Teldec recorded the complete Bach sacred cantatas under Leonhardt and Harnoncourt between 1971 and 1989; it has reissued the series on ten midprice 6-CD sets as well as on 1- and 2-CD sets. James Oestreich writes of its "sustained novelistic prose and epic poetry," and says the "series was made all the richer, of course, by the infusion of two separate and strong directorial personalities, often exasperating but always deeply involving."[32] An admiring Nicholas Kenyon exemplifies critical response when he says that "on the whole, there is more coherence in Leonhardt's quiet un-self-advertising performances,

---

28. Kemp, "Quarterly Retrospect," *Gramophone* 71 (September 1993), p. 34.
29. *Gramophone* 73 (March 1996), pp. 78–79.
30. Towe, in *Choral Music on Record*, ed. Alan Blyth (Cambridge University Press, 1991), p. 22.
31. Lueken, recording review, *Historical Performance* 3 (Fall 1990), p. 89.
32. Oestreich, "Why the Bach Cantatas? Because They're There," *The New York Times*, 3 November 1996, Sunday Arts and Leisure section, pp. 33–34.

and more exuberance and a greater hit-or-miss failure rate in Harnoncourt's occasionally brilliant offerings."[33] A good one-disc sampler of both conductors is Teldec 42615, featuring Cantatas Nos. 124–127. For those wanting a sampler of Leonhardt alone, Sony Classics (SK 68265) recorded him in 1995 leading three great Bach cantatas—Nos. 27, 34, and 41—all of which had been assigned to Harnoncourt in the Teldec series.

Leonhardt brings insight and feeling to the *St. Matthew Passion* (Deutsche Harmonia Mundi 7848-2-RC, 3 CDs). Like the cantata recordings just mentioned, it is sung entirely by male voices, and the boy choristers and soprano soloists in this recording are excellent. I have to admit, though, that in profound arias like "Aus Liebe" my heart is more thoroughly rent when the soloist is a grown woman with the expressive depths of, say, Herreweghe's Barbara Schlick. Leonhardt's *St. Matthew* avoids one of the problems of much early-music performance, that of breathlessly fast tempi. Such tempi were perhaps a necessary corrective to the ponderous ones chosen for Bach by, say, Otto Klemperer; but according to Malcolm Boyd, there may be indications of a "general retreat" from the excessive speed often adopted since[34]—a trend he thinks "will be welcomed by many." According to Wye J. Allanbrook, in the opening chorus of the *St. Matthew* the meter suggests "the slow progress of Christ into Jerusalem riding on an ass (Matthew 21), or . . . the agonizing limp of his walk to Calvary."[35] These images suggest "slow, limping rhythms," she says, so the waltz tempos and "loose, swinging rhythms" found in many early-music renditions are inappropriate.[36] Leonhardt, I think, gets this movement right. Leonhardt's Bach recordings show the kind of articulation—the chopping up of words, etc.—that makes choral conductors wince, or at least raise their eyes heavenward, but that for some listeners has come to represent a true Bachian style. It does enhance transparency.

The choral directors I know have nothing but praise for Philippe Herreweghe's choral finesse. The same seems to be true of critics. In Edward Rothstein's *New York Times* survey of *St. Matthew Passion* recordings, Herreweghe's (Harmonia Mundi 901155) is the clear favorite: in Herreweghe's hands, Rothstein says, "The Passion becomes a genuinely weird and moving story, avoiding the innocent graciousness that once characterized the early-music movement while retaining the gravitas of pre-authentic Bach."[37] Simi-

---

33. Kenyon, "Bach's Choral Works: A Discographic Survey, Part 2," *Opus* (February 1986), p. 54.

34. Boyd, "J. S. Bach: Two Choral Masterpieces," *Early Music* 22 (August 1994), p. 525—which praises Thomas's Mass in B Minor.

35. Allanbrook, "The Sleep of Sin: A Note on an Aria from Bach's *St. Matthew Passion*," in *Essays in Honor of Robert Bart*, ed. Cary Stickney (Annapolis, Md.: St. John's Press, 1993), p. 19. Her argument is part of an analysis of how Bach tries to illustrate texts in this work musically.

36. Allanbrook, personal communication, 1996.

37. Rothstein, "CDs in the Spirit."

larly high praise has greeted Herreweghe's Easter Oratorio (on Harmonia Mundi 901513, with Cantata 66), motets (to Graham Sadler, "much the most successful of those I have heard";[38] Harmonia Mundi 901231), and, in fact, most of his Bach recordings. I have been unable to find a negative review of Herreweghe's Bach; the complaints I've heard have been spoken, from some (as it happens) British early-music performers who believe that Leonhardt and Harnouncourt take the right approach to articulation and that Herreweghe is too smooth.

It may not surprise those performers that Herreweghe's forays into nine-teenth-century music have been especially successful (though Paul Hillier is not alone in admiring Herreweghe's recordings of pre-Bach composers like Schütz). An example of Herreweghe's nineeenth-century recordings is the Beethoven *Missa Solemnis* (Harmonia Mundi 901557), a work that John Deathridge calls "perversely difficult to perform." Deathridge, in a BBC Radio Three survey of all available recordings (28 January 1996), calls Herreweghe's "by far the most interesting," and backs up the judgment in detail. Michael Tanner, in *Classic CD*, comes to the same conclusion: Herreweghe "has come nearer to solving the problem [of performing the work] than anyone else, even Karajan or Toscanini."[39]

FOR FURTHER READING

Bach's choral works have been at the center of the revolution in Bach scholar-ship that has been in progress since the 1950s. This revolution is described in Christoph Wolff's *Bach: Essays on His Life and Work* (Cambridge, Mass: Har-vard University Press, 1991), esp. chap. 1. The book also contains some help-ful chapters on the choral works, as does Robert Marshall's *The Music of Jo-hann Sebastian Bach* (New York: Schirmer 1989), Part 2. Marshall's Part 4 includes an interesting essay on the Teldec cantata series, entitled "'Authentic' Performance: Musical Text, Performing Forces, Performance Style" (pp. 229–39). John Butt's Cambridge Handbook *Bach: Mass in B Minor* (Cam-bridge University Press, 1991) is an especially good guide to form and compo-sition in Bach's choral works.

An important and original discussion of the one-per-part controversy, by a performer who favors Rifkin's position, is Andrew Parrott, "Bach's Chorus: A 'Brief yet Highly Necessary' Reappraisal," *Early Music* 24 (November 1996), pp. 551–80. Parrott reviews the evidence thoroughly but concisely, and con-cludes, "Rifkin's thesis deserves to be regarded as beyond reasonable doubt. The burden of proof lies squarely with those who hold to the notion of an 'ideal' 12- (or 16-) strong Bach choir."

38. Sadler, *Early Music* 15 (May 1987), p. 303.
39. Tanner, "Herreweghe Triumphs in Beethoven," *Classic CD*, December 1995, p. 86.

∞ IV ∞

CLASSICAL AND ROMANTIC

Few artists have ever described their own work as "classic"; it is a term reserved for the dead. Mozart, Haydn, and Beethoven never dreamed that they were writing in the "Classical style." Nobody else seems to have thought so either, until the 1830s—much later in Beethoven's case. This problem here is more than semantic.[1] Robert Levin, Malcolm Bilson, and Roger Norrington, though they don't try to reform our terminology, all suggest ways in which we enfeeble these composers by crowning them with that particular laurel, and (to use Norrington's image) mounting them on smooth marble pedestals.

The term "Romantic" also has problems, but at least it was in use when the music we apply it to was written. Where it may confuse us is in the realm of performance practice. Composers may not call themselves "classical," but, as we'll see, some early-music performers describe their playing style that way. Yet we'll also see that the assumption that "Classical" playing styles were strict is, in various ways, questionable. It is also characteristic—but of us, and perhaps not of history.

Nonetheless, in contrast to the pre-Baroque interviews, the following ones rarely raise the idea that it's "impossible" to recover a historical performing style. They do, however, spend a good deal of time on the historicist/mainstream "turf wars." That's because these wars are fought mainly over composers who were already part of the active concert repertory when the early-music revival began—or so I wrote in the introduction, and you will find evidence for that in these interviews. I also said that the turf wars seem to be

---

1. Wye J. Allanbrook sees the term as an essentially Romantic notion that continues to mislead commentators on Haydn and Mozart. See the fifth lecture in her *The Secular Commedia* (Berkeley: University of California Press, forthcoming).

subsiding; you will find less evidence for that in Robert Levin's distaste for the unhealthy alliance of competitions, record companies, and agents, in Malcolm Bilson's reservations about modern style, or in John Eliot Gardiner's concerns about overstandardized orchestral playing.

However valid these critiques may be, they raise the issue of differing tastes. Monica Huggett told me that as a student she felt straitjacketed by the big sound, lush tone, and constant vibrato of the violin school of Ivan Galamian and Dorothy DeLay;[2] but Itzhak Perlman, perhaps the most distinguished product of that school, calls period string players' non-vibrato phrasing "sterile" and "totally lacking in warmth." Robert Levin argues below that Mozart benefits from being played in a historical style, but Perlman says, "I'm certain Haydn and Mozart would have adored our modern approach to phrasing and vibrato."[3]

Of course, we'll never know what they would have adored; and even if we did, as I wrote in the introduction, some believe that we shouldn't care about that so much as about what *we* adore. But Perlman does not make that argument. Like most mainstream musicians, he is just as concerned with the composer's intention as, say, Bilson is (a fact that Bilson discusses in his interview). Where the two differ is in their understanding of Mozart's intentions. Perlman implies that those intentions transcend the accident of how people played the violin at the time—but Bilson and Levin argue below that some details of the era's playing style are crucial to Mozart's intentions.

Whichever side you take, it should be noted that if Perlman prefers more vibrato, few historical performers nowadays would insist that he suppress this taste when, say, playing Brahms merely because Brahms might not have shared it.[4] And of course, we can't know that Brahms wouldn't have adored the best of Perlman's Brahms playing any more than we can know the opposite.

We do know, however, that the Galamian approach stokes Perlman's artistic fires, while the historical-performance approach stokes those of Huggett and Anner Bylsma (who can't bear too much vibrato in Brahms). The following discussions tell us a great deal about the music, and about musical life today and in the past—after all, it's the abundance of historical evidence that quiets the objection that historical fidelity is not possible even in part—but in the end, what matters most about this evidence may be that it serves my interviewees as kindling.

2. Bernard D. Sherman, "Monica Huggett," *Strings* 10 (March/April 1996), pp. 54–61.

3. Ross Duffin, "Performance Practice: Que me veux-tu?" *Early Music America* 1 (1995), p. 35.

4. Spare-vibrato playing sounded *better* to the ears of Brahms's close associate Joseph Joachim, who said, among other statements, "A violinist whose taste is refined and healthy will always recognize the steady tone as the rule" (in his *Violinschule* [with Andreas Moser; Berlin, 1905], II, p. 94). Brahms might well have agreed.

16

Restoring Ingredients

Malcolm Bilson on
the Fortepiano

"[T]he time will come, I believe," wrote Andrew Porter in 1976, "when audiences—and pianists—having once discovered the tone colors and clarity and alertness of wooden-framed pianos with thin strings and buckskin-covered hammers, will want to hear more of them."[1] That time has yet to come. Even in the early-music world, the fortepiano has fewer friends than we might expect. The harpsichordist Christophe Rousset speaks for many when he calls it "an imperfect instrument, [which had] yet to evolve."[2] Part of the problem is that in a large modern concert hall the instrument becomes little more than a tinkling symbol; but even in the small rooms it was designed for, its limited dynamic range and short tone life can seem desiccated to many who grew up with a Steinway. Malcolm Bilson, who mastered the Steinway long ago, argues below for the advantages of that short tone life.

In making a case for the older instrument, Bilson addresses a more basic issue, still a touchy one for fortepianists: why might historical instruments matter at all? He also discusses changes in playing style, involving approaches to articulation and phrasing that are diametrically opposed to what has become the standard modern practice (though how recently it became "standard" is not always recognized, as he also points out).

Even for the generally unconverted, Bilson offers a specific corrective. It's often said not only that Beethoven was dissatisfied with the pianos of his day

1. Porter, "Pianists and Pianos," from the *New Yorker,* 23 February 1976, reprinted in *Music of Three Seasons: 1974–1977* (New York: Farrar, Straus and Giroux, 1978), pp. 299–300.
2. Stephen Pettitt, "Virtuosity with Heart," *Gramophone* 71 (September 1993), p. 16.

(true, though perhaps exaggerated), but that in his mind he sometimes heard a piano image "not unlike that of the modern Steinway concert grand."[3] Yet as William S. Newman has shown, and as Bilson discusses below, Beethoven's piano ideal differed profoundly from the modern one.[4] Beethoven would probably have been at least as unhappy with our pianos as he was with those of his day. This is not to say we should abandon the concert grand (I'm not throwing away my CDs of Schnabel, Goode, or Brendel, nor would Bilson say I should[5]); but we shouldn't dismiss Beethoven on the fortepiano *a priori*.

In fact, my conversation with Bilson preceded a remarkable Beethoven recital. In it, he proved to be so communicative a Beethoven player that he got a large portion of the audience to laugh out loud at some of the musical jokes in the Op. 33 Bagatelles, a response I had never encountered before at a Beethoven concert. I interviewed Bilson at the site of the sponsor of the concert, the Ira F. Brilliant Center for Beethoven Studies in San Jose; we were surrounded by shelves packed with books, documents, manuscripts, and rare Beethoveniana. The Poletti fortepiano used in his recital was in the room, and at regular intervals Bilson walked over to it to make musical points.

My questions made Alfred Brendel—a pianist and thinker whom Bilson admires greatly—serve as Bilson's antagonist. A few months after I met with Bilson, I heard Brendel, in a radio interview with the pianist Sarah Cahill, say that he now thinks that parts of some early Beethoven sonatas are served better by the fortepiano than by the modern grand. He said that the opening of Op. 7 is hard to play at a suitably fast tempo on a modern Steinway, but that the tempo is easier to achieve on the fortepiano, with its incisive sound and shallow action. This is not to say that Brendel is a convert. He holds that early piano music is rarely composed to exploit the sound of the fortepiano *per se*, but uses it to suggest other instruments; he therefore thinks it unnecessary to bother reviving the vintage piano. Bilson brought up this argument at the beginning of our conversation.

Alfred Brendel says that when you play Beethoven on a modern piano you're playing a transcription.[6] Yet he also argues that the modern piano does more justice to Beethoven.

3. Edward Greenfield, Robert Layton, and Ivan Marsh, *The New Penguin Guide to Compact Discs and Cassettes* (London: Penguin, 1988), p. ix.

4. Newman demonstrated in 1971 that throughout Beethoven's life his piano ideal remained the light, responsive Viennese fortepiano. This research, which has never been seriously challenged, is summarized in chap. 3 of Newman's *Beethoven on Beethoven* (New York: Schirmer 1988).

5. Though his older writings suggest a position less tolerant than the views presented in this interview; see his "The Viennese Fortepiano of the Late 18th Century," *Early Music* 8 (1980), pp. 158–62, esp. pp. 161–62.

6. Brendel, *Musical Thoughts and Afterthoughts* (New York: Farrar, Straus and Giroux, 1976), p. 16.

May I rather refer to Brendel's notes on the Mozart concertos,[7] which I think are really quite wonderful? In fact, I agree with virtually everything Brendel says, until he comes to the question of the instrument. He dismisses Mozart's piano, and cites the Sonata in A Minor, K. 310, as an example. His point, if I understand it correctly, is that pianos *per se* are not really so important anyway. The first movement, says Brendel, is symphonic (I'm not sure I really agree with that, but let's buy it for the sake of argument); the second movement imitates a voice, a cantabile, singing line; and the third movement is clearly a wind divertimento. But the minute I accept Brendel's categories, it seems clear to me that Mozart's piano does each of them better than a modern piano!

How?

Well, if the first movement is symphonic, it does not seem natural to put the most important part of the music into the background, which is what one is forced to do on a modern piano. One cannot play those opening left-hand chords full out on a modern piano, because it is simply too bombastic; and it is virtually impossible to give them rhythmic pulse (strong, weak, strong, weak—as required by all the tutors of the late eighteenth century), so what one hears—from everybody—is a melody with chords in the background.

The second movement, says Brendel, is a vocal line, and I agree completely. But in Mozart's time a vocal line meant clear inflection between strong and weak syllables, strong and weak beats, stressed versus unstressed. This is spelled out clearly by Mozart's careful slurring and articulation marks—but do you know any performance or recording that slurs as Mozart asks? Look at the beginning of the movement:[8]

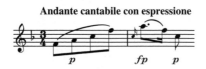

Andante cantabile con espressione

The slur and the *fp* between the A and the F in the right hand reinforce the "sighing" aspect of the little figure; and of course, the F must be released, not carried over legato to the C—Mozart knows very well how to write three-note slurs when he wants them. Have you ever heard anyone play this the way it is so clearly written? On the contrary, one hears a "long, singing line"—a much later concept. The modern piano is very good at achieving such a line, but very poor at achieving what I believe Mozart associated with singing, namely declamation and inflection of the syllables of the text. (In music without text, the tutors tell us, one should always inflect as if the text were there; otherwise it is not natural. And Leopold Mozart tells us that a

7. Brendel, *Music Sounded Out* (New York: Farrar, Straus and Giroux, 1991), pp. 3–11.
8. Mozart, Sonata in A Minor, K. 310, second movement.

group of notes under a slur should be played with a slight diminuendo[9]—a point with expressive significance, I've come to feel.) The modern piano, with its long tone life, has great difficulty playing the F sufficiently softer than the A; it becomes inaudible due to the long singing of the A—and releasing the F will invariably sound like a hiccup, because again the tone of the modern piano wants to continue.

So the more rapid decay of sound on the fortepiano lets you convey that fp on the top A, whereas the slow decay on the modern one prevents that?

Right. Then regarding the third movement, the wind band, I completely agree with Brendel, but once again you have the difficulty that one cannot play all the voices equally, due to the cross-stringing of the modern grand.

The bass strings being crossed under the other strings?

Yes. I'm beginning to think more and more that while cross-stringing has some virtues, it has many more drawbacks. Do you know why they crossed strings on the modern grand?

To save space?

Curiously, even someone from Steinway gave that answer; it's a widespread belief. But after about 1800 the standard length for grands was eight feet; Steinway's first grands in the 1850s were straight-strung, and they were eight feet long. When Steinway crossed the strings, they went to nine feet to get back the extra length they had lost.

So length isn't the reason. What is?

To pull the bridges in toward the center of the soundboard, where the board is most resonant. Think of a violin with the strings running right across the center; on modern pianos, the soundboard is "crowned," as the violin belly is. In addition to the cross-stringing, the grain of the wood on all modern pianos runs diagonally from the keyboard treble to the tail bass. What that achieves is to bring every tone to the center of the soundboard, and it gives the modern piano an enormously concentrated tone, a wonderful virtue. But there are drawbacks as well, compared to the old straight-strung, straight-grained construction. The following passage, as I understand it, is unplayable on a modern piano:[10]

---

9. Leopold Mozart wrote that the first note of a group of "two, three, four, and even more [slurred notes] must be somewhat more strongly stressed, but the remainder slurred on to it quite smoothly and more and more quietly." I quote it from the discussion of the slur in Sandra Rosenblum's *Performance Practices in Classic Piano Music* (Bloomington: Indiana University Press, 1988), chap. 5, p. 159; see especially the subsection "Do All Slurs Indicate Attack and Release?" on pp. 172–83.

10. Mozart, Sonata in Bb, K. 333, opening.

There are two voices here, and the left-hand voice is, if anything, even more interesting than the right; he could have written a simple Alberti bass, but he didn't. Now, if we had a modern piano here, I simply could not give equal weight to both voices.

Why not?

Because the tone is so concentrated that all the sounds slap at each other. One can do it, but it *sounds* very bad: only a very poor pianist would do that. And so, what you'll hear, invariably (listen to any recording), is a beautiful singing right hand, with the left hand in the background. Most listeners are used to hearing it that way, but to me it sounds like a violin–cello duo in which the cello is put at the back of the stage!

Actually, the "slapping at each other," as I call it, this clashing of the sounds together, is something jazz pianists use very much [plays a jazz progression]. There we are used to it; indeed, it is a major component of the jazz piano sound. But we generally don't like it in "serious" music.

And so you lose the independence of voices. [Plays the beginning of the finale of K. 310.] There's a lot going on in the middle voices, but listen to any recording—you'll hear the top voice—just as in K. 333. But on this fortepiano, you can give each voice its due—all the strings are running parallel and the grain of the wood is running parallel, so in a sense each note is independent, whereas on a modern piano there's a conglomeration of sound.

How about Brendel's belief that the modern piano serves Beethoven better?

I think the modern piano serves Beethoven far worse than it does most of the other Classical composers, because Beethoven was extremely interested in the piano and really wrote quite differently for the piano than for strings or for orchestra.

For example?

Well, one thing I consider enormously important in Beethoven is the sforzandos. The modern piano doesn't have a sforzando, it only has loud notes. Because, again, the tone life is so long, it doesn't have the punch in the shoulder that Beethoven would know.

Brendel discusses how difficult it is to play Beethoven's sforzando on a mod-

ern piano, and you suggest it's partly the instrument. You've also written[11] *about the way in which Beethoven's bass figuration depends on the fortepiano's transparent bass.*

Yes, left-hand transparency is an essential part of Beethoven's piano writing, and it is almost impossible on a modern grand, once again because of cross-stringing.

To move to the next generation in Vienna, Brendel argues that most of Schubert's piano music isn't conceived with the piano in mind, with the exception of the Impromptus. *Do you think Schubert benefits from period pianos?*

I personally think that Schubert's piano music is very much tied to these instruments.

Why?

Well, one thing that is very important in Schubert but that one doesn't hear much in modern performances is rhythmic inflection. Now, you know the *Wanderer* Fantasy, don't you? Sing me the opening bar.

[Interviewer sings: TUM! ta ta TUM! ta ta TUM! diddle-diddle-diddle tum ta ta TUM TUM!]

That's terrific! Ask anyone who knows this piece, and they will sing just what you sang, with strong accents on the downbeats (which are also marked by Schubert in the score). Now, go to any recording, and what you will hear is quite even beats. If you try to produce on a modern piano the inflection you just sang, the after-beats sound weak and *very* peculiar. [Plays opening of *Wanderer* with strong accents on the downbeats.] Anyone sitting down at this fortepiano would, I believe, play it that way; but not on a modern piano. All this is very much at the heart of what I think is important in Schubert.

That applies not just to *fortissimos*, but also to *pianos* and *pianissimos*. Listen to any recording of the opening of the B♭ Impromptu, Op. 142, No. 3. Everyone plays the two eighth notes of the second beat evenly, or even a little louder than the downbeat. Yet Schubert's articulation markings clearly indicate the second beat as weaker than the first, an approach reinforced by all the tutors of the time.

What is especially interesting here, I think, is that whereas a weaker second beat is not natural to the tone of the modern piano, the four recordings I have heard on fortepianos *also* crescendo across that second beat. "Pianos," says the wag, "don't make music—people do," and there seems to be a lot of truth in

11. Bilson, "Keyboards," in *Performance Practice: Music after 1600*, ed. H. M. Brown and S. Sadie (London: Macmillan, 1989, and New York: Norton, 1990), p. 232.

that statement. The concept of the long, continuous line was drilled into all of us in every conservatory in the world. We have to learn a new language; sympathetic instruments won't do it all for you, but they can help.

The wag might ask another question: do these matters make a great performance?

Of course they don't. A great performance is obviously a function of how deeply one understands the music. But if you read Türk—Daniel Gottlob Türk's *Klavierschule* is the most important keyboard tutor of the late eighteenth century—his chapter on *Performance* is divided into two parts: *Execution* and *Expression.* I think that most musicians would agree with what Türk says about expression, namely that what counts is depth of feeling, and how well one plays one's instrument, and how well one can transmit one's inner understanding of the music to the audience. But when one comes to execution (which embraces just the matters we've been discussing, such as inflection or stress and release), not only does one not hear these aspects in modern performance, but actually very often one hears just the opposite.

Let's explore that, first regarding meter and metrical articulation. Schnabel said that if he were rich enough he would have all his music printed without bar lines. And Karajan said it should sound as if there were no bar lines at all. On the other hand, the consensus seems to be that in Beethoven, Haydn, and Mozart bar lines are very important.

Very important, *and* heavier down beats, which I was told by at least one Schnabel student—possibly two—to always avoid. When I talk about this, one of the pieces I like to demonstrate with is the first movement of K. 332, which has slurs within each measure:[12]

Mozart has clearly set off each measure from the others with its own slur, and that gives what I perceive as the lilt. When I was demonstrating this recently, a Schnabel student sprang up onstage and said, "What you're saying is completely wrong. Schnabel always taught us to accentuate the *third* beat, in order to keep the long line going." There is a CD out now of Schnabel playing K. 332, and you can hear that very clearly. Now, Schnabel was in a way a wonderful Mozart player, but his basic aesthetic—thus his execution—is diametrically opposed to what any eighteenth-century musician would think was normal.

12. Mozart Sonata in F, K. 332, first movement.

Some people say that Schnabel was right—one scholar wrote that when Mozart wanted continuous legato he would slur "each bar separately, but intended no audible break between them."[13]

Did Mozart *ever* want continuous legato in the sense that it is practiced nowadays—that is, without inflection? I believe that Mozart's slurs mean just what we discussed before, a gradual tapering from first note to last (subject, of course, to other rules of stress, such as high notes, dissonances, etc.). "Diminuendo," by the way, might seem too strong a word for what happens. Normally we use it to refer to going from *forte* to *piano;* that's not what I mean. I mean diminuendo within *piano,* so that you end up weaker than you started, albeit in the same overall dynamic. In any event, I think the reason many modern-day musicians find it difficult to let go of the concept of continuous legato is that most, in order to "keep the tone going," do not make this diminuendo under the slur, as in K. 332 or the Schubert B♭ Impromptu. If one is going ahead full steam with a good, rich tone, an articulation break will always seem intrusive and unnatural. If, however, the last note is softer, a break is quite natural.

Genuine long legato slurs did, of course, exist at the time; the composers of the London school used them, and they are found frequently in Beethoven. They perhaps find their apogee in Chopin, who often wrote a single slur over a page or more and is reported to have phrased that way. Mozart would doubtless have found his playing very original!

Let me reformulate the wag's question. Your point that Schnabel's continuous legato in that phrase differs radically from Mozart's lilting slurs convinces me—I'm thinking of Czerny saying that Beethoven didn't like Mozart's playing because it was "choppy, with no legato."[14] *But one could still argue that both*

13. Robin Stowell, "Leopold Mozart Revisited," in *Perspectives on Mozart Performance,* ed. R. L. Todd and P. Williams (Cambridge University Press, 1991), p. 138. Paul and Eva Badura-Skoda say the same in their pioneering *Interpreting Mozart on the Keyboard,* trans. Leo Black (New York: St. Martin's, 1962), pp. 54–55; they distinguish between "articulating slurs" (the kind Bilson speaks about) and "legato slurs" (the kind Stowell mentions). However, in *The Pianist as Orator* (Ithaca, N. Y.: Cornell University Press, 1992), p. 110, George Barth challenges Eva Badura-Skoda on this issue and shows that her long-line interpretation of one-bar slurs is based on a misreading of Türk's chap. 6. Barth's arguments would apply also to a passage in Leopold Mozart (chapter 1, section 3, paragraph 17, footnote) that has been used to support the "legato slur" concept. By the mid-nineteenth century, however, the endings of slurs may no longer have indicated breaks in articulation: see Nicholas Temperley, "Berlioz and the Slur," *Music and Letters* 50 (1969), pp. 388–92. But Temperley, too, argues that they did not indicate breaks even for Classical composers: see his Cambridge Handbook *Haydn: The Creation* (Cambridge University Press, 1991), p. 116.

I side with Bilson on this issue, but I am at fault for not pursuing another question: whether *all* of Mozart's slur marking should be understood as intentional, or whether some might result from habit or convention.

14. Quoted in Rosenblum, *Performance Practice,* p. 23; see also her discussion on pp. 149–52 and her chap. 5. Czerny's report is widely but not universally assumed to be true.

Schnabel's and Mozart's executions are valid and effective. In other words, the wag might say that Mozart's way of playing it was not inherently the best or ideal way. How would you answer that?

I would be the first to say that it's not necessary to be concerned with Mozart's intentions; and if you're not, that's fine. If you *are*, though, I think these slurs and other markings are perhaps even more important than the notes—in some passages the exact notes weren't crucial to Mozart. Now, Mozart wrote great notes, and you can play them in many different ways and produce great music. I've heard wonderful Mozart from Rachmaninoff and Schnabel (and Schnabel was very concerned with Mozart's intentions but understood them within a later aesthetic). I certainly don't claim that I or other fortepianists play Mozart better than such artists. And I'm not a purist. I can, if I like, choose to ignore a crescendo or slur mark sometimes; that's my right as a performer. But my concern is that I think very few musicians today know what these markings signify. Most haven't been taught how to read these scores, which contain so much information. There are six Urtext editions out, but I have heard no modern pianist try to make these slurs in K. 332 audible. This reflects neither their lack of interest in Mozart's intentions (*pace* the wag) nor their instruments (which can sound these slurs) but the enormous change in musical aesthetics across the nineteenth century.

To understand that change, let me begin by asking about influences on the older aesthetic.

I think it has a lot to do with the prestige that poetry had at the time. In every eighteenth-century source, music is compared to language, and there are no languages I know of that don't have inflection. If you want to learn to speak any language like a native, you have to learn not just the accent but also the inflection. I think that's the most difficult thing when English actors try to do American or American actors try to do English; the "can't" and "cahn't" part is simple, but they *inflect* very differently from the way we do.

We say gar-age and they say gar-age.

Right; and if music is like speech, then inflection is very important in it, too, and the rules of inflection are very clear in all these sources. There are things the sources don't agree about, but on these inflection rules they all agree. Stronger downbeats, stronger accents on dissonances—hold these notes longer and those notes shorter. Consider how we say "Mother"—the second syllable must be shorter and weaker. If you say "MO-THER" [giving the word two equal stresses] you sound like a foreigner. But then of course this is the way most modern singers sing. They sing [sings two long notes in operatic style] "MO-THER" and they make it to the Metropolitan Opera!

This change, away from an aesthetic of music being like speech to the long, sustained line, is often attributed by early-music players to Wagner, above all, with his "endless melody."

That's the generally accepted wisdom. But George Barth, in his fascinating book *The Pianist as Orator,* accuses Beethoven's student Czerny of already changing many of Beethoven's short slurs to longer ones.[15] For example, Czerny puts slurs over the opening bars of the *Pathétique* Sonata, changing what would clearly have been perceived as detached chords (the so-called French Overture style) to the legato style we are accustomed to nowadays.

What aesthetic influences made Czerny do that?

Well, for one thing, the later the pianos get, the less susceptible they are to doing this kind of inflection. In 1991 I played the Schumann Concerto with John Eliot Gardiner on a replica of an 1830 Graf piano. A year later I had the chance to do it again with the Cayuga Chamber Orchestra, in Ithaca, New York, where I live, this time on an 1855 Bösendorfer, still a straight-strung Viennese piano. But the 1855 piano, with its much larger hammers, was a quite a bit heavier than the Graf I was used to, and it was not available for me to practice on, so I practiced on the Steinway in my studio at Cornell. It was curious how much less *sensitive* the 1855 Viennese piano was than the Graf, but how *far* less sensitive the Steinway was than either of them!

Now, I realize that most of your readers will just about hit the ceiling—an 1830 piano is more sensitive than a Steinway? The Steinway (or Bösendorfer or Bechstein) has such an enormous range of color; could an old piano compete with that? But with all the color possibilities, fine nuances of inflections are lost—the best modern pianists do virtually everything with color, and little with articulation or inflection, which have come to be so important in my way of hearing all this music.

For example, in the first statement of the Schumann's opening melody by the piano, there's a sforzando on the high E that nobody plays. I realized, when practicing on the Steinway, that I couldn't play it either, because there was no way to get it to decay fast enough to make the proper inflection between it and the following resolution on D (which should be much softer). It's quite easy for anyone to sing that very expressively, by the way, but our standard modern pianos won't deliver that kind of expression.

You know, both Brendel and Charles Rosen criticize the older pianos for their shorter tone life; but when you think about it, the decay of tone (as it is so sweetly referred to in our language) is the *only* musical characteristic the piano can call its own. The best composers are very sensitive to that, and know how to turn it into a virtue (as we saw when we were talking about Beethoven's sforzandi a while back).

So are you saying that part of the change in the aesthetic, to a more long-

15. Barth, *The Pianist as Orator,* pp. 94–95.

line, less inflected style, came about as a result *of pianos getting louder and heavier—rather than as a cause?*

It's partially true, although I cannot imagine that the "long-line" approach is purely due to the larger tone of the later pianos;[16] that would surely be imputing to pianos a bigger role than they deserve, although the piano had certainly become, by the mid-nineteenth century, the main instrument for European music. It must be remembered that English pianos of the late eighteenth century already had a very long tone life, and, as I said, one sees very long slurs in the works of the important London composers (Clementi, Cramer, Dussek, et al.). This was the wave of the future; Vienna was conservative by comparison.

So the modern piano has its real roots in London and not Vienna?

That is certainly true to a great extent. The difference between the Viennese-style pianos and the English-style pianos, and the two schools of playing associated with them, continues until very late in the nineteenth century. The English school is taken up in Paris and is well represented by the piano music of Chopin and Liszt. The Viennese school goes on through Schubert and into Schumann and, indeed, right up through Brahms to the end of his life. Compare Schubert's *Moment Musical* No. 3 in F Minor to the B Minor Capriccio of Brahms, Op. 76, No. 2. It's virtually the same kind of piece. Only, Brahms was afraid the Viennese tradition of playing was getting lost, and so he indicated small accents on the after-beats in the left hand; that wasn't necessary for Schubert, but they are surely the same kind of inflection, where the "pah" of the "oom-pah" is given a slight lift. And in the first piece of Op. 119, Brahms still writes one slur over each bar—the same notation Mozart used in K. 332! We know that Brahms complained late in his life that players were no longer observing the two-note slur, which he still seems to have considered a "sigh."[17] Does *anyone* play Op. 119, No. 1 that way, lifting at the end of each measure?

16. The enormous popularity of Italian *bel canto* opera at the time was perhaps another factor; for a discussion of its influence on Chopin, see Charles Rosen, *The Romantic Generation* (Cambridge, Mass.: Harvard University Press, 1995), pp. 334–51. More significant may have been the "newly systematic" use of the four-bar phrase as the basic time unit of music (*ibid.*, pp. 258–78). As Rosen says, this "gave a larger sense of motion to long works" (p. 278); it also made it important "to avoid giving a similar emphatic accent on the first bar of every group, as if one were accenting a downbeat" (p. 267).

17. Brahms wrote to Joachim, in May 1879, that a slur over a pair of eighth notes indicates that the second note is shortened, losing some of its value. Moreover, "To apply this to larger note groups would mean an execution marked by liberty and delicacy, which nevertheless is appropriate most of the time." Quoted by Max Rudolf, *The Grammar of Conducting*, 3rd ed. (New York: Schirmer, 1994), p. 408, who notes that "this kind of phrasing calls to mind eighteenth-century performance practices." The English pianist Florence May, after studying with Brahms in 1871, noted that "he made very much of the well-known effect of two notes slurred together, whether in a loud or soft tone, and I know from his insistence to me on this point that the mark has a special significance in his music." May, *The Life of Johannes Brahms* (London: Arnold, 1905), p. 18.

[Plays it.] At the slow speed Brahms asks for, it is quite easily realizable, even on the richest modern piano.

It is illuminating to see that Chopin and Liszt (although they were by no means the same) were doing in Paris something different from what Schumann and Brahms (also not the same, of course) were doing in Germany, and that a great deal of this has to do with piano aesthetics, so different in those two places. Mendelssohn seems to be somewhere in the middle; both types of pianos were important for him and play a role in his keyboard music.

That covers the differences among instruments. But to return to the relationship between aesthetics and understanding what the markings in the scores were supposed to mean, I'd like to ask you about some details of "execution," beginning with articulation markings. For example, the "portato," the marking ⁀·····

I was taught that it was called the "portamento," which I no longer think it should be called. I was also taught that it meant you should play the notes half length, whereas I now know that half length is the *normal* length for notes that are not otherwise marked. Instead, it seems that according to Türk, Leopold Mozart, and others, notes played portato should be held as long as possible.

Suppose you have four notes descending. If these notes are not marked, then they're to be played detached, at half their length. Though Leopold Mozart and Türk qualify that: both say that the length of the note depends on the context of the music. In a scherzo, unmarked notes would probably be shorter than half length; in an adagio of a heavier nature, they would be longer, though still detached from one another. Now, if you put a slur over those notes, they're not just connected but, as we've seen, have an inherent diminuendo—it's as if you come to the end of a bow-stroke, then start afresh with a new one.[18] However, if you have portato, the slur with the dots under it, it's a continuous sign—it's as if you either bow on each note or tongue on each note.

Again, you have to decide on what the context of the piece is. This is something I always try to get students to understand. The first thing you have to understand is that whatever your teachers tell you is probably wrong—even if it's me! We have what Beethoven gave us, but when Beethoven writes a portato marking or a sforzando, do we really know what to do? Does a sforzando mean to play longer? Does it mean to play louder, and if so, how much? All of these are really open questions. And it seems to me that any young person who's starting out should doubt everything and try to make his own decisions

---

18. Bilson points out that the German word *Bogen* means both "slur" and "bowing." Regarding this, Monica Huggett pointed out to me that on Mozart's violin just changing the bow's direction creates an audible articulation; this, she said, reflects "both the old bows and the gut strings." By contrast, "with a modern setup . . . you have to make a kind of hard articulation for it to register." Bernard D. Sherman, "Monica Huggett," *Strings* 10 (March/April 1996), pp. 54–61; quote, p. 58.

about such things. And investigating instruments and how they react to such markings as sforzando is very much part of this questioning.

So we decide just what contemporaries understood by "execution" based, ultimately, on our own educated judgment?

Of course. You know, we do not have recordings of Beethoven or Schumann or Chopin or Liszt or Bach or Mozart playing, but we do have recordings of Prokofiev, Bartók, Rachmaninoff, and Elgar. Get a score of one of these composers, and sit down and listen to one of those recordings. It can be quite illuminating, but *not* as is often done, through asking, "How does Bartók play this piece?" Rather, try it from the point of view of listening to what Bartók plays, and then asking *How did he write this down on the page?* In other words, do it backwards. And this might help understand what Beethoven might have heard that would make him mark the page as he did. It gives you a fresh perspective.

Well, one element of these recordings is often rubato. Let's talk about rubato, as an example of execution. What about the contrametric rubato that Mozart is said to have used, where the left hand kept steady time while the right hand moved more freely?

I very much believe in the left hand not knowing what the right hand does, and I try to do this in Mozart. In one of the Mozart concertos I recorded with John Eliot Gardiner, in the middle section of the slow movement I made a great effort to realize this: the orchestra was playing a beautiful, lilting accompaniment, and I was wandering around and weaving in and out. But in the finished product you don't hear much of it. I think that what happened was that when they were editing the tapes they threw all those takes out because they *weren't together!*

Will you tell me which concerto it is?

I'm sorry, I'd rather not. But, you know, Chopin talked a lot about this kind of rubato, and I've been trying to do it in Chopin lately.

Isn't it difficult?

Chopin himself said it was difficult. He made his students practice the left hand with two hands till they had it just right—because the accompaniments must always be inflected as well—before he'd let them try to add the right hand.

I don't know of many pianists who do much with that kind of rubato now.

Horszowski did: listen to his recording of the D♭ major Nocturne. Of course, he was old; he was probably trained that way. Recent training shuns such things.

How about the agogic rubato—the usual kind—where both hands speed up and slow down together. Do you use that in Mozart and Beethoven?

I think the agogic rubato should be used, and I'm sure that I do. It's very clearly shown in Barth's book that Beethoven did it.

I'm sure Mozart did, too. Now, there's a well-known quotation by Mozart from a letter that so-and-so didn't play "im Takt."[19] That's usually translated "in tempo," but that's not really the proper translation of *Takt*. *Takt* means "time," it means "beat," it means "measure," it means all kinds of different things. I think what Mozart was saying, in effect, was that the music didn't sound as if it was proceeding properly through time. I *don't* think that Mozart was thinking that something should accommodate a metronome. The difficulty with a metronome is that it doesn't distinguish between beats, bars, and gestures. And all of the sources say that this beat is more important than that beat, that this should be longer and that should be shorter, that this should be heavier and that should be lighter.[20] For instance, in the way you sang the *Wanderer*, the two eighth notes were probably *not* exactly twice as fast as the quarter notes. This belongs to a natural execution. Now, if you exaggerate that, and make the eighth notes conspicuously slow or fast, then of course I'd say that you were playing out of time, because these things have to have some relation to each other. As a basic rule, the sources tell us that the long notes should be held longer and short notes played a little faster;[21] this is not done nowadays, but I think it makes perfect sense, as long as it is "im Takt."

Again, the basic way to play—including the differing strengths and lengths of equally notated notes—is not expression, but rather merely execution?

That's right, although of course expression and execution are always connected. When I gave a lecture on this, I used a recording of Bartók playing a piece called *Evening in the Country*, the first section of which is marked "with rubato." He plays enormously freely—some eighth notes are more than twice as long as other eighth notes. Then there's a rhythmic section marked "non-rubato," but he plays the little figure ♫. faster than written. The music is strict, but the little figure isn't. That's execution. He's not accelerating, he's not decelerating, but he inflects the rhythm. It's like playing a Viennese waltz; there's a little lilt to it, otherwise you're giving it the wrong execution.

And you say that people don't do such things nowadays?

One of the things that are missing in most modern playing is that there are not enough ingredients in it. For example, I always tell pianists that they do a

19. Letter of 23–24 October 1777, mocking the playing of Nanette Stein, daughter of the fortepiano maker: quoted in Rosenblum, *Performance Practices*, p. 23. Bilson draws a different conclusion about Mozart's rubato than Rosenblum does, on pp. 383–84.

20. Türk, for example, wrote about this, concluding, "In poetry, no one has yet introduced as desirable a meter which consists of nothing but one-syllable feet": discussed in Barth, *The Pianist as Orator*, pp. 16–18.

21. This remained standard practice until after World War I, as shown by old recordings. See Philip, *Early Recordings and Musical Style*, chap. 3.

great deal with color and almost nothing with length. Even the greatest pianists play virtually every note full length, connected to the next (unless they're playing staccato). But length is an extremely important ingredient.

Another important ingredient is vibrato. String players even sixty years ago used various different vibratos, or none, depending on the music. Today they employ a single, constant vibrato. To me, it's not just a little bit crazy, it almost verges on lunacy. One hears a cellist in string quartet playing a low B♭ as an organ point—and vibrating on it! This is something that I can never understand. They vibrate the same way on everything. But unlike the older string players, they rarely use another ingredient, portamento (sliding). Singers don't slide much either nowadays. To have a word like "Liebe" [love] and not slide between the two syllables is very hard for me to understand.

Another ingredient in piano playing which has disappeared, and which is very important, and which you still hear in pianists early in this century, is not playing all chords together but rather rolling some of them.

Bartók did that.

Bartók did all these things—rolling chords, playing rubato, not having the hands together.[22] All of these are important ingredients that can be used and, of course, abused.

Can't modern instruments execute in the old way?

Many of the fortepiano techniques are difficult to do on modern pianos. They're difficult to do on all modern instruments, basically, because modern instruments are set up for long tones. But some could be done easily.

I'm teaching one day a week at Eastman this year, and I'm having a very good time there. Very few of the students who play for me play on the old piano I brought there—I never push them to. But one very talented young woman who is playing Mozart is trying to, and I hope when she goes back to the modern piano she'll bring something with her. But it's not because she sat down to try the piano; it's because I said, "Look: look what's on the page here." And she tried to play it on the Steinway and couldn't, and then she went over to the smaller piano and found she could, and easily.

Because with a piano, once you've struck the tone, you can't really do anything further. A violinist can learn to use his modernized violin and his Tourte bow differently, and wind players can learn to do different things. But with the piano, the one thing that's "set at the factory" is the aftersound; you can't do anything about it, you can only adapt to it.

So does that imply that the piano repertoire most needs period instruments?

Well, when you say "period instruments," do you mean turn-of-the-century Bechsteins with soft hammers for Debussy, and Steinways for Prokofiev?

22. László Somfai, *Béla Bartók: Composition, Concepts, and Autograph Sources* (Berkeley: University of California Press, 1996), pp. 279–95.

That's an interesting question too. I hadn't meant that, but what do you think?

I think that's true. People think of period instruments as meaning only old ones, but it also means modern ones.

So what should a modern pianist do? A modern violinist might try to incorporate Baroque style, but do you have any specific suggestions for modern pianists?

It's very difficult to discuss these things in the abstract. I realize that when I learn these pieces, and then hear them in concert or hear records of people playing them on modern pianos, I just read what's on the page so differently. So, therefore, the overall interpretation comes out very differently as well. But I think that what's being done with fortepianos might teach modern players to play differently; I hope it will.

When I was a kid there would be a tough technical passage and I would say, "This is not playable. I've been practicing this for three months and nobody can play that!" Then I would get a record and hear somebody play it, and I would be able to play it too—immediately! After three months of not being able to play it and considering it unplayable. Many pianists talk about imitating bassoons, and imitating voices, and imitating strings; now maybe some of them can learn to imitate a piano!

SELECTED DISCOGRAPHY

Bilson was the first fortepianist to record the complete Mozart concertos, between 1983 and 1989. According to Joseph Kerman, "one can only admire his responsiveness to the shades of expression called for in this amazing and amazingly diverse repertory. . . . He has to be the exemplary Mozart pianist for our time."[23] Richard Taruskin particularly admires the concertos recorded after 1986 (Nos. 20–27, and 6 and 8); as the series proceeded, he says, Bilson displayed "new poise and depth."[24] Quoting an interviewer, Taruskin says Bilson increasingly explores "'worlds of fortepiano color as yet undreamt of'"; further, he embellishes more, and his rubatos, "once virtually nonexistent, are becoming a trademark" (Bilson's comments above suggest that this may have been in spite of the producers).

In the following year, 1990, Hungaroton recorded Bilson in the complete Mozart sonatas. These performances take up from the high level on which the concerto set left off; sample the audacious treatment of the left hand in the opening of K. 310 (which Bilson discusses early in our interview) and of the

23. Kerman, "Mozart à la Mode," *New York Review of Books,* 18 May 1989, pp. 50–52; quote, p. 52.

24. Taruskin, "A Mozart Wholly Ours," originally printed in *Musical America* (May 1990, pp. 32–41), reprinted in *Text and Act* (New York: Oxford University Press, 1995), pp. 273–85; quote, pp. 283–84.

harmonic progressions in the opening of the Fantasia, K. 475—the list could go on at length. Bilson's rhythmic liberties reflect his concerns with speech-like inflection, with slur markings, with the metrical hierarchy (see John Butt in Chapter 9), and with the "psychological reaction" discussed in Robert Levin's interview. In an essay about K. 475/457, Gretchen Wheelock praises Bilson's recording for capturing "the enormous rhetorical range of the work," and for exploiting "the expressive range of [the instrument] in a spirit of improvisatory freedom and discovery."[25] Listening to the Fantasia and K. 310, I was reminded of what Nicholas Anderson wrote about Anner Bylsma's Bach suites:[26] if these two Mozart recordings had been released in 1965, they would have been decried as self-indulgent and romantic.

Precisely such complaints greeted the first releases of Bilson's complete Schubert series for Hungaroton (HCD 31587, featuring D. 537 and 959; and especially HCD 31586, featuring D. 850 and D. 568). Susan Kagan, a discerning critic and respected pianist, objects to the "romantic" liberties Bilson takes; she believes that Schubert should be played in a "more classical style."[27] There is evidence for and against her view; but as Bilson explains in his interview, and as I hope emerges in later chapters, the equation of "Classical" with "strict" may be a twentieth-century one. Other critics have found much to praise in these Schubert releases. Nicholas A. Rast says of D. 959 that "Bilson's blend of spontaneity and distinctive contrasts of tonal colour in all movements winningly conveys both the music's potently dramatic use of motivic material and its large-scale psychological spans."[28]

Bilson and some of his students are, as I write, recording the complete Beethoven piano sonatas for Claves. The only Bilson Beethoven recording I've heard is a set of the cello sonatas with Anner Bylsma on Elektra-Nonesuch (79152 and 79236). Its music-making, says David Fanning, is "creative, spontaneous, and uninhibited," with "true Beethovenian drama."[29] Those who dismiss the idea of Beethoven on the fortepiano should hear it; the period instruments solve balance problems that modern pianos create in these works, making it clear that Beethoven would have written the piano parts differently for a modern grand. Fanning writes that Bilson's "first entry in the C major Sonata sounds for all the world as if his partner is triple-stopping."

FOR FURTHER READING

Sandra P. Rosenblum's *Performance Practices in Classic Piano Music* (Bloomington: Indiana University Press, 1988) is a thorough, balanced exposition of many of the issues discussed above. William S. Newman's *Beethoven on*

25. Wheelock, "Recovering Mozart's Fantasy," *Early Music* 24 (May 1996), p. 351.
26. And which I quoted to Bylsma in his interview.
27. Kagan, *Fanfare* 19 (May/June, 1996), p. 263.
28. Rast, *Gramophone* 74 (August 1996), p. 76.
29. Fanning, *Gramophone* 69 (April 1992), p. 93.

Beethoven (New York: Schirmer, 1988) is an outstanding discussion of performance practice in Beethoven's piano works. George Barth's *The Pianist as Orator* (Ithaca, N. Y.: Cornell University Press, 1992) is an insightful analysis of tempo flexibility and articulation in Beethoven, and of the eighteenth-century rhetorical tradition in music, in which Beethoven was steeped. For a subtle discussion of the "ingredients" lost in modern playing, and of how they became lost, see Robert Philip's *Early Recordings and Musical Style* (Cambridge University Press, 1992). Alfred Brendel's two books of essays (*Musical Thoughts and Afterthoughts* and *Music Sounded Out* [New York: Farrar, Straus and Giroux, 1976 and 1991]) contain fascinating insights into the Viennese Classical composers' piano works from one of their finest interpreters. As Bilson mentions, another distinguished interpreter and important thinker, Charles Rosen, has attacked the ideas behind the use of period pianos. A particularly subtle exposition is the first chapter of his *The Romantic Generation* (Cambridge, Mass.: Harvard University Press, 1995), which does not discuss the fortepiano in isolation, but mentions it in the context of a larger discussion of the relationship between sound and music. His comment on Beethoven's pianos is typically thought-provoking; he explains that Beethoven worked with the gap between idea and realization, and that the strain this puts on the listener's imagination is an essential element of his music. Rosen then concludes, "The best argument for using the pianos of Beethoven's time . . . is not the aptness of the old instruments but their greater inadequacy for realizing such an effect, and consequently the more dramatic effort required of the listener. The modern piano, however, is sufficiently inadequate to convey Beethoven's intentions" (p. 3).

17

Speaking Mozart's Lingo

Robert Levin on Mozart
and Improvisation

Robert Levin became a fortepianist by accident. As a concert pianist and Mozart scholar, he had met Malcolm Bilson at several conferences. Though he had enjoyed their exchanges, he was astonished when Bilson asked him to participate in recording Mozart's four-hand piano music. "But I don't play the fortepiano," Levin said. "Ah," said Bilson, "You'll learn fast."

He did, though he still performs on the Steinway at least as often as on the fortepiano. That kind of back-and-forth is becoming common among historical performers. What makes Levin uncommon is another element of accident, one that he introduces into the Mozart works he performs: he doesn't play the same notes at each performance but makes some of them up on the spot.

We now think of music in terms of a division of labor: the composer writes it, the performer plays it. In earlier eras, as some previous interviews have indicated, the labor was less divided. The performer was expected to contribute a significant amount to the composing process; and, of course, the performer often *was* the composer. In Mozart's time, genres like the opera aria and the concerto still called for a good deal of performer input. In these works, Mozart didn't write down all of the passagework, lead-ins, and cadenzas, but often played (as he wrote to his father) "whatever occurs to me at the moment." This leads to the paradox in the quest for "authentic" performance that Lawrence-King spoke about: how can we apply the movement's original concern with fidelity when we're dealing with composers who composed their music anew at every performance? If you want to play the way Mozart played—*really* the way Mozart played—you had better learn to *compose* the way Mozart did, and be able to do it "at the moment." As far as I know, Levin is the first modern performer to have managed that. In an attitude that flouts standard modern practice, he follows period practice by *not* being faithful to the score. Levin even improvises fantasias in Mozart's style on themes submitted by the audience—a feat that never fails to amaze.

Mozart's improvisations reflected an ethos that, as Levin points out, also reached into what was then a relatively new institution, the concert hall. To Mozart, playing a concerto was not an act of communion with a hallowed masterpiece; it was show biz. His letters show that he expected a kind of audience response that would be found today at a jazz club but might get you thrown out of some classical concert halls.

When did the ethos change in classical music to our current one—when, in other words, did the music become "classical"? This question, too, features in our discussion. To what Levin says I would add only that the growing emphasis on sticking to the score went hand in hand with a growing concern with integrated musical structure[1]—since improvisation challenges the supremacy of both. As I'll discuss in the "For Further Reading" section at the end of this chapter, some musicologists have objected to improvising in Mozart concertos because they believe the structure is too tight to allow for it.

It would be a mistake, by the way, to think that improvisation reduces the need for rigor in musical training. On the contrary, Levin argues that to improvise successfully one needs far more rigorous training than is customary in musical education today. (He had the good fortune to have five years of study with the legendary composition teacher Nadia Boulanger, who had earlier taught Aaron Copland, Elliott Carter, Dinu Lipatti, and many other great musicians.) Perhaps it's relevant that we spoke by telephone when Levin had just returned to his alma mater, Harvard, to join its faculty. He hopes that renewed interest in improvisation might foster a revival of higher standards of theory teaching—that is, a return to the tradition of teaching performers how to compose.

It's been said that the musical culture of Mozart's age was (ironically, given the rigid class structure of his day) more like our popular than our "classical" culture.

There's no question that the boundaries between popular and—how should one say it?—artistic culture, what's sometimes called "serious" music, were

1. Charles Rosen, *The Romantic Generation* (Cambridge, Mass: Harvard University Press, 1995), pp. 68–78, discusses the change to seeing musical works as abstract, independent aesthetic objects in the late eighteenth and early nineteenth century. Lydia Goehr argues for a far-reaching change in the basic concept of music and art in this period; her work is discussed briefly in the "For Further Reading" section of this chapter. See also Joseph Kerman's "A Few Canonic Variations," *Critical Inquiry* 10 (1983), pp. 107–25, reprinted in his *Write All This Down* (Berkeley: University of California Press, 1994), and Carl Dahlhaus's "The Metaphysics of Instrumental Music," in his *Nineteenth-Century Music*, trans. J. Bradford Robinson (Berkeley: University of California Press, 1989), pp. 88–96.

much narrower in the past than they are now. In the late eighteenth century, people were more comfortable with going back and forth. A man of the soil like Joseph Haydn shows this most remarkably, but Mozart, who probably identified more with the aristocracy than did Haydn, was certainly able to write in the popular style when he chose to do so. It's seen in pieces like the Divertimento K. 287, where he quotes several folk tunes, and just as openly in *The Magic Flute*.

Also, in our culture today it's the popular musicians, the vernacular musicians, who command not only untrammeled adulation from the public but also vast sums of money, and have to deal with meteoric rises and equally sudden falls from public grace. That's not unlike one aspect of Mozart's career, and from that point of view your comparison is well taken. Mozart made fabulous sums of money during the period when he was the darling of the Viennese and Prague public, and he seemed to be making a comeback in 1791 before his life was cut brutally short.

How about the culture of the concert hall itself? The modern concert, where one is supposed to sit silent until the end of a piece, seems worlds apart from Mozart's concert hall, where people would applaud during the piece after a striking passage, like a jazz audience.

Correct, and that reflects a concept of history that developed in the nineteenth century, but was not at all a part of the concert scene when Mozart was presenting his works to the public. The only kind of music that really absorbed the public then was contemporary music. With the exception of some sacred music, the Viennese didn't take much interest in anything more than two weeks old. They did not want to hear the piano concerto that Mozart had written three weeks or (heaven forfend) a year ago; they wanted to hear something that was brand new. This kind of appetite seems remarkable in light of today's attitudes toward contemporary music, but the comparison is not entirely fair, because the musical language of the late eighteenth century was much more accessible to a well-educated listener. With this appetite for something current comes a zest for it, and an audience that is seeking not to enjoy time-sanctioned masterpieces but to be challenged, to be stimulated, to be astounded, to be confounded, to be overwhelmed with grief or ardor. That kind of public has an attitude much more like that of the public that goes to, as you said, a jazz or rock concert—or to the movies.

With the growing attitude that music is a continuum with a glorious historical tradition worth preserving came a more museum-like attitude toward performance. The first of the great European orchestras, created in 1828 in Paris, was called into being by François-Antoine Habeneck for the purpose of performing the symphonies of Beethoven—who had died the year before. This shows that the bounds of interest were slowly shifting from a nearly exclusive preoccupation with the present to this idea of a heritage. Along with the heritage comes the sense of etiquette. And the sense of etiquette is a dangerous one, because it can lead sooner or later to ossification, which it has, to a substitution of mores for content, which it has, and to a kind of obsession with accuracy and responsibility, which it has—and not only among performers but also, in some ways willfully and in other ways involuntarily, in the profession of musicology. We have developed something which the Germans call *Werktreue,* faithfulness to the text, and also a sense that it's necessary in establishing the text to strive to find the so-called *Fassung letzter Hand,* the composer's definitive version.

But it's almost impossible to imagine a *Fassung letzter Hand* for Mozart. He lived in an age of spontaneous performance, improvisation, embellishment, and the inescapable demands that economics imposed on musical activities; all this created performances that were constantly in flux. When Mozart revived an opera and some singer couldn't do this or that passage, he revised the aria. He added certain arias because a singer wanted more; and if it was a different kind of voice, he changed or replaced extensively. These things were not seen as beneath his dignity, because he lived in an age when composers still felt that if the performers looked good, then the composer looked good.

As opposed to the mid-twentieth-century composer's idea of, "Who cares if you listen?"[2] When did the attitude start to change?

It changed in a critical way with Beethoven, who even said that his music was not like the old music. Mozart's music was very often sight-read, which was possible when people played in only one kind of musical style. Even orchestras seemed to have done this reasonably well, since Mozart did speak about good and bad performances with orchestras—although in terms of intonation and ensemble we might perhaps consider what he considered bad performances execrable and what he called good performances mediocre. Against that background, it's very important to realize that Beethoven wrote music that could not be sight-read. If Beethoven's music is sometimes awkward, it's not because he didn't know how to write for the instrument, but because that was what he wanted—and, for artistic reasons, had—to do. Berlioz is another example of an astonishing innovator whose music certainly ought not to have been sight-read if it was to make any kind of impact.

So the trends of our century—new music that's difficult,[3] respectful treat-

2. Milton Babbitt, "Who Cares If You Listen?" This 1958 essay has been anthologized often, including in *Contemporary Composers on Contemporary Music,* ed. Elliot Schwartz and Barney Childs (New York: Da Capo Press, 1978), pp. 244–50. The title was not Babbitt's—he wanted to call it "The Composer as Specialist"—but many people think it captures an attitude of his era.

3. Rosen says in *The Romantic Generation* (p. 72) that the "impetus behind avant-garde ideology [arose] at the very end of the eighteenth century. When the work of art is initially rejected by the public, this provides its moral credentials; it demonstrates that the work was not created for popularity or money, and justifies its success with posterity."

ment of a canon of works—had their seeds, more or less, with the coming of the nineteenth century?

Of course, Mozart was considered difficult by his contemporaries; and some early Romantics saw him as one of the first Romantics. But by and large his stock fell at around 1830 or so, and rose again only in our own century.[4] Why do you think this happened?

That is a fascinating thing. One of the reasons why Mozart did so badly in the past was that he was always known as a precursor of Beethoven, and since Beethoven had to be the greatest, Mozart could only be pretty good. Beethoven's unforgettably obsessive rhythmic figures, a cellular way of getting beneath the skin of the audience until he smashes atoms, is something we do not regard as a Mozartian quality. Mozart's virtue was more the spinning out of the line, with infinite rhythmic variety and flexibility, so that it always sounds like the thing is being made up in front of you. Neither one of these is better than the other—that's not the point—but previous generations seem to have needed to rate people.

Mozart's "rising stock" also shows what happens when we begin to emerge from the penumbra of this Romanticized view of things, which cast a very long shadow. In it, Mozart continued to be regarded as a divine freak of nature whose music, like a Hummel porcelain figurine, was always in exquisite taste but on a somewhat limited scale, and whose claims to greatness had to be qualified in light of the monumental and overwhelming achievements of subsequent generations. Now, this is not to say that people like Furtwängler, Walter, Schnabel, Rubinstein, or Edwin Fischer didn't give transcendent Mozart performances. One of the more brilliant of Taruskin's many contributions is his observation that the historical-performance movement reveals less about the eighteenth century than it does about our age. This sudden fascination with the re-institution of original bowings and so on is as much a phenomenon of the twentieth century at its end as Furtwängler's performances were of the twentieth century in its first half. And it's not possible to predict what fifty years from now will qualify as representative performance of any of this literature, because it's in the nature of things that very often we do not see our own prejudices and our projections of our own values onto this music—you can call them limitations if you wish to be negative. And I think that a composer such as Haydn and Mozart might be astonished that everyone is so careful about doing it like this or like that. Most likely they weren't careful about doing things; they just did them.

But they did not have the problem that we have of two hundred intervening years of music with performance styles and instruments so radically different. To my ears, as long as Mozart was being played in the same performance style as Schumann, his distinctive personality and its aesthetic un-

4. Leon Botstein, "Nineteenth-century Mozart," in *On Mozart*, ed. James Morris (Cambridge University Press, 1994), pp. 204–26.

derpinnings were likely to be washed over. Beethoven is for me a Classical composer, but because his music was looking in a direction that the later music represents, it didn't suffer in the same regard, except that the monumentality led to a drastic disregard of Beethoven's tempos, and to sacrifices in the liveliness of the surface.

Why do you think the historicist approach benefits Mozart's music?

Because in the case of Mozart, the baby was virtually thrown out with the bath water. Those very sweet, long, legato lines served the purpose of showing how tasteful and Olympian and perfectly balanced Mozart was. They did not show how his music, like Haydn's, depends on a constant amazement, a perpetual inconsistency with mercurial transformations from the flirtatious to the grand, from the grand to the teasing, from the teasing to the beseeching to the charming to the lyrical to the lamenting and back and forth—and often four or five of these things within the space of eight bars. The music is this way—here we come back to the beginning of our conversation, about popular culture—because it was designed to make an enormous impact on first hearing, because there was not expected to be a second one.

Malcolm Bilson said this also reflected a new expressive need: "One essence of the old 18th-century style is musical development [the "spinning out" of a musical motif]; in the new style this is replaced by psychological reaction. What comes in bar 2 comes there because it fits psychologically after bar 1, whether or not it is motivically derived from that bar." [5]

Well, Mozart was a dramatist. He was an opera composer first and foremost, and everything he wrote has to be understood in that regard. The concertos are a more polarized and evident example of that, but the dramatic principle in his rhetoric is not missing from the piano sonatas or string quartets or vocal music. And Mozart, being a man of the theatre, was constantly aware of what is necessary to advance the plot, to entertain at the local level without sacrificing the larger design. It is no coincidence that Mozart's music has such an extraordinary variety of motivic material but that, in spite of the profligacy of this richness, it never uses a theme without a hierarchical purpose. Architecturally, his is one of the most complex musics that Western culture has produced, rivaled only by a small number of works—one of which is Schoenberg's First Chamber Symphony, Op. 9—but not by Brahms or Haydn or Beethoven, who were not temperamentally suited to this kind of composition.

Still, here again we can trace the boundaries between vernacular and art music in a very effective way. From the moment the overture of *Figaro* begins it's a smash hit, and after each act you go out singing the tunes, as you do at a great Broadway show. Now, of course, the music is much more sophisticated

5. Malcolm Bilson, "Interpreting Mozart," *Early Music* 12 (November 1984), p. 520.

than Broadway in many respects; but in *Figaro* there is rarely an aria or ensemble that doesn't advance the plot. And that kind of localized and long-term development—which is also, by the way, reflected in Mozart's choice of keys for successive numbers in an opera—is not the kind of thing that many other composers were interested in. For instance, Mozart is the only composer in the pantheon who took care in all of his mature operas to end in the key he began in. This is not to say that doing so is good whereas not doing so is bad, but rather that Mozart's structural hierarchy and his dramatic control are not coincidences but are part of the same personality, and these things, along with the extraordinary impulsiveness that Malcolm Bilson describes, all connect to the need to grab the public immediately, to beguile them, to lure them, to seduce them, to charm them, as I said before, and leave them no room to let go. The concertos, like the operas, were supposed to involve the combination of theatricality and improvisation in terms of embellishments, and what they lack in a specific plot they nonetheless make up for in the very careful delineation of character that one can read underneath the musical surface.

How is character delineated in concertos?

Tonality is a major factor. A piece in A major by Mozart could never be confused with one in C major; if you know his language well, you could tell that there was something wrong with a piece in A that was transposed to C. Take the Piano Concerto No. 23 in A, K. 488, and play it in C major. It won't sound right, because A major in Mozart is a key that's lyrical, sunny; we associate it with a special kind of radiance, a real iridescence often referred to as autumnal because the clarinet works have such ineffable coloristic and expressive feelings about them. On the other hand, C major and D major are much more normal keys, D major being the standard trumpet and drum key and C major being the majestic key.

Now, interestingly, none of the great composers used such a small range of *principal* tonalities as Mozart did: there is not one piece Mozart ever wrote whose principal tonality has more than four sharps or flats—none. But on the other hand, the modulations within those tonalities in Mozart are more audacious than those of just about any composer, with the possible exception of Schubert. The conflict, the daring, the dislocation of such far-flung modulations occur relative to a home turf that remains within bounds. It shows we're dealing here with a remarkable kind of societal code; in Mozart these tonal wanderings have a sociological aspect to them. Thus, the delineation of character: for Mozart, these tonalities represent ways of portraying people and types of people. Heroes, anti-heroes, protagonists who are more delicate, or more vulnerable, assertive, grander—the decision to write a piece in a particular key is already making a major statement. And because he was enormously conservative in his choice of keys, the way the artist represents the protagonists within this frame is all the more riveting, because there's at least this external attempt to stay within these conventions. The straitjacketing of these conventions, the pressures they bring to bear, can be all the more telling.

Does this choice of specific keys communicate anything to a listener who doesn't have absolute pitch?

His audience was helped to a good sense of *relative* pitch by the use of asymmetrical tunings, non-tempered tunings (on recordings I've used various historical tunings). I won't say they're indispensable, because we're no longer used to them, and a lot of people nowadays would think the instruments were out of tune. But when Beethoven brings back a false reprise in the wrong key, people then knew it wasn't right because all the intervals sounded weird.

Even with these tunings, though, I wonder how much Mozart expected his audiences to understand his system of key associations. After all, different people had different associations.[6] But one other way by which Classical composers delineated character, as Leonard Ratner and Wye J. Allanbrook emphasize, is through reference to a large body of musical "topics"—musical features (rhythmic, melodic, etc.) that by convention were associated in everyone's minds with certain types of characters. The various dances each had well-known associations to class and character; so did hunting horns, church styles, and so forth.[7] So, for example, K. 456 in Bb begins with four bars on a "military" topic, but K. 595, which is also in Bb, begins with a "lyrical singing" topic. Would you comment on the relationship between Mozart's key choices and his use of topics?

6. Rita Steblin, *History of Key Characteristics in the Eighteenth and Early Nineteenth Centuries* (Ann Arbor, Mich.: UMI Press, 1983) shows that this was a popular subject among music theorists of the era, but that there was little consensus: different theorists' views of key characteristics often conflicted.

7. See Allanbrook's *Rhythmic Gesture in Mozart* (University of Chicago Press, 1983), especially its introduction and first two chapters, and Ratner's *Classic Music* (New York: Schirmer, 1980). If the idea of a repertoire of widely understood musical "topics" seems far-fetched, consider our own musical culture. By alluding to rap, heavy metal, Sousa marches, cool jazz, college fight songs, slow blues, show tunes, Dixieland, and numerous other musical topics, a composer can instantly make us think of the associated types of characters. Film and TV composers allude to such topics particularly frequently.

The idea of a system of topical associations may remind us of what Page, Thornton, and Hellauer say in this book about Gregorian modes, which may have communicated emotions through a system of associations that people had internalized.

One question is whether the late-eighteenth-century topics still communicate in that way to us. To at least some extent, I think, Allanbrook is right in saying that some of them do: we still recognize a descending chaconne bass in the minor as lamenting, and a gigue as light-hearted. Some of this may reflect our having learned some "topical" conventions through our exposure to them; but it is also possible that some musical topics relate to the thing they signify in a way that doesn't entirely depend on convention. For example, the "funeral march" (yet another topos) may imitate the slow, heavy way we move when we grieve; the gigue may imitate the way we move when we're joyful.

Perhaps an appropriate analogy might be made between tonality in music and locality in drama. In choosing to set a play or an opera in a specific place the dramatist invokes the color, the mores, the dialect of its denizens. But the choice of venue, whether exotic or familiar, scarcely limits the potential types of characters. What it does is to put nobles, peasants, lovers, libertines, ingenues, murderers or conspirators into a geographical context that provides an overall frame. There are some kinds of activities or patterns of behavior that are endemic to certain places. So it is with Mozart's choice of tonalities: B♭ major encompasses both lyrical and sprightly characters. But just as choosing Paris as a setting excludes mountains or a seaport, Mozart's B♭ major excludes the majesty of trumpets and drums.

Even in his era, other composers did not equal Mozart's consistency and conservatism in choosing tonal settings. And one could say that with the evolution from Classical to Romantic music there is a motion away from these kinds of sophistication, that delicacy of hearing, to—again—an ever more monumental sort of style.

To help regain that delicacy of hearing, you've done research on Mozart's style, and one of the methods you've used to study Mozart's language is statistical analysis: for example, in your reconstruction of the Symphonie Concertante for Four Winds.[8] Haven't some people found this a soulless, antiseptic way to approach something as subtle and alive as music?

That's exactly right, but even with certain Mozart specialists whose knowledge may exceed mine, I'll say, "Look at this harmonic progression or this melodic figure; that's something which does not occur anywhere in Mozart." And they'll answer back, "Sure, but he could have done that." And I'll say, "Well, wait a minute; on the theoretical level he could have done anything, but when you have close to a thousand pieces, including fragments, and something never happens, then aren't you safer arguing that that thing lies outside of the language?" If the idea is to try to define the language, you have to say, "Well, they could have done that, but they didn't."

Weren't you criticized for being too objective by people who preferred the idea of a composer as an intuitive genius?

The idea of being objective about these things flies in the face of why anyone gets involved in art in the first place: they love the music, and they're very subjective about it. If you get into a case of attribution, which is what the contretemps with the Symphonie concertante for winds is about, nobody wanted

8. Levin's book *Who Wrote the Mozart Four-Wind Concertante?* (Stuyvesant, NY: Pendragon Press, 1988) makes a convincing case that the Symphonie Concertante in E♭ has come down to us not as Mozart wrote it but in a nineteenth-century arrangement (K. 297b/Anh. C 14.0) for a slightly different group of instruments, in which the work is recomposed in a "dialect" later than Mozart's own.

to be told on a statistical or analytical basis that a piece they hated was conforming to Mozart's plan, or that a piece they loved was not.[9] They wanted to be left alone with their prejudices. I was continually being confronted by people who couldn't understand how I could write a 500-page book about the wind concertante and say nowhere in it from beginning to end whether I liked the piece or couldn't stand it. But I wasn't interested in my own feelings about the piece.

It seems to me that if you wish to be a linguist the first thing you do is document. You go out in the field, you listen to people talk in a particular part of northwestern Kentucky, and you listen to the color of their vowels and the aspiration and pronunciation of their consonants. And then you say, "We found this in this corner of the state, but if you go a little bit north, you begin to hear the r's a little more like that." That's considered legitimate; but when you start talking about Schubert that way, people get mad. But Schubert spoke, he had a dialect. It was a sublime dialect, but once you want to find out what the dialect is, then speaking of it as being great or inspired or the product of genius is not the point. The point is to try to decide what it is and what it does, and to try to decide what its social fabric is, the kinds of conventions it observes and the ways those conventions are violated, and whether any kind of code can be drawn up that will account for the conventions and their violations. That will never make you able to compose music of the greatness of that composer, but it gives you a lot of insight. And if you want to improvise, to the extent that you're capable of isolating the conventions and the exceptions you will be able to fabricate music out of these mores and conventions that will sound to most ears like a good replica of that music. It's as simple as that.

I mean, look what happened when they made *Gone with the Wind*: there was such an enormous fracas because Scarlett was going to be played by an Englishwoman. The elocution lessons and everything else that went on before Vivien Leigh could take that part and not be the laughing-stock of everybody south of the Mason-Dixon Line—these were all considered absolutely necessary. Well, why is it necessary in Hollywood and not in Carnegie Hall?

Perhaps it's that the aesthetic mode of film is realism, and all that period detail helps us to suspend disbelief and forget that those are just actors up there. Traditionally, people would say that instrumental music is more abstract than film—its referents are less specific and "realistic," so the musical characters you've described needn't look so exact in order for it to work. Besides, people miss the musical subtleties more easily—most of us wouldn't notice if one of Mozart's musical "characters" had a wrong accent.

Well, the funny thing about it is that it's like 'enry 'iggins. In some people's cadenzas I can hear many things that are un-Mozartian; and, unlike someone

    9. See Levin's exchange with Nancy Miller in *Opus*, August and November 1985.

who might have a hunch and be correct, I can even tell you why—but there are undoubtedly sins that I'm committing that somebody with more knowledge than I currently possess would point out immediately. And Mozart isn't around to say, "Hey, you really got my lingo down!" or "Idiot! You don't understand a thing!"

Let me ask you about an area where you might apply your analysis of the language. Virgil Thomson criticized Schnabel for playing the passagework in Beethoven too expressively, rather than treating it as neutral background material;[10] Paul Henry Lang made the same criticism of Leon Fleisher in Mozart. How articulate should passagework be in Mozart and in Beethoven?

I'm working on the "Emperor" Concerto right now, and it's always revealing to see the differences between Mozart and Beethoven in this respect. Very often there are arpeggio passages in the "Emperor" that could be part of an etude. They're relatively mechanical, and the middle-term scaffolding is also an arpeggio. It's very rare to find something like that in Mozart. Mozart's passagework is rarely devoid of melodic content. He's too much of a vocal, operatic composer. Some pieces have more mechanical passagework than others, but there usually is a cellular idea which fits into a middle- and long-term shape. It doesn't mean that Beethoven is bad and Mozart is good. It shows that Beethoven was explicitly interested in that mechanical element because he could get something from it. It's a much more overt kind of thing, just like Beethoven's cellular repetition of rhythmic ideas. I think it can be an irritant at times—it jars, it excites, it has a causticness, it has a willfulness— whereas there is always in Mozart (at a certain level) a perception of elegance. Even when the music is decidedly angular, there's always an architectural sense of harmony, of consistency of disclosure and rhetoric. And that's why the passagework usually has a suave as well as a mechanical side to it. There are exceptions, but they're few.

Regarding articulateness, also recall that if you open up the Breitkopf & Härtel edition of Mozart (reprinted by Dover), every time there are sixteenth notes for one or two bars there's a slur over them, and if there are more than that it says "legato." Mozart never used the word "legato" in his scores in his life; that was put in by Carl Reinecke, who edited the concertos. According to Reinecke's values Mozart had to be balanced and beautiful and well-modulated, and so he played it in the legato style. I play non-legato in Mozart because there is strong evidence that the premise of that period was that everything is played non-legato unless marked to the contrary. I should point out that this is an issue of clarity, definition, and balance. If you play legato on a fortepiano with oodles of pedal, you'll never be heard. If you have an orches-

10. In a 1944 column, reprinted in *A Virgil Thomson Reader* (New York: E. P. Dutton, 1981), pp. 248–49.

tra of any size, the sparkle, the crystalline speaking of the fortepiano will be enhanced by non-legato. People who are of an open mind have said that they're surprised at how they took to non-legato performance, because they found it so lively in comparison to the other.

I wonder what you think about the use of the continuo in Haydn and Mozart. In Charles Rosen's view,[11] "in Baroque music the setting in relief of the rate of change of the harmony [is] essential," because that's where the motor impulse and energy come from—so the continuo playing is essential. But in the Classical style, energy is based not on those sequences of harmonies but on larger phrases and modulations; so he concludes that the continuo's "emphasis of the harmonic rhythm is therefore not only unnecessary but positively distracting" in Haydn and Mozart.

Charles Rosen is one of the most brilliant people of our age, and it's always rewarding and provocative to read him. The distinction he makes between those two styles is certainly relevant. But I wonder how Mozart or Haydn would have responded to that comment. They might have said, "Oh, really? Oh, well, maybe so!" This is not to denigrate what he says. The point that Rosen really makes is that the music was evolving in new directions and the composers didn't notice what that implied for performance.[12] This leads, he says, to the question, Does the composer know how his piece is to sound?[13] Rosen seems to suggest that the composer might not, but I cannot imagine that *anyone* would know better how his music is to sound than a composer like Mozart, who was no mere abstract thinker: he had continual involvement in performance (including leading the orchestra in opera and symphonic concerts).

But Rosen's viewpoint relates to something you've said in public several times—that we can probably do better than the composer's contemporaries in reconstructing the language because we're more familiar with it, having spent so much time with it.

11. *The Classical Style* (New York: Norton, 1972), pp. 189–96 ("continuo" is defined in the Alan Curtis interview, p. 135, n. 6). According to Neal Zaslaw, it appears that "under many circumstances and in many repertories, the continuo instrument remained a part of concert and opera performances": Zaslaw, *Mozart's Symphonies* (Oxford University Press, 1989), p. 466. There is, however, heated controversy over whether they were used in non-theatre symphony performances in late-eighteenth-century Continental Europe; see James Webster, "On the Absence of Keyboard Continuo in Haydn's Symphonies," *Early Music* 18 (November 1990), pp. 599–608.

12. Rosen says that the use of continuo put Mozart and Haydn with "other *performers* of their day, whose idea of performance had not yet caught up with the radical changes of style which had occurred since 1770, and for which Haydn and Mozart were so largely responsible." He says later, "there is no reason to assume that the composer or his contemporaries always knew with any certainty how best to make the listener aware of [the significance of the music's meaning]." *The Classical Style* , pp. 195–96.

13. Rosen asks, "does the composer know how his piece is to sound?" and eventually concludes, "the composer's idea of his work is both precise and slightly fuzzy." *Ibid.*, p. 195.

We've heard Mozart pieces a thousand times instead of once. And *because* we're separated by a chasm of intervening styles, it's much easier for us to be objective about things that people of that time would not have noticed at all. Now, I play continuo because we know Mozart did it; he explicitly calls for it. Still, we could say that it doesn't matter that Mozart played along with the orchestra in tuttis of a concerto; we don't need to do that any more, so let's not do it. And it doesn't matter that Mozart used the fortepiano, we have a Steinway, let's do it. It doesn't matter that Mozart's articulation was very much designed around the instruments he had, which had consonants that spoke with precision and a fast decay that produced a lively surface; we now have something which produces a smoother, more continuous surface, so let's do that. You know—we now have cinderblock, so we don't need granite. I come back to a culinary analogy: that's the cake that Mozart baked. That's the sauce he concocted. And in that sauce, he says at the beginning of every single line of every piano concerto, with exceptions that are as remarkable as they are important, that the piano is to play with the string basses when it's not soloing. That's what he says. And in the early concertos the bass lines have continuo figures. Admittedly the figures are mostly not in his hand, they're in the hand of his father; but there's no chance—none—that his father didn't know what his son had in mind; he was doing the mechanical stuff that could save his son time. So there's no doubt that Wolfgang played continuo.

Again, you could say that he played continuo to keep the orchestra together; we have a conductor, so we don't need that any more. Now, I wouldn't want what I'm about to say to be misinterpreted, because I have had so many rewarding experiences working with conductors, but in fact as soon as you have a conductor you surrender the responsibility for the performance into the hands of that conductor. When you play without a conductor and you have a concertmaster and a fortepiano (or Steinway) player, and they're seated in an intimate circle around one another, they all listen because they have to make that ensemble by themselves. The result is a performance that is likely to be much tighter, much more active, and much more engaged than one with a conductor, because there's collective responsibility. The pianist behaves like the timpanist, keeping the orchestra rhythmically together in certain key sections, and the violinist leads in the melodic sphere—though sometimes there can be an overlap of those functions. That also shows psychologically that Mozart's music is never simply a conflict between a protagonist and the masses.

That brings us to Rosen's next point—that if the soloist plays continuo, it reduces the effect of the soloist's entrances, which in his concertos are dramatic events.

I'm rather surprised that a musician of Rosen's sophistication projected that nineteenth-century conception upon Mozart. There are places where Mozart flings down the gauntlet just like Beethoven: that occurs in the C Minor Piano Concerto, K. 491, in the [first-movement] development, and it's thrilling when it happens. But how many times does it happen? Mozart has the piano accompanying the orchestra as often as the orchestra is accompanying the piano. His solo-tutti relationships are much more sophisticated, involving symphonic, concerto, and chamber-music elements. And the idea of a piano sitting in the middle of the ensemble being an equal in the orchestral texture who at a given pre-arranged signal rises up and becomes a personality in his own right is something I find enormously attractive. Also, I don't have to play "cold" when I get to the first solo entry. (When one plays continuo with a Steinway, though, one has to be careful not to play too loud.)

Rosen also says that in continuo playing the emphasis on the change of harmony is the only important thing—the doubling and the spacing of the harmony are secondary considerations.

Well, even in the Baroque era voice-leading and spacings were not secondary but *primary* considerations—otherwise a text on thorough-bass could be a fraction of the length of actual Baroque treatises on the subject: there is little art in plunking out chords, but a great deal of finesse required to connect them adroitly in a texture sensitive to the character prescribed by the composer, complementing and deepening its meaning.

When playing continuo, I find it not very interesting to play just chords; and I've been attacked for not playing just chords. But far from finding it disturbing, I think it's wonderful for the audience to hear a roulade or a trill and to know that there's something simmering in the pot. And I can't imagine the world's greatest keyboard genius, with all we know about him, sitting at the piano for 70 bars plunking chords. I suspect a rapscallion glint in the eye; he was probably just jamming like a great Dixieland player.[14]

That brings us to the subject of improvisation, the most striking example of which is that you don't write cadenzas out beforehand but improvise them on the spot—the ultimate in getting away from the Fassung letzter Hand. *Why?*

Well, I assume that most of these pieces were written for Mozart's own self-expression, so to that extent whatever we know about his personal style ought to illuminate what we do now. Otherwise I wouldn't improvise. Mozart's students didn't improvise; they played prepared cadenzas, so I could do that. But I don't find that nearly as stimulating, and the unanimous reaction of the audience whenever I've played improvised cadenzas is that when the orchestra stops after the 6-4 chord before the cadenza, the audience gets very quiet. For the first time in most of their lives, they're at a classical concert where—despite

14. See Levin's "Instrumental Ornamentation, Improvisation and Cadenzas," in *Performance Practice: Music after 1600,* ed. H. M. Brown and S. Sadie (London: Macmillan, 1989, and New York: Norton, 1990), p. 288. But see also Tibor Szász, "Beethoven's Basso Continuo," in *Performing Beethoven,* ed. Robin Stowell (Cambridge University Press, 1994), pp. 11–13, for a somewhat different viewpoint.

their familiarity with the piece—they don't know what's going to happen next. On the other hand, it won't be a piled-on set of crashing dissonances, so they can judge for themselves as well as anybody whether what happens succeeds or fails. And that's a very hot seat for the performer. For me it's a place where I use about as much adrenaline as I do throughout the rest of the concerto. It takes a vast amount of concentration and coordination, and if the mind and body are not perfectly synchronized there'll be a calamity.

The cadenzas are perhaps the clearest example of your methods of mastering Mozart's language. You've written that the cadenza is "less a prolonged virtuoso display than a decorated cadence"—a way to create harmonic tension before the final resolution—and you mention that a Mozart cadenza has three sections—well, I'm reading back to you what you've written.[15]

It doesn't mask the fact that there are Mozart cadenzas which don't do those things. The cadenza in K. 488 uses a tiny snippet of material from one of the least noticeable places in the concerto, just a little passagework, which shows up in the beginning of the development; all of the big tunes are neglected. That cadenza, revealingly enough, is not preserved on a separate piece of paper, as was Mozart's usual practice, but is written into the autograph score itself; that may suggest that this concerto is a unique case. But it's marvelous to have that cadenza, because it shows that the harmonic principles are inviolable even though the question of how much motivic stuff you need isn't. You can improvise a great cadenza that has just about nothing in it in terms of tunes but keeps the harmonic juggling act going. What you *can't* do is write a cadenza that is harmonically stable but obediently reminds everyone that "and then I played, and then I played . . ."

You said earlier that you can hear things in other people's cadenzas that aren't Mozartian; in an essay you give examples that have what you call "foreign accents"—stylistic features that are not in Mozart's language—in some published embellishments of Mozart concertos.[16]

When you hear great Mozartians play, you can often hear a little Brahms, a little Beethoven that creeps in. What's fascinating to me, though, is that musicians have never been concerned about this kind of temporal cleanness, the kind of historicity we've been discussing in terms of linguistics and so on. It has never been considered a sin to have Beethoven or Brahms present in a

---

15. In "Instrumental Ornamentation, Improvisation and Cadenzas," pp. 279 and 283, which gives a technical analysis of the Mozart cadenza.

16. *Ibid*, pp. 277–78. That Mozart's music would have been embellished in, for example, the returns of a rondo theme or in many sparsely notated passages in concertos, has been clearly demonstrated. See *ibid*., pp. 269–79, and especially Levin's article "Improvised Embellishment in Mozart's Keyboard Music," *Early Music* 20 (May 1992), pp. 221–33. See also this chapter's "For Further Reading" section.

Mozart concerto. When Brahms wrote cadenzas to the Mozart concertos they sounded as much like Brahms as like Mozart, and the same principle applies to Beethoven's or Clara Schumann's or Artur Schnabel's cadenzas. After all, Beethoven was not concerned with this in his *own* music—his cadenza to his Second Concerto seems to have been written around the time of the "Emperor" and sounds like it, and it can't be played on the instrument for which the Second Concerto was written. Beethoven was not interested in that kind of thing. He'd probably say, "Well, why should I play on that old rattle-trap?"

Yet, as I was saying, could you imagine a Hollywood director doing a movie that takes place in Chicago in 1930 with 1959 Chevrolets driving around? It's interesting to me that this one so distinctly American idiom, the movies, is the one place where these kinds of historical niceties are observed to the last T— but not in Beethoven and Schubert. We can say, "Well, it doesn't matter." Well, it didn't in the past. Maybe it doesn't matter if the cadenza is completely different. But for me it has been an enormously revealing challenge to test one's real ability to speak the language of the composer idiomatically. In the cadenza you show that what you have been saying throughout the body of the concerto is a personal utterance, whose legitimacy is proved by how idiomatically you speak the language when you are no longer being fed the lines.

How do you translate the improvisation into the recording studio?

It's very difficult, because there has to be a primary version set down. Even in the main body of the concerto, away from the cadenzas, there are many passages that Mozart assumed would be embellished. And the beauty of those embellishments lies in their spontaneity, perishability, and uniqueness. But when you listen to that record fifteen times you may grow to like those embellishments, and you may then not like some other ones, even by the same performer, and even though those new embellishments might be, from the performer's (or anyone else's) point of view, better than the ones on the record. So there is something about recording which is antithetical to the freedom of improvisation. Nonetheless, in my first recordings with L'Oiseau-Lyre I recorded without regard to the microphone, in the sense that each take had its own embellishment, and the producer selected among them. And when it came to the cadenza, every time we had a take I improvised a different one. So a number of improvised cadenzas were available for each place in this recording.

However, keeping in mind that a recording also has archival value, the people at L'Oiseau-Lyre were worried about reviewers grouching that this recording would be at a disadvantage to other performances because it does not use Mozart's cadenzas. And I understand that; I have never claimed that improvised cadenzas are going to be up to Mozart's standard. The idea is that something spontaneous sounds different from something that is not, and that the audience benefits from that in a performance. And, in a sense, a recording that you know to be of a live concert will always have an excitement that a studio recording does not. Nonetheless, to be on the safe side, in a separate session I recorded all of Mozart's own cadenzas.

So we can just program the CD player.
Exactly; the person who wishes to have all of the variants will presumably have access to them. I have talked to the engineers about looking to the future when a kind of random generator could select among a panoply of cadenzas. I think we're on the verge of being able to do that. We decided that in doing what we did we would be keeping abreast of subsequent technological developments; we wanted to see how a new technology could be used to refresh an old performance style. For once, new developments do not undercut old values.

On that point, Robert Philip's Early Recordings and Musical Style[17] *argues that recording itself changed playing styles, among other things fostering our taste for precision.*
Well, naturally, we rehearse, which they didn't do much; we use marked bowings, which they did not do in that contemporary-oriented musical culture of theirs. We are very much concerned with hygiene; you get a third take that is musically inspired but has five wrong notes, and most recording engineers will insist that you fix them. So we do takes over and over again to get things perfectly in tune, and then things are spliced together. I know an artist who confessed to me that on one of his recordings there were 621 splices in about 50 minutes of music. Well, you can figure out how much spontaneity and how much of an architectural arch is going to be found in something like that. We live in an age that glorifies technical achievements of an Olympic sort above everything else. Having done that, we reap the reward, which is that we now get people who can play louder and faster than ever before, and better in tune, but we do not have a generation of risk-takers; and this goes straight back to improvisation. You rule out the idea that the performer is a creator, and turn that person into a reproducer (which by the way did not need the great danger of recordings, but was already coming into place; the recordings merely cast the die in a more unequivocal way). Once that happens, the training of our musicians becomes achievement-oriented.

And that's what happens today. I was the head of the theory department at the Curtis Institute for five years and continued to teach theory for almost fifteen years, and I saw it very clearly. All of the students, with the smallest of exceptions, fought tooth and nail the idea that they had to understand how the musical language functioned. They wanted to practice and practice and do nothing else so that they could win this and that competition and have a major

---

17. Cambridge University Press, 1992. Neal Zaslaw argues, by the way, that we may underestimate the technical standards attainable in Mozart's time (*Mozart's Symphonies*, pp. 504–06); but Philip's data strongly suggest that verbal reports of precise playing, like those Zaslaw mentions, were made relative to standards that we would now consider low.

career. It never occurred to them that once you stood in front of an audience and began to speak and had nothing to say, it wouldn't be so good.

Now, they must be assuming that their instincts are powerful enough that they would be able to do these things right. But instinct is a very tricky business. It lies on a bedrock of cultural accretion, and that cultural accretion comes about through being involved in the *real* events of the culture and its evolution—not on the skyline of mimicry. Now we have a generation of people who have grown up learning music through recordings. A young aspiring violinist listens 95 times to Heifetz playing the Sibelius concerto, and before that person is even aware of it, out of veneration for Heifetz's indisputably unique achievement he or she is using fingerings and bowings that Heifetz used, absorbing these not by choice but automatically through mimicry. Then she or he hears another marvelous artist play the Sibelius and doesn't like it because Heifetz's ritard or portamento is missing, and another one appears somewhere else. So we've become people who are less and less literate in our art—people who often can't "speak" a word of it, who have no idea grammatically what a musical sentence is, who don't know that a parallel fifth is not something that is grammatically acceptable in a work, who will change a passage to make it more effective instrumentally and turn it into something grotesque and illiterate—even though they may be some of the most famous performers before the public today. And I speak of experiences I've had as a member of the audience.

That is something that fifty years ago would have been inconceivable. George Szell and Artur Schnabel were composers; we may not know them as composers, but that was how they were trained. There was no way that they or a man like Wilhelm Furtwängler, who was also a composer, could possibly be guilty of this kind of thing. They were architects within the music. Their views of how the music goes may have been stylistically at odds with what we now claim to know from the eighteenth century, on the basis of documents that in some cases are really quite unequivocal; but nonetheless, the alleged sins of that prior generation are as nothing compared to the lack of integrity of a musician performing in front of the public when the language has been absorbed only through instrumental lessons and the habit of listening, rather than through knowing what tension and release are and knowing how the music really functions in a palpable way.

It's like speaking a language phonetically, syllable by syllable, rather than mastering it.

It's exactly like that. If one has any doubts about that, one only has to go to the *Neue Mozart-Ausgabe* and look at the three sets of lessons we have from Mozart as a theory teacher. We see there that regardless of what instincts and intuitions he had, despite all of the fabled genius that we know and respect, when musicians came into Mozart's care and he had to teach them, he taught them with the same principles that are hated today by students who say that theory is boring. He made them realize figured basses, and harmonize melodies, and write species counterpoint. He wrote the first half of a minuet and asked them to write the second half. He made them write canons and various exercises in free composition. We can see what the students wrote and what Mozart corrected. And we see that then, as now, the idea was (as Renoir said), "First become a good craftsman—this will not prevent you from becoming a genius." The fact is that these things were regarded as matters of course by musicians until recently.

This is a societal thing. We now live in an age in which people think you don't have to play by the rules. Getting by is a creed. People think, "You don't have to go to school—you can drop out and still become a football player or supermodel or rock star and make millions of dollars." The old assumptions about the work ethic and being scrupulous and honest and fair—those things, if anyone watches television, are laughed at. In music it transposes to, If you can play fast on your instrument and thunder your octaves, then it doesn't matter how ignorant you are—you're gonna get the jobs. So we have this unhealthy alliance between concert managers, recording companies, and competitions. And the result is that it's such a product/achievement-oriented thing that very often the differences between the first-prize winner at competitions Y and Z, or between the first- and fourth-prize winners, are tiny.

So in part, this reflects a change in the classical-music culture—to the performer being merely a reproducer—but also a weakness in the overall culture. How do you relate these trends to your research and your work with improvisation?

One of the things that frustrate me the most, when I give lectures here and there on improvisation, is that somebody comes up to me and would like me to tell them the trick to doing, it in five sentences, so that they can go home and do it immediately. That's our society at work. You don't have to sit down and learn theory, you don't have to analyze music, you don't have to study music; all you have to do is listen to five sentences and go out and start doing it right away. I can only tell such people, "Too bad: it doesn't work that way." I couldn't do it if I hadn't had those years studying with Nadia Boulanger, who taught me to a fare-thee-well to listen and refine my hearing and my palate to distinguish chord spacings and voice leadings and harmonic progressions and structural articulations. I thank her for all of that. For years and years I tried to teach this stuff with the same fervor because I think the survival of the art depends on it.

Do you think that what you're trying to do could give rise to increased interest in learning music theory?

I would hope so. Look, in spite of all the pessimism I've voiced, there is no question that there are young people around who are doing marvelous things, very imaginative things, who are less nailed to tradition and self-consciousness than we ever were. Such people give me many grounds for hope. But I say to the garden-variety conservatory student, You'd better learn how to do this, but you'd also better learn what it means to do it; and it may mean that your mindless practicing ten hours a day is going to have to be curbed if you're going to find out what it is you really need to do.

Regarding the direction of causality, do you think the decline in playing standards has contributed in the decline of the size of the audience for classical music?

I would be tempted to make that kind of accusation, but it's not quite fair. I *would* say that something about our concert life has become more and more ritualistic and less and less healthy, and that invites desertion on the part of the public. However, this must be qualified by the fact that in the United States culture was transformed by the diaspora precipitated by the Nazi cataclysm in Europe; the wholesale immigration of artists and their audience from Europe to America in the 1930s changed the American cultural landscape. That generation is now passing from the scene, and their children, born in an American environment, are shaped by the values of that society.

And in Europe, with the Americanization of culture there, the young people, who drink Coca-Cola and eat Big Macs and listen to American pop music, are as disengaged or disengaging from European art music as their American counterparts. The danger is worldwide. When Richard Taruskin said in one of his reviews that saving *both* vernacular and serious music was dependent on finding some kind of bridge between the two cultures,[18] that song of Cassandra is not limited in its poignancy or its urgency to our country. So there is cause enough for alarm.

Now, in every age there have been incandescent performances by visionary artists, and we have our share of those artists today, whom I believe in without reservation, across the board—keyboard players and instrumentalists and vocalists. Nevertheless, the overall pattern is distressing. We musicians have to earn those dollars of philanthropic support. We have to earn those souls coming and listening to us, and we're not going to do it by giving stuffy performances that are just warmed-over Backhaus or Heifetz or Szigeti.

SELECTED DISCOGRAPHY

Antony Hopkins called the cadenza "the orchestra's favorite part of a solo concerto." It has never been mine. A musicologist friend identified the reason—and at the same time the appeal of Levin's improvised cadenzas. In my (and her) usual experience, cadenzas are often the parts that we hope will end

---

18. At the end of "A Mozart Wholly Ours," originally printed in *Musical America*, May 1990, pp. 32–41, reprinted in *Text and Act*, pp. 273–91.

quickly so that the real stuff can begin again; but if I knew I were hearing an improvisation, it would more likely keep me on the edge of my seat.

Recording, of course, is antithetical to that sort of experience, but the first discs in Levin's Mozart concerto series capture some of it (they include K. 271 and 414, L'Oiseau Lyre 443 328; and K. 413, 415, and 386, L'Oiseau Lyre 444 571). Reviewing K. 413, Stanley Sadie praises the performance's "hints of the opera house in its characterization and its surprises," and calls Levin's playing of the slow movement "very expressive and it brings out the latent rhetorical quality in the piano line very effectively." As for the improvised cadenzas, he writes, "Dare I say that in K413 his is as good as Mozart's?"[19]

No critic has yet complained about the improvisations in Levin's Mozart, but some have objected strenuously to improvised ornamentation in Levin's Schubert sonata recording (Sony SK 53364).[20] These critics are, I believe, mistaken when they call it historically unjustified. We have firm written evidence that Schubert's favored singer embellished the songs in just this way when he sang them (accompanied by the composer), and that this was standard practice at the time;[21] it is inconceivable that Schubert himself would have felt more constrained. Even these critics, however, sometimes praise Levin's Schubert playing, and other critics have been unequivocal. For example, Nicholas Rast says that in the A Minor Sonata, D. 537, Levin "delights in the varied tonal characteristics of the 1825 Fritz fortepiano which he plays with a freer, more flexible response to gesture [than András Schiff in the same work]."[22]

Levin's recording of the last four Haydn piano trios (Sony SK 53120)—four of Haydn's greatest works—with Anner Bylsma and Vera Beths is one of my current favorite CDs. Sadie writes of Levin's "great vitality and delightful crispness," and the way he "puts across the intellectual force and the argumentative character of the music."[23] Sadie does find the slow movements of Nos. 42 and 43 too hard-pressed, but he praises the "eloquence and expansiveness of Levin's playing" in No. 44 and especially delights in No. 45.

Levin is recording the complete Beethoven piano concertos with John Eliot Gardiner on Archiv. The first release, the "Emperor," is distinguished by its freedom and its vivid sense of rhetoric (Archiv 447 771). Erik Tarloff loves the playing but says that to perform this concerto on the fortepiano "seems almost perverse"—and concludes that had Levin "chosen to play his 'Emperor' on a Steinway or a Bösendorfer, he might have given us one of the greatest recordings of the piece ever put on disc."[24] As a fortepiano fancier, I think Levin has

---

19. Sadie, *Gramophone* 73 (September 1995), p. 63.

20. Susan Kagan, *Fanfare* 19 (November/December 1995), p. 363; Nicholas Toller, "Schubert in a New Light," *Early Music* 23 (August 1995), p. 524.

21. Walther Dürr, "Schubert and Johann Michael Vogl: A Reappraisal," *19th-Century Music* 3 (1979–80), pp. 126–40.

22. Rast, *Gramophone* 74 (August 1996), p. 76.

23. Sadie, *Gramophone* 72 (June 1994), p. 70.

24. Tarloff, "Beethoven on Original Instruments," *Slate* (www.slate.com), 1 October, 1996.

done exactly that. In it, by the way, Levin plays keyboard continuo, as all the evidence suggests Beethoven would have.[25]

Levin's completion of Mozart's unfinished Requiem has been recorded by Martin Pearlman on Telarc 80410; Elliot Hurwitt places the performance "among the best . . . now available."[26] (Helmut Rilling has also recorded Levin's version [Hänssler Classics 98979], but I failed to obtain a copy for review.) When William Christie recorded the Requiem, he used the version prepared by Franz Xaver Süssmayr, a student of Mozart, because it is "perhaps the closest thing we'll ever have to truth . . . [Süssmayr] after all was there with [the] dying composer."[27] But Levin argues that Süssmayr's completion suffers from "grammatical and structural flaws that are utterly foreign to Mozart's idiom."[28] This brings up a question raised in Levin's interview—whether we, at 200 years' distance, might be able to gain a more idiomatic command of Mozart's musical language than his near contemporaries did.

Finally, Levin continues to play music of our own contemporaries: he is recording the complete piano works of John Harbison and has made some remarkable discs with the violist Kim Kashkashian on ECM.

FOR FURTHER READING

Music critics have had no qualms about Levin's improvised embellishments and cadenzas in Mozart; but some musicologists have been skeptical. The debates between those favoring such additions and those opposing them reflect, in certain ways, more basic aesthetic positions.

The strongest case for improvisation is made in Levin's own writings—the best available introductions both to how ornamentation and improvisation should be done in Mozart, and to why it is historically justified. The essay "Instrumental Ornamentation, Improvisation and Cadenzas," in *Performance Practice: Music after 1600*, ed. H. M. Brown and S. Sadie (London: Macmillan, 1989, and New York: Norton, 1990), is especially useful, as is "Improvised Embellishments in Mozart's Keyboard Music," *Early Music* 20 (May 1992), pp. 221–33.

The opposition is best represented by Frederick Neumann's encyclopedic study, *Ornamentation and Improvisation in Mozart* (Princeton University Press, 1986). The cataloguing of historical data here is unmatched, and if you are serious about this subject you must read this book; but be certain also to read Levin's review of it in the *Journal of the American Musicological Society* 41

---

25. Szász, "Beethoven's Basso Continuo."

26. Hurwitt, *Fanfare* 19 (January/February 1996), p. 266.

27. Christie, quoted in Joel Kasow, "An Interview with William Christie," *Fanfare* 19 (January/February 1996), pp. 72–74.

28. Levin, "The Editor's Perspective," booklet note to Pearlman's Mozart Requiem, Telarc 80410.

(August 1988), pp. 355–68. Neumann's conclusions are, as I implied, opposite to Levin's—he would forbid improvisation and anything more than minimal ornamentation. Another member of the opposition is Christoph Wolff (who, like Levin, is a professor at Harvard). In "Cadenzas and Styles of Improvisation in Mozart's Piano Concertos,"[29] Wolff argues that Mozart prepared his written cadenzas for his own use, not his students', and that he wrote out many other cadenzas for his own use that have since been lost. Some critics have complained that Wolff cannot document either claim, and also that he offers no concrete evidence for his explanation that Mozart's comment about playing "whatever occurs to me at the moment" applied mainly to his early concertos.[30]

The evidence he provides, in fact, is his belief that Mozart's mature cadenzas were too "motivically and metrically tightly controlled" to allow genuine improvisation and, moreover, that they gave Mozart a chance to continue the process of making "adjustments to a work." This plays into Richard Taruskin's argument (which one can acknowledge regardless of which side one takes) that both Neumann's and Wolff's arguments are attempts to defend a more basic concept, which Levin also discusses in his interview—*Werktreue*—and behind it the concept of the unified, perfected musical work.[31]

As Levin suggested in his interview, these concepts have not always been common coin. The evolution of the modern concept of the musical "work"— of musical pieces being integral works of art like paintings or sculptures—is the subject of Lydia Goehr's fascinating book *The Imaginary Museum of Musical Works* (Oxford University Press, 1992) and her related paper "Being True to the Work," *Journal of Aesthetics and Art Criticism* 47 (1989), pp. 5–67. She argues, to quote the latter (p. 5), that "the concept of a musical work first fully emerged in classical music practice at the end of the eighteenth century and that, since that time, it has been used pervasively in the world of music"; as she often says, it began to "regulate musical practice" around then. One can think of various examples of the work concept "regulating musical practice" before 1800, and of numerous examples of later Western art music to which the work concept is only partially relevant; but Goehr recognizes that such ex-

29. In *Perspectives on Mozart Performance*, ed. R. Larry Todd and Peter Williams (Cambridge University Press, 1991), pp. 228–38

30. See Richard Maunder's review in *Music and Letters* 73 (November, 1992), p. 591, and Taruskin's comments in *Text and Act*, pp. 287–89. On the subject of Mozart and ornamentation and improvisation, see also: Katalin Komlós, "'Ich praeludirte und spielte Variatonen': Mozart the Fortepianist," in *Perspectives on Mozart Performance*, pp. 27–54; Eva and Paul Badura-Skoda, *Interpreting Mozart on the Keyboard*, trans. L. Black (London and New York, St. Martin's Press, 1962), chaps. 8 and 11; Malcolm Bilson, "Some General Thoughts on Ornamentation in Mozart's Keyboard Works," *Piano Quarterly* 24 (1976), pp. 26–28; and Henry Mishkin, "Incomplete Notation in Mozart's Piano Concertos," *Musical Quarterly* 61 (1975), pp. 345–59.

31. Taruskin, *Text and Act*, pp. 287–89.

ceptions exist. Whether or not one accepts her ideas, it is unlikely that either *Werktreue* or the work concept wholly regulated the performance (or creation) of Mozart's concertos or operas[32]—although even if Wolff and Neumann's adherents were to accept that, they could plausibly maintain that the concept *should* have regulated the performances, or that they should now.

Wye J. Allanbrook's research on musical "topics" in Mozart sheds fascinating light on the evocation of character that Levin speaks about. It's probably no exaggeration to say that there is no more important book on Mozart's musical language than her *Rhythmic Gesture in Mozart* (University of Chicago Press, 1983). Her forthcoming *The Secular Commedia,* to be published by the University of California Press, places topicality in a larger aesthetic framework. Also, her mentor Leonard Ratner's *Classic Music* (New York: Schirmer, 1980) is the groundbreaking study of the musical topics of this era.

More than other biographies I've seen, Maynard Solomon's *Mozart* (New York: Harper Collins, 1995) gives the composer three convincing dimensions and says interesting things about his music (notably in the chapter on the Salzburg divertimenti). Solomon's Freudian interpretations are usually handled tactfully, though at times they feel Procrustean or strained, and they are always stimulating, even when one disagrees.

32. Charles Rosen, *Sonata Forms* (New York: Norton, 1980), pp. 9–10, argues that the forms and techniques of composition that Haydn, Mozart, and Beethoven developed in certain genres led to a work of music existing as "an independent . . . object"—independent, that is, of text or virtuoso additions, or of primarily extramusical purposes. By contrast, the concerto and the aria still served "extramusical purposes."

18

Taking Music Off the Pedestal

Roger Norrington
on Beethoven

Was Beethoven the first great Romantic or the last great Classic? If you believe
the movies, or the booklet notes for certain mass-market CDs, he was the ultimate Romantic, the rebel who burst the chains of Classicism. But if you believe most modern scholars, he was "the culminating composer of the Classical style." Yet recently, some Beethoven scholars, such as Maynard Solomon,
have argued that focusing entirely on Beethoven's "derivation from eighteenth-
century traditions" can oversimplify matters, by understating Beethoven's "radical modernism" and the "overlapping of Beethoven and Romanticism."[1]

Solomon concludes that "Beethoven's masterworks—like his life—arise out
of a perpetual tension between archaic sources and utopian possibilities." Perhaps it's this tension that allowed even Beethoven's disciples to put their own
spins on him. His students Carl Czerny and Ferdinand Ries described a
Beethoven who played "strictly in time"; yet some other musicians who knew
him reported a Beethoven who, to quote his self-styled Boswell, Anton
Schindler, played "without any constraint as to the rate of time." That may
sound like the birth of the Classical/Romantic dichotomy, but the issue gets
more complex: some argue that Czerny's "strict" Beethoven reflects the long
legato style of the *nineteenth* century, and that Schindler's apparently Romantic Beethoven is rooted in the "speaking" style of the previous century.[2]

When "historically informed" players forged ahead to record the Beethoven

1. Maynard Solomon, *Beethoven Essays* (Cambridge, Mass.: Harvard University Press,
1988), p. x.
2. On this point see the "Postscript" at the end of this chapter.

symphonies in the 1980s, they had no doubts that Beethoven should be played Classically—which to them meant strictly. That they'd take this stand could have been predicted by the least competent bookmaker in London. After all, these pioneers—primarily the Hanover Band and Christopher Hogwood's Academy of Ancient Music—came to Beethoven from an English early-music style characterized by energetic strictness. In addition, some of their spokespersons expressed the view that in Beethoven's day, limited rehearsal time and the lack of a conductor disallowed today's "wider variety of nuance and tempo modification" in orchestral playing: the symphonies had therefore been given "uncomplicated, rhythmical performances."[3] In addition, some of the performers claimed that such approaches allowed them to give performances that were "accurately old."[4]

Anyone could also have predicted that such claims would provoke Richard Taruskin. Taruskin argued that these players, in propagating what he called the legend of "Beethoven: Preserver of the Eighteenth-Century Tradition," were really making the music suit their own objective twentieth-century taste. Their idea of Classical style, he said, is a historical fiction, fabricated by moderns as a stick to beat the Romantics with. As for the musical results, he described one of these musicians, Hogwood, as re-dedicating the *Eroica* "To Celebrate the Memory of a Great Nebbish."[5]

At the time, Hogwood's goal was, apparently, to play music just as it was played at the first performances. But when you apply that goal to Beethoven symphonies, you run into its contradictions. In Beethoven's Vienna, everyone agreed that orchestral standards had declined alarmingly;[6] to re-create them would be to re-create something no one had liked at the time. To be true to Viennese practice, the principal players would have to send substitutes to the rehearsals and show up only for the performances. And to consider the resulting under-nuanced, under-rehearsed performances as reflecting the composer's ideals is to ignore what we know about Beethoven's own conducting. Recall Robert Levin's remark about how Beethoven was the first Viennese composer to write orchestral music that "ought not to have been sight-read"; then consider that when he rehearsed an orchestra he was "very particular" about trying to get the players to realize "expression, the delicate nuances, the equable distribution of light and shade as well as an effective *tempo rubato*."[7] This

3. Clive Brown, notes to Hogwood's CD of Beethoven's first two symphonies, L'Oiseau-Lyre 414 338.

4. Christopher Hogwood, "Hogwood's Beethoven," *Gramophone* 63 (March 1986), p. 1136.

5. "Beethoven: The New Antiquity," in Taruskin's *Text and Act* (New York: Oxford University Press, 1995); originally published in *Opus,* October 1987, pp. 31–41, 43, 63.

6. See Clive Brown, "The Orchestra in Beethoven's Vienna," *Early Music* 16 (February 1988), pp. 4–20, esp. pp. 4–6

7. According to an eyewitness, Ignaz von Seyfried; other accounts support him (see Brown, "The Orchestra," p. 17).

doesn't sound like a man with a strong preference for uncomplicated, rhythmical performances.

In Taruskin's view, the only historically minded conductor to do something honest and artful with Beethoven was the leader of the third British period-instruments Beethoven cycle to be recorded: Roger Norrington. Norrington, too, claims Beethoven for the "Classical," but as our interview shows, he has hardly lacked an interpretative point of view—a controversial one to this day, but an influential one. Of the three cycles, only his has become a best-seller, has won industry awards, and has affected the way many musicians and audiences—including mainstream ones—approach Beethoven.

I spoke to Norrington in early 1994 when he was in San Francisco to conduct the San Francisco Chamber Symphony. Our interview took place on a spring-like January morning at the mansion where he and his wife were houseguests. Norrington couldn't have been further from the dictatorial maestro stereotype. With his warm, open temperament, he has a gift for putting people at ease. More importantly from an interviewer's standpoint, he is full of original opinions, colorfully expressed—though he emphasizes that he is a performer, not a scholar. He shared his views generously and met my occasional disagreements with his natural civility and humor. Lurking behind much of our conversation was the question whether Beethoven was Classical or Romantic.

It's been said that you've influenced Beethoven playing more thoroughly than anyone since Toscanini. A more recent ideal was Karajan, who was criticized for being too smooth and refined. One thing he said was that one should not be able to detect the presence of bar lines—it should be as if no bar lines are there at all.

I couldn't disagree with Karajan more. Bar lines are terribly important in Classical music—though, of course, not all are of the same importance. One of the keys to determining their importance is the dance element, what's called the "periodicity" of the music:[8] is it in four-bar phrases? two-bar phrases? three-

---

8. Norrington is referring to the grouping of measures into multi-bar phrases—imposing, as Charles Rosen says, a "steady, slower beat over the beats of the individual bars." Four-bar periodic phrasing "was already in frequent use in the early part of the eighteenth century," he says, and by the last quarter of the eighteenth century "it dominated almost all composition." In spite of the "slower" beat this imposes, "the music of the late eighteenth century actually seems to move faster than that of the Baroque"—he compares this to how in high gear the motor of a car turns over more slowly but the car moves faster. He later says, "For Beethoven the four-bar rhythm takes on an even greater effect of motor energy than for the composers of the previous generation, propelling the music forward; his deviations from it seem almost always like an act of will": Rosen, *The Romantic Generation* (Cambridge, Mass; Harvard University Press, 1995), p. 261; in a larger discussion of four-bar phrases, pp. 258–278. (In his *The Frontiers of Meaning* [New York: Hill and Wang, 1994], p. 44, Rosen mentions Beethoven's "insistent attempts to attack the rhythm of the bar line and to affirm it at the same time.")

bar phrases? And where are the irregular shapes, the five-bar and six-bar phrases and so on?

Beethoven himself was totally aware of this, of course. For example, in the middle of the Scherzo of the Ninth Symphony he suddenly writes, "Ritmo de tre battute" and then "Ritmo di quattro battute": he expects you to beat in three-bar periods, then go back to four later. Now, this relates to another element of Beethoven—upsetting the expectations of bar lines.[9] But all his music is written with reference to bar patterns.

And this is related to the dance element?

Absolutely. When I prepare a score that is an actual dance—the *Prometheus* ballet music of Beethoven, or *Les petits riens* of Mozart, or the ballet in his opera *Idomeneo*—the position becomes even clearer. My wife, Kay Lawrence, is a choreographer of early dance, and we often work together. The lines I draw in these scores to show phrase lengths are precisely where she sees the dance changing direction—where the dancers go around one way and then the other way, for instance. We're listening to the music, and she says, "there," "there," and "there." Her "there"s as a choreographer correspond exactly to my bar patterns as a conductor.

And there are similar patterns even in the symphonies?

Yes.[10] You don't actually dance to symphonies and concertos, of course, but the structure of the music is related to dance music. Dance was the public's primary relationship to music of most kinds.

Would you say any movements in the Beethoven symphonies are in actual dance style, other than scherzos?

You mean a first movement or a last movement. Well, let me see. We know the *Eroica* finale theme is a contredanse, because he had already published it as one. But many of his other movements have the flow and spring of *potential* dances.

What about other elements in Beethoven's thinking? For example, Leonard Ratner identifies a number of "topics" in the Classical composer's "thesaurus":

9. Donald Francis Tovey points out that Beethoven is most likely to upset or break bar patterns in his dance movements: "it is just where Beethoven's rhythms are most dance-like that we encounter ambiguities and positive changes of stress . . . the most vivid examples of [this] are in Beethoven's scherzos. . . . [in many places in Beethoven] the bar is still a typographical device rather than a constant rhythmic unit" (*Beethoven* [Oxford University Press, 1965 (1944)], pp. 69-72).

10. Leonard Ratner, in *Classic Music* (New York: Schirmer, 1980), writes that in music of the Classical era that isn't an actual dance but uses dance elements, "the typical dance rhythms are employed, but the length of sections does not conform to choreographic patterns of symmetry" (p. 18). Norrington said, when I sent him this passage, "That's what I'm *saying!*"

one was dance styles, but there's also the "singing style," military and hunt music, the learned style (what might be called the stile antico), *and several others.*[11] *And there's been a lot of discussion lately of how central the rhetorical tradition was to Beethoven's approach to music.*[12]

Of course, and you haven't mentioned dramatic declamation and recitative, two more topics. The greater the music, the larger will be the frame of reference, and the more the ideas that will be clothed in passion. It is simply that dancing was the strongest and most widely understood of these elements. Our danger is that we don't think of Classical music as something that is useful anymore. We think of it as awe-inspiring. We've sent it terribly up-market, put it on a pedestal. People like Toscanini and Karajan very much put it on a pedestal. It eventually became a replacement for religion, didn't it?

Yes, although I think it's been shown that both placing it on a pedestal and exalting it like a religion go back to Beethoven's time, and that he played a key part in spreading these ideas.[13] *On the other hand, it's been said that the character of Beethoven comes across differently in your performances—in a way that counters our mythic image of him.*

A deeper implication of Norrington's point is that the preoccupation of Baroque and especially Classical composers with large-scale symmetry and "periodic" phrasing results from the influence of dance music, whose prestige (and, therefore, influence on serious composition) increased owing to the prestige of the French court in the seventeenth and eighteenth centuries. A clear discussion of the larger influence of dance on Baroque form can be found in John Butt's Cambridge Handbook *Bach: Mass in B Minor* (Cambridge University Press, 1991), chap. 6. Regarding the Classical style, see Charles Rosen, *Sonata Forms* (New York: Norton, 1980), chap. 3, and Wye J. Allanbrook, *Rhythmic Gesture in Mozart* (Chicago: University of Chicago Press, 1983), chap. 2.

11. Ratner, *Classic Music,* pp. 9–24. He also lists the French Overture, the brilliant style, the fantasia, so-called "Turkish music," the pastorale, and the *Sturm und Drang* style. However, he does say that "Dance topics saturate the concert and theater music of the classic style; there is hardly a major work in this era that does not borrow heavily from the dance" (p. 18). Ratner details the dance elements that Classical composers used as "topics" (pp. 9–16).

12. George Barth's *The Pianist as Orator* (Ithaca, N.Y.: Cornell University Press, 1992) is the most complete discussion of this topic. Other discussions include, for example, William S. Newman, *Beethoven on Beethoven* (New York: Schirmer, 1988), chap. 6.

13. In this development—closely related to the emergence of the "work concept" discussed in the Levin interview—Beethoven was a crucial transitional figure. Carl Dahlhaus, in *Nineteenth-Century Music* (Berkeley: University of California Press, 1989), pp. 94–95, and 183, cites late-eighteenth-century German discussions of the "religion of art" and of music as the true revealer of religion; he also cites an E. T. A. Hoffman essay of 1814 (which Beethoven almost certainly read) describing Beethoven's symphonies as the modern counterpart to Palestrina in revealing metaphysical truth. Dahlhaus also explains how the new bourgeois concert audience sacralized art in a way the aristocracy had not; Beethoven not only suited this new attitude, but helped catalyze it. An example of Beethoven placing music on a pedestal is his remark, made to Bettina von Arnim, that "I despise the world which does not intuitively feel that music is a higher revelation than all wisdom and philosophy" (reported in her letter to Goethe on 28 May, 1810).

Yes, I badly wanted to restore the *human* side of his music, the vivacity, the humor, the craziness, the elegance, the vulgarity—the exuberant *range* of expression which Beethoven's own contemporaries were already comparing to Shakespeare. I felt that this "physical" side was essential both to his nature and to his position as a survivor from the eighteenth century. What Beethoven and Wagner meant as "mythic" were very different things.

In life, too, Beethoven was plentifully human rather than wrapped in divine mist. For instance, when he was writing the first eight symphonies he was quite young—he finished the Eighth when he was 42, and was still quite boisterous. He was a bit shy of company because of his deafness, but when with friends he was very good company, full of wit and repartee. If he had not lost his hearing, he would have been very . . . well, you know, he loved dancing and being in company. He wasn't merely some sort of reclusive scholarly figure. He had many sides. He was mortal.

It reminds me of one pianist's remark that Beethoven's music "is 85 percent cheerful." But what about his shaking his fist at fate?

Well, he might well have shaken his fist when he went deaf—who wouldn't? We all shake our fists occasionally. And clearly he was a person of exceptional musical integrity. He wasn't an ordinary person. But he did have ordinary tastes—eating and drinking. We tend to forget that, because we idolize him. "He couldn't possibly fart, could he?" We've got these reverential views.

But that's part of how I think about him—virility, energy, dance; a tremendous brain for putting together this amazing music, and an incredible performer on the piano. And an improviser, like all those great guys were—Beethoven's improvising must have been staggering. And that's in the symphonies too.

Improvisation?

Don't let me exaggerate. Classical music is not really improvisation. But improvisation lies near its creative heart. Beethoven could extemporize a sonata form or a fugue. Any good performance, of course, wants to sound as if it's being composed that moment, but a good development section must *sound* like an improvisation—otherwise it seems too planned. I mean, if you think about some nineteenth-century symphonies, the development sections are not terribly convincing—they say it in the key of A, and then say it again in D, and then again in G. You can tell what's going to happen a few bars on. With Beethoven, you can *never* tell what's going to happen next.

A symphony may be a great structure, but it wants to *sound* as if it's being made up—particularly last movements. First movements are more about structure and argument—that's what the sonata form *is*, after all.[14]

14. The sonata form—a way of organizing music, really, rather than a fixed form—is at the heart of what musicians call the Classical style of Haydn, Mozart, and Beethoven. In a

That brings up the topic of dramatic structure.

. . . the structure of drama, the architecture of feeling. These were big pieces. They were much the longest single movements that anyone was writing. You don't get a single span of one tempo like that anywhere else, even in opera finales. But they combined lightness and drama, I think.

But Beethoven's concern for complex, tightly integrated structure, where every note plays a part in the design—it did have a big impact. On this point of unity and tight structure, most commentators have put great emphasis on, for example, how he organized music dramatically, with a movement being built around a dramatic conflict between two different keys (an approach he got from Mozart and Haydn).

Sure. And of course the tonality generally fits the same bar patterns.

So you see them as integrated—the dance-based aspects and the tonal drama.

Yes, they naturally go together: key and shape, speed and harmonic rhythm [the rate at which important harmonies change]. The speed of the harmonic rhythm is what I'm so constantly trying to elucidate in my performances: particularly in "slow" movements, because there, if you don't take care, the harmonic rhythm moves unbearably slowly—a so-called Wagnerian idea, which has been much in fashion since his time. Because conservatory-trained conductors were used to it in later music, they naturally made their Beethoven go slowly. That's how they felt it. Slower for them was more "profound."

Wagner and Liszt were noted for conducting Beethoven slow movements more slowly than had been done before. Wagner said that an adagio can't be too slow.

Yes, although he frequently complained that his own music was taken too slowly, he always looked for drama and seemed to think that a slow movement in Beethoven should be *very* slow, and the pauses should be very long; no diminuendo, and a lot of sostenuto. He also made a big change of tempo for

---

sonata movement, the composer first establishes a home key (say, D major) and then creates a dramatic conflict by moving the music into a second key (in this case, probably A major) in a dramatized way. The two conflicting keys are often represented by contrasting themes ("subjects"). All of this takes place in the movement's opening section, which today is called the "exposition." A second section (the "development") intensifies the sense of conflict; and the third, final section ("recapitulation") resolves it, reconciling the conflicting material in the home key.

Some historians say the sonata style grew out of symmetrical dance forms, expanding them to a larger scale, turning their harmonic design into a drama, and increasing their range of internal contrast and variety. Charles Rosen's *The Classical Style* (New York: Norton, 1972, esp. the chapter "The Coherence of the Musical Language") and his *Sonata Forms* are important books on the classical sonata style.

the second subject. It could be very exciting. People liked it, and it became very popular. Some people still like it!

I just find that it's not appropriate to the origins and gestures of the music. And Beethoven's metronome marks bear that out. His metronome marks are clearly in the Classical tradition. They're not "Wagnerian" at all, which is why so few people follow them today.

Your fast tempos were the first thing everyone noticed about your Beethoven set.

That was the scandal!

Although it wasn't really unprecedented—Toscanini, for example, often was right up there. He was faster than you in the first movement of the Ninth. But the slow movements had often been a lot slower. What's your view now on metronome markings?

I do them the same, I don't think I've changed. I suppose some people felt I was just trying to stick to a rigid, outmoded code. But I just find them inspiring, you see. The only reason I do music in a particular way is because I'm excited about it, not because it's morally "superior" or "politically correct." It was crucial for me to take seriously any *facts* about Beethoven's music. But since I had such an eighteenth-century training, I found his speeds as inspired as they were comprehensible.

I must admit, I had a tussle with the Ninth. One does, because there are one or two very strange tempos, and my performance may not be right—may not be what he intended. It was an honest attempt to make those tempos work, and they could be wrong. It's the first eight symphonies that I would swear by, because he metronomized them together, in a block, seven or eight years after he'd written the Eighth.[15] So he really knew those symphonies well. But when he metronomized the Ninth he'd never heard it. He was guessing. He hadn't had the experience, which everybody needs, of hearing the piece.

15. Arguments for the validity of Beethoven's metronome markings have shown that his metronome was in good working order (Peter Stadlen, "Beethoven and the Metronome," *Soundings* 9 [1982], pp. 38ff.) and that he was consistent in the types of markings he gave for similar movements (see note 20, below). One argument against their accuracy is that tempo is influenced by acoustics and orchestral size, so that the tempo musicians "hear" when reading a score is often different than the tempo that works in real performance. Further, Beethoven, by the time he metronomized his symphonies, could barely hear real performances; and he never had the opportunity to test the marked speeds in performance, something that has often led composers to modify their scores. It's also argued that a composer's sense of what tempo to take in a piece can vary with mood, age, and other factors; Beethoven himself changed the metronome mark for the first movement of the Ninth from "108 or 120" for the quarter note to a much slower (though still fast) 88. Recordings by composers like Stravinsky and Bartók of their own works support all these arguments—composers do not necessarily follow their own metronome markings, nor are their tempos in a work consistent from one year to the next.

All the same, it's reasonable to say that the metronome markings give a general sense of Beethoven's tempos, and indicate that they were fast by modern standards, especially in the

One of your metronome-based tempos that people had trouble with was in the slow movement of the Ninth.

That one I'm absolutely sure of. The two that are really questionable are the trio of the Scherzo, because he says "faster" and the metronome mark appears to say "slower," and the march in the finale. So those two are more foggy, really.

It's been argued that he meant those to go twice as fast as the metronome marks.[16]

Yes. Ben Zander's recorded it that way, and it's exciting, but pretty wild. I can't say I'm altogether convinced, but I'm not sure that I'm right either. Those are two tempos I'd like to ask Beethoven about! The slow movement I wouldn't even bother to ask him about, because I'm sure it's right.

It's different in character from what we're used to.

He marks it "Adagio molto e cantabile." No doubt he meant it to be heard in two main beats per bar; the feeling is "in two." If he had calculated a metronome mark just for those two beats, it would have been "half note = 30"—that is, each of the two main beats would have been heard 30 times a minute. But 30 was not on his metronome, so he marked it quarter note = 60. That's how I would match the "Adagio" description with the metronome marking.

Secondly, in all his symphonies there are no "slow" movements, any more than there are in Haydn or Mozart—"adagio" is very rare in Haydn, and the Italian word *adagio* doesn't even mean "slow"—it means "easy." People at the time usually referred not to "slow movements" but to Allegrettos, Andantes, and so on.

The metronome marks for Mozart by Hummel, his student, and those for Haydn and Mozart by Czerny, Beethoven's student, support you—the slow movements aren't very slow.[17] *The same is true of the metronome markings Czerny left for Beethoven's piano sonatas, and the markings Beethoven left for the "Hammerklavier."*[18]

slow movements—which is not to say that it's "wrong" to play them more slowly if we prefer them that way.

16. Clive Brown, "Historical Performance, Metronome Marks and Tempo in Beethoven's Symphonies," *Early Music* 19 (May 1991), pp. 247–58. Jonathan Del Mar makes a third suggestion. He argues that the metronome marking half note = 116 results from a mis-hearing by Beethoven's scribe; Beethoven, he suggests, may have said "160" (the two words sound alike in German as well as English). Another possibility is that Beethoven was giving the metronome marking for the Scherzo (which is 116), not the trio. See Del Mar, "The Text of the Ninth Symphony," Appendix 2 of Nicholas Cook's Cambridge Handbook *Beethoven: Symphony No. 9* (Cambridge University Press, 1993), pp. 110–17.

17. William Malloch, "Carl Czerny's Metronome Marks for Haydn and Mozart Symphonies," *Early Music* 16 (February 1988), pp. 72–82.

18. Sandra Rosenblum, "Two Sets of Unexplored Metronome Marks for Beethoven's Piano Sonatas," *Early Music* 16 (February 1988), pp. 59–71.

Right. So, at 60, the Ninth's Adagio fits right into the Classical tradition.

Thirdly, you didn't make a mistake about 60. Even if you were deaf, you *knew* 60. It was the tempo you were brought up with in the eighteenth century. At home, you wouldn't hear the air-conditioning, or the fridge, or the telephone, or television, but there was one mechanical noise you would hear, and that was the pendulum of the grandfather clock. And they all went at 60. And if you were deaf, you could *see* the pendulum ticking at 60. I mean, you just don't make a mistake about it—60's the one tempo that we can rely on. If he'd put 48, that would be one thing; but 60, no.[19]

Besides, it's a typical slow movement, and it sounds beautiful at 60, in my view. If you think of the finale of the "Pastoral," it's that sort of world, isn't it? The last movement of the "Pastoral" is also 60. So it doesn't surprise me in the Ninth. Even some quite well-known Beethoven scholars say they can't quite manage it. But I certainly don't find it difficult.

It's hard to adjust to if you're used to its being slower.

I suppose it *is* hard to adjust. It would be interesting to know how many people have adjusted. On the other hand, my daughter, who hadn't heard it any other way, heard a performance at the "old" tempo last year, and she didn't recognize the piece! It was on the radio, and she said, "What the hell is this music? It sounds vaguely familiar." Her contemporaries, the kids who write to me from school, don't say, "You've changed my life": they say, "Why do other people take these funny slow tempos?"

So it's a question of what you're used to. One tends to forget that new people come out of school every year used to the alternative methods. It happens very quickly, this change of tastes. And as I said earlier, aside from the two tempos about which I am unsure in the Ninth, in the other symphonies all of the tempos are just wonderful speeds.

Some of the fast movements are faster than we're used to, also.

That's right. The first movement of the "Eroica" is 60, too. It's fantastic at that speed. And when Beethoven was metronomizing, in some of the notebooks there are cross-references. He'll say, "Oh yes, that's allegretto, that's 90, like my trio in a certain other work." And you think, Yes, he's got a

---

19. Max Rudolf gives two other arguments for the approximate correctness of the metronome mark for this movement. He says that the second part of the tempo marking, "e cantabile" ("and singing") was "a modifying afterthought." Says Rudolf, "*Cantabile* held a special meaning for Beethoven, who once said, 'Good singing was my guide; I strove to write as flowingly as possible.' When played at ♩ = 40, as the *Adagio* has often been performed, the melody is no longer singable in terms of human song. Moreover, the second subject of the movement [*Andante moderato*] is marked ♩ = 63, leaving no doubt that Beethoven felt little difference in the pacing of the two themes." In his *The Grammar of Conducting*, 3rd ed. (New York: Schirmer, 1994), p. 398.

clear idea about these tempos.[20] As opposed to, "Beethoven's a hopeless old dotard, who doesn't know anything about his music. We know better." It's an amazing viewpoint, isn't it? He died when he was—what—57? He was younger than me, and we get instead [mimes a caricature of an old man on his deathbed]. I mean, what is this?

That gets back to what you said about our reverential view of his character. Another aspect of that view is the notion that Beethoven was always deadly serious. But together with Haydn, he was one of the greatest musical humorists.

And how! I'm surprised at how much humor there is. For instance, people don't expect to find humor in the "Eroica," but the last movement is hilarious, absolutely *hilarious*. It's as funny as any of the Haydn symphonies. Some people think, "Oh, no, if it's heroic it couldn't be funny. Heroes don't have a nice time." But to me, the hero is a *person*, and he's having a tremendous time, in Heaven or wherever it's supposed to be, until the slow section where he seems to be remembering the funeral march. We're in the middle of the celebration, at the end of the battle, and we're remembering the people who didn't make it—that seems to be what's going on. But then the humor comes back again. It's hilarious in a very superior way. After all, humor does not have to be silly. It can be revealing and inspiring.

Charles Rosen has written of instances of Beethoven's humor being based not on a comic manner but on content.[21] Few, however, have applied the term "hilarious" to that finale. Could you give an example of a joke from the "Eroica" finale?

Some of the jokes, perhaps the kind Rosen's referring to, are very up-market—expecting one key and getting another, or setting up a particular kind of rhythm and then changing it. So the more you know about Classical style, the more you enjoy that kind of high-table joke. But in the "Eroica" finale, you also have this frenetic introduction, which sounds as if it's going to be incredibly important and dramatic. And then you hear the pizzicato strings, and you think, "What is this?" It's clearly absurd, but it's another 50 measures before you discover that it's the *bass line* of the tune, not the tune it-

---

20. This is supported by Rudolf Kolisch, *Tempo and Character in Beethoven's Music*, reprinted in *Musical Quarterly* 77 (Spring and Summer 1993; originally published in *Musical Quarterly* 29 [1943], pp. 169–87; 291–312). It shows that similar tempo marks and time signatures in different works tend to get similar metronome marks. Better still is the summary of Hermann Beck's research on this subject, in William S. Newman's *Beethoven on Beethoven*, pp. 90–97.

21. Regarding the finale of Op. 101, which Beethoven tells the performer to play "with decision," Rosen says the humor is based not on manner but on "contrasts and surprises." Rosen, notes to his 1971 recording, *The Late Beethoven Sonatas* (Columbia M 30939–41), p. 3.

self. And the tune is one Beethoven had already used three times in other works:[22]

So you can guess that he expected his audience to know it by then. They'd heard it as piano variations, they'd seen it in a ballet, in the finale of *Prometheus* [where it probably represented Bacchus], and he published it as a dance to be used during Carnival. They'd danced to this damn thing before hearing it in the "Eroica." So suddenly they have this sort of *Evita* tune coming up, and they knew it was a fun tune, because contredanses were fun dances. They were not like aristocratic minuets; they were family dances, jolly middle-class dances.

The "Eroica" middle-class? Surprise! But he was showing what a nice guy the hero was. He wasn't stuffy. He was a man of the people, the way all heroes should be. All the great heroes, all great gentlemen in the eighteenth century, like Washington, for example, had the "common touch." They didn't make servants feel uncomfortable. They had a way of dealing with their farmers and their staff; people were admired for that. They weren't all up on huge pedestals, you know.

It ties in with Beethoven's tearing up the dedication to Napoleon when he heard he had crowned himself emperor.

Right, it's for the common man as well. And Beethoven, above all, would be somebody who would prefer that the hero be accessible. So in the finale there's this jolly contredanse and all these larks. There are lots of jokes. The fugues too are jokes, aren't they? Incredibly overcomplicated and hilarious. It's very exciting—it's like skiing at high speed through a forest. You've got to think fast and you've got to listen fast, and it's a lot of fun. So why shouldn't music be fun? Mozart and Haydn showed how it could be done.

Maynard Solomon says that Beethoven's heroic works, for all the frightening emotions they let into music, are not "conventionally tragic, let alone death-haunted," because they usually close on "a note of joy, triumph, or transcendence." He relates this ultimately to "the essential features of high comedy."[23]

Beethoven wrote ten operas, didn't he—*Fidelio* and the nine symphonies. I

---

22. Beethoven, Symphony No. 3 in E♭, Op. 55, "Eroica," fourth movement, bars 77–81.
23. Maynard Solomon, *Beethoven* (New York: Schirmer, 1977), p. 194.

think they're all incredibly operatic. There are the comic operas, the Second, the Fourth, and the Eighth, or the rescue operas, the Fifth and the Ninth. The Seventh is more about dance—I think Wagner is right—but let's face it, *dramatic* dance. And the Sixth is the oddball, because it's so pictorial.

Every symphony is different from every other, amazingly different, but he was a naturally *dramatic* composer. He had a hard time writing his first opera, and he never got around to another. But he wrote very dramatic symphonies. The Second Symphony finale is a hilarious comic-opera finale, the Fifth a heroic-opera finale.

After all, symphony and opera came to power at the same time. The time when opera houses really opened to the public, outside Italy, Hamburg, London, and a few other places, was the mid-eighteenth century, just when the symphony was coming up. The symphony is a naturally operatic animal. The two genres seem to me to be totally allied. They share the same language, and that language is Italian.

Rosen argues that the timing of the Classical language is that of Italian opera.[24] *I wanted to ask you more about performance practice issues. When you developed your interpretations, it obviously wasn't just a matter of using period instruments and following the metronome markings. You wrote in your CD booklet that orchestra size and pitch were not crucial to the era's style—they varied from place to place, even in one town—but that other factors like bowing and phrasing were crucial. Would you describe some of them?*

Let's see. To begin with, they didn't seem to use much vibrato in orchestral playing (though soloists did use some vibrato—some more than others). That gives you much cleaner textures, so you hear more—it's more transparent when there's no vibrato.

And that would aid transparency at the fast tempos.

At any tempo! So does the fact that the woodwinds are all different in sound from each other—they're less homogeneous than today, so that makes a difference. Returning to the strings, Spohr (Beethoven's contemporary, who knew him and played under him in at least one early symphony, and wrote a book on violin playing) didn't use spiccato at all [the technique, much used today, of repeatedly bouncing the bow slightly off the string]: it clearly wasn't part of his style.[25] Beethoven may have intended some spiccato, but probably much less than we are taught today. The basic bowstroke, even for shorter notes, was on

24. Rosen, *The Classical Style*, chap. 3, "The Origins of the Style."

25. Spohr claimed that spiccato "went against the Classical tradition in German violin playing." See Clive Brown, "Bowing Styles, Vibrato, and Portamento in Nineteenth-Century Violin Playing," *Journal of the Royal Musical Association*, 113 (1988), p. 106.

the string, not spiccato. So we have a definitely on-the-string style for quite a lot of the time.

Then we use a style of bowing which derives ultimately from Baroque practice. We tend to use down bows for strong notes and up bows for weak ones, more so than is done today. For instance, the beginning of each bar is a down-bow normally,[26] unless there's a specific reason for it not to be.

Does that make the music more metrically accented?

It makes the music a bit more dancy. Then note length seems to me equally important. We don't play staccato on notes unless Beethoven says to do so. We don't just play all the short notes short, which is what modern orchestras tend to do. We play the staccato pretty hard, because it's clear from the manuscripts that he doesn't show dots, he shows daggers—really sharp-looking things. Often they're reproduced in modern editions as dots, rather gentlemanly-looking things (you know, put them in a club without raising eyebrows). But they were clearly something much stronger.[27]

In general, when there weren't dots or daggers on the notes there was a smoother style of playing. The slur is the smoothest; the portato is smooth;[28] the notes with no markings are separate but long. If you had just one rehearsal (the norm in those days) these small markings were crucial.

Are you saying that the articulation of notes in Beethoven tended actually to be smoother?

Some smoother, some rougher: a big variety—and side by side.

How about the phrasing?

It was shorter than today, I think. But many short phrases can be beautifully modulated into one long one. And the clarity and *amount* of the phrasing make a huge difference. There are two reasons for a different approach to phrasing. The first is that Beethoven's musicians had a whole series of conventions, which came from the Baroque (and which every musician was taught), so that they knew where to play loud and soft without being told. They had

---

26. This practice (known as the "rule of the down bow") is first reported in the 1590s, and was especially dominant in eighteenth-century France, as Anner Bylsma observes in his interview. Although some important eighteenth-century Italian virtuosi—Geminiani (1751) and Tartini (1771)—opposed it, and it was not applied rigidly in Italy as it had been in Lully's orchestra, the principle continued to have relevance to orchestral playing in Beethoven's Vienna and, for that matter, has relevance even to modern mainstream playing. See Robin Stowell, *Violin Technique and Performance Practice in the Late Eighteenth and Early Nineteenth Centuries* (Cambridge University Press, 1985), pp. 303f.

27. See Clive Brown, "Dots and Strokes in Late 18th- and 19th-Century Music," *Early Music* 21 (November 1993), pp. 601 and 607.

28. The portato marking is discussed in detail by Malcolm Bilson in his interview, p. 308. Also see Clive Brown, "Dots and Strokes," p. 607.

this whole system of what they called "good notes" and "bad notes."[29] You inflected everything; music is a language with inflections in it. People like Leopold Mozart taught that right from the start you must stress one note and lighten another. If you have two notes, one of them *has* to be louder than the other. You have to decide. You can't just have *uh-uh* [illustrates two equal stresses], which Stravinsky often expressly calls for—that's his style. With Haydn, Mozart, and Beethoven that's impossible. So phrasing is absolutely built into the way we play, and the lengthening and shortening of notes comes into that, too, and accentuates it.

This system of "good" and "bad" notes reminds me of the Kodály method of music education in Hungary, where the first thing you sing is your own name. Not *duh-duh*. It always has an inflection, like somebody calling, "MAH-mee."

That example seems to reflect the Baroque/Classical idea that music is like oration.

Right. But the second reason for that different type of phrasing takes us back to the dance. Rhythm does not constitute dance; *phrasing* constitutes dance. Phrasing is what makes you want to dance. Rhythm—*uh-uh-uh-uh-uh*— isn't dance. Nowadays, we have consciously "primitive" dance rhythms—but it isn't what *they* thought of as a dance. They had to have ONE-two-three, ONE-two-three. If you play for that kind of dance, you have to propel the music by phrasing. ONE-TWO-THREE doesn't make you want to dance. You have to play ONE-two three. It elevates the first beat. They felt that in their bones.

Don't forget, there wasn't one single musician in Vienna who didn't play in a dance band for some part of the year. The court orchestra played at the court balls for the whole of Carnival. The theatre orchestra played for balls at the theatre and in the Redoutensaal. If you were a fiddler you played for a danc-ing master. You couldn't be a musician and not play for dance. And if you play for dance (as I was lucky enough to do for country dancing, when I was young) you get to know how to *move* people to dance. When you reach the end of a phrase you've got to take the music forward [sings wonderfully, with an irre-producible lilt, an English folk-dance theme]. You've got to keep them amused, to keep their feet going. It's the same in the concert hall—you keep their minds and their feet amused. Keeping the sense of onward movement is done with phrasing, not with tempo.

And this relates to making sense of Beethoven's tempos?

This relates to making sense of the tempos—the tempo's success or other-

---

29. Downbeats, for example, were "good" notes; second beats were "bad." See the inter-view with John Butt, Chapter 9, for further explanation.

wise is in the *flavor* of how you make the music move. When you get to a very fast tempo, by showing the periodicity of that phrasing you can give it a poise. Consider the "Eroica" opening: DUM de dum-dum, DUM de de dum [he accents the first beat of the first and third bars of the phrase]. That feels slow because it's a two-bar phrase:[30]

Whereas DUM de DUM duh [accenting the first beat of each bar] will sound more hurried. Mozart and Beethoven are constantly playing with that ambiguity. Of course, it is particularly important in slow tempos. A slow movement has lots of small periodicities that keep it going. If you play them too slowly, those periodicities turn into a series of chains around your ankle. Even in the Adagio that you heard on Monday, the opening of the Haydn Forty-ninth, I said, "Don't think of six beats, just because there are six eighth notes in the bar. Don't even think in three—think in one. Although it's Adagio, you can easily let it fall to bits." It's the *phrasing* of the slow stuff which helps you dance to it, and stops it from being boring.

A related issue is rubato and tempo fluctuation. This has been a source of controversy surrounding your recordings. What do you think about tempo fluctuation in Beethoven?

In Beethoven I don't vary the tempos very much at all. I may be completely wrong, and he may have varied it much more. I believe he may have played more freely in solo sonatas, but not nearly so much in public, symphonic works. It would have been a very difficult thing to do, anyway. People didn't conduct much—there weren't virtuoso conductors around yet, in the modern sense. And, then, fluctuation is not so relevant to a big public piece. A sonata was to be played in a salon, so it's free; it's like an intimate conversation. But when the king was addressing his people, he didn't slow up for the second subject. A symphony is just such a public occasion. It's a difference we no longer observe today, because all of our music has become public, but it's an important difference.

The main reason, though, is that for me tempo fluctuation just doesn't *feel* necessary in Beethoven. As soon as I get to Mendelssohn, I feel it necessary to vary the tempos. I *feel* the need to do it. That's guessing too, of course. We

---

30. Beethoven, Symphony No. 3 in E♭, Op. 55, "Eroica," first movement, bars 3–6. Notice how Beethoven's slur marks support Norrington's approach: the two-bar slur discourages an accent on the first beat of the second bar.

know Mendelssohn didn't do it very much—Wagner thought he was a bit of a prissy Kapellmeister, didn't he?[31] But it seems to me necessary. In the second subject of the "Reformation" Symphony, for instance, I slow down quite a bit. I just can't go straight on. But in Beethoven I feel a need, on the contrary, for a kind of Classical uniformity, as in Haydn. Performance must always be information *and* feeling. The information is there, if you like, to help *educate* the feeling.

There are reports of Beethoven slowing down and speeding up in his playing, and some about his use of tempo rubato in conducting;[32] but Rosen argues that in orchestral pieces, the structure doesn't call for much rubato inflection, reflecting performing conditions that made it hard to do rubato.[33]

Yes, one rehearsal was normal for a concert. Of course, I don't adhere *rigidly* to each tempo. If you listen to the slow movements of the "Eroica" and the Ninth, you'll find a lot of changes of tempo, but they are slight and (hopefully) well modulated.

Many of these issues reflect the fact that this was a transitional period, both in performance practice and in society's views of the artist and the arts.

Yes. And Beethoven was full of new ideas. The fact that I keep talking about him as an eighteenth-century composer doesn't contradict the fact that he was looking forward. He was incredibly inventive.

Solomon has emphasized his "radical modernism."[34] Nonetheless, it seems that you're trying to approach the music in terms of its historical antecedents rather than its consequents.

31. Donald Mintz's article "Mendelssohn as Performer and Teacher," in *The Mendelssohn Companion,* ed. Douglass Seaton (Westport, Conn.: Greenwood Press, forthcoming), argues that Wagner's *On Conducting,* with its attacks on Mendelssohn, was "in the first instance an anti-Semitic tract and only in the second a treatise about conducting." But while Mintz supports Norrington's view that extreme tempo variations within a movement came in only with Wagner's conducting, he also shows that moderate tempo flexibility (relative to a single underlying tempo) was part of nineteenth-century conducting style before Wagner.

Interestingly, Joseph Wilhelm von Wasielewski, a conductor and a student of Mendelssohn, wrote in 1883 that Mendelssohn "was exceptionally free in conducting his own work but very strict in everything else" (David Fallows, personal communication, 1995). This speaks well for Norrington's instincts with this music; it also points out "that composers tend to feel more free to interpret their own works in their own way" (*ibid.*).

32. Beethoven's use of tempo rubato in conducting was reported by various people; I discuss this in detail in this chapter's Postscript.

33. Rosen, *The Classical Style,* pp. 144–45.

34. Solomon, "Beethoven: Beyond Classicism," in *The Beethoven Quartet Companion,* ed. Robert Winter and Robert Martin (Berkeley: University of California Press, 1994), pp. 59–75.

Yes, that's essential. And only by setting the eighteenth-century scene does one most forcefully realize his modernity. People reacted strongly at the time, too, of course. I read a lot of the contemporary criticism, for instance, which is very revealing, because it mentions some things we wouldn't have thought of, and it doesn't talk of other things at all. For instance, regarding the Ninth Symphony, contemporary critics tended to talk one minute about key change and the next minute about something quite fantastical, fairies-marching-through-the-undergrowth stuff. They tended to think in literary imagery, which today you're not "supposed" to do.[35] Back then it was absolutely normal. Berlioz did it to Beethoven's Fifth. He clearly thought that was how you listened to music: pictorially. So that's one thing that surprises us—what they *did* put in.

One of the things that affected contemporaries was the roughness of Beethoven's music. Solomon describes his heroic works as incorporating such elements as "death, destructiveness, anxiety, and aggression, as terrors to be transcended within the work of art itself."[36] It was more violent than what they were used to.

It is, though I think we sometimes underplay Mozart and Haydn, too. I don't think Mozart should ever sound rough, but he goes very near the edge. Haydn comes close, too (in the opening of *The Creation*, or the drinking chorus in *The Seasons*). Clearly, Beethoven *did* go over the boundary; they must have enjoyed going very near the edge, but Beethoven went over it. So, yes, I agree, it must have been more violent than usual. And they did think it was wild. Schubert at first didn't like a lot of Beethoven—he thought it was too rough. Weber said of the Beethoven Seventh (that repeated bit at the end of the first movement) that Beethoven was ripe for the madhouse. So clearly there was a feeling that he was too violent for words. Beethoven was wild, in any case. He might not have been quite so wild if he hadn't been deaf, I suppose, and fighting it—sometimes the myth is right. Railing against fate—that's what you do if you're a musician and you lose your hearing. You either go under or you fight it.

---

35. Some of these writings can be found in Nicholas Cook's Cambridge Handbook *Beethoven: Symphony No. 9* (Cambridge University Press, 1993). For example, the staccato runs in the woodwinds in the Scherzo of the Ninth are compared to "Columbine tripping with her Harlequin, who springs in bold leaps from one modulation . . . to another" (p. 32). As Norrington says, we tend to smile at such descriptions today; but Scott Burnham's *Beethoven Hero* (Princeton University Press, 1995) argues for the "kinship of the 'highly technical structural analyses' of the twentieth century and the picturesque stories that critics in the nineteenth century made up to account for works of music." (I quote Charles Rosen, "Beethoven's Triumph," *New York Review of Books*, 21 September 1995, p. 54; he calls Burnham's demonstration "brilliant," and also argues that technical analysis of music is "fundamentally metaphorical" [p. 53].)

36. Solomon, *Beethoven*, p. 194.

Perhaps that relates to what you were saying before about his character. Railing is a robust response.[37]

That's good! Yes, it was Beethoven who was the hero of his own "Eroica." That's why he could afford to tear up the dedication!

Anyway, the things critics wrote about music at the time are very important to me. We can't always understand them, of course, because we don't have their second-nature thoughts about it. But at least it helps to break the mold of what our teachers taught about it, which is often very different. And then, having used the old information to change your viewpoints, in the end you have to go on your own instincts. Mine are instinctive performances. The information is just information; however much background you discover about a piece, that doesn't tell you how to *play* it.

Someone praised your Beethoven performances for not feeling pedantic.

Thank God! And if that's really true, it's because although they were fifty percent informed, they were also fifty percent instinctive, organic. That's very important to me. In the end you're doing the music for now, absolutely for now. People get a bit confused about that. They think that because we're being historically informed, we're trying to be historical or "authentic." I *never* use the word "authentic." There is no such thing. I'm trying to get away from performances that have seemingly rather irrelevant gesture, and replace them with gesture that does seem likely to suit the music. But in the end we're doing it for now.

The extreme case, though, might be whether you would flat-out contradict the historical evidence, if it didn't feel as artistically right to you as doing something anachronistic?

I guess the right answer is "Yes." I have to believe in what I'm doing, and believe it at an instinctive level. But as I said before, I try to train the instincts so that they will create gestures entirely in keeping with the mode of a particular epoch, while keeping an eye out for the unique and the extraordinary in a particular piece.

I was saying that Toscanini and, nowadays, people like Charles Mackerras and David Zinman have done the symphonies at the fast tempos on modern

37. But, perhaps, not ultimately the healthiest. Maynard Solomon's enlightening essay "The Quest for Faith" concludes that in his late period "Beethoven had become strong enough to set aside the armor of heroic self-sufficiency which had to some degree impoverished his middle years. He found a new ability to call for help, to pray, to give thanks, to reveal weakness, and even provisionally to accept his dependence upon an immaterial and unknowable deity" (in his *Beethoven Essays* [Cambridge, Mass.: Harvard University Press, 1988], p. 229; first published in *Beethoven-Jahrbuch* 10 [Jahrgang 1978/1981], ed. Martin Staehelin [Bonn: Beethovenhaus, 1983], pp. 101–19).

instruments. What is your view on using historical instruments versus modern ones?

I just like old instruments very, very much. They teach me such a lot about the music. When a modern orchestra is playing superbly, with control over vibrato, with an awareness of phrasing, and beautifully together, I must admit that I do sometimes wonder why I bother with old instruments, because the effect is so good. But in the end I don't think that early music is about instruments; it's about the music. You could do a historically informed performance of a Bach suite on a steel band. It would be historically informed in the sense that it had the right speed, the right phrasing, the right feel. It wouldn't be a *sound* that Bach had heard before, but it could be historically appropriate. And modern instruments are a lot nearer than a steel band, of course, and are in fact quite similar to the old ones. All I have to do is to try to make their playing *relevant* to the music.

I inhabit both worlds. About half my time is spent with early instruments, the other half with modern ones. That's perhaps a little unusual. But I have a very pragmatic approach to the whole thing. I'm a musician, not a scholar. I like to play early music with old instruments because it *sounds* so good, not because it's politically correct! It isn't a question of its being more "moral" somehow—that it's immoral to play with vibrato, for instance. I take a more hedonistic viewpoint. The sound of the old instruments is so beautiful; that of the new ones so rich and strong.

SELECTED DISCOGRAPHY

Richard Osborne praises Norrington's keen "feel for the everyday dress and furnishings of period Beethoven," and adds that Norrington's Beethoven symphony cycle, "for all its several oddities, has something of the evocative power of a Balzac novel"[38]—an interesting comment in view of the priorities Norrington discusses in this interview. If you want to sample the set, you might try its "first and finest entry," as James Oestreich calls it, the Second and Eighth Symphonies (EMI 47698). Oestreich praises their élan, and adds that "Norrington's zippy, electric performances largely vindicate Beethoven's long-disputed metronome markings."[39] The other most-often-praised excerpt from the series includes the First and Sixth Symphonies (EMI 49746). The remaining performances in the cycle have been more controversial—with strong detractors and supporters, and few neutral parties.

Indeed, Norrington's conducting never fails to challenge preconceptions; he may or may not please you, but he will never bore you. In other repertory (all on EMI), some of the more highly praised CDs are his Rossini Overtures (which

38. In a review of Gardiner's Beethoven symphony cycle, in *Gramophone* 72 (November 1994), pp. 65–66.
39. "Beethoven Ever After," *The New York Times*, 1 March 1996, p. C27.

Osborne called "perhaps the cheekiest, most shocking, most uproarious, and in some ways the most revelatory"[40] recording of these works; EMI 54091); Weber symphonies and *Konzertstücke* (55348); and his Purcell *Fairy Queen* (55234), which is well cast and "richly stylish," according to Eric Van Tassel—though he thinks it has a few "excessively fast" tempos.[41] Norrington's Brahms *Ein deutsches Requiem* (EMI 54658) has been called "stirring and moving,"[42] though it has detractors, some of whom object to its baroque-influenced phrasing and articulation and to its unusually quick tempos. (Contrary to what some admirers have written, most of these tempos are substantially faster than the original score's metronome marks—a fact that could be taken as evidence against the charge that Norrington follows such markings slavishly.)

As these examples illustrate, faster-than-usual tempos have been a controversial aspect of Norrington's style. Several of them figure in his widely praised *Don Giovanni* (54859), though it also has a couple of unusually slow tempos. It declares its iconoclasm from the opening Andante: the meter is *alla breve* (two beats per bar), which Norrington says meant to Mozart a tempo "twice as fast" as the same tempo marking with four per bar. Regarding its use in this overture he differs from Wye J. Allanbrook, who sees this passage as an *alla cappella*—i.e. slow—form of *alla breve*.[43] I can't tell you who is right, but while I still prefer the slower tempos I'm used to, Norrington does make his approach work.

FOR FURTHER READING

In addition to the Barth and Stowell books discussed in the Postscript below, William S. Newman's *Beethoven on Beethoven* (New York: Schirmer, 1988) provides a good starting point for investigating performance practice in Beethoven, as do the relevant parts of Sandra Rosenblum's *Performance Practice in Classic Piano Music* (Bloomington: Indiana University Press, 1988). Max Rudolf's *The Grammar of Conducting*, 3rd ed. (New York: Schirmer, 1994), devotes seven wise, informative pages to Beethoven issues (pp. 397–403). Some important bar-by-bar guides for conductors of the symphonies include Norman Del Mar, *Conducting Beethoven* (Oxford University Press, 1992), and Heinrich Schenker, *Beethoven's Ninth Symphony*, trans. and ed. John Rothgeb (New Haven, Conn.: Yale University Press, 1992); both are very much worth exploring. Del Mar comments on historical-performance issues—rarely with approval, but always with intelligence.

Regarding Beethoven's music, Donald Tovey's *Essays in Musical Analysis* (Oxford University Press, 1935–39), *Beethoven* (Oxford University Press,

40. *Gramophone* 68 (April 1991), p. 1842.
41. Van Tassel, "Collection: Purcell on Record," *Gramophone* 73 (November 1995), p. 65.
42. Lionel Salter, *Gramophone* 70 (April 1993), p. 106.
43. *Rhythmic Gesture*, p. 198.

1944), and other writings contain illuminating discussions. The best introduction to Beethoven's musical context may well be Charles Rosen's *The Classical Style* (New York: Norton, 1972); it also has a brilliant, original discussion of Beethoven's style. Regarding his sociocultural context, some good introductory discussions are the first four essays in *The Beethoven Quartet Companion*, ed. Robert Winter and Robert Martin (Berkeley: University of California Press, 1994).

Norrington's remarks about Beethoven's jovial side are clearly meant as a corrective, not a summation of his complex personality. Maynard Solomon's *Beethoven* (New York: Schirmer, 1977) is one of the most successful psychological biographies of any composer, even for those of us who don't share Solomon's Freudian perspective. Scott Burnham's *Beethoven Hero* (Princeton University Press, 1995) is an especially important discussion of the heroic style in Beethoven, how it has influenced our image of him, and how it relates to the trends of thought of Beethoven's era.

Postscript: "Classical" and "Romantic" Performance Practice in Beethoven

Did Beethoven play "Romantically" or in a strict "Classical" style? George Barth's *The Pianist as Orator*[44] (already mentioned by Malcolm Bilson) is one of several recent publications that put a surprising twist on this question. Barth attempts to reconcile the conflicting testimony about Beethoven's "strictness" and his "freedom from constraint" in tempo, and concludes that the opposing witnesses actually describe the same style—but that this becomes clear only when you read them from the standpoint of late-eighteenth-century German writers like C. P. E. Bach and D. G. Türk. These writers preferred a declamatory "speaking" style, which treated rhythm in music rather as we treat rhythm in speech: it could emphasize an important note not only by playing it louder (which is how modern performers do it) but also by holding it a little longer. Also as in speaking, this style tended to pass a little hastily over unimportant short notes, a practice modern musicians avoid. This was the style that Beethoven grew up with, and plenty of written discussions of it have survived. But how might it have sounded? We can hear what this style sounded like, says Barth, in the Beethoven recordings of Béla Bartók.

To most modern critics that assertion is as disorienting as the news that polyunsaturated fat is worse for your heart than other types. We had assumed that Bartók's recordings, with their flexible rhythm, were anachronistically Romantic, and that the true historical style is found in stricter, low-fat recordings like Norrington's. The Bartók example would not, however, surprise another

---

44. Ithaca, N.Y.: Cornell University Press, 1992.

author, Robert Philip. In his essay "Traditional Habits of Performance in Beethoven Recordings,"[45] he argues that "in fundamental ways, musicians from early in our century were closer to the traditions of Beethoven's day than we are now"—and in "we" he includes Norrington, Gardiner, and Co. as well as their mainstream colleagues. Philip does not say that the styles of early recordings are identical to Beethoven's, but he does indicate that they are closer with regard to such seemingly un-Classical "ingredients" (to use Bilson's term) as flexibility of tempo, non-literalness of rhythm, and use of portamento.

These assertions gain support from other writers. Clive Brown tells us that by 1811 "a number of Viennese string players were using portamento liberally, not only in their solo playing but also in the orchestra";[46] its popularity was due to the prestige of the French "Rode/Viotti" school of violin playing, which involved "a highly expressive cantabile often involving the use of prominent portamento."[47]

As for tempo flexibility, although we have a good deal of evidence about Beethoven's and even his predecessors' practices,[48] the evidence is conflicting. But the overall picture suggests that, as Philip puts it, "the idea of a constant tempo in extended movements is an invention of the late twentieth century." I've already quoted Ignaz von Seyfried, conductor at the Theater-an-der-Wien (where various Beethoven premieres took place), on Beethoven's concern with "an effective tempo rubato" when rehearsing. Schindler quotes a 21-bar excerpt from the Second Symphony detailing the rubato that he says Beethoven used when leading it. He shows the composer speeding up in crescendos and slowing down for soft passages—a practice common in early recordings.[49] Though Schindler is known to have forged some of his "evidence," the gist of this account is affirmed by Ignaz Moscheles, who also heard Beethoven con-

45. In *Performing Beethoven*, ed. Robin Stowell (Cambridge University Press, 1994), pp. 195–204.

46. Brown, "The Orchestra in Beethoven's Vienna," p. 18. In 1811 Salieri wrote a letter strongly attacking this trend in orchestras; he wrote a similar letter four years later, which suggests that the first letter had had no effect.

47. Clive Brown, "Ferdinand David's Edition of Beethoven," in *Performing Beethoven*, p. 119; see also pp. 130, 132–36 in the same essay. But David Watkin's "Beethoven and the Cello," pp. 112–15 in the same volume, says that although the treatises by cellists connected with Beethoven recommend using portamento, they suggest fairly moderate use; he argues that "the influence of the Viotti school was strongly felt by cellists during Beethoven's lifetime, but it was [Bernhard] Romberg who inspired a school of cello playing," and his school used portamento "sparingly." Watkin also reports that the *c.* 1825 treatise by Dotzauer, a pupil and follower of Romberg, says that portamento should be used less in orchestral playing than in solo playing—though Salieri's letters make one wonder how many players took this advice.

48. See Brown, "The Orchestra in Beethoven's Vienna," pp. 17–18; and Barth, "The Pianist as Orator," pp. 53–86.

49. In old recordings, rising volume is often marked by acceleration, and falling volume by retardation. Will Crutchfield notes that there's something natural about this: "A crescendo is an expression of heightened energy; so is an acceleration. Is it so bizarre that they should coincide?" ("Brahms by Those Who Knew Him," *Opus*, August 1986, p. 21).

duct.[50] Even Carl Czerny, who insisted that students play Beethoven to a metronome, writes of the cello sonatas that "there occurs in almost every line some notes or passages, where a small and often imperceptible relaxation or acceleration of the movement is necessary."[51] He also gives rules for when one *should* slow down which, when applied to Beethoven, sound Schindler-like.[52] Finally, Beethoven himself writes in the score of his song *Nord oder Süd* that the metronome mark applies only to the first few bars; after that, "feeling has its own tempo."

Beethoven's large movements include contrasting themes and textures, so it is at least conceivable that a movement's different themes might work best at somewhat different tempos. Robert Martin, for example, tells of a string quartet finding that the very fast metronome mark for Op. 95's first movement works perfectly for the opening theme, but makes the second theme sound "terribly rushed and out of character."[53] The group eventually decided to compromise with a "somewhat slower [overall] tempo," because "most modern quartets feel uncomfortable about changing tempos markedly within a movement. . . . Nowadays it seems objectionably self-indulgent to change tempos (except very subtly) to accommodate the second theme." But would it have seemed that way to Beethoven? As Martin's wording implies (and as Taruskin and Barth argue), perhaps this has more to do with modern taste than with history. In teaching the piano, Beethoven "rarely said anything" about wrong notes, but if a student "lacked expression [in] the character of the piece he became angry";[54] what flexible tempos emphasize is the different sections' differing characters, while an unchanging tempo emphasizes their underlying structural unity. Of course, Beethoven's large movements *are* amazingly unified, and of course he worked hard to unify them; and of course, flexible tempos can distort his music when exaggerated or mishandled (I think of some of the Russian "new subjectivist" pianists). But the best of the old (and, for that matter, new) recordings show that conveying unity doesn't require as extreme a suppression of diversity as we sometimes hear today.[55]

A final characterful "ingredient" of old recordings is their speech-like rhythm and phrasing. Philip shows that Bartók was not unique; early in our century musicians often accented a note by holding it longer and by hastening

50. Schindler's excerpt and Moscheles's comment can be found in Taruskin, "Beethoven: The New Antiquity," pp. 256–59.

51. Watkin, "Beethoven and the Cello," p. 112. See also Barth, pp. 74–86.

52. Barth, pp. 85–86.

53. Martin, "The Quartets in Performance: A Player's Perspective," in *The Beethoven Quartet Companion,* p. 120.

54. According to Beethoven's student Ferdinand Ries; see *Beethoven Remembered: The Biographical Notes of Franz Wegler and Ferdinand Ries,* trans. Frederick Noonan (Arlington, Va.: Great Ocean Publishers, 1987), pp. 82–83.

55. See Barth, *The Pianist as Orator,* p. 64.

less important short notes—as we've seen was done in Mozart's and Beethoven's day.

In replying to these arguments, Norrington could note that six of the symphonies pre-date the portamento vogue that Brown describes—though evidence suggests that Beethoven was on to the new French violin style by 1800. Addressing another topic, Norrington might point to testimony, such as that of Ferdinand Ries,[56] about Beethoven's keeping a steady tempo, as well as to evidence that Beethoven's playing grew freer as he aged (that is, after many of the symphonies were written). He could also note Schindler's comment, "That orchestral music does not admit of such frequent changes of tempo [as piano music] is an understood fact," and could mention Charles Rosen's view that "even the late orchestral works like the Ninth Symphony clearly imply a performance with few of the individual refinements of tone, accent, and tempo of the sonatas and quartets."[57] And Norrington stands on unshakable ground when he says that Wagnerian tempo fluctuations were more extreme than Beethovenian ones. Besides, to return to a leitmotif of mine, how much diversity of tempo is needed is ultimately a matter of taste—and Norrington says that his preference for a unified tempo is based on his feeling. Lord Menuhin says, "the dramatic build-up of Beethoven's rhythms has the inevitability of a tidal wave. . . . As soon as you change the pace you lose that inevitability."[58] Note that, like Norrington's "feeling," this is the artistic judgment of a first-rank Beethoven interpreter, rather than an appeal to historical practice.

In general, though, Philip believes that "period performers have got away with the unspoken assumption that late-twentieth-century neatness and cleanness are somehow 'authentic' in Beethoven." That assumption, he concludes, can't hold much longer. And doubting it may bring musical rewards. My reservations about some early-instrument Beethoven may reflect the performances' relative lack of interest in the ingredients Philip lists. It is these matters that can make a fast tempo breathe and feel natural. They can also heighten expression, by letting a great moment register or an important modulation tell. Some historical performers seem to agree; many others may disagree. For myself, I believe that Barth and Philip et al. give historical performers valuable new information to work with.

---

56. "[Beethoven] usually kept a very steady rhythm and only occasionally, indeed, very rarely, speeded up the tempo somewhat. At times he restrained the tempo in his crescendo with a ritardando, which had a beautiful and most striking effect" (translation from Barth, p. 54). Ries studied piano with Beethoven from 1801 to 1805.

57. Rosen, *The Classical Style*, p. 144.

58. Brian Hunt, "A New Challenge," *Gramophone* 73 (April 1996), p. 22.

19

Reviving Idiosyncrasies

John Eliot Gardiner on Berlioz and Brahms

Since the 1960s, John Eliot Gardiner has spent much of his career conducting two groups he founded in his native England, the English Baroque Soloists and the Monteverdi Chorus. It has become obvious, though, that to categorize him as an "English choral conductor" and "early-music specialist" would be unfair. Not only was he conducting opera at Sadler's Wells in 1969; he has performed such composers as Bizet and Chabrier with the opera of Lyon (whose orchestra he founded), and he has more recently turned his attention to even later music. From 1991 to 1994 he was Principal Conductor of the North German Radio (NDR) Symphony Orchestra, with whom he recorded Rachmaninoff, Mahler, Weill, and Britten, and he has recorded Lehár's *Merry Widow* with the Vienna Philharmonic.

When I approached Gardiner about this book, he was at Tanglewood rehearsing the Boston Symphony Orchestra in Berlioz. Our topic was the use of early instruments in Romantic music. Some observers have dismissed experiments in this field as simple empire building by the historical-performance movement. Yet Berlioz himself wrote that "at no period in the history of music has there been greater mention made of instrumentation" than in his own. These words appear in his treatise on orchestration—apparently only the second (by just a few years) ever written on that subject. And Carl Dahlhaus notes that "this 'emancipation of tone color,' initiated by Berlioz, freed tone color from its subservient function of merely clarifying the melody, rhythm, harmony, and counterpoint of a piece, and gave it an aesthetic raison d'être and significance of its own."[1] If that is so, then a case could be made that period instruments might be more significant in Berlioz or Liszt than in most earlier music.[2] As we'll see, though, the case does not convince Gardiner.

It may seem odd that a book on "early music" should include Berlioz; yet Berlioz might be considered a patriarch of period instruments. As Hugh Macdonald writes, Berlioz was among the first to put forth the view that when we perform music of the past it "should be enshrined in its own period and not brought up to date."[3] For example, Berlioz decried the "ravagers of works of art"[4] who altered the orchestration of earlier composers. True, in reviving a Gluck opera in 1859, he discreetly retouched the orchestration—but only, he said, "solely in order to render it precisely as it was composed by Gluck."[5] This concern with the composer's instrumentation can be said to have led eventually to the use of period instruments in our century.

Brahms and Berlioz were in some ways polar opposites—Brahms the exemplar of "absolute" music, Berlioz of literature-based music; Brahms, unjustly derided for "gray" orchestration, Berlioz the unquestioned master of color. Yet both were children of an era whose historical awareness was unprecedented. According to Peter Burkholder, Brahms was the first composer to be "obsessed with the musical past" and with his place in musical history; in our century, such obsession became the norm.[6] Brahms's obsession with the musical past meant that he knew far more about early music than most of his predecessors. He studied Schütz, Bach, Palestrina, and many others in depth; he considered their works to represent a lost golden age, and sometimes wrote in their long-outmoded forms himself. The related feeling of nostalgia is sometimes underlined in modern performances of Brahms—perhaps because (as I discussed in this book's introduction) we share that feeling. Yet Gardiner and others who are experimenting with historically informed Brahms performance often de-emphasize the nostalgic quality in favor of vigor; it's another example, perhaps, of historical information being used to make old music sound new. Whether it benefits the music is, of course, a matter of debate, on which Gardiner expresses clear opinions.

1. Carl Dahlhaus, *Nineteenth-Century Music*, trans. J. Bradford Robinson (Berkeley: University of California Press, 1989), p. 243.

2. See for example the review by Julian Rushton, *Early Music* 17 (November 1989), p. 623.

3. Macdonald, *The New Grove Dictionary*, vol. 2 (London: Macmillan, 1980), p. 601.

4. In Berlioz's "Instruments Added by Modern Composers to Scores of Old Masters," from his *À travers chant* (Paris, 1862). A modern translation is *The Art of Music and Other Essays*, trans. and ed. Elizabeth Csicsery-Ronay (Bloomington: Indiana University Press, 1994); the essay is on pp. 148–49. See also José A. Bowen, "Mendelssohn, Berlioz, and Wagner as Conductors: The Origins of the Ideal of 'Fidelity to the Composer,'" *Performance Practice Review* 6 (Spring 1993), pp. 77–88.

5. See Joël-Marie Fauquet, "Berlioz's Version of Gluck's *Orphée*," in *Berlioz Studies*, ed. Peter Bloom (Cambridge University Press, 1992), pp. 189–253.

6. Burkholder, "Brahms and Twentieth-Century Classical Music," *19th-Century Music* 8/9 (1984), pp. 75–83.

We began by discussing a trend that's affecting orchestras around the world: standardization. Many orchestras are losing some of their region's traditional orchestral sound and style. One factor behind this is jet-age maestros who, says Nicholas McGegan, spend more time in the first-class lounges of airports than in front of orchestras; another is the international distribution of recordings. Yet technology is only part of the equation; attitude, as I think emerges in our talk, is another. I hope Gardiner's attitude doesn't prove quixotic.

You recently founded the Orchestre Révolutionnaire et Romantique (ORR), recruiting freelance period-instrument players in Europe and the USA, to focus on nineteenth-century music. The skeptic might ask why it's needed, when this music has been part of the repertoire since it was written.

I feel uncomfortable with the implication that one has to look to the outside to find a gap that requires filling, rather than respond to one's inner creative impulses. Although I enjoy working on nineteenth-century repertoire with modern symphony orchestras (with whom perfectly valid and convincing interpretations are of course possible), there is an added dimension to the work we do in the ORR: it feels far more like a voyage of discovery than an act of regurgitation. The coming into existence of such an orchestra is an antidote to the monochrome sound quality that is fast becoming the norm nowadays in international orchestral playing. It seems to me that this is due in the first place to the phenomenon of a small posse of "star" conductors going around to a small number of orchestras in different countries and creating a somewhat standardized sound. That's an exaggeration, of course, but there is some truth to it; and it is a phenomenon reinforced by the major recording companies, whose producers have been known to insist on replacement players for, say, woodwind soloists with pronounced national or regional timbres which do not conform to the accepted norm. This standardization process has tended to blur the local, regional, and national characteristics of orchestras, and arrest the evolution of idiosyncratic performing styles.

For example, if you listen to recordings of Russian orchestras between the world wars or even in the post-war years, but certainly way before perestroika and glasnost, you get a very strong sense of their location and provenance, as well as of the individual flavor of their music-making. When, for example, the Leningrad Philharmonic with Mravinsky performed Tchaikovsky symphonies, the style, the sound spectrum, and the emotional range were arresting and distinctive—utterly different from the same symphonies as played by, say, Karajan and the Berlin Philharmonic.

Today, even the Czech Philharmonic and the Dresden Staatskapelle, two of the great Eastern European orchestras, seem to me to be under threat: their integrity and ability to continue to evolve and develop along their own lines are in jeopardy because of insidious pressures to make them sound like all the other orchestras. But it's not a totally bleak picture, because you do of course get individual sounds still—the Vienna Philharmonic is immediately recognizable, I would say, and particularly in their own special repertoire of the late nineteenth century they are an inimitable living embodiment of a forgotten style of playing. I recently recorded Lehár's *Lustige Witwe* with them and their playing was utterly magical. It was also obvious to me that they are *the* period-instrument orchestra for that repertoire!

I recall reading that the Czech Philharmonic players themselves, after hearing recordings by the Berlin or the Chicago, wondered whether international listeners would be able to accept their style. So they felt pressured to modify it when they recorded. The pressures toward standardization might be said to result largely from technology—the jet planes that the conductors commute on and the hi-fi systems the musicians listen on.

It's also partly to do with the instruments themselves. A lot of instruments have national or regional characteristics, like the Viennese oboes and horns, or the French woodwind instruments, in particular their bassoons and cornets. The tendency now is towards a Germanization and, even more, an Americanization of instruments. And I feel it's to be deplored, because we're not getting the diversity we had. Modern French orchestras, for example, have generally become rather Germanized, but that is perhaps more to do with the influence of their principal conductors (predominantly non-French) and the repertoire these conductors tend to favor.

A lot of the sounds in your recording of the Symphonie fantastique *with the ORR remind one of the sounds that French orchestras produced until a generation ago—those orchestras' small tubas sounded more like your ophicleides than large-bore modern tubas do; the bassoons and trombones were more narrow-bored, like yours; and so on. That fits with part of the justification you gave for the ORR—to be, as you put it, an antidote to the standardizing trend. After all, early-music experiments often influence the mainstream: Beethoven playing, for example, has been changing in the last five years or so.*

It has. Period-instrument Beethoven has lost a layer of self-consciousness and gained in technical fluency to the point where I can legitimately hope that, say, our recording of the complete symphonies will be judged not in a sectarian category ("the newest period-instrument recording") but on its own musical terms. As to whether the mainstream orchestras have been influenced by period-instrument orchestras in this repertoire, I have my doubts. There is still a lot of resistance, dismissive jibing, and ignorance. Yet the sort of cross-fertilization that Harnoncourt, for one, has been able to achieve with a brilliant modern-instruments orchestra like the Chamber Orchestra of Europe is an example to mainstream orchestras of what can be achieved given the required will and flexibility by the management and players alike. And it seems to me there are hopeful signs around. It wasn't all that long ago that I conducted the Philharmonia Orchestra in London in an all-French program, and the principal bassoon asked me if I minded if he and his colleagues played French bassoons in *La mer*. They'd never done so before in public, but they'd been working away at these instruments privately and wanted to try them out. I think it's very encouraging when standard-instrument orchestral players take that sort of initiative. To be able to choose according to the repertoire between French and German bassoons—totally different systems with different fingerings and embouchures—seems admirable to me. This is one of the most hopeful signs, which might help to guarantee the survival of the standard symphony orchestra into the next century.

But yes, certainly, one of the *raisons d'être* of the ORR is to combat the tendency to make the whole repertoire sound the same. This is again an insidious tendency, to homogenize the playing of music from Beethoven (or earlier) to Richard Strauss in an all-purpose style—which is, for the most part, the *Zeitgeist* of the 1920s and 30s, frozen in time but suited to the increasingly clinical tastes of a technically obsessed age, for which gramophone recordings bear a heavy responsibility. And I think that one of the reasons for a certain public disillusionment with symphonic music could be the rather routine, homogenized way of trotting out the same old pieces in the same old style. That—together with some fairly unadventurous programming and an old-fashioned formality of presentation—has made the concert hall somewhat predictable and dull.

No doubt most conductors sense that there is an obligation to present a work—of whatever period or style—as though for the first time, with a sense of re-creativity, if not creativity. And in that context it helps enormously to try to re-create and rediscover the idiosyncrasies and individuality of isolated and individual composers, and of national styles evolving in a particular country. That, in turn, is tied up with the function for which the music was composed and the kind of social context within which it was written. It leads you to examine not only the original source material, but the crucial matter of instrumentation—the types of instruments, the style they were played in, in what proportions, in what layout, and so on.

In this context, let me ask you more about Berlioz, whom you've recorded with the ORR and the Opéra de Lyon. He was, obviously, fascinated with the orchestra.

It seems to me that Berlioz was a key figure, because if anyone was centrally placed to influence the way the nineteenth-century orchestra developed, it was he—by his enthusiasm, imagination, and technical mastery—although he was often mocked and despised (but not ignored) by his fellow composers. Later on, of course, Mahler was a seminal figure. But both of them in their different ways (and not always different ways, obviously) celebrated the virtuosity of the newly evolving orchestra, the kaleidoscopic colors that could be obtained from the orchestra, and above all its expressive potential. Take *Roméo et Juliette,* for example. It's significant that Berlioz decided that he had no need to use singers for the character of either Romeo or Juliet. The orchestra on its own was quite capable of expressing their separate characters and emotions. Berlioz actually says at one point that he relished the expressive potential of a symphony orchestra more than any composer before him. I'm sure that's the case. He was using instruments that had not changed much in form and sonority and shape since the Baroque, alongside the newest instruments like the *cornet à piston*—and he was exploiting the tension that exists whenever you juxtapose the new and the old. His was a very transitional period: for example, string instruments were being converted by violin makers like Vuillaume to be more powerful and to project into larger halls, and therefore they needed to have their necks reset at a steeper angle to the table and their bass bars made thicker, and so on. So in experimenting with and against traditional usage, Berlioz was every bit an avant-garde composer. He took a great interest in all these developments and made sure that he was *au courant* with the technical difficulties and capacities of all the orchestral instruments. From his contact with people like Baillot and Paganini he learnt the most up-to-date techniques and sonorities of modern violin playing, which he then required his orchestral players to emulate—and he gave those players far more specific instructions as to what he expected of them technically than any previous composer.

And then he brought much more fantasy and imagination to orchestral writing than anybody hitherto, including Beethoven: he seemed to rejoice in the distinct personalities of musical instruments—there's so much more dialogue and dialectic within the Berlioz orchestra than in any of his contemporaries or his predecessors that the instruments seem almost to be real people conversing, so that with Berlioz's orchestra you're dealing with a far bigger organism put to far greater expressive ends than ever before.

In the example you refer to, he has the tenor instruments represent the voice of Romeo (cellos and violas, and horns in the tomb scene) and the violins and high winds represent the voice of Juliet.[7]

And remember how Berlioz justifies his treatment of the love duet in *Roméo et Juliette*: "If the duets of love and despair are given to the orchestra, the reasons are numerous and easy to comprehend. First, and this alone would be sufficient, it is a symphony and not an opera. Second, since duets of this nature

7. The observation is from D. Kern Holoman's *Berlioz* (Cambridge, Mass.: Harvard University Press, 1989), which has a valuable analysis of *Roméo et Juliette,* especially the love scene, on pp. 262–66.

have been handled vocally a thousand times by the greatest masters, it was wise as well as unusual to attempt another means of expression." And the following observation is a crucial one: "It is also because the very sublimity of this love made its depiction so dangerous to the musician that he had to give himself the imaginative latitude that the positive sense of the sung word would not have given him, resorting instead to instrumental language, which is richer, more varied, less precise, and by its very indefiniteness incomparably more powerful in such a case."[8]

This is a tremendous manifesto for the powers of the nineteenth-century orchestra. It's something that an opera composer like Verdi wouldn't have agreed with—nor would many of his contemporaries—but Berlioz certainly pushed the expressive powers of the orchestra far beyond the limits set by his great hero, Beethoven. And I would have thought it a breakthrough that Mahler would have admired. By the way, both Berlioz and Mahler wrote wonderfully for voices—it's not that being "pro-orchestra" they were "anti-voice."

So people might say, Fine, why can't a modern orchestra play them?[9] Well, of course, a modern orchestra *can* play them brilliantly; but the question is, do we get the full force of the originality of these compositions when played on standard modern instruments? There's so much to be gained and to be learnt from trying to reconstruct Berlioz's orchestra. When we recorded the *Symphonie fantastique* with the ORR in the hall of the old Conservatoire in Paris, the site of its premiere, along with the thrill of assembling the instruments known to or specified by Berlioz came the matter of their deployment. We used the layout proposed by François-Antoine Habeneck, the first conductor of the Société des Concerts du Conservatoire, who conducted the premiere in 1830: a steeply raked series of steps for the orchestra, and a most unusual layout with (for example) the harps out in front, behind the conductor, and the double basses and cellos paired off or arranged in threes and fours on a huge staircase. You get a totally different kind of sonority—dryer, more intimate, and far more vivid.[10] Well, again, people can say, that's possible to do with a modern orchestra. Yes, perhaps, up to a point; but it is surprising how conventionally and unadventurously music is often performed in concert halls today.

---

8. From the Preface originally printed in the libretto for the 1839 performance.

9. Gardiner wrote about this question in the ORR's privately printed "Manifesto for a New (Old) Orchestra": "I am not implying that two or three generations of great interpreters have 'got it wrong' up to now. That would be not merely impertinent but to deny the valid creative tension which undoubtedly exists between the conception of a musical work and its realization; in other words the way a composition can survive history and not merely tolerate but be enriched by changes of instruments and styles of performance."

10. Berlioz wrote at length about orchestral placement in his 1843/1855 *Traité d'instrumentation*, pp. 293–94 and 310. See Holoman's discussion in *Berlioz*, pp. 354–56.

Various critics have been calling for years for a return to one of the things you did, putting the first and second violins on opposite sides of the stage— as most orchestras did until the Second World War—as an aid to transparency.

Right. That almost goes without saying for *any* music from eighteenth-century concerti grossi onwards, where the violins are used antiphonally; and several other arrangements are possible, too. I recently conducted Mahler's Fourth on tour with the NDR Symphony Orchestra and we split not only the violins left and right, but the cellos and basses as well, with just the violas in the middle. For the slow movement, the individual strands of the string lines were more beautifully separated and over a wider spatial spectrum than I had ever heard before. That is just one example of what can be done with a modern orchestra setup (though in this particular case I had no first-hand evidence that Mahler himself deployed his strings this way; it just seemed natural!). But with a period-instrument band, in composers as diverse as Schumann and Brahms and, above all, Berlioz, there is the potential for even greater contrasts as a result of the instruments themselves. To return to Berlioz as an example, there's the side-by-side juxtaposition of natural trumpets, which had not evolved very much really since Monteverdi's or Bach's day, with brand-new *cornets à piston*. Then you have dinosaur-like period instruments like the serpent and the ophicleide, which Berlioz used in his early scores to give a specifically raucous sound.

Julian Rushton writes that in the Dies irae episode in the Fantastique *when modern bass tubas replace the ophicleides it "turns a harsh parody into a Falstaffian romp."*[11] *He also complains that modern bassoons sound too gentlemanly and damp the work's fire somewhat.*

Exactly. Overall, with period instruments in this repertoire you get a more vivid and sharply defined palette of colors beyond that of a standard symphony orchestra, where modern cultivated sounds tend to assimilate and merge rather than to retain distinctively separate strands of instrumental lines.

The example of the ophicleide might answer another objection from the skeptic: vivid, specific, unstandardized tone colors may be fun, but are they important musically? In a lot of earlier music, after all, tone color is clearly not central to the conception—you can play the Fourth Brandenburg with a harpsichord instead of a violin soloist (and in fact most of Bach is transcribable), and lots of Baroque chamber pieces can be played on a range of different instruments. But Berlioz comes closer to using a specific tone color as a central element. The ophicleides in the Dies irae section give an effect that's part of the expression, and even a very similar instrument like the tuba

11. Rushton, *The Musical Language of Berlioz* (Cambridge University Press, 1983), p. 89. Berlioz did sanction the substitution of a tuba later in life, but Gardiner, who calls this tuba/bassoon pairing "ill-balanced," makes a strong musical case for the original.

just can't re-create it.[12] *So using original instruments might be far more significant in Berlioz than in Bach.*

Not quite. Both benefit from removing the film of later anachronistic instrumental tissue. But Bach's music is incredibly robust and seems to withstand all manner of treatment: look how incredibly illuminating some of Glenn Gould's recordings have been. Bach even emerges recognizably on the Moog synthesizer.[13]

Another composer you've begun to explore with the ORR is Brahms, who is usually thought of as hardly needing period performance practice.

It seems to me that Brahms, more than any other composer from that period, has suffered from being interpreted if not in a Wagnerian way, then by applying the Wagnerian ideal of the endless, long-line melody, and the weighty sound and texture of the Wagner orchestra.

Malcolm Bilson gives an example of the Wagnerizing of Brahms in one of the late piano works, the Intermezzo Op. 119, No. 1. As he says, everyone now overrides the two-note slurs—"sighs," as in Mozart[14]—*and connects them into a long Wagnerian line. Apparently Brahms protested against this trend as it emerged in his own day.*

12. Charles Rosen discusses this in *The Romantic Generation* (Cambridge, Mass.: Harvard University Press, 1995), especially in chap. 1, where he says, "orchestral color is not one of the fundamentals of form before the Romantic generation; tone color was applied like a veneer to form, but did not create or shape it . . . It was the Romantic generation that introduced it directly into the initial stages of strict composition . . . they altered the relationship between the delight in sound and the delight in structure" (pp. 39–40).

As to how this applies to Berlioz, Leonard Ratner, in *Romantic Music* (New York: Schirmer, 1992), contrasts Liszt and Berlioz: "Berlioz's point of departure is the song. . . . around this firm basis of syntax, Berlioz's orchestra plays with sound to loosen some of the edges, to digress, to displace momentarily, to isolate figures. . . . For Berlioz, the point of reference is syntax, colored by sound; for Liszt, it is sound, put into order by syntax" (pp. 216–17). Julian Rushton argues that "with the exception of a few outstandingly coloured passages, it may be safely said that the substance of Berlioz's music is separable from its instrumentation" (*The Musical Language*, p. 74). Holoman has shown that orchestration didn't take place until late in Berlioz's compositional process. Thus I may overstate the importance of period instruments in Berlioz's music. After all, as Gardiner himself says, Berlioz works well with modern instruments. But the examples discussed in the interview show that period instruments do make a big difference in at least some parts of Berlioz's music.

13. For further discussion of this, see the interview in Chapter 9 with John Butt. More qualifications may be added to the previous note: Howard Mayer Brown, for one, has noted that some Baroque music—for example, much of the French Baroque—depends more than Bach does on "nuances of sonority." See his essay "Pedantry or Liberation?" in *Authenticity and Early Music*, ed. Nicholas Kenyon (Oxford University Press, 1988), pp. 29–30. And Rosen, on p. 39 of *The Romantic Generation*, qualifies the remark quoted above by saying that "Delight in instrumental color for its own sake is not new with Liszt." He finds a few exceptional examples in which sound is of primary importance in pre-Romantic music, but the examples mainly involve music that aims "at an illusion of improvisation," such as organ toccatas and unmeasured preludes.

14. See the discussion in Bilson's interview.

The same is true of his orchestral music. Take the second movement of the First Symphony: how often, if ever, do you hear the slurred dotted rhythms of the first-violin melody [bars 7 and 8] played with the appropriate inflection? Again, these are "sighs," and it is difficult for sighs to penetrate a caramelized *legato perpetuo*:[15]

The same is true of the great oboe melody in the slow movement of the Violin Concerto: are the devices of "circular breathing" which modern oboists adopt really appropriate or necessary to bring out the pathos of that heavenly inflected melody?

And as for Mahler and Wagner, I suspect that both are more sinned against than sinning, in the sense that they had such a strong influence on the way that the orchestra developed and the way conductors conducted that it spilled over into Brahms interpretation. I am sure that Brahms should be de-Wagnerized. And the effect of the instruments in my recording of the *Requiem* is, I think, at least a step in the right direction, towards something that is not only more transparent but more distinctive in its sound world—even if the string sound is as yet too lightweight.

The orchestral music of Brahms lends itself to a weightier sonority than he himself probably envisaged. It is more gratifying for musicians to play him in a grandiose and syrupy way; but it seems to me that often this is wide of the mark. To my mind, his music calls for a particular depth and breadth of sonority, but not weighty or syrupy in the modern fashion, and a "breathing" sound capable of subtle inflection, ebb and flow. It is a sonority quite different from, say, the taut, almost abrasive sounds that Beethoven seems to have required of his players at full stretch or, again, from the kaleidoscopic switches of color that Berlioz elicits from *his* orchestra. It takes a lot of skill on the part of the individual player to control the broader, deeper sound required by Brahms without its either becoming mannered, in a crypto-Baroque way, or else having all those wonderful subtleties of inflection and cross-rhythm ironed out. Like all techniques, it has to be worked at, once the appropriate sound concept has been defined and transmitted to the players in such a way that it fires their imaginations. I feel we are only at the very beginning of our process of reappraisal with regard to the orchestral music of Brahms; but the potential rewards here are immense.

15. Brahms, Symphony No. 1, second movement, opening.

There is plenty of evidence of a sparing use of vibrato and of a more generous use of portamento in the performance styles of both Berlioz and Brahms—though in different ways.[16] I would imagine that the ORR would have little difficulty with limiting vibrato, coming as they do from Baroque music, but great difficulty with portamento.

Actually, both practices are very difficult to introduce for purely expressive ends, rather than merely to fulfill instructions, and are therefore hard to achieve without self-consciousness.

Regarding vibrato, remember that in each generation there are those who advocate more vibrato and those who prefer less. It's a matter of taste. Along these lines, some critics assume wrongly that the ORR and the English Baroque Soloists don't use vibrato. They do, at varying rates and places, and if it doesn't obtrude to the extent that it detaches itself from the expression then we've achieved our goal.

The whole challenge consists in precisely this: finding the perfect meeting-point of heart and mind, instinct and knowledge. But we should beware of instinct as a bottleable commodity. It changes with habit, usage, and redefinition of stylistic parameters.

SELECTED DISCOGRAPHY

Gardiner considers the juxtaposing of old and new instruments crucial to Berlioz's conception of the *Symphonie fantastique* (Philips 434 402); Peter J. Rabinowitz observes that the instruments that sounded "old" to Berlioz's audiences sound "new" to us, and vice versa.[17] Still, Rabinowitz thinks that "many of Berlioz's local [instrumental] effects come across exceptionally well" with Gardiner's period instruments—though he believes this stems "more from Gardiner's interpretive discernment" than from the instruments. Rabinowitz praises Gardiner's responsiveness to detail and says that "many of the nightmare qualities emerge clearly," though he feels there is a little too much "clear-headed control." K. Robert Schwartz has no such reservations, and praises Gardiner for realizing "the full emotional range of the symphony."[18]

16. According to Robin Stowell, Berlioz's contemporaries Habeneck and Baillot both prescribed tasteful portamento "especially in slow movements and sustained melodies when a passage ascends or descends by step." They advised that the ascending stepwise portamento be accompanied by crescendo, and descending portamento by diminuendo. (In Stowell, "Strings," *Performance Practice: Music after 1600,* ed. H. M. Brown and S. Sadie [London: Macmillan, 1989, and New York: Norton, 1990], p. 399). A more liberal use of portamento in Brahms is demonstrated in the recordings by his close collaborator Joseph Joachim and by other evidence. See Clive Brown, "Bowing Styles, Vibrato, and Portamento in Nineteenth-Century Violin Playing," *Journal of the Royal Music Association* 113 (1988), p. 117. Orchestral vibrato appears to have been an infrequently used special effect before World War I: see Robert Philip, *Early Recordings and Musical Style* (Cambridge University Press, 1992), chaps. 4 and 5.

17. Rabinowitz, *Fanfare* 17 (November/December 1993), pp. 185–86.

18. Schwartz, *Classical Pulse,* April/May 1994, p. 17.

The *Symphonie* is the most familiar of Berlioz's works, but Gardiner/ORR's second Berlioz release is of the least familiar Berlioz work—the newly recovered *Petite Messe Solennelle*. Gardiner directed the modern premiere in London. That performance, recorded by Philips (442 137), reveals the work to be far more than juvenilia. Gardiner/ORR's third Berlioz CD, *Harold in Italy* (446 676), may be their best so far; Edward Greenfield, who finds it thrilling, praises its "white heat" of intensity, attained, he says, without excessive speed.[19]

As Gardiner notes, modern instruments work well in Berlioz—as is shown by his recordings with the orchestra of the Opéra de Lyon in pieces that reflect a gentler side of the composer. The Berlioz scholar David Cairns concludes a survey of recordings of *L'enfance du Christ* by calling Gardiner's "near to being the answer to one's prayers"[20] (though he dislikes a few tempos, such as the very slow one chosen for the Shepherd's Chorus;[21] Erato 45275, 2 CDs). The Gardiner/Lyon *Nuits d'été* (Erato 45517), in the original keys and with the voice types specified, is outstanding.

Critics have been divided about the Gardiner/ORR Beethoven symphonies (complete, Archiv 439 900–2AH5; also available singly). Erik Tarloff calls the set "to my ears, the one to own,"[22] but Barrymore Laurence Scherer says the performances "reveal Beethoven's architecture, his energy, his muscularity, but they offer little of Beethoven's heart."[23] Even Scherer likes the Seventh; Richard Osborne calls it "glorious."[24] Osborne begins by praising the introduction's "ideal blend of weight and anticipation," and has similar praise for the remainder of the work. I can't recall a more nuanced performance of the Sixth's "Scene by the Brook": listen, for example, to the perfectly judged rubato when the bassoon makes the transition into the second subject in bar 32 (2:36–2:41 in the CD track). A little more of such nuance might have benefited the rest of the "Pastoral" ("brisk efficiency," says Osborne), the "Eroica" (according to Alex Ross, the performance mutes the "frenzied dissonances and funereal despair"[25]), the Fifth (though Ross considers this "the best in the set . . . a shock"), and the Ninth. In the first movements of Nos. 3, 5, and 9, Gardiner builds up terrific climaxes; but in quieter passages, some people find Gardiner not always as responsive.

In the ORR Brahms *Ein deutsches Requiem* (Philips 432 140), Gardiner avoids what he calls the "lugubrious and pompous" feeling of many performances. His performance is, Lionel Salter writes, "notable for its intensity and

19. Greenfield, *Gramophone* 74 (August 1996), p. 44.
20. In *Choral Music on Record*, ed. Alan Blyth (Cambridge University Press, 1991), p. 185.
21. It is taken at little more than half of Berlioz's metronome mark.
22. Tarloff, "Beethoven on Original Instruments," *Slate* (www.slate.com), 1 October 1996.
23. Scherer, "Letting Beethoven Be Beethoven," *The Wall Street Journal*, 21 February 1995, p. A15.
24. Osborne, *Gramophone* 72 (November 1994), p. 66.
25. Ross, "Crossed Paths on the Rocky Road to 'Authenticity,'" *The New York Times*, 9 April 1995, Arts and Leisure Section, p. 44.

fervour (not mere ferocity)."[26] Virginia Hancock, whose research has clarified our understanding of what Brahms learned from early music, praises the recording with many detailed observations.[27] Her criticisms are just as interesting: some of them are of *non legato* that is "presumably intended to avoid 'Wagnerian sostenuto' in the choral parts, [but] sometimes create[s] an impression of over-fussy articulation." Hancock would also like a larger chorus—though the singing throughout strikes her as superb—and sometimes finds the string section too small to balance the winds. Although it was a first attempt at Brahms, what John Steane says of the sixth movement applies to the whole—"one is caught up in the power of it."[28]

Most critics have agreed that Gardiner's *Merry Widow* (with the Vienna Philharmonic; Deutsche Grammophon 439 911, 2 CDs) is "utterly magical": a typical comment is that of Scherer, who says it "comes as close to perfection as I can imagine."[29]

FOR FURTHER READING

Donald Tovey thought that Berlioz was a better writer than composer; he underestimated the music, but not the prose, which D. Kern Holoman praises for its "fetching combination of insight and wit." Berlioz's *Memoirs* are a literary classic, demonstrating that of all the great composers, he would probably have been the most entertaining dinner companion; David Cairns's translation is published by Gollancz (London, 1969). The memoirs are no more trustworthy than the average autobiography, of course; you might supplement them with Holoman's excellent *Berlioz* (Cambridge, Mass.: Harvard University Press, 1989).

As Tovey's comment shows, Berlioz's musical style has sparked controversy since its own time, mainly because of his idiosyncratic treatment of harmony and counterpoint. Today his music has won general esteem, thanks in part to some perceptive analyses. The most impressive is Julian Rushton's *The Musical Language of Berlioz* (Cambridge University Press, 1983). Holoman's biography also sheds a great deal of light on the music.

An excellent discussion of historical Brahms performance is Will Crutchfield's article "Brahms by Those Who Knew Him," in the late, lamented magazine *Opus* (August 1986, pp. 12–21 and 60). I discuss issues of early-music Brahms performance in *Early Music America*, Spring 1997 and *Early Music*, August, 1997. Robert Philip's book *Early Recordings and Musical Style*, to which I've referred so often, is again an invaluable resource (Cambridge Uni-

26. Salter, *Gramophone* 68 (April 1991), p. 1881.
27. Hancock, "Brahms in Better Balance," *Historical Performance* 5 (Spring 1992), pp. 37–39.
28. Steane, *Gramophone* 69 (January 1992), pp. 81, 84.
29. Scherer, *BBC Music Magazine*, December 1995, p. 69.

versity Press, 1992). The best current biography is Malcolm Macdonald's *Brahms, The Master Musicians* (London: Dent, and New York: Schirmer, 1990). Good discussions of Brahms's music include Michael Musgrave's *The Music of Brahms* (Oxford University Press, 1985) and, on a more advanced level, Walter Frisch's *Brahms and the Principle of Developing Variation* (Berkeley: University of California Press, 1984). Norman del Mar's *Conducting Brahms* (Oxford University Press, 1993) is a fascinating guide to conducting the works for orchestra.

20

Reinventing Wheels

Joshua Rifkin on Interpretation
and Rhetoric

Joshua Rifkin's career as conductor, harpsichordist, and pianist has taken him from Busnoys to Bach, from Schütz to Stravinsky, and from Josquin to Scott Joplin—with, along the way, the spoof *The Baroque Beatles Book* and some lovely instrumental arrangements for Judy Collins. The Bach Ensemble, which he founded in 1978, has recorded a number of Bach works and has toured throughout the USA and Europe; he has also appeared as guest conductor and keyboard soloist with many modern orchestras.

Rifkin is also a scholar, who has specialized in Renaissance and Baroque music, with particular emphasis on Josquin and Bach. His controversial argument about the size of Bach's "choral" forces is discussed in Chapter 15. Our conversation touched on more basic issues of historical performance, though, going beyond the specifics of scholarship to the foundations of the whole enterprise.

How much "interpretation" and inflection should go into a performance of, say, Bach or Mozart? Some early-music performers have advocated a great deal of these, others far less.

There's a soft underbelly to a lot of what we do in historical performance, in that there are profound discrepancies between our modern interpretative practices and what we can determine about musical practice in the eighteenth century and earlier (and somewhat later, for that matter). By calling attention to these discrepancies, I don't mean necessarily to criticize what we do, but merely to try to heighten some awareness and promote some reflection.

It's pretty obvious and well known that "interpretation," as we have inherited this idea in the performance of standard repertory in the twentieth century, was foreign to most earlier music-making. I think it was Nicholas Kenyon who said that, by all the evidence we have, music-making in the eighteenth century was more like what we would call "readings" than what we would call "interpretations." Except for operas, we know that they were lucky to have two rehearsals of a piece, or even one, and a rehearsal basically meant a read-through. When I try to imagine how this all went, I think of the jingle session— a modern situation in which musicians come in to a performing space of some sort, are handed a newly written piece of music, read it once or twice through, play it more or less flawlessly with a sense of its basic stylistic assumptions, and then go home. Of course, this notion is quite distant from the way we think of performing the great masterpieces, which we imagine to require much more profound insight born out of years of reflection.[1]

This much is easy and obvious enough, I think, but there are aspects that are less easy and obvious. To get at these I would refer to an experience I had a couple of months ago, when I recorded several of the "London" Symphonies of Haydn.[2] I was dealing with an extremely good period-instrument orchestra, very experienced, technically very capable; yet we all found this music exceedingly difficult. I myself had underestimated its difficulty, not simply in terms of the individual parts (particularly the violin parts) but also in terms of the ensemble demands and even the directorial demands that they posed. In the course of the sessions the producer and I had a conversation which led to some further thought. He asked, "What must this have sounded like in London at its first performance? Given the lack of rehearsal, what kind of effect could it have made?" In fact, by all evidence, it made an absolutely stunning effect, and people just loved it. The reviews were enthusiastic beyond measure.

In part that may reflect our much higher expectations today for technical perfection.

Partly, but there's more to the issue than that. As I was thinking about the

---

1. A good discussion of this topic can be found in Donald Mintz's "Mendelssohn as Performer and Teacher," in *The Mendelssohn Companion*, ed. Douglas Seaton (Westport, Conn.: Greenwood Press, forthcoming). Mintz gives references to the most important German discussions of this issue, especially that of Hermann Danuser, in his *Musikalische Interpretation* (Laaber: Laaber Verlag, 1992), Section 1. It appears that musical "interpretation" in the modern sense began to be discussed only as recently as the 1840s.

It could be argued that the second half of the eighteenth century saw the publication of numerous books on musical performance, and that these sometimes indicate something that sounds a lot like "interpretation." These books, and the music of such treatise writers as C. P. E. Bach, may well represent the first sproutings of the concept of interpretation. But it's likely that concept postdates J. S. Bach, at any rate—which does not mean we should avoid interpretation when we play his music.

2. Nos. 96, 97, and 99, with the Capella Coloniensis.

Haydn premieres, I was recalling that I had recently heard the premiere of the new *Partita for Orchestra* of Elliot Carter. In the talk before it Carter praised—quite rightly—the accomplishments of the Chicago Symphony Orchestra and its conductor, Daniel Barenboim. But then Carter said that as his pieces live and are performed and re-performed (he's one of the few contemporary composers to have the good fortune to see his music develop a performing tradition), performers continue to find more in them, and find ways of playing not just the notes but really the music—to find a personal slant on the pieces. He has, at least in principle, clearly welcomed this. And I know from other circumstances that Carter has felt the performance of his music to improve regularly. Every ten or twenty years most of his pieces get freshly recorded and, he tends to feel, better recorded.

Well, this is where our Haydn question and what Carter was talking about started to meet. There's no question that a lot of first performances are very bad, but not all are that bad, and a lot of pieces have triumphed at their premieres, as did the Haydn symphonies and, in fact, the Carter *Partita*. But in a sense, the quality of the first performance is not really at issue, because no matter how bad or how good it may be, subsequent performances are going to change things. Subsequent performances are going to assume an increasing familiarity with the work and its language, and are thus going to be able to achieve a naturalness that first performances cannot achieve. And it is precisely on the basis of this, of really speaking the language, that one begins to develop insights into the particular utterance of the language and begins to develop interpretations as opposed to simple readings.

The dilemma I want to return to is that in the general practice of the eighteenth century they didn't yet have a standard, regularly repeated repertoire, and thus could rarely have reached the interpretative phase. We, by contrast, can't avoid interpretation—given the increasing familiarity of the works, both in our own performances and in our inherited traditions of performances and composition, even if they are traditions from so-called mainstream practice. Moreover, we may *need* interpretation in a way that the original audiences did not, because we have heard the pieces so often. Mozart's audience was hearing the "Jupiter" Symphony for the first time, so a competent run-through was sufficient for them; but we have heard it a hundred times, so a mere run-through would bore us.

The example you gave of Carter comes from our century, in which there has been no central musical style that all composers use; in learning a new piece, we often have to learn not only the piece, but also its unique style—what you called its "language." By contrast, in the eighteenth century composers had a more unified style, or language. Would that common style mean that even with limited rehearsal there could be not only more insightful performances but also more interpretation?

It would have improved certain things without question. I think in principle we can imagine that performers would, in general, understand the significance of a lot of musical gestures, expressive devices, and so forth, in ways that modern performers dealing with contemporary pieces might not. It's perhaps akin to how jazz musicians today can take a chart and know how the written lines are to be realized without being told—or, to mention it once again, the jingle session. I think this can stand as an example of a larger sense of "speaking the language." I think what familiarity with the language does make possible is giving a much better *delivery* right off the bat. But delivery and interpretation are not exactly the same thing, although locating the boundary between them is a difficult matter. I think we can probably imagine a good level of delivery, even if the technical level sometimes may have been problematic, as in the Haydn. I think in many instances this could have taken care of a lot of the issues. With much of the repertory it would have taken care of *all* the issues; there are pieces that we generally accept are not the most profound under the sun but that with the right performance can be quite wonderful. Well, there you have delivery pure and simple, unclouded by these other issues. But for the great pieces, the issue remains.

So the historical performer is facing a contradiction. The questions with which he or she has to grapple are, How far does interpretation take us from the original, how much of that is legitimate, how much is not legitimate, and what means do we have for deciding? At the same time we have to reckon with not only how far this is taking us from the original, but to what extent we can reconcile all this with the supposed and, in part, actual foundations of the use of "historical" instruments, practices, etc. There is an interesting set of muddles.

One response to the dilemma you mentioned—how much to interpret, how much that is related to the original practice and how much not—has been to develop a common style of playing Baroque music. David Fuller describes it as "a kind of generalized rubato intended to clarify the metre and highlight important notes and events. . . . Its salient characteristic is an exaggerated lengthening of the downbeat—sometimes every downbeat, no matter how clear it may already be from the harmony or other factors of its context. Further rhythmic distortions may emphasize dissonant or climactic notes, thematic entries, or any feature the performer fears his audience may miss. Sometimes all sense of the beat, far from being clarified, disappears in a fog of nuance.

"It is true that liberties far beyond overdotting and inequality were cultivated in certain Baroque styles. The few mentions doubtless only hint at a wider reality. . . .

"What is certain, however, is that the 'audible analysis' practised by modern players of Baroque music has nothing to do with notes inégales. . . . Any

*connection with old performance is purely speculative—which is not to say that
it may not have corresponded exactly to the way some players performed."*[3]
Could you comment?

It's a very well-taken point. Let's turn it around for a second. Let's give this
phenomenon its most charitable explanation. We could say that we have
learned something about this music. It's wonderful that people know something
about what the harmonic points of a piece are, where the phrases are going,
and so forth. This is a level of knowledge that's not to be gainsaid. I remember coaching a chamber music masterclass in a serenade of Max Reger that is
basically tonal but is not as familiar in its syntax as other late Romantic pieces
might be. These were very capable performers, extremely gifted; any one of
them could render a dazzling Brahms fiddle concerto or its equivalent. But they
made hash of Reger's music, because they didn't know where the phrases were
falling, where the weight lay, and so forth. It had to be painstakingly pulled
out of them by consideration of questions like, How are we going to make this
palpable, and how are we going to project this? Now, in repertories where this
has not been so self-evident—and even Bach may be considered as being such
a repertory—the fact that musicians have become sensitized to these things, so
that they really have a sense of how the language is working, is something to
celebrate.

*What you've just described sounds like, essentially, good "delivery." Where
does interpretation fit into understanding this style that Fuller describes?*

Well, the next question is, of course, What do you do with this knowledge
of how the language works? Here opinions may differ, and here again we're
entering this dimension where the historical evidence leaves us in the lurch. It's
a very subjective matter, because one person's violently stretched-out, meterless
performance is another person's weighting of the proper moments in time; one
person's well-proportioned performance is another person's dull, uninflected
reading. We have no way, really, of telling. And here is where we become very
personal, and have very little choice but to be so.

Although here again is where we might want to ask about objective foundations, at least in the interest of keeping in touch with them. To take a simple, trivial enough question, does it make a difference whether the kind of thing
that Fuller describes is happening in a solo harpsichord piece or in a piece for
large ensemble? If it's happening in the latter instance, is it reconcilable with
what we know about the sources of the time—about the orchestral parts of the
time, with their minimal performance instructions, and about the performance
practices? Is it reasonable to assume that a bunch of even extremely skilled mu-

---

3. Fuller, "The Performer as Composer," in *Performance Practice: Music after 1600*, ed.
H. M. Brown and S. Sadie (London: Macmillan, 1989, and New York: Norton, 1990), pp.
138–39.

sicians very familiar with the style would have sat down in real time in the eighteenth century, with real eighteenth-century performance practices, and produced the kinds of results that Fuller described? If not, does that mean it's a bad thing to do so now?

That brings us back to the initial point of departure about interpretation. These pieces have progressed and changed through performance, and through the way that they gradually divulge secrets to performers, and the way that performers gradually find new secrets to tease out of them. Where does one call a halt to this process? I don't know the answer. In a way it's akin to what happens to folk music—you can never keep it in its pure state. I think I've tended to become something of an extreme relativist on these issues, in principle. In actual practice, I hate many of these performances, but that's just my private taste, and I try to do my own performances.

Behind many of these performances is a particular way of understanding the concept of musical rhetoric, which looks upon it as involving a kind of musical lexicon. One major proponent said that in the Baroque era "a repertory of formulaic expressions (musical figures) was available for portraying emotions and for figures of speech; a vocabulary of musical possibilities, so to speak." Through such means, music "was always expected to speak."[4] Could you talk about the current use of this idea of rhetoric in Baroque performance?

Rhetoric is one of these areas where we have to clear out the stables a little bit. Rhetoric should be a very simple matter. The first point is that the treatises from the late fifteenth century to the eighteenth are addressed to composers, not performers or analysts; they have to do mainly with composing pieces of music, not usually with performing them. The second point is that their significance has been misunderstood; indeed, it is a sign of misunderstanding that they are thought to have such significance.

Rhetoric has, first of all, almost nothing to do with content and meaning. The use of rhetorical terms in music theory was simply a way of labeling certain devices in compositions for which there was not a commonly accepted terminology. This is obvious if one reads the treatises. So-called compositional theory up until the late sixteenth century was in fact contrapuntal instruction, concerned with the relationship of notes against each other, and with the basic contrapuntal devices—canonic writing and the like. What is never addressed in

---

4. Nikolaus Harnoncourt, *Baroque Music Today: Music as Speech*, trans. Mary O'Neill (Portland, Oregon: Amadeus, 1988), p. 119.

An influential source on the relationship of music to rhetoric is the article "Rhetoric and Music," by George J. Buelow, in *The New Grove Dictionary*. A skeptical voice is that of Peter Williams—see, for example, his discussion in *The Organ Music of J. S. Bach*, vol. 3 (Cambridge University Press, 1984), pp. 69–72, and his essay "The Snares and Delusions of Musical Rhetoric," in *Alte Musik/Praxis und Reflexion*, ed. Peter Reidmeister and Veronika Gutman (Winterthur: Amadeus, 1983), pp. 230–40.

the theoretical literature of the time is how actual pieces behave, even in such simple descriptive terms as "here there's a bit of imitation, here there's homophony, there the line rises and the line falls." Now, the first great musical treatise to look at rhetoric, Joachim Burmeister's *Musica Poetica* [1606], undertakes the praiseworthy enterprise of trying to come up with descriptive terms for what actually happens on the surface of musical pieces. Lacking a terminology of music, such as the technical terminology that we have, he simply goes to the sister discipline that already has a developed terminology for describing surface phenomena in a performance medium, and that is rhetoric. Rhetoric is not grammar, and it's not the basic tools of speech; the basic tools of musical speech were already part of traditional compositional theory. Rhetoric dealt with delivery, and with the shape of sentences in terms not of grammatical parts but of whether you repeat words for emphasis and so forth. It is a kind of taxonomic business, on the level of the sentence, and also in terms of the parts of an oration, showing how B follows A and how C follows B. First you have this theme, then you have that theme, then you have the development. Burmeister, needing terms for this kind of thing in music, simply appropriates the terms used in rhetoric. A line goes up? Well, in rhetoric you have a term to describe a climactic situation. A line goes down? You have a term to express this. The voices come together in what we would call homophony? Well, you could borrow rhetorical terms for that. Two significant things about this are that it has only tangentially anything to do with meaning, and that the terms themselves have absolutely no significance. Indeed, if you look at the history of rhetoric in musical theory you discover that different terms are used by different authors, and that even the same author will borrow different terms from rhetoric at different times trying to get to a closer analogy. But there's absolutely no mystical significance to the terms themselves. You could just as easily call them Ginger and Fred as *anabasis, catabasis,* or any of them.

Now, let's go to the end of the rhetorical tradition and consider the most famous example, in which Mattheson says a piece of instrumental music is like a *Klangrede,* "oratory in sound."[5] This became the title of a famous book, *Musik als Klangrede,* by a very famous conductor who cut his teeth in the early-music world.[6] There the proposition is made (and it's very widely held among modern performers of Baroque music) that somehow there is a fundamental difference between music before the French Revolution and music in later eras. Later music is held to be just notes and their relationships, but early

---

5. Mattheson, *Der vollkommene Capellmeister* (Hamburg, 1736; facsimile, Kassel: Bärenreiter, 1954); English translation, *Johann Mattheson's "Der vollkommene Capellmeister": A Revised Translation with Critical Commentary,* trans. Ernest C. Harriss (Ann Arbor, Mich.: UMI Research Press, 1981), p. 425.

6. Harnoncourt, *Baroque Music Today:* the original title is *Musik als Klangrede.*

music—ah! that's an *oration!*[7] Well, come on. You read Mattheson, and he's saying, Look, a piece of music has a beginning, a middle, and an end. And that's *all* he's saying. It shows that Mattheson was no dummy about music. If, as Birnbaum says,[8] Bach could expound on the relationship of music and rhetoric, it would also suggest that he understood that a piece of music had to be coherent and well made. But let's not kid ourselves that it means anything else. Again, none of this has anything to do with some different style of performance. The kind of "rhetorical" performance that we have been blessed with over the last twenty years—which sometimes milks every little gesture for all it's worth, and finds deep meaning in rhetorical terms that really just describe standard musical phenomena—has no historical basis.

In some ways performers are not to blame, because they have been misled by the scholars. There is a pernicious tradition of German scholarship that has created the fiction of rhetoric and meaning in music—Hermann Unger, Arnold Schering, Arnold Schmidt, and in our country Ursula Kirkendale[9]—and it's widespread. It certainly has created the notion of a kind of secret language. Performers have turned to them as scholarly authorities. And let's face it, it's an attractive idea. We are all attracted by secrets and hidden meanings, meanings that are more profound than what has been accessible to all of us (and might *now* be accessible only to *some* of us). It's understandable; but, as Dorothy Parker said, there's less there than meets the eye.

I think sensitive musicians, when they heard under-inflected, motoric playing of Bach, intuited that "we're not getting at something; there is more to this." Reading some treatises, and hearing things from some musicologists, they found that in a way the rhetoric idea, even if it was misconstrued, reinforced and helped them come to grips with this thing that they were intuiting. And

7. Many do believe that music changes, around this time, from a mimetic ideal (art as a mirror up to nature or to emotion) to an expressive one (art as expressing one's unique inner feelings). This differs from but is not unrelated to the change Harnoncourt argues for.

8. In his second (1739) defense of Bach against the attacks of Scheibe (discussed in John Butt's interview, Chapter 9), Bach's friend J. A. Birnbaum, a Leipzig rhetoric teacher, writes: "[Bach] understands so thoroughly the parts and benefits which the composing of a piece of music has in common with oratory that not only does one listen to him with a satisfying pleasure whenever he directs his profound conversation to the similarity and conformity between the two, but one also admires the clever application of the same in music." Translation from Peter Williams, *The Organ Music of J. S. Bach*, vol. 1 (Cambridge University Press, 1980), p. 91.

9. Kirkendale, "The Source for Bach's Musical Offering: The *Institutio oratoria* of Quintilian," *Journal of the American Musicological Society* 33 (1980), pp. 8–141, argues that Bach structured the work to follow the parts of an oration as set out by Quintilian. Christoph Wolff and Peter Williams deny her claim; see Wolff, *Bach: Essays on His Life and Music* (Cambridge, Mass.: Harvard University Press, 1991), pp. 421–22, Williams, "Encounters with the Chromatic Fourth," *Musical Times* 126 (1985), pp. 276ff, and Williams, "Snares and Delusions," pp. 235–38.

then perhaps they produced some ridiculous performances, but nevertheless that served as a means to help understand the speech better.

Of course, while acknowledging the ridiculous performances, some would say it also produced a few great performances.

Indeed, it may seem that I think no profound truths about the eighteenth century were being discovered in this emphasis on rhetoric. On the contrary: if one can understand rhetoric properly, not as it has been misapplied to musical performance, then one can in fact find it rather meaningful—although basically it should be telling us nothing that we do not already know. Rhetoric is simply effective speech—good public speaking, if you will. I've referred often here to the idea of knowing the language—knowing how, say, Haydn's or Carter's language functions. That is precisely what rhetoric is supposed to deal with— not with hidden meanings or anything like that, but with knowing, when I want to make an effective statement about something, how to make it clear, how to set it off from something else, which words carry a certain affective weight in themselves, and so forth. It is what any native speaker knows, and what any good actor knows, and what any good musical performer performing his or her native "language" of music knows. In that way *any* good performance is rhetorical, be it Toscanini conducting Beethoven's Third, or Horowitz playing the Liszt Sonata, or Stravinsky conducting his own music. You listen to Stravinsky conducting his music and it sounds coherent, while with a certain level of conductors it doesn't always. In that unchallenging sense, rhetoric is very much at the basis of all that we do, but it's at the basis of what any decent musician in any repertory does.

I have to stress that for the most part the significance of these things is purely musical and syntactic. It has a semantic dimension, but not one you can put your finger on. An unusual leap, a chromatic fourth, or a special chromatic alteration—it's something that you have to understand has a certain meaning because it's not the everyday plain occurrence in a piece. Because it is an elaboration effect, an unusual construction, it means that you have to be aware of its unusualness, its relationship to the usual, and that you have to have some understanding of how you might project this, how you might make this make sense.

I'm reminded of a story I heard from Chris Krueger, the flautist in the Bach Ensemble, about having coached in the Berg Chamber Concerto under Rudolf Kolisch. He said that what was striking about Kolisch when he would sing them examples from this piece is how highly inflected the singing was, in an unmistakably Viennese fashion. It was instantly clear, when you heard Kolisch sing it, what Berg had in mind with all these lovingly detailed markings of his, which are so often just completely wrongly played today because they are played without any understanding of what lies behind the notes. Berg's was a Viennese dialect, and Kolisch spoke that language, so he inflected naturally in that style. Again, it's knowing where Max Reger's cadences fall, knowing where he's interrupting and evading a cadence, knowing that you have to project both the sense that it is going towards something and that it is evading it. All that is linguistic understanding—all that is, in the true meaning of the term, rhetorical: it's how to put the point across. But much of this other stuff—treating each little pattern of a few notes as a meaningful rhetorical gesture whose meaning is coded in a Latin term—is without foundation.

For that reason, I would prefer just for a while at least to avoid the word "rhetoric" until it can be shorn of this extraneous baggage. At which point I'd be very happy to use it once more, because, properly understood, it's something that every good performance has and needs.

Let me pursue some qualifications. John Butt writes that rhetoric was an aspect of German Baroque performance as well as composition, and in a way that did differ from later styles of playing. In the performance sphere, he says, it had to do with using ornamentation to increase the eloquence and emotional power of the presentation. But he agrees with you that the various ornamental elements had no specific meanings or connections to sung texts.[10]

He writes elsewhere that the added ornaments, musically, were elaborations of a fundamental structure—there was a hierarchy—and that these figures were therefore given some form of delineation in performance.[11] *How do you respond to the idea that in the earlier Baroque—the text-centered post-Monteverdi style, which we still find echoing in early Bach—rhetorical performance was different from performance later, and that it involved some kind of articulation of smaller units for added effect?*[12]

If one qualifies the meaning of the word "rhetoric" carefully here, so that it doesn't suggest the esoterica we've just discussed, I can agree with him. Nevertheless, even when one says, "This is the elaboration of a simpler figure, and therefore it must be delivered in that way," the question of course is *how?* If you don't understand it at all, you will probably ride right over it. But in the

10. See Butt, *Musical Education and the Art of Performance in the German Baroque* (Cambridge University Press, 1994), pp. 46–51. See also his interview in Chapter 9 of this book.

11. "When it is considered that Bernhard and Walther viewed the added figures as the elaboration of a fundamental *prima prattica* structure—in other words there is a hierarchy of diminution within the music—and further that such a style resembled a rhetoric, it is not unreasonable to infer that figuration in performance would have been given some form of delineation" (Butt, *Bach Interpretation* [Cambridge University Press, 1990], p. 19).

12. David Schulenberg, "Musical Expression and Musical Rhetoric in the Keyboard Works of J. S. Bach," in *Johann Sebastian Bach: A Tercentenary Celebration*, ed. Seymour Benstock (Westport, Conn.: Greenwood Press, 1994), pp. 95–109, sees Bach's style changing in this regard. He says that Bach's early cantatas, written in the language of Buxtehude, illustrate important words musically, declaiming them in a rhetorical way; Schulenberg also finds elements of this approach in Bach's early instrumental music. In later Bach, though, he says that formal architecture becomes more important than such rhetoric, and the response to text is less detailed.

first flush and joy of discovery, you may think that you really have to communicate your discovery and enthusiasm to the listener, i.e. pump it for all it's worth. Again, real speech lies somewhere in between, even in highly rhetorical actor's speech. Again, much of the stuff in rhetoric is just making conscious to us what good speakers and good musicians do. As musicians we are like Molière's Monsieur Jourdain—we're constantly discovering that we're speaking prose, or even poetry perhaps. Any halfway sensitive musician does this. In a sense, the awareness of this can heighten your doing it. But I wonder if there's an obligation to make it noticeable.

Even if there's no obligation, an artist may prefer the result.

Absolutely, and that of course is their prerogative. But it's another question when people speak of what happened in the past. We can never know, of course, but I like to think that the best performers in those days did it intuitively. I really do not believe that there was any conscious notion of this in performance. What theorists were saying about it, insofar as it had any applications to performance at all, was in a sense more descriptive: they were putting a magnifying glass to what happens in a good performance, just as the science of rhetoric was fundamentally putting a magnifying glass to what good orators did.[13]

George Barth writes that Beethoven[14] played much of his music in a "declamatory" style, delivering the phrases like someone declaiming, rather than someone singing a long, mellifluous line or maintaining a moto perpetuo. He relates it to the more detailed, "speaking" articulation that many people see in pre-nineteenth-century music. He believes that the speaking style lost some footing in the course of the nineteenth century and has been neglected in much Beethoven playing in recent decades. Do you have any comments?

It strikes me as, on the face of it, a well-taken point. In a sense, though (and I'm sure George would be the first to agree with this), all good singing is declamatory and all good declamation sings. I suppose my personal idea of good performance style, which is of course purely subjective, is always wanting somehow to gain the advantages of everything at once. Good singing speaks; there's Callas. And if you don't speak well, you end up with Monty Python's parody of a BBC announcer, with uninflected sentences starting and stopping in mid-sentence. So, it's a question of emphasis, or of being aware of a side of it of which we perhaps had not been aware—of developing a sense of how intelligibility is a matter of seeing what the gestures are, what the moves are. Very often these things have been lost.

13. Another consideration, as far as historical foundations go, may be nationality. Butt suggests in Chapter 15 of this book that German singers articulated the figures more than did Italians.

14. *The Pianist as Orator* (Ithaca, N.Y.: Cornell University Press, 1992).

I'd add that it's not just in the performance of Beethoven. Where George Barth and others might use the word "declamation," I tend to use the word "inflection." It is my sense that this "declamation" or "inflection" was more characteristic of all musical performance before the Second World War. You listen to Kreisler or Furtwängler, and you hear highly inflected performances; Schnabel's Beethoven always seemed to me a very speaking kind of playing. All three are in many ways examples of what a lot of people in the so-called early-music business have been trying to rediscover and recover. The music-making of these pre-war artists is indeed speaking, saying things. In that sense I think that we are reinventing a particular wheel—which I don't say as criticism, because wheels constantly roll out of sight and have to be reinvented. But maybe what all this is about is that while we may need all the historical apparatus and all the PR, in a sense we're just trying to plug into some home truths.

The problem, I think, is that we all like structural cohesion and continuity, we all like detail, we all like declamatory speaking, we all like beautiful sounds, we all like guts, we all like sensitivity—but we can't do full justice to any one of these elements without glossing over another one. In practice, what happens is that each of us likes these elements in various proportions at various times; and similar shifts take place, from decade to decade, in the fashions of musical reception. There are many ways of slicing it; every era will slice it differently, and so will every performer, each time he or she performs. I was just reading some interview comments I made eight years ago. I was astonished to see myself saying some of the things I said. Whether I have really changed my beliefs or fashion has dragged me out of them I don't know; but one comes to other places—thank God.

SELECTED DISCOGRAPHY

Rifkin's 1982 recording of the B Minor Mass (Nonesuch 79036, 2 CDs) was the first to use the one-per-part approach he advocates. Critical responses vary widely to this day. The disc won the 1983 *Gramophone* Award; its strongest advocate, Teri Noel Towe, calls it "intensely powerful [and] revelatory," adding that the participating musicians have "the guts to sing and play with vigour and sensitivity, warmth and understanding."[15] By contrast, Nicholas Kenyon says that Rifkin "just lets the music happen . . . and to my mind misses many of the opportunities offered by one-to-a-part performance."[16] Peter Williams, occupying middle ground, agrees that "the singers simply sing: no rhetoric, no showmanship," but he likes the result more, saying, "the chamber performance, quiet and undemonstrative, brings out the wonderful inherent melodiousness of

15. Towe, "J. S. Bach: Mass in B Minor," in *Choral Music on Record,* ed. Alan Blyth (Cambridge University Press, 1991), pp. 57–58.
16. Kenyon, "Bach's Choral Works: A Discographic Survey," Part 1, *Opus,* December 1985, pp. 14–17; quote, p. 16.

Bach's music most beautifully." Still, he thinks the performance is undermined by the instrumental work, which "in rejecting Harnoncourt's constant cresc-dim effect . . . replaces it with nothing."[17] I will say only that the tempos, which in 1983 often seemed too fast, today (after years of hearing early-music Bach) seem reasonable throughout, with the exception of the speedy Sanctus.

According to John Butt, in Rifkin's 1985 recording of Cantatas 147 and 80 (L'Oiseau-Lyre 417 250-2) the advantages of one-per-part "are manifold. . . . balance and ensemble are superb throughout."[18] Butt also says that the alto aria in 147 is "beautifully interpreted." Many feel that Rifkin's finest Bach record is of the Mühlhausen cantatas numbers 106 and 131 (L'Oiseau Lyre 417 323).

Scott Joplin's revival in popularity was effectively launched by Rifkin's Nonesuch recordings; in his latest contribution in this genre, a collection of rags by Joplin contemporaries and tangos by Ernesto Nazareth (*Rags and Tangos*, Decca 425 225), Malcolm Macdonald finds deep insights that are "aided and abetted by [Rifkin's] exceedingly resourceful piano-playing."[19]

FOR FURTHER READING

Richard Taruskin's seminal writings on authenticity and historical performance, referred to so often in this book, are collected and updated in *Text and Act* (New York: Oxford University Press, 1995). Another significant collection features various authors: *Authenticity and Early Music*, ed. Nicholas Kenyon (Oxford University Press, 1988). Peter Kivy's *Authenticities* (Ithaca, N.Y.: Cornell University Press, 1995) is an important philosophical discussion of the topic.

17. Williams, *Early Music* 12 (February 1984), p. 139.
18. Butt, *Early Music* 15 (November 1987), pp. 575 and 577.
19. Macdonald, *Gramophone* 69 (April 1992), p. 120

EPILOGUE

Nicholas McGegan described the current early-music scene to me in these terms:

> The sense of protest has gone out of it, which I think is potentially very helpful. In other words, we're doing it because we enjoy it, not because we don't enjoy what other people are doing. The other thing is that we are no longer wrapping ourselves up in this cloak of being—unlike modern players—"correct," which of course is something you can never be in the arts. Also, once you get obsessed with style at the expense of content, things are just as much out of whack as when people are obsessed with content at the expense of style.

There's a lot of truth to that, and yet some of the interviews in this book (not McGegan's) do convey a sense of protest and of being more "correct" than mainstream players. In this and many other respects, the interviewees' motives, creeds, and methods vary. The interviews bear out Michelle Dulak's comment, "Never has historical performance been stronger than today, and never has it been harder to say exactly what it is."[1]

Still, to facilitate discussion we can divide the interviewees into three broad types. Placing an artist in any one camp may be (unintentionally) insulting—I apologize if so—and it usually oversimplifies, making what's ambiguous seem definite; but it might be useful in picking out trends.

Artists of my first type uphold what we might call the central early-music tradition: they adhere firmly to the ideal of trying to play music as it was played in its own time. Their most explicit statement comes from someone whose schedule didn't allow a full-length interview—Andrew Parrott, a British conductor whose recordings have received deservedly warm reviews:

> To argue that we need not concern ourselves with earlier performing conventions simply because our ears are (necessarily) "modern" is, effectively,

1. "The Early Music Movement Circles Its Wagons Again," *The New York Times,* 11 June 1995, Sunday Arts and Leisure section, p. 25

a self-fulfilling prophecy: we can listen in only one way (a "modern" way), so that is how we shall listen. Unfortunately, this is a popular viewpoint, perhaps because most classical musicians are temperamentally more conservative than they care to admit, but also because many react against any apparent preoccupation with "rules" and against anything they perceive as prescriptive or restrictive. I have never seen performance practice that way. The more I learn—and there is so much more to discover than many begin to imagine—the richer, the more fascinating, and, often, the easier performance becomes. The challenge of absorbing new information, rather than constricting and limiting the performer, acts as a stimulus to the creative imagination and can also prove positively liberating. It does not so much dictate what *not* to do as offer us new ideas of what we might choose *to* do. New possibilities emerge, even if old ones fall by the wayside. Surely it is only the complacent, over-cautious or unimaginative musician who cannot be bothered to rethink aspects of performing style in this way.

One could question that last sentence. We wouldn't consider a Furtwängler or Beecham complacent, over-cautious, or unimaginative, but they probably didn't think about performance practice very much. They certainly didn't accept the early-music movement's view of style as something you choose; what they focused on was content. (This can be related to Robert Morgan's idea, cited in this book's introduction, that musicians in the past believed themselves part of a living tradition stretching back to Bach, and therefore felt free to play him in their own current style.) One could also argue that for some early-music performers—though not for Parrott—the "rules" have in fact been prescriptions, which serve to reduce the need to make subjective decisions. All the same, Parrott's program *is* likely to stimulate, liberate, and give new possibilities—at least when it is joined to Parrott's level of artistry. And his unapologetic conviction does not bear on his artistic success.

Nonetheless, the interviews show that historical evidence doesn't inspire everyone in the same way. The second type of artists I identify *rejects*, at least partially, the core ideal of historical authenticity. Such artists aren't complacent—they know their history and have rethought their styles. But unlike Type Ones, they flout history openly when they prefer something else. We might assume that these artists have been emboldened by the skeptics' battering at the historicist ideal; on the whole, though, it seems to me that both Types One and Two reach their positions not through the intellect but through temperament or artistic need. Presumably Type Twos, unlike Parrott, believe themselves either constrained or ill served by historical strictness. I think here of Peter Phillips, who was arguing his viewpoint in 1978, and of Jeffrey Thomas and others that I place in this group.[2]

2. According to Taruskin, my Type Ones, the early-music mainstreamers, aren't *simply* try-

The third type is often a subset of Type One, sharing the dedication to history that Parrott commends; but it uses history radically, to undermine a more basic assumption, one that the first two groups share with the mainstream. This assumption is *Werktreue*—fidelity to the work—and, behind that, the concept of the fixed, perfected work itself.[3] In the introduction to *Text and Act* (p. 13), Richard Taruskin complains that "The whole trouble with Early Music as a 'movement' . . . is the way it has uncritically accepted the post-Romantic work-concept and imposed it anachronistically on pre-Romantic repertories." What draws his censure "is not the anachronism but the uncritical acceptance—and the imposition." Whether you agree with him or not, the interviews show that a growing segment of the "movement" neither accepts the work-concept "uncritically" nor always imposes it, anachronistically or otherwise. I'm thinking above all of improvisers like Andrew Lawrence-King, Julianne Baird, and Robert Levin, who are being faithful to the historical practice of *not* being faithful to the work. Baird speaks explicitly about changing the balance of power between composer and performer, and restoring the performer's role in the compositional act—that is, of returning to a pre-*Werktreue* philosophy. She has chosen a repertory that allows this, and so supports Dulak's view that "early music" has come to mean, above all, a place where musicians are allowed to experiment with approaches that are discouraged in the mainstream. (I should add, though, that Levin's improvising is meant to fulfill Mozart's intention.)

Another possible undermining of *Werktreue* is found among those artists, like John Butt, McGegan, and Paul Hillier, who praise rougher, less perfect, less polished playing—who might say, with Anner Bylsma, "To hell with the perfection of the highway tarmac!" Today's emphasis on flawless execution might reflect (among other causes) the recording-studio ethos and, also, *Werktreue*—being so true to the work that every one of its notes is audible and in just the right place. While many musicians regard modern technical perfection as a straightforward example of progress, others take a more Luddite view. I know of a musicologist who prefers to hear Classical string quartets played by ama-

---

ing to play music as it was played when it was new. Taruskin would argue that Type Ones, like Type Twos, also use history selectively, in order to produce a result they and their audiences like. He argues, however, that this is not a conscious process: unlike Type Twos, they usually won't violate what they have concluded was the historical practice, except when they must (using mezzos or countertenors instead of castrati, for example) or in rare cases where the historical practice is clearly harmful to the music. But unconsciously, he thinks, Type Ones tend to deal with evidence according to their biases. Readers may decide whether the interviews support his hypothesis.

3. Lydia Goehr recognizes this: "More than any other movement currently existing within the European tradition of classical music, the early music movement is perfectly positioned to present itself not only as a 'different way of thinking about music,' but also as an alternative to a performance practice governed by the work-concept." Goehr, *The Imaginary Museum of Musical Works* (Oxford University Press, 1992), p. 284.

teurs; the modern professional quartets have such perfect ensemble, he believes, that they obscure the identity of the four parts in a way never imagined by the composers. It sounds as if one person is playing all four instruments, rather than a conversation of four distinct individuals.

In its early days, the early-music movement was sometimes a caricature of a poorly polished approach and was often derided for its amateurism; musicians hadn't yet learned to play old instruments well, so they were often out of tune and out of sync. It wasn't until they could play old instruments with all the polish of the mainstream that they became accepted (and at the same time, controversial—they could no longer be laughed off). The trend I see in my few Type Three interviews is a turnaround: now they *can* play perfectly, but these artists aren't sure it's always worth the price. Various performers today are questioning the ideal of technical perfection, and the majority of them are in the early-music sphere (mainstreamers who share such questions might be less likely to get away with acting on them).[4] This is logical on historical grounds: although performers in past times could be highly virtuosic, the evidence indicates that our concern with studio perfection didn't arise (usually) until some decades into the twentieth century. Before then, for example, uniform orchestral bowing was rare, and what musicians call "ensemble" was looser (as we hear in early recordings of quartets, for example). This historical argument has sometimes been raised to excuse the amateurism of early-music performers of the previous generation: that logic is questionable, but I don't think it motivates the artists I mention. I think their concerns represent, once again, temperament—in this case, a temperament that finds clockwork perfection an artistic straitjacket.

Again, there are qualifications. Peter Phillips and Christopher Page are hardly alone in the aesthetic pleasure they take in perfect ensemble; and perhaps Page is right that this ideal was shared in the distant past. It seems to have applied in the orchestras of Lully and Corelli as well, and perhaps elsewhere.

That, then, is my typology, although (as I said at the outset) it's far too schematic. Leonhardt might seem a classic example of Type One, but not only has he become less so in his statements, he is also known to have been a great closet improviser all along. My Type Threes often make reference to jazz, but so does William Christie, who is hard to classify. A single artist may fit all three of the above types at various times; as I've said, the historical-performance movement has never been harder to define.

---

4. I may be wrong about this. When *The New York Times* mentioned "wrong notes and bobbled entries, which were by no means infrequent" in a recent Berlin Philharmonic Brahms cycle in New York, it added that "they were the inevitable byproducts of risks being taken by players however consummately skilled, a part of the overall exuberance of the performances. . . . In the way he marshals this excitement . . . Abbado seems to have attached to something more primal in the orchestra." James Oestreich, "Abbado, Making Berlin Philharmonic His Own," *The New York Times,* 9 October 1996, pp. B1, B5.

In the introduction I said that even when you believe that historical practice matters, you still have to decide whether each specific practice is essential to performance, or not important, or even harmful. My "typology" could be understood as three different angles on those decisions: Type Ones consider more of historical practice essential than Type Twos do; Type Threes value a different set of information. In any event, the three-part typology may dramatize the most obvious implication of this book: that to refer to historical performers in the aggregate as "they" (as some critics still do) is too vague to be useful.

My grouping also seems to call out for some crystal-ball gazing. I think many people would agree with Robert Levin that the improvisatory approach of some Type Threes is likely to prosper, simply because it offers so much excitement to audiences and performers. Many people, too, would agree with those who see Type Two as representing an advance: when Harnoncourt decides to conduct modern orchestras with only a few specific historical instruments, it shows that for him historical performance has become not a recipe but an option, which he can exercise for artistic reasons. Still others believe that the Type One approach yields the most progress (Parrott is not the only Type One whose performances are especially admired—some others are Reinhard Goebel and Sigiswald Kuijken, both of whom try to be uncompromising about historical veracity). Parrott is not alone in fearing that the Type Two approach could lead to laziness. It would be easier to choose sides if one of the three types were to produce consistently better artistic results than the others, but none do; it all depends on the artist.

Part of my explanation of why Type Three will prosper—audience appeal—relates to another issue. Although marketers still make claims about "Verdi as Verdi would have heard it," few artists do anymore; more and more of them seem preoccupied with the concerns that Anthony Rooley, Peter Phillips, and others express about giving the audience a meaningful—and even an enjoyable—experience. For various reasons, some today[5] see this as a healthier direction for performing artists than Romantic disdain for audience approval—an ideal sometimes at least claimed by classical musicians. But a less theoretical factor may also bear on this change in orientation. Demand for classical music has been shrinking, as younger audiences desert it for, essentially, American popular culture.[6] The reasons for the desertion are too complex to go into here,

---

5. See Taruskin's "Why Do They All Hate Horowitz?" *The New York Times*, 28 November 1993, Sunday Arts and Leisure section, p. 31, for an example of this viewpoint.

6. Edward Rothstein ("The Tribulations of the Not-So-Living Arts," *The New York Times*, 18 February 1996, pp. E1, E14) reports on a study commissioned by the National Endowment for the Arts, "Age and Arts Participation with a Focus on the Baby Boom Cohort: 1982–1992," by Judith A. Balfe and Richard A. Peterson, which was based on interviews with 10,000 American adults. It shows a "massive shift in taste and tradition" over the generations to pop music and mass culture and away from the fine arts. This is hardly a unique finding.

but what is relevant is that it might especially affect early music, which has usually been even more marginal and specialized in its appeal than mainstream classical music.

It's not surprising, then, that the rare early-music hits of the last few years have often involved some form of popular culture. Several have involved the dominant styles of our day—witness the Hilliard Ensemble's jazz collaboration. Others have resulted from association with the dominant medium of our day, film—witness Jordi Savall's heartrending soundtrack to *Tous les matins du monde*—though film tie-ins are hardly a new phenomenon (think of the 1940 cartoon *Fantasia*). The Hilliard and Savall examples arose from artistic conviction, but their lessons have not been lost on marketers. As Erato undertook Ton Koopman's Bach cantata series in 1995, it tried to interest a Hollywood studio in a film about Bach, featuring Koopman's playing. Polygram released a pair of Gardiner's Beethoven symphonies to capitalize on the film *Immortal Beloved*; the CD cover featured the following blurb:

> You gotta have it! The full, incomparable thrill of Beethoven's most revolutionary symphonies in white-hot performances. The Fifth, that cosmic tale of tragedy leading to triumph, is the "Star Wars" of symphonic music. And the Third is a swashbuckling thriller which for sheer passion, romance, and gusto had to wait for Indiana Jones in "Raiders of the Lost Ark" to find its visual counterpart.[7]

This may not seem much of an improvement over "Beethoven as Beethoven imagined it," but the marketers know what works: this release sold well. We can expect them to remember that.

We can also expect to see more performers trying to build bridges to mass culture through their own presentations. I think of the ensemble Bimbetta, which bills itself as "Five Babes Who Go for Baroque," and whose concerts embed seventeenth-century music in hip, postmodern theatre. I've heard good reports but haven't seen the group. I won't speculate on the general merits of such approaches, beyond predicting that some will work and some will turn the stomach—as when a young American maestro "bounds on stage dressed as Superman or in a Mozart wig," which led Leon Botstein to say, "This is so horrendous it bears no description."[8] (Of course, anything, including standard concert etiquette, will turn the stomach of someone, somewhere.) Some believe that such approaches are a necessity; the American Symphony Orchestra League has, for example, suggested that orchestras play more pop and ethnic music to attract larger and younger audiences (I think they used the adjective

7. DG Archiv 445 944.
8. Audrey Choi, "Modern Maestros Conduct Themselves in Offbeat Fashions: To Sell Seats, They Will Dress Like Batman or Mozart; Riding in on an Elephant," *The Wall Street Journal*, 8 January 1996, pp. 1, 4.

"diverse"). I'm not sure how one would apply that particular recommendation to early music, but the need is at least as real. The reconciliation of popular and classical cultures that Robert Levin called for in his interview is happening in several areas today, and early-music crossover is one. Its successes needn't necessarily be hip ones, by the way: Anonymous 4 has managed, for example, to touch large audiences deeply without making its concert presentation even slightly pop. Still, the group's market success results not from its concerts, memorable though they are, but from its recordings. These have clearly tapped into popular trends (even if that doesn't reflect the artists' intentions) and have reached the market through popular media. It's not for nothing that the *New Yorker* called the group "the fab four of medieval music."

Mention of Anonymous 4 brings us to another forecasting question: what will the few media hits do for the great majority of early-music performers? It's possible that the hits may boost demand for early music as a commodity. But it has also been argued that, in general, mass media and telecommunications tend to drive up demand only for the few market-preferred "superstars," and that this tends to drive *down* demand (and fees) for the non-superstars.[9] It can't be assumed that the success of the media's chosen few will rub off on the remaining body of worthy artists—the opposite is just as likely. People who spend good money on Jordi Savall CDs and concerts may be less inclined to come out to hear a local gambist, or at least to pay a lot of money to do so. (And obviously, electronic media like CDs are a major factor behind the shrinking of concert-hall audiences—music lovers stay home rather than go to concerts.[10])

This brings us to another prognostication factor: the classical recording industry, which, by all accounts, is in financial straits. Sales of the standard repertory have flattened, and even major orchestras are losing their recording contracts.[11] Early music's rise to popularity depended critically on recordings, so the poor health of the record industry will be unwelcome news. Record companies may become less willing to take chances with early-music recordings that require large ensembles or that feature unusual repertory. They may also be less

9. This is the "superstar model" of income distribution, proposed by the University of Chicago economist Sherwin Rosen in 1981; for an explanation, see Paul Krugman, *Peddling Prosperity* (New York: Norton, 1994), p. 149. Rosen applies the model not only to entertainers but also to top lawyers, business executives, and others. On this, see Robert Frank and Philip Cook, *The Winner-Take-All Society* (New York: The Free Press, 1995).

10. Rothstein writes, "The NEA report notes . . . that 'video consumption' of classical music is high for the same age groups that show declines in attendance at concerts. Recordings have also become more important as a replacement for the live experience" ("The Tribulations"). He adds that this news is even worse than it may seem at first glance, because classical record buyers often use the music as background, rather than as something to listen to with serious interest. This, as noted early in this book, is certainly true of currently popular medieval music.

11. Allan Kozinn, "Strike in Philadelphia: What Stopped the Music," *The New York Times*, 17 September 1996, p. C1.

willing to risk money on unknowns, even gifted ones, which would tilt the scale even further toward the superstars.

However that plays out, it is fair to say that an artistic scene generally thrives when those who want to practice the art can afford to do so. Economic viability is not a sufficient condition for "an abundance of musical genius" to emerge, but historical studies suggest it may be a necessary one.[12] A poet like Wallace Stevens may have overcome conditions that wouldn't let him devote time to writing poetry, but especially among performing artists, who need to practice and rehearse together, such adverse conditions tend to reduce output and thin the ranks. This brings us to another economic factor clouding the crystal ball. The degree of non-box-office financial support available to artists—whether from private donors or from governments—is likely to affect any non-popular art. Early music has usually had limited box-office appeal; even in its era of origin, "private" patronage was typically paid for out of various forms of hidden or direct taxation, whose revenues were spent by and for aristocrats rather than the general population. We can't safely predict the extent of government support in coming decades, but we can note that in France and the Netherlands the generous government support, though probably not the key to the thriving early-music scenes there, has probably been a non-trivial factor. It has made it possible for hundreds of musicians to develop and pursue their art full-time. We can also note that in the USA such support has been a whole order of magnitude less per capita,[13] and that this may have been one reason why so many leading US early-music artists have migrated to Europe,[14] and

12. "Although suitable economic circumstances are in themselves hardly sufficient to elicit an abundance of musical genius, they may constitute a necessary condition for that result." William and Hilda Baumol, "On the Economics of Musical Composition in Mozart's Vienna," in *On Mozart,* ed. James Morris (Cambridge University Press, 1994), p. 87. The article discusses Elizabethan theatre, and music in the Hapsburg empire in the late eighteenth century. There was high demand for theatre in Elizabethan London and for music in late-Hapsburg states, and general wage levels were low in both eras; these factors combined to create a great deal of attractive employment opportunity in the respective arts. "[S]urely it is plausible," write the Baumols, "that many of those entering the labor market would turn to careers for which they thought themselves suitable in professions where there existed opportunities for employment." Such reasoning might encourage modern youngsters to seek careers in pop music, TV, or film (and of course in medicine and dentistry), but not in classical music.

13. The most recent international study, done by the London-based Policy Studies Institute, found that in 1987 the Netherlands and France spent ten times as much per capita on the arts as the US did (these figures sum arts spending from all levels of government, then divide the total by population size). Similar studies from other sources have found similar ratios. Other indirect factors—welfare and educational benefits, government support for churches, universities, and classical-music radio—tend to exaggerate the difference rather than diminish it; differences in private philanthropy and corporate support do not alter it significantly.

14. For example, Benjamin Bagby, William Christie, Sarah Cunningham, Alan Curtis, Bruce Dickie, Laurence Dreyfus, Jonathan Dunford, Elizabeth Gaver, Nancy Hadden, Sterling Jones, the members of Project Ars Nova, Skip Sempé, Hopkinson Smith, Stephen Stubbs, Barbara Thornton, Glen Wilson, and many others. Joshua Rifkin's home base is in Massachusetts, but most of his performing is done east of the Atlantic.

why so few leading Europeans have migrated to the US (my book gives disproportionate coverage to those few, for practical reasons). The demise of US federal arts and humanities spending, and the possible reduction of tax incentives for private donors, may therefore have implications for early music. Even if these prove dire, the question remains of whether they should be a matter of concern for US policy makers; I will not discuss that here. Obviously, if governments pay people to do something (as those of the Netherlands or France do for early music), more people will do it, and some of them will do it well; but it may not be something a society values. Clearly the US citizenry, by and large, does not value early music. Proving that it should do so is not as easy as I would like, though I would argue (were it less tangential to this book) that the arts and humanities in general deserve the country's support.

We could try to read plenty of other tea leaves. Howard Gardner suspects that "we are reverting to a period in which creative activity will be less individualistic and less iconoclastic, more communal and more continuous with its past"[15]—an interesting prediction, but I'll refrain from speculating on it, except to say that such a development might suit some forms of early music well (and others poorly, such as that archetypal individualist/iconoclast, Beethoven). Besides, I've yet to be convinced that it's happening, attractive though it sounds. Bimbetta raises the issue of how early music might be affected by the "postmodern condition." This book may or may not demonstrate Brad Holland's remark that "if you're confused about [postmodernism], that's probably because you're beginning to understand it";[16] but I agree with John Butt, who sides with "critics who are sceptical of postmodernism as an ideal."[17] Butt adds, though, that the term "is certainly acceptable—indeed useful—as a description of the condition we happen to be in" (I'd add that some of its theoretical concerns are important ones). Still, Butt finds fault in seeing postmodernism "as the answer to all the evils of modernism, as the way for the future, even as a happy utopia in which all differences will live side-by-side in a pluralistic flux." To pursue his point, consider what happens when you try to apply postmodernism to early music. If modernism implies a disdain for one's audience, then those seeking to win popular audiences might be considered postmodern—but Butt points out that when pleasing the

---

As for the European expatriates who appear in my book, two (Butt and Hillier) have university positions, so don't rely on performing for their incomes (this is true of the few other expatriates I can think of, who are, by the way, mostly British)—and Butt will be moving back to England at about the time this book is published. The third, McGegan, spends as much time performing in Europe as in the US. Many American artists who remain in the USA—such as Baird, Bilson, and Levin—typically depend on university posts, not concerts, for their living.

15. Gardner, "How Extraordinary Was Mozart?" in *On Mozart*, p. 50.

16. Holland, "Express Yourself: It's Later than You Think," *The Atlantic*, July 1996, pp. 66–68; quote, p. 66.

17. Butt, "Acting up a Text," *Early Music* 24 (May 1996), p. 327.

audience becomes a musician's overarching goal, it can create just as many aesthetic dilemmas as disdaining the audience does. If by modernism we mean what some call "reification" and "sacralization" of the work of art, then post-modernism may be the term for those who embed music in hip theatre or otherwise take it "off its pedestal"; but while Monteverdi sung in the context of hip theatre may be fun and may reach new listeners, it may not necessarily be a greater human experience than Beethoven played to a rapt audience by Schnabel. And if by modernism we mean a preoccupation with form and structure, then some of the improvising Type Threes could be classified as postmodern (as well as pre-modern); but the achievement of a Beethoven in using form for expressive ends may be truly great. A happy pluralism, whether it's postmodern or something else, might be a good development— and it *is* safe to say that we're getting more of it today than we used to.

The historical-performance movement is the child of an unlikely union—that of scholarship and art. It would bring this book to a nice conclusion if I could say that it is reaching adulthood. Pronouncements like that should be made with caution, but a case can be made for this one. Of course, recordings from thirty years ago by David Munrow, Thomas Binkley, Michael Morrow, Leonhardt/Brueggen/Kuijken, and Harnoncourt preserve music-making that is anything but immature. And there have been some dull and some bizarre performances in recent years; and, as Laurence Dreyfus argues, commercial success has led to institutionalization and to some formulaic, thoughtless playing.[18] Still, there is a much larger pool of thoroughly accomplished musicians in the field now; their technical standards have risen markedly; they indulge in less mannerism and exaggeration; fewer "demonstration" performances take place, whose main goal is to show that something can be done rather than to make music. It can also be said that various groups of artists are maturing. Rooley's discussion of his own artistic odyssey exemplifies one such group: musicians of a more literalistic, polite background who have learned to step out and become freer and more expressive. A mirror example involves certain Continental musicians whose extremely inflected, sometimes overwrought playing has become more mature and integrated, and thus even more exciting. It is also safe to say that the discourse about historical performance is more mature and sophisticated. McGegan's view that the sense of protest and correctness has gone out of it is, to a large extent, valid, even among Type Ones.

Of course, there is no reason to assume that artistic movements like this one necessarily evolve to ever higher states of maturity. Artists often do; movements may or may not. As it happens, so far the movement *has* matured. There are

18. Dreyfus, in his section of "The Early Music Debate," *Journal of Musicology* 10 (Winter 1992), pp. 114–17.

a number of exciting artists at work today who have evolved wonderfully in their own playing, and many of them have learned tremendous amounts from their teachers' experiments or their own long experience. For this reason above all, historical performance has never been stronger—or harder to define, partly because it interacts with the mainstream in so many ways, yet still maintains the separateness of its niche. It wouldn't surprise me if in the future historical performance becomes even harder to define and, not coincidentally, even stronger.

INDEX